*WAYSIDE AND WOODLAND SERIES*

# BIRDS
## OF THE BRITISH ISLES
## AND THEIR EGGS

PLATE 1
*Above :* Mallard, p34
*Below :* Teal, p36

*Above :* Scaup, p45
*Below :* Garganey, p38

# BIRDS
## OF THE BRITISH ISLES
## AND THEIR EGGS

*Edited and revised by*
### J. A. G. BARNES, M.A. (Oxon.)
*From the three-volume work by*
### T. A. COWARD, M.Sc., F.Z.S., F.R.E.S., M.B.O.U.

★

WITH 177 PLATES
INCLUDING MANY COLOURED ILLUSTRATIONS
BY ARCHIBALD THORBURN AND OTHERS
AND REPRODUCTIONS FROM PHOTOGRAPHS BY
J. B. & S. BOTTOMLEY, ERIC HOSKING ETC.

FREDERICK WARNE & CO. LTD.
*LONDON · NEW YORK*

ISBN 0 7232 0999 5

Text printed in Great Britain by
William Clowes & Sons, Limited, London, Beccles and Colchester

Plates printed by Morrison & Gibb Ltd., Edinburgh
Birds' Eggs illustrations printed by
Lowe & Brydone (Printers) Ltd, Thetford

295.874

# CONTENTS

Preface     vii

Introduction   *Classification and the British List; Bird Protection; Birds Recorded in the British Isles less than 5 Times*     ix

Orders

GAVIIFORMES   Divers     1

PODICIPITIFORMES   Grebes     6

PROCELLARIIFORMES   Petrels, Shearwaters     12

PELECANIFORMES   Gannets, Cormorants     19

CICONIIFORMES   Herons, Storks     24

PHOENICOPTERIFORMES   Flamingoes     33

ANSERIFORMES   Ducks, Geese, Swans     34

FALCONIFORMES   Birds of Prey     76

GALLIFORMES   Game-birds     96

GRUIFORMES   Cranes, Rails     106

CHARADRIIFORMES   Waders, Sea-birds     116

COLUMBIFORMES   Pigeons     202

CUCULIFORMES   Cuckoos     208

STRIGIFORMES   Owls     211

CAPRIMULGIFORMES   Nightjars     220

APODIFORMES   Swifts     222

CORACIIFORMES   Kingfishers     224

PICIFORMES   Woodpeckers     229

PASSERIFORMES   Perching Birds     234

Index     349

# PREFACE

Thomas Alfred Coward was one of the outstanding figures of a very important period in the history of British ornithology. During his lifetime he saw the study of birds develop from being the pastime of a very small leisured élite, consisting mainly of sportsman-collectors, to something like its present status as an absorbing hobby for thousands of people of the widest possible range of age and occupation, and Coward himself, by his writings, lectures, and example, played no small part in bringing about this change.

He was born at Bowdon in Cheshire in January 1867, and lived there most of his life, though he also travelled widely in the British Isles and on the Continent to acquire first-hand knowledge of birds unfamiliar in his native county. He was personally in charge of the famous Dresser collection of skins in Manchester Museum and took careful notes of the plumage, 'soft parts' and measurements of any bird that came into his hands in the flesh. He did valuable work for bird protection, and in his thoughtful attitude towards what is now known as nature conservation he was far ahead of most of his contemporaries. But first and foremost Coward was a field naturalist, with a profound interest in every aspect of a bird's life and an exceptional gift for close and accurate observation. His most important contribution to British ornithology was his original work on field recognition and his careful recording of the details of bird behaviour.

Although he produced three volumes of collected essays on ornithological topics the essence of his life's work was concentrated in the two volumes of *The Birds of the British Isles and Their Eggs*, first published in 1920, and in the supplementary Series III added in 1926. In this work Coward showed not only an encyclopaedic knowledge of British birds but also a remarkable talent for producing a highly readable character sketch of a species in two or three pages of print. His descriptions of the Starling and the Dunlin might be taken as examples. This combination of accurate information with readability in a compact form gave this book a unique position in British ornithological literature.

The coloured illustrations of birds for the book, taken from Lord Lilford's *Coloured Figures of the Birds of the British Islands*, many of them from paintings by Archibald Thorburn, made a worthy counterpart to Coward's lively prose. Thorburn, son of the Scottish miniature painter Robert Thorburn, was an elder contemporary of Coward, born near Edinburgh in 1860. Few would question his right to be considered one of the greatest of bird artists. The suggestion of movement in the figures and the deft hints of habitat in the background are well shown in the plates of ducks, waders and raptors in this book.

Coward died in 1933, and the last full edition of his book, edited by that other great Cheshire naturalist, Arnold Boyd, was published in 1950. Since that date the numbers, distribution, and even the habits of many British birds have changed, and there has been a vast increase in the quantity of published information about them, so it became inevitable that some parts of Coward's text would have to be extensively revised in order to produce a reliable modern reference book. My aim in this new single volume has been to retain as much as possible of his original descriptive essays, while bringing up to date the statements on the distribution of each species and incorporating, in a brief and simplified form, the results of some of the most important recent studies on population and behaviour. To a very limited extent I have drawn upon personal observation to modify or supplement Coward's text.

In a popular work of this kind it is not possible to name authorities for all new material or attempt a bibliography, but I should like to acknowledge my special indebtedness to the series of articles by J. L. F. Parslow in *British Birds* vols. 60–1 on 'Changes in status among breeding birds in Britain and Ireland', and to the *Field Guide to the Birds of Britain and Europe*, by Peterson, Mountfort and Hollom for their clear and succinct notes on identification. I have also constantly referred to Witherby's *Handbook of British Birds*, Dr Bannerman's *Birds of the British Isles*, *Ireland's Birds* by R. F. Ruttledge, James Fisher's *Thorburn's Birds*, and to the periodicals *British Birds*, *Bird Study* and *Ibis*.

Coloured illustrations of birds' eggs used in this edition are by H. D. Swain; other new illustrations, Leach's Petrel (Pl. 9), Canada Goose (Pl. 33), Collared Dove (Pl. 97), Carrion Crow (Pl. 114) and Willow Tit (Pl. 118) have been provided by Robert Gillmor, and the Raven (Pl. 113) by Ernest C. Mansell. Thanks are also due to the photographers, whose names are given on the black and white plates, for their kind permission to reproduce their photographs. Some of these have been selected as an aid to identification, others for their intrinsic interest or beauty. Finally I should like to acknowledge with gratitude the advice of I. J. Ferguson-Lees on matters of nomenclature and classification (though he is in no way responsible for any errors of fact or judgment), and also the guidance of John Clegg at all stages in the preparation of the book, and the assistance of my daughter, Helen Caldwell, with proof-reading and indexing.

J. A. G. BARNES

# INTRODUCTION

## Classification and The British List

'The title of a bird to rank as British is a matter of personal opinion.' This was the opening sentence of Coward's Introduction. Today most amateur bird-watchers will be content to leave this decision to the British Records Committee of the British Ornithologists' Union, and few will envy them their task of pronouncing whether some new sight record refers to mis-identification, a bird escaped from captivity, a case of assisted passage or a genuine wild vagrant. Older records, too, must be subject to critical scrutiny, as is shown by the recent exposure of the unreliability of a whole series of occurrences of rarities, previously accepted, in the Hastings district. Nevertheless Coward's forecast that many New World species would be found to have reached Britain unaided has been fully justified. With the establishment of coastal bird observatories and regular watching of likely wader haunts the satisfactory identification of rare vagrants has become much more frequent than it was in Coward's time, and every year now adds new birds to the 'British List'. At the same time introduced species, chiefly waterfowl, are becoming established as feral breeders, and several exotic birds may soon have to be accepted, as the Canada Goose has been, as British.

However, although a single occurrence qualifies a bird for inclusion in the British List, and the discovery of a specimen of a new species must provide excitement for the finder and interest for students of migration, the average bird-watcher will not regard these extreme rarities as 'British birds' in any ordinary sense. Accordingly in this volume species with less than five accepted British records have been excluded from the main text and relegated to a simple list at the end of this introduction. Some of these will no doubt soon achieve their fifth record, but this arbitrary criterion does serve to indicate the most exceptional vagrants.

The problems of classification, nomenclature and sequence of species are an even more fruitful source of disagreement than the composition of the British List; yet they affect every bird-watcher at least in the practical task of finding his way about in a reference book or county list. Coward's *Birds of the British Isles and Their Eggs* arranged the species in the '*Handbook* order', starting with the crows and finishing with game-birds. This order was generally accepted in Britain until the publication in 1952 of the B.O.U. *Check List*, which was based on the Wetmore sequence, starting with divers and ending with sparrows. However, *The Birds of the Palaearctic Fauna* by Charles Vaurie (1959) shows considerable differences from the *Check List* sequence, especially in re-grouping the passerine species in a new system of families and sub-families. Both English and scientific names of several birds have been altered in recent publications. At the time of going to press (December 1968) there is no general agreement on these matters, so it has seemed advisable in this book to retain the familiar sequence of the 1952 *Check List*, but to adopt the English and scientific names now in general use in *British Birds* and other periodicals.

The scientific name of a bird consists of the name of its genus, spelt with a capital initial letter, followed by the specific epithet, both in a more or less latinised form. The genus is a group of very closely related species. The family is a larger group with a scientific name ending in -IDAE, and may include several genera; some taxonomists divide certain families into sub-families with the suffix -INAE. The largest grouping is the order, with a scientific name ending in -IFORMES. The species may be regarded as a unit with an objective reality, since birds of even closely similar species hardly ever interbreed in the wild; but the other groupings are human abstractions intended to show evolutionary relationships.

A species may have recognisable geographical races, or subspecies, and these races are indicated by trinomial scientific names. For example, Lesser Black-backed Gulls breeding in Scandinavia have noticeably darker mantles than native British birds: the former are distinguished as *Larus fuscus fuscus*, the latter as *Larus fuscus graellsii*. In most cases these subspecific differences can only be detected by careful study of the bird in the hand, or of its skin on the table, and often there is a gradation, or 'cline', from one geographical race to another. In this book subspecies are only mentioned and described when they can be satisfactorily identified in the field, for example the Pied Wagtail, *Motacilla alba yarrellii*, and the White Wagtail, *M.a. alba*. In a very small number of instances the distinction between a geographical race and a full species is not beyond doubt; the Hooded and Carrion Crows and the Bean and Pink-footed Geese come into this category.

Coward emphasised in his Introduction that the popular classification of British birds into residents, summer and winter visitors, passage migrants and irregular visitors is a very rough and ready one, as many birds would appear in more than one category and several in three or four. However, the following rounded figures give an idea of the comparative numbers of each group in the British List: residents 130, summer visitors 60, winter visitors 25, passage migrants 30, vagrants 215.

For the study of geographical distribution the world has been divided into zoological regions, now usually accepted as six or seven well-defined areas. The Palaearctic embraces Europe, Africa north of the Sahara and Asia north of the Himalayas. The Nearctic is America north of Mexico, and the two together the Holarctic Region. The remainder of Africa and southern Arabia is the Ethiopian, whilst the Oriental or Indian Region includes southern Asia and the Malays. Australia, New Guinea and the southern Pacific form the Australasian Region. South and Central America are the Neotropical Region. The British Isles lie on the western boundary of the Palaearctic, and are influenced by that region, the Nearctic, and in summer by the Ethiopian.

The chart, mapping the topography of a typical bird, will explain the terms used in descriptions. This book gives the salient characters noticeable in birds in the field rather than detailed descriptions of plumage. The measurements supplied at the end of each description are merely to indicate size; birds of one species vary greatly in measurements as well as in plumage. The length,

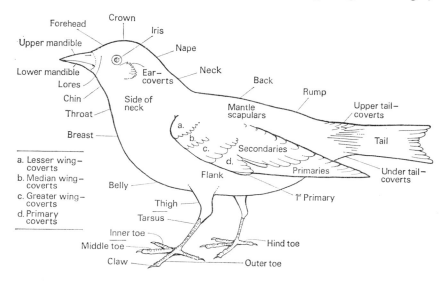

THE TOPOGRAPHY OF A TYPICAL BIRD

measured from the tip of the bill to the tip of the longest tail feather, is only a rough guide. Wing measurements are taken from the angle of the closed wing, the 'shoulder', to the tip of the longest flight feather.

## Bird Protection

In a section of his Introduction under this heading Coward gave an interesting and critical account of the history of legislation to protect wild birds in Britain. The successive Acts and Orders up to the date of Coward's death were highly complicated and generally ineffective, and it was not until 1954 that a simpli- fied comprehensive Act was passed, providing protection for all birds and their nests and eggs, with certain specified exceptions. Four lists of species were appended to this Act. The First Schedule gives extra protection, by special penalties, to over sixty birds and their eggs. The Second Schedule lists about twenty common birds considered harmful to agriculture or fisheries which can be killed or taken by authorised persons at any time. This list in- cludes the big gulls, several birds in the crow and pigeon families, Cormor- ants, House Sparrows and Starlings. The Third Schedule names sporting birds which may be killed outside the Close Season; and the Fourth Schedule specifies birds which may not be sold alive unless close-ringed and bred in captivity.

An important feature of the Act is that any species not mentioned in the Schedules is automatically protected. Other clauses in the 1954 Act or the amending Act of 1967 give the Secretary of State power to establish sanctuaries where all birds and their eggs are protected, and arrange for the issue of licences for taking birds for certain scientific and other purposes. There are restrictions on the methods that can legally be used to 'kill or take' any wild bird, and these are of special concern to bird-ringers. A section of the amending Act has made it an offence wilfully to disturb any 'First Schedule' bird on or near a nest containing eggs or unflown young. This clause naturally affects bird photographers, ringers and nest-recorders, who now require a permit from the Natural Environment Research Council if they wish to photograph or 'wilfully disturb', for scientific purposes, species on Schedule 1. A licence is also required for ringing or colour-ringing any wild bird.

The Secretary of State for the Home Department has recently proposed further amendments to the Protection of Birds Act. These appeared in the national newspapers on November 27th 1968, but at the time of going to press the proposals have still to be approved. A list of birds protected under the First Schedule of the 1954–67 Act, and the new amendments, are given below. Copies of the Act may be obtained from H.M. Stationery Office.

### First Schedule—Part I

*Wild birds and their eggs protected by special penalties* AT ALL TIMES

Avocet
Bee-eater (all species)
Bittern (all species)
Bunting, Snow
Bustard
Buzzard, Honey
Chough
Corncrake (Landrail)
Crossbill, Common (England and Wales only)
Curlew, Stone
Diver, Black-throated
Diver, Great Northern
Diver, Red-throated
Eagle (all species)
Goshawk
Grebe, Black-necked
Grebe, Slavonian
Greenshank
Harrier, Hen
Harrier, Marsh

Harrier, Montagu's
Hobby
Hoopoe
Kite
Merlin
Oriole, Golden
Osprey
Owl, Barn (England and Wales only)
Owl, Snowy (Scotland only)
Peregrine
Phalarope, Red-necked
Plover, Little Ringed
Quail, Common
Redstart, Black
Roller
Ruff *and* Reeve
Shrike, Red-backed (England and Wales only)
Sparrow Hawk (England and Wales only)
Spoonbill

| | |
|---|---|
| Stilt, Black-winged | Tit, Bearded |
| Stint, Temminck's | Tit, Crested |
| Swan, Whooper | Warbler, Dartford |
| Swan, Bewick's | Warbler, Marsh |
| Tern, Black | Wren, St Kilda |
| Tern, Roseate | Wryneck |

## *First Schedule—Part II*

*Wild birds and their eggs protected by special penalties* DURING THE CLOSE SEASON

| | |
|---|---|
| Brambling | Common Scoter |
| Godwit, Black-tailed | Garganey |
| Grey Lag Goose (England and Wales only) | Goldeneye |
| | Long-tailed |
| Whimbrel | Scaup |
| Wild Duck of the following species: | Velvet Scoter |

## *Further changes to the Schedules, proposed in 1968*

1. Bustard, Roller, Bewick's Swan and St Kilda Wren to be removed from the First Schedule. These birds would remain protected under the general provisions of the Act, but the special penalty would no longer apply.

2. (a) Fieldfare, Firecrest, Kingfisher, Redwing, Serin, Snowy Owl, Spotted Crake, Wood Lark, Wood Sandpiper, and Savi's Warbler to be added to Part I of the First Schedule.

(b) Brambling and Black-tailed Godwit to be transferred from Part II to Part I of the First Schedule. The effect of this would be to afford these birds special protection at all times.

3. Velvet Scoter and Grey Lag Goose to be removed from Part II of the First Schedule and added to the Third Schedule. These birds would remain protected during the close season, but the special penalties would no longer apply.

4. References in the First Schedule to:

(a) 'Quail, Common' and 'Crossbill, Common' to be amended to 'Quail, European' and 'Crossbill' respectively;

(b) 'Diver, Black-throated', 'Diver, Great Northern', and 'Diver, Red-throated' to be replaced by 'Diver (all species)';

(c) 'Harrier, Hen', 'Harrier, Marsh', and 'Harrier, Montagu's' to be replaced by 'Harrier (all species)'.

However, as Coward pointed out, 'bird protection can never be accomplished by legislation alone'. It has become increasingly clear in recent years that the survival of a rare species is often threatened more by the destruction or contamination of its habitat than by deliberate human persecution. The disastrous effect upon certain birds of persistent toxic chemicals used in agriculture and the constant menace to sea-birds of oil discharged at sea are only two examples of the way in which man is affecting his natural environment and the bird life that forms part of it. The draining of marshes, clearing of wasteland and destruction of hedgerows are other obvious factors influencing our bird population. Fortunately there is increasing co-operation between the Natural Environment Research Council and voluntary organisations such as the Royal Society for the Protection of Birds and the British Trust for Ornithology in research on these problems. Nature Reserves, many of them with special ornithological interest, have been established by the Nature Conservancy, the R.S.P.B., local authorities, or County Naturalists' Trusts, and these sanctuaries and wildfowl refuges are playing a valuable part in maintaining our bird population. The R.S.P.B. 'wetland' reserves, with their control of water levels and experiments in providing artificial nesting and feeding habitats, serve the double purpose of conservation and of education in its widest sense. Every year thousands of people enjoy close views of undisturbed birds, rare and common, from carefully sited hides, and although a few diehard individualists may disdain this kind of organised bird-watching there is no doubt that many visitors to the reserves are awakened to a new appreciation of the beauty and interest of bird life. Television programmes have also done much to stimulate public interest in natural history. The Young Ornithologists' Club, sponsored by the R.S.P.B., is training young bird-watchers, by its literature and field courses, to make and record worthwhile observations. The British Trust for Ornithology and the Wildfowl Trust are enlisting large numbers of amateurs in national enquiries on problems of bird population and distribution, and many local societies are engaged in similar activities on a regional basis.

Yet in spite of these encouraging developments it is still true that when a decision has to be taken about the use of land the views of the naturalist and conservationist usually carry little weight against those of a government department or a commercial or sporting interest. There is no shortage of naturalists' organisations. The need now is for more effective co-ordination of their efforts and a stronger and more influential public opinion to support them. We still need a wider realisation of the truth of Coward's dictum: 'The wild bird is a national asset.'

### Birds Recorded in the British Isles less than 5 Times
#### (to 31st December, 1966)

The figure in brackets is the number of accepted records.

Pied-billed Grebe, *Podilymbus podiceps* (3)
Madeiran Petrel, *Oceanodroma castro* (3)
Frigate Petrel, *Pelagodroma marina* (1)
Bulwer's Petrel, *Bulweria bulwerii* (4)
Kermadec Petrel, *Pterodroma neglecta* (1)
Collared Petrel, *Pterodroma leucoptera* (1)
Capped Petrel, *Pterodroma hasitata* (1)
Magnificent Frigate Bird, *Fregata magnificens* (1)

Black Duck, *Anas rubripes* (3)
Egyptian Vulture, *Neophron percnopterus* (1)
Griffon Vulture, *Gyps fulvus* (3)
Pallid Harrier, *Circus macrourus* (4)
Purple Gallinule, *Porphyrula martinica* (1)
Caspian Plover, *Charadrius asiaticus* (1)
Western Sandpiper, *Calidris mauri* (3)
Stilt Sandpiper, *Micropalama himantopus* (4)
Laughing Gull, *Larus atricilla* (1)
Slender-billed Gull, *Larus genei* (2)
Ross's Gull, *Rhodostethia rosea* (4)
Bridled Tern, *Sterna anaethetus* (4)
Royal Tern, *Sterna maxima* (1)
Great Auk, *Alca impennis* (Extinct since 1844)
Rufous Turtle Dove, *Streptopelia orientalis* (3)
Black-billed Cuckoo, *Coccyzus erythrophthalmus* (4)
American Nighthawk, *Chordeiles minor* (2)
Red-necked Nightjar, *Caprimulgus ruficollis* (1)
Egyptian Nightjar, *Caprimulgus aegyptius* (1)
Little Swift, *Apus affinis* (1)
Needle-tailed Swift, *Hirundapus caudacutus* (4)
Blue-cheeked Bee-eater, *Merops superciliosus* (1)
Calandra Lark, *Melanocorypha calandra* (1)
Bimaculated Lark, *Melanocorypha bimaculata* (1)
White-winged Lark, *Melanocorypha leucoptera* (3)
Penduline Tit, *Remiz pendulinus* (1)
Brown Thrasher, *Toxostoma rufum* (1)
Dusky Thrush, *Turdus eunomus* (3)
Black-throated Thrush, *Turdus ruficollis* (3)
Eye-browed Thrush, *Turdus obscurus* (3)
Siberian Thrush, *Turdus sibiricus* (1)
Olive-backed Thrush, *Catharus ustulatus* (1)
Pied Wheatear, *Oenanthe pleschanka* (3)
Isabelline Wheatear, *Oenanthe isabellina* (1)
Black Wheatear, *Oenanthe leucura* (4)
Red-flanked Bluetail, *Tarsiger cyanurus* (4)
Cetti's Warbler, *Cettia cetti* (2)
River Warbler, *Locustella fluviatilis* (1)
Pallas's Grasshopper Warbler, *Locustella certhiola* (3)
Thick-billed Warbler, *Acrocephalus aedon* (1)
Paddyfield Warbler, *Acrocephalus agricola* (2)
Booted Warbler, *Hippolais caligata* (4)
Orphean Warbler, *Sylvia hortensis* (2)
Sardinian Warbler, *Sylvia melanocephala* (2)
Dusky Warbler, *Phylloscopus fuscatus* (4)
Brown Flycatcher, *Muscicapa latirostris* (2)
Olive-backed Pipit, *Anthus hodgsoni* (2)
Red-eyed Vireo, *Vireo olivaceus* (4)
Black-and-White Warbler, *Mniotilta varia* (1)

Parula Warbler, *Parula americana* (1)
Yellow Warbler, *Dendroica petechia* (1)
Myrtle Warbler, *Dendroica coronata* (2)
Northern Waterthrush, *Seiurus noveboracensis* (1)
Yellowthroat, *Geothlypis trichas* (1)
Bobolink, *Dolichonyx oryzivorus* (1)
Baltimore Oriole, *Icterus galbula* (4)
Summer Tanager, *Piranga rubra* (1)
Citril Finch, *Serinus citrinella* (1)
Rufous-sided Towhee, *Pipilo erythrophthalmus* (1)
Rose-breasted Grosbeak, *Pheucticus ludovicianus* (4)
Slate-coloured Junco, *Junco hyemalis* (1)
White-throated Sparrow, *Zonotrichia albicollis* (4)
Fox Sparrow, *Passerella iliaca* (1)
Song Sparrow, *Passerella melodia* (2)
Pine Bunting, *Emberiza leucocephala* (2)
Rock Bunting, *Emberiza cia* (4)
Spanish Sparrow, *Passer hispaniolensis* (1)

# Order GAVIIFORMES

## Family GAVIIDAE Divers

*Powerful diving birds; bill strong and straight; legs set far back, toes webbed, tarsi flat and capable of rotation.*

## Black-throated Diver *Gavia arctica*

The Black-throated Diver ranges over northern Europe. It nests in the north of Scotland, the Outer Hebrides and the Orkneys, and it has recently begun to breed regularly in south-west Scotland, but numbers are small in all areas. Some birds remain all winter in Scottish waters, but there is a general southerly movement in autumn, when, as on the return in spring, the bird is not infrequent off our coasts and on inland waters; it is scarce in English seas in winter.

There is little difficulty in distinguishing the three divers when in summer plumage; the fourth is very rare. In size the Black-throated Diver is intermediate and may be known by its sharply defined, shield-shaped, purple-black throat, bordered on either side by wavy white streaks. There is a half-collar of black and white dashes above the shield, whereas the Great Northern Diver has in addition a second and larger streaked collar. The throat of the smaller species is red, from which it takes its name. The winter and immature plumages are more difficult, but the ashy-brown upper parts of the Black-throated are usually more uniform than in the Great Northern, and are sprinkled with a few white spots, but not so profusely as in the Red-throated. The best distinction is in the bill, which is less massive than that of the larger bird, and lacks the slight but perceptible uptilt of the Red-throated.

Compared with its bulk, the short wings of the Black-throated Diver look feeble, yet it can fly with speed and power; it flies straight, close to the surface or at a considerable altitude. The neck is outstretched in flight, but looks short and thick, for there is little difference between the width of the head and neck; on the wing the bird is cigar-shaped. It swims low, often with the lower neck awash, and forges forward with great speed, turning its supple neck from side to side. At the least suspicion of danger it further submerges the body, and after a dive will expose head and neck only until sure that the coast is clear; it often raises itself high in the water, flapping its wings, and sometimes points the bill upward as if stretching. Quick though it is on the surface or in the air, its best speed is under water, when it can outstrip swiftly swimming fish, its main food. Many good observers say that it uses its wings as well as its feet when making a spurt, and though it has been seen flying under water, the greatest speed is probably attained when, with wings held close to its sides, it shoots forward with strong lateral and simultaneous strokes. The legs, set far back, move like those of a grebe, and are turned, so as to 'feather' and offer little resistance, when brought forward. The freedom with which the tarsi can be revolved is shown by the habit of raising one foot above the back.

A dive of two minutes has been recorded, but a duration of thirty to fifty seconds is more usual. If the bird is diving to a depth it takes a header, first springing up in the water, but often it sinks with hardly a swirl.

After a dive it almost invariably sips water, and often turns its head and wipes the side of its face and probably the bill against its lower back. The call of the divers is discordant and weird; Seebohm likens it to the scream of a tortured child; it is a melancholy wail, an 'uncouth shriek'.

The nest, for convenience, is close to water, often on a small islet in an inland loch, for the bird cannot really walk; it shuffles on its tarsi and toes, raising its body and throwing it forward an inch or two at a time. Yet if chased on land it can travel fast in a series of quadrupedal bounds, making use of the wings as hands. The eggs, two as a rule, are laid in May in a simple depression, usually without nesting material. They are dark brown or olive, sparsely spotted with black and brown. The nestling has long, sooty-brown down and, like the young grebe, is frequently carried on the back of the parent bird.

In summer the crown and nape are bluish-grey, cheeks sooty and chin black; below the chin is an evenly striped black and white cravat, and below that the black throat, showing a purple or green sheen. On either side of the neck are black and white wavy lines, and the blacks extend to the sides of the breast as a series of lines or dashes. The back, scapulars and wings are blue-black; on the scapulars are rows of rectangular white spots, forming distinct broad bars; on the coverts are a few round white spots. The abdomen is white. The strong bill is blackish, paler in winter; legs black; irides crimson. In winter the head and upper parts are ashy-brown and the underparts white; all the neck decoration is lost, but the top of the head is paler than the back and wings; there is a brownish patch on the side of the neck. Length, 25 in. Wing, 12·8 in. Tarsus, 3·1 in. *Plates 2, 3 and 162.*

## Great Northern Diver                                    *Gavia immer*

As a winter visitor to British seas the Great Northern Diver is not uncommon; it has not been proved that it breeds in the British Isles, even in the Shetlands, though a few non-breeding, apparently mature birds occasionally remain in northern waters for the summer. Iceland is the nearest breeding station to Britain. Birds have been seen off the English coast in August, but usually they do not appear until October, and most have returned north before the end of April, stragglers only passing in May.

Seebohm's 'as big as a goose' gives a very rough idea of the size of this handsome diver, yet it certainly is the size which commands attention when it appears, as it often does, on inland waters and swims amongst more familiar fowl. The bird in breeding plumage, which is usually lost in September, differs from the Black-throated Diver; its head is glossy black, not slate-grey, and it has two half-collars of white spots on the neck instead of one, the lower and additional one being the larger. Though, when in winter dress, the large size and heavy, dagger-shaped bill are striking, such characters are of little use when it is solitary, and the bird frequently travels alone. The majority of the birds which visit inland waters in winter are immature, and those at sea give few opportunities of close observation as they bob about on the waves. A mature winter Great Northern is less uniform than the Black-throated on the upper parts, and has a more barred appearance. The crown looks dark. It can be told from the rare White-billed Diver by the colour of the bill, which even in winter is darker, and by the slight downward curve towards the tip of the upper mandible, which is straight in the White-billed and appears to tilt upward.

Except when on migration the 'Loon', as it is called on the east coast as well as in America, is little on the wing, but owing to its large size its appearance in flight is even more remarkable than that of the Black-throated. The wings, set far back, look inadequate to carry the torpedo-shaped body, yet the bird travels with speed. The thick neck, pointed bill, and position of wings prevent confusion with a goose, and even with its nearer but much smaller relation, the Great Crested Grebe. The short legs are trailed and usually point inward, and are only exceptionally extended on either side of the tail. The normal swimming position is deep in the water, the lower neck awash; if the bird is alarmed the back vanishes also, but when unsuspicious it will ride buoyantly, rolling like a grebe as it preens its plumage, nibbling at the feathers after moistening its bill. Often it raises itself upright in the water to flap its wings. When indolently floating, the short thick neck is carried in a graceful curve, or rests on the shoulders; frequently a foot is raised above the back and shaken in the air. If swimming fast it holds the neck and head well forward, and occasionally extended along the water, a position assumed by the Great Crested Grebe during nuptial display. In ordinary slow progression on the surface the leg strokes are alternate, but when diving or swimming at great speed they are simultaneous and lateral, in the same plane as the body. The dive is its highest accomplishment; its existence depends upon great speed under water, the power to overtake swiftly swimming fish. The method differs according to circumstances: it may spring forward, almost clear of the water, to take a deep header, and at other times submerge its body until the head and neck alone are visible. Then, dipping these, it slides forward, hardly disturbing the surface. As a rule, during the dive, the wings are held close to the sides. The average duration of dive is about forty seconds, but Coward recorded dives of two and three minutes. Large fish are brought up to be eaten and are swallowed head first. Crustaceans and cephalopods are also eaten. A little water is usually sipped immediately after the dive. Rising from the surface is only accomplished after thrashing the water with its wings, and it has not been seen to rise from the land, where indeed it can only shuffle along in a prone attitude. The Loon has the same distressful wail as other divers, and a milder, more musical love-call, as well as a deep guttural growl, which may be uttered by winter birds.

The spring moult begins in December, but full dress may not be attained until May. The head and neck are then black, glossed with purple and green; under the chin and on the sides of the neck are bands of white streaked with black, and below the black on the sides of the white breast are wavy slate-grey lines. The upper parts are glossy black, plentifully spotted with white; on the mantle the spots are large and square, arranged in regular bands. The quills and tail are black. The bill is blackish, paler in winter, legs black and irides crimson. In winter the only indication of the throat adornment is a dark patch on the side of the neck; the head and nape are sooty, and the upper parts ashy-grey with obscure spots, giving a mottled appearance. The tail is tipped with white. Young birds have the crown and nape grey, the face suffused with brown; the feathers of the upper parts show pale edges, often as regular but indistinct bars. Length, 31 in. Wing, 14 in. Tarsus, 3·6 in. (*Plates 2 and 4.*)

## White-billed Diver                                    *Gavia adamsii*

This rare vagrant from arctic Russia and Siberia has been recorded about twenty times on or near the east coast of Britain between Shetland and Yorkshire. The green and purple gloss on the head varies individually, and the number of neck streaks is not constant, but the primary shafts are, as a rule, whitish in this bird and brown in the commoner species. This bird is, however, larger, and has a deeper and more massive bill, which at all seasons is yellowish-white; the colour alone is not enough, since many winter Great Northerns have very pale bills, but in the White-billed bird the upper mandible is straight, and the lower inclines sharply upward from the well-marked 'angle', giving the whole bill a suggestion of uptilt. Length, 33 in.

## Red-throated Diver                                    *Gavia stellata*

The Red-throated Diver breeds in the north of Europe and is a common winter visitor and passage migrant to the British Isles. It nests in the north of Scotland and many Scottish islands, and one or two pairs breed annually in the north of Ireland.

Much commoner than the other divers, this bird can be identified at any season by its smaller size and slender uptilted bill; it is about the size of a Mallard. The vinaceous red patch on its throat, from which it gets its name, is sufficient for identification in summer, and in winter the white speckles on its back set it apart from other divers. Many of its habits, though in the main similar to those of its congeners, approach those of grebes; it is a graceful, active, playful bird when on the water, assuming quaint but never distorted attitudes as it rolls and gambols. Though it swims low and when anxious submerges its body, it floats buoyantly, resting with the head on its back, the bill pointed towards its tail. It is sociable, and high flights of small parties are not unusual; from these it descends obliquely, sometimes almost vertically, hurtling down with turns and twists, but changing the angle of descent before it strikes the water, ploughing up a wave. The flight is rather grebe-like, and its head is carried a little below the level of the long axis of the body. The wings are sometimes, but not always, used under water, and the speed and skill when chasing fish is little inferior to that of more powerful divers. Dives of a minute and a half have been recorded. Fish are its chief food, though crustaceans and other aquatic animals are eaten; large numbers of medium-sized fish have been found in the gullet. All the divers have one habit, which is also common to the Cormorant: as they swim on the surface they sink the head below, and thus avoid the confusion of surface ripples. When they sight the prey they at once dive and follow it.

The usual barking *kark, kark* is distinct from other diver notes, but it has a loud wailing cry, and a guttural note of alarm. The Red-throated, more frequently than other divers, assumes the upright pose, though its normal method of progression on land is with breast to ground. It frequently stands when turning the eggs. The largest numbers pass northward in April and May, and even in March some have advanced far towards nuptial dress. The date of the assumption of summer or winter plumage is irregular; even late in October many still show red on the throat. In June and July few remain off the English shores, but some appear about the middle of August, and immature birds have been known to linger through the summer.

The nest, often on an island in a freshwater lake or pool, is never far from water, and, as is also the case with the Black-throated, there is a well-flattened pathway from the landing place to the nest, smoothed by the bird's advancing breast, which during the breeding season is stained with peaty soil. The egg is smaller but similar to that of the Black-throated Diver, the spots on its dark ground being few; two are often laid, late in May or in June, but single eggs are occasionally found. Untidy nests of grass or other vegetation are not infrequent, though the eggs may be in a mere depression in the herbage. Sitting birds, if scared, crouch on the nest with head and neck extended, and are wonderfully inconspicuous. The nestling, clad in dark grey down, has a small white patch above and in front of the eye, and a short triangular bill.

The plumage of the adult bird in summer is singularly beautiful; its graceful movements show off the white and black lines on the back of the sinuous neck. The head and neck are soft, pale blue-grey, streaked on the crown and nape; the throat is red; back and wings ashy-grey, slightly spotted with white, and underparts white. The bill is grey, the legs black, the irides ruby-red. In winter the chin, lower part of the face, and front of the neck, as well as the underparts, are white, and the upper parts are a browner grey, profusely speckled with white. Immature birds have throats and flanks mottled with grey. Length, 22 in. Wing, 11 in. Tarsus, 2·6 in. (*Plates 4, 5 and 162.*)

# Order PODICIPITIFORMES

## Family PODICIPITIDAE Grebes

*Slender diving birds; bill straight; legs posterior, no visible tail; toes lobed; tarsi flat, capable of rotation.*

### Great Crested Grebe                                    *Podiceps cristatus*

Few once-persecuted birds have made more rapid recovery than the Great Crested Grebe; it was at one time slaughtered for its satin breast, 'grebe-fur', and was almost exterminated. It has not merely increased in its old haunts but has extended its range. Censuses taken in 1931 and 1965 showed that the population in Great Britain had risen from about 2800 to about 4500 in the thirty-four years. The most densely populated counties in 1965 were Cheshire, Staffordshire, Warwickshire, Norfolk and Essex. No Great Crested Grebes were found in Cornwall, Devon, Cambridgeshire and Northumberland, in several counties in Wales and in the north of Scotland. In Ireland numbers are found in the north, especially on Lough Neagh, but over much of the country it is scarce or absent. Some of the increase in England, especially in the southern counties and midlands, is due to the creation of new reservoirs and flooded gravel pits.

In autumn there is a movement of migrants along our coasts and many inland waters are deserted in early winter; but unless they are frozen out some birds will remain on fresh water through the winter. Passage birds in small flocks appear as late as May, when the residents are nesting.

At any season this bird is distinctive; the erectile 'ear-tufts' and frill of summer have no counterpart, and in winter its slender build and large size prevent confusion with other grebes. It swims low in the water, often with the lower neck awash. Though the bird frequently rests its head well back on the shoulders, gracefully curving the neck, the usual position of the slim neck is rather stiffly erect; it appears slender below the ample frill. It can swim fast on the surface, the head forward, the straight neck inclined at about 45°, but if speed is necessary the bird dives; underwater progression, when the legs strike out simultaneously and laterally, is wonderfully swift. Except during courtship, when it takes frequent short flights, it is little on the wing, though it travels from mere to mere, or to the sea, flying high. In flight a white wing-bar is very conspicuous. The outstretched neck sags a little, but is raised, as are the feet, when the bird alights, striking the water with its breast. Grebes resting on the water frequently shake a leg above the back, or roll, their satiny underparts flashing, as they preen their feathers. The dive is almost invariably easy, a quick slip under water with little surface disturbance, though occasionally the bird makes a forward spring. The dive usually lasts from twenty to thirty seconds. The leg action is quick, but its power is more impressive than its speed; in the forward stroke the lobed toes lie together and the flattened tarsi are turned so as to cut the water; in the back stroke both expanded toes and flat tarsi grip the water. Newts, molluscs and insects are eaten, but fish are the mainstay, and on fish the young are fed. The Grebe is little on land, but it walks easily and gracefully on the nest, its body well forward, and its tarsi raised at an angle.

The Great Crested Grebe is a noisy bird, especially in the pairing season. The most frequent call is a repeated *jik, jik, jik*, often *jicker, jicker*, uttered by either sex, and a loud discordant *gorrr* is common. This is often uttered by a male when, thrashing the water with its wings, it chases a rival. There is also a pleasant twanging banjo note and a rasping whirr. The hunger-cry of the young is a wheezy and insistent *tcheep, tcheep, tcheep*. Strange courtship antics begin in January, even before the frill is developed; the ear-tufts are never really lost; the ruff is most pronounced in the male. Often two birds approach with necks stretched along the water, then rear themselves, breast to breast, stretching the necks to full extent and spreading wide the frills, whilst they gently fence with their bills. One or both will dive for weed and dangle it at the other, suggesting nest construction. During the upright caress both will suddenly dip their necks until the crown nearly touches the back; the head is usually vigorously shaken after the fencing. When the male approaches the female with head depressed, the ruff is closed and the ear-tufts at times loll over like wattles. Eggs normally are laid from April until August; second broods have been recorded, but first broods frequently come to nought. The nest is usually a floating mass of wet decaying weed, moored amongst reeds, lilies or other aquatic vegetation, but where reed cover is lacking eggs may occasionally be laid on a dry bank. The green or blue tinge of the elongated egg is hidden by a chalky outer covering, which soon is permanently stained with vegetable juices. When disturbed the sitting bird raises itself, and with rapid right and left pecks covers the eggs with nesting material, then slides into the water and dives. Four is the normal number of eggs. Both birds incubate and tend the young, carrying them at first in a cradle formed by the slightly upraised wings; the pose of the parent is then distinctly higher than usual. The nestling has close cinnamon down striped with glossy black, the stripes most distinct on the neck; the crown is pinkish-buff surrounded by black, and in front is a small bare vermilion triangle.

The adult bird is greyish-black on the top of the head and back of the neck; the upper parts elsewhere are greyish-brown, and the under silky-white. There is a white wing-bar. In summer the tippet is rich chestnut shading to deep brown. The bill is yellowish, the legs olive-green, and irides crimson. The frill is lost in August, leaving a white face and eye-stripe, and begins to show again in December. Immature birds are ashy-brown with longitudinal stripes on the neck. Full plumage is attained in the second winter. Length, 19 in. Wing, 7·5 in. Tarsus, 2·5 in. (*Plates 5, 7 and 162.*)

**Red-necked Grebe**  *Podiceps grisegena*
The Red-necked Grebe is a regular but not numerous winter visitor from

eastern Europe, scarce on the west side of Great Britain and in Ireland. It is not known to have nested in Britain and is a less frequent visitor to inland waters than its congeners; during winter it is usually a salt-water grebe. A few reach us in August, but it is, on the whole, a cold-weather visitor. Most return in March or April, when some are in full nuptial dress.

In summer dress the distinctive characters are the warm chestnut neck, and the grey cheeks, bordered above by white, just below the eye. The bird is a little smaller than the Great Crested, and considerably larger than the Slavonian, the next in size. In winter, when it looks very black and white, the lower part of the face is still a good character, the white in strong contrast to the dark cap which extends to the eye. The neck is grey, whereas in the Great Crested there is a white stripe above the eye, and the throat and neck look white. It is a stockier, less slender bird than the Great Crested, and its stout, short neck is carried well erect. A broad white border to the wing is very conspicuous in flight, and the forward edge of the wing is pale as far as the carpal joint. The swimming, diving and feeding habits closely agree with those of the Great Crested Grebe, and its voice, seldom heard in Britain, is at breeding time peculiarly strident and loud; it is less averse to terrestrial progression and has been seen to walk and hop in an upright posture. The food consists of crustaceans, molluscs, fish and aquatic insects. It often brings its food to the surface before swallowing it.

The upper part of the head and back of the neck are glossy black in summer, when the ear-tufts are prominent; there is no ruff. The chin and cheeks are suffused with pearl-grey, bordered from bill to eye with pure white. The upper parts are greyish-brown, sides of neck and breast rich chestnut, flanks rufous-grey, and the rest of the underparts silky white with underlying grey mottles. The bill is black, yellow at the base; the legs greenish-black. The ear-tufts are much reduced in winter, though the bird retains a flat-headed appearance, and all the neck colour is lost. For some time young birds show traces of the neck streaks. Length, 17 in. Wing, 7 in. Tarsus, 2 in. (*Plate 6.*)

### Slavonian Grebe          *Podiceps auritus*

The Slavonian or Horned Grebe, which has a northern range in Europe, Asia and America, breeds regularly in small but gradually increasing numbers in the north of Scotland. As a winter visitor it may occur anywhere in the British Isles. The autumn passage lasts from September to November; from April to June return movements are in progress.

The Slavonian Grebe likes calm water, inland or in estuaries and sheltered bays. It swims rather high in the water with the neck erect, and if uneasy, glances nervously right and left. This is especially noticeable in birds near their nests, when the straight neck is often slightly inclined backwards. The erectile horns are tufts of chestnut feathers, extending from the eye and projecting above the nape; some of these are long and silky in texture and look golden or straw-yellow in sunlight. The neck and back in summer are deep chestnut, coppery in strong light, the cheeks and chin are velvet-black, and there is a frill or tippet, shorter than that of the Great Crested Grebe, and frequently expanded. When swimming away from the observer, glancing over its shoulder, the bird shows a yellow nape divided by a dark line.

In winter both the Slavonian and Black-necked Grebes look black and white on the water and may be confused, but the bill of the former is stout, and though the culmen is straight it bends down at the tip, whereas in the Black-necked the slender bill has a distinct upward tilt. Late in March some are in winter dress, though early in the month others have attained nuptial plumes. Mature birds in winter have very white cheeks, giving the dark head a capped appearance; in the Black-necked Grebe the cheeks are dusky below the eye, and the contrast less striking.

The Slavonian Grebe readily takes wing, and in flight the neck may be carried straight or sag slightly, like that of the Great Crested. The wing-bar— the innermost secondaries are white, there is no white on the primaries—is broad and conspicuous on the open wing, but usually shows only as a white line when the bird is swimming. The dives are quick and expert. In the breeding season the male has a varied vocabulary, including a rippling trill rather like that of the Little Grebe. The nest is a mass of decomposing weed, often built in *Equisetum* or other aquatic vegetation. Four eggs, laid in June, are usual; they are greenish-white at first, drab later. The young are striped brown and white and have a bare red patch on the forehead.

The adult in breeding plumage has a black head with a broad golden stripe through the eye, forming projecting horns at the back of the head, chestnut neck and flanks, dark brown back with a broad white bar on the wing, silky-white underparts. In winter upper parts are blackish, underparts white; the black cap does not extend below the eye. The bill and legs are blue-grey. Length, 13 in. Wing, 5·5 in. Tarsus, 1·75 in. (*Plates 6 and 8*.)

## Black-necked Grebe                                         *Podiceps nigricollis*

The Black-necked Grebe nests in central and southern Europe and is partially migratory. In the British Isles it is a winter visitor, passage migrant and resident. It breeds regularly in very small numbers in central Scotland and has nested sporadically in widely separated localities in England and Wales. It no longer breeds in Ireland, although there was a large colony there earlier in this century.

The Black-necked Grebe is slightly smaller than the Slavonian, and when swimming is, like a Dabchick, very broad in the stern, but carries its neck more erect. The distinctive summer characters, in addition to black neck and upper parts, are the silky golden-straw feathers which extend across the ear-coverts, fanned out over the cheeks, and the rich copper flanks. In winter the slender, uptilted bill distinguishes it from the Slavonian Grebe. Further characters are the slightly duskier neck and the black of the crown extending below the eye. The bird swims buoyantly, unless alarmed, sitting high; the erectile feathers of the crown usually rise abruptly from the bill, giving the appearance of a very high forehead, but there are no distinct ear-tufts. The duration of timed dives ranges from nine to fifty seconds. Molluscs and aquatic insects are eaten, and small fish are sometimes given to the young. Insects are captured on the surface with the rapid right and left snatches of a Phalarope. When feeding on caddis worms the bird bites and shakes the case until the larva is ejected. The calls are soft, and the trill is not unlike that of the Slavonian Grebe, but not so loud. The hunger-cry of the young is milder and quieter than that of the Great Crested. The nuptial display has much similarity to that of the larger bird; there is the same upright pose, breast facing breast, gentle toying with one another's bills, dipping of the head and neck, and approach with necks outstretched on the water.

The nest, similar to that of the Dabchick, is a large collection of decaying weed moored amongst pond-weed, bog-bean or other aquatic vegetation. Three or four eggs are normal; they are of the same blue tint as those of the Great Crested, and are coated with a chalky deposit which is speedily stained with brown and green. They are laid in May or June. The nestling is ashy-grey above and white below; the neck and head are streaked, there is a bare patch on the crown and the bill is lead-blue. At first the parents carry the young, though they are often shaken off, and Coward saw one old bird repeatedly duck a nestling, as if trying to induce it to dive; they will, when young, dive a little for food.

In summer the head, neck, breast and back are glossy black, and the wings have a greenish sheen; the cheeks are crossed by silky straw-coloured plumes; the flanks are coppery chestnut, and the underparts white. The male is distinctly larger and has more pronounced ear-coverts. The bill is blue-black, pinkish at the base, the legs blackish-green, irides red. In winter the head, often to below the level of the eye, the back of the neck, and mantle are brownish-black and the flanks mottled with grey; except for a dusky band on the lower neck the underparts are white. In the young in autumn the cheeks and necks are dusky. Length, 12 in. Wing, 5·7 in. Tarsus, 1·5 in. (*Plate 6.*)

### Little Grebe                                              *Podiceps ruficollis*

Dabchick is a widely used name for the Little Grebe, a familiar resident in most parts of the British Isles. It ranges through central and southern Europe, and is partially migratory, though it may be that its frequent collision with lighthouse lanterns is due to nocturnal wandering rather than regular migration. Frost drives the Dabchick to the coast, but it also visits estuaries and tidal gutters for food, independently of weather.

The smallest of the grebes is much rounder and squatter than its congeners, and usually swims with the neck curved; it is, however, the absence of tail, and its habit of fluffing up the feathers of the hinder end—tail-coverts by courtesy—which give it a characteristically bluff finish. In flight its large feet project beyond its 'blunt end'. Its bill is short and stout. The bird is browner than the Black-necked Grebe, and has neither tufts nor frill; in winter it is still browner on the upper parts. It flies frequently, with a quick flutter of short, rather rounded wings, and if disturbed near the bank, will fly for a dozen yards and dive immediately it drops. The white on the inner webs of the secondaries hardly shows in flight, and not at all when swimming; it is concealed by the overlap. It is a persistent diver, slipping under without surface disturbance, or with a vigorous plunge, kicking up a little shower of spray with its lobed feet. Dives may last twenty-five seconds, or the bird may reappear immediately. In clear and shallow water its movements may be observed; the wings are not used, even when turning; they are tightly held to the sides. On the surface, when not hurried, the foot strokes are alternate, but under water it progresses in a series of rapid jerks, vigorously rowing itself along. At the beginning of the stroke the feet are at right angles to the body; at the finish they almost meet behind the so-called tail, and the half rotation of tarsi and toes, already described, is very distinct. So lateral is the stroke that a bird swimming at the bottom does not stir the mud. Air bubbles clinging to the feathers give it a silvery, filmy appearance under water.

After a dive a Dabchick, if nervous, protrudes the head and body only, and often swims to the side, sheltering under the bank with the bill alone above the surface, where it holds itself in position by gentle circular strokes. Birds thus hiding may be taken from the water. Little Grebes can stand and walk well, with the tarsi slightly bent. Freshwater molluscs, crustaceans and insects are the main food, but small fish are captured, and occasionally unwisely: more than one bird has been found dead with the gill spines of a bull-head, *Cottus gobio*, embedded in its mouth. The call is short, a soft, subdued note, not unlike the whistle of the Teal, but the rippling trill is loud and clear, a rapidly repeated double note, which begins suddenly and runs down the scale.

The nest, sometimes floating, is a large collection of weeds, mostly brought from under water, and the eggs are normally covered when the bird is absent. Four to six white, but soon stained, eggs of the usual grebe type are laid in April; but second broods are common. The young have brown and black down streaked with white, and can dive as soon as they take to the water, but prefer to snuggle under the parental scapulars. The old birds dive when the young are on their backs, but the little ones rise like corks and anxiously look for the reappearance of their bearers, when they scramble back over the parent's tail.

The head and upper parts are dark greyish-brown, almost black, in summer; the chin and breast are black, cheeks, throat and sides of the neck warm chestnut, and the flanks brown. The underparts below the breast are variable, blackish but with a silky, silvery sheen which gives the impression of grey. The bill is blackish horn, pale at the tip and base, and a fold of skin at the gape is greenish-yellow. The legs are dark olive. The upper parts are lighter and browner in winter, and the underparts, including the lower face, are silvery-white, suffused with brown on the lower neck and breast. Young birds have dusky streaks on the head and are an even lighter brown. Length, 10 in. Wing, 4 in. Tarsus, 1·25 in. (*Plates 6, 8 and 162.*)

# Order PROCELLARIIFORMES

## Family DIOMEDEIDAE Albatrosses

*Large; wings very long; semi-tubular nostrils on sides of long bill; anterior toes webbed, no hind toe.*

### Black-browed Albatross                                        *Diomedea melanophrys*

This rare vagrant from southern seas has occurred in the British Isles about a dozen times. One frequented the Bass Rock through the summer of 1967. It is distinguished from commoner British sea-birds by its size, with a 6- or 7-ft. wing-span, and gliding flight, and from other albatrosses when adult by its yellow bill. In the mature bird the back and wings are brownish-black, the tail is grey, and the head, neck, and underparts are white. A blackish band above the eye, less conspicuous in young birds, is the 'brow'. The bill is yellowish, as are the legs in old birds. Length, 29 in. Wing, 19 in. Tarsus, 3·3 in.

## Family HYDROBATIDAE Storm Petrels

*Small, long-winged, web-footed birds; bill short, hooked, nostrils in one double tube.*

### Wilson's Petrel                                               *Oceanites oceanicus*

Wilson's Petrel inhabits the Antarctic and migrates north at the approach of the southern winter; thus, when it reaches our islands, which it does on very rare occasions, its visits are in summer. Most occurrences have been in the south, but it has reached the Hebrides and Ireland. It is a long-legged, square-tailed petrel with yellow-webbed toes pattering over the waves. Its alternate gliding and fluttering flight is distinctive. Its plumage is black, with the white lower back of other petrels, but the longer legs and yellow webs on the black toes are distinctive. The tail is variable, usually square, sometimes slightly forked. Length, 7 in.

### Leach's Petrel                                               *Oceanodroma leucorrhoa*

The North Atlantic breeding range of Leach's Petrel is more to the north and west than that of the next species, the Storm Petrel. In the British Isles it breeds in the Outer Hebrides and Shetlands, and sporadically on a few islands off the west coast of Ireland. Yet the bird, on the whole, is more frequently seen off our shores, for a number pass south in autumn over our seas; westerly gales often drive them inshore, and not infrequently whirl them helplessly far inland. The great 'wreck' at the end of October 1952 caused several thousand casualties.

The species was formerly known as Leach's Fork-tailed Petrel, for it is the decidedly forked tail which distinguishes it from the Storm, though not from all its congeners. It is larger, but in the main its sooty dress and white back patch agree with those of the Storm; the median wing-coverts are pale brown, and show on the flying bird as two brown patches converging above the white rump. The habit of picking food from the water, holding its long wings elevated above its back as it almost alights, paddling with its feet, and the nature of its oily planktonic food agree with those described for the Storm Petrel below, but its bounding, erratic flight is distinctive, and it does not follow ships. Purring and crooning sounds are heard at night in the breeding colonies.

The nest hole is generally excavated by the male bird, though a natural hollow under a boulder may be used. The nest chamber is usually lined with grass, roots or moss. The single egg, laid in June, resembles that of the Storm Petrel but is larger. Both parents incubate, in shifts of three or four days each, for a period of fifty days or more, and the fledging period is even longer. The nestling has long sooty-black down, darker than that of the Storm.

Both adults and immatures have upper parts sooty-brown, but not so dark as the Storm Petrel; lower rump and upper tail-coverts white, but central feathers greyish. A pale band on the wing-coverts is noticeable in flight. The bill and legs are black. Length, 8·5 in. Wing, 6 in. Tarsus, 0·9 in. (*Plates 9 and 162.*)

### Storm Petrel                                          *Hydrobates pelagicus*

The sailor is well acquainted with the Storm Petrel for the bird follows in the steamer's wake in any weather. During the greater part of the year the ocean is the Petrel's home; it is a bird of the eastern Atlantic. Its British breeding colonies are on islands off the Scottish and Irish coast, and on some in Wales and the Scillies. There is a general southward movement in autumn, but the bird is scattered far and wide in winter, and only continuous bad weather brings it to land. Strong gales not only drive it ashore sometimes in such numbers as to be classed as 'wrecks', but often carry it far inland, dropping it, storm battered, in towns or other unlikely spots for an oceanic bird, where starvation hastens the end.

The Storm Petrel is a small sooty bird with a white patch above and below the base of the tail; the tail is square, not forked as in its nearest allies. Its wings are long and narrow; its flight buoyant, swift and erratic; as it follows a steamer, a frequent habit, it looks like a long-winged House Martin, the white back patch helping the resemblance. It swerves and twists, and occasionally lowers its long legs and patters on the surface; from this the sailors coined the name Little Peter striving to walk on the waves. During this pattering, half-running flight it dips its head for food. It will eat oily matter, skimming it from the surface. One bird was kept for a few days, and fed on oil floating on water in a saucer; the bird flew over it like a Swallow and skimmed off the oil. The chief oceanic food, however, consists of small crustaceans and cephalopods, and for these, churned up by the screw, it follows a steamer, and not, like a gull, hoping for scraps. In a rough sea it swims easily, rising on the advancing wave and apparently glissading to the trough. Its wing-beats are not hurried, it skims and glides, beating deliberately, more like a tern than an auk. It is nocturnal in its movements on land, where it progresses by fluttering flight with toes just touching the ground. It rests on the full length of the tarsus.

R. M. Lockley has given a careful account of the nesting habits of the Storm Petrel on Skokholm. The birds arrive late in April or in May, and eggs are laid towards the end of that month or in June, in burrows in turf, cracks in rocks or walls or amongst boulders. The nest, when any is made, is a small collection of grasses. The chalky-white egg is usually zoned with fine reddish specks. Though the birds sometimes call on the wing, most of the nocturnal sounds come from the nest—'a harsh, purring, ūrr, long sustained, and ending abruptly with chikka, almost, indeed, a hiccough'. Incubation lasts nearly six weeks and the fledging period averages nearly nine. The young birds are not always fed by the parents every night; they can starve for six days, and when fully fledged are deserted by their parents and find their own way to the sea. When incubating, the old birds leave the nests for nocturnal exercise or for food. The food for the young is regurgitated oily matter, probably half-digested squid. An oily smell pervades the colony, and the bird itself reeks of oil; if handled, its first act of retaliation is a jet of oil, squirted from beak or nostrils.

The plumage of both adults and immatures is sooty-brown, paler on the flanks and under wing-coverts; the lower rump and upper tail-coverts are white. A narrow whitish wing-bar is visible on birds in fresh plumage. The bill and legs are black. The long down of the nestling is sooty-brown above, hoary on underparts. Adult length, 6·5 in. Wing, 4·7 in. Tarsus, 0·9 in. (*Plates 9 and 162.*)

## Family PROCELLARIIDAE Petrels and Shearwaters

*Long-winged petrels; bill with united tubular nostrils.*

### Manx Shearwater                                         *Puffinus puffinus*

The Manx Shearwater breeds in the Scilly Isles, on several islands off the coasts of Wales and Scotland, including the Orkneys and Shetlands, and on some islands and a few headlands on the coast of Ireland, as well as in Iceland and the Faeroes. British birds, and probably passage migrants from further north, are common off our shores in autumn, and numbers are sometimes picked up inland. Southward migration is a well-marked movement; few birds are seen in British waters in midwinter.

The Manx Shearwater, no longer an inhabitant of the island from which it gets its name, is nevertheless a common bird in the Irish Sea; indeed, it is well distributed and often common in most of our coastal waters in summer, even at a distance from any known breeding ground. Its black upper and white underparts are a little like those of an auk, but its long, slender bill, with a strong hooked tip, and its narrow pointed wings are those of a petrel. Even on the water it looks more slender, has finer lines than the stout Guillemot or Puffin, and on the wing it is a very different bird as it skims or shears the waves. It glides upward, cants over at right angles, swoops with one wing just missing a crest, then skims the surface, rising and falling with the waves, then up again, now right wing up, now left. There is little wing-beat, but an easy loitering glide; it does not hurry. Often, however, strings of Manx Shear-waters pass, bent on business; these birds fly straighter and with greater speed, but their longer wings are never rapidly moved like those of auks; the birds swing along and glide with easy grace, undulating just above the waves.

Breeding birds may travel five or six hundred miles from the nesting colony to feed, and R. M. Lockley's homing experiments have shown the bird's astonishing navigational ability over distances of hundreds or even thousands of miles. The bird is diurnal in its feeding habits at sea, but strictly nocturnal at the breeding colony. Large rafts of adults assemble offshore in the evening and fly in to the nest holes about two hours after sunset. The food, which consists of small fish and molluscs, is either picked off the surface as the bird paddles over the water like a petrel, or is caught by shallow dives.

The nests are in burrows in turf, often on steep slopes, in cracks or caves in rocks, or amongst the debris of scree and fallen rock. The single egg is white and measures about 2·3 by 1·6 in.; it is usually laid in May. Some eggs are within easy reach, others fully 5 ft. from the entrance. The old birds peck at an intruding hand with chortling expostulation, but when taken from the hole utter no complaint; they bite, the hooked nail giving a powerful nip, and the sharp claws painful scratches. The young are fed on oily regurgitated food, and are fat balls of long blue-grey down, with a fluffy tuft on the head. When placed on the ground the young crawl on all fours, using the wing stumps and the weak tarsi.

The bird is generally silent at sea, but at night it is noisy at the nesting colony. The calls vary, some being harsh and scolding, others soft and crooning: *It-y-corka, kitti-koo-roo, kok-a-kok* (very quick), *kok-a-roo-roo, It-is-yor folt*. At the end of August departure begins, and from the first week in September many are moving in strings along our shores, and large numbers cross the land, dropping weaklings in places far from the coast. R. M. Lockley's observations on Skokholm show an incubation period of about fifty-two to fifty-four days, and fledging lasting seventy-two to seventy-three days. The last young leave about the middle of October, after being deserted by their parents for about a fortnight.

The adult Manx Shearwater is sooty-black above and white beneath; the bill is blackish; the legs pink. Length, 16 in. Wing, 9·5 in. Tarsus, 1·75 in. (*Plates 9 and 162.*)

The Balearic Shearwater, the west Mediterranean race of the Manx, which occurs off our coasts in autumn and winter, has the upper parts browner and the underparts dusky.

### Little Shearwater                                    *Puffinus assimilis*

About a dozen examples of this species have been recorded in the British Isles, mostly belonging to the race breeding in the Azores, Canaries and Madeira. This shearwater resembles the Manx but is smaller, has bluish, not pinkish feet and the black crown does not extend below the eye. It has a rapid, fluttering flight between short spells of gliding. Length, 11 in.

The West Atlantic race, *P.a. l'herminieri*, regarded by some authorities as a separate species under the name of Audubon's Shearwater, has been recorded once in Sussex. It is slightly larger than the eastern form and has a longer, heavier bill.

### Great Shearwater                                    *Puffinus gravis*

So far the only known breeding place of the Great Shearwater is the Tristan da Cunha group in the south Atlantic. In our spring—the southern autumn—the bird migrates north and occurs throughout the Atlantic, even to the Greenland seas. Apparently the northward movements of this oceanic bird are even further from the shore than on its return, for in June and July it is fairly frequent off the Outer Hebrides, St Kilda and Rockall. From August until November it passes south, usually well offshore; it is commoner off the western than eastern coasts, though an almost annual visitor off Yorkshire. The Great Shearwater looks dark brown on the back and shows a clearly defined dark brown cap with white cheeks and an almost complete white collar. White shows at the base of the dark tail. As they careen a dusky patch is visible near the vent; otherwise the underparts are white. The back is distinctly brown, not black like that of the Manx Shearwater. The flight resembles that of other shearwaters, with long glides, sometimes of a mile or more. It alights on the water or plunges into it to feed. Squids form an important part of its diet.

The upper parts are ash-brown, except for the white tail-coverts; the quills and tail-band are blackish-brown, and the sides of the face and underparts white, mottled with brown on the abdomen; the under tail-coverts are sooty. The bill is blackish, the legs dark brown. Length, 18 in. Wing, 12·7 in. (*Plate 9*.)

### Cory's Shearwater                                    *Procellaria diomedea*

Cory's Shearwater breeds chiefly in the Mediterranean and appears, usually singly or in very small numbers, off the coasts of south-west England and Ireland in autumn, more rarely off other coasts and at other seasons. It is a large, heavily built bird, lighter in colour than the other shearwaters seen in British seas. Its grey-brown hood merges gradually into the white throat, and it lacks the white collar of the Great Shearwater. The underparts are white,

PLATE 2    *Above :* Black-throated Diver, p1

*Below :* Great Northern Diver, p2

PLATE 3

Black-throated
Diver, pl

Photo: J. B. and S. Bottomley

PLATE 4

*Above:* Great Northern Diver (winter), p2

*Below:* Red-throated Diver, p4

Photo: Sidney J. Clarke

PLATE 5    *Above :* Red-throated Diver, p4

*Below :* Great Crested Grebe, p6

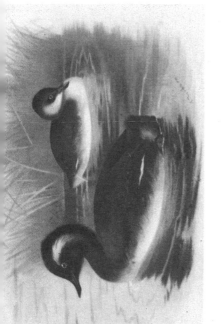

PLATE 6

*Above left :* Black-
necked Grebe (summer
and winter), p9
*Above right :* Red-
necked Grebe (summer
and winter), p7

*Below left :* Little Grebe
(summer and winter),
p10
*Below right :* Slavonian
Grebe (summer and
winter), p8

Photo: *J. B. and S. Bottoml*

PLATE 7     Great Crested Grebe, p6

Photo: J. B. and S. Bottomley

*Above*: Little Grebe, p10

PLATE 8

*Below*: Slavonian Grebe, p8

Photo: J. B. and S. Bottomley

PLATE 9

PLATE 10     *Above :* Shag, p22

*Below :* Cormorant, p21

PLATE 11
Fulmar, p17

*Photo :*
*J. B. and S. Bottomley*

Photo: *J. B. and S. Bottomley*

PLATE 12

*Above :* Cormorant (immature), p21

*Below :* Shag (immature), p22

Photo: *J. B. and S. Bottomley*

PLATE 13

*Above :* Squacco
Heron, p27
*Right :* Fulmar,
p17
*Below :* American
Bittern, p30

PLATE 14

*Above :* Gannet, p19

*Below left :* Heron, p24

*Below right :* Purple Heron; p26

Photo : Eric Hosking

PLATE 15    Heron, p24

Photo : Eric Hosking

PLATE 16     Bittern, p28

PLATE 17
*Above :* Night Heron, p27
*Below :* Bittern, p28

*Above :* Little Bittern, p28
*Below :* Spoonbill, p31

with no dark smudges on the flanks. Its flight has been described as resembling that of the Fulmar.

The upper parts are grey-brown, back and sides of neck greyish, flanks and belly pure white. The bill is yellowish; the legs flesh-coloured. Length, 18 in. Wing, 14·3 in.

## Sooty Shearwater                                                *Puffinus griseus*

The Sooty Shearwater is a world-wanderer which breeds on islands in the seas round New Zealand and the south Pacific. At the end of its breeding season this southern shearwater migrates northward, in our spring, and must be looked upon as an annual visitor to our shores. It has been seen, usually in small numbers, from August to October at several points off the coasts of Great Britain and Ireland. Off the Yorkshire coast it is so well known as to be named the Black Shearwater by the fishermen, for at a distance it looks very black as it flies with typical shearwater flight, skimming and swinging, now the upper, now the lower parts in view. Its food and habits are very similar to those of the Great Shearwater, with which it often associates.

The general colour is deep brown, darkest on the upper parts; there is a paler line on the underside of the wing. Length, 16 in. Wing, 12 in.

## Fulmar                                                         *Fulmarus glacialis*

Until 1878 the only known British breeding place of the Fulmar was St Kilda; then a colony was established on Foula, and at first gradually and then more rapidly the bird spread as a nesting species round the coasts of the British Isles. By 1959 there were 486 breeding colonies and 222 'prospecting stations' round the coasts of Britain and Ireland, and the number of occupied nest sites was probably over 100,000. The increase probably began in Iceland over 200 years ago, and the biggest colonies in the British Isles are still found in the north. James Fisher, who has studied and recorded this remarkable expansion so thoroughly, believes that it is due to the provision of trawler offal within range of all these colonies. This explanation is confirmed by the fact that the rate of increase has declined since 1950, corresponding to a reduction in the amount of trawler offal available. It is interesting that Fulmars are now breeding on a Yorkshire cliff ten miles from the sea. Beyond our islands the range extends northward to the Arctic seas. Except during the nesting season —roughly May to August—the bird comes little to land; it is an oceanic wanderer, but during winter a few may be seen well offshore in our southern seas, and occasionally a bird is storm-driven inland. Some birds return early to the neighbourhood of the colonies, or even linger in the north all winter.

The Fulmar, with its grey back and white head and underparts, is not unlike a large gull, but the bill, with its tubular nostrils, is that of a petrel. But the most skilful gull cannot compete with it, for 'the Fulmar flying free' is one of the easiest, most graceful and powerful of sea-birds. From time to time it takes a few strong strokes, but for the most part its flight is clever steady unwavering sailing with wings more outstretched than those of any gull, steady as the wings of an aeroplane. It sweeps round in huge arcs, catching the wind with the fine, almost imperceptible adjustments of the soaring bird, yet rising to no great height. Without effort it sails in the teeth of a gale that drives the great Atlantic rollers shoreward; it swoops into the trough, sweeps up the crest and swings over at right angles, the tip of one wing just clearing the wave. Its neck looks short; it is compact and well proportioned, gleaming white against a green sea or lowering sky.

St Kilda used to exist more upon Fulmar than any of its other fowl; the bird provided oil and feathers for rent, food for winter consumption, and, when the islanders realised that collectors would pay, eggs for dealers. For centuries the bird was exploited, but in spite of the annual Fulmar harvest the area was congested. The food of the Fulmar consists of fish, any floating oily refuse, cuttles and, near the nest, sorrel; sometimes food is picked up as the bird swoops, but often it settles on the water to feed. The young, plunging the head into the parent's mouth, feeds on regurgitated oil; both old and young are so full of oil that they eject it on the slightest provocation, squirting it, often at an intruder, for three feet or more. The oil is a beautiful clear amber colour, and has a penetrating but not unpleasant smell. St Kilda reeks of the smell, as do skins and eggs of the bird; blown eggs, twenty years old, retain this persistent odour.

The single egg is laid on the rock, in a rough scratching in soil, or in an apology for a nest—a few bits of grass or thrift, or on a slight lining of small flat stones. The white egg is rough in texture, and measures on the average 2·9 by 1·9 in.; incubation begins about the middle of May. At the nest the Fulmar has a low crooning note, and a loud '*ek, ek, ek*', when visited by the mate. The usual resting position is on the foot (tarsus), and the bird will shuffle in that attitude on the ledge, but the bird can and does very occasionally walk on its toes, chiefly when stirred by sexual excitement. The nestlings have greyish-white down and dark bills.

The adult Fulmar has two phases, but the dark one, sometimes called the Blue Fulmar, in which the blue-grey extends to the underparts and head, is rare in British colonies, though common further north. The lighter or normal bird is white on the head, neck and underparts, though usually with a slight yellowish tinge; the back, wings and tail are blue-grey, faintly tinged, rather than mottled, with pale ashy-brown; the quills are darker. The bill varies in colour from brown to grey or yellowish; the legs may be pale blue, grey, pinkish, green or yellow. Length, 19 in. Wing, 13·25 in. Tarsus, 2 in. (*Plates 11, 13 and 162.*)

# Order PELECANIFORMES
## Family SULIDAE Gannets

*Birds with the four toes connected by membrane.*

## Gannet
*Sula bassana*

Apart from the British Isles, the main stronghold of the species, the Gannet has only a few crowded breeding places on the shores of the North Atlantic. In the British Isles it nests in the Orkneys, Shetlands and Outer Hebrides; Ailsa Craig, the Bass Rock and Scar Rocks (Wigtownshire); Grassholm, Wales; three sites in Ireland and two in the Channel Islands; and lately a few pairs have nested on Bempton Cliff, Yorkshire. The breeding population of the British Isles is steadily increasing and is now probably almost 100,000 pairs. In winter it is pelagic, occurring off both east and west shores of the North Atlantic.

Off our shores, at almost any season, some of these grand white birds with black wing tips may be seen floating easily with wide-spread pointed wings, tacking and sailing, without apparent effort, adjusting their aerial pose to benefit by every wind. Some birds look black, or black and white, for the plumage varies greatly with age. In mastery of the air even the Eagles, Kite and Buzzard cannot excel it, nor is the Falcon's stoop more impressive than its headlong plunge into the sea. Its great expanse of wing, exceeding 6 ft., carries it lightly, high above the waves as it watches for fish below; with half-closed wings it shoots down obliquely, then closing them entirely, plunges into the water with a mighty splash; the dive may start a hundred feet or more above the water; at times, however, it will mount but a few feet before again turning and diving. It brings no fish to the surface; the prey is captured and swallowed before it reappears, and, flapping heavily for a few yards, catches the breeze and sweeps easily upward. Herrings and other shoal-swimming fish are its main food, but it will swallow the spine-armed gurnards without difficulty.

The Gannet is noticeably most plentiful in spring and autumn, for there is a distinct southward migration for winter, especially of immature birds. After the breeding season, from August onward, most of the Gannets wander southward; they are pelagic but go where fish are abundant. The bird travels regularly on both passages along our west and east coasts. The northward passage is, as the spring advances, more direct and purposeful; small parties stream past the Northumberland shores all day long, flying low, undulating over the waves, doubtless heading for the Bass. In spite of these migrations and oceanic wanderings, when the birds remain on or above the water day and night, the breeding haunts are only entirely deserted for a few weeks; in February, even at the end of January, a few reach the rocks, and laggards remain until December; the majority, however, arrive in March and April and depart in September and October.

In spring and summer a Gannet colony is a wonderful sight; the ledges of the precipitous crags are lined with birds, the rocks are whitewashed until an outcrop like Stack Lee, in the St Kilda group, looks one great white pinnacle. Fifty miles or more from the rock, birds pass to and fro, some fishing, others hastening with food for the young. As one draws nearer the crowd becomes denser until thousands are passing overhead or diving on all sides; above the rock is a swirling cloud of birds. When leaving a cliff face they launch themselves out into horizontal or upward flight, but they have some difficulty in taking off from a level surface. The take-off is often preceded by vertical stretching of the neck and beak and a snoring call. The arrival of incoming birds at a cliff colony is striking: their speed and weight brings them with such velocity that one expects them to dash themselves against the rock, but throwing the wings well forward they grip the air and check momentum. In the typical courtship display paired birds stand face to face with raised or waving wings and heads wagging from side to side; often the bills clash or are stropped against each other. Hoarse calls are used in various contexts at the breeding colony, but at sea the Gannet is a silent bird.

The nests are made of seaweed, turf or vegetation torn from the cliff-top, and decorated with all sorts of odds and ends; golf-balls, paper, a parasol and candle-ends have been found in the nests. Like Rooks and other colonial nesters, the birds are not above petty larceny, and frequent squabbles are caused by nest robbing; sometimes a fighting couple will fall over the crag into the sea and there settle the dispute.

The single egg is bluish-green beneath its chalky outer deposit, and is usually stained by its wet surroundings. The brooding bird covers it with both feet before lowering its body upon it. Both birds build and incubate; incubation lasts six weeks. The eggs are laid from April onward, a second egg being laid if the first is destroyed. When first hatched the dark slate young bird is blind and naked, but patches of down soon appear, and grow in volume into a thick woolly covering. It feeds by plunging its head and often most of its body into the huge gape of the parent, groping for disgorged fish. In a few weeks feathers show, at first on the back, and by degrees replace the down, until, in first plumage, the bird is dark brown, speckled with white. After remaining three months on the rocks it departs in this dress. Storm-driven Gannets in this plumage are not uncommon inland, and occasionally, after a gale, a fagged and starving mature bird is picked up in a field or more unlikely situation miles from the sea. When twelve months old the head and neck are mottled with white and the underparts lose most of their brown colour. After the second autumn moult the entire head is white and patches show on the upper parts. After the third and fourth moults the dark colour is gradually replaced by white. There may be irregularity in the duration of immaturity, but individual variation in the distribution of dark and light in birds of the same age may have caused confusion.

The mature bird is white, tinged with yellow on the head and neck; the quills are dark brown. The skin round the eye is dark steel-blue, the bill slate-blue with a horn-coloured tip. The legs are slate-blue, the irides greyish-white. The juvenile has upper parts brownish-black flecked with white, under-parts paler, spotted with dark brown. Length, about 27 in. Wing, 19 in. Tarsus, 2·25 in. (*Plates 14 and 163*.)

## Family PHALACROCORACIDAE Cormorants

**Cormorant**                                              *Phalacrocorax carbo*

The Cormorant is found almost everywhere in northern seas and inland waters of large size. In the British Isles the breeding range is in many places coincident with that of the Shag, but in the north and west of Scotland and in the west of Ireland the smaller bird predominates; elsewhere, as a rule, the Cormorant is the more abundant species.

There is much that is ungainly, awkward and uncouth about the Cormorant, yet it is a handsome and interesting bird. Its breeding haunts are rocky coasts, but it may be met with anywhere along the shores, far up tidal estuaries, on broad rivers and inland waters. On the wing, at a distance, it can only be told from the Shag by its size, but at close quarters the thicker bill, the white on cheeks and chin and the browner wings and back are distinctive. In the hand the fourteen tail feathers, as against twelve in the Shag, are an unfailing feature. As a rule it flies low over the waves, with long neck outstretched and feet trailed behind, but when crossing land, rises to above gunshot, and occasion-ally, in sport, soars to a height, wheeling and floating with wide-spread primaries. The wing-beats are quick, strong and regular; occasionally it will skim with motionless wings. It swims low, holding the bill pointed upward at an angle of about 45°, not at right angles like a grebe or downward like the Swan; its head is frequently turned from side to side. If alarmed it sinks the body until the back is awash, swimming with head and neck alone exposed. It paddles like a duck, moving the legs alternately, but beneath the surface they strike together. It dives well, usually springing slightly from the water with wings fast closed and submerging with a graceful curve; often a spurt of water is kicked up as it goes down. Under water it swims with feet alone, progressing in rapid jerks, driven forward by the simultaneous action of the legs, its neck slightly curved, its head held back, ready to strike at its prey. In the up stroke the webbed toes are gathered together, but are expanded and slightly curved so as to grip the water when it is propelling itself forward. When the bird is turning, checking speed or rising to the surface the wings are slightly, very slightly, opened, but it does not use its wings for swimming under water.

Though an occasional young Guillemot, Puffin or other bird may find its way down the Cormorant's throat, it is really a fish-eater. It out-swims fish under water, and as a rule, at any rate, brings them to the surface before swallowing them. There, if they prove troublesome, it worries and shakes them as a terrier shakes a rat; it will beat them on the surface, carry them below and bring them up again, until their struggles are subdued; then they are gorged, swelling first the extensive gular pouch and later the thin but elastic neck. The dives are irregular in duration, but not so sustained as in some birds; often they last less than half a minute. Exaggerated ideas of the voracity of Cormorants have been corrected by recent studies, which show an average daily consumption of about 1½ lb. of fish. Many species are taken, including especially flat-fish and eels. After fishing the Cormorant delights to stand upon some rock or post, drying its outspread, sharply angled wings, looking like a long-necked heraldic eagle. Numbers ascend estuaries with the tide and line the shores at the ebb, and many are found on inland waters. Roosting in trees is regular in some places. On the Dee marshes they will sit in rows on the wire sheep railing, their big inward-turned toes wrapped round the wire; in spite of a stiff breeze they maintain their balance. As they sit they gape, as if blasé; probably they are striving to eject the pellets of undigested food. The note, seldom heard except near the nest, is a deep harsh croak. On rocks the Cormorant stands fairly erect with straight tarsus, but it walks awkwardly, swaying its neck from side to side. In courtship both will raise and dip their necks, a common nuptial action of water birds.

The nests are usually on ledges of a steep crag facing the sea, often many together. In Ireland and Wales there have been a few inland nests on isolated rocks, and exceptionally in trees. On the coast nests are built chiefly of sea-weed and are often of great size. Nesting material is added after the eggs are hatched. Three or four eggs are laid late in April or in May; they are elongated, rough and chalky-white, but blue if the outer covering flakes off. The young are at first naked, blind slate-grey little monsters, which squeak as they plunge their bills into their parents' mouths to obtain half-digested food. The down which grows in about a fortnight is woolly and sooty.

The adult is black, glossed purple and green; the slightly elongated feathers of the nape form a ragged mane. The mantle is bronze-brown with dark margins forming a network pattern. The lower face and chin are white. From February until about July white filaments are sprinkled over the head and neck, and silky-white patches on the thighs; in some British and most Continental birds the head and neck are white with only faint dark flecks. The bill is horn-coloured, yellower at the base, and the bare skin surrounding it and the gular pouch is yellowish; the legs are black. In the brown first plumage the dull white underparts are mottled; later the breast is streaked and the belly almost white until mature plumage is attained. Immature plumages are irregular and are complicated by the frequent occurrence of a white-breasted phase, in which dress the bird has been known to breed. Length, about 36 in. Wing, 14·75 in. Tarsus, 2·8 in. (*Plates 10, 12 and 163.*]

**Shag**                                              *Phalacrocorax aristotelis*

The range of the Shag is restricted to Iceland and the western shores of

Europe; a closely allied form occurs in the Mediterranean and Black Seas. In the British Isles it breeds freely in the north and west of Scotland, the Orkneys and Shetlands and the west coast of Ireland, and is fairly common along the shores of Wales, Isle of Man and the south-west of England. Its numbers have greatly increased recently in north-east England and south-east Scotland.

In its breeding plumage, the distinctive feature of which is a short but conspicuous recurved crest, it can always be distinguished from the Cormorant, but this head-dress is only worn during the first six or seven months of the year. At other times the adult bird may be told by its smaller size, green plumage and absence of white on the face. The twelve tail feathers are the safest character in young birds. The habits of the Shag or Green Cormorant differ little from those of the larger bird, but it less frequently visits inland waters, although the bird does at times occur inland when there is no evidence of its having been 'storm-blown'.

Although occasionally standing erect, its usual pose is less upright and more graceful than that of the Cormorant; the body is inclined at an angle, the neck curved like that of a Swan. This same curve is seen when the bird is swimming, though the bill is carried pointing up at an angle; the body is often awash. When the bird rises to the surface after a dive it frequently raises the head and neck, looking round cautiously, before exposing the whole back; if it suspects danger it at once dives again, but without the graceful curving leap out of the water. It leaves the water with some difficulty, splashing with its wings and feet, but when once on the wing flies with steady beats close to the surface. Fish of various kinds are captured by speed under water, the method of progression being the same as in the Cormorant. It is voracious and will kill and devour large-sized fish. At the nesting colony the male has an aggressive croaking call, but the female is silent except for hissing and clicking sounds.

The Shag is a gregarious nester, building on cliff ledges, among boulders or in wave-washed caves. The nests are built of seaweed and other vegetation collected by the male and usually built in by the female. The eggs, two to five in number, resemble those of the Cormorant except in size, and are, like them, blue beneath their rough chalky covering. The sitting birds are difficult to dislodge; they sit on the ledges, swinging their heads from side to side if approached. Both sexes incubate. April is the usual month for eggs, but later clutches are common. The young, after their naked stage, are quaint little objects in sooty-brown down.

The adult is glossy oil-green, darkest on the head and neck, and in the breeding season has a short upstanding crest. The slender bill is blackish, paler on the under mandible and yellow at the gape; the legs are black. In the first plumage the general colour is brown above with some white beneath, mottled with brown. After the first autumn moult the neck is faintly speckled and the upper parts slightly glossed. Probably in both Shag and Cormorant the fully mature plumage is not attained until after the third moult. Length, 30 in. Wing, 10 in. Tarsus, 2·25 in. (*Plates 10, 12 and 163.*)

# Order CICONIIFORMES

## Family ARDEIDAE Herons

*Wading birds with long legs and strong, straight bills; toes on same level; claw of middle toe with a comb.*

## Heron
*Ardea cinerea*

The Common Heron has a wide Old World range. In the British Isles it is a resident, though numbers of immigrants reach us from Scandinavia in autumn and a few British-bred birds emigrate. Herons breed in nearly all counties in the British Isles. A census in 1928 showed a nesting population of nearly 4000 in England and Wales; annual counts of sample areas over the following thirty-five years indicated no general increase or decrease. Numbers drop sharply after a severe winter, as in 1963, but normally recover within a few years and remain stable until the next hard winter. There were signs, however, of a serious and more permanent decline in the north of England in the 1960s. After the breeding season there is a general dispersal from the heronries, but although a few birds may cross the English Channel there is no regular migration of our native Herons.

The specific epithet of the Heron is descriptive; when it stands patiently in the shallows it looks a grey bird, and greyer still when it perches, as it often does, on the dark branch of some fir. Its French-grey mantle, dark slate, almost black flight feathers, white forehead, head and neck with black markings and trailing black crest, its filamental bushy breastplate, and stout yellow bill, are unlike those of any other British bird. In many parts it is called the Crane. The Heron is a water bird, but whether fresh or salt, clear or muddy does not matter as long as it will yield something worth waiting for. It does not, however, always wait for its quarry, but stalks through the water with long, deliberate strides, ready to dash its pick-axe bill upon any unsuspecting fish, frog, beetle or other animal. Young wild-fowl are killed, and indeed in hard weather full-grown birds; a Water Rail has been found whole in its stomach. Mice, rats and moles are eaten, and, judging by the fur in cast-up pellets, large numbers of water-voles, but fish, especially eels, form the staple diet in most places. In its nesting habits the Heron is gregarious, and though a solitary Heron is a common sight, it is often sociable; three or four will feed close together or stand in a group on the bank as they preen their feathers.

In its characteristic resting position the bird stands very upright, often on a mooring post, stump, or dead branch, with its neck drawn in and its head sunk between its hunched-up shoulders; when feeding the carriage is less upright, the head and neck and even the body tilted forward. If prey is sighted the dart downward, swinging as if hinged on the legs, is very rapid. The bird stabs its prey, sometimes several times, to 'knock it out', and large fish are carried to the bank and the flesh picked from the bones. The Heron will wade until the body is afloat and even swim for a short distance. Occasionally it dives from the air. The head and neck of the bird shoot up at once on the least suspicion of alarm, and the great wings are unfolded, but the actual launch is slow; the flight is deliberate, but the strokes are so powerful that the speed attained is considerable; in a few seconds, croaking in alarm, the bird is far away. Almost immediately the head is drawn back and the long legs trailed, the normal position in flight. The call, a resounding *frank*, differs only slightly from the cry of alarm; it is frequently uttered on the wing.

The nuptial dances of cranes are well known, but in the Heron they are only seen in a rudimentary form: a bird may sometimes take a few prancing steps with raised wings on the gathering-ground near the heronry in early spring. Greeting and courtship display on or near the nest is much more striking and elaborate. In the typical greeting ceremony the head and neck are stretched upwards and then brought back over the body with the bill still held in a vertical position. The presentation of a stick by the male to the female is often a preliminary to coition. A curious feature of the early stages of the breeding cycle is a temporary change in some adults in the colour of the bill and sometimes of the legs: they become suffused with varying shades of red and pink. Mr F. A. Lowe, who has made a special study of this species, has found that the change may be a momentary one at times of sexual excitement.

On the sides of the breast and in other places the Heron has patches of 'powder down', the use of which has caused discussion; they are powdery brittle feathers of a waxy nature. The powder, which is liberally applied to the plumage in preening, coagulates the slime of eels and other fish, and this can then be removed by the pectinated claw.

The nests are usually in a colony, huge platforms with shallow cups, in the branches of tall trees; occasionally they are built on the ground, on rocky cliffs, or in marshes. Large sticks are used, with smaller but seldom soft material for lining. By the middle of February or early in March the four to five pale greenish-blue eggs are laid, and a few weeks later the heronry is lively. Most of the nests are so large that the old birds look small when they alight upon them, uttering a deep growling *gwrronk*, answered by a feeble pipe from newly hatched young. The hunger call of older nestlings is an incessant chittering *tac, tac, tac*, very much like the roosting note of the Blackbird. The nestlings are quaint, half-naked little objects, with short, thick, blunt bills, showing a trace of yellow, and stout lead-coloured legs. They are 'handy' with their bills when climbing amongst the branches, hooking them over twigs when foothold is insufficient. The young are fed by regurgitation, which they stimulate by grasping the parent's bill. Second broods are quite exceptional: the late young sometimes found among the trees well into the summer are usually the result of replacement clutches.

The adult has head and neck white, except for a black line through the eye, ending in a pendent crest and black markings down the front of the neck. It has elongated white feathers at the base of the neck. The upper parts and tail are ash-grey, quills blackish; underparts greyish-white with some black on the flanks. The bill is yellow; legs brown. Immatures have grey head and neck and only the rudiments of the black crest. Length, 36 in. Wing, 17·25 in. Tarsus, 6·75 in. (*Plates 14, 15 and 163.*)

## Purple Heron                                    *Ardea purpurea*

The Purple Heron nests in many parts of Europe, even as near England as Holland and France, but in our islands is only known as an uncommon visitor on migration, mainly to the east and south of England in spring and autumn.

In general build it resembles our Heron, but is smaller and more richly coloured. In flight the wing looks an almost uniform slate-blue compared with the clearly defined light and dark pattern of the Grey Heron's. Our Heron is shy, but the Purple Heron is skulking; indeed, in its love of dense cover it resembles the Bittern more than the Heron. It has a very long, thin neck, lined with black, and as it stands amongst reeds, is difficult to detect; its feet are large in proportion, well fitted for marsh walking. In flight the neck hangs lower than in our bird. It feeds after dark as well as in daylight. Its diet is very varied and includes small mammals, frogs, fish, insects, crustaceans and molluscs. The Purple Heron sometimes adopts a bittern-like protective posture with head and neck stretched obliquely upwards. The call is softer and less raucous than that of the Common Heron.

The adult's crown and crest are purplish-black. Its back and wings dark slate-grey, the neck rufous, strongly striped with black, but the elongated plumes on the back are chestnut; those overhanging the reddish breast are black, white, grey and chestnut. The belly and under tail-coverts are black. The bill is yellow, legs brown and yellow. The immature bird is dark brown above, mostly buff below and lacks the adult's plumes and black markings on head and neck. Length, 31 in. Wing, 14 in. Tarsus, 5·2 in. (*Plate 14.*)

## Little Egret                                    *Egretta garzetta*

In recent years an average of four or five Little Egrets have been recorded annually in the British Isles, usually in May, June or July, and chiefly in the southern counties of England. It breeds in southern Europe and Africa.

This small, pure white heron feeds in shallow water in the open. It is distinguished from the Great White Egret by its much smaller size and from the Cattle Egret by its black bill, yellow feet and long slender neck. Two long slender plumes project beyond the nape in summer, and on its back and breast are soft filiform plumes. The young bird is greyer and plumeless. Length, 21 in. Wing, 11·25 in. Tarsus, 4·5 in.

## Great White Egret or Great White Heron                                    *Egretta alba*

This bird breeds in eastern Europe and central Asia and winters further south. About a dozen vagrants have been recorded in England and Scotland. This pure white heron is much larger and slimmer than the Little Egret and has a very long, thin neck. It lacks the Little Egret's long crest and has blackish, not yellow feet. The bill is yellow or yellow and black. Length, about 35 in.

## Squacco Heron                                              *Ardeola ralloides*
The Squacco Heron breeds in southern Europe and in Africa, where it also winters. Over ninety, mostly immature, have occurred in our islands. It is described as skulking, hiding in aquatic herbage by day and feeding at night, but it also feeds both in the morning and long before dusk. Its diet is varied, but it is said to take more insects and crustaceans than most herons. The rather heavy flight is varied by long glides on steady but slightly drooping wings. The general plumage in summer is buff and white, yet in flight the bird looks remarkably white; the buff is inconspicuous.

In summer the adult's head and neck are lightly streaked and it has a long drooping crest of black-edged white feathers. The neck, elongated breast feathers and mantle are buff, wings and tail white. The bill is blackish, legs yellowish-green. In winter the bird is browner and has dark streaks on head and neck. Immatures resemble winter adults. Length, 18 in. Wing, 9 in. Tarsus, 2·6 in. (*Plate 13.*)

## Cattle Egret                                                  *Bubulcus ibis*
The Cattle Egret, formerly known as the Buff-backed Heron, is a resident in the Iberian Peninsula and southern Russia as well as many parts of Africa and Asia and has been accepted as a very rare vagrant to Britain. However, the bird is not infrequently kept in captivity and some records are probably attributable to escapes. Unlike the Little Egret, it feeds in fields among grazing cattle, and it is a stockier, thicker-necked bird with buffish tufts on crown, breast and mantle. The rest of the plumage is white; the bill is yellowish, the legs reddish in summer, dusky in winter. Length, 20 in.

## Night Heron                                             *Nycticorax nycticorax*
The Night Heron is a summer visitor to central and southern Europe. It has visited all parts of our islands and appears almost regularly on the east and south coasts of England both in spring and autumn. It has been recorded in every month of the year, but as numbers of free-flying birds are kept in zoological gardens some reports may refer to 'escapes'.

Standing at rest, with its head sunk in its shoulders, the Night Heron, about a third shorter than the Common Heron, looks a stout, dumpy bird. Long, narrow, white nuchal plumes hang over the back, usually three in number though more are recorded. The general colour scheme is dark above and light below; as the bird flies the dark upper parts are in striking contrast with the grey on wings, neck and tail. It flaps deliberately, and takes frequent long glides, the wings then held amost horizontally; in flight, with head drawn well back and legs trailed, it is noticeably short and stout. Usually it feeds at night, remaining silent, perched on a branch and concealed by foliage, during the day, but at dusk becomes lively and noisy, uttering a loud, harsh croak.

A Cheshire man, whose father shot a Night Heron, remembered hearing the bird in the evening 'at hay-making time, making a noise like a man vomiting' —not at all a bad simile.

The adult has crown, nape and mantle blackish with a blue or green sheen, wings and tail grey, and brow and underparts greyish-white. Three long white plumes hang from the nape. The bill is dark green, legs yellow, irides red. The juvenile has brown upper parts with pale buff spots and streaks; buff underparts with brown streaks. Length, 24 in. Wing, 11·25 in. Tarsus, 3·15 in. (*Plate 17.*)

### Little Bittern                                              *Ixobrychus minutus*

The Little Bittern breeds in central and southern Europe and Asia and winters in Africa. To the British Isles, where it has occurred in all parts, including the Shetlands, it is now a regular visitor on migration in small numbers, and though actual proof is lacking, has probably nested in eastern and southern counties of England.

The small size—a heron about as big as a Lapwing—should prevent confusion with any other bird, but it is not an easy bird to see, for it skulks all day in the herbage and feeds at night. The creamy patch on the wing is conspicuous in flight, especially in the male. Apart from nocturnal habits, it is an expert at camouflage. Heron-like, it stands motionless with its head sunk in its shoulders, but if approached turns its buff breast towards the intruder, and pointing its bill skywards, slowly stiffens itself upward. As it stretches it becomes attenuated, gaining several inches in height, until it is hardly distinguishable from a dead reed blade. When feeding or protecting itself, it can dart its head and bill forward with dangerous speed, but this lengthening trick is slow; so also is the rotation of its body as it keeps its breast towards and its eyes upon the moving observer. The bird will allow itself to be caught by man or dog, trusting to being missed as long as it remains still. It can, however, run swiftly through dense herbage. In flight its wing-beats are more rapid than in the larger herons.

The nest is not unlike that of the Moorhen, and though occasionally in a low bush, is usually in a reed-bed. The eggs are muddy white. The male has a call which corresponds to the boom of the Bittern. It is sometimes described as a grunting croak, but Lilford calls it 'a sort of deep guttural cough'.

The crown, hind neck and back of the male are greenish-black, the primaries and tail browner, and the face and underparts rich buff; on the breast and flanks are dark streaks. The wing-coverts and underparts are buffish-white. The bill and legs are greenish-yellow. The female and young bird are brownish-black on the crown, brown on the back, and have the hind neck rufous and the underparts buff streaked with dark brown. Length, 14 in. Wing, 6 in. Tarsus, 1·75 in. (*Plate 17.*)

### Bittern                                              *Botaurus stellaris*

The Bittern, which is found in suitable habitats throughout most of Europe, became extinct as a British breeding bird in the second half of the 19th century and re-colonised East Anglia in the first quarter of the 20th. In spite of setbacks after severe winters, it is now well established in the marshes of Norfolk and Suffolk and breeds in smaller numbers in four other English counties. From three to six pairs nest regularly in north Lancashire. It is a regular winter visitor to Ireland and has occurred in winter or on passage in many parts of England and Wales and occasionally in Scotland.

The only bird with which the mottled and barred Bittern can be confused is its American representative (page 30). It is a large heron, rich buff, barred, mottled, and vermiculated with black and brown. During the day the Bittern hides in reeds or other vegetation, and unless disturbed is rarely seen on the wing until the young require attention. When approached, it assumes protective attitudes, pointing the bill upward so as to expose to view the thin buff neck with its irregular brown streaks, which, in reeds, confuse the eye. It will crouch amongst the dead and broken litter in winter, with its long neck outstretched, or flatten itself out with the head resting on the shoulders and the bill alone pointing up. In this position, with crest erect and breast frill spread, it is prepared to defend itself; it is unwise to handle it without caution, for a Bittern can shoot up to full height with great suddenness and aim for the eyes. When feeding young the female is less cautious, flying to and fro all day between the nest and the feeding ground. On the wing the bird looks light brown, cinnamon in sunlight, compact and short-necked. The flight is slow and owl-like, though direct; the wings move faster than the measured beats of the Heron. Some individuals fly fairly high, calling a deep *agh, agh*, but others hardly clear the reed tops and are difficult to see. In spring high pursuit flights, involving two or more birds, are not uncommon. In the vegetation the Bittern walks or runs, if disturbed, with the shoulders high and the head lowered; it slips with ease out of sight. On alighting it will stand for a few moments, bill up and neck stretched, as it turns its head in all directions, before sinking out of sight.

The boom of the Bittern, familiar in literature and fable, is the call of the male—a deep, bovine, resonant note, certainly audible for over a mile. He begins to boom in January and continues until the young are hatched in June. The boom is repeated three or four times in succession, with a one- or two-second interval between each note, then a pause of variable duration. At close quarters, two or three preliminary grunts or coughs are audible, followed by a sound like an inspiration; the boom bellowed only a few feet away is not very loud; it is its carrying power that is so remarkable. The Bittern feeds on the smaller animals of the marsh, and is a great eel-catcher. When the young are hatched the female makes frequent journeys to some dyke, deep bog, or other selected feeding ground, perhaps a mile from the nest, where for half an hour or more she collects food, returning with her gullet visibly distended.

The nest is usually built in reeds and of reeds, but it may be placed in sedge. The eggs, usually five in number, are olive-brown and match the dead reeds or sedge; they are laid from the end of March until June. The young when first hatched are quaint little 'animated golliwogs'. The young frequently leave the nest when four or five days old. Later they have a curious bubbling call.

Adults have crown, nape and moustachial stripe black, back and wings rich brown, barred and mottled with black, underparts buff marked with brown. Young birds are paler and have more uniform quills. The bill is greenish-yellow, legs pale green. Length, 30 in. Wing, 13 in. Tarsus, 3·8 in. (*Plates 16, 17 and* 163.)

### American Bittern                                *Botaurus lentiginosus*

Of some fifty records of the American Bittern in the British Isles, about half are from Ireland and nearly all between October and March. The bird is found throughout North America and in winter in the West Indies. Its food, voice and habits are generally similar to those of our bird, but it is more frequently seen in open meadows. It is noticeably smaller than our bird.

The upper parts are finely speckled with black, not barred and mottled as in the Common Bittern. The crown is chestnut-brown instead of black, and the quills are greyish-brown with black tips, not barred. The bill and legs are yellowish-green. Length, 26 in. Wing, 12 in. Tarsus, 3·5 in. (*Plate 13*.)

## Family CICONIIDAE Storks

*Long-legged, strong-billed birds; slight membrane at base of front toes; no pectination on middle claw.*

### White Stork                                        *Ciconia ciconia*

The White Stork was formerly common in Holland, Germany and southern Scandinavia, but, though protected and encouraged to nest on or amongst houses, is now scarce. It was a useful scavenger.  To England it is a rare vagrant, being most frequent in East Anglia, though it has reached Scotland and Ireland. Some records may refer to 'escapes'.

Familiarity with pictures may cause error; Herons are often called Storks. The White Stork is a tall, stately bird, dignified in movements, white with black flight feathers, and with very red bill and legs. In Europe the arrival and departure of the Stork commands popular interest. The bird moves by day, usually at a great height, flying with slow and measured wing-beats, but on the wing can immediately be distinguished from the Heron, for it carries its neck outstretched, and though the red legs trail behind, they sag a little and are not in a straight line with the long axis of the body. The Stork, a silent bird, has no flight call: in the breeding season and when excited it claps or clatters its bill, often producing a roll or trill. It frequents marshes and water meadows and perches on trees, buildings, poles or fences. Frogs form a major part of its diet.

The plumage is all white except for black quills, scapulars and greater coverts; the bill and legs are red. The juvenile is browner on the wings, and its bill and legs are duller. Length, 40 in. Wing, 23 in. Tarsus, 8·8 in. (*Plate 18.*)

## Black Stork                                                    *Ciconia nigra*

The Black Stork, which breeds chiefly in eastern Europe, has occurred as a rare vagrant in the British Isles, chiefly in the southern counties of England and mainly in May and June. In carriage, flight and food it differs little from the White Stork, but it is shy and solitary in its habits; it shuns houses and frequents wild, partly wooded country.

The whole plumage, except for white lower breast and abdomen, is black with a variable metallic sheen. The bill and legs are bright red. Length, 38 in. Wing, 22 in. Tarsus, 7·5 in. (*Plate 18.*)

## Family THRESKIORNITHIDAE Spoonbills and Ibises

*Heron-like form; long bill, decurved or spatulate; neck extended in flight.*

## Spoonbill                                                *Platalea leucorodia*

The summer range of the Spoonbill extends over central and southern Europe. It nests in Holland, but bred in East Anglia and some southern counties of England until the 18th century. One of the earliest birds to receive legal protection, it was even unlawful to take its eggs, but these efforts failed to save it. Today it is a more or less regular visitor to Norfolk and Suffolk, and parts of the south coast on spring and autumn migration, sometimes appearing in small flocks. To other parts of our islands it is a casual visitor.

Tall, white, crested, and with a long bill broadly spatulate at the tip, the Spoonbill is unlike any other bird, yet confusion has arisen through duplication of names. Its old name was Shovelard or Shoveler, and the Shoveler Duck is still called the 'Spoonbill'. When feeding it scoops for molluscs or crustaceans, moving its bill round with a circular motion. In deeper water the bill is immersed to the base, but the same circular sweep from side to side is made. Small fish and frogs as well as worms and insects are eaten. The flight is slow but easy and buoyant. The bill is straight in the direction of flight and the neck curves slightly downwards, sagging a little; the long legs trail in line with the body. The bird will soar on motionless, widespread wings, sweeping gracefully round, and when at a great height, a mere speck in the sky, it flickers white or vanishes as its varying angle reflects the light. The Spoonbill is not a secretive bird; it feeds in open marshes and shallow lagoons, especially near the sea. Breydon flats and Minsmere pools are just to its taste. Like the Heron, which it resembles in gait and stance, it will perch freely in trees. Its feet are slightly webbed, and it occasionally swims.

In summer there is a tinge of yellow on the drooping crest and upper breast of its otherwise white plumage. The bill is blackish with yellow tip, and at the base is a yellow patch; the legs are black. In the juvenile the crest is absent and the primaries have black tips. Length, 34 in. Wing, 14·5 in. Tarsus, 5·5 in. (*Plates 17 and 19.*)

## Glossy Ibis                                           *Plegadis falcinellus*

The Glossy Ibis breeds in central and southern Europe, Asia and Africa, migrating far south in winter. It is an occasional vagrant to our south and east coasts and sometimes reaches Scotland and Ireland. Its visits have become less frequent in recent years. To wildfowlers it is known as the Black Curlew, from its curved bill and dark plumage; against the light it looks black, but in a good light at close quarters it shows brilliant metallic gloss.

In flight the Ibis resembles neither Curlew nor Heron. The legs trail, but the neck is neither outstretched nor drawn far back. It carries the head well up, the neck gracefully curved, the head lower and curve less pronounced when it is travelling fast. The rounded wings move rapidly and at intervals the bird glides. The Ibis is sociable; parties usually travel in lines or chevrons. Resting on branches is a common habit. The illustration shows its frequent habit of sunning itself with one wing raised. The food consists of worms, crustaceans and molluscs, picked up by the tip of the bill and swallowed with a single upward jerk; the bird also probes in mud like a Curlew. The note, seldom uttered, is a guttural croak.

The mature bird in summer is dark maroon on head, neck, back and underparts; the head is burnished green, and the blackish wings are glossed with green and purple. The bill, 5 or 6 in. long, is brown, and on the lores and round the brown eyes the skin is green; the legs are greenish-grey. In winter the plumage is duller and streaked with white, and the brown young shows little gloss. Length (average), 22 in. Wing, 11·75 in. Tarsus, 4 in. (*Plate 18.*)

# Order PHOENICOPTERIFORMES
## Family PHOENICOPTERIDAE Flamingoes

*Long-legged stork-like birds with many duck-like characters. Serrated bill much bent.*

### Greater Flamingo                                          *Phoenicopterus ruber*

The Flamingo nests in Spain and southern France; it is an occasional wanderer to Britain, but as it is often kept in confinement the history of birds observed is uncertain.

It is a very tall pinkish-white bird with black quills and rose-pink or scarlet coverts, very noticeable in flight. The neck is long, the heavy bill curiously bent downwards. When feeding in the shallows the Flamingo will droop the head and drink or scoop for food with the bill reversed, the posterior ridge of the culmen actually scraping the bottom. The bird has a duck-like chuckle, and a loud honking trumpet, similar in tone to the call of certain geese. The plumage of the adult is pinkish-white, except for black primaries and secondaries and rose-pink wing-coverts. The bill is black and pink; the legs are pink. The bill and legs in the young, whose wings are barred, are leaden. Length, about 50 in., but the size is variable. Wing, 16 in. Tarsus, 13 in.

# Order ANSERIFORMES

## Family ANATIDAE Ducks, Geese and Swans

*The Anatidae, all swimming birds, have the three toes in front connected by membrane; they are web-footed.*

**Mallard**                                             *Anas platyrhynchos*

The Mallard is our most abundant and best-known duck; it occurs throughout the Holarctic region. Resident throughout our islands, it is also an abundant migrant, winter visitors arriving in autumn.

The really masculine name Mallard is more distinctive than the older comprehensive Wild Duck, and is now applied to both sexes. The drake is not difficult to identify when in full dress, with glossy bottle-green head, white collar, grey scapulars and flanks, and the perky upcurled feathers on the tail. His breast is warm brown, whilst that of the dark-headed Shoveler drake is white above a chestnut band. The duck, in mottled browns and buffs, is less distinctive, and may be confused with the Gadwall, Shoveler, or even Pintail; in summer, when the drake has donned his extra or 'eclipse' dress, a protection during the moult, he is more sombre and feminine. In flight drake or duck may be told by the wing pattern, a purple green-shot speculum, bordered above and below with black and white—two distinct white bands, one the outer edge of the wing. The white borders of the wedge-shaped tail are also plain.

The haunts of this duck are varied; in winter it abounds along our shores and on marshes, on large or small sheets of water in the lowlands, and on reservoirs and moors on the hills. Its usual feeding-time is from dusk to dawn, and during the day it rests in packs or scattered flocks on open water, swimming idly with head drawn back or snoozing with its bill tucked amidst the feathers of its back. It will sleep on the bank or dawdle about, picking a scrap here and there, and at times a few birds will feed at the water's edge; but it is not until the evening that 'flighting' takes place. Then the birds go off to the ponds, ditches or fields to seek food, returning at dawn. Food, animal or vegetable, for it is omnivorous, is sifted from the mud which passes through its laminated bill. In the fields it picks up grain; in the woods acorns, and worms, snails, slugs and insects are all accepted; it plucks ripe berries from the brambles or the seablite seeds on the marsh, and on the sandbanks devours cockles and other shellfish. In frost the majority retire to salt water, but some will linger, roosting on the ice; should snow fall the oblong, half-thawed patches mark their chilly beds. At all times gregarious, the winter flocks of Mallards, especially on the coast, are sometimes immense, and even when the ducks are sitting the drakes form little bachelor groups on the water. During the diurnal rest the birds are alert; if disturbed, all rise in a body with a rush of wings, and, splitting into twos and threes, fly to and fro high above gunshot.

The flight is swift; the wing-beats, rapid and strong, produce a swishing whistle. The bird springs clear of the water when disturbed, shooting upwards, and when about to alight comes down with head well forward but with the body upright, striking the surface with the feet and tail, ploughing up the water as it checks its pace with open wing. In some localities diving for food is regular. When at play a number will splash together and take short superficial underwater excursions, and a wounded bird will try to escape by diving.

Immigrants arrive from August onward, but the largest numbers collect on inland waters in December and January; many remain until April and May; parties of migrants are about long after our resident birds have begun nesting. Marking birds has demonstrated that some of our immigrants come from Russia, Scandinavia, Lapland, Iceland and Holland; British birds have been found in the Baltic and France. The voice of the drake is a low, conversational chuckle during the breeding season, with an occasional sonorous quack. But when the birds are startled it is the duck which quacks in alarm, but in a different tone. Seebohm spells the male note *quork*, and the female *quark*, a good distinction. When pairing the drake also whistles. Pairing begins early; display may be seen in October. A number of drakes swim round a duck, posturing in various ways, but the sequence of actions is not always the same. The bird sits up in the water, as if making its seat more comfortable, and dipping the head, strokes its breast with its bill. It raises and fans its tail, showing off the white, and stretches its neck along the water as a final compliment to its selected mate. In late spring aerial pursuits of single females by parties of drakes are common.

Incubation often begins in March. The nest is usually at a short distance from the water, in thick vegetation, in woods, dry reed or willow beds, hedgerows, or in heather on the moors. Sometimes it is in the fork of a tree or the deserted nest of some large bird. Grass and dead leaves are the usual materials used, and as incubation proceeds, a lining of dark brown down is added with which the eggs are covered when the duck leaves them; when she is sitting her sombre dress is sufficient protection. The eggs, eight to fourteen in number, are variable—greenish-blue, olive-brown, cream or white. The normal moult begins in August, and by the end of September most drakes are in full dress. In June or July the drakes assume the so-called eclipse plumage and moult the flight feathers.

The downy juveniles are brown and buff, with a few white patches and a noticeable dark streak through the eye beneath a stripe of buff, also a dark mark on the ear. They are carefully guarded by the duck alone, and if threatened she strives to lure away the intruder by an extravagant performance of 'injury-feigning', flogging the water with her wings, taking short rushing flights and quacking vigorously. The ducklings scatter: some dive in the rushes or grass and hide; others run out over the water, their light bodies unsubmerged, and dive when well clear of the bank; when they reappear they show only head and neck and again go under.

The drake in winter has a bottle-green head, white collar, purple-brown breast, grey flanks, and black tail-coverts; the tail is white with curled black central feathers. The female is mottled brown. Both sexes have a white-bordered purple speculum on the wing. Young males and drakes in eclipse resemble females, but their heads and backs are darker. The drake's bill is yellowish, the duck's olive; legs orange. Length, 23 in. Wing, 11 in. Tarsus, 1·75 in. (*Plates 1 and 163.*)

## Teal                                                                *Anas crecca*

The Teal, our smallest duck, is resident in varying numbers throughout England, Wales and Ireland, commonest in the north, and in Scotland it breeds freely. As a winter visitor it is abundant, large numbers reaching our shores in August and September. Abroad it nests throughout northern Europe, and ranges south in winter into Africa.

The most noticeable mark on the drake is the long white line on the wing, emphasised by the black line below it, showing as a longitudinal streak on the swimming bird, and as two lines down the back when in flight. At closer quarters a conspicuous buff-framed metallic-green patch, from the eye to the neck, is visible on the rich brown head; the finely vermiculated back and flanks are seen, and a prominent black-bordered warm buffish triangle below the tail. The open wing exhibits a broad band of white above the velvety-black and metallic-green speculum, and a narrower rim of white at the edge of the flight feathers. The brown and buff duck has less distinctive colouring, but her white-bordered green speculum distinguishes her from the Garganey, and her small size from the Mallard.

Though in winter it is found in considerable numbers in tidal estuaries, the general haunt of the Teal is fresh water; it frequents lakes and quiet pools, especially where there is abundance of cover. In autumn and winter the numbers increase as the coast birds move inland, and there is some emigration of our home-bred stock in autumn. There is a southward movement in mid-winter if the weather is severe. The return passage in spring begins in March.

In its feeding habits the Teal is by no means always nocturnal, though where it is much persecuted it feeds at dawn and dusk. On inland waters it spends some time dozing on the bank or open water, but it also upends in the shallows, and sifts the plankton from the water with its laminated bill. Rotifers and minute crustacea form a considerable part of its varied diet, and vegetable substances are not neglected. In flight the Teal is distinctly swifter than the Mallard; when put up, Teal keep together, flying to and fro in a compact flock, turning and twisting with the precision of waders. No birds leave the water with greater skill and velocity than the Teal, shooting directly upward; a flock may well be called a 'spring' of Teal. At full speed a flock will suddenly and with unanimity take a short corkscrew dive of a few feet and instantly resume horizontal flight. As the birds turn with one accord their light under-parts flash like those of waders. These dives do not necessarily mean a change of direction; indeed, a swiftly flying Teal will turn its head, and even look behind it without losing speed or altering the line of flight. When the flocks intend to alight they will often shoot downwards with great speed, almost falling obliquely, but when near the water they throw the feet and tail forward and check their pace with widespread fluttering wings.

There are few more talkative ducks than the Teal; birds in the winter flocks chuckle conversationally, and on the meres the loud clear call, a short sweet whistle, rings out incessantly. When the drakes are courting the low double whistles run into a musical jumble, a delightful chorus. The duck, especially when alarmed, has a short harsh quack. In nuptial display a favoured duck, ready for admirers, is surrounded by several drakes, who constantly raise themselves in the water, shooting up the head and neck and lowering it at once, with an action that suggests a hiccough; for a second the facial glories are displayed, and as the bird resumes its normal pose it exposes the long white side streak. During this competitive exhibition the whole flock will rise for a flight round the lake, and after wheeling, turning and twisting, return to the display; both rival drakes and ducks from time to time chase one another with open bill, but there is no serious fighting. These displays may be witnessed in autumn, but from January to April the birds are really busy.

The nest, which is of the ordinary duck type, may be in a marsh, a dry wood, or amongst heather on a moor; it is lined with very dark down with hardly noticeable pale tips. The creamy eggs are often tinged with green; they are usually eight to ten, but sometimes more in number, and are laid between April and June. The young have light chocolate down, yellowish-buff beneath, and a dark line passes from the eye to the ear and thence down the side of the neck, and a second borders the cheek. When the duck is alarmed for the safety of her brood her behaviour is often extravagant. In her short flights with head curiously held back, her almost upright body hangs heavily, and she repeatedly drops on the water, flogging it with her wings. The white bars on her wings show more conspicuously than usual, as if exhibited to catch the eye.

In winter the drake has a brown head with green eye-patch, grey back and flanks with a white line conspicuous even on the closed wing, and noticeable buff patches near the tail. The white breast is spotted with black and the abdomen is white. The bill is blackish-brown, the legs dusky. In eclipse a plumage not unlike that of the duck is assumed, but the back is darker and the underparts more spotted. In the brown duck, mottled and barred with buff, the white breast and underparts are spotted after her spring moult. Both sexes have bright green speculum. Length, 14–15 in. Wing, 7·25 in. Tarsus, 1 in. (*Plates 1 and 163*.)

The American subspecies, the Green-winged Teal, is now recorded in the British Isles almost annually, chiefly in the spring months. The drake lacks our bird's distinctive white streak above the wing, but has a whitish crescentic band between the breast and flanks. The female cannot be distinguished from the European Teal.

# Garganey                                    *Anas querquedula*

South of the arctic circle the Garganey breeds throughout the Palaearctic region, and in winter visits tropical Africa. Its range is rather more southerly than that of the other surface-feeding ducks. It is a summer visitor to England, for it breeds regularly in some eastern and southern counties, and has, within recent years, nested in other counties, and also in Wales, Scotland and Ireland. But throughout most of the British Isles it is a rare and irregular visitor on spring migration. Comparatively few are noticed on the return passage, when it is less easy to identify them, and in winter they are very rare.

The strikingly beautiful plumage of the drake Garganey cannot be confused with that of the Teal, a bird of about the same size. The noticeable features of the drake are the broad white stripe, shown up by a dark crown, which passes from above the eye in a graceful curve to the nape, and the blue shoulders, blue as in the Shoveler. Indeed, from a distance the whole wing appears to be blue-grey; this is noticeable in birds on the wing as well as on the ground. Long pointed black and white feathers droop over the wing, and one commanding character is that the warm brown of the breast ends abruptly and does not shade into the white of the abdomen. A metallic-green speculum, often concealed by the grey flanks, is bounded by white bars, also present in the duck, though the speculum itself lacks lustre. The brown duck has less character, but as she usually travels with her mate he does the advertising. Pale edgings to her feathers, however, give her a much lighter appearance than the duck Teal.

The migratory Garganey usually reaches the Kentish coast in March, and departs about August. In habits it differs little from other surface feeders, but is certainly not exclusively nocturnal. On the wing it is even swifter than the Teal. In flight the wings look lightish, but do not show clean patches or bars as do those of the Goldeneye and Tufted Duck. When scared it springs clear from the water with the agility and velocity of the Teal. Several observers assert that the bird sits high in the water, swimming buoyantly, but this is not always so; not infrequently it swims low, and with neck extended 'bibbles' along the surface like the feeding Shoveler (see page 44), a bird with which it has much in common. Both animal and vegetable matter is consumed, and in addition to crustaceans and aquatic insects it has been known to catch small fish. Although both sexes have a sharp quack, it is the distinctive male breeding note that has earned it the name of 'Cricket-Teal'. This is a rattling or clicking note, likened by Saunders to the whirr of a child's rattle.

In England the nest is usually in a marsh, a depression amongst thick herbage thinly bordered with grass; the down, added as incubation proceeds, is blackish tipped with light buff. The creamy eggs, six to thirteen in number, are laid in the latter half of April or in May. The duck attends to domestic duties.

In winter and spring the drake has a dark brown crown, emphasising the tapering white superciliary streak, and chestnut cheeks. The brown neck and breast are pencilled with black. Below the sharp line of demarcation the abdomen is white and the greyish flanks finely vermiculated. The forewing is blue-grey, speculum green, the long drooping scapulars black and white. The bill is black, legs leaden. The duck is brown and buff, her markings bolder than in the drake. The eye-stripe is buff, and the chin and underparts white faintly suffused with buff, the face speckled with brown. The wing-coverts are greyish, and the absence of a distinct speculum distinguishes her from the duck Teal. The brown drake in eclipse retains the blue shoulders and speculum; young birds are at first like the duck. The down of the ducklings is rich brown and buff, shading to dirty white. A dark stripe passes through the eye, and another across the cheek. Length, 15–16 in. Wing, 7·8 in. Tarsus, 1·3 in. (*Plates 1 and 163*.)

## Blue-winged Teal                                                            *Anas discors*

This American duck breeds in Canada and the northern States and winters as far south as Peru. About twenty examples have been recorded in the British Isles; all are considered to have been genuine wild birds. The distinctive mark of the drake is a prominent white crescentic patch in front of the eye on its grey-brown head, and in both sexes the China-blue shoulder differs from the blue-grey of the Garganey. The clove-brown back of the drake has U-shaped buff marks and the sepia rump is bordered with white. The buff-and-black-streaked scapulars are glossed with green and the metallic-green speculum bordered with white. The bill is black, the legs yellowish. The female is a brown and umber bird, pale on the speckled head and neck, and white on the chin. Length, 16 in.

## Gadwall                                                                     *Anas strepera*

The breeding range of the Gadwall is almost as wide as that of the Mallard, practically the northern temperate regions south of the arctic circle. It now breeds in some numbers in East Anglia and there are smaller numbers nesting regularly in a few other counties of England and Scotland, either by introduction or natural colonisation. A few pairs breed in northern Ireland. For the most part, however, the Gadwall is a scarce and irregular but widespread winter visitor to all parts of Great Britain and Ireland.

Superficially the Gadwall resembles a rather dark female Mallard, but may always be told by the black and white speculum; the overhanging scapulars or the fluffed-out flanks often almost conceal the white. Ducks, if watched long enough, usually rise in the water to flap their wings, and then the white flashes into view. As it frequently swims with Mallards, opportunity is given of comparing size; it is distinctly smaller and greyer than the ducks, and in flight its wings look more pointed. Crescent-shaped marks, grey in the drake and brown in the duck, show on the head and neck. It swims buoyantly and flies swiftly, its wings whistling, but its feeding and other habits differ little from those of other surface-feeding ducks. Normally nocturnal, it may, however, be seen feeding in the day, paddling gently as it holds itself vertically in the water with its foreparts immersed. Migrants, which reach our shores from the end of August onwards, may be noticed at sea, but the favourite haunts are freshwater lakes and pools, where, shy and retiring, it seeks the shelter of the aquatic vegetation. The note of the drake is described as a chuckling croak. The duck has a mallard-like quack.

The nest, seldom far from water, is as a rule well concealed by its surroundings; it is built of grass or other dry plants, and is lined with dark greyish-white down, lighter than the nest-down of the Mallard. The eight to thirteen eggs are buffish-white, and are usually laid in May. The down of the juveniles is similar to, but a little darker than that of the Mallard.

The adult drake, in winter, has the head and neck greyish-brown with darker speckles and most of the upper parts dark brown with crescentic grey markings; the wing-coverts are dark chestnut shading to black, the speculum black and white, upper and under tail-coverts conspicuously velvet-black. The breast is dark brown with pale markings shading to the whitish abdomen; the grey pencilling of the flanks is noticeable. In May an eclipse dress is assumed, approaching that of the duck, but the chestnut coverts are retained. The bill is lead-blue, nail black, legs dark orange. The duck is a browner bird, and the feather centres and markings are more pronounced; she lacks the chestnut on the wing and her under tail-coverts are speckled with grey and brown. Her bill is banded laterally with dull orange. Immature birds have streaked underparts. Length, 20 in. Wing, 10·5 in. Tarsus, 1·8 in. (*Plates 20, 21 and 164.*)

### Wigeon *Anas penelope*

As a regular nesting species the Wigeon occurs in Scotland, chiefly in the north, but though odd pairs have nested in England, Wales and Ireland, it is in most parts of the British Isles a common winter visitor. Abroad it nests in northern Europe and Asia and in winter visits Africa.

On the water an old drake Wigeon is a conspicuous bird, his large white wing-patch never concealed; a yellowish-buff or creamy crest forms a wide parting on his warm burnt-sienna head, and his back and flanks, divided by the white line, are finely pencilled with black on grey. His pinkish breast shades somewhat abruptly into white, and as he swims with pointed tail a little elevated, the white contrasts noticeably with the velvet-black of the under coverts. The more sombre duck shows only a little white on the wing when swimming, but her rufous head, well-marked back and white underparts separate her from the much larger Mallards and the smaller Teal, her frequent companions on inland waters. When the birds rise, white shows distinctly on the wing of either sex: on the drake it is a great oblong patch, 3½ by 2 in., formed by the black-tipped greater wing-coverts; on the duck a conspicuous double bar.

A few Wigeon reach our shores and inland waters in August, but they are seldom numerous until mid-October. Though often abundant on meres and lakes at some distance from the coast, sometimes up to 1000 on reservoirs in the very centre of England, the Wigeon is chiefly a salt-water duck; in muddy and sandy bays and inlets it feeds in thousands, and floats offshore in great packs and lines, looking from the land like undulating collections of floating wrack as the birds rise and fall on the waves. Even in a rough sea they sleep peacefully, and where their feeding grounds are liable to be disturbed they spend the day at sea, flighting inward at dusk. Although on the banks the bird picks up molluscs, crustaceans and marine worms, its main food is the sea-grass *Zostera*, which grows on tidal flats. When unmolested it will feed by day, and its times are to some extent regulated by the tides. The weed is dragged up by the roots, the bird swimming or wading in shallow water and only dipping the head and neck; it seldom feeds in the vertical reversed position common to most surface-feeders. It rarely dives for food, but it will, like most ducks, dive and splash in play, and a wounded 'cripple' dives with great activity. It will eat grain, and birds have been found in autumn crammed with black-berries which they had doubtless gathered on the edge of ponds and ditches.

The Wigeon is perfectly at home on land, walking with ease and running swiftly; the drakes race after one another, open-mouthed, on the grass or sand. On the wing it is quicker than the Mallard, though hardly as swift as the Teal. A flock will turn and twist in flight, but the evolutions are less erratic than those of the last-named bird. The call of the drake is a long musical whistle, *whee-oo*. Throughout the winter this call is constantly uttered; the bill is opened wide when the bird calls. The contented purring note of the duck is very different from her quack of alarm, a harsh growling *kraak, kraak*. During courtship, when the drake is most musical, his neck is carried stiffly erect, and he frequently sits up in the water to flap his wings, advertising the glory of his white patch.

The majority depart north at the end of February or early in March, but passage flocks are met with in April and May. Several Wigeon recovered in the British Isles have been ringed as juveniles in Iceland, and many more marked in Britain in winter have been reported from eastern Europe.

The nest, built in grass, heather or other herbage, is seldom far from water; the down is dark with pale centres. The eggs, six to ten, are creamy-white, similar to but lighter and a little larger than those of the Shoveler; they are laid from April to June. The duckling in down is almost uniform brown above with rufous cheeks and neck, and lacks the distinctive eye streak of the infant Mallard and Teal.

The adult drake in winter has a chestnut head, buff forehead and crown, pinkish breast, vermiculated grey back and flanks, black under tail-coverts. A broad white patch on the wing-coverts is conspicuous in flight and visible at rest; the speculum is green and black. The bill is lavender-grey, legs olive-grey. The duck's head is pale rufous spotted with black; her upper parts generally are brown barred with buff; her wings, smoke-grey on the shoulder, have a white border to the green speculum. The flanks are rufous, the belly white. In eclipse in summer the drake is more rufous than the duck, but he loses most of his masculine characters. Immature males are at first like the duck in winter, but by November and December they are in very intermediate dress. Length, 18 in. Wing, 10 in. Tarsus, 1·75 in. (*Plates 21 and 164.*)

## American Wigeon                                      *Anas americana*

Although there is often the possibility that records of rare waterfowl may relate to escapes from captivity, there is definite proof that this North American duck does sometimes cross the Atlantic: a juvenile ringed in New Brunswick, Canada, was shot in Shetland in October 1966. One or two individuals are reported in the British Isles in most winters. The most marked differences between this bird, which is known in America as the Baldpate, and the Wigeon are on the head of the drake. The central crest is yellowish-white, and below it is a dull green stripe from the eye to the nape; under this again the whitish face and throat are speckled with black. The rest of the plumage corresponds in pattern, but is browner and more vinaceous. The head of the duck is yellowish-white speckled with black. The bill is greyish-blue, the legs brown. Length, 18·5 in.

## Pintail                                               *Anas acuta*

The Pintail breeds regularly in small numbers in Scotland and also nests in a few widely scattered localities in England, and occasionally in Ireland. It is a regular but not abundant winter visitor, more frequent on the sea than inland. It nests throughout Europe and in winter reaches Africa.

The Pintail is just as slender and elegant as the Shoveler is bluff and heavy. Naturally the two elongated central tail feathers of the drake are his most distinctive character, but his long neck and high forehead give him a somewhat misleading short-billed appearance. A narrow white stripe passes down each side of his long neck, starting at the back of the face and extending to and joining the pure white breast and underparts; the rich brown of the head and upper neck throw this streak into prominence, and it catches the eye, even when the bird is at a distance. The pointed tail of the duck is shorter, but her speckled head and slender neck, and long narrow wings give her character in flight. Immigration begins in September, and most appear to leave in March and April. November to January is the period of greatest abundance. Though uncommon far inland, the Pintail is partial to fresh water near the shore. It is a shy and cautious fowl, spoiling the sport of the fowler, straining its long neck over the low banks and sighting his approach.

The Pintail is quick on the wing, pulling ahead of its companions, Mallards and Wigeon, and its pinions move with unusual rapidity. On the water it is buoyant and graceful, carrying its tail slightly elevated. It certainly often feeds by day, though it has been described as nocturnal, and when it tips its body and immerses head and neck to secure food from the bottom, the long tail is depressed as if to preserve the balance. Crustaceans and molluscs are eaten, but its main food is vegetable; it will visit the stubbles for grain. As a rule it is a quiet bird, though it has a quack of alarm, especially when looking after its brood, and a low chuckle when undisturbed, but during courtship it utters a musical double *quuck, quuck*. The courtship of the Pintail, noticeable in January and February, is an interesting performance; several drakes will swim round the duck, their necks stiff, bills depressed, and tails elevated skyward. With that quick rise and fall, as if settling themselves more comfortably in their aquatic seat, they posture before the apparently bored female, repeating the mellow, deep pairing call. Sometimes, with open bill, the duck drives away a too importunate admirer. If this performance is disturbed every tail goes down at once, for when alarmed the bird carries it horizontally.

The nest in Scotland is usually on dry ground, and is not always carefully concealed; it is lined with sooty-brown down as incubation proceeds. The eggs, seven to ten in number, are yellowish-green as a rule, and are smaller than those of the Mallard; they are laid in April or early May. The duckling in down is whiter beneath than the juvenile Mallard.

The drake in winter has chocolate-brown head and neck, with a curving white line up each side of the neck, back and flanks vermiculated with grey on white, and long-pointed, black-centred, buff-edged secondaries; the sides of the abdomen are buff, showing distinctly against the velvet-black of the under tail-coverts. The speculum is glossy bronze-green, bordered above with buff, and below with black and white bands. The mottled duck is light on the underparts; her breast and abdomen are speckled and flanks boldly marked with dark brown. Two white bars cross the wing, but the space between is dull. The drake's bill is blue-grey with a black central stripe, the duck's grey-horn; the legs are slate-grey. In eclipse, from July to October, the drake is brown, though duskier than the duck, and the speculum does not lose its brightness. The brown immature drake is duck-like at first. Length, 28 in. Wing, 11 in. Tarsus, 1·75 in. (*Plates 21 and 164.*)

## Shoveler                                                             *Anas clypeata*

The handsome Shoveler increased rapidly as a resident in all parts of our islands in the first half of the 20th century, but its position is now more stable. It is well distributed in the north and east of England, but is rather scarce in the south and in Wales. It breeds widely in the east and south of Scotland and in most counties in Ireland. As a passage migrant and winter visitor it is common on many inland waters. It has a wide breeding range in Europe and in winter it reaches tropical Africa.

The long, broad, spatulate bill of the Shoveler is its most noticeable feature; but the bluff white breast of the drake, followed by rich chestnut on the lower breast and belly, make it a conspicuous bird, even on a pool crowded with other fowl. A nearer view reveals a glossy green head and neck, light blue shoulders and, a rare character of surface-feeders, a yellow eye. Except for her blue shoulders, duller than those of her mate, the mottled brown duck differs little from the female Mallard, but the slimmer, long-necked Mallard should never be confused with the stocky, short-necked, big-billed Shoveler, which, even when at rest, floats down in the bows, with its heavy bill resting on its breast. From March to May, when the passage birds are bound north, and again from August to November, the numbers are greatest; far more pass through our islands than remain to nest or winter. Britain is its half-way house, a food-providing hostelry; April and September are the busiest months. Though its wings move with great rapidity the flight of the Shoveler is neither so swift nor strong as that of the Mallard; the flying bird looks what it is, heavy and unwieldy. Yet the flight is not always straight; the Shoveler will swoop and change direction like the Teal, though with much less skill. On the ground it is less agile than many species, for, in proportion, its feet are small and weak. The flight call is a repeated *tuk, tuk,* but both drake and duck have a deep quack, lower than the resounding note of the Mallard.

On the water the bird is often remarkably active, swimming in short rushes this way and that as it scoops the water with its spoon, 'bibbling' as the fowlers call it. Water, especially when full of weed or mud, is passed rapidly through the bill, and visible and invisible contents are sifted and retained by the well-developed lamellae; the bill of the Shoveler is an effective sieve. It by no means confines itself to planktonic feeding, well equipped though it is for this form of diet. The bird is most excited when catching insects, either on or just above the water, cleverly intercepting those that fly near. The assumption of the vertical pose, head down and tail up, is not popular with the Shoveler, nor does it dive often. It feeds at night and by day, though it often spends hours asleep on the water, its head tucked in its scapulars, its white upper breast puffed out, as it swings slowly round and round. In some districts it is found regularly on salt water, but small pools, bogs and marshes, be they ever so dark and muddy, fresh or brackish, are its favoured haunts.

The nest is often in a marsh, and where the ground is wet it is a large structure of grass and rushes, but in a dry site, which it prefers, it is not above the level of the ground, though well concealed by surrounding vegetation. In the Cheviots it is often in heather or dwarf willow. The nest down is blackish-brown with faint white tips. The eight to twelve eggs, usually greenish, are laid in April or May. The nestling is clad in yellow and brown down like that of the Mallard, but without the buff on the wings. At first the small bills show little lateral expansion. When the young have passed the flapper stage, they and the old birds leave many of the nesting haunts, though on some bogs and pools Shovelers may be met with all the year round.

In winter the adult drake has dark green head, white lower neck, breast and scapulars, chestnut flanks and belly, black under tail-coverts. The forewing is pale blue, speculum green with white borders. The duck is mottled brown like the female Mallard, but the blue forewing shows in flight. In the drake the bill is slate-grey, the legs orange-red, and the irides yellow, but in the duck these are respectively olive-brown with orange at the base, dull orange, and dark brown. In eclipse the drake closely resembles the duck, but the belly is tinged with rufous. The shoulder blue, which is retained, is brighter than in the duck. At first the plumage of all young is feminine. Length, 20·5 in. Wing, 10 in. Tarsus, 1·4 in. (*Plates 21, 23 and 164.*)

**Red-crested Pochard**                                    *Netta rufina*

Those ducks which habitually obtain their food by diving are collectively
known as the diving ducks, as opposed to the surface-feeders. The Red-
crested Pochard, an uncommon visitor to Britain, is one of this group. The
majority of its occurrences have been in the eastern and southern counties,
especially in Essex, where autumn visits have become regular in recent years,
following the extension of the bird's breeding range to Denmark, Holland and
north-west Germany. It has also occurred in many other parts of the British
Isles, though it is impossible to say how many of these birds have been escapes
from waterfowl collections.

Compared with the familiar Pochard this bird is large, but apart from that
it has several distinctive characters. The adult drake has a crimson bill, chestnut head, shading to golden on the crest, black breast and white flanks. The
duck has whitish cheeks contrasting with a dark crown and she shows some
red or orange on her bill. Her body plumage is much paler than that of the
female Common Scoter which has a similar head pattern. In flight both sexes
show a broad white patch extending almost the whole length of the wing.

Its habits roughly correspond with those of its congeners; it is a diurnal
feeder, diving for its animal and vegetable food in fresh water. It rises from
the water with apparent labour, and flies with rapidly whirred wings; on the
ground it is not as good a walker as most of the surface-feeders, for the feet of
all diving ducks are better fitted for underwater progression than for exercise
on land. Its note is harsh and grating, another common character.

In winter the adult drake has chestnut head shading to golden-yellow on the
erectile crown feathers; black neck, breast, underparts and upper tail-coverts;
brown back and wings with a wide white bar on the flight feathers; white
flanks. The duck has dark brown crown, whitish cheeks and sides of neck,
light brown body plumage and dull white wing-patch. The drake's bill and
legs are red, the duck's reddish-brown. Drakes in eclipse and young males
resemble females, but the crest is visible. Length, 22 in. Wing, 10·5 in. Tarsus,
1·5 in. (*Plate 22*.)

**Scaup**                                                *Aythya marila*

Although the Scaup has occasionally been discovered nesting in Scotland and
the northern Isles, it is mainly a winter visitor, often abundant, to our coasts.
Its European breeding range is a northerly one, extending from Iceland
through Scandinavia to northern Russia. It seldom appears on inland waters,
but when it does so it consorts with other diving ducks.

The Scaup is as partial to salt water as the Pochard is to fresh. Its black
head and breast, grey mantle, and white flanks show up well on quiet water,
but when at a distance, tossed on a rough sea, it is not so easy to distinguish
from the much larger Scoter or even other marine ducks. It is a typical diving
duck, short and squat, and, as in the Pochard, its bill slightly uptilts. The drake
Scaup can be distinguished from this bird by its black, green-shot head and

the distinct white bar on its wing, very noticeable in flight, and the female by a broad white mask surrounding her lead-blue bill. It can be told from the black-backed drake Tufted by its larger size, grey back and absence of crest, but with females more care is needed. The immature Tufted Duck often has a patch of white at the base of the bill. The wing-bar is present in both; indeed, the main difference is in the size of this frontal patch, which in the Scaup reaches to the level of the eyes. On rising from calm water the bird splashes along the surface, paddling with its feet, but from the crest of a wave it has less difficulty in getting on the wing. It is sociable, but usually swims in small parties, a dozen or so together, though at times these little gatherings are scattered everywhere, thousands of birds in sight at once. Except when resting on the banks it seldom packs closely like the Wigeon. Being a deep-water feeder it can obtain food in rough weather and is not forced ashore by storm; it feeds where the depth is not too great for it to reach bottom to hunt for molluscs, worms and crustaceans. The name is supposed to be derived from the habit of frequenting the 'mussel-scaups' or 'scalps', the rocks or estuarine mud-banks where these bivalves live. Cockles and other 'shell-fish' are eaten. The bird is very silent in winter, but sometimes utters a grating alarm call. Cooing and crooning notes are used in courtship.

Scaup congregate to rest on exposed banks in estuaries and bays, and are then difficult to approach, but the small parties met with near the shore are not so shy. The usual time for arrival of migrants is from the middle of September onwards, but birds are often noticed in August. Passage birds are most numerous in October. Many return north in March, but some linger until May or even June. The immediate neighbourhood of water is usually selected for the nest; the eight to eleven eggs, greenish but darker than the Pochard's, average 2·43 by 1·71 in. Eggs in Scotland have been found in June.

The adult drake has the head, neck and breast black with a green sheen, the upper parts white with fine vermiculations of black and grey, and the flanks and underparts white. On the wing is a white bar. The black parts in the drake are chocolate in the duck, except the facial patch, which is white. The upper parts are dark brown with grey pencilling, the sides dull brown and also lined, and the underparts tinged with brown. In both sexes the bill is greyish-blue, darker in the female, and the legs lead-blue; the irides at all ages are yellow. The drake in eclipse resembles the duck, but lacks the white mask. The broad mask of the young birds is suffused with brown, but still is distinct, and in immature drakes the head is sooty. Length, 19 in. Wing, 8·5 in. Tarsus, 1·5 in. (*Plate 1.*)

### Ring-necked Duck                                      *Aythya collaris*

This North American diving duck has occurred four or five times in the British Isles since the first record in 1955. The male is rather similar to a Scaup, but has a black back and white in front of the pale grey flanks. There are two white bands across the bill. The female resembles the duck Pochard, but has white round the eyes and base of the bill. Length, 17 in.

**Tufted Duck**                                              *Aythya fuligula*

The increase of the Tufted Duck in the present century is more striking than that of the Pochard; in almost all parts of the British Isles, including Ireland, where the Pochard is only feeling its way, the Tufted Duck has established itself as a permanent resident, though it is still scarce in north-west Scotland, Wales and south-west England. It is a freshwater species with a breeding range extending across northern Europe and Asia. Many Continental birds winter in Britain.

The black and white Tufted Duck, black above and white below in the drake, is not a difficult bird to tell; the long, graceful crest in winter sets it apart from other ducks. The female and young birds are less distinctive; they are dark brown above, and have dull white underparts, while the crest is only slightly developed. It is not, at first sight, always easy to separate them from Pochards, especially when their lavender-tinted flanks obscure the white wing-bar. On the wing, however, this white bar is very plain, though less noticeable than that of the Goldeneye. On account of the Tufted's golden-yellow irides, it is sometimes called the Golden-eye, leading to confusion with the other diving duck known by that name. The residents receive large additions from overseas in autumn, October being the month when most arrive or visit our waters on passage. From then onwards there are flocks of varying size on all the larger waters, but these diminish from March to May, and in June and July the only birds in evidence are the breeding stock and others which for some reason show neither inclination to nest nor to migrate. Non-breeding birds often spend a few summers on a water before nesting begins there.

Undoubtedly the Tufted is our best-known diving duck, and it is expert at the art. The Tufted may take a header or merely slip out of sight, but like the Pochard it usually kicks up a parting jet of water. In clear water the bird may be watched swimming easily at a depth of 10 ft. or more, but the usual depth of dive is from 2 to 6 ft. Normally the dives do not exceed fifteen seconds in duration. The Tufted's habits are fairly regular; as a rule most of the day is spent idly on the water, the birds slumbering with the blue bill tucked into the black back, floating lightly, like small black and white buoys swinging in the wind. Others attend to the toilet, rolling on one side and showing the white underparts to perfection, as they scratch neck or flank with a foot. The social habit is well developed, and flocks of considerable size consort with Pochards; the bird is seldom met with in any numbers on the sea. Towards evening the flocks fly or swim to the feeding ground, which may be on another lake or the shallower parts of that on which they have spent the day, and again in the early morning the birds usually feed. Tufted Ducks, however, may be seen diving for food at all hours, often in little groups close inshore, vanishing one after the other until the water swirls and eddies. Aquatic weeds, molluscs and insects are taken. If alarmed the birds sink the body, stiffen the neck, and make for open water, but are slow to take wing; when they do they splash with wings and feet. Flocks on the wing flash as they turn, but aerial gymnastics are not frequent; at times a flock will suddenly drop diagonally to a lower level and at once resume horizontal flight, and the descent to the water is swift and accompanied by a loud rushing sound. The flight and alarm note are similar—a growling *currah* or *kurr*, but the breeding call is a soft, liquid *puk*, with a little of the Pintail twang. As the drake calls he rises vertically in the water and jerks his head upwards. A duck, if uneasy when conducting her brood, utters a frequent short grunt.

The nest is placed in various situations, usually dry spots near water, and is well concealed by rushes, reeds, heather, or other herbage; it may be in a hollow or beneath a bush, but is occasionally exposed. It is formed of dry grass, sedges and leaves, and the dark down varies in quantity. The eight to ten eggs are large, greenish or olive-brown. They are laid late in May or in June, and it is often well into July before the sooty-brown little balls of down venture out into the open. The duck in charge shows her anxiety by her stiffly upright neck, and though prior to sitting she was constantly attended by her mate, she is usually left to take all family responsibilities. Drakes in eclipse swim together well away from the brood. The juveniles crowd after their mother, often pressing against her flanks, and if alarmed she by no means always lures them to deeper water, but will lead them into the shelter of the aquatic fringe. As the young grow, the down becomes browner—less sooty— and the eyes, at first brown, change to dull white, and much later to yellow. Many birds in first plumage have a marked white patch at the base of the bill, and adult females at times retain a few white feathers.

The drake in winter has all black plumage except for pure white flanks and belly and a white bar across the flight feathers; he has a pendent crest. The female and juveniles are dark brown, though the duck in winter may show some dull white on the flanks; they may show white feathers at the base of the bill. The drake in eclipse is like the duck but blacker above and whiter below. The bill and legs are grey, with a bluish tinge in the male; irides golden yellow. Length, 17 in. Wing, 8 in. Tarsus, 1 in. (*Plates 22 and 164.*)

## Pochard                                                     *Aythya ferina*

Within recent years there has been a marked increase of the Pochard as a resident species in the British Isles, but it is still rather scarce and local, especially on the western side of Great Britain, and in Ireland it is only a sporadic breeder. It breeds in eastern and central Europe and migrates to the west and south in autumn. Great numbers visit our islands in winter, congregating in flocks on the larger waters inland. Unless these are frozen over only occasional birds appear on salt water.

The Pochard is not a difficult bird to identify, for the head and neck of the drake are rich chestnut-red, and most of the upper parts lavender-grey, finely pencilled with undulating black lines. It has no central paler crest as in the Wigeon, nor any distinct wing-patch. The back of the Scaup is vermiculated like that of the Pochard, but the former has a black head, and the absence of wing-bar prevents confusion with the rare Ferruginous Duck. Probably it is

PLATE 18
*Above left :* White Stork, p30        *Above right :* Black Stork, p31
*Below :* Glossy Ibis, p32

PLATE 19

Spoonbill
(immature), p31

Photo:
J. B. and S. Bottomley

PLATE 20
Gadwall (male
and female), p39

Photo: *Eric Hosking*

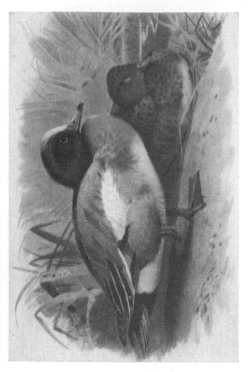

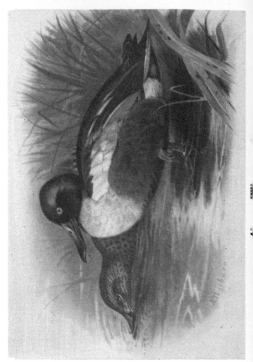

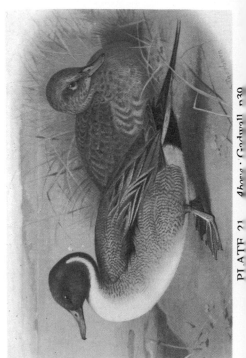

PLATE 21.    Above : Gadwall. p.30

PLATE 22

*Above left:*
Tufted Duck, p47
*Above right:* Red-
crested Pochard,
p45

*Below left:* Long-
tailed Duck (male
and female,
winter), p52
*Below right:*
Pochard, p48

*Photo : Eric F*

PLATE  23

*Above :* Pochard, p48

*Below :* Shoveler, p43

*Photo : Eric F*

PLATE 24

Red-breasted
Merganser
(female), p58

Photo: Eric Hosking

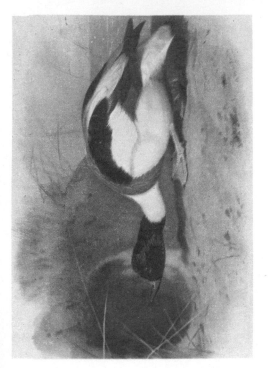
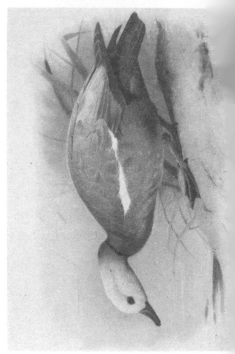

PLATE 25

*Above left:*
Ferruginous
Duck, p50
*Above right:*
Shelduck, p63

*Below left:*
Goldeneye, p51
*Below right:*
Ruddy Shelduck,
p65

PLATE 26     *Above*: Eider, p56
                 *Below*: King Eider, p58

*Above*: Common Scoter, p54
*Below*: Velvet Scoter, p53

PLATE 27    Goosander, p60

PLATE 28    Grey Lag Goose, p65

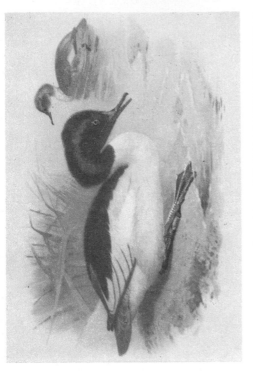

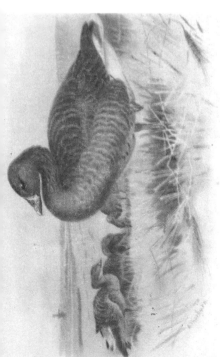

PLATE 30    *Above* : Grey Lag Goose, p65
*Below* : Bean Goose, p68

*Above* : White-fronted Goose, p67
*Below* : Pink-footed Goose, p68

*Photo: J. B. and S. Bottoml*

PLATE 31

*Above:* Whooper Swan, p73

*Below:* Bewick's Swan, p74

*Photo: Eric Hoskir*

PLATE 32    Buzzard, p77

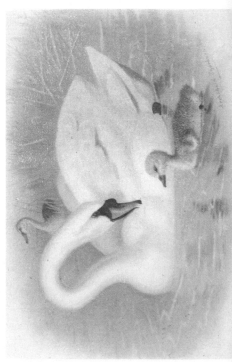

the carriage of the head and neck of the Pochard which causes the impression that the bill has a slight but distinct upward tilt, for in the hand this is no more noticeable than in several other species.

September and October are the months in which the immigrant Pochards reach most districts. From year to year the number of winter visitors varies, and during the season there is much fluctuation on any particular water, at one time only a few small parties being present, but at others hundreds or even thousands of birds. The Pochard is sociable, and flocks move from water to water. The flight is fairly quick and direct, but the rapid movements of the short wings give the impression of greater speed than is actually attained. When about to alight, the whole flock will suddenly slide down diagonally at great speed, the wings producing a startling rushing sound, skim above the surface, and enter with a splash. Diving ducks do not spring clear like surface-feeders when rising, but beat along the water for some distance like Coots, striking with wings and running feet. The bird is, as a rule, in no hurry to rise, and when approached, draws off into open water, sinking its body until the wavelets wash across its neck, and glancing back over its shoulders as it swims swiftly away. With a little care it is possible to get close to a party feeding inshore. The manner of diving varies individually, probably according to the depth the bird desires to work; at times the bird springs up and with a graceful curve takes a header, but frequently it slips below the surface, often kicking up a little shower of spray, and swims so superficially that its underwater progress can be followed by a ripple on the surface. It is difficult to estimate the size of a feeding flock, for the birds bob up and go under again at once; two or three, a dozen, or none may be visible at any moment. Weeds are dragged from the bottom, vegetable food being preferred, but molluscs and water insects are also taken. Most of the feeding takes place at dawn and dusk; the birds usually rest well out from the shore through the hours of full daylight. The alarm note is a guttural *qu-a-a-a-ak*, but the flight call is a harsh *currah*. When courting, the drake extends his head along the water and whistles softly to the duck. On land the Pochard is ungainly; its large feet, set far back, are adapted for subaqueous progression. The hind toe in the diving ducks is lobed.

The nest is usually in a very wet or boggy situation, never far from and often actually over water; in consequence it is a bulky structure of rushes, reeds, or flags, raised well above the surface like the nest of the Coot. The quantity of blackish down, acquired in the spring moult, varies considerably, and in some nests, even when the young are hatched, is scanty. The eggs are remarkably large especially when compared with those of Mallard and other large-sized surface-feeders. They are greenish, six to ten in number, and are laid from April to June. The nestling is olive-grey above and buff beneath, and has a buff eye-stripe and small patches on the wing.

The drake in winter has a chestnut head and pale grey wings and body with fine black vermiculations. Below the chestnut there is a black band, narrow above and broad on the breast; the lower back, beyond the grey, and the under tail-coverts are also black. In the duck the head and neck are a darker brown and the cheeks and chin greyish-white; the breast and upper parts are reddish-brown, the latter shading into greyish-brown, crossed by undulating grey lines. The browner male in eclipse is indistinctly barred with grey. Young males resemble the ducks, but soon show grey feathers on back and wings; the black breast is not gained during the first year. The bill is black, crossed by a band of slate-blue, much broader in the drake than the duck; the legs are slate-grey. Length, 19 in. Wing, 8·25 in. Tarsus, 1·5 in. (*Plates 22, 23 and 164.*)

### Ferruginous Duck *Aythya nyroca*

The Ferruginous Duck or White-eyed Pochard is a bird of southern Europe and western Asia which occasionally wanders northwards, and in most years two or three appear in our eastern and southern counties, and more rarely in the west, or in Scotland and Ireland. This duck is commonly kept in captivity, and some at least of the recent records probably relate to escaped birds.

This species may be confused with the female Pochard or Tufted Duck, for its general colour pattern is similar, but birds of either sex or at any age may be told by the combination of a white wing-bar and white under tail-coverts. In addition the drake has a much browner head and neck than the drake Pochard, and his back is umber, not grey with vermiculations like that of the commoner bird. The white iris, from which he gets the alternative name, is very noticeable; in the duck it is tinged with brown, and her plumage is duller, whilst young birds are even more dingy.

The Ferruginous Duck is an expert diver, seeking its food—weeds, aquatic insects, molluscs and crustaceans—in freshwater pools, in marshes and other quiet spots, for it is shy and retiring, and even when kept on private waters lurks in those parts where vegetation is thickest. Its call on the wing is similar to that of the Pochard, a harsh, growling *kurr*. It is not specially quick on the wing, leaving the water with much splashing, and on land is decidedly awkward.

Adults have dark chestnut head, neck, breast and flanks, duller in the female, white underparts and under tail-coverts; back and wings are dark brown with a broad curved white bar on the flight feathers. Bill and legs are blackish; the iris is white in the drake, brown in the duck. The drake in eclipse resembles the duck; juveniles are similar but lack the white under tail-coverts. Length, 16 in. Wing, 7·75 in. Tarsus, 1·2 in. (*Plate 25.*)

### Bufflehead *Bucephala albeola*

This lively little duck is a native of North America and has been recorded in the British Isles some half-dozen times. It is a smaller bird than our Goldeneye, and both drake and duck may be recognised by the white patch or band which runs upwards from *behind* the eye to the crest. In the drake this mark is larger and more distinct on his glossy green head than on the more soberly coloured duck. Females and immature birds, in addition to showing this mark, are browner than Goldeneyes in similar dress. Length, 14–16 in.

## Goldeneye                                          *Bucephala clangula*

The smart Goldeneye is a well-distributed, though not very abundant winter
visitor to salt and fresh water; it has twice been proved to have nested in a
wild state in Cheshire. It normally nests, however, in Scandinavia and across
arctic and sub-arctic Europe and Asia. Its winter wanderings do not, as a rule,
extend as far south as those of other diving ducks. In our islands immature
birds are much more abundant than fully mature drakes.

The adult drake Goldeneye is a very black and white bird, with a large white
spot at the base of the bill, below and in front of the eye, which shows clearly
on his glossy green head. The female and young are brown on the head, grey,
mottled with darker brownish-grey, on back, wings and flanks, and the females
have a white collar. They have a broad white wing-bar divided by a black
line; the white on the back and wings of the adult drake is in three parts. There
is, however, little difficulty in identifying the Goldeneye of either sex at any
age, once we have become familiar with its short squat shape and 'buffel
head'. It swims with head well up, the long mane-like feathers of the nape
standing out, giving it a peculiarly big-headed appearance; on the wing this is
just as prominent, for the feathers stand out round the short, thin neck. The
difference in size between the females and males is very remarkable, but the
young drakes do not look as big as the old pied birds. As a winter visitor the
Goldeneye is regular and locally abundant, especially in parts of Scotland and
northern England. It also occurs as a passage migrant. The first birds usually
reach the inland waters in August, and some linger until May or even June.
The Goldeneye is nervous, and unsociable as far as other species are concerned;
it swims and feeds by itself or with a few of its own kind, but seldom consorts
with other ducks. When a man approaches the lake it is the first to rise, and is
quicker in getting on the wing than other divers, though it often scutters
across the water, splashing with its feet. Once on the wing it flies swiftly, often
close to the surface, and does not drop until it reaches the farthest extent of
the pool. The noise it makes in flight—more of a whistle than a rattle—is far
louder than that produced by other ducks; it suggests the ring of thin ice
cracking under the bows of a boat. In favourable conditions it may be heard
across water from fully half a mile away. Vocally the bird is not demonstrative,
though a startled female may utter a harsh grunting expostulation, deeper
than that of the Pochard, but with the same guttural suggestion of *kr*. The
display of the Goldeneye is remarkably vigorous. The drake throws back his
head, often striking his tail, jerks it forward, and at the same time kicks up
jets of water with his feet.

The Goldeneye is thoroughly at home on the water; it seldom comes to
land; ashore it stands in a more upright position than most ducks. Even where
there are a number of lakes in one district the bird usually shows partiality for
certain waters, probably because they provide some particular food. In
Lakeland Macpherson found it the commonest diving duck, and this is still
the case. As an expert diver it is distinctly ahead of its relatives; Coward's
notes give an average of twenty-three seconds below the water, and of three

or four seconds on the surface between each dive. Thus when the bird is busily feeding it is much longer invisible than visible. Often if surprised it dives, swims out for a distance and takes wing when it comes to the surface, and does not sink its body and draw off from the shore like Tufted or Pochard. It is almost entirely an animal feeder, diving for molluscs and crustaceans, and, in fresh water, aquatic insects. In its nesting habits it differs from other ducks, for choice selecting a hole in a tree; it can be induced to make use of nesting-boxes.

The adult drake has a black head with greenish sheen, a round white patch between eye and bill, black back and tail, white breast, flanks and underparts. The wings are black with a broad white patch near the body, conspicuous in flight. The duck has a chocolate-brown head and white collar, brownish-grey back and wings and white underparts; the white wing-patch shows even at rest. Juveniles are similar but browner and lack the white collar. The drake in eclipse resembles the duck but has a blackish head and white breast. The bill is blue-grey, the female's with yellow tip; drake's legs are orange, duck's brownish-yellow; irides yellow. Male: Length, 18 in. Wing, 8·25 in. Tarsus, 1·5 in. Female: Length, 16 in. Wing, 7·75 in. Tarsus, 1·4 in. (*Plate 25.*)

**Long-tailed Duck**                                                *Clangula hyemalis*

The breeding range of the Long-tailed Duck is circumpolar and mainly arctic; it is abundant in Iceland. It has nested once in the Orkneys and probably once or twice in the Shetlands. It is a winter visitor all round our shores, though more plentiful in Scotland and on the east coast of England.

There is always something characteristic about the Long-tailed Duck whatever plumage it is in; it is small and squat and its bill is noticeably short. It swims buoyantly, and when the bill does not show clearly it may be confused with the young Smew. In both winter and summer dress, which markedly differ, the drake has the two central tail feathers 4 or 5 in. longer than the others, and as a rule he carries his tail proudly erect. In winter his plumage is mainly dark brown and white, with a pronounced brown mark on the side of the neck. His head and neck are otherwise white. Much of the white is retained on the face in summer, but the crown and practically all the upper parts are rich brown. In winter the scapulars and inner secondaries are elongated and white, but in summer they have black centres and broad rufous edges. The brown females have no very salient characters, but a brown patch shows plainly on the greyish-white cheek. In old females the head is often very white. Long descriptions of the immature plumages are apt to confuse, for no two birds are exactly alike, and the drake is often in a curious mixture of winter and summer dress. The usual time of autumnal arrival off our shores is September, and of departure, March or April.

The Long-tailed Duck is perfectly at home on the sea, apparently rejoicing in a rough day. Facing the wind it rides buoyantly up the advancing wave, breasts the breaking crest, and glides into the hollow; from the shore we see the small bodies for a moment, then they vanish to appear immediately on the next crest. Its feeding grounds are, as a rule, well offshore; it dives in the troubled water above some sunken reef, seeking molluscs on the rocks and crustaceans in the tangle. The Long-tail is a noisy bird, especially in winter and early spring, and it is from its oft-repeated musical cry that it has earned the Scottish name Calloo. The lively conversational calls may be heard at any time, and often through the night; when it calls it throws the head upward and opens wide its bill.

The bird is a lively and neat diver, and swims underwater in the shallows, using the feet alone, opening the wings when turning, but in deeper water the wings are used vigorously and continuously. Nearer inshore, where the water is very shallow, it swims with the back exposed, its head beneath the surface. If suddenly alarmed on reaching the surface the bird rises more cleanly than other diving ducks, and on dropping to the water it will sometimes go under at once. The average duration of dives has been estimated at over forty seconds. The courtship attitudes of the drakes include extending and lowering the neck and throwing the head right back before uttering the call. The display is frequently interrupted by squabbles, though these slight differences of opinion are not confined to the breeding season. In display the long tail is carried almost at right angles to the back. The duck has a low note which is drowned by the clamour of the drakes. The eggs are elongated, greyish-green to buff, and average 2·1 by 1·5 in.

The difficulty of describing the plumage is complicated by the varying phases due to season and progress towards maturity. The adult drake in winter has head, neck, scapulars, inner secondaries, flanks and underparts white, the rest of the plumage brownish-black, the most noticeable mark being the large oval brown patch on the side of the neck. The elongated tail feathers are black, the others white. The short bill is rose-pink, black at base and tip; the legs are grey. In summer the drake is reddish-brown on head and back. The female in winter has brown head, back, neck mark, breast band and wings, white cheeks and underparts. Both sexes have a duller eclipse plumage in late summer. Juveniles resemble females but are dingier and have brownish, not white throats. Male: Length, 20–23 in. Wing, 9 in. Tarsus, 1·2 in. Female: Length, 16 in. Wing, 8 in. Tarsus, 1·1 in. (*Plate 22.*)

## Velvet Scoter                                                    *Melanitta fusca*

The Velvet Scoter breeds in northern Europe and probably nested in Shetland in 1945. In winter it visits the Atlantic and Mediterranean. To our shores it is a winter visitor in small numbers, but is sometimes numerous off the east coast of Scotland.

The broad white wing-bar of the glossy black Velvet Scoter shows well on the flying bird, or when, raising itself in the water, it flaps its wings, but, as in other wildfowl, it is commonly concealed by the secondaries or fluffed-out flank feathers when the bird is on the water. Distance—for scoters keep well offshore—adds to the difficulty of identifying species, but in a good light the Velvet may be told by its superior size, the broader band of orange on the bill, the white spot immediately below the eye of the drake, and the two almost white patches, one behind the eye and the other at the base of the bill, on the face of the brown duck. In habits, time of arrival and departure, and general behaviour, this bird differs little from the Common Scoter, its frequent companion at sea. Pairs are said to swim more together, but in the huge flocks of Common Scoters, as in packs of Mallards, this marital constancy is little evident until the birds rise, when the pairs often fly together; sometimes, however, Velvets fly in little parties. The flight is quick and near the water. Unlike the Common Scoter it is generally a silent bird. Young and non-breeding birds, probably immature—though the less glossy summer dress of old drakes is hard to distinguish from that of nearly mature males—sometimes linger through the summer off our northern shores. One point in which it differs from the Common Scoter is that the plumage of the young bird is not strikingly different from that of the duck.

The amount of yellow on the bill of the drake Common Scoter varies considerably, but in the Velvet Scoter the pattern is different. The bill is orange and red with the basal knob black, and a black line running through the nostril towards the light nail, where it meets the black line along the edge of the upper mandible. The bill of the duck is leaden, and the basal knob but slightly developed. In both sexes the legs are orange-red, but much brighter in the male. Length, 22 in. Wing, 11 in. Tarsus, 2 in. (*Plate 26.*)

**Surf Scoter**                                                  *Melanitta perspicillata*

This North American marine duck has been recorded much more frequently in recent years, and one or two are now reported almost annually in the winter months, chiefly from Scotland.

As in the eiders, a triangular feathered tract runs down the centre of the swollen and rather massive bill towards the nostrils. The basal protuberance is long and sloping and not a knob. In the drake the bill is showy, shading from deep red to orange and pale yellow; on the sides are white spaces and large squarish black patches. Even more distinctive and conspicuous are a rectangular white mark between the eyes and triangular white patch on the back of the neck; the rest of the plumage is glossy black. The duck is a brown but variable bird, sometimes showing the neck mark more or less clearly and occasionally two whitish spots on her pale brown cheeks. Young males and old females have much in common, but the distinctive male marks appear before the birds attain glossy dress; young birds of either sex have white underparts mottled with brown. The female may be told from the duck Velvet by the absence of the white wing-bar, and from the Common Scoter by the neck marks and facial spots. Length, 21 in. (*Plate 29.*)

**Common Scoter**                                                      *Melanitta nigra*

The Common Scoter nests regularly in the north of Scotland, and has now become well-established in north-west Ireland. It is, however, best known as an abundant visitor to our shores, not merely in winter but at all seasons, for many immature or otherwise non-breeding birds remain during summer. The breeding range extends across northern Europe and Asia, and in winter the is bird abundant along the Atlantic coasts.

The black Scoter, blacker than any other duck, is a heavy-looking bird, even when, like a cork, it rides buoyantly on the waves. It is seldom very near shore, therefore difficult to see clearly, but in a good light its one colour spot, an orange patch upon its bill, is conspicuous; it is the drake only who sports this label, and the base of his bill is much swollen; the duck is a grey-cheeked brown bird. Drake and duck alike, when swimming at ease, carry their pointed tails elevated like the Pintail; this pose catches the eye when the birds are with other diving ducks. When swimming fast the tail is lowered. The absence of white marks on the head prevents confusion with the Velvet Scoter; the absence of the wing-bar is less reliable, since that of the Velvet is often concealed by the flanks of the swimming bird. The majority of the winter birds reach our seas in September; in that month and in April there are large passage movements. All winter the birds are common, and, at any rate off the Lancashire, Welsh, Northumberland and Yorkshire coasts, numbers of immature or other non-breeding birds remain the whole summer. Parties of flightless moulting birds may sometimes be found on shore in early autumn.

The Scoter is certainly a salt-water duck, but it breeds by freshwater lochs and pools and frequently occurs on some inland waters at other seasons. Not only are these visits in April, when there is an occasional and possibly regular overland migration, but little parties appear from time to time in June and July. Off the North Wales and Lancashire coasts the bird is frequently found in immense numbers, and the sea, as far as the eye can reach, is dotted with ducks, or lined with little strings flying swiftly close to the waves. The birds will feed on a falling tide, those farthest out rising to fly shorewards over their companions and dropping where the waves are breaking. They may also be seen flying in long lines far out, undulating like distant steamer smoke, their numbers countless. At close quarters the buoyancy of the swimming bird is very noticeable; it constantly uplifts itself to flap its wings after its frequent dives and shakes a shower of drops from its bill. If disturbed it swims quickly, the head well forward, bobbing like that of the Moorhen, and utters a low *tuk, tuk*. In flight, when its wings whistle, it has a harsh, grating call, but the courtship note is more melodious.

The duration of timed dives varied from sixteen to forty-nine seconds. Molluscs of various kinds are the chief food. Summering birds in North Wales regularly pass in flocks in the morning and afternoon between their feeding grounds near shore and some night haunt at sea, suggesting that they are normally diurnal feeders.

Usually in wet surroundings, the nest is a slight grass-lined hollow, well concealed; the five to eight creamy-white eggs are laid in June, and surrounded with very dark down. They measure about 2·5 by 1·8 in. The duckling is dark brown above and on the breast, and white beneath.

The drake is glossy black above, very dark brown beneath, and his bill is lead-blue, with an orange line on the prominent basal knob and a wider mark below; the legs are brownish-black. The brown plumage of the duck is relieved by the pale cheeks and whitish chin, and the young have the underparts white mottled with brown. Length, 19 in. Wing, 9 in. Tarsus, 1·75 in. (*Plates 26 and 164.*)

## Harlequin *Histrionicus histrionicus*

The drake Harlequin, as the name suggests, is a gay, parti-coloured bird, utterly unlike any other. The sombre duck is apt to be confused with the female Long-tailed Duck, but has much less white on the cheeks and neck. The Harlequin is a resident in Iceland and breeds in Greenland and the north of Canada. It has been recorded about ten times in winter and spring off the coasts of Scotland and northern England. The drake is blue-black in general colour of the upper parts, rich chestnut on the flanks and with a streak of the same colour on either side of the crown, boldly marked with white on the sides of the face in front of the eye, on the cheeks and sides of the nape, and with a white collar, incomplete breast band, and patches on the wings. The female is almost uniform brown above, and on the throat and underparts brownish-white with darker mottlings. In front of and behind the eye are dull white patches. Length, 17 in.

## Steller's Eider *Polysticta stelleri*

This beautiful little duck has occurred about half a dozen times in the northern isles of Scotland and on the east coast of England. It is a circumpolar species which does not normally breed in Europe but is found off the shores of Norway, and in the Baltic in winter. The drake has the head and neck white, the chin black, and a glossy purple-shot black collar joins its black back; the wings are black and white, the lower breast and flanks rich chestnut and the abdomen dark. It is much smaller than the other two eiders, but has the same art green on the head—in front of the eye and on the nape. The duck is dark brown mottled with buff, and has a brown-black speculum narrowly bordered with white. Length, 17 in.

## Eider *Somateria mollissima*

The Eider nests abundantly in Iceland, Scandinavia and the western Palae-arctic region generally. On the Scottish coasts, in the Shetlands and Orkneys, and some of the Hebrides, the Eider is a resident, and on the north-east coast of England some numbers nest annually, most plentifully on Holy Island and the Farnes. There is a flourishing colony in north-west England on Walney Island; a single pair first nested there in 1949 and now there are over a hundred pairs on the island. It also breeds in several places in Ireland, chiefly in the north, but it has spread southwards and greatly increased its numbers in recent years. There has been a marked extension of the winter range of the Eider, which was formerly scarce away from the breeding areas, but now occurs frequently off many of the coastal counties of England and Wales.

The Eider is a large, heavy duck, with a bill sloping from the forehead. Down the centre of the bill, about half-way to the nostrils, is a feathered peak, but even more noticeable than this is the angular tract of feathered skin that runs forward on each side of the bill, dividing the upper mandible, as far as the nostrils, into two portions. The handsome drake, white above, except on the crown and lower back, which, like most of the underparts, are black, can hardly be confused with any other species, for the King Eider has an entirely different bill.

The brown duck, mottled and barred with black, has little beyond her size and shape that can be called distinctive when she is seen at a distance. The female King Eider has a longer peak on the bill, but this is not easily seen on a bird tossing on the waves. The sea, and usually a restless sea, is the place where we are most likely to meet with the Eider, for no duck, not even a Scoter, is more maritime; an Eider inland is exceptional. Offshore, especially at high tide, fleets of Eiders cruise in any weather; the birds lift on the waves, ride through the curling crests, and dip into the troughs without raising their sleepy heads from their breasts. Birds in these flocks are often in puzzling plumage, old white drakes and brown females, and in between young males in various stages of immaturity, mottled, streaked and banded with white, black and brown. When white foam indicates sunken reefs the birds draw in to feed, diving in the rough water for molluscs on the rocks or crustaceans in the weed. They swim close to the exposed rocks, without apparent effort, floating back when a wave threatens to dash them on to the reef. As the tide sinks some mount to rest upon the reef, and others, with head and neck below, but not with the body uptilted, investigate the sand in shallow pools. Small molluscs are swallowed whole, but larger ones and crabs are crushed in the powerful bill; starfish and small cuttles are also eaten.

On the wing the Eider looks heavy, but its speed is considerable; it often flies straight, just above the waves. In flight it has a harsh grating call, but this is less noticed than the low coo, which the drakes utter with head thrown up with a jerk, as if gulping. During courtship this note, frequently repeated, becomes a crooning love-song as, bobbing and jerking, the amorous drakes swim round the duck. The nest, constructed of grass, heather or seaweed, is placed in various situations, sometimes in heather or thrift in the open, but often under the shelter of a wall or rock, and in some parts of Scotland regularly in woods. The large greenish eggs usually number four or five, but much larger clutches are recorded. Fresh eggs may be found from May to July, but late broods may be due to the earlier eggs having been taken for food. Where the bird is protected it is a close sitter and absurdly tame; it is possible to stroke the sitting 'St Cuthbert's Duck' on the Farnes. Captive Eiders have sat for twenty-eight days without taking food or water, and apparently never left the nest. Long before the eggs hatched the old duck was 'buried overhead, nest and all, in a mass of luxuriant chickweed'. The young in down are brown with grey or yellowish eye-stripes and underparts, and their bills and feet are blue-grey. The duck leads them to the water at an early age, and sometimes joins forces with other old birds. The drake usually deserts the female during incubation, but some individuals have been seen anxiously keeping guard. Mixed broods of ducklings of various ages may be attended by a single duck.

The forehead, crown, a stripe on either side of the bill, lower back, and underparts of the drake Eider are black; a white stripe divides the crown, and the neck, face, upper parts generally, and a patch on either side of the abdomen is white. The breast is a beautiful rose-buff, but the most delicate colour is the pale green on the nape and cheeks and the yellow of the elongated inner secondaries. In eclipse plumage, which is developed in July, the drake is blackish on the upper parts with pale breast and white forewing. The duck at all seasons is brown with black barred markings on the body. Young males resemble females at first and develop mature plumage by irregular stages over about three years. Both sexes have bill and legs various shades of greenish-brown and grey. Length, 25 in. Wing, 12 in. Tarsus, 1·75 in. (*Plates 26 and 164.*)

### King Eider *Somateria spectabilis*

The arctic and circumpolar King Eider travels south in winter and consorts with the commoner Eider; in the British Isles it is a rare vagrant, most frequently observed in the Orkneys and Shetlands, though it has also occurred on the east coast and in Ireland.

Rather smaller than the Common Eider, the drake can without difficulty be recognised by the prominent orange boss or lobe on its flesh-coloured or orange bill; a fringe of black frames the knob, showing it up. The drake is also blacker on the wings and back than the Common Eider. The duck cannot easily be distinguished on the water, but in the hand the length of the wedge in the centre of the bill is a good character—it reaches to the nostrils. The habits and food, as far as they have been observed, differ little from those of the Eider; it is ungainly, especially on land, but flies quickly, close to the water. Off the Farnes and in other places drake King Eiders have remained with other birds until June or even July.

The head and neck of the adult drake are white, with black round the knob on the bill and a strong black chevron on the chin; the crown is lavender, the cheeks suffused with delicate green. The upper back, a patch on the wings, and another on the sides of the abdomen are white, the breast is buff, and the rest of the under and upper parts, including the elongated secondaries, are blackish-brown. The duck is brown, palest on the head and neck, and redder than most female Eiders. Length, 22–24 in. (*Plate 26.*)

### Red-breasted Merganser *Mergus serrator*

The Red-breasted Merganser is a breeding bird of northern Europe. In many parts of Scotland, the Scottish islands and Ireland it is a common resident, and it is now nesting in increasing numbers in several localities in north-west

England and North Wales. Elsewhere it is only a winter visitor and regular bird of passage, more abundant on the west than the east coast.

The handsome drake is smaller than the Goosander, from which it may at once be told by its chest band, reddish-brown streaked with black, by the noticeably longer crest, and the conspicuous white and black patch on the shoulder. When swimming it shows a creamy streak on the wing. The female closely resembles the duck Goosander, but when with Mallards looks smaller, whereas the Goosander is larger. She shows a much darker and more distinct bar across the wing-patch than the female Goosander, but as she swims low in the water the bar is often hidden and only visible when she flaps or takes wing. When swimming she moves her head forward and backward, after the manner of the Moorhen, a trick that is not noticeable in the other bird. The Merganser is far more a sea duck than the Goosander in winter, but it commonly frequents estuaries and the lower course of some rivers, and it nests by lakes and streams as well as near the seashore. Its food, fish of various kinds, is hunted below the surface, but in shallow gutters it will swim with the head alone below, picking up small flat fish and crustaceans. Captured fish are sometimes brought to the surface to be eaten, but probably this is only when the captive is too large to be at once swallowed, and is so lively that it has to be subdued. When the fish has been swallowed a sip of water is taken, a common habit of fish-eaters. Sand-eels are favourite food; for these the birds dive excitedly near the shore.

If disturbed the Merganser sinks its body or dives, but when it rises it scutters along the surface for some yards. On the wing it is quick, flying straight and usually low. It has a grating flight call, not unlike that of the Goosander, but as a rule it is not noisy except when pairing, when it constantly coos as it stretches its head upwards, after the fashion of the Eider. Some of the winter visitors arrive in September, and the largest numbers are passing in October and throughout May. In spring the drakes go through display long before they leave the coast. There is a family likeness in all duck displays, but they differ according to the colour or pattern adornment of the drake; he strives to exhibit his best points. Thus the Merganser slightly raises his wings so as to extend the black-barred white secondaries, and stretches up his neck to show his collar; when he raises himself in the water, as if seating himself more comfortably, the breast band is exhibited. Drakes will force themselves suddenly through the water when striving to frighten away a rival. The habit of rising in the water, with or without wing flapping, is by no means confined to the pairing season.

The nest in most cases is well concealed by brambles or other bushes, or by rank herbage; the bird sits closely. It is a slight structure, well lined with grey down when the clutch of eight to twelve drab or slightly greenish eggs is complete at the end of May or in early June. Sometimes many nests are in a small area. The ducklings, brown with white spots on wings and sides and with rich chestnut cheeks, are led to the nearest water, and a few days later to a lake or the sea. In the estuary or on the shore the ducklings share the strange habit of the Shelduck and Eider; some of them leave or are left by the parents, and join forces with other broods; thus a single old bird may be seen tending two or more families.

The drake's head and neck are glossy green-black, his crest long and tufted; a line down the back of the neck passes through the white collar to the black upper back, and the lower back and flanks are finely pencilled with grey. The wings are black and white, the white crossed by two black bars, and on the shoulder is a patch of black and white feathers. Beneath the breast the under-parts are white. The duck has a pronounced crest, brown head and neck, grey-brown back, white wing-bar divided by a dark line, and white under-parts. Both sexes have red bill, legs and irides. The drake in eclipse shows white on the forewing but otherwise resembles the duck, as does the greyer-backed juvenile male. Length, 23 in. Wing, 9·5 in. Tarsus, 1·5 in. (*Plates 24, 29 and 165.*)

## Goosander                                                   *Mergus merganser*

Although several ducks will occasionally eat fish, the 'saw-billed ducks' are the only ones that habitually fish for a living; their long, narrow, serrated bills are well fitted for catching and holding slippery prey. The Goosander, the largest of the group, inhabits northern Europe and Asia, migrating south in winter, and regularly visits estuaries and inland waters in Scotland and England, especially the big London reservoirs. In the north of Scotland a number nest annually, and it has now spread as a regular breeding species to south-west Scotland, Northumberland and north Cumberland.

The Goosander shares with the Red-breasted Merganser the popular name of 'Sawbill'. The handsome drake, with glossy green-black head, black and white wings, grey lower back, and salmon-pink underparts, cannot be confused with the long-crested and ruddy-breasted Merganser drake, but the brown-headed, grey-backed females are very much alike. The Goosander is the larger bird, but size is of no value when the two are not together. Perhaps the best distinction is in the mane-like crest, which in the Goosander is graduated from the nape to the lower neck, whereas in the Merganser it is long at its highest and lowest point and short between; when it stands out it looks more ragged. The chestnut head and neck are sharply divided from the clear grey body, whereas in the Merganser the brown merges gradually into the grey-brown back. The Goosander is far more of a freshwater duck than the other; it seldom appears on the coastal waters where the Merganser is common. Breeding pairs tend to colonise the headwaters of a river rather than its lower course. Immigrant Goosanders reach England in October, but in the northern counties numbers are small until December. Flocks of forty or more are not uncommon in February and March. April is the month of emigration, but birds on passage will linger for a few days, even in mid-May.

The elongated, cigar-shaped body is well adapted for rapid progress in the air, on or under the water; the bird swims with great speed, easily forging ahead of Mallards, even when not hurried. With neck awash and head well forward it slides through the water, its rounded back just showing like a small submarine travelling on the surface, but if suspicious it sinks its deck and leaves only its periscope visible. When resting on the water its attitude is similar to that of the sleeping Great Crested Grebe, the head and neck laid back between the wings; the white coverts and flanks then hide the dark portions of the wing, and the back merely shows as a crescentic line above the white side. The rosy-tinged underparts show when the bird raises itself and flaps its wings, and when it rolls to scratch its blood-red bill an orange leg appears. The ducks, both when swimming and flying, look much darker than the drakes, although their backs are ashy-grey, for the white underparts on breast and flanks are tinged with grey. Goosanders rise heavily, splashing like diving ducks, but when clear of the water fly straight at great speed; they will fly high above an inland water. The only note heard in winter is a harsh *karrr*, but in spring the drake is said to utter a 'soft, low croak'. When a party is fishing, the water swirls as the birds pop up and dive again one after the other. Fish are, frequently at any rate, swallowed under water. The duration of the dives varies, ranging from ten to 110 seconds. A minute below is common, and the bird will often travel fifty yards or more before reappearing. It is neither as upright nor awkward as a Cormorant on land, but is easy on its feet and, considering the far back position of the legs, remarkably horizontal in pose. The courtship performances differ little from those of other ducks; there is the same head throw and gulp as the competing drakes swim round the duck, the same occasional squabbles, and now and then the bird forces itself forward with a strong stroke, after the manner of the cob Swan.

The Goosander nests in holes, often in hollow trees, under rocks or in peat banks, and but little nesting material is collected. Eight to twelve creamy eggs, not unlike those of the Shelduck, are surrounded with light down, and the clutches are often complete early in May. The average size is 2·7 by 1·8 in. When the ducklings, brown above, white on wings, sides and underparts, and with chestnut heads, hatch out, they are led to the water; if the nest is in an elevated position, the young require help in descending. The duck has been seen to bring down some in her bill, others pressed against her breast.

The drake has bottle-green head, black back, grey rump and tail. The lower neck, breast, flanks and belly are white suffused with pink. The wing in flight shows the basal half white, the outer half blackish. The duck has chestnut-brown head and upper neck, with short mane rather than crest, white throat, grey back and flanks, white breast and underparts. In flight the wing looks dark at the tip but white on the rear edge near the body. Both sexes have red bill and legs. The drake in eclipse resembles the duck but has darker mantle and white wing-coverts. Juvenile males have browner upper parts than the duck. Male: Length, 26 in. Wing, 11 in. Tarsus, 1·9 in. Female: Length, 24 in. Wing, 9·5 in. Tarsus, 1·7 in. (*Plates 27, 29 and 165.*)

## Smew                                                            *Mergus albellus*

The Smew, the smallest of the mergansers, is a native of north Europe and

Asia and visits western and southern Europe in winter. Although most abundant as a winter visitor to south-east England, especially the London reservoirs, it occurs from time to time in all parts of Britain, visiting bays, estuaries and inland waters. It is scarce in Ireland. Immature brown-headed birds are commoner than old drakes.

The adult drake, about an inch and a half longer than the duck, is, without being really white, one of the whitest looking of our birds, for the velvet-black markings enhance the snowy appearance. The 'White Nun', as it is called to distinguish it from the female and immature 'Red-headed Smews', has a drooping white crest with two converging green-black lines; as the bird swims with all its feathers in place and with the finely grey-lined flanks concealing most of the black on the wings, the general effect is of a white bird with fine and regular black lines. The back shows as a black line above the scapulars, another narrow line marks the edge of the wing, and two inward curving lines cross the side of the white breast. When, however, the drake raises itself and flaps its wings the black on back and wings shows plainly; the effect is black and white instead of white and black. The female is, at first sight, a little like the Long-tailed Duck, but her head and neck are bright chestnut and she has a decided crest. The points which attract the eye are the very white cheeks and chin.

When swimming, if unsuspicious, the Smew is buoyant and carries the neck gracefully arched, but if alarmed, at once straightens the neck and sinks the body; it swims rapidly away or rises, sometimes splashing with its feet for a few yards, but sometimes shooting straight up from the water. Its flight is very swift, and the bird is generally shy and quick to take alarm. The flight note and call of alarm have the family grating character. Although the legs are set far back the bird takes the water feet first like other ducks. The Smew is a quick, neat diver, though the dives seldom last more than fifteen seconds. It will sometimes dive in very shallow water, so superficially indeed that its back is exposed. It hunts for small crustaceans and insects as well as fish.

The male is mainly white, with a black back and eye-patch and black on the crest and wings and two fine black lines on each side of the breast; the flanks have grey vermiculations. The female has a grey body and tail, chestnut cap and white cheeks and throat; her black and white wing pattern resembles the drake's. The immature is like the female but the wing patches are dingy white. The bill and feet in both sexes are slate or blue-grey, the irides red in old birds, but browner in the young. Length, 16–17·5 in. Wing, 7·6 in. Tarsus, 1·25 in. (*Plate 29*.)

### Hooded Merganser                                    *Mergus cucullatus*

The Hooded Merganser is a North American bird which on five occasions has appeared in Scotland, Wales and Ireland. The head and neck of the drake are black glossed with green and purple, and with a fan-shaped white patch from the eye to the nape. The head is a little like that of the Bufflehead, but the white patch in that bird is not edged with black, nor has it the breast marks or merganser bill. Otherwise the Hooded Merganser is mainly black and white, with grey vermiculations on the brown flanks. The female is brown above and on the breast, and the buff crest—without any white—is smaller and more of the merganser shape. The underparts are white. She is darker, especially on the head and neck, than the female Red-breasted Merganser. The bill is black, the legs yellowish. Length, 18 in.

## Shelduck                                                *Tadorna tadorna*

The Shelduck breeds near suitable shores round the coasts of Europe. Its distribution in the British Isles is general but uneven; it is a sand- and dune-haunting species, locally abundant on the east coast and in the Bristol Channel and exceedingly plentiful in some parts of north-west England, Wales, Scotland and Ireland. There has been a marked increase in numbers during the present century, especially on the east and south coasts of England.

This large and handsome duck has certain goose- and swan-like characters, and is not easily confused with other species. When flying over the distant banks it looks black and white, but at closer range, the broad chestnut band across the white chest is conspicuous, and the scarlet bill with its prominent knob is characteristic. The drake Shoveler when sleeping shows the same stout white breast and chestnut band, but is a squatter, short-necked bird with a lower pose on the water. The name means pied, and has no connection with shield.

Tidal flats, whether of sand or mud, are favoured feeding grounds. It feeds both by day and by night, for its times are regulated by the tides. It is gregarious, but the 'droppings', the sporting term for the flocks, are seldom large, though in late summer and winter it may congregate in thousands. The birds scatter over the banks hunting for molluscs, worms or crustaceans, even racing after sand-hoppers. Mussel-beds are frequented, and some marine weeds are eaten. Like gulls, the Shelduck will mark time or paddle in shallow water to bring worms or other animals to the surface, but much of its food is obtained when swimming by dipping the head and neck, and upending like other surface-feeders. On dunes and marshes, frequented at high tide and during the breeding season, land molluscs and other animals are eaten. The bird walks easily, and its flight is slow and regular, suggestive of a goose rather than a duck. The drake has a low whistling call, and the duck a subdued barking quack, which when rapidly repeated has a laughing ring. The drake may be distinguished by his superior size and the large knob on the bill. The bird swims lightly, sitting high on the water; the adult seldom dives unless wounded or in courtship or coition.

Occasionally the nest is in a hole in a tree or rocks or in undergrowth; the normal site is in a burrow, generally that of a rabbit. A small collection of grass, moss and often bracken, with a plentiful lining of pearl-grey down, is placed in a hollow at a variable distance, 2 to 12 ft., from the entrance. Occupied burrows may be told by the footprints left by the birds. In early spring the birds collect for pairing display; the drakes stretch up their necks and dip them suddenly, and walk round the ducks, their necks depressed and bent, their shoulders hunched up. When rivals meet there is a short tussle, the combatants spring clear from the ground, but one soon gives in and is chased away on foot or wing by the victor. These parliaments meet long after incubation has begun, the members resting, preening themselves and chattering softly on the grassy levels amongst the dunes. Many paired birds do not actually breed.

The eggs, usually laid early in May, are creamy-white, and measure about 2·6 by 1·9 in. The usual clutch is seven to fifteen; the large numbers occasionally reported are doubtless produced by two ducks. The nests are often in colonies. On Brean Down and in some Welsh localities the bird nests on high ground—on Puffin Island on the cliff 100 ft. or more above the sea—but as a rule sandhills and links are favoured.

Inland nesting, especially since the marked increase of the species, is not uncommon. Shelduck have nested round the shores of Windermere since 1918, and breeding is now regular even in Nottinghamshire and Cambridgeshire. Within a day or two of leaving the egg the ducklings are usually taken to the sea by their parents, and an annual attempt is made to conduct these inexperienced pedestrians from their nest-hole. It is said that the ducklings are sometimes conveyed in the beak or on the back of the old birds, but walking is the usual method. On the shore they run with wonderful speed; on the water they dive with skill, and a brood can tire out an energetic retriever and never be in danger.

Both parents attend the brood at first, but after a few days two or more families often combine into packs, which may include over sixty ducklings, under the care of one pair of adults, and later often of a single bird. The caretaker adults are usually aggressive towards other adults either with or without young. Later in the summer the packs break up into smaller independent parties. The apparent reason for this abandonment of families is the approach of the moult. It is now known that the great majority of adult Shelduck from the British Isles migrate to the North Sea coast of Germany to accomplish their moult. On fine clear evenings in July large flocks of Shelduck can be seen leaving many of the west coast estuaries of England by well-defined routes leading to the North Sea. The only known moulting place in Britain is Bridgwater Bay in Somerset, where one or two thousand adult Shelduck moult each year. These may perhaps be immigrants from Ireland, as many locally bred birds migrate up the Severn towards the Wash.

The adult has a metallic green-black head, but the plumage generally is white and black; a white neck collar is followed by a broad, rich chestnut band; the back, coverts, and flanks are white; primaries and scapulars black. On the wing is a chestnut and bronze-green speculum; a black band passes down the centre of the belly. The bill is scarlet, the drake's with a prominent knob; legs pink. Immature birds have blackish crowns, white cheeks and underparts, showing no breast band at first, and hair-grey backs and mantles; their bills are flesh-coloured. The grey edges of the greater wing-coverts of first-year birds distinguish them from adults, in which the wing is pure black and white. The duckling is clad in white down with a sepia band from crown to tail, crossed by a band at the shoulders and another, less complete, to the thighs. The bill is lavender-grey, legs olive-grey. Length, 25–26 in. Wing, 13 in. Tarsus, 2·3 in. (*Plates 25 and 165*.)

### Ruddy Shelduck                                                   *Tadorna ferruginea*

There is always a suspicion that any Ruddy Shelduck that is seen in Britain in an apparently wild state may have wandered from private waters, for the bird is a favourite ornamental fowl much addicted to wandering. On more than one occasion the bird has spread northward and westward throughout Europe, and numbers have invaded our island. It is an occasional but irregular visitor.

Even those who do not know the Ruddy Sheldrake in captivity cannot fail to identify the bird; its orange-brown and buff plumage, and the square white patch which shows plainly on its open wing, are distinctive. On the water it swims with the breast and foreparts low and the stern high, showing a raised and rounded lower back above the deep counter of its black tail and coverts; the neck is carried well erect. On the wing it is heavy and slow. It has a loud double call and a barking cry. In our parks and public gardens it walks easily, cropping the grass like a goose; insects, worms and frogs are also eaten.

The general colour of the adult male is orange-brown, paler below; the head is buff, there is a black neck collar, and the wing-coverts are white. When the bird is swimming the white is hidden by the scapulars, but in flight it shows plainly in a large square patch. The speculum is bronze-green. The legs are blackish, the bill lead-grey. The female and young male have no black collar. Length, 25 in. (*Plate 25*.)

### Grey Lag Goose                                                       *Anser anser*

Of the five species of 'grey geese' which occur in Britain the Grey Lag is the only one that nests with us; the others are winter visitors. A century and more ago the Grey Lag bred on moors and marshes in various parts of England; now it nests in a fully wild condition only in the north of Scotland and some Hebridean islands. However, Grey Lags have been introduced to some parts of England in recent years, and considerable numbers are now breeding in Norfolk and the Lake District in a feral state. Grey Lags breed in northern and eastern Europe, most of them migrating to the south and west in autumn.

Grey geese are exceedingly variable in size and plumage; the assertion that any species may infallibly be identified by certain characters is apt to mislead. Passing 'skeins' of grey geese usually fly too high and fast for identification, and 'gaggles' feeding or resting are too alert to permit close scrutiny. Even in the hand a bird, especially if immature, may puzzle an expert by its variation from type.

The typical characters of the Grey Lag are lavender-grey shoulders, lower back and rump, thick white-nailed bill and pink legs. It is the biggest of the grey geese.

The general habits of all grey geese are similar; they are normally diurnal feeders, cropping grass and gleaning grain. When, however, the fields are disturbed by farmers or others, or on moonlight nights, they adapt themselves to circumstances, and after spending the day on the banks or tide-line, flying inland at dusk. On the coast the uncovered banks are their usual nocturnal haunts, and inland the gaggles sleep in some open country or quiet water; at daybreak they go off to feed, flying in ordered lines or in chevron formation. If forced to remain in the estuary or on the shore during the day they are unsettled and restless, skeins repeatedly taking short flights to reconnoitre. Grain, grass, clover and other vegetable substances are their regular food; in many places they can find sufficient grass on the saltings without risking trips to the cultivated land.

Migratory Grey Lags reach us from mid September onwards, and remain until April or even May. Certain localities attract the bird. Some hundreds regularly visit certain favoured haunts in south-east and south-west Scotland, north-west England and widely scattered districts in Ireland. Elsewhere it is a scarce visitor. The call in flight is loud and sharp, a deep sonorous *ackh*, *ackh*, almost exactly the note of the domestic goose, of which it is probably the most direct ancestor; when the birds settle, the clonking clamour resembles that of other greys. During the breeding season the pair converse in familiar language, the contented undertones of the farmyard. On land it walks with ease and dignity, without the waddle of the overfed domestic bird; it swims lightly, and if threatened during the moult, when through the simultaneous loss of the flight feathers the bird is helpless, it dives with skill. Diving also occasionally takes place during communal bathing, some birds performing complete somersaults in the water. In flight the slow, measured beats betoken strength, and the speed attained has astonished many an inexperienced sportsman.

The nest is large, placed in thick heather, rushes or other vegetation. Little or no lining is provided when, in mid April, the four to six yellowish-white eggs are laid, but the goose constantly adds down until the eggs are concealed. The average size is 3·4 in by 2·3 in. The sitting goose is shy and nervous, turning her head from side to side, her neck feathers dividing in sinuous creases; she is on the alert to sight danger. The down-clad yellowish-brown and yellow goslings are usually hatched in May; their under surface is at first a wonderful golden-yellow.

The head and neck of the adult are light brown, upper parts greyish-brown, darkest on the wings and scapulars; shoulders, lower back and rump bluegrey. The ashy-grey tail is tipped and bordered with white; the upper and lower tail-coverts are pure white. The breast is suffused with brown, and the belly dull white with a few dark blotches and bars. There are often some white feathers at the base of the bill. The white-nailed bill is pink or orange, the legs flesh-coloured. The immature bird is darker and lacks the spots and bars on the underparts and the white above the bill. The gander is the bigger bird, but the size varies greatly, and all measurements of this and other grey geese must be treated as averages. Length, 30–34 in. Wing, 18 in. Tarsus, 3·3 in. (*Plates 28, 30 and 165.*)

## White-fronted Goose                                    *Anser albifrons*

The White-fronted Goose is a winter visitor, often numerous, especially on the west side of Great Britain. In Ireland, where it is much the commonest wild goose both inland and near the coast, only the yellow-billed Greenland race is found. The pink-billed race breeds in northern Russia and Siberia.

The White-fronted Goose, at any rate when mature, is easy to identify; it is smaller than the Grey Lag and the white at the base of the bill is a broad and conspicuous band. The beak is pink or orange with a white nail, distinguishing this species from the Bean and Pink-foot, and the legs are orange-coloured; the only species with which it can be confused is the smaller and darker Lesser White-fronted Goose. There are broad dark bars on the breast and belly, and the note is distinct, louder and harsher than the metallic cry of the Pink-foot. When the two are flying together the White-fronted can be picked out by its frontlet and dark flanks. Immature birds, however, have less white on the forehead, and in some there are no bars.

The habits are similar to those of other greys; it feeds on grass and clover, but is perhaps more of a marsh than cornfield species, and may be seen in estuaries moving with the tide, flighting to the marshes and fields at high tide and returning with the ebb. It arrives and departs at the same seasons as other greys, and is not infrequent in inland marshes and river valleys; the bird is most abundant in December and January.

The plumage is ashy-brown with pale edges to the back feathers and a white patch at the base of the bill. Underparts are crossed by black or dark brown bars and blotches; the flanks are dark brown, under tail-coverts white. The legs are orange, the bill of the eastern race pink with white nail. Birds of the Greenland race are darker and have orange or yellow bills. Immatures lack the white forehead and dark bars on the belly. Length, 27–28 in. Wing, 16–17 in. Tarsus, 2·6 in. (*Plate 30.*)

## Lesser White-fronted Goose                           *Anser erythropus*

The Lesser White-fronted Goose breeds in northern Scandinavia and Russia and migrates south in winter. Two or three birds appear in Britain in most winters, notably on the Severn estuary, in Norfolk and sometimes on the Scottish side of the Solway. It associates with White-fronted Geese and resembles them in habits; its voice is described as being squeakier than theirs. Diagnostic characters are the small size, white frontal patch extending to the crown, and yellow ring round the eye.

The adult's plumage resembles that of the White-fronted, including the dark bars on the belly, but is rather darker; the white on the forehead is more extensive. A yellow ring surrounds the eye. Immatures lack the white front. The bill is pink with white nail, legs orange. Length 21–26 in. Wing, 15·5 in. Tarsus, 2·5 in.

**Bean Goose** *Anser fabalis fabalis*
**Pink-footed Goose** *Anser fabalis brachyrhynchus*

The Bean Goose and Pink-footed Goose are now usually treated as geographical races of one species, but in favourable circumstances they are readily distinguishable in the field and are accordingly described separately below.

The Bean Goose is a rather uncommon winter visitor to Great Britain and Ireland, though it may be seen in some numbers in south-west Scotland. It breeds far north in Europe and Siberia.

The black bill, crossed by an orange band, and the orange legs serve to identify the typical Bean; the legs of the Pink-foot, which has a somewhat similar, though shorter bill, are flesh-coloured. The general colour, especially on the shoulders and rump, is darker and browner than that of the Grey Lag; on the wing its head and neck look very dark, darker even than the Pink-foot, and the white upper tail-coverts show up against the brown rump. The call, *honk, honk*, is softer and more bell-like than the note of the Pink-foot. The flight is strong and direct, the wing-beats slow; on the water the bird looks large but rather slender, and its weak bill long; as in other greys, the feathers on the nape and back of the neck stand out in a mane. When the bird is feeding the neck is not curved as in the swans, but has a sharp kink or angle; this is noticeable in any greys when, with neck stretched and beak open, one bird attacks another in play or anger.

Immigrant Beans arrive in September and October, and some linger until April or later. They share the field-feeding habit with the Grey Lag, and both near the coast and inland the bird is a gleaner of the cornfields.

The adult's upper parts are greyish-brown, darker than the Grey Lag's, and the pattern on wings and scapulars, due to pale edgings of the feathers contrasting with the brown, is more distinct. Underparts are pale brown on the breast, shading to dirty white. The bill is black at base and tip, crossed by an orange or yellow band; legs orange or pinkish-yellow. The immature is darker. Length, 31–34 in. Wing, 17·5–19 in. Tarsus, 3 in. (*Plate 30.*)

The Pink-footed Goose, a winter visitor to the British Isles chiefly from Iceland, is in many parts the best known of our grey geese. It is the most numerous goose on the east coast and is now wintering in some thousands on the Solway and the Lancashire coast. A few are found each winter in Ireland.

The bird may be recognised by its short bill, black at base and tip and with an intermediate pink rather than orange band, usually smaller than that on the bill of the Bean. The legs are flesh-coloured or pink. Although it is a brownish bird, the body looks very light in sunlight, this being partly due to the blue-grey shoulders and greyish back, darker than those of the Grey Lag. The head and neck are dark.

The Pink-foot is gregarious; the gaggles are frequently huge. The skeins fly in lines, Vs, or double chevron formation; the birds call constantly as they fly; their metallic voices carry for great distances. The quality varies: some are harsh, others shrill and musical. When following the tide the birds alight

69                                                                    BRENT GOOSE

on the uncovered banks and stand alert with necks uplifted. When satisfied
that they are secure, they rest or preen their plumage, but when driven off
by the tide immediately begin to call and rise with a mighty rush of wings and
babel of voices.

Many birds reach the west coast about the third week in September, but
the skeins come in gradually and it is usually the end of October before the
winter flocks are complete. Emigration begins in March, and nearly all have
left before the end of April. As soon as they arrive the birds visit the fields,
gleaning in the stubbles in the early morning and at dusk, but when forced by
circumstances to avoid the cultivated land, they crop the grass on the saltings;
they are always shy and nervous, and the approach of a man sends them off
'honking' to the banks.

The head and neck are seal-brown, the upper parts greyish-brown, darkest
on the wings and scapulars, and with bars formed by the pale feather tips.
The rump and breast are brown, the belly suffused with grey, shading to pure
white. The young bird is darker. The bill is pink with black base and tip; the
legs pink. Length, 27–28 in. Wing, 16·5–17·5 in. Tarsus, 2·8 in. (*Plate 30*.)

## Snow Goose                                            *Anser caerulescens*

As a winter visitor from the arctic of eastern Asia and western America the
Snow Goose has not infrequently been reported from various parts of the
British Isles, occasionally in flocks of a dozen or more, but there is always the
possibility that odd individuals may have escaped from captivity.

The Snow Goose, white with black wings, is conspicuous and unlike any
other wild goose; its black flight feathers and short neck prevent confusion
with the swans, and the only other large white bird that in any way resembles
it is the Gannet, whose thick neck, long, powerful bill, cigar-shaped body and
easy sailing flight are distinctive. The flight of the Snow Goose is strong; its
call is a monosyllabic *kaw*. Its visits to Britain have usually, but not invariably,
been in exceptionally hard weather.

The adult bird is white with black primaries. The legs and bill are red. The
young bird is brownish-grey on the upper surface; its bill is almost black, and
its legs grey. Length, 25–30 in.

## Brent Goose                                             *Branta bernicla*

The Brents and Barnacles are collectively known as black geese to distinguish
them from the grey group. They are more maritime in their habits than the
grain-eating greys and feed largely on *Zostera* and other marine plants. They
are highly gregarious. The Brent is a winter visitor to the Atlantic and North
Sea coasts of Europe from the high arctic. It used to visit the east coast of
England and parts of Ireland in huge packs, but there has been a serious
decrease during the present century. However, since the bird has been given
legal protection there has been some recovery and numbers have recently
increased, especially in Ireland and parts of Scotland.

The Brent is, on the wing, a small dark goose, stumpy and almost duck-like.

The small white patches on its neck, and the white tail-coverts and abdomen show conspicuously in contrast with the black head and neck and general dusky plumage; the white stern is specially noticeable, for the coverts above and below almost screen the dark tail. Some Brents arrive in September and October, but the main influx reaches English coasts in midwinter. Most leave in March or April, but stragglers may remain until May or even later. The Brent feeds by day, but it rarely leaves the shore, finding its vegetable, and occasionally animal food—molluscs and worms—on or in the ooze of tidal estuaries. Naturally its movements are largely regulated by the tide, and it occasionally feeds in the dusk. The birds, in long lines, follow the receding water, their angled necks bent as they gobble the sea-grass, or are slowly driven back by the flood, still feeding; in shallow water they swim and dip their heads to drag up the weed, or upend like ducks, their white sterns alone visible. The Brent walks gracefully, can run fast, and flies with considerable speed. A disturbed pack flies hither and thither, taking ordered formation only when travelling for a distance. The flight call is loud and metallic, a double note frequently repeated. It also has a guttural croak. At high tide the birds swim in the open, avoiding the shore, but return as soon as the banks are exposed.

Adults have head, neck, upper breast and back slate-black, with a small white patch, in which black is often mingled, on either side of the neck. The lower neck is slate-grey; sides of rump and upper tail-coverts white. In the dark-breasted form underparts below the breast are slate-brown, showing distinct whitish bars on the flanks; in the paler form the lower breast is brown and the rest white or suffused with grey. The bill and legs are almost black. Immatures are browner, and the neck spot is hardly visible. Length, 23 in. Wing, 13·5 in. Tarsus, 2 in. (*Plate 34.*)

**Barnacle Goose** *Branta leucopsis*
The Barnacle Goose nests in Greenland and Spitzbergen, and in winter is found locally on northern European shores. It is more frequent in the Hebrides than the Brent, and is plentiful on the west coast of Scotland and the west of Ireland; in the Solway it is much more numerous than formerly, but though it used to visit the Cheshire Dee in some numbers it is now only a rare straggler. Its winter quarters are more northerly than those of the Brent.

The Barnacle, though a marine feeder, is less strictly addicted to salt water than the Brent, for it will feed on marshes and cultivated land bordering bays and inlets. Larger and paler than the last species, its black crown and neck and white face are its noticeable features; its under surface is greyish-white. The first Barnacles arrive towards the end of September, but the bird is seldom numerous until late October; they leave in March and April, but emigration is often delayed in the north. It is a nocturnal feeder, at any rate on the pastures; during the day it usually rests on flats or marshes, but it will sometimes also feed by day. Its call has been likened to a 'coughing grunt', and a gaggle can raise a clanging clamour of sharp yelping cries. Not only is the bird easy on its feet, but it can run swiftly, scampering across the flats with outstretched neck after a companion in anger or play. The flight is powerful and often at a height. The name is not derived from its food, though, like the Brent, it will eat molluscs and crustaceans, but from the ancient myth that the ship-barnacles gave birth to geese.

The adult has white face and forehead, black cap and neck, and a black mark from the bill through the eye. The upper back and breast are black, lower back and rump brown, but upper parts generally lavender-grey barred with black and white. The underparts, the sides of the rump and upper tail-coverts are white; on the flanks are faint grey bars. The bill and legs are black. Blacks in adults are replaced by brown in the young, and whites suffused with buff and spotted. Length, 25 in. Wing, 16 in. Tarsus, 2·2 in. (*Plate 34.*)

**Canada Goose**                                                    *Branta canadensis*

The Canada Goose was formerly denied a place in the British avifauna on the ground that when it has been recorded it must have 'escaped from captivity or from ornamental waters', but it now has as good a claim as the Mute Swan or the Pheasant to be regarded as a British bird. It is a native of North America, migrating as far south as the Gulf of Mexico. A few vagrant birds have appeared in the Hebrides and Ireland, but the resident breeding stock, some of them descended from birds introduced over two centuries ago, are generally sedentary. Numbers have greatly increased in recent years and there has been much artificial redistribution, so that breeding pairs or colonies are now found over much of England and parts of Wales, southern Scotland and northern Ireland.

The Canada differs from the smaller Barnacle in the pattern and extent of the white on the face and the smaller amount of black on breast and neck. The upper parts are brown, not grey. It nests on the shores of pools, reservoirs, and the banks of rivers as well as on artificial lakes. The nest is a large structure of reeds and other waterside plants, thickly lined with down. Five or six eggs are laid in April and are incubated by the female.

The normal migratory instinct appears to have been lost, but some individuals or flocks wander during the winter, and the numbers to be met with in any particular haunt vary greatly. When the young are on the wing in July the Cheshire birds, in flocks, flight nightly towards the hills, returning to the meres in the early morning, but whether the object is to roost on the reservoirs or to feed at night on the moors is uncertain. Normally the birds feed by day on the borders of the meres, cropping the grass, and they also visit cultivated fields. These passing flocks of 'wild geese' are frequently noticed in the first half of July, but seldom later, though the birds move freely during autumn and winter. There are indications of a late summer 'moult migration' to a Scottish sea loch. The note is a resounding *honk, honk*, sounded if the feeding birds are approached, and as they walk towards the safety of the water; they take wing if followed.

The face, to behind ear-coverts, and chin and throat are black; the sides of the face are white. Upper parts are brown, pale feather edgings forming bars;

the light brown flanks and belly are faintly barred. Legs and bill are black. Length, 36–40 in. Wing, 19·5 in. Tarsus, 3 in. (*Plate 33*.)

### Red-breasted Goose *Branta ruficollis*

The Red-breasted Goose is a western Siberian bird which visits the Caspian and other waters and occasionally wanders westward. It is a rare vagrant to the British Isles, occurring singly and usually in company with White-fronted Geese. About twenty records have been accepted, but as large numbers have been introduced into the Netherlands some recent reports may not refer to genuine wild vagrants. The upper parts are black, and the sides of the face and neck and the breast are rich chestnut bordered with white. There is a large white patch at the base of the bill, separated from the cheeks by a black line which passes through the eye from the crown to the chin. The belly is black; the flanks and tail-coverts are white. The short bill and the legs are dark brown. The immature bird has less rufous on the face. Length, 21 in.

### Mute Swan *Cygnus olor*

The wild Mute Swan nests in northern Europe and migrates in winter to the Mediterranean and northern Africa. Some of the birds which visit our shores in winter may be wild migrants, but the Swan has been so long domesticated or semi-domesticated, and so many live a free and independent life, that the origin of any particular bird is obscure. Native British swans were probably all reduced to a semi-domestic state from medieval times, but many have now become feral. Ringing has shown that long flights, for example from the Thames to north Lancashire, are not uncommon. Censuses held in 1955 and 1961 showed that the population of Great Britain had remained stable at about 19,000 birds. In winter large herds are found in many places, especially on rivers and estuaries in towns, and there is a large proportion of non-breeding birds in summer.

The Mute Swan may at once be known by the black knob or 'berry' at the base of its orange bill; this tubercle is smaller in the female. It may also be recognised by the graceful S curve of its head and neck, and its frequent habit of swimming with the wings half raised and the tail pointed slightly upwards. Young birds as a rule carry the neck straighter. In flight the wing strokes are deliberate but very powerful, and throb rather than whistle; the noise recalls the sound of horses galloping on hard ground. The name Mute is misleading, for the bird, especially the male or 'cob' when guarding the nest, has a defiant trumpet note—an explosive grunt. The sitting bird will hiss defiance. The food consists largely of aquatic plants; on private waters the bird is a useful check to the troublesome Canadian Pondweed, *Elodea canadensis*. Insects are eaten, and, it is said, frogs, but these and toads it will worry and discard, and it will kill but not eat the young of other water fowl.

In courtship display both birds repeatedly dip head and neck into the water. The pen submerges as the cob mounts, and after coition the pair may rise up breast to breast in a posture like that of Great Crested Grebes in their greeting ceremony. The nest is a large structure of rank vegetation lined with down, and is usually placed near water, on an islet if one is available. The five to twelve greenish-white eggs, laid as a rule in April, average in size 4·3 by 2·9 in. The bird pairs for life, and the cob shares in incubation, but usually guards the nest, 'busking', as it is called, when approached. In this terrifying performance the wings and scapulars are further raised, and neck is drawn back until almost hidden by the wings; the bird forces itself forward in rushes with simultaneous strokes of its feet, ploughing up the water. The ash-grey downy young are at first carried on the parent's back. The male will at times monopolise domestic duties, refusing to allow his mate to relieve him during the long incubation.

The adult has white plumage, orange bill with black at base and tip and along the cutting edge, and black legs. The juvenile is usually grey-brown with grey legs and grey bill, but white cygnets occur. Length, 60 in. Wing, 27 in. Tarsus, 4·5 in. (*Plate 33*.)

**Whooper Swan**                                                     *Cygnus cygnus*
Three swans are on the British list, but only two, both winter visitors, can be counted as really wild: this and the next species. The Whooper breeds in northern Europe and Iceland and moves south in winter. One or two pairs have nested in the north of Scotland from time to time, but normally it is a winter visitor there and on coastal and inland waters in Great Britain and Ireland. It has become both more regular and increasingly numerous in most districts during the present century, and especially since about 1948, though it is still commoner in the north than elsewhere. Numbers wintering in Ireland have greatly increased in recent years and it now outnumbers Bewick's Swan in nearly all parts of the island.

Size, when there is no chance for comparison, is insufficient as a means of identification in the field, and there is little difference between the Whooper and Mute. The best character is the beak. In the Mute this is black at the base, where there is also a prominent knob or tubercle; the rest, except for a black line along the cutting edge, is orange; the black reaches to the eye. In both Whooper and Bewick's the pattern is reversed and the lemon-yellow extends from the eye to the nostril; in the former, however, the patch is larger and more angular, a wedge passing forward into the black tip beyond and below the nostril. A curious optical illusion is caused by the pattern of the Whooper's bill; when the bird is some distance away the black tip appears to overhang.

The Whooper appears on English waters in late October or in November. Numbers vary from year to year, but it can no longer be regarded as a hard-weather visitor, as it was in the earlier part of the century. Family parties of four or five birds are common, but herds of twenty or more are by no means unusual; in Scotland numbers are much larger and hundreds may be seen in favoured places such as Loch Leven. There is often a good deal of movement during the winter from one water to another. The Whoopers leave England in March or April, but a few non-breeding birds may remain in Scotland through the summer.

On the water the shy bird carries its neck stiffly erect, its bill at right angles as it turns its head sharply from side to side; its wings rest flat upon its back and are not arched as in the Mute. From behind, the wings show like two smooth cushions; the short pointed tail is carried horizontally. When the head is lowered to feed, the neck has a goose-like angle and not the graceful curve of the Mute. Like other swans the bird upends, submerging the head and fore-parts, paddling slowly to hold itself in position; its wing-tips are slightly raised. The food, aquatic weeds, molluscs and other animals, is mostly obtained from the bottom, but in recent years Whoopers have been increasingly grazing on land, and even feeding on potatoes like grey geese. When the bird rises, head to wind, it flogs the water for some distance. Once under way it flies with great speed and power, its neck extended, the swish of its long wings producing a whistling sound quite distinct from the throb of the flying Mute. The English name is derived from the note, a distinctive character. The call is variously described as a deep-toned whistle, a trumpet, bugle or bass trombone sound. There is variation both in pitch and volume, the calls sounding louder when the bird is on the wing than when it is on the water.

The adult's plumage is white, its bill black with a yellow wedge reaching from the feathers to beyond the nostril; the legs are blackish. The juvenile is grey-brown, paler than the young Mute Swan; its bill and legs are flesh-coloured. Length, 60 in. Wing, 25 in. Tarsus, 4·3 in. (*Plates 31 and 33*.)

### Bewick's Swan                                            *Cygnus bewickii*

Bewick's Swan breeds further north in arctic Europe and Asia than the Whooper, and in winter, though it is found in various parts of the two continents, its range is more northerly. It is a winter visitor to our islands, especially the eastern counties of England, where it has become much more common. In Scotland and Ireland, however, numbers have declined sharply in recent years.

Although much smaller than the Whooper, the shape and size of the yellow patch on the basal portion of the short bill of Bewick's Swan is the best mark for identification. This patch is somewhat rounded in front and does not extend as far as the nostril. One distinction between the two wild swans, not always clearly shown in figures and seldom mentioned, is that there is one patch in the Whooper and two in Bewick's; that is to say, the black on the bill of the Whooper only reaches part way up the culmen, whereas in this bird it normally extends to the forehead. The black line bordered on either side by yellow is usually but not invariably noticeable when the bird faces the observer; in some birds it does not quite extend to the feathers of the forehead. In the Whooper a band of colour crosses the base of the bill. Other useful distinguishing characters of the Bewick's Swan are the comparatively short, thick neck and shorter bill, which give the bird a more goose-like appearance than the graceful, slim-necked Whooper.

In general habits, food, flight and appearance Bewick's resembles the larger bird, with which it was long confused, but on the average its visits are shorter. November is its usual month of arrival in Scotland, but as a rule it is in December, January and February that we see it; it seldom remains after March. It frequents salt-water lochs and inlets, and though it often wanders inland, is on the whole more maritime than the Whooper. In recent years its visits to English inland waters have been far more frequent than they used to be. Like the Whooper, it will sometimes graze like a goose on dry land, though it normally feeds on submerged or exposed aquatic vegetation. Its flight call is quite distinct, a sharp, repeated, barking note, loud and metallic; a puntsman described a herd as yelping 'just like a lot of poodle puppies'. The reddish or ochreous tinge frequently seen on the head and neck of adult swans is due to staining from peaty or other discoloured water.

The adult has white plumage, black bill with a rounded yellow patch on each side, and black legs. The juvenile is pale brown, its bill patches flesh-coloured. Length, about 50 in. Wing, 21 in. Tarsus, 3·8 in. (*Plates 31 and 33.*)

# Order FALCONIFORMES

## Family FALCONIDAE Falcons

*The Falcons are the diurnal birds of prey; the bills are strongly hooked, the raptorial feet, with three toes in front and one behind, are armed with curved talons, and are fitted alike for clutching prey or perching.*

### Golden Eagle
*Aquila chrysaetos*

The Golden Eagle, which is widely distributed in Europe, is resident in the Highlands of Scotland, the Hebrides and one district in south-west Scotland. From 1953 to 1960 a pair nested in Antrim, Northern Ireland, and since 1955 one or two non-breeding birds have appeared regularly in the Lake District of England. Elsewhere in the British Isles the Golden Eagle is a rare vagrant. There was an increase in the numbers nesting in Scotland in the middle of the 20th century, but a sharp drop in breeding success became apparent from about 1960. This has been attributed to toxic chemicals in sheep dip affecting carrion-eating adults.

The Golden Eagle in romance is fierce, terrible and a robber of infants— in reality a large, powerful, magnificent bird with a cowardly vulturine character. Noble in appearance, especially in its marvellous airmanship, it is ignoble in habits, stealing an occasional sickly lamb, but not daring to try conclusions with a full-grown ewe, and carefully avoiding encounter with its enemy, man, even when he is robbing its eyrie. Flapping its huge wings at intervals, it sails majestically at immense heights, the wing-tips curved upward, the strong pinions spread like fingers. It does not dash on its quarry with the splendid stoop of the Peregrine, but drops suddenly upon the unsuspecting hare or Ptarmigan, gripping its life out with cruel talons. It will sight the long-dead sheep and gorge upon the putrid flesh. Sport, not sentiment, saved the Golden Eagle from extinction, and on some of the Scottish deer-forests it became almost common; had the shepherd had his way he would have harried it out of existence. The hare and perhaps the Ptarmigan and Red Grouse are annoying to the deer-stalker, warning the stags by their rushes or flights when disturbed, and these the Eagle keeps down. On the ground the Eagle is ungainly and waddles rather than walks, but when standing on its favourite look-out, some rock or pinnacle from which it can command the district round, its massive beak, heavy brows and piercing eyes give it a truly regal mien; small wonder that it has been so often selected as a national emblem. As a rule it is a silent bird, but has a loud yelping scream.

The nest of the Golden Eagle, though occasionally built in a tree, is generally placed on some steep though by no means inaccessible crag; many nests may be reached without a rope. The birds, if permitted, return again and again to the same place, though not annually to the same nest; each pair has two or three alternative nests which are probably used in turn. One of these old nests is patched up each year and fresh material added, so that in time they become huge structures, perhaps 6 ft. across at the base, and consequently requiring a broad ledge for their support. Branches, twigs and heather are piled to a height of perhaps 2 ft., and the cup of the nest is from 12 to 16 in. across, lined with heather tufts, moss and grass, and usually a quantity of the great woodrush. At the end of March or early in April two or exceptionally three eggs are laid; they are white or marbled and blotched with reddish-brown and violet. A single brood is reared, and, almost invariably, if the eggs are destroyed the bird makes no effort to nest again that year. The young are fed at first on liver, and later on carefully prepared food, birds plucked and headless and rabbits denuded of their fur, and finally on furred and feathered victims which they learn to tear up for themselves. Until the eaglet is eleven weeks old it cannot fly, and just before this feat is accomplished the nestling begins to screen its food with its wings when it stands upon it, rending it with its beak. This is the habit of all raptorial birds.

The Golden Eagle has the legs feathered to the toes, a character that distinguishes it from the White-tailed Eagle. It is dark brown above and below, more tawny on the head, and the long yellowish feathers on the nape are golden in bright light. The beak and claws are blackish-brown, the cere and toes yellow. In young birds the feathers have white bases, and the basal part of the tail is white. Male: Length, 32 in. Wing, 24 in. Tarsus, 3·7 in. Female: Length, 35 in. Wing, 27 in. Tarsus, 3·9 in. (*Plates 37 and 165*.)

### Spotted Eagle                                                     *Aquila clanga*

The Spotted Eagle is a casual wanderer to the British Isles, which has occurred about a dozen times. Its range extends eastward from the Baltic into Siberia and central Asia, and in winter it is met with in southern Europe, Africa and India.

It is in the immature dress, that of most if not all wanderers to Britain, that the bird deserves its name 'spotted'; the brown plumage is then spotted with buffish terminals and edges to the feathers of the wing-coverts and inner secondaries, and the underparts are marked with pale streaks. In mature birds the plumage is darker than in the Golden Eagle, and there is no barring on the tail; the head and bill are smaller, the wings proportionally broader. It is also a smaller bird. Length, 26–29 in. Wing, 20·5–21·5 in.

### Buzzard                                                           *Buteo buteo*

During the 19th century the Buzzard was almost exterminated in England by game preservers, but a marked increase began about 1914, and by 1950 Buzzards were well distributed and locally abundant in Scotland, Wales and the western half of England, though still absent from most eastern counties. With the virtual disappearance of rabbits after the spread of myxomatosis in 1954 there was a sharp drop in the Buzzard population of Wales, the midlands and south-west England, but the reduction was less marked in the Lake District and Scotland. There has been a recovery in most districts since 1957.

A few pairs have nested in northern Ireland since 1950, but its survival there is in doubt. It breeds throughout most of Europe. British birds are sedentary.

Though heavy in build, and apparently indolent in habits, the Buzzard is handsome; its size and appearance are often responsible for its death, for it is mistaken for an eagle. It rises with slow 'lumbering' flight, but when well on the wing is a master of aerial locomotion, graceful and easy. It sails, moth-like, with round wings well forward, no angle visible at the carpal joint, and with flight feathers splayed out. With motionless wings and expanded squared tail, it tilts to suit the wind, lifting and tacking, wheeling and soaring without visible effort. Two or three will play together with plaintive mewing cries, crossing and recrossing one another's course as they rise higher and higher until mere specks in the blue. They drift over a crag; then the wings are bowed and they sweep down the slope, rising again with a long curve to top the next obstacle; sometimes the downward rush is checked suddenly by the outspread wings and the bird banks smartly, but often with half-closed wings it drops diagonally until close to the ground, when with slight change of poise it skims to rock or tree and alights. When hunting it flies at a greater height than the harriers; like them it seldom attempts to chase its prey, but pounces suddenly upon an unsuspecting victim. Though it will kill a wounded Grouse and drop upon helpless young birds, it does little damage to game; indeed small mammals and insects rather than birds are its victims. It will kill mammals up to the size of a young rabbit, but its pellets prove that beetles, especially large dors, are hunted for, and it is known to devour earthworms. In Wales Buzzards have frequently been seen following the plough. It has no objection to feeding on even offensive carrion, and frequently eats the dead lambs on the fells, but no one can accuse it of sheep slaughter.

In mountainous country it often nests on a broad ledge on crag or cliff; too frequently these sites are easily accessible; but where there are trees it constructs a bulky nest amongst the branches. Now that the Buzzard has extended its range into many well-wooded districts, tree nests are much more common than crag ones. Sticks and large branches, heather roots and stems form the framework, and the lining is of grass with, as a rule, a plentiful addition of green-leaved branches or twigs; these, as if it rejoiced in decoration, are added after the eggs are laid and even when young are in the nest. The number of eggs varies, but two or three seem the normal complement; they are dull or tinted white, blotched, streaked or faintly marked with red, brown and violet. They are laid at intervals of some days, and the bird or birds, for both are said to incubate, sit when the first egg is laid. When the white down-clad young are in the nest the old birds occasionally protect them with courage, dashing at and even striking a passer-by, but as a rule, mewing piteously, they keep at a safe distance.

The Buzzard is a very variable bird, but the normal plumage is dark brown, except on the lower breast and belly, which are whitish, boldly barred or occasionally streaked with brown. The tail is barred with brown and black. The cere and legs are yellow. Females, except for their superior size, resemble the males, but immature birds are paler. Male: Length, 21 in. Wing, 14·5 in. Tarsus, 3·1 in. Female: Length, 23 in. Wing, 16 in. (*Plates 32, 37 and 166.*)

## Rough-legged Buzzard                              *Buteo lagopus*

The Rough-legged Buzzard breeds in northern Europe and Asia, and is an irregular migrant, its movements apparently being regulated by weather. To the British Isles it is a winter visitor and passage migrant; the majority of those which visit us are immature. It has been met with in all parts, but only in the north and east of Scotland and on the east coast of England with any degree of regularity. More than twenty birds have been recorded from Ireland.

The feathered tarsi of the Rough-legged Buzzard explain its name, but are not often visible to aid identification in the field. When the bird is overhead the whitish underside of the wings is conspicuous, and the larger size and longer, narrower wings are noticeable if a Common Buzzard is visible for comparison. The white patch on the tail is noticeable when it turns; in a good light its head appears almost white. It has a clear ringing *mee-oo*, louder than that of our bird; a gamekeeper described it as 'screaming like a cat'. It frequently hovers almost like a Kestrel, its wings vibrating rapidly, its depressed tail spread, when the white base and sub-terminal bar are very conspicuous. Quicker and stronger in flight than the Common Buzzard, this bird prefers larger game; in England, where it avoids woodlands, it will remain, as long as it is unmolested, in the vicinity of a rabbit-warren, and has been known to kill leverets and to devour Grouse, though it is not proved that it struck these down in flight. In Scandinavia it feeds largely on lemmings, but is not particular about its meat being fresh, and will devour carrion.

The upper parts of the adult are dark brown; the whitish head and neck streaked with brown; the feathers of the coverts and scapulars have buff margins, showing as pale bars in flight. The tail-coverts and basal half of the tail are white. The underparts are mostly white, with dark patches on the belly and at the carpal joint of the wings. Length: Male, 23 in. Female, 26 in. Wing, 17·5–18·5 in. Tarsus, 2·8 in. (*Plate 37.*)

## Sparrow Hawk                                    *Accipiter nisus*

The Sparrow Hawk is resident in wooded parts of the British Isles. In the north of its European and Asiatic range it is a migrant, and in autumn considerable numbers reach our eastern shores, and probably some are birds of passage. Until about 1955 it was, with the exception of the Kestrel, the commonest bird of prey in most parts of the British Isles, and with the lapse of game-keeping during the 1939–45 war numbers had increased considerably in many places. But a sudden decrease was noticed from about 1955 and within ten years the species had become virtually extinct in several eastern counties of England. The decline was less severe but still noticeable in north and west England, Wales, Scotland and Ireland. The evidence strongly suggests that the use of toxic chemicals in agriculture was the cause of the severe drop in the population of this species. Ten years later there were signs of recovery in some districts, following the application of restrictions on the use of certain insecticides.

The Sparrow Hawk's short wings give it a long-tailed appearance in flight, and when perched it stands higher and looks a more leggy bird than the Kestrel. Its manner of hunting is different, for it flies low, beating along hedgerows and seldom rising to do more than skim over to the far side. It will fly up a road or lane, frequently topping the hedges, and searching each bramble patch or furze bush for victims; it threads its way amongst the trees in a wood, quickly but silently, dashing suddenly upon any unsuspecting bird. When about to perch it will cross a field, a few feet above the grass, and suddenly rise to a high branch when near the foot of a tree. It will pick out one bird from a flock and chase it, without heeding the cries and occasional mobbing flight of other birds. When Black-headed Gulls and Lapwings assault it, however, it simply avoids their attacks, dodging skilfully, for it turns and twists with ease and grace. The quarry is eaten on the ground; the Hawk stands with both feet on its victim, droops its wings so that they form a tent, spreads its tail as if to give support, and rips off the feathers or fur. The blood-stained remnants of its feast remain to mark the scene of the tragedy. Small passerine birds are its chief food, but it will kill birds as large as Wood Pigeons, and not infrequently raids the farm for chickens. Careful observers find it does little harm to game. Mice, frogs and insects are also eaten. If disturbed at a meal it rises with a chattering cry of alarm or defiance. In the excitement of the chase the Sparrow Hawk often gets into difficulties, for it will blindly dash after its terrified victim into a room or crash to death against a window.

The Sparrow Hawk builds a substantial nest in a tree, generally selecting a conifer, but it likes a foundation and usually starts on an old nest or squirrel-drey. On this it makes a large flattish nest of fir-twigs, and as a rule the lining consists of bits of fir bark and down. The four to six eggs, generally laid in May, are bluish-white, strongly blotched and splashed with dark reddish-brown. The eggs in a clutch often vary considerably; the marks may be massed at either end, forming a solid patch, or in a zone; often one or two eggs have few marks. Both birds help in building, though the hen alone incubates the eggs. One brood is normal, but if eggs are destroyed the bird will lay again. Both male and female have been known to breed in their immature dress. If the nest is visited the birds usually keep at a safe distance, flying round with chittering cries.

The adult male has dark greyish-slate upper parts, with a whitish spot on the nape; the flight feathers and tail are dark brown barred with grey. The bill is bluish horn, cere and legs yellow, irides orange. The male's underparts are more or less rufous barred with reddish-brown; the female's white with brown or dark grey bars. The female is larger and browner on the back. The young bird is dark brown above, with rufous margins to the feathers, and the white underparts are more streaked than barred with brown. In both sexes there is considerable variation in size. Male: Length, 13 in. Wing, 7·9 in.

PLATE 34

*Above :* Brent
Goose, p69
*Right :* Barnacle
Goose, p70
*Below :* Honey
Buzzard, p83

PLATE 35     Red Kite, p81

PLATE 36    Marsh Harrier, p84

PLATE 37    *Above:* Golden Eagle (immature), p76
            *Below left:* Buzzard, p77
            *Below right:* Rough-legged Buzzard, p79

PLATE 38    *Above left :* Sparrow Hawk (male), p79
            *Above right :* Sparrow Hawk (female), p79
            *Below :* Goshawk (first year), p81

PLATE 39
Osprey, p87

Photo: Eric Hosking

*Above:* Montagu's Harrier, p86

PLATE 40

*Below:* Hen Harrier, p85

Photo: Eric Hosking

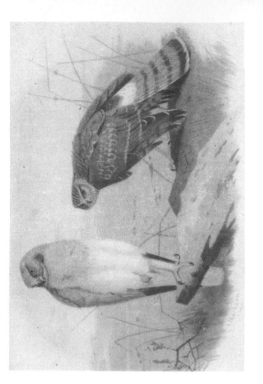

PLATE 42

*Above left:*
Montagu's
Harrier (female
and dark male),
p86
*Below left:*
Montagu's
Harrier (adult
and immature
males), p86
*Right:* Peregrine
(adult female),
p89

Photo: *J. B. and S. Bottomley*

PLATE 43

*Above:* Kestrel, p94

*Below:* Peregrine, p89

Photo: *Eric Hosking*

*Photo: Eric Hosking*

PLATE 44    Black Grouse (female), p98

PLATE 45

*Above :* Gyr Falcon (Iceland form),
    p91
*Below :* Merlin (male), p91

*Above :* Gyr Falcon (Greenland
    form), p91
*Below :* Merlin (female and
    immature male), p91

*Right* : Red Kite, p81

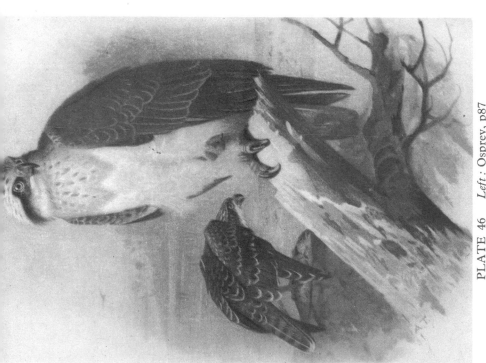

PLATE 46　　*Left* : Osprey, p87

PLATE 47
Red-legged
Partridge, p101

PLATE 48
Water Rail, p106

Photo:
J. B. and S. Bottomley

PLATE 49
*Above :* Hobby (male), p88         *Above :* Kestrel, p94
*Below :* Red-footed Falcon, p93

Tarsus, 2·1 in. Female: Length, 15 in. Wing, 9·2 in. Tarsus, 2·4 in. (*Plates 38 and 166.*)

## Goshawk                                                    *Accipiter gentilis*

The Goshawk is a sporadic breeder in England and an occasional autumn and winter visitor, chiefly to the eastern counties of England and Scotland. It is a widespread breeding species in continental Europe. Whether the nesting pairs in England have been genuine wild birds or have escaped from captivity is doubtful. In former days of falconry, according to literary historical evidence, falconers intentionally released Goshawks in order that they might breed in Britain and obtain the requisite degree of ferocity and skill, but game-preservation prevented the permanent establishment of the species.

The short-winged, long-tailed Goshawk, in plumage and habits, is a large fierce Sparrow Hawk; it beats for its quarry, then dashes suddenly upon it, turning and twisting with great agility, but does not stoop with the skill of the Peregrine or other falcons. Mammals as large as hares, and birds of the size of Mallard and Partridge are killed by this powerful hunter; it is not popular with the gamekeeper. It breeds in a secluded wood, preferably coniferous, and builds a large nest, or adopts another bird's old one.

The adult has ashy-brown upper parts and a whitish superciliary stripe; its tail is boldly banded with dark brown and tipped with white. The underparts are barred black and white, the under tail-coverts white. The bill is bluish-black, the cere, legs and irides yellow. The immature bird is brown above, with pale margins, and the tail is banded with dark grey; the underparts are buff, spotted and striated with dark brown. Male: Length, 20 in. Wing, 12 in. Tarsus, 3·1 in. Female: Length, 23 in. Wing, 14 in. (*Plate 38.*)

## Red Kite                                                          *Milvus milvus*

The Red Kite is found in most parts of Europe, though not in the far north. In Britain it is a sedentary species; an occasional straggler, usually immature, reaches our shores, but these visits are very irregular. The story of the Kite as a British resident is one of at least moderate success for conservationists. In the 18th century the bird was common in all parts, a woodland species constantly visiting the towns and villages, though apparently never resident in Ireland. In this century the number of breeding pairs has fluctuated, sometimes dropping to as few as four, but by 1965 there were fifteen to twenty pairs breeding in central Wales. The future of the birds will depend upon the survival of deciduous woodlands and open country to provide breeding and feeding habitats as well as upon protection from direct interference.

Also called the Glead, a name derived from its gliding flight, it is a magnificent bird on the wing, when it may be recognised by its forked tail and reddish plumage. When hunting it flies low, with steady deliberate wing-beats and easy glides, but when it soars it has all the grace and swing of the Buzzard, and will perform in strong wind and storm. It is not a noisy bird, but has a weak, high-pitched Buzzard-like mew or *wheeo*. It is not a valiant hunter and feeds on small mammals, birds, reptiles and amphibians which it picks up from the ground; its habit of lifting the young of Grouse, Pheasants, and chickens and ducklings in the farm was certainly responsible for its decrease. It picks up offal and eats carrion; indeed it was known at one time as a useful scavenger. Its present restricted Welsh haunts are the slopes of wooded valleys, and though it feeds at the edge of the moors, it is by no means a moorland or, normally, a hill bird.

In Wales, though not in all parts of its range, the Kite nests in a tree. It usually, though not invariably, builds an entire nest; occasionally it modifies one of a Crow or other species. The nest is a rubbish heap, for all kinds of litter, turf, grass with its roots, wool, rags and paper are stuffed in amongst the branches which make the main structure. The cup is flattish and the lining mainly sheep's wool, but here again miscellaneous articles are introduced: rags, paper, string, and indeed anything it can pick up. Shakespeare knew the Kite when he said that where it 'builds, look to lesser linen'. It is acquisitive. Both sexes collect this rubbish, but apparently only the female broods. The two or three eggs are dirty white streaked, smeared and lined with reddish-brown, and are usually laid in Wales about the middle of April. The young are clothed in white and pale brown down.

The head of the adult is white, streaked with black, the rest of the upper parts reddish-brown with paler edgings to the feathers; the underparts red with dark streaks. A pale patch on the underside of the wing is obvious when the bird flies overhead. The bill is bluish horn; the cere, legs and irides yellow. The young bird is duller and has a brown head. Length, 25 in. Wing, 20 in. Tarsus, 2·3. (*Plates 35, 46 and 166.*)

### Black Kite *Milvus migrans*

The Black Kite, a bird of south and central Europe and north-west Africa which migrates in winter to tropical Africa, has been recorded in Britain seven or eight times. It has the same habits of hunting for offal and food as our bird. Its tail is less forked and it looks a darker and blacker bird on the wing than the Red Kite, but its plumage is similar. It is not so white on the head, is browner and less rufous, especially on the tail, and the adult lacks the light feathers on the underwing. Length, 24 in. Wing, 18 in.

### White-tailed Eagle *Haliaeetus albicilla*

In the 19th century the White-tailed Eagle was more abundant than the Golden Eagle in the British Isles; now it is extinct, except as an occasional straggler in autumn and winter; most of these wanderers are immature. It breeds in Greenland and northern Europe and Asia. Formerly the White-tailed Eagle occupied many eyries round our coasts and a few inland; it was found in the Lake District, Isle of Man, Lundy and the Isle of Wight, and until 1910 or thereabouts at least one eyrie existed in Ireland, where it was at one time common.

Also known as the Erne or Sea-eagle, it is more of a coast-haunting species than the Golden Eagle. Its eyries were usually on some precipitous sea cliff, its favourite perch a rocky, wave-washed pinnacle. Its slow, flapping flight and majestic aerial sailing resemble those of the Golden Eagle, but it can be distinguished at all ages by its shorter wedge-shaped tail. Its yelping call is shriller than that of the Golden Eagle. Both eagles are frequently mobbed by much weaker birds; yet the White-tailed Eagle will kill ducks and other large birds, though fish forms a fair proportion of its food. The bird sometimes plunges for fish like an Osprey, but this is not its only method of catching them, for it has been seen dropping on trout in the shallows. It will eat any mammal or bird that it can capture and overcome, and it will not refuse carrion. As is the case with all eagles, and indeed with many raptorial birds, the young tend to wander, but adults are generally sedentary.

At all ages the unfeathered tarsi distinguish this bird from the Golden Eagle. The upper parts of the adult are brown, and the head is lighter, grey or almost white in very old birds; beneath it is darker brown. The whole tail is white. The beak, cere and legs are yellow. In the darker immature birds the tail is at first brown, but later becomes mottled and greyer, but is never barred as in the Golden Eagle. The cere and legs are duller yellow, the bill black. Male: Length, 36 in. Wing, 24 in. Tarsus, 4 in. Female: Length, 40 in. Wing, 27 in. Tarsus, 4·5 in. (*Plate 41.*)

## Honey Buzzard                                          *Pernis apivorus*

The Honey Buzzard is a summer visitor to northern and central Europe and winters in Africa. It is now mainly known in our islands as a rare spring and autumn visitor on passage, but is also a scarce summer visitor. It continues to breed in very small numbers in the south of England and has probably once nested in Scotland.

The Honey Buzzard is a bird of the woods, seldom apparently indulging in the long flights and aerial performances of its congeners, though Gilbert White, who knew it well, says it 'skims about in a majestic manner'. It delights to sit, sunning itself, and when seeking food walks and runs on the ground with ease. As its favourite food is the larvae of wasps, it certainly is not honey that it seeks, and though it attacks nests of wild bees it is the grubs it devours. It has no fear of wasps and will scratch out the 'cakes', entering so far into the hollow as to be almost hidden. A woodman in Salcey Forest actually pulled one out of a wasps' nest when he saw its tail protruding. Although it feeds mainly on insects it also kills small birds and mammals and robs nests of eggs. In flight the Honey Buzzard may be distinguished from the Common Buzzard by its comparatively long tail with dark bars near the base, and its narrower, projecting head. Its call, a high-pitched *kee-er*, is also characteristic.

The nest is usually built upon the old nest of some other species or on a squirrel-drey; its chief characteristic is the lining of fresh green leaves and twigs which are sometimes woven into the outer fabric and renewed from time to time. The eggs, usually two or three in number, are very handsome: they are white, boldly blotched and smeared with rich chestnut or red; sometimes the markings almost obscure the white.

Most raptorial birds are variable in plumage, none more so than the Honey Buzzard. A usual type is grey on the head, brown on the back, white spotted and barred with brown beneath. The barring on the tail varies in width and number of bars. Some birds, described as a dark form, are mostly brown on the underparts. The young have a whitish head and feathers of the upper parts edged with pale brown. In other immature birds the head is brown. The bill is black, the cere lead-blue, the legs and irides yellow or brown. Length, 22–25 in. Wing, 15–17 in. Tarsus, 2 in. *Plate 34.*)

**Marsh Harrier** *Circus aeruginosus*

The Marsh Harrier precariously maintains its status as a British breeding bird. It was temporarily exterminated towards the end of the 19th century, but was re-established in Norfolk in the 1920s. By 1958 a dozen pairs were nesting in Norfolk and Suffolk and a few pairs in Dorset. There had been occasional nests in other parts of England and one in North Wales, but there was a sudden decline in the next few years and the total British population was reduced to about six pairs, half of them in the reserve of the Royal Society for the Protection of Birds at Minsmere, Suffolk. The Marsh Harrier has not nested in Ireland since 1917. Non-breeding birds, usually immature, occur with some regularity in spring and summer on a marsh in north Lancashire and occasional vagrants or passage migrants elsewhere.

The Harriers are variable birds; no two birds seem exactly alike. On the wing, however, when details are hidden, the male Marsh Harrier looks a large brown and grey bird with black wing-tips in marked contrast to the grey of the wing. The head appears paler than the back. The female looks larger and much darker; her browner wings do not show up the blacker primaries. The young bird, shown on the colour plate, is easier to recognise, for the pale head appears almost white against the rich brown of the rest of the plumage. Dense reedbeds or luxuriant marshes are the haunts of the Marsh Harrier; it flies low just above the reeds, quartering the ground with strong, purposeful flight. It takes a few deliberate powerful strokes, then sails with wings uplifted, held at an angle of 30 to 45° above the plane of its body. A Coot or Moorhen, a vole, frog, or even a dragonfly catches its eye, and instantly it drops upon its prey, but it does not attempt to fly a bird down in the open. In spring it subsists largely upon eggs and nestlings of marsh birds, and on these it feeds its young; it is indeed a harrier of the marsh. On this level expanse, where tail reeds obstruct the view, the low-flying bird is not easily seen. Occasionally the bird soars to a great height, rising with wide sweeps, almost like a Buzzard; the tips of the wings recurve, the primaries stand apart.

The nest, a large platform raised above the water or soaking marsh, is built of sticks, reeds and sedges, lined with smaller blades of aquatic plants; it is usually in a dense bed of reeds or other vegetation. Three to five whitish or pale blue eggs are usually laid in May. The fierce little nestlings are clothed in white down. The female is said to incubate and the male to feed her, and both birds hunt for the young. The male will feed the female before the eggs are laid. The Marsh Harrier is, as a rule, a silent bird, and the only regular note is a high-pitched *tli-keeah*.

The adult male Marsh Harrier is, usually, dark brown on the back and mantle, rufous on the rump, neck and wing-coverts, with dark brown centres to the feathers. The primaries are brownish-black, the secondaries and tail ashy-grey. The buffish head and face are surrounded by a frill, a partial facial disc. The underparts are reddish-brown, buff or almost white, streaked with dark brown; the thighs noticeably rufous. The bill is brownish-black, the cere and legs yellow. The female is a browner bird, lacking the grey on wings and tail, and her head is darker. The young are even more variable than the mature birds, but in their first year they are dark chocolate-brown, as shown on the plate, with paler heads. There may be only a yellowish-white spot on the nape, or the crown, nape, chin and cheeks may be buff, creamy or almost white. Male: Length, 21·5 in. Wing, 16 in. Tarsus, 3·4 in. Female: Length, 24 in. Wing, 16·75 in. Tarsus, 3·5 in. (*Plates 36, 41 and 166.*)

## Hen Harrier                                                     *Circus cyaneus*

At the beginning of the 20th century the Hen Harrier was practically restricted, as a regular British breeding species, to the Orkneys and Outer Hebrides, although one or two pairs continued to nest in northern Ireland. From 1940 an increase began, and this continued for the following twenty-five years. Several localities on the mainland of Scotland have been re-colonised, there has been a considerable extension of range in Ireland, and a few pairs breed in England and Wales. In several districts young conifer plantations provide undisturbed nest sites. However, in most parts of Britain the Hen Harrier is still only known as an occasional spring and autumn passage migrant or winter visitor. It has a wide distribution in Europe.

Although wandering birds, mostly immature, are met with in wooded districts, the usual haunts of the Hen Harrier are moorlands, hillsides, marshes and open wastes. When seen at close quarters the white patch above the tail is noticeable. The silvery-grey dress of the male and the black primaries might be confused with those of Montagu's Harrier, but the underparts of the Hen Harrier are unstreaked and there is no dark bar on the wing. The barred or 'ringed' tail of the female is a good but not distinctive character. Sharing with other Harriers the habit of closely and diligently quartering the ground with buoyant easy flight, the Hen Harrier more frequently interrupts its progress by hovering, though not like the Kestrel. The wings beat more slowly and the pose is different. The tail is not usually spread, though when the bird swerves from side to side, careening gracefully, the expanded tail acts as a rudder. When rising or soaring the long wings curve upwards, the flight-tips separate; the bird will at times undulate, rising and falling as it flies. The Hen Harrier is a silent bird, but when angry has a quick, chattering cry, a weak imitation of the *hek, hek, hek,* of the Peregrine. The female utters a squealing wail when the nest is threatened. Small mammals—voles, mice, rats and young rabbits—birds, frogs, lizards and insects are its food, and it is a persistent robber of the eggs and young of other species. As a rule it drops suddenly upon its unsuspecting prey, but Coward saw one chase a small wader with dogged determination. The wader saved itself from the pouncing stoops of the Harrier by dropping to the water and diving as the pursuer shot past; swooping round, the Harrier hovered above the small bird until it emerged from the water, and stooped, though missing, as the fugitive again took the water. It will eat Starlings and larger birds, including Coot and Teal.

The nest is always on the ground, amongst heather or on a small space trodden down by the birds amongst thick vegetation; it is built of heather, sticks, rushes, grass or any convenient material, and may have a full soft lining of finer bents or be practically unlined. It varies considerably in size and finish. The four to six eggs are usually laid in April or early May, and only one brood is reared, but late clutches, the result of accident to the first, are frequently found. The eggs are dull white or tinged with blue, and in damp situations are frequently stained; rarely, they are faintly marked with brown. The female sits closely and is fed by the male; he will hover above her and drop his gift, which she will spring for and catch in the air.

The male is pearly-grey with almost black primaries; the grey on his breast shades into white on the belly; the upper tail-coverts in both sexes are white, though sparsely spotted in the female. The bill is blackish; the cere and legs yellow. The female is a larger bird and her facial disc, bordered with buff, is more noticeable. She is brown above with paler markings on the wings, buff tips on the coverts forming bars; the crown is streaked with dark brown. The tail is barred with bluish-grey and brown. The underparts are warm rufous, streaked with dark brown. The immature bird is similar but more rufous. Length, 19 in. (male), 21 in. (female). Wing, 13·4–14 in. Tarsus 2·6 in. (*Plates 40, 41 and 166.*)

### Montagu's Harrier                                       *Circus pygargus*

Montagu's Harrier, a migratory species, is a summer visitor to Britain and to many parts of Europe, though not to the far north. The breeding population in the British Isles has fluctuated during the present century, but has recently declined to a total of about twenty pairs in England and Wales, and one or two pairs in Ireland. It has occasionally nested in the south of Scotland. Young conifer plantations are a favourite breeding habitat for this species as well as for the Hen Harrier. Though it is the smallest of the three harriers the proportionately long wings give an impression of size, and Montagu's Harrier is not easy to distinguish from the Hen on the wing. It has the same habits of closely quartering the ground, swerving from side to side, canting its wings, and pouncing suddenly upon its quarry. When skimming over reed-beds its flight, slow and uneven, is buoyant and easy; with uplifted wings it sails gracefully, its extended open primaries rounding the otherwise pointed wings. Soaring flights are common, the bird drifting in wide sweeps and circles at a great altitude; as it turns the light falls on its blue back and dark flight feathers, reminding one of the Hen Harrier, but at close quarters the band on the wing and brown streaked underparts are noticeable; the pale red spotted thighs and grey upper tail-coverts distinguish it from the male Hen Harrier. The brown females and immatures are difficult to identify, but the unstreaked underparts of the juvenile Montagu's are diagnostic. The Montagu's also shows rather less white on the rump and is a little smaller than the Hen and more buoyant in flight.

Montagu's Harrier reaches its breeding haunts in April, and though now rare and thinly distributed is, normally, a gregarious bird, travelling in companies and, in Spain and North Africa, where it is common, nesting in colonies. Even here four pairs have been known on one marsh. If undisturbed it remains throughout the summer, leaving in October or even later. Its food is similar to that of other harriers, though as a rule smaller game than that of the Hen; it seldom chases its victims unless they are disabled. Eggs and young birds form a large proportion of its spring diet. During incubation the male waits on and feeds the female; she often takes food from him in the air.

The nest varies in size and finish according to its situation; it may be on a moor, heather or gorse-clad common, young plantation, rocky waste or marsh. At times a mere hollow, with a slight rim of nesting material, suffices, but some nests are a mass of twigs, reeds and grasses. It is usually on the ground in beaten-down vegetation. Eggs, four to six, are laid late in May; they resemble those of the Hen Harrier, but are smaller. Young in down are white.

The male is blue-grey above, with black primaries and a dark bar across the wing; the upper tail-coverts are ashy-grey; the grey tail has the outer feathers barred. The white underparts have strong rufous streaks. The bill is blackish, the cere and legs yellow. The female is dark brown, streaked on the paler head and neck, white above the eye and on the chin, and with a pale-edged facial disc; the tail is barred. Underparts are buff, streaked with rufous. Young males resemble the female, but upper parts have buff edges to the feathers and the underparts are almost unstreaked. Dark, sometimes almost black, forms of this variable bird occur; one is shown on the colour plate. Length, 18 in. (male), 19 in. (female). Wing, 15 in. Tarsus, 2·3 in. (*Plates 40, 42 and 166.*)

## Osprey                                            *Pandion haliaetus*

Early in the present century the Osprey became extinct in the British Isles as a breeding species. It has a wide distribution in northern and eastern Europe and winters in the Mediterranean countries and Africa.

However, since 1955 a pair has nested on Speyside, where the Royal Society for the Protection of Birds has combined protection with publicity in a daring and successful annual exercise. By 1967 two more pairs were breeding elsewhere in Inverness-shire. In other parts of the British Isles the Osprey is an occasional passage migrant and non-breeding summer visitor, occurring on both inland and coastal waters.

The Osprey can be recognised at a distance by the contrast between its dark brown upper parts and white underparts, and when in flight by its long, narrow wings, noticeably angled at the carpal joint. In Britain it is purely a fish-eater, though not particular whether from fresh or salt water; it will capture surface fish at sea, flounders from a muddy estuary, lazy bream in the meres, or trout in the clear streams. It flies with slow, powerful strokes and frequently poises and hovers, its head slightly bent as it scans the water beneath. After these hovering pauses, if nothing moves below it will glide on, or will plunge headlong with a mighty splash and emerge with or without a captive in its claws, for by no means every dive succeeds. The talons strike deep into the flanks of the fish, which is then carried, head pointed to the front. The Osprey, when fishing, sails at about 30 ft. above the water, but will soar and circle at a great height. It likes to perch on a dead branch or rock, to which it returns with its prey. In courtship display the male circles high overhead, uttering a rapid *chee-chee-chee*; but the commonest call is a musical piping *pew-pew-pew*.

The birds arrive at their breeding quarters in Scotland in April and immediately begin to repair the nest or build a new one. It is a bulky structure of large sticks with a lining of grass, moss and bark. Three eggs, with bold brown blotches on a creamy ground colour, are laid; they are incubated chiefly by the female, but the male relieves her for short periods, especially in the early morning. When the young birds are hatched the male fishes for the family, while the female remains at the nest and distributes the food to the young. The young birds take their first flights in August.

The adult Osprey is dark brown above; the head is white, streaked with brown, and there is a broad band of brown from eye to nape. The underparts, except for a brown breast band, are white. The bill and claws are black, the cere and legs blue. In immature birds the dark feathers have pale edges and buff tips, as shown in the plate. Male: Length, 22 in. Wing, 19 in. Tarsus, 2·2 in. Female: Length, 24 in. Wing, 21 in. Tarsus, 2·4 in. (*Plates 39 and 46.*)

**Hobby**                                                    *Falco subbuteo*

The Hobby breeds in north and central Europe and winters far south in Africa and Asia. Spring immigrants arrive in England early in May, and in southern counties the bird nests regularly, though it is now scarce and local. The breeding population of England has been estimated at seventy-five to 100 pairs, with the largest concentration in Hampshire. Further north it is rare, and in Scotland and Ireland is known only as a straggler on migration.

It is distinctly the falcon of the woodlands, spending much of the day perched in a tree, but hunting with remarkable activity in the early morning, late afternoon and evening until dusk. When perched, and it is not a very difficult bird to approach, its long red shank feathers are very characteristic. It has proportionately long, narrow wings and a shortish tail, and though it will hover for a moment over a bush, its swift gliding flight is quite distinct from that of the Kestrel; the bird with which it is most likely to be confused is the Merlin, from which it can be told by the thighs and moustachial streaks, as well as by its longer wings. Like the Peregrine, its wings winnow quickly before each floating glide. It will kill small birds, Sky Larks being frequent victims, but it also feeds upon insects, catching dragonflies with a swift stoop from above, then rising at once and devouring them as it flies. Insects are caught in the foot and transferred to the bill. It nips up the booming dor beetle in the evening, and will capture the white cabbage butterfly which most birds ignore. Its wonderful speed enables it to strike down or chase and capture the Swallow and Martin, and it can out-fly the Swift. At times it will circle high above the Swifts and Swallows, stooping at them in play rather than with fell intent, for it delights in aerial exercise. In spring a pair will mount together, circle, swoop and dodge in nuptial enjoyment. A characteristic call is a chattering *ki-ki-ki*.

The Hobby does not build for itself, but appropriates the old nests of crows or other birds. The number of eggs is usually three, and they are often similar to the mottled and blotched red-brown eggs of the Merlin, though many have a yellower ground. They are not laid as a rule until June, and a single brood is reared, second layings following disaster. Emigration takes place in September, but there are records of stragglers in November.

The upper parts of the adult bird are slate-grey; the ear-coverts and strong moustachial stripe are black, contrasting with white cheeks and chin. The underparts are rufous-white, boldly streaked with black; the thighs and under tail-coverts orange-rufous. The bill is blue; cere and legs yellow. The thighs of the female are slightly streaked. The young birds are brown above, with pale margins to the feathers, and the underparts are washed with yellow; the red of thighs and tail-coverts is pale. Male: Length, 12 in. Wing, 10 in. Tarsus, 1·25 in. Female: Length, 14 in. Wing, 11·25 in. Tarsus, 1·4 in. (*Plates 49 and 166.*)

**Peregrine**                                                      *Falco peregrinus*

The handsome Peregrine is the largest and most powerful of our resident falcons. In spite of persecution and the repeated harrying of nests by farmers and egg-collectors, the breeding population of the British Isles remained stable for the first half of the present century, but a catastrophic decline began about 1955. Most of the sea-cliffs in the south of England were deserted and there were drastic reductions in the number of breeding pairs in Wales, the Lake District and parts of Scotland and Ireland. Of those that laid eggs, few succeeded in raising young. D. A. Ratcliffe has shown strong evidence that this decline was due to persistent toxic chemicals used in agriculture and carried in sub-lethal strength in the bodies of the Peregrine's prey. However, there were signs of a possible slight recovery from 1965.

There is a dash, neatness and finish in the flight of the Peregrine which is purely its own. The wings move rapidly, beating the air for a few moments, and are then held steady in a bow whilst the bird glides forward, sometimes rolling slightly from side to side. The legs, as in other raptorial birds, lie under the tail and are not held forward, except when striking; at times one leg will be dropped and shaken during flight. When seen from above the bird looks blue, from below, red or rufous, but if at a distance or high in the air it looks a black arc or swiftly moving crescent. The bend of the bow varies with the speed and inclination of flight; during descent, when the wing-tips point backward, it is a sharp curve. Near a coastwise eyrie the bird will sail out over the water, easily and gracefully, rising to a great height, then with wings almost closed shoot seaward, recovering itself near the water and after a low flight above the waves mount once more. Tiercel and falcon, as the male and female are called, join in aerial gambols, sporting together as one or the other playfully mounts and stoops at its consort. The 'stoop' of the Peregrine is its swoop or downward rush with almost closed wings, seen to best advantage when hunting. An aerial fight between two tiercels is a sight to be remembered; the stoops and dodges are no play then; the birds rise to a great height, each striving to get above the other to gain advantage for the stoop, which is avoided often by a sudden upward rush of the lower bird, accompanied by a scream of rage or fear. The usual cry of the Peregrine when its eyrie is approached is a sharp, quickly repeated *hech* or *hek*; that of the tiercel is a distinct *hak, hak, hak,* but in the falcon it is quicker and runs into a fierce chattering scream, *hek, hek, ek-ek-ek.*

Near the eyrie the birds have look-outs, some jutting rocks or pinnacles on the cliff face. Here a bird will perch for hours, with head sunk into its shoulders, and its breast turned outward, showing white against dark rocks, but hardly visible on the chalk cliffs of the south coast. Occasionally the head, set off by the black moustachial streaks, is turned sharply to watch the flight of some passing gull or wader. On the cliff-top, near the eyrie, are the shambles or slaughter-house, scattered litter of blood-stained feathers and the rejected remnants of many a victim. The Peregrine will kill birds large or small— ducks, gulls, Curlew and even small waders; it will kill and eat Jackdaws and Rooks, Grouse, Partridge and Pigeon; indeed it is specially fond of the Stock Dove and domestic Pigeon, stopping the return of many a homer. As a rule the quarry is killed in flight, struck down by the 'bolt from the blue' and sent hurtling earthward, headless or with back ripped open, amidst a cloud of feathers. Immediately after giving the fatal blow with the hind claw, the destroyer shoots upward, descending later to enjoy its meal. The rush of a stooping Peregrine when heard at close quarters is like the sound of a rocket.

No nest is made; the two to four richly coloured orange-red or deep brown eggs are placed in a rough hollow scraped on some ledge of a steep crag or cliff. They are usually laid in April, and though normally single brooded, the bird will lay again if the first eggs are destroyed. Both sexes sit, but the falcon is far fiercer and noisier in defence of the nest than her mate. Until the downy white young are fledged they are fed upon plucked and usually headless food. When very young they lie prone and motionless as long as watched, but when the new feathers are appearing, they scramble about restlessly on the ledge, with a cheeping food call.

The adult male has upper parts slate-grey with dark bars, crown and cheeks very dark, and the black moustachial patch conspicuous. The underparts are buffish-white, deepest on the breast, and are barred with black, the amount varying individually. The bill is blue; the cere and legs yellow. The female, a larger bird, is darker and the bars are heavier. In immature plumage the upper parts are greyish-brown with buff margins to the feathers, and the yellowish underparts are streaked and not barred. The cere and legs are livid blue-grey. Male: Length, 15 in. Wing, 12·5 in. Tarsus, 2 in. Female: Length, 18 in. Wing, 14 in. Tarsus, 2·3 in. (*Plates 42, 43 and 166.*)

**Gyr Falcon**                                                    *Falco rusticolus*
There are three geographical forms of the Gyr Falcon with marked plumage differences. Birds of the very white type, breeding in northern Greenland, regularly visit western Europe and are almost annual birds of passage in spring and autumn in Scotland and its islands. There are over eighty records from Ireland and from time to time birds are seen in England and Wales. The darker form, mainly nesting in Iceland, is much less frequent, and the very dark European Gyr Falcon has very rarely been recorded in the British Isles.

In bearing when perched, in dash and ferocity when stooping on its prey and in angry cries the Gyr Falcon differs little from our Peregrine, but it is larger, has broader wings and lacks the facial markings. Large birds and mammals are attacked, the main food being hares, gulls, Guillemots, Puffins and waders, Grouse, Ptarmigan and rabbits in Britain. The white plumage of the Greenland Falcon may be said to be 'protective', not that so powerful a bird needs protection from enemies, but that its plumage in a land of snow gives it a degree of invisibility which enables it to approach its prey and so obtain food. Owing to its magnificent powers of flight, the visiting Gyr Falcon avoids the gun more easily than some of the other birds of prey; it is not uncommon to hear of 'white' Falcons seen but not 'obtained', most of which were, probably, Greenland birds.

The plumage of the Greenland race is mostly white, except for its dark primaries; on the back are a few blackish-grey bars, on the flanks a few spots, but no bars. The Iceland birds are much darker, brownish-grey on the head and back, and spotted and barred on the creamy-white underparts; the bars on the flanks are distinctive. In both forms the tail is barred. The bill is bluish horn; the cere, eye-rims, and legs yellow. Immature birds of both races are much browner, and their markings on both upper and under surface browner and broader. Male: Length, 21 in. Wing, 14·5 in. Tarsus, 2·75 in. Female: Length, 23 in. Wing, 16 in. Tarsus, 3·0 in. (*Plate 45.*)

**Merlin**                                                      *Falco columbarius*
The range of the Merlin extends from Iceland across north and central Europe. Northern birds move south, and many winter in Mediterranean countries. In the British Isles it is resident, and to some degree a winter visitor and bird of passage.

As the Hobby is the falcon of the southern woodlands, so the Merlin is the bird of the northern moors. As a breeding species it is hardly known in the south, though it breeds sparingly on Dartmoor, but from North Wales, Derbyshire and Yorkshire northward to the Shetlands, and in Ireland, it nests on suitable moorlands, but it is nowhere abundant and numbers have decreased during the present century, especially since about 1950. Though the smallest of its group, it is active and predatory, lording over the lesser fowl of the uplands. In winter, when most passerine birds desert the bleak moors, it is more widely distributed, but never regularly haunts coverts and woods. Swift on its long narrow wings, it glides less than other falcons, and seldom employs the wonderful downward stoops of Peregrine or Hobby, but following every turn, twist and double of its quarry, fairly flies it down. When it has gained on its victim it rises above it to strike it down with its foot. Gamekeepers say that, except for picking up an odd 'cheeper', it does little harm to Grouse, though it will, in sport, chase and stoop at an adult bird. Meadow Pipits, Wheatears and Larks are its favourite victims on the moor, but it will kill as large a bird as Thrush, Snipe and even Lapwing. On the coast it will put up and dash into a dense cloud of Knots, Dunlins and other waders, single out its quarry and follow it relentlessly as it dodges close above the waves. Fearlessly it assaults any large bird that ventures near its nest, driving the Crow and Black-headed Gull away; it even makes bold attacks on the Short-eared Owl and Peregrine, and once a pair of birds harried a passing Heron until it squawked in terror. Beetles and moths, especially the large-bodied oak-eggar, so common amongst the ling, are eaten, the latter captured on the wing. The call of anger and alarm has much in common with that of the Peregrine, a hurried shrill *kik, kik, ik-ik-ik-ik*, but when a pair, with many aerial gymnastics, sport together the cry loses its ferocious tone. Various softer calls are used by both sexes at the nest.

On the moors the Merlin nests amongst the heather or coarse upland grasses, making no real nest, but laying its eggs in a hollow scraped in the ground or a depression amongst the vegetation; at times it is fully exposed, though often screened by bracken, ling or crowberry. The bird is not confined to the hills, but haunts the coast and low-lying marshes. On the Welsh coast it nests on the cliffs, often at the top, where the ground is flat, and frequently close to a turf bank or wall, but sometimes on a ledge in a gorge or on the grassy slope some distance below the edge. It may nest amongst the marram on the sand-dunes and under a tussock in a deep inland bog. Rarely, the Merlin occupies an old nest in a tree. Year after year, even when the nest has been disturbed, a pair will return to the same spot, even to the original 'scrape' if it can be recognised. Not far from the nest is the look-out, a rocky outcrop or boulder, a post, wall or grassy mound; this, too, is often the slaughter-house or shambles, streaked with blood-stains and surrounded by feathers and bones of the carcases plucked and prepared for the young. The eggs are laid in May, usually in the second half. Four is the ordinary number, though five is not un-common, and many nests contain only three. They are much like those of the

Hobby and the denser spotted eggs of the Kestrel, and are usually closely freckled with reddish-brown and almost black spots.

For a very short time the newly hatched young are quiet fluffy white weaklings with ivory, pink-tinted beaks, but they rapidly gain courage and ferocity, and whilst still too feeble to sit up, will throw themselves on their backs in resentment at familiarities, defending themselves with beak and claw. Even when just out of the egg they will call, a whispered echo of their parents' angry *kik, kik, kik,* and before the pink flesh is hidden by the thickening greyish down, will scream defiance. When the first dark grey feathers, spotted with yellowish-brown, replace the down, they will, though still too weak to walk, fight gamely if handled.

The adult male has upper parts slate-blue with fine black shaft streaks, underparts rufous with broader striations; the tail barred with black, a broad band near the white tip. The bill is blue; cere and legs yellow. The female is brown, has pale margins to the feathers of the back, and broad mottles and streaks on the underparts; her tail is distinctly barred black and brown. The young are like the female, but redder. Male: Length, 11 in. Wing, 7·8 in. Tarsus, 1·45 in. Female: Length, 12 in. Wing, 8·6 in. Tarsus, 1·5 in. (*Plates 45 and 166.*)

### Red-footed Falcon                                    *Falco vespertinus*

The Red-footed Falcon is a summer visitor to eastern Europe; it winters in Africa. On migration, usually in spring and summer, it not infrequently occurs in the British Isles. In most years two or three are reported, mostly from the east and south of England, but it has been met with in the west and in Wales, Scotland and Ireland.

The Red-footed Falcon has more of the Kestrel than the Hobby in its manner of flight. It is not quick in its sailing and it frequently hovers; it shares with the Hobby one habit, that of hawking for crepuscular moths; the specific name indicates these evening flights. Mice and lizards are eaten as well as insects, but it is not swift enough to capture many birds. Its call is a repeated *ki,* not unlike that of the Kestrel, with which it has many things in common.

The male's upper parts, as also the tail, the breast and under wing-coverts, are slate-grey, darkest on the head and lightest on the quills. The feathers round the eye are almost black. The thighs, belly and under tail-coverts are rich chestnut. The bill is dark horn, cere and legs red, and the claws almost white. The female has head, nape, underparts, and under wing-coverts rufous rather than chestnut, and the slate back is mottled and barred with blackish-grey; the tail is distinctly barred. Immature birds are browner above and the general colour is redder and paler; the forehead and throat are almost white. They may be distinguished from young Merlins by the absence of distinct striations on the thighs. Length, 11·5 in. Wing, 9·8 in. Tarsus, 1·15 in. (*Plate 49.*)

## Lesser Kestrel
*Falco naumanni*

The gregarious Lesser Kestrel is a bird of the Mediterranean basin; in winter it migrates to tropical Africa. It has frequently wandered north and west in Europe, and a few have been recorded in the British Isles. Most of these have been mature males, from which we may guess that the visits of the species are commoner than is supposed; males are easier to identify, and probably females have been overlooked. The bird is mainly an insect-feeder, catching grasshoppers and other insects on the wing. The male resembles our Kestrel, but has no spots on the back, and the secondaries are slate-grey. The female closely resembles our bird except in size, but in both sexes one character is distinctive—the claws are white. Length, 12·25 in.

## Kestrel
*Falco tinnunculus*

The Kestrel is both resident and migratory. It has a wide range, embracing most of Europe; the more northern birds winter further south. Even from Scotland and the north of England there is a marked southward movement in autumn, and at this time immigrants reach us to winter or pass further south. Although there was a marked drop in the breeding population in eastern counties of England about 1960 the Kestrel is still the most abundant diurnal bird of prey in Britain.

In addition to its chestnut dress and broadly barred tail, the flight of the 'Wind-hover' is a sure sign of its identity, for though other hawks hover none has so perfected the art. It hangs 20 to 30 ft. above the earth, poised in the air with quivering wings and wide-spread, depressed tail, then slides forward, often without a wing-beat, to halt once more over a fresh patch of ground. For a second or two the swiftly winnowing wings may be held motionless, the bird supported by an air current. High, soaring flight is unusual; it seldom moves at a great altitude unless on migration. Passages from field to field are easy, steady, and never hurried; the Kestrel obtains its food by quickness of eye, not of wing. The smartest actions are when, having sighted quarry while hovering, it dives headlong with almost closed wings, checks itself close to the ground, seizes its victim and mounts again. Other birds frequently mob it. As a rule it pays little attention, sliding away sideways to avoid impact, mounting suddenly upward or dropping to a lower level. The call is a clear *kee, kee, kee* or, especially in the spring, a double-noted *kee-lee, kee-lee*.

The bird is catholic in its haunts. It frequents moors and rocky crags, woodland and field, and the coast, and will nest on buildings in towns as well as on mountain crags over 2000 ft. above sea level, indeed anywhere it can find small mammals and insects. Voles and beetles are its staple diet. It kills few birds, probably because it cannot catch them. Although it may snatch up an occasional Pheasant chick the real attraction to the rearing-field is the host of mice which glean the scattered grain. Nevertheless individual Kestrels have been proved to feed their young mainly on birds, especially Starlings, and others take surprisingly large prey. A male, bearing a heavy load, had twice to stop to rest and then just managed to clear a hedge, but had to drop its quarry, a warm but headless leveret.

No real nest is made by the Kestrel. It lays on a ledge of rock, in a scratched hollow, in a quarry or ruin, church tower, or in the deserted nest of some other species. When disturbed the sitting bird will often slip away without a sound, but sometimes it will fly round at a safe distance expostulating. Coward records that once when he was near a nest the female hovered above him and stooped repeatedly for at least ten minutes. When about 40 ft. above him she closed her tail, slid forward slightly and dived with almost closed wings, shearing off with an angry scream when about 10 ft. above his head. The eggs are usually four to five in number, though six or more are sometimes found; they are laid in April and May. They vary, but are generally thickly mottled or smeared with red or tawny-brown, frequently obscuring the yellowish ground colour. Both birds take some share in incubating, and unless the first eggs are destroyed only one clutch is laid. The young at first are clad in greyish down, and though they will squeal feebly if handled, seldom show fight.

The head, rump and tail of the male are slate-grey; the tail has a broad black sub-terminal band and white tip. The back is pale chestnut or rufous, spotted with black; the underparts more buff, with black streaks and spots. The bill is blue; cere and legs yellow. The female is rufous, paler below, barred on the back and striated beneath; her grey tail has, in addition to the sub-terminal band, several dark bars. The young, until a year old, are like the female, but browner, especially on the tail. Unlike most other raptorial birds, there is little difference in the size of the sexes, both showing great variation. Length, av. 14 in. Wing, 9·5 in. Tarsus, 1·6 in. (*Plates 43, 49 and 166.*)

# Order GALLIFORMES

## Family TETRAONIDAE Grouse

*Ground birds; bill short, stout; wings short, round; tarsi feathered; toes four, hind toe small.*

### Red Grouse

*Lagopus lagopus*

The Red Grouse is a British insular form of the continental Willow Grouse. It is generally distributed in Scotland, Wales and England as far south as Shropshire, Derbyshire and Yorkshire, and a few pairs breed on Dartmoor and Exmoor, where the species was introduced in the 19th century. The Red Grouse of Ireland have paler plumage than British birds; their numbers have greatly declined during the present century.

The Red Grouse is a moorland bird, but is not confined to those which are heather clad; indeed, on the Pennines and in other parts there are well-stocked moors where it would be difficult to find heather or ling. On such moors, however, the crowberry, often confused with the heaths, is usually plentiful. The altitude of the moor matters little if other conditions are favourable, but though Grouse are found at sea level, most of their haunts are above the 1000-ft. contour. The appearance of the 'Moor-fowl' is familiar, though generally as a shot-battered corpse, or as a possible recipient for shot as it comes, a stout, short-winged bird, whirring and gliding over the shoulder of the moor, toward the turf batteries. Though richly coloured, it is well hidden amongst the irregularities and varied shades of the rough moor; it lies low, rising when disturbed with a startling whirr, and flies just above the heather, turning sideways as it takes advantage of the undulations or steep slopes of the cloughs or corries. Its call, a loud crow, is used as a challenge as it stands, head erect and red wattle raised, on some tussock or mound, but its alarm, when flushed, is a rapid *kok, kok, kok*, as it flies, and a clear *goback, goback, goback*, when it alights at a safe distance and runs amongst the tussocks. The young feed largely on insects, especially caterpillars, though they take a few leaves and shoots of ling and other plants; the old birds subsist mainly on shoots, leaves and seeds of heather, ling, crowberry, bilberry and other plants of the 'tops', and in autumn on the abundant moorland fruits. Seeds of grasses and rushes are eaten, but raids on cornfields are exceptional. When, in winter, the moor is snow-clad for weeks at a time the Grouse usually descend to lower ground; in some parts there is apparently regular local migration from the higher to the lower ground. Sometimes, however, the Grouse tunnel under the snow to obtain their food and are thus concealed from view. Water, easy to obtain on the hills, is necessary for the bird. Grit, too, is essential to aid digestion, as indeed it is with most birds, and it is common to see Grouse on the unfenced moorland roads picking up grit or enjoying a sun or dust bath. Research by biologists of the Nature Conservancy on moors in

Scotland has shown that the population of Red Grouse is dependent upon the quantity and quality of food available; the effects of predation and disease seem to be negligible. In particular the mortality of chicks has been correlated with the die-back of heather in the preceding winter. Properly controlled heather-burning, which increases the production of new shoots, is an important factor in maintaining the number of Grouse on a moor.

Although satisfied with one mate, the cock Grouse will fight even after he has paired, but as in other species the sexual spars are not serious. In winter the bird is gregarious, but the packs do not 'jug' close together like Partridges, and by the end of March they have mostly broken up. The nest is a simple hollow in the ground, often sheltered by ling or other plants, and lined with a few sprigs of heather and dry grass. Seven to ten, or even more, richly coloured red or yellowish eggs, closely mottled and blotched with reddish-brown, are laid late in April or in May, the date varying according to the severity of the season. The colour is at first 'loose', and smeared eggs are not uncommon. 'Cheepers', clothed in mottled and streaked yellowish-brown and chestnut down, rapidly get the power of short-distance flight, and when no bigger than thrushes will whirr for a few yards after their parents, but soon learn that there is safety in remaining still.

The typical winter and spring plumage of the male is chestnut-red, barred with wavy black lines; the markings are least conspicuous on the coppery-red throat and neck. The bill is blue-black, and above the eye is a vermilion erectile wattle or comb. In summer the bars are wider and more pronounced and there is more buff in the general plumage. The female is often a more spotted bird, but when barred shows strong buff and black markings. The feathers on legs and toes are thin and worn in summer, but thick and long after the autumn moult. Length, 15 in. Wing, 8·25 in. Tarsus, 1·8 in. (*Plates 50 and 167.*)

## Ptarmigan                                                   *Lagopus mutus*

The mountain ranges of Europe, from Scandinavia to the Pyrenees, are the home of the Ptarmigan; with us it only occurs in the highest mountains of Scotland, including those of Skye and Mull, seldom breeding below the 2000-ft. contour.

There is no difficulty in distinguishing the Ptarmigan from other grouse, although its zone overlaps that of the Red Grouse occasionally, for at all ages it is not only a whiter bird but when mature has white quills in each of its three seasonal phases. It is not a bird of the heathery moor but of the rocky summits, where lichens and mosses replace more luxuriant vegetation, and where, on northern slopes, the snow will linger through the summer. The ordinary note is a low croak, but more varied calls are used in courtship and care of the young. When running on snow, these grey birds look very much like the stones in motion, and in winter dress they are almost invisible, even to the keen eye of the Golden Eagle or the hill fox. The Ptarmigan runs and hides rather than take wing, but in flight is wonderfully swift; it will cross at a great height from peak to peak. Its food is on the whole similar to that of the Red Grouse, though naturally of a more alpine nature; it eats mosses and lichens as well as berry-bearing, low-growing plants and dwarf willows. In autumn, sometimes early, the birds pack, and in winter usually descend to a lower zone, but like the Red Grouse it will at times seek food by burrowing in the snow. The packs break up in spring, but the nest, an unlined or scantily lined hollow, is not scratched until May. The seven to ten eggs are not unlike pale eggs of the Red Grouse, and are often laid in June. Young in down are rather darker than those of the last species, especially on the head. They fly at a very early age, and are carefully guarded and boldly defended by their parents. The hen, and sometimes the cock, will feign injury and the latter will attack a dog, and it is said a man, if the young are threatened.

The Ptarmigan has three moults. In nuptial plumage from about April to July, the male is barred on the upper parts with brown, grey and buff; the underparts below the breast are mostly white. Black, white-tipped outer tail feathers and white, black-shafted quills are constant in all phases. The more tawny female has black barring. From August until about October the upper parts are grey, vermiculated with black, and the female is rather browner. In winter both sexes are white, except for the black on tail and quill shafts; the lores and a streak through the eye are black in the male. Above the eye of both sexes there is a scarlet comb, more pronounced in the male; the bill is black. Until the first autumn moult the primaries of young birds are brownish. Length, 14·5 in. Wing, 7·6 in. Tarsus, 1·5 in. (*Plates 53 and 167.*)

## Black Grouse                                                 *Lyrurus tetrix*

The Black Grouse, which is found in northern and central Europe, has a wide but rather uneven distribution in Scotland, northern England and Wales. A few pairs still breed in Somerset, but otherwise the species is extinct in the southern counties of England. In Scotland and Wales numbers have increased in the new forestry plantations. The Black Grouse is unknown in Ireland.

Though common in some northern woodlands, the usual haunt of the Black Grouse is the sparsely wooded fringe of the moor, hilly country where there is a variety of feeding ground—moors, woodlands and cultivated land. The Black Cock differs from other grouse in his glossy blue-black plumage and lyre-shaped tail; the Grey Hen, his mate, is a less distinctive brown bird, smaller than the female Capercaillie, and differing from her in having the tail forked and not rounded, and in showing two rather faint pale wing-bars in flight. The strong, swift flight is typical of all grouse, but in the semi-arboreal habits and in polygamy the bird especially resembles the Capercaillie. The food varies according to locality and season, and though insects or other animals are eaten, is largely vegetarian; the tender tops of moorland plants, especially ling, heather, crowberry and bilberry, as well as moorland fruits and berries, are appreciated, and buds, leaves and fruits of trees are included. Conifers suffer from the Black Grouse, and when the corn is ripe grain is freely devoured.

The annual display and competitive performance of the males take place in spring, usually in the early morning. The males gather to 'lek' or compete in some open space, and fight, dance and show off, and the females come to look on with more or less evidence of approval. The actual fights look more serious than they are, for little more than a trial of strength results; there is much of the game-cock in the threatening preliminaries, but the blows are mostly with the wing, the feet, though used, being unarmed. Fighting changes to an exhibition of competitive dancing when the hens arrive at the tilting ground; with hoarse cries the excited birds leap into the air, posture and dance. More deliberate and sedate exhibition of plumage charms includes many extraordinary attitudes; with drooping wings and elevated wide-spread tail, the contrast of white wing-bar and under tail-coverts with the dark plumage produces striking effects. The outward and even forward spread of the gracefully curved tail feathers, and the snowy expanse of fluffy feathers beneath, are the more conspicuous feature. The exhibition is accompanied by a curious whirring note. It is not, by any means, proved that regular harems are selected and retained, and the separation or mingling of the sexes after the young are able to look after themselves may vary in different localities.

During summer, when the cock loses his fine tail for a time, and has a browner dress, especially on the head, he takes little interest in the female, and in winter several males and females will feed together without jealousy. Hybrids with other species, such as Pheasant, Capercaillie and Red Grouse, are not infrequent, but there is much variation in the plumage of mature birds, as well as rather complicated age changes, and the parentage of some reported hybrids has been challenged.

The nest is usually on the ground in thick herbage, and the six to ten, or even more, eggs are rather thinly speckled with reddish-brown on a yellowish ground. Nestlings have buff or yellowish down, mottled with black and chestnut, and reddish black-banded heads. They are tended by the hen only.

The normal plumage of the male is glossy blue-black, browner on the wings; the under tail-coverts and a bar on the wing are white, and above the eye is a large vermilion wattle, very prominent during the period of display. The bill and toes are blue-black. The female is rufous-buff, barred and mottled with black, and the wattle above her eye is smaller. Young birds at first resemble the hen, but young males show a mixture of brown, black and white in autumn, and early an outward curve of the short tail feathers, though the full tail is not acquired until the third year. Male: Length, 19·75 in. Wing, 10 in. Tarsus, 2·25 in. Female: Length, 18 in. Wing, 9 in. Tarsus, 2 in. (*Plates 44, 50 and 167.*)

**Capercaillie**                                                    *Tetrao urogallus*
Although the handsome Capercaillie was re-introduced to Britain as recently

as 1837, the bird is indigenous, and in remote ages made excellent meals for our ancestors, who left its bones amongst other evidences of their feasts in 'kitchen-middens' and cave deposits. Abroad the bird is a native of most European pine forests, and it was from Sweden that the ancestors of the present thriving Scottish birds were obtained; from Perth, where they were turned down, they have colonised the conifer woods in many parts of the Highlands.

The cock is a large, heavily built bird, with strong, curved, whitish bill, grey-black plumage, and legs feathered to the toes. Across the breast is a metallic-green gorget. The hen is a smaller, much browner bird, rather like a Grey Hen with a more rounded tail. She also has a reddish patch on the breast and otherwise pale underparts. Now that the 'Cock of the Woods' has increased, it has even extended its habitat to woods of deciduous trees, and apparently the hens regulate the extension of range, wandering to new woods, where, not infrequently, an amorous Black Cock selects one for its harem, and interesting hybrids result. Both Capercaillie and Black Grouse are polygamous. The Capercaillie has the strong, swift, but not long-sustained flight of the grouse family: a series of rapid wing movements with intervals when the bird glides with the wings steady, the primaries curved downward. It perches freely, and feeds in the branches on young leaves, buds, shoots and pine needles, and does not refuse caterpillars or other insects which it finds; fruits and berries of all kinds are taken in their season. The 'song' of the cock Capercaillie, normally heard only in spring, consists of a variety of clucking, popping and grinding noises and is delivered with upstretched neck and fanned tail. The male's display, in which leaping and wing-flapping is interspersed with bursts of song, may be communal, with both males and females present, or may be territorial, occasionally leading to actual fighting. One notorious cock near Brechin, Angus, regularly attacked humans, sheep and even vehicles each spring from 1958 to 1961, pecking fiercely and battering with its wings. A few similar cases have been reported elsewhere.

The nest is a hollow lined with pine needles and moss, in which six to eight eggs, yellowish in ground and speckled with red, are laid late in April or in May. The young have buff down, are mottled and striped, especially on the head, with black, and have a bare red patch behind the eye.

The male has upper parts and much of the underparts black, dusted and speckled with grey; the breast has a greenish gloss; the feathers of the neck are elongated and are spread during display; the coverts are reddish-brown with white speckles and tips, and both primaries and secondaries, as well as the feathers of the flanks, show a good deal of white. Above the eye is a long vermilion wattle; the heavy bill is yellowish-white. The female is reddish-brown, mottled on the upper parts with black, buff and white; the underparts are barred with buff, black and white, with a rufous patch on the breast. Young birds closely resemble the hens. Male: Length, 33–35 in. Wing, 14·8 in. Tarsus, 3 in. Female: Length, 22-25 in. Wing, 12 in. Tarsus, 2·2 in. (*Plates 50 and 167.*)

Family PHASIANIDAE Partridges and Pheasants

*Ground birds, with short, rounded wings; bill short and stout, toes four.*

**Red-legged Partridge**                                    *Alectoris rufa*
The range of the Red-legged Partridge does not extend beyond south-western
Europe. It is not a British native, and was introduced for sporting purposes in
the second half of the 18th century. In the north and west, where a few
attempts have been made to establish it, no colonisation has been accomplished, but in eastern and midland counties of England it has settled, multi-
plied and spread. Under the impression that determined colonisation was
detrimental to the resident Partridge, sportsmen, regretting their haste, strove
to wipe it out, but it refused to be evicted, and in places where driving has
replaced shooting over dogs, it is tolerated rather than encouraged. As
exhausted birds have been found upon the shore, and others noted at sea, it
has been argued that migrants may reach us from time to time, and that our
birds may attempt to emigrate, but so far there is no suggestion of regular
migration.

The plumage of the French Partridge, as it is still called in East Anglia, is
more striking than that of the common bird; the strongly barred flanks and
black-framed face and throat are its most conspicuous features. On grass or
dark soil its light brown upper parts are noticeable; it looks a larger, paler
bird than ours. The natural habitat is stone-strewn or sandy waste, and the
chalky undulations of Norfolk suit it well; it delights in a sunny spot where it
can lie on its side and enjoy a dust bath. It is, perhaps, more of a runner than
the Partridge; it certainly seeks safety by foot rather than on the wing if long
grass or other concealment is near; its speed on the ground is remarkable.
When put up it flies swiftly, whirring its wings, and rising just high enough
to skim the hedges. Armed with blunt spurs, the males are ready to fight for
their rights, marital or territorial, but a weak bird speedily knows when the
odds are against it; the Red-leg, however, is the more powerful and pushful
bird and monopolises food supplies and suitable nesting sites. Grass, clover,
buds and shoots, as well as insects, spiders, molluscs and worms, are its food,
and for the greater part of the year the bird is sociable, visiting the feeding
grounds in little parties or coveys. The note is a crake-like *chuk, chuk,
chuk-ker.*

The nest is a hollow, often in a hedgerow bottom or beneath a bush,
sparsely lined with grass and leaves. Large clutches of eggs are common, and
nine is a small number; a full nest may contain double. The egg is yellowish-
buff with fine reddish spots or blotches; late April and May is the time for the
first eggs. Nests on the top of a haystack have been recorded several times;
in its ordinary life the bird rather likes an elevated stand, perching on walls
and even branches. The nestling has reddish down, pale and unspotted on the
head, but mottled with blackish-brown on the back, where there are three
yellowish longitudinal streaks.

The mature bird has the upper parts hair-brown, tinged rufous on the back and grey on the forehead; the white face and throat are framed by a black line, which starts at the bill, runs through the eye, and then curves down the neck to form a gorget. Below this the lavender breast is speckled with black; the flanks, also lavender in ground, are barred with white, black and chestnut. The bill, eye-rims and legs are bright red. Length, 13·5 in. Wing, 6·25 in. Tarsus, 1·7 in. (*Plates 47, 53 and 167.*)

**Partridge**                                                      *Perdix perdix*

The sportsman is mainly responsible for the abundance of the Common or Grey Partridge, a bird of Europe and western Asia which is resident in the lowlands of Great Britain and Ireland, though decreasing in nearly all districts. Distinctly a bird of cultivation, it is most abundant on farmland, though thinly distributed on upland pastures and occasionally nesting on the moors. From the point of view of the sportsman who wants big bags, it is a delicate bird, yet hardy enough to hold its own in small numbers where little protection is afforded. Coveys on sand-dunes and marshes are by no means rare.

The Partridge, like the Pheasant, is too familiar to need much description. It is a ground bird, running swiftly, and lying squat until we are upon it, then rising with a curious sound, a mixture of its creaking voice and whirring wings. Its aerial spurts are rapid and not long sustained; its flight an alternation of quick vibrations of its short, rounded wings, and glides with still wings bowed. The tail is spread when the bird rises, plainly showing the chestnut outer feathers. The family parties not only keep together through the winter, but join forces with others, and as coveys roost and feed together, the social habit gives some protection from many enemies. Pairing begins in February, sometimes earlier, and for some weeks there are constant running fights and much challenging, before mating difficulties are solved. There is little or no bloodshed in these contests, but much healthy exercise. By the end of the month the covey has split into pairs, and the creaky calls, which cannot be expressed by any combination of letters, become infrequent. Though coddled less than the Pheasant, the Partridge gets protection by the removal of its predatory foes, and doubtless its habits are thereby influenced. Yet to a great extent it retains the protective colour which on certain soils and in herbage aids concealment, and has not lost the instinct to lie still and benefit by this gift. In a root-field it is entirely screened, and even on the stubbles it is not unlike a clod of earth when viewed from a distance; it is most active in the early morning and towards night, lying in quiet little groups during most of the day. Though not so catholic in its tastes as the Pheasant, it is fairly omnivorous, and is a great devourer of insects and other small invertebrates, but grain, grass, fresh shoots and seeds of all kinds give variety.

The nest is well concealed, a hollow in thick vegetation in a hedgerow or beneath a bush; it is lined with grass and leaves, and these last are used to cover the ten to twenty olive-brown eggs when the sitting bird leaves them. Eggs are seldom laid before the end of April or in May, and summer nests, even in August, are not uncommon. The 'cheepers' have buffish-brown down, spotted and striped with black, and brownish bills and legs. They are carefully tended and defended by the old birds who will boldly attack a threatening foe, even a dog. Alternatively the parents, especially the male, may 'feign injury'.

The Partridge is a variable bird. The typical male is slate-grey with fine vermiculations of black, and bars and streaks of chestnut and buff, most pronounced on the wings and flanks. The forehead, cheeks and throat are chestnut, and there is a large chocolate horseshoe-shaped patch on the pale greyish breast. The female's head is more streaked than the male's, and the horseshoe, if present, is smaller. The bill and legs are blue-grey; behind the eye is a small red unfeathered patch. Buffish-brown replaces the grey in young birds, and there is little chestnut on the face. Uniform or nearly uniform grey and reddish-brown birds are not uncommon. Length, 12·5 in. Wing, 6·5 in. Tarsus, 1·4 in. (*Plates 53 and 167.*)

## Quail                                                          *Coturnix coturnix*

The Quail, our smallest game-bird, occurs throughout Europe, and is a scarce summer visitor to the British Isles. The majority arrive in May and depart in October, but occasionally a few remain all winter. Numbers greatly decreased from about 1870, until there were few localities where it bred regularly. In Ireland the Quail was a common resident in the middle of the 19th century but had practically disappeared by 1920. More recently, however, there has been a marked recovery in Britain and western Europe generally, and in suitable habitats, especially on calcareous cornland and in the Scottish islands, four or five can be heard calling within earshot of each other in a good year.

The Quail is a diminutive sandy-buff Partridge, and the two birds have many common habits. As a ground bird it keeps well in cover, its small size an advantage in scant herbage; if flushed by a dog, for a man seldom walks it up, it flies with whirr and glide like the larger bird, and drops again almost immediately. Indeed, the only sign of its presence is, as a rule, its liquid trisyllabic call, *whit, whit, whit,* which gives origin to its vernacular names, 'Wet-my-lips', or 'Wet-my-feet'. This is the call or challenge of the male, and there is a low double note common to the sexes. That Quails migrate in hordes is known, and nocturnal travel seems usual, but when the birds are nesting they are less sociable; the autumn 'bevy' is often no more than the family. The food differs little from that of the Partridge.

The nest is a scratching in herbage, lined with dry grass; the eggs, seven to ten in number, are variable, the ground being buff or yellowish, and the deep brown markings either blotches, smears or fine speckles. They are laid as a rule late in May or in June. The young at first have buff and yellow down and are streaked with black.

The general colour of the old bird is sandy-buff, blackish on the back, broadly streaked on the wings and flanks with yellowish-white; the dark brown crown has a central buff stripe, and there are pale superciliary streaks.

The male has a double blackish-brown collar, from the dark ear-coverts to a brown stripe on the throat. The female's throat is uniform buff, and her breast is more profusely speckled than the male's. Young males resemble the female. The bill and legs are brown. Length, 7 in. Wing, 4·4 in. Tarsus, 1·1 in. (*Plates 57 and 167.*)

## Pheasant                                                    *Phasianus colchicus*

Only as a long-established alien can the Pheasant be admitted as a British bird, though the date of introduction is unknown; it is first mentioned in 1059. More recently various pheasants have been introduced, and have been inter-bred with the older stock; it is impossible to meet with a pure descendant of the original *P. colchicus*, though some of the characters survive. The Chinese *P. torquatus*, first introduced about two hundred years ago, has also left its mark, notably in the white neck-ring, but we can only look upon the semi-domestic Pheasant of today as a mongrel. *P. colchicus* hails from the Black Sea area of western Asia, but many closely allied forms occur in other parts; the Romans, Phoenicians, or whoever first traded the bird on sporting Britain, may have brought different races. *P. colchicus* is figured in the colour plate.

The cock Pheasant has erectile ear-tufts and a featherless red face; it is a gorgeous bird, but would it be here at all were it not almost sacred? The habits of this carefully tended bird have, undoubtedly, been influenced and altered by artificial conditions. It is a woodland species, thriving best in protected coverts, but it also feeds and rests on marshy ground and in reed-beds. It roosts in trees for protection, but is, in other ways, a ground bird, nesting on the level and running swiftly to escape an enemy, unless forced to take flight, when it rises with a whirr of round wings, often 'rocketing' over the tree tops; it is then swift, but incapable of really sustained flight. If it can sneak through the herbage with lowered head it tries this dodge, and will crouch in cover; the plumage of the female then gives her protection. Young birds, if alarmed, will run from the coops and crouch in the grass. The bird is omnivorous, eating vegetable and animal food. One bird's crop may be filled with germinating grain, and another with wire-worms. A favourite but apparently trivial food is the spangle gall on the oak, a mixture of animal and vegetable.

In spring the male indulges in display, showing off his charms as he runs round the hen with much of the sideling, wing-trailing action of the domestic cock. He is pugilistic, ever ready to use the spurs with which his feet are armed; before a fight the rivals face with lowered heads and ruffled necks, and strike like game-cocks with the back of the feet. The loud, sudden crow of the cock is immediately followed by a rustle of the plumage and flapping of the wings, a familiar woodland sound in spring. It is well known that thunder, an explosion, or other loud noise will start the Pheasant's crow. The bird is normally polygamous. The nest is a hollow in cover, lined with a little grass and a few leaves; the olive eggs vary in number—ten or twelve are common—and are laid in April and onward. Occasionally the eggs are in old nests of other birds in trees. The eggs are incubated and the young tended by the hen only.

The plumage of the cock varies greatly owing to the mixture of races introduced. The head is dark with green gloss, short ear-tufts and scarlet wattles on the face. Most birds have a white collar. The body plumage is generally rich chestnut, barred and streaked with black; the back is patterned with black and buff on a chestnut, greenish or creamy ground colour. The long pointed tail is boldly barred. The hen is a brownish bird mottled with buff and dark brown. Her barred tail is shorter than the cock's but still conspicuously long. Length, 24–36 in. Wing, 9·5 in. Tarsus, 2·5 in. (*Plates 53 and 167.*)

# Order GRUIFORMES

## Family GRUIDAE Cranes

*Tall birds with long, straight bills; hind toe elevated.*

### Crane
*Grus grus*

The tall and graceful Crane nests in the north and east of Europe and winters in Africa. In Britain, where it bred in the 16th century, it is now a rare passage migrant, though occurrences have been more frequent in recent years. So many of these birds are kept in private parks that some records may refer to 'escapes'.

The Crane is long-necked and heron-like in build, but has little else in common with the group. Its general colour is slate-grey, relieved by a white streak on the side of the face and neck, but the most striking character is the large bunch of drooping blue-black plumes—the inner secondaries—which gracefully curves over the wings and tail. It walks sedately, as a rule, and flies with neck extended and legs trailing, but below the line of the body. Migrating flocks keep regular order, flying in V and W formation, or with a line leading from the apex of the chevron, an inverted Y. The loud trumpet blast of the bird is sounded as it flies, and also when on the ground. In its quaint dance it will trip lightly with uplifted and slightly fanned wings, leap into the air and stop, point the bill skyward and sound its horn. In this dancing habit, as well as in other ways, the Crane shows similarity if not relationship to the Rails. The Crane eats anything from grass and grain to insects, small birds and mammals.

The adult's plumage is grey, except for black round the base of the bill and on the secondaries drooping over the tail, and white on the cheeks and sides of the neck. On the crown is a warty red patch. The bill is greenish; the legs green. Immature birds at first have no red patch, but their heads are rusty and the grey is mixed with brown. Length, 45 in. (*Plate 54.*)

## Family RALLIDAE Rails, Crakes and Coots

*Short, rounded wings; bills variable; feet large; toes long, with (Coot) or without (Rails) swimming membranes.*

### Water Rail
*Rallus aquaticus*

The Water Rail is present at all seasons in parts of England, Wales, Ireland and the south of Scotland, but it is a local species and is absent from many counties. Occurrences at coastal lights in spring and autumn show that there is some migration, though the extent of this is still unknown. It has a wide distribution in Europe.

The presence of the Water Rail is often unsuspected by those who are unfamiliar with its habits, do not know its voice, and fear to wet their feet. It is a bird of the marsh, hiding effectively from view in dense aquatic vegetation. Its laterally compressed body, for it has a remarkably narrow sternum, enables it to slip between closely set stiff reeds which would hold up a Moorhen. It can be recognised from other rails by its long, slightly decurved, red bill, and by the black and white transverse streaks on its flanks. These streaks aid concealment when the suspicious bird stands motionless in vegetation; instinctive 'freezing' is common. Anxious and nervous, it hesitates to take wing, but if surprised flies heavily with its long legs limply dangling. That it can fly fast and for long distances is proved by its death against lighthouse glass, and the loss of a wing or other injury when, during nocturnal migration, it has struck a wire. Its gait is graceful; it lifts its long, wide-spreading toes, useful when tramping a quaking bog, with delicate, cautious deliberation. When unaware of human presence it holds its head up, and elevates its tail, frequently jerking it like a Moorhen, exposing the yellow and white under tail-coverts; but if alarmed the head and tail are depressed, and with a swift run the bird vanishes into cover. It swims well, swimming in preference to flying over water. Its calls are varied; one is half groan, half squeal, and another, *tchif, tchuf*, has a contented tone, and is rather deliberately repeated. But the most noticeable sound is a loud explosive yell, like the cry of an animal in mortal agony; this it will utter when startled by any sudden sound, and also, apparently, for the pleasure of making a noise. Both male and female utter a curious purring note and a wide variety of other sounds. Insects, worms, molluscs, berries, seeds and, occasionally, grain are eaten. In winter Water Rails have frequently been seen feeding on the carcases of other birds.

The nest is composed of flags, reeds, sedges, or whatever vegetation is handy, and is supported on a platform of bent and broken stems, almost invariably in a very wet and treacherous situation; it is often raised 6 in. or more above the water. The bird approaches by well-trodden but narrow tracks, and always with a suspicious carriage. Seven to twelve light buff or brown, rather sparsely spotted eggs are laid in April, and both birds sit. The nestling is a downy, blue-black ball with absurdly big feet and a short bill; it has a feeble cheeping cry. Miss E. L. Turner photographed a female removing eggs and newly hatched young in its bill from a discovered nest.

The upper parts of the Water Rail are chestnut streaked with black, but the crown is tinged with olive. The sides of the face, neck and breast are lavender, and the flanks strongly barred with black and white, above the buff abdomen. The bill is red, blackish at the tip; the legs are greenish-brown. In winter the bill is duller, and the general colour browner. Young are tinged with olive above and are buffer below. Length, 11·5 in. Wing, 4·75 in. Tarsus, 1·7 in. (*Plates 48, 54 and 167.*)

## Spotted Crake                                             *Porzana porzana*

The Spotted Crake breeds in most of Europe and winters in Africa. It is decidedly migratory, and though a few pairs nest most years in England or

Wales and, rarely, in Scotland and Ireland, it is best known as a regular passage migrant. A few occasionally remain all winter.

Much smaller than Water Rail or Moorhen, this bird may be distinguished by its spotted olive-brown plumage and brown barred flanks; the other small crakes are not spotted on the face and neck. Even more skulking than the Water Rail, the opportunity it affords for observation is usually brief—a fleeting vision of a running form which might just as well be a rat. Even a dog finds difficulty in flushing the bird from the deep bogs and marshes that it normally frequents, but it is a vigorous nocturnal migrant, and when it meets with a telegraph wire or other obstacle, or is attracted by the rays from a lighthouse, it comes to grief. The 'wired' corpse is more familiar than the living bird. When swimming it looks small, like a diminutive Moorhen, bobbing its head in time with its spasmodic forward jerks. Its food is both animal and vegetable, similar to that of the Water Rail. The Spotted Crake has various cries, but the most characteristic is a high-pitched *whitt-whitt-whitt*, persistently repeated. It is commonly heard at dusk. Coward describes how at 3.30 on a May morning he heard a low *tick, tack*, rather like the note of a Snipe, which rose quickly in pitch and volume until it throbbed like a piston—*tchick-tchuck, tchick-tchuck*, every second. It stopped suddenly, and after a pause again began low, ascending until the air seemed to vibrate. This throbbing repetition, with its sudden end, was continued for about half an hour.

The nest is in a marsh or bog, on a tussock or platform of broken stems; it is built of aquatic plants, and often has a concealing bower of living stems bent over it. The eight to twelve eggs, buff with dark red and sepia spots as a rule, are laid in May. The down of the nestling is black.

The crown of the adult is dark brown, and the upper parts are chestnut, streaked with black and speckled with white; the underparts and the side of the face are greyer, the spots most abundant on the face and neck. The flanks are barred with brown and white. The bill is yellow, red at the base; the legs yellowish-green. Length, 9 in. Wing, 4·75 in. Tarsus, 1·25 in. (*Plate 54.*)

### Sora Rail                                         *Porzana carolina*

The Sora Rail, or Carolina Crake, breeds in Canada and winters in South America. Two have been found in the Hebrides and one each in England, Wales and Ireland. The adult has a black forehead, face, chin and throat, and its upper parts are streaked, rather than spotted, with white. The cheeks, neck, and breast are blue-grey and unspotted, and the flanks are barred with black and white. The bill lacks red at the base, but otherwise resembles the Spotted Crake's. Length, 7·5 in.

### Baillon's Crake                                   *Porzana pusilla*

This bird is a central and southern European species which also occurs in Africa and western Asia. In the northern part of its range it is migratory and passage birds have occurred in the British Isles from time to time. Only two were recorded between 1946 and 1966, but the small crakes are so shy and skulking that many may go unrecorded. A few have been observed in winter; rather more in summer. Indeed it is said that nests were taken in Cambridge and Norfolk in the 19th century.

Baillon's Crake differs from the Spotted in size, being even smaller than the Little Crake, and in the fact that its neck, breast and face are unspotted, and that its under tail-coverts are barred. Its flanks also are barred, though in the Little Crake they are uniform grey. Though usually silent by day, it has a trill not unlike that of the Little Crake. The upper parts are brown, streaked with black and white, the white being on back and scapulars and sometimes on the coverts; the underparts, including a stripe above the eye, are slate-blue, except on the flanks and under tail-coverts, where they are black, barred with white. The female is a lighter brown, and the young bird has the underparts buff, indistinctly barred. The bill is green, the legs flesh-coloured. Length, 7 in. (*Plate 57*.)

## Little Crake                                                                *Porzana parva*

The Little Crake breeds in Europe from the Baltic southwards, and winters in the southern part of this range as well as farther south. It has occurred occasionally, chiefly on passage in spring and autumn, in various southern counties and, very rarely, in Scotland and Ireland.

The male is distinguished from the even smaller Baillon's Crake by its olive-brown upper parts without white streaks on the wings, its unbarred flanks and green legs. The female has buff underparts, while those of the female Baillon's are blue-grey. It has a varied vocabulary, but its most characteristic utterance is a repeated mono-syllable followed by a trill. Its habits are very similar to those of other small rails. The male's upper parts are olive-brown with dark streaks, and a few white dashes on the back; the rump is black. The underparts are slate-blue, and only the under tail-coverts are barred in mature birds. The female has the underparts buff, and her throat is white; the young bird is similarly coloured, but shows indistinct barring of brown on the flanks. The bill is green, red at the base; the legs are green. Length, 7·5 in. (*Plate 57*.)

## Corncrake or Land Rail                                                        *Crex crex*

The Corncrake is found throughout Europe and is a summer visitor to our islands. During the present century it has rapidly decreased in numbers, particularly in the second and third decades, the decrease starting in south-east England and spreading to the north and west. An inquiry in 1938 and 1939 established the fact that except in north-west Ireland and the Scottish islands, where there had been no change, this decrease had been general. The decline has continued, and there is now no part of England or Wales where breeding is regular, though occasional nests are still found, chiefly in the northern counties, where single birds are not infrequently heard craking for a few days. Mechanical mowing is almost certainly responsible for the Corn-crake's disappearance as a breeding species.

Although its rasping voice was so well known that the Corncrake was once a familiar bird, few who noted its arrival in late April or early May had ever really seen it. They may have noticed its head above the growing grass, but like others of its kind it shows itself but little. Most leave during October, though a few remain all winter; instances of wintering, though occasionally recorded from the south, are more frequent in western counties, Ireland and the Scottish islands. The Corncrake is a slender, brown, short-billed bird with barred flanks and rich chestnut wings, very noticeable in flight. Though really nocturnal in habits, the males in spring are so obsessed by nuptial instincts that they call by day and night. If startled they will at times take wing, and occasionally fly from field to field, though apparently with labour, the wings moving rapidly and the legs dangling loosely. In longer flights, however, the legs are trailed. The Corncrake can fly fast and at an altitude, and is a long-distance traveller; it is known as a winter visitor to South Africa. It is, how-ever, fair to state that, like other rails, it can swim, and thus could rest on water.

The Corncrake walks with the head rather low and the neck drawn in, lifting its feet high like other rails, but it is a cautious, suspicious bird, and at the least sound cranes its neck for a better view, before running for cover. At times, like the Water Rail, it stands still when anxious, allowing a near approach before it darts for shelter, and if captured will, at any rate occasion-ally, simulate death, hanging limply with closed eyes, but recovering instantly if opportunity of escape presents itself. Even when calling, it keeps well hidden, though its head shows above moderately short grass when, pointing its bill upward, it calls its rasping *crek-crek*. In the Hebrides it often calls from a wall, but the habit is not common where there is long grass. The tone and appearance of the bird when craking suggest challenge rather than love-call, for the males fight fiercely. It has other notes; a grunting sound accompanies courtship, and an angry bird, attacking a rival or striving to drive away a predacious foe, will give a loud squealing threat.

The nest is commonly in a grass field, and often suffers when mowing begins, but it is sometimes in wet situations. It is a grass-lined hollow, and at times the surrounding blades are bent over to help concealment. The eggs, usually eight to ten, or even more, are pale buff, sparsely spotted or splashed with reddish-brown; they are laid from May onward, and though many nests are destroyed, it is probable that second broods are normal, for late nests are common. The nestling has long brown-black down, and is fed on insects, the chief food of the old bird, though worms, slugs, snails and seeds are eaten.

The adult bird in summer is yellowish-buff, streaked and spotted with dark brown; the wings are rich chestnut. The cheeks and a stripe above the eye are slate-grey, underparts buffish-white with rufous bars on the flanks. In winter yellow replaces the grey on the face, as it does in immature birds, which have the flanks tawny and with only indistinct bars. The bill is yellowish; the legs fleshy brown. Length, 10 in. Wing, 5·25 in. Tarsus, 1·8 in. (*Plates 57 and 168.*)

## Moorhen                                       *Gallinula chloropus*

The Moorhen has a wide range in Europe and is partially migratory. It is an abundant resident in the British Isles, and there are indications of passage migration.

Any water—lake, pond, river or ditch—suits the Moorhen, the size regulating the number present in spring, for it is jealous of territorial rights, and two pairs cannot exist peacefully on one small water. The only birds with which it can be confused are the Coot, larger and with a white frontal plate, and the Spotted Crake, smaller and with no plate; in fact the vermilion bill and frontal plate give the bird its distinctive character. It has a perky, high-stepping gait, and a habit of flirting its tail and bobbing its head. It bobs and flirts when swimming as on land, progressing in a series of short jerks, usually holding the tail level with the water, but often raised so as to show the white under tail-coverts and the black line which centres them. If disturbed it scuttles over the water, half flying, half running, leaving a troubled trail behind as its toes splash the surface. Its long, slightly flanged toes enable it to walk over lily-pads and other floating weeds, and aquatic plants provide it with food, for it is practically omnivorous. Grain and seeds are sought for in the fields, even in the farmyards, at some distance from water, and berries, including garden fruit, are eaten. Animal food, however, is welcome, and the moorhen has been accused of destroying eggs and young birds.

The Moorhen dives well, and uses the wings under water, not fully extended but held near the sides, half open. Its power of partial submergence is well developed; it will swim under water to the bank, keep the body submerged, and protrude the bill only. Even newly hatched young will slip over the edge of the nest and submerge. The vocabulary of the bird is varied, and when males are fighting—a frequent occurrence—angry and explosive. The loud, metallic call, which sounds like *fulluck*, and another softer note, *tcheco*, are common. One cry, *tit-a-tit*, quickly uttered and not unlike a call of the Barn Owl, is usually, though not always, a flight note. It is heard when the bird indulges in nocturnal wanderings, especially in spring and autumn, for the Moorhen has a curious habit of flying at night, even amongst houses, without apparent object. The most noticeable form of display is the exhibition of the white under tail-coverts, as the bird swims with the foreparts low and the lower back and tail raised. Rival males fight like game-cocks, striking with both feet, even when on the water. Serious damage is sometimes done, and after pairing quarrels, defeated males may be seen limping with broken toes and dislocated thighs.

The nest is a rather well-woven platform of flags, reed-blades or rushes, lined with grass, usually near the water's edge in low vegetation, or in the branches of an overhanging bush. Sometimes it is in a tree at a considerable elevation and away from the water, its foundation being the old nest of some other species. Though the Moorhen looks rather awkward amongst branches, it keeps its balance well, even when on swaying twigs; indeed, it often roosts on a branch. Supplementary nests and platforms are constructed, though second broods are often in the first-used nest. The number of eggs varies, usually six to ten; they are buff or clay-coloured with red and purple spots. Eggs in the middle of March have several times been recorded, but April is the usual month, and two or even three broods are reared; young of the first brood will, it is said, help to feed later nestlings. Exceptionally the bird covers the eggs when it leaves. The down of a newly hatched chick for the most part, is black, though hoary round the eyes and on the chin and throat. Above the eye is a black line, and the crown is livid blue, passing through pink to orange on the nape. The sealing-wax red frontal plate tops an orange bill with a yellow tip and canary-yellow nail, and the legs are olive-green, much darker than in the adult bird. On the bastard wing is a distinct nail or claw, which, like that of the Hoatzin of South America, is used in climbing. Coward saw a tiny bird scramble into the nest, using its wings as hands, and C. B. Moffat watched a nestling climb from the water up a steep bank, 3 or 4 ft. high, clutching the herbage with its wing-claw.

The adult is slate-black with deep brown wings, white under tail-coverts, and a white line on the flanks. In first plumage the bird is rusty-grey, whitish-grey beneath. The shield and base of the bill are vermilion, and the tip yellow in mature birds; the juvenile's is greenish without a shield. The legs are green with a red and yellow 'garter' above the 'knee'. Length, 13 in. Wing, 6·75 in. Tarsus, 1·75 in. (*Plates 58 and 168.*)

## Coot                                                      *Fulica atra*

The Coot is found throughout Europe; it is resident in all parts of the British Isles, except some of the Scottish islands, but in the northern parts of its range it is migratory, and there is some movement south from Scotland and the northern isles. Its haunts are the larger waters, including slow rivers, and in winter some seek the coast.

The Coot is a heavy, rather clumsily built bird, slate-grey with a white bill and spear-shaped frontal plate; this plate is responsible for the name Bald Coot. Swimming Coots may be told from dark ducks by the bobbing movements of their heads; if disturbed they run along the surface, splashing vigorously before getting clear, and this same splashing rush is common when one bird chases another. The wings move rapidly in flight, and the bird gets up some speed, flying straight, but always looks heavy; its legs trail behind its tail. It frequently feeds on grass or grain on the banks, but seldom ventures far from the water, and runs quickly with head low and with beating wings if it fears danger. Hard frost drives it to the sea, but it will remain on fresh water after all grebes and ducks have left, and if then it attempts to alight on the ice, slides forward on its breast, and falls sideways when it attempts to walk on the slippery surface. Its method of alighting differs from the feet-foremost drop of a duck and the breast plunge of a grebe, for it alights on the breast with the feet lowered; it is intermediate between the two. It is a constant

*Right:* Capercaillie, p99.

PLATE 50    *Above:* Red Grouse, p96
*Below:* Black Grouse, p98

PLATE 51
Oystercatcher,
p116

PLATE 52
Lapwing (male),
p117

Photo:
J. B. and S. Bottomley

*Above* : Water Rail, p106
*Below* : Spotted Crake, p107

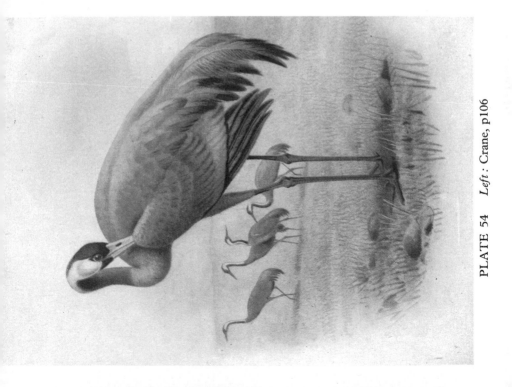

PLATE 54    *Left* : Crane, p106

PLATE 55
Turnstone, p127

Photo:
R. B. and S. Bottomley

*Photo: J. B. and S. Bottomley*

PLATE 56     Golden Plover, p124

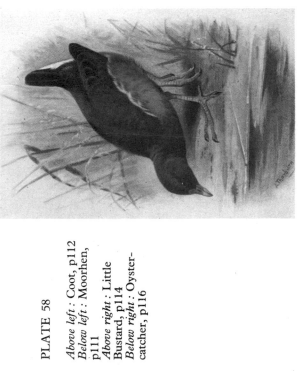

PLATE 58

*Above left* : Coot, p112
*Below left* : Moorhen,
p111
*Above right* : Little
Bustard, p114
*Below right* : Oyster-
catcher, p116

Photo: *J. B. and S. Bot*

PLATE 59    Long-billed Dowitcher, p128

*Photo: J. B. and S. Bottomley*

PLATE 60     Common Snipe, p129

*Above* : Turnstone, p127
*Below* : Lapwing, p117

PLATE 62    *Above* : Dotterel, p125
*Below* : Kentish Plover, p122

PLATE 63
Curlew, p133

PLATE 64

Black-tailed
Godwit, p138

Photo:
J. B. and S. Bottomley

but not neat diver: it jumps from the water and plunges, going down with a splash, but quickly reappearing. Yet it can swim fast under water, striking with both feet at once—not alternately as on the surface—more under the body than those of the grebe, though visible when viewed from above. The lobes on the toes fall back and present little resistance to the water when the feet are brought forward, but automatically open out during the propelling back stroke. The object of diving is to obtain the fleshy stems of weeds and aquatic molluscs, for both vegetable and animal food are taken.

If the Moorhen is quarrelsome, the Coot is a prize-fighter; it swims with head and neck low, shoulders hunched and wings slightly raised, threatening a rival. Combatants sit high in the water, apparently balanced on their tails, and strike with both feet and wings. The battles are accompanied by war-cries and much splashing, but seldom result in serious injury. The bird is bold in defence of eggs or young. In spite of its apparent bad temper it is sociable, and in winter gregarious; possibly augmented by immigrants, the numbers on favoured waters are very large; there are often hundreds, and sometimes thousands, in a single flock. Its calls are varied and difficult to express on paper. A bell-like *kwong*, and a softer *tnewt* are common, and a clinking metallic note is a warning or alarm when the nest is approached. As it swims from the nest, looking back apprehensively over its hunched shoulders, it utters an explosive *tizz*, a regular splutter. The hunger-cry of the young is a wheezy squeal—*queep*, and the nestling has a faint whispering pipe. The Coot flies at night, but is less noisy than the Moorhen. In April one alighted on a green-house, probably mistaking it for water, and in February one dropped in a town back-yard; both these may have been migrants or the night flight may have had nuptial significance. A captured bird will peck and scratch viciously when handled.

The nest, a large structure of flags, reeds, sedge and, rarely, twigs, is built in aquatic vegetation, but is seldom actually floating. If the water rises additions are made until a big stack remains when the water subsides. The stone-grey, black-speckled eggs number from six to ten as a rule, and are laid in April or May. They are not normally covered when the bird leaves the nest, but Coward saw one partly covered. The head colour of the nestling in its early days is more vivid than that of the juvenile Moorhen. The bill is black at the extreme tip, the rest dead white, shading to vermilion at the base and on the plate; round the bill the down is bright red, the sides of the face are orange, the crown is livid blue or ultramarine, and the nape may be orange, flame or black, like the rest of the hairy down. The remainder of the down is sooty with hoary filaments.

The mature bird has a narrow white wing-bar, the rest of the plumage different depths of slate-grey, but velvet-black on the head and neck. The bill and frontal plate are white; the legs are olive-green, and the irides crimson. The back is rusty-grey in first plumage, and the underparts, including the sides of the face and front of the neck, grey to white. Length, 15 in. Wing, 8·5 in. Tarsus, 2·3 in. (*Plates 58 and 168.*)

# Family OTIDIDAE Bustard

*Long-legged running birds with three toes, united at the base and fringed with membrane.*

## Great Bustard  *Otis tarda*

Up to the end of the 18th century the Great Bustard nested in wild open spaces in England and south-east Scotland, and the 'droves' which roamed over the Yorkshire wolds, Salisbury Plain and similar uncultivated areas were often immense, but the bird was too big and edible to survive. Early in the 19th century it vanished from Salisbury, and though a few pairs lingered in East Anglia and Yorkshire until the late 'thirties, spread of cultivation, increase of population and, perhaps more than either, improvement in sporting guns, swept them away. So today the Great Bustard is a very rare vagrant to Britain. In central and southern Europe and in western Asia, it survives locally. It is not, apparently, a regular migrant, but an occasional wanderer.

The size of the Great Bustard renders it easy to see and identify, a tempting mark for the gunner. A male, big and tasty as a Turkey, may weigh over 30 lb. The Bustard walks with 'stately and deliberate gait', the body horizontal and head erect, but in corn or tall herbage it is often partially hidden. It feeds largely on grain and other vegetable substances, but also eats insects, especially grasshoppers, worms and other small animals. It seldom runs, even when pursued, for its feet are small; if alarmed it takes a few quick steps and unfolds its ample wings, flying quickly, though with slow, strong beats. There is so much white in the bird's wings and on its underparts that when flying at a distance it looks as white as a gull.

The male is much larger than the female. His head and neck are slate-grey, and on his chin are tufts of long whitish bristles; his upper parts are yellowish, barred with black, but with the coverts mostly white. The breast is brown and barred; the rest of the underparts are dead white. The female has no bristles and her breast is white. The young resemble her, but there are black bars on the coverts. The bill is slate, dark at the tip; the legs brown. Male: Length, 44 in. Female: Length, 30 in.

## Little Bustard  *Otis tetrax*

The Little Bustard used to be an almost annual winter visitor to Britain in very small numbers, but its visits have become less frequent and it can now only be described as a very rare vagrant. Its range extends from western and southern Europe to western Asia and North Africa.

In winter dress the Little Bustard is yellowish-brown, delicately vermiculated, barred and streaked with black, and with white underparts. It looks like a game-bird, and has many game-bird habits. It runs like a Partridge, and when flushed rises high, eluding the sportsman; flocks will wheel at a great height with plover-like evolutions. On the wing it looks even whiter than the Great Bustard. The rapidly moving wings make a loud swishing sound.

In summer the male's chin and upper throat are lavender; lower throat and neck almost black, crossed obliquely by two white bands on either side. The sandy head is striated; the back and upper parts finely marked with wavy black and brown lines. The outer wing-coverts and underparts are white. In autumn the neck ornamentation is lost, and in distribution of colour the male agrees with the female, though her back is at all times more boldly blotched, and her neck and breast are barred and speckled. Length, 17 in. (*Plate 58.*)

**Houbara Bustard**                                    *Chlamydotis undulata*
The Houbara or Macqueen's Bustard is a native of western Asia which sometimes wanders into Europe. Five examples have been recorded from the east side of Britain in autumn. The black and white crest and the drooping frill or ruff, partly black, partly grey, are sufficient to distinguish it from other bustards. The neck and tail are long and the wings darker than in the Great and Little Bustard. Length, 28 in.

# Order CHARADRIIFORMES

## Family HAEMATOPODIDAE Oystercatchers

*Bill long, stout, laterally compressed; toes united at base; hind toe absent.*

**Oystercatcher** *Haematopus ostralegus*

The Oystercatcher is resident in Europe, but a large number move southward in autumn; many reach the British Isles, where there is also a southward migration, but on most of our shores, whether rocky or sandy, birds are present at all seasons. It nests freely in north-west England, Wales and Ireland and very abundantly in Scotland, but is thinly distributed on the east and south coasts of England.

The long, stout and compressed orange bill, the pink legs, and black and white plumage make the 'Sea-pie' an easy bird to recognise. At all seasons it is sociable, and little parties of non-breeding birds feed on the shore when the residents are nesting; in winter, when the migrants have arrived, the flocks are often immense. With the advance of the tide they pack on the lessening banks, or crowd on reefs and islets, and when forced to move rise with a chorus of calls, *kleep, kleep, kleep,* and fly, low over the water, to a drier refuge. When they settle, the clamour rises in volume for a few seconds and then dies away. At any time of year small groups may be seen performing the 'piping display', standing or walking round with heads lowered and bill-tips almost touching the ground and piping excitedly. This activity reaches a climax with the approach of the breeding season and is used both as a courtship and a hostility display. When the tide falls the birds scatter over the ooze or rocks, plunging the bill deeply for cockles or worms, or wading over the still-submerged mussel-beds to catch their victims before they close their valves. The bird occasionally opens small oysters, but much more important items in its diet are the mussel, cockle and *Tellina*; these bivalves are skilfully opened and limpets are knocked smartly off the rocks. Crabs and other crustaceans are eaten. In recent years Oystercatchers have been feeding increasingly in pastures, both near the coast and further inland, at all seasons.

The call is a clear, ringing *feet, feet,* and the alarm a sharply emphasised and repeated *pic, pic, pic.* Nesting birds are bold, mobbing human beings as well as avian visitors.

The choice of nesting site varies, as do the quantity and quality of the nesting material. In most of England and in Wales the nest is usually near the shore, but in Scotland and northern England it may be found by rivers and lochs. The river valleys of the north of England have only been colonised during the present century, and the spread is still continuing. Nests may now be found on farmland a mile or more from sea or river. They may be in fields, on cliff edges, on rocky reefs or islands, on sandhills, pebble ridges, salt-marshes or railway embankments; they may be unlined or with a plentiful lining and wall of bents or seaweed, and in some cases with a selection of small pebbles and broken shells. Three is the usual number of the yellowish, blotched or streaked eggs; they are laid as a rule in May. The down of the newly hatched chick is close and plushy, light grey with darker stripes and mottles down the centre of the back, on the head and stumpy wings. The bill is short and dark, reddish at the base, and the legs blue-grey. The behaviour of birds when guarding eggs or young varies individually, but at the least suspicion of danger the sitting bird slips silently away, and the first evidence of the vicinity of a nest is the monotonous *pic, pic,* of the pair, standing on rocks, mounds or walls some distance apart.

In summer the upper parts, except the lower back and upper tail-coverts, a patch on the wing, and a small streak below the eye, are black, as are the neck and throat; these exceptions and the rest of the underparts are white. In winter there is a half collar of white on the throat. Immature birds, which are browner on the back and wings also have white on the throat. The bill varies from orange-red to vermilion, the colour of the narrow rim round the blood-red eye; the legs are pink. Length, 16·5 in. Wing, 9·75 in. Tarsus, 1·8 in. (*Plates 51, 58 and 168.*)

## Family CHARADRIIDAE Plovers

*Stockily built wading birds with characteristic bobbing action when feeding; bill shortish; hind toe absent or elevated and short.*

### Sociable Plover                                                   *Vanellus gregarius*
This native of southern Russia and central Asia has been recorded in the British Isles, including Ireland and the Orkneys, eight times. It has been seen consorting with Lapwings, and like them it is a round-winged plover. The adult bird is ashy-brown, with a black crown and a streak through the eye, and between these a conspicuous white stripe from the forehead to the nape. The primaries are black, the secondaries white, the tail mostly white with a subterminal black-brown band. The cheeks and throat are buff, the lower breast brown, shading to black on the belly, the abdomen and flanks rich chestnut. The under tail-coverts are white. The crown of the young bird is brown and its superciliary stripe buff; the underparts are buffish-white, with a few dark markings on the breast. The bill and legs are black. Length, 13·5 in.

### Lapwing                                                              *Vanellus vanellus*
As a nesting species the Lapwing is found throughout the British Isles, but except in the north of Scotland the breeding population has decreased seriously since about 1940. The chief cause is probably changing methods of farming. In autumn and winter numbers are greatly increased by immigrants from Europe, where it has a wide breeding range.

The erectile crest, round wings and call, and seemingly black and white dress, are well known, but the Lapwing or Green Plover is not really black and white; at close quarters in sunshine the glossy green back and the rich chestnut patches above and below the tail are wonderfully beautiful. Marshy fields and rough upland pastures are typical haunts, but its choice of habitat is catholic; it feeds, a shore bird, on the tidal flats; it flocks on cultivated land; it is companion of the Curlew and Golden Plover on the bleak moor. It is a bird of open spaces, where the soil is either bare or only covered by light vegetation. Trees and buildings are avoided. In the nesting season it is scattered, large lowland fields usually having their pair or pairs of birds, but as soon as the young can fly they form small parties, and from June onward the bird is gregarious. In autumn immigrants arrive from the north and east, and throughout the winter the flocks are often immense, though there are frequent southward movements after the usual time for passage. The bird is capricious, and weather conditions or over-abundance in any place may cause extra and erratic migration. Recoveries of ringed birds show that there is considerable immigration in autumn, especially from Norway. Although some British-bred Lapwings are almost sedentary, many from Scotland and the north of England move to Ireland in autumn, and there is a considerable movement from the midlands and south of England to France and the Iberian peninsula. The extent of the emigration is much affected by the severity of the winter.

The Lapwing is useful, destroying more wireworms, tipulid and lepi-dopterous larvae than carnivorous insects and worms. Like the Ringed Plover it often patters on the ground with an extended foot when feeding. In flight the broad round wings flap slowly; the bird moves fast, but without the dash of the sharp-winged plovers; Lapwings flying high flicker black and white. The birds travel, when changing ground, straight, but without the ordered formation of many waders; lines are rare, and leaders frequently alter. Towards dusk in autumn and winter the flocks indulge in aerial exercise, wheeling and changing direction, as they rise and 'tremble up to cloud'. Their evolutions, though concerted, are without the quick turns and swaying swoops of sharp-winged waders. The air mastery of the Lapwing is seen in its nuptial flight. It is often active at night, especially by moonlight.

The ordinary call is a wheezy *pee-wee*, from which the bird gets the name Peewit, with many local variants, but in February or early March both note and actions change. Before the winter flocks have dispersed, the males begin their erratic aerial dances, accompanied by a long, undulating, wild, but musical whistle, utterly impossible to put into words; the bird rises almost heavily, sweeps round in a wide circle, suddenly dashes upward, and calls. As suddenly it hurtles earthward, turning and twisting, throwing its broad wings anywhere, but never losing control, and often with the last excited *hoo-oo-ee*, it drops lightly and runs forward with crest erect. During aerial display the Peewit often flies round in curves and circles, swinging from side to side and beating the air with a loud humming or soughing sound. This is not all the performance; the male scrapes and sits in imaginary nests, turning in them as he scratches the hollow in frenzied haste, or bending forward, breast to ground, raises and exhibits the chestnut coverts and banded tail.

As long as the site is open the nest may be anywhere, a shallow scrape in grass, on the ridge between furrows, in moorland ling, even on a cinder spoil-bank. A few bents or straws are collected as decoration by the sitting bird, and occasionally mild efforts at nest construction are made. Four olive or dark buff eggs, richly mottled, are arranged with points in the middle; clutches of five are rare. They are often laid in March, but the first half of April is more usual. The sitting bird leaves the nest silently, running for a few yards, and goes through the motions of feeding; then the pair will fly overhead, wailing, and if the nest is threatened, dashing with a loud, angry *peet* at the head of the enemy. The rufous, black-marbled down of the nestling is protective, and at the first warning call the chick crouches with head back, but not always hiding the white collar. Nestlings disturbed in the open will run for shelter. The parent birds will swoop at and strive to drive away a man, a dog or even a cow which crosses their domain; very occasionally they will lure an enemy away by 'injury-feigning'.

The crown, crest, face, throat and breast of the male Lapwing in summer are black; the back and wings are metallic-green glossed with bronze and purple; the sides of the neck and underparts below the breast are white. A broad black subterminal band crosses the white tail, and the upper and under tail-coverts are bright chestnut. The bill is black; legs fleshy red. The female has a shorter crest, and a less clearly defined black gorget, and her wings are narrower and less rounded. In winter the throat is usually white, and the upper parts show buff margins. The crest is shorter on the still buffer young, and their chins and throats are white. Length, 12 in. Wing, 8·75 in. Tarsus, 1·6 in. (*Plates 52, 62 and 168.*)

## Ringed Plover                                    *Charadrius hiaticula*

The Ringed Plover breeds in northern and central Europe, and some winter in Africa. As a nesting species it occurs on all our coasts and in a number of inland localities; probably most of our birds are resident, though there is an extensive autumnal immigration and at the same time emigration from the south coast. The breeding population on the coasts of England and Wales has been increasingly affected by human disturbance.

On the shore there is no more familiar wader than the lively Ringed Plover; it is a little larger than its constant companion, the Dunlin, and has distinctive black markings on its head and face, framing a prominent white forehead. On a pebble beach these markings and its sandy-drab back are by no means conspicuous, but on mud or grass the bird shows up well. Except in the breeding season the Ringed Plover is eminently sociable, and even in its nesting it shows a tendency to colonial habits. Sociability is not limited to its own species; it consorts freely with Dunlins, Sanderlings, Stints and other waders, flying and feeding with them. In April and May, when large numbers are on passage after the residents have settled down, and on the return in autumn, wonderful flights of these mixed waders may be witnessed when the birds are awaiting the turn of the tide. The Ringed Plover is as skilful and agile in its turns and twists as any and its white plumage as silvery, when with sudden swoop the flock showers earthward. At a distance these suddenly rising and dropping flocks look like showers of sunlit spray. When little parties sweep past along the beach, skimming low over the sand, the noise of wings sounds like the rustle of silk. The wing-beats are regular, rather deliberate, and when about to alight the bird glides, and finally trips forward with uplifted wings; the speed is never slow, but when amorous pairs indulge in nuptial flight, or when the Merlin strives to fly it down, few birds can excel it. Its actions on the beach when feeding are more energetic and spasmodic than those of the Dunlin; more erratic than the Sanderling's. Its legs twinkle as it runs for a few yards, stops and tilts forward to pick up some tiny crustacean, worm or mollusc, and at once is off for another run. It sometimes halts for a moment to patter rapidly on the sand with its foot. It will stand, observant, jerking its bullet-head, or for a second raise its wings straight above its back, when the great length of the pointed flights magnifies its size. If nervous it utters a low, musical, but querulous *tooe*, or *tooli*, and when numbers are calling together in a flock, this becomes a long, harmonious *tooli, tooli, tooli, tooli*, which, though often running into a trill, is the nuptial song, usually uttered on the wing. On migration it frequently visits the banks of rivers, meres and lakes, and is common on sewage farms. It also nests inland, commonly in Scotland and locally in England, Wales and Scotland.

When the nesting site has been selected, and a few preliminary scrapes made in the sand, the male tempts the female to sit, and trilling the breeding call, will run and sit in one of the hollows. Rivals are boldly attacked then and even after the young are hatched; the guardian male, with lowered head, trailed wing, tail expanded and depressed, and the feathers of his back raised like the dorsal crest of an angry dog, will boldly attack all comers. In the site and decoration of the nest the bird shows variety and decided aesthetic taste. The pebble ridge above high-water mark is favoured, and there, when eggs are in the depression, the nest is hard to see, but without eggs the lining or paving of smaller stones or bits of broken shell often gives it away. On sand or grass this lining is even more conspicuous, but often none is used, or only a few bits of weed or chips of wood are collected. The bird is an anxious and fussy parent, often betraying the presence of eggs or young by its persistent plaintive pipe; the sitting bird slips from the nest at the first hint of danger, runs with head low, and joins its mate at the water's edge. The young in grey and sandy down has a broad white collar and black band above its white nape, but as it crouches, an expert at 'freezing', the drawn-back head hides these marks. If handled it will at first remain still, but if it feebly pipes the old birds become wild with excitement, and after flying round will fall and tumble with simulated disablement. The three or four greyish, brown-spotted eggs are only conspicuous when laid on grass, but more usual surroundings are sand or shingle.

The general colour of the upper parts of the adult bird is mouse-grey to drab, of the underparts white. A black band passes through the eye, and another crosses the top of the head, framing the white forehead; below a white collar is a black gorget, deepest in front. A white streak above the eye and a white wing-bar are conspicuous. The bill is orange at the base, blackish at the tip; the legs chrome-yellow. The young bird is hair-grey, and the brown gorget is incomplete in front; the face stripe is brown, and the band across the crown absent. The bill is black, lighter at the base, and the legs are brownish-yellow, but always light enough to distinguish it at any age from the Kentish Plover. Length, 7·75 in. Wing, 5·25 in. Tarsus, 1 in. (*Plates 61 and 168.*)

## Little Ringed Plover                              *Charadrius dubius*

The establishment of the Little Ringed Plover as a British breeding species is a most interesting example of the exploitation by a bird of an artificial and temporary habitat. Until 1938 the Little Ringed Plover, although breeding throughout most of Europe, was known only as a very rare vagrant in the British Isles. In that year a pair reared a brood on the bed of a partly dried reservoir at Tring, and from 1944 a steady increase and expansion took place. By 1965 all the eastern and midland counties of England had been colonised, with a total population of about 170 pairs. The great majority of these have nested in gravel pits while they were actually being worked, in spite of the inevitable disturbance; the growth of vegetation in a disused pit soon makes it unattractive to the birds. More recently a few pairs have nested on natural shingle banks, but so far the expansion of breeding population seems to have been dependent on the availability of suitable artificial sites. Non-breeding birds now appear regularly in north-west England, and nests have been found in Cheshire and south Lancashire.

The Little Ringed Plover is a summer visitor to England, moving south in August and September. In its movements and general habits it resembles the Ringed Plover. The most obvious diagnostic character is the lack of white on the wing in flight, but the white line above the black on the head and pale legs are also distinctive. The difference in size is obvious when the commoner bird is present for comparison, but may not be noticeable otherwise. The usual call is a high-pitched *tiu*.

The nest is a scrape, with little or no lining, in gravel, sand or dried mud. The eggs, normally four, are laid in late May or June. Their markings are similar to those of the Ringed Plover's but smaller. The nestlings are also similar but rather warmer in colour.

The colour and pattern of the plumage resemble the Ringed Plover's with the following exceptions: there is a thin white line above the black on the forehead and a yellow ring round the eye; the inner primaries are uniform brown. (In the Ringed Plover the inner webs are white, and show as a white patch when the wing is closed and as a bar when it is open.) The bill is black, only slightly yellowish at the base of the lower mandible, and the legs are paler. The black of the adult bird is replaced by brown in the young, and the upper parts are buffer. Length, 6 in. Wing, 4·5 in. Tarsus, 0·9 in. (*Plate 61.*)

# Kentish Plover
*Charadrius alexandrinus*

Although the Kentish Plover is widely distributed round the coasts of Europe and there are still one or two pairs in the Channel Islands it is now extinct as a breeding species on the mainland of Great Britain. It used to breed in small numbers on the coasts of Kent and Sussex, but there has been no record of a nest there since 1956. Egg-collecting and the increasing disturbance of beaches by holiday-makers have been major factors in its disappearance. It is now known as a scarce passage migrant on the south coast and a rare vagrant elsewhere.

The Kentish is smaller than the Ringed Plover, and may be distinguished by its incomplete pectoral band and its black bill and legs. The bird, especially the female, looks more sandy than the Ringed Plover; there is, too, something distinctive in the flight. Young Ringed Plovers have an interrupted breast-band, but their legs are yellowish. The female Kentish is browner than the male, the black patch on the lower neck being noticeably brown. The habits and food differ little from those of the last species; the note is shriller and more flute-like, and the bird has a soft plaintive *whit* when alarmed.

The nest is usually a depression in sand or amongst shingle. The yellowish-buff or stone-coloured eggs are as a rule curiously streaked with black; they are generally three in number and are laid in May, and often placed vertically, their smaller end deeply buried in the sand, a method at times adopted by the Ringed Plover.

The male in summer is sandy-drab on the upper parts; the crown has a rufous tinge. The forehead and a streak above the eye, the collar and underparts are white. There is a black mark above the forehead, and a streak through the eye to the cheeks, and a black patch on each side of the breast. In the female this patch is brown, and the black on the forehead is absent. In winter adults show practically no black or rufous, and immatures have similar plumage. The bill and legs are black. Length, 6·25 in. Wing, 4·25 in. Tarsus, 0·9 in. (*Plates 62 and 168.*)


# Killdeer
*Charadrius vociferus*

Both specific and popular names of this common North American plover refer to its loud, clear note, *kill-dee*; it is a noisy bird. It is found throughout North America, and in winter Central America and Peru. It has occurred in England, Scotland and Ireland about sixteen times. Its colour-scheme closely resembles that of our Ringed Plover, but it has two bands across the breast, the upper one forming a collar. The general colour of the upper parts is browner, and this is specially noticeable on the facial streak and cheeks. The lower back and wedge-shaped tail are rufous-brown, with a subterminal black band to the latter. It is a rather larger bird than our Ringed Plover, with legs and tail longer in proportion; the bill is black and the legs yellowish-green. Young birds have rufous margins to the feathers of the upper parts. Length, 10 in.

**Grey Plover**                                                 *Pluvialis squatarola*

The arctic breeding range of the Grey Plover is circumpolar, and its winter travels take it as far as the Cape and Australia. In the British Isles it is a regular and plentiful passage migrant and winter visitor, and has been met with in every month of the year. It is rare in the north of Scotland and is more plentiful on the east and south coasts of England than on the west, but it is by no means uncommon on the shores of Lancashire, Wales and Ireland.

The Grey Plover is a shore bird, infrequent inland, and though its flocks are not as large as those of the Golden Plover it is often present in great numbers. On favoured feeding grounds such as the Humber 'clays' the birds are scattered over a wide area with nowhere more than two or three in a group. The old bird is always greyer than the Golden Plover, and in summer well deserves the name Silver Plover, but the young, washed with yellow, are less distinctive, unless in the hand, when the presence of the small hind toe settles the matter. But, like the Golden, this bird frequently raises its wing, and will even run with uplifted wings, and then the black or very dark axillaries show plainly on the under surface; these dark marks may be seen on the flickering wings of a passing bird. Further points are the whiter rump and upper tail-coverts, and the black- and white-barred tail. The Grey Plover is as a rule a lively and noisy bird, running quickly when feeding and constantly calling from the ground or on the wing. Its note is less liquid than that of the Golden, and is shrill and penetrating. Its wing-beats are rather deliberate, but it is swift and strong in flight. It is not always nervous, and young birds are at first absurdly tame, a common fault of arctic nesters. If approached they will run for a few yards, turn to see if they are followed, and seem reluctant to fly; old birds, too, will stand solitary, resting but not asleep, when waiting for the tide to turn, and not pack with other waders.

The majority of the autumn birds come in September and October, but many arrive towards the end of August and some even in July. August birds are often in breeding plumage. Most of the September immigrants are immature, and the adults in winter dress soon follow. The bulk of the visitors move south, but a fair proportion winter, and from March until the middle of May and exceptionally until early June, parties are constantly passing.

In spring the upper parts are chequered brownish-black and greyish-white; the underparts to the lower breast are deep black. The colour pattern is as in the Golden Plover, but the white band separating the black and grey is broader; the forehead and abdomen, as well as the under tail-coverts, are white, and there is a good deal of white on the quills and wing-coverts. The black is lost in winter, and the upper parts are browner; the sides of the face, neck and breast are streaked and mottled on a pale ashy-brown ground. Young birds have much pale yellow on the upper parts; the underparts are streaked with brown. The axillaries, though dusky-brown, are still distinctive. The bill is black, the legs blue-grey. Length, 11 in. Wing, 8 in. Tarsus, 1·9 in. (*Plate 61.*)

## Golden Plover                                    *Pluvialis apricaria*

The Golden Plover is a resident, passage migrant and winter visitor in the British Isles. A few pairs nest on Dartmoor, and it breeds in Wales, chiefly in the north, extensively on the Pennine moorlands, but only very locally on the Lake District fells. It nests throughout the mainland of Scotland and on some of the islands, but only locally and in decreasing numbers in Ireland. As a passage migrant and winter visitor it occurs in thousands in many districts, both coastal and inland.

The Golden Plover is a typical plover, far more so than the round-winged Green Plover or Lapwing; it has sharply pointed angled wings and rapid flight, and is a plump, bullet-headed, short-billed bird with a high forehead, and runs lightly over pastures or coastal mud. It is a more inland bird than the Grey Plover, its nearest relative, from which it can be distinguished by the absence of the hind toe. In the field, apart from its yellower dress, it may be recognised by its white axillaries; when it raises the wings and holds them for a second stiffly, which it frequently does when stretching, and also when it alights, the Golden shows a white under surface, but in the Grey the axillaries are a dark patch on a dusky ground.

During spring and summer the moors are the haunt of the 'Whistler', a a name given from its frequently repeated liquid call. On the shore and in the lowland fields in February some birds show traces of the black underparts of summer, and by April nearly all have attained full breeding dress. The birds move to the hills in March, but long after this, even until May or June, certain lowland fields are visited by passing flocks, replaced by fresh arrivals as soon as one lot leaves for the north. These flocks often consist mainly of birds of the race breeding in northern Europe with very clearly defined black and white markings on the face, breast and underparts. The Golden Plover is partial to particular feeding grounds, seldom visiting other fields in the immediate neighbourhood. By the end of July the first adult birds are returning, still with their underparts mottled with nuptial black; in September the white-breasted young appear. Most of these flocks pass south, but in October and November the wintering birds join forces with the Lapwings. On the wing the species usually separate, the sharp-winged Plovers out-flying the slowly flapping Lapwings.

The gregarious Golden Plover whistles frequently when on the wing, but is silent when at rest. The normal call is a clear *tlui*, heard at all seasons. Towards evening the flocks indulge in elaborate aerial performances, turning, twisting and diving in pure enjoyment of air mastery. When all descend, and for a moment their white underwings flash in the light of the setting sun, the settling flock warbles a low, murmuring, long-shore chorus, and then as the wings are closed the yellow birds melt into their surroundings and vanish. On ploughed land the Golden Plover is almost invisible. On the moors the male trills a love-song as he sweeps round above his mate, and in March birds on the ground may suddenly raise a trill of welcome to a party passing over— *ri, toori, toori, toori*—but relapse into silence when the visitors move on. When changing ground or on migration the V-formation is common; nocturnal migration is often detected by the calls of the bird, but diurnal movements have often been observed, even at a great altitude. The animal food is that of other waders, varied with a few moorland seeds and berries.

The upper moor, bare or clothed with coarse grass and stunted ling or crowberry, is the usual nesting site, and the nest itself is often exposed, but by no means easy to find, for when the four mottled eggs are laid, the sitting bird slips quietly off and runs for some distance before taking wing. One of the pair, usually the male, though both are known to sit, stands sentinel on the skyline, and gives a long warning *tooee* if any one appears within sight. When the mate is at a safe distance from the nest it answers the call, and both will fly round the intruder with plaintive cries, and long after the danger zone is passed will stand watching, repeating a single mournful *too*. The eggs are generally laid in May, and by the end of the month the downy nestling crouches in the herbage. When first hatched the little bird is a wonderful golden-yellow, with dark mottles and whitish streaks.

In summer the upper parts of the British adult are mottled with black and golden-yellow, and the tail and coverts are barred with brown and yellow; the underparts to the abdomen, and usually including the cheeks, are black or dark brown, but the extent of this dark area varies and is generally less on the female. In the northern race the black extends above the eye and bill and the whole black gorget is bordered by a broad white line. The under surface of the wing and tail-coverts are white. The bill is blackish-brown; the legs blue-grey. The black portions are white in winter, the colours are less golden, and the cheeks, grey-tinged breast and flanks are mottled with brown and yellow. The plumage of the young resembles that of the adult bird in winter, but the flanks are more mottled and back more spotted with yellow. Length, 11 in. Wing, 7·5 in. Tarsus, 1·6 in. (*Plates 56, 61 and 168.*)

**Lesser Golden Plover**                                    *Pluvialis dominica*
This plover breeds on the arctic tundra of Siberia and North America and migrates far south in both continents. Vagrants sometimes reach Britain, occasionally even in small flocks. It is a smaller and more lightly built bird than our Golden Plover, with longer legs and narrower wings which extend beyond the tail when closed. The plumage is generally similar to that of the Golden Plover, but its underwings are buff and axillaries grey, not white as in the Golden Plover. The immature has a whiter face and eye-stripe than the young Golden Plover. Length, 9·5 to 10 in.

**Dotterel**                                              *Eudromias morinellus*
The Dotterel breeds in northern Europe and Siberia, and winters in north Africa and western Asia. In the British Isles it is a summer visitor and passage migrant, regular in its visits, but never numerous. It still breeds regularly but in decreasing numbers in the central Highlands of Scotland. An occasional pair has nested on mountains in the north of England up to the middle of this

century, but it is now only known there as a scarce spring passage migrant. Elsewhere in England and Scotland it occurs in small numbers on spring passage, much more rarely in autumn. In Ireland it is a rare vagrant.

The plumage of a Dotterel in a specimen or picture looks very conspicuous, but in its favourite haunts, wild barren uplands, the bird is most difficult to see. It is a squat and plump, round-headed, short-billed plover; its most characteristic markings are the curved white streak above the eye which meets its fellow on the nape, and the white band that divides the slaty-brown upper breast from the chestnut and black below. What the bird gains from the protection of its coloration it loses through its stupid tameness; it is one of our easiest birds to approach. Towards the end of April or early in May 'trips', as the small parties are called, arrive in England; some, probably passage birds, travel slowly along the coast, but others follow ancient inland routes, halting at certain oft-frequented spots to feed or rest. The trips comprise from five to a score of birds, and their arrival is, or was, watched for keenly, for the Dotterel has always had a high money value, originally for its flesh, but later for its plumage; certain feathers are used for artificial flies. The travellers are tired and stupid, and if shot at will settle again at once; it was not uncommon for the whole trip to be wiped out. Egg-collecting is responsible for further diminution in numbers, but is less to blame than the wholesale destruction of the recently arrived immigrants. The return passage is in August and September.

The food either on the hills or the rough pastures, when on migration, mainly consists of insects and their larvae, though worms and molluscs are also eaten. Like other plovers, the Dotterel runs for a foot or two, then stops and tilts forward to pick up its food, and between its runs often stretches its long wings above its back. On the wing the bird is not unlike the Golden Plover, swift and graceful, with powerful strokes. Its notes vary according to circumstances; a low, plaintive whistle and a harsh call of alarm are the best known, but at the nest there is a soft, parental twitter.

Typical Dotterel ground is barren, stone-littered, and almost without vegetation; the bird nests on the black soil near the wind-swept tops, seldom below the 2000-ft. contour. The three buff or stone-coloured, brown-blotched eggs, less pyriform and more tern-like than those of most waders, are placed in a shallow scrape, usually lacking lining or decoration. Eggs are sometimes laid before the end of May, but the middle of June is the normal time for incubation. Though the sitter will sometimes rise with a cry of alarm it usually slips away quietly, and at once begins by spreading and trailing wings and tail, and falling as if disabled, a varied exhibition of 'injury-feigning'. But if the eggs or young are handled the parent returns to within arm's reach and falls about in apparent frenzy. If, however, the nest is undisturbed the bird will return and brood eggs or young at the very feet of the observer. The down of the nestlings is grey, mottled and streaked with buff, chestnut and black; there is a white band on the nape. The back and wings of the adult are brownish-grey, neatly patterned on the coverts with rufous margins. The top of the head is brownish-black, and below this is the curved white stripe from the forehead to the nape; the face and throat are white, and a dark streak passes through the eye and widens on the sides of the neck. The upper breast is slaty-brown, bordered below with bands of black and white; the lower breast is bright chestnut, shading to black on the abdomen and white on the under tail-coverts. In winter this bright pattern is lacking though a pale pectoral band can be distinguished. The heads of young birds are more rufous and streaked on the crown, the eye-stripe and the blacker upper parts are tinged with buff. The underparts, buff on the breast and flanks, and white on the abdomen, are mottled with brown. The bill is black; legs dull yellow. Length, 9 in. Wing, 6 in. Tarsus, 1·4 in. (*Plates 62 and 168*.)

**Turnstone**                                                    *Arenaria interpres*

The Turnstone is circumpolar in summer and cosmopolitan in winter. It breeds as near to Britain as Iceland and southern Scandinavia, but though it has often been suspected of nesting in our islands no nest has ever been found; it may be called a non-breeding resident, since it is present at all seasons. It is a common passage migrant and winter visitor, and many birds, even in breeding dress, linger on our shores all summer.

The Turnstone is a wader of the rocky shore, though on sandy beaches it may be seen hunting along the tide-wrack. In full summer dress it is a tabby, short-legged, brightly coloured shore bird, very black and white about the head and neck, with noticeable orange legs and a short, slightly uptilted bill. In immature and winter plumage it is more indefinite in its coloration, suggesting irregular black, white, grey and brown markings; it looks more variegated than other waders. When consorting with other birds it may be recognised by its actions as well as appearance. The pose is characteristic when a flock rests, often accompanied by Purple Sandpipers, on some rock just out of reach of the waves. Immigrants begin to appear in July and August, but before the end of September the wave of passage migration has spent its force, for many of our visitors may be bound for the southern hemisphere. From the latter half of April until June northward passage causes increase on our shores. The bulk of the birds which remain to winter, and also those about in summer, are immature.

Although, on passage, the Turnstone occasionally visits inland waters, its favourite haunts are at the edge of the waves, either on tide-washed reefs or rocks. In its feeding habits it proves the value of its short pick-axe bill, using it as a lever to tip up and throw over large stones, hence its name, and with an upward sweep jerk the long strands of tangle aside, and quickly pounce on the exposed sand-hoppers, small crabs and molluscs. Its movements are deliberate when it feeds among the surf churning over the rocks, but on the litter at high-water mark it runs quickly, its keen eye detecting any stone or bit of weed beneath which crustaceans may be sheltering. Never, it seems, is a stone turned a second time. There are well-authenticated stories of co-operation or mutual aid when a stone or dead fish was too heavy for the efforts of one bird.

On shingle the variegated plumage is a useful protection; the bird is almost invisible. It is tame or indifferent, and will permit close approach before it takes wing with a short, Redpoll-like trill; as it flies the white on the wing and lower back is conspicuous, the bird flickering black and white. In several places Turnstones have become increasingly tame in recent years and are even found picking up crumbs on seaside promenades among pigeons and sparrows.

In summer plumage, attained by the end of April, the head, lower back and underparts are white, banded and blotched on the cheeks, neck and breast, and streaked on the crown with black; the back and wings are variegated with black and warm chestnut. The bill is blackish-brown, the legs bright orange. In winter the bird is darker and browner, the blacks replaced by greyish-brown, and the whites on head and neck much suffused and speckled with brown; the legs are duller. Immature birds resemble adults in winter, but are buffer, and their upper parts are speckled with greyish-white. Length, 9 in. Wing, 6 in. Tarsus, 1 in. (*Plates 55 and 62.*)

## Family SCOLOPACIDAE Snipe, Curlews, Godwits and Sandpipers

*Long legs; long, slender bill; wings usually pointed.*

### Long-billed Dowitcher                                    *Limnodromeus scolopaceus*

The very similar Long-billed and Short-billed Dowitchers were first distinguished as separate species in 1932; both birds were previously known in Britain as the Red-breasted Snipe. The Long-billed Dowitcher breeds in the far north-west of Canada and north Alaska and has several times been identified in Britain in autumn. The Dowitchers are rather short-legged, long-billed waders about the size of a Redshank. In winter plumage they are grey above and whitish below, with barred or spotted flanks and whitish eye-stripes. In summer the plumage is chestnut and cinnamon-red. The flight pattern is not unlike that of a Greenshank, with white rump and lower back, but the pale-tipped secondaries give the wing a whitish trailing edge. The flight call is a prolonged *keek*, sometimes repeated several times. Although there is some overlapping of measurements the Long-billed Dowitcher normally has a longer bill, body and leg, but a shorter wing (not reaching the end of the tail) than the Short-billed, and the under tail-coverts are barred, not spotted. The juvenile is greyer and paler on the breast and underparts than the young Short-billed. Length, about 11·5 in. (*Plates 59 and 65.*)

### Short-billed Dowitcher                                        *Limnodromeus griseus*

This species breeds in sub-arctic parts of Canada and southern Alaska, and has recently been identified in Britain more often than the Long-billed

Dowitcher. Differentiation of the two species in the field is very difficult. The spotted, not barred, under tail-coverts and the buff underparts of juveniles are the chief plumage differences. The call is described as a metallic *küt-küt-küt*. (*See* Long-billed Dowitcher.) Length, about 11 in.

**Common Snipe**                                          *Gallinago gallinago*

The Common Snipe breeds over large areas in Europe and throughout the British Isles. From autumn until spring our resident stock is greatly increased by winter visitors, and there is also a passage migration.

The Common Snipe is a bird of moor and marsh, perhaps most remarkable for its very long, sensitive bill. A bird in the hand, provided that it is neither mutilated nor moulting, can be told by its tail; the Great Snipe has sixteen tail feathers, and the greater part of the outer ones is white towards the tip; the Common Snipe has the basal portion of its fourteen feathers black, and the tips red, only the outer pair having white ends, and all the feathers are marked with a subterminal black band. The twelve feathers of the Jack Snipe, especially the central pair, are pointed; they are dark brown with rufous margins. In the field such distinctions are seldom of value, but the behaviour of the Common Snipe differs from that of the Jack. When disturbed, it dashes into the air with a loud, harsh call—*scaap*—and immediately begins a rapid zigzag flight, which often saves its life; its dodges are irregular and not always in the same plane; when just out of gunshot it straightens its route, but does not alight until some distance away. The Jack, on the other hand, often rises silently; its turns and twists are more moderate, and it drops into cover within a few yards; it may be put up again and again.

The Snipe spends the day in some marsh or thick cover near water, and at dusk 'flights' like a duck. One by one, or in 'wisps', as the small parties are called, the birds shoot up from the marsh, calling, and vanish in the dusk, making for muddy ditches, the edges of ponds, oozy bogs, or other spots, where, probing the mud, they can feel for worms. The slightly swollen, pitted tip of the long bill is a wonderfully useful and flexible pair of forceps; the last inch of the upper mandible can be raised or depressed at will. Worms are the main food, though insects and, in hard weather, some seeds are eaten. Large numbers of 'foreign' Snipe arrive in October and November, and some of our home-bred birds go south; a hard frost or heavy snow causes westward movement, filling the Irish bogs with refugees. Return migration begins in March and lasts until after our birds have begun to nest. Display usually begins in March, but the strange 'drumming', frequently heard during display, is not entirely confined to the breeding season, nor is it exclusively masculine. The displaying bird rises with strong, rapid wing-beats in towering circles, alternated with sharp descents, volplaning steeply with wings half open and tail widespread. As it shoots down, the outer tail feathers stand out at an angle of about 45°, and the rush through the air causes these to vibrate with a booming note like the bleat of a kid. No doubt the vibration of the stiff primaries helps the sound, though the two tail feathers are mainly responsible. Often in the air and on the ground the Snipe has a vocal note, a deliberate *chip-per, chip-per, chip-per;* this is often uttered from a post, rail or other elevated perch, when the rhythmical movements of the head can be seen. Perching in bare trees is not uncommon. On sewage farms the birds feed all day; the food is often swallowed without the bill being withdrawn from the sludge.

The nest, a grass-lined cup, is well concealed in rushes, long grass, or on the moors, in cotton-grass and ling. The pyriform eggs, usually four, placed with their small ends inward, have oblique dark smears and blotches; clutches are usually complete about the middle of April. The nestling is a ball of reddish-brown down, barred and streaked with darker brown and black, and plentifully frosted with specks of silvery-white. Trusting instinctively to its colouring for concealment, it crouches silent and motionless, even if threatened by a boot or taken in the hand. Though the young can run as soon as they are dry, the parents continue to feed them; it is said that at times they carry them to the feeding-place, but certainly they sometimes conduct them on foot, calling to them as they strut ahead with flirting tail and slightly drooped wings.

The adult has the head dark, with a median stripe and two lateral stripes of buff; there is a dark streak from the bill to the eye. The back is dark brown, with lighter streaks on the mantle; the wings are mottled and barred with black, buff and brown, and the flanks barred with brown and white. The bill is horn, browner towards the tip; the legs greenish-brown. Length, 10·5 in. Wing, 5 in. Tarsus, 1·25 in. (*Plates 60, 65 and 169.*)

## Great Snipe · *Gallinago media*

The Great Snipe nests in northern Europe and north-western Asia and winters from the Mediterranean southwards to the Cape. In the British Isles it is a very scarce passage migrant or vagrant. It has usually been observed in autumn and winter; in spring it is infrequent. It has been found in all regions, but most frequently in the east and south of England.

There is often confusion between this bird and the Common Snipe, for the markings and colour are similar on the whole, but as the tail is usually spread in flight the white terminal portion of the more outer feathers of the Great can generally be seen. These are not so white in immature as in mature birds, and most of those which visit us in autumn are birds of the year; but at any age the underparts, even the abdomen, of the Great are more barred and speckled than those of the Common. Its usual haunts are drier than those of either the Common or Jack Snipe; it may be found in fields, amongst bracken, or even in woods. It is slower on the wing, and flies heavily without zigzags; indeed, it looks a bulkier bird than the resident species, though its actual length on the average is about the same, for the bill is proportionately short. As far as is known, it feeds rather more on what it can pick up than upon worms, for which it has to probe; insects and their larvae have been found in its stomach. In Britain it is a silent bird, rising without any call of alarm.

The plumage closely resembles that of the Common Snipe except in the points already mentioned—the tail and underparts. The bill is brown, almost black at the tip; the legs are greenish-brown. Length, 11 in. Wing, 5·5 in. Tarsus, 1·35 in. (*Plate 65*.)

**Jack Snipe**                                                    *Lymnocryptes minima*

The Jack Snipe has a northern and eastern breeding range in Europe; it winters in southern Europe and north Africa. It is a regular winter visitor and passage migrant to Britain, usually arriving during September and leaving in March or April, but occasionally a few non-breeding birds remain all summer.

'Jack' is a diminutive, and thus well applied to this very small snipe; indeed, its size alone is sufficient for identification. But when seen on the ground—no easy matter, for it loves thick cover—the absence of the central buff streak on its dark brown head separates it from the other two snipe. Its twelve pointed, dark, pale-edged tail feathers are an even surer distinction, and its bill is short, nearly 1½ in. shorter than that of the Common Snipe. Though most sportsmen affirm that the bird rises silently and does not zigzag, neither statement is strictly correct. It may utter a low, weak, but perfectly distinct call as it rises. It is slower on the wing than the Common Snipe, and its uncertain dodges do not appear to have such sharp angles; it changes direction more deliberately. It nearly always rises singly even if other Jacks are present on the marsh; wisps, however small, are very rare. It seldom flies far, often not more than twenty yards, before it drops abruptly into cover, and, unless again forced to take wing, remains in hiding. Indeed, it will sometimes crouch so as to baffle the searcher, and even allow a dog to pick it up.

The head is dark brown with a broad buff stripe above the eye but not on the crown; the back is dark brown with a green or purple gloss. The flanks are not barred and there is no white on the tail feathers. The buff and chestnut longitudinal streaks on back and wings are even more distinct than in the Common Snipe. The bill is yellowish with black tip; the legs light blue-grey. Length, 7·5 in. Wing, 4·25 in. Tarsus, 0·8 in. (*Plate 65*.)

**Woodcock**                                                      *Scolopax rusticola*

The literature of the Woodcock is extensive; it is *the* bird of the sportsman. In the British Isles it is a resident, a winter visitor, and a passage migrant from northern Europe to winter quarters further south. As a breeding bird it is common in woodlands in the north of England and much of Scotland and Ireland, but is scarce or absent in the south-west of England, west Wales and most of the Scottish islands. Statements that all British-bred birds winter here or that all migrate do not cover the ground; the only conclusion that can be reached if we examine the reports of recovery of ringed birds is that there is no fixed rule, and that the Woodcock, like many other species, shows individuality. Some young birds remain near the place of birth; others wander in autumn, even travelling north, and others again go abroad. Many birds marked in England and Scotland are found in Ireland.

The Woodcock has a noticeable character—a big eye set far back on a round head; this, coupled with a long bill, a dark stripe from bill to eye, black bars on head and neck, and soft marbled and barred buff, brown and black plumage, are a combination which even the novice cannot mistake. As a matter of fact, however, our visions of the living Woodcock are as a rule fleeting. By day it shuns the open, crouching quietly in the woods, its colour and markings in such harmony with its surroundings that it is invisible unless disturbed. Then, rising with a swish of wings, it dodges through the trees, to drop at a safe distance. We may come upon it again, squatting in a ditch with long bill depressed and eye upon us, but the chances are that we shall not see it until it again takes wing. The sound, as the bird rises, resembles the sharp ripping of stiff paper. The flight varies; it is swift and dodging when the bird is scared, but it can be slow, uncertain and owl-like as the birds return from their nocturnal feast to the shelter of the wood. The bill is carried pointed downwards. At times the speed is great, for on migration a bird once crashed through the lantern at the Flamborough light.

A few immigrants reach the east coast in September, but the biggest flights are in October and November, and hard or rough weather abroad brings the laggards later. In winter westward movements to Ireland are common. At dusk the bird leaves the wood, usually by some well-used glade, to feed in the marshes or muddy ditches, and even in hard weather finds some soft spot in which to push its sensitive bill to feel for worms, its main food. A captive Woodcock stamped to bring worms to the surface. It turns its probe from side to side, and can evidently tell when it touches its victim, which is then gripped by the curiously prehensile portion of the upper mandible and dragged out. When its head is turned sideways it is not listening for the sound of worm movement; the lateral position of the eyes of many birds causes them to turn the head when they concentrate upon one spot. Doubtless the Woodcock has good hearing; though exactly why the position of its ear, which is in front of and below the level of the eye, differs from the normal has never been discovered. In autumn the Woodcock is a silent bird, and often it rises without a sound; but it will, at times, utter a short *pier*, resembling the winter flight note of the Skylark. In spring, when the males are 'roding' in the early morning or at dusk, they have more to say. The bird gives 'a deep, constantly repeated croak—*croho, croho*—varied at regular intervals by a shrill screech—*chizzic*'. The roding flight, usually just above the tree tops, covers a regular beat. The bird's wing action looks slow and owl-like. If roding males meet, erratic, twisting pursuits may follow. When displaying on the ground the cock struts with uplifted and spread tail, drooped wings and puffed-out feathers.

In the winter wood the colour of the plumage hides the Woodcock; on the nest it is almost invisible. The nest in itself is little more than a depression in the fallen leaves, often of oak or beech, still plentiful in March when the four brown-blotched eggs are laid, for the Woodcock is an early nester; our breeding birds are usually sitting before the emigrants have left. The nestlings are rich buff with dark longitudinal bands on head and back, and a dark band crosses from eye to eye; the down is flecked with white. It is not certain that the old bird carries them to and from the wet feeding ground, but she will carry them away if the nesting site has been discovered. As to how this is accomplished is one of the ever-fruitful themes for ornithological squabbles. Woodcock have been reliably reported carrying the young between the thighs, between the feet, supported under the body by the bill or the tail or both, and even on the back.

Variation in the plumage of Woodcocks is common, but the broad black bars across the back of the head and the lighter bars on the underparts are constant. The colours are a wonderful combination of black, buff, chestnut and grey in bars, mottles, and fine wavy lines. The bill is reddish horn, browner at the tip, the legs flesh-coloured. There is no difference between the sexes, and young birds cannot be distinguished in the field. Length, 14·5 in. Wing, 7·5 in. Tarsus, 1·5 in. (*Plates 66 and 169.*)

## Upland Sandpiper                                          *Bartramia longicauda*

As a vagrant to the British Isles the Upland Sandpiper, a North American species well known to wander on migration, is rare and irregular, but it has appeared about fifteen times in widely scattered localities in Great Britain and Ireland. Most occurrences have been in autumn or early winter. It is a large sandpiper somewhat resembling a Ruff, but its movements when feeding are those of a plover. Its habit of holding up the wings, showing the barred under surfaces, is characteristic. The dark brown upper parts are barred with black. The rump is blackish-brown, the rather long tail buff, barred with black, and white tipped. Conspicuous arrow-head marks show on the buff breast and bars on the flanks; the chin and abdomen are white. Winter birds are yellower, and the young more rufous. The bill is blackish; the legs dull yellow. Length, 11 in.

## Curlew                                                        *Numenius arquata*

The Curlew has a wide range in northern and central Europe, and in winter reaches South Africa. It has greatly extended its breeding range and increased its numbers in the British Isles in the 20th century. It now breeds throughout Great Britain and Ireland, with the exception of the Outer Hebrides and some counties in south-east England. The Curlew was formerly regarded as a typical moorland bird, but since about 1930 breeding pairs have increasingly occupied lowland pastures and farmland, and it is this remarkable change of habitat that has enabled it to colonise large areas of England and Wales which were quite unsuited to its requirements at the beginning of the century. The reasons for this extension of breeding habitat are not clear. There is little evidence of overcrowding of the moorland areas; indeed, in several districts the population of the uplands has declined as that of the lowlands has increased.

The long, curved bill, which varies from 4 to 7 in. in length, the bulky brown body, and the wild whistle, make the Curlew a familiar shore bird; the smaller Whimbrel has a much shorter bill and distinctive dark streaks on its crown. At all seasons suitable feeding grounds are frequented, and as the bird is catholic in its tastes it may be seen amongst rocks as well as on mud or sand. It is as well known to the shepherd as to the fisherman, for in spring and early summer its haunts are moors and pastures, often at a great distance from the coast. Early in March the resident birds repair to the hills, leaving behind immature and non-breeding individuals and winter visitors from more northern haunts. Northward passage reaches its height in April and May. By July the breeders are returning from the hills, and at the end of this month there is at times noticeable passage movement; from August until October passage and the arrival of winter visitors continues. Many English and Scottish birds winter in Ireland. The Curlew is at all times gregarious and sociable, crowding on banks and rocks when the tide is full, but when on migration its numbers are often immense. It frequently migrates at night, when only a feeble estimate of the passing hordes can be guessed at from the babel of voices of invisible travellers. On estuary banks where the flocks have been roosting one can pick up pellets, often composed of cow-dung, grit and the wing-cases of beetles, and also an occasional crumpled yellow gizzard-lining.

At all times the bird is noisy; its call—*kour-lee*—is perhaps the best-known wader note, but this cry has a number of modulations and variations. On the moor the call of the 'Whaup' may have an amorous inflection, or, as it rises to a startled and startling scream, it may mean that our presence has been suddenly detected. From the guardian of the nest, standing sentinel on the skyline, it is a warning to the sitting mate, who silently slips from the nest and suddenly makes his or her presence known from a different quarter, and the two birds, as long as an intruder is about, keep up an incessant *whoo-wee, whoo-wee, who-wee*, distinct from the other notes. On the moors, before the eggs are laid and even when birds are sitting, the male indulges in a nuptial flight, a rising and falling aerial dance, accompanied by a trilling song, which has much in common with that of the Redshank. Here, too, may be heard the long, liquid bubbling call, which has no resemblance to the ordinary cry, but which is by no means only a breeding note, and is sometimes uttered by birds in winter on the flats. When the young are crouching in the heather the parents have two other notes, the first, a warning, very similar to the titter of the Whimbrel, and the other a savage bark of anger as the bird flies and sometimes hovers overhead.

The flight of the Curlew is more gull-like than that of most waders; it rises rather heavily, but is quick on the wing, though its slow and measured beats do not suggest speed. Flocks, especially when travelling for a distance, adopt the chevron formation or fly in well-ordered lines. The bird has been met with far out at sea, but as it can swim well it would have no difficulty in taking rest. On the coast the bird feeds with the tide, either by day or night. The sickle-shaped bill can be thrust into the mud, but often the bird delicately picks up a mollusc or other animal, jerks its head, and so passes the food up to the gape. On the moors insects and worms are eaten, and berries—blackberry, whinberry and crowberry, for instance—are appreciated.

Although the Curlew now nests on a low-lying heath or meadow, or in the upland pastures, its true home is 'the tops', where cotton-grass, crowberry, and stunted ling crop out amongst the sphagnum. The nest, often a mere apology, is placed amongst the tussocks, and the three or four large eggs brooded in April and May. The bird on guard, after warning its mate with a loud *cour-lieu*, will run towards a man, when the young are hatched, and strive to draw him from the danger zone, but a passing Raven, gull or hawk is fiercely assaulted and driven away with angry barks. The down of the nestling, pale brownish-white, mottled with chestnut and a few rich brown blotches, is inconspicuous in certain surroundings, but does not always hide the crouching bird. It has a short, straight, lead-blue bill.

The adult bird in summer is streaked on the head, back and breast with dark brown and buff; the wings and tail are barred with dark and light brown, and the white lower back has a few dusky streaks, while on the flanks are sagittate spots. There is a distinct pale eye-streak, and the chin, abdomen and under tail-coverts are white with a few dark markings. In winter the colours are paler, and the immature bird is more tawny. The bill is brown, reddish at the base of the under mandible; the legs green. Length, 23 in. Wing, 12 in. Tarsus, 3·25 in. (*Plates 63, 66 and 169.*)

## Whimbrel                                                    *Numenius phaeopus*

The breeding range of the Whimbrel is more northerly than that of the Curlew; it extends from Iceland and the Faeroes to north-western Siberia, and its winter range to the Cape. A few pairs nest in the Shetlands and Outer Hebrides, and, rarely, an odd pair elsewhere in the north of Scotland, but to most parts of the British Isles it is a regular and common passage migrant. A few non-breeding birds linger through the summer, and occasionally wintering is recorded.

The Whimbrel differs from the Curlew in having a shorter, rather less curved bill, and in its much darker crown, which is not brown with narrow streaks, but has two broad brown bands divided by a median narrow buff stripe. Though a bird of the shore, the passage, especially in spring, is often overland, and the distinctive rippling or tittering call of the incoming birds may be heard at night in April as well as May. Though passing inland, the bird does not often stop to feed by inland waters in England, though numbers do so regularly in Ireland. Return migration begins in July and continues until October, very few lingering until November; from December onward the bird is very rare. When travelling, small flocks of Whimbrel often adopt the line or V-shaped formation; the flight is steady and straight, but the wing-beats are quicker than those of the heavier bird. Low rocky shores are as much frequented as mud-flats; the brown bird, often almost invisible on the tangle, feels with its bill amongst the weed for molluscs and crustaceans, or hunts in the rock pools for prawns, gobies or butterfish; it will test the size of crabs, swallowing the small ones and reluctantly throwing aside those which are too large. On the flats it eats the usual marine creatures, and inland adds berries to its diet of worms, land snails and insects. The bird is by no means shy; when the wary Curlew warns other waders, the Whimbrel will continue its meal unmoved.

The nest is a slight hollow in the moss or amongst rough grasses, lined with a few bents or bits of moss. The three or four eggs, similar to small eggs of the Curlew, are not usually laid until June. At the nest the alarm note resembles that of the commoner species, and the Whimbrel is just as plucky in its assaults upon possible foes. The nestling plumage closely resembles that of the Curlew.

The adult has a dark brown crown divided by a pale streak down the middle; otherwise the neck, back and breast are streaked brown and buff but are darker than the Curlew's. The rump, lower back and abdomen are whitish. The young show both blacker and buffer mottlings than the adult. The bill is brown, the legs pale slate-blue. Length, 17 to 19 in. Wing, 10 in. Tarsus, 2·2 in. (*Plates 66 and 169.*)

### Eskimo Curlew *Numenius borealis*

The arctic American Eskimo Curlew migrates to, or used to migrate to, South America, reaching Patagonia and the Falklands, and has been obtained in England, Scotland, and Ireland seven times. The species is now almost extinct. The last recorded for Britain was one which reached the Scilly Isles in 1887. The Eskimo Curlew resembles a small Whimbrel with dark lower back and tail-coverts, and with sagittate marks on the breast. Length, 14 in.

### Bar-tailed Godwit *Limosa lapponica*

The Bar-tailed Godwit is a passage migrant, winter visitor and non-breeding resident in the British Isles. It nests in the far north of Europe and Asia and migrates as far as Africa in winter. In spring and autumn it is often numerous on our coasts, but numbers vary widely from year to year. Considerable flocks winter in Britain and some non-breeders stay through the summer. It seldom occurs inland.

The Godwits are tall waders, distinguished, when at a distance, from Curlews by their straight, actually uptilted and not downward curved bills. There are no other shore birds like them, but it is not always easy to tell one from the other when they are on the ground. The tail marks, as implied by the names, are good characters, if visible, but a bird on the shore makes no special effort to advertise its salient points; the tail of the present species is not always barred, the actual tail feathers are grey in winter, but the black tail of the other is constant and usually conspicuous. If the two species are together there is no difficulty, for the legs and, usually, the bill of the Black-tailed Godwit are longer than in the other; it towers above its companions. In flight the conspicuous white wing-bar, black tail and long trailing legs of *limosa* make it possible to distinguish immediately between the two species. Even in winter, however, the upper tail-coverts of the Bar-tailed show bars, and the young birds, which form the bulk of the autumn flocks, have decided bars. The bills of Bar-tailed Godwits vary greatly: as a rule from 3 to 5 in.

In East Anglia the Godwit seldom appears in numbers until early May, but on the Lancashire seaboard very large numbers appear in April, and the regular winter flocks are by no means small. In June there are few left, though a sprinkling of non-breeders often remain until in August the buff-breasted young of the year appear. From then until well into October Godwits abound on all suitable parts of our coasts; often flocks number thousands of individuals. Tidal ooze or sandbanks are the favourite feeding grounds of the Godwit. The food, marine invertebrates, may be picked up with the tip of the bill and rapidly jerked up until swallowed, may be intercepted as they seek to hide themselves in the sand, or may be probed for nostril-deep. The upward tilt of the bill, as well as its length, varies, but it is always visible; at times the bird sweeps its bill through the shallow pools like an Avocet. As the tide rises Godwits congregate with Knots and Oystercatchers along the sand at the edge of the water, and until the ebb, rest in dense packs. As a rule they keep on the sea side of the crowd, their long legs allowing them to wade deeply; they will stand on one leg, slowly hopping sideways up the shore as the water rises. When the tide turns the pack rises with a great rush of wings and flies, with strong wing-beats and with neck bent and head sunk in the shoulders, to the exposed banks, and there, walking rather deliberately with bill more or less horizontal, scatter to feed. Before alighting the flock will often perform rapid and complicated evolutions, turning and twisting, and shooting diagonally towards the beach with an angular twist before alighting. Reefs and rocky islets are often crowded with Godwits at high tide, and as the birds are driven from the banks, become congested areas; yet fresh arrivals come in and, lowering their long legs, drop into the mob. Those on the outskirts leap into the air, and with a flicker of wings drop where the crush is already great, so that these 'resting' packs are in a continuous state of disturbance. A few red birds, in almost full summer dress, are in the grey packs in April. Even in September a few have not lost the summer red, for, like the Knot, the Godwit is irregular in its changes. The birds on the rocks and when feeding keep up a wheezy undercurrent of notes, quite distinct from the rather harsh double flight-call. None of the many attempts to describe this barking note is satisfactory.

In summer the upper parts are a mixture of blackish-brown and reddish-chestnut, the underparts chestnut-red. The head is streaked, the coverts greyish, and more decided streaks show on the back than in the Black-tailed Godwit. The upper tail-coverts are white streaked with brown, and the tail is barred with brown and white. In winter the upper parts are ash-grey, underparts white; brownish streaks show on the mantle. The tail is partly grey, upper tail-coverts barred with brown. Most birds in the early autumn flocks are immature, more tawny-yellow than the winter old birds; the breast is buff and slightly streaked, upper tail-coverts white blotched with brown, and tail barred with brown and white. The bill is delicate rose-pink at the base, shading to black at the tip. The legs are grey. Length, 14 to 17 in. (according to length of bill). Wing, 8 in. Tarsus, 2 in. (*Plate 69.*)

### Black-tailed Godwit                                                    *Limosa limosa*

The breeding range of the Black-tailed Godwit extends from Denmark and Holland across central Europe to western Asia, and in winter it occurs in northern Africa. It became extinct as a British breeding bird about the middle of the 19th century, but thanks largely to the care of the Royal Society for the Protection of Birds it became re-established in the middle of the 20th. There is a flourishing colony of over thirty pairs in East Anglia and there has been sporadic breeding elsewhere since 1937. As a passage migrant and winter visitor it is most plentiful on the east and south coasts, but since 1940 has become increasingly numerous in the west, and there has been a similar increase in Ireland.

The Black-tailed Godwit is an easy bird to recognise when alongside its shorter-legged relative, but when by itself may be known by its white wing-bar—less distinct in young birds—and by the long legs extending far beyond the tail in flight. When feeding it is a slender, graceful bird, stalking deliberately, and bending its noticeably long neck in almost swan-like curves. It wades into deep water and often immerses most of its head when probing for food. Its flight is strong and less erratic than that of the Bar-tail. The nest, a simple depression in the ground, with a lining of dead grass and rootlets, may be near a marsh, but is usually on firm ground and often in quite short grass. On the breeding ground the Black-tailed Godwit is noisy, constantly calling in its display flight. It has also a rapid, chattering flight call, *kak, kak, ka,* and a repeated *wikka,* and when on the ground an anxious *kee-ah* or *kee-veek.*

The summer plumage is reddish-brown mottled with black on the upper parts; the lower back is black, and upper tail-coverts and base of the tail white, but the distal portion of the tail feathers is crossed by a single broad black band. The underparts are reddish-brown on the breast, and flanks and abdomen are whitish with bars of black and brown. In winter the bird is ashy-brown above and whiter below, the breast and neck being grey. Young are not unlike the adult in summer on their upper parts, but the underparts are paler. The bill is pinkish, darker towards the tip, the legs greenish-black. Length, 16 to 18 in. Wing, 9 in. Tarsus, 3·8 in. (*Plates 64 and 66.*)

### Green Sandpiper                                                    *Tringa ochropus*

As a passage migrant the Green Sandpiper occurs in all parts of the British Isles, though it is scarce in the west of Scotland. It breeds throughout northern Europe and winters in Africa. It is a rather uncommon winter visitor, and, rarely, remains all summer; indeed, it has occurred in every month in the year. Breeding in Britain has been recorded twice, in Westmorland and Inverness; it has been suspected elsewhere.

The Green Sandpiper is larger than the Common and can, even when at rest, be told by its white upper tail-coverts and strongly barred tail. On the wing the white lower back shows very clearly; this, contrasted with the dark back and wings, makes the bird look black and white. In flight it may be distinguished from the Wood Sandpiper by the sooty under surface of the wing; in the Wood it is greyish-white. The Green Sandpiper seldom frequents the open shore; it is an inland species, haunting the borders of rivers and small streams, lakes, and even small ponds or pools on a saltmarsh. Easily flushed, it rises high, towering to a great height with strong beats of its sharply angled wings, and with many Snipe-like turns and careens. Almost invariably it calls on rising, a loud, clear *toie, toie, toie*, with a rounder, fuller *o*-sound than the call of the Redshank. Though it does not as a rule alight within sight, it will return to the same spot when the coast is clear, sometimes in less than half an hour; day after day it frequents one pond or river reach. Occasionally two or three birds will feed close together, but as a rule it is solitary; flocks, very rarely large, are seen only during migration.

In May and June, August and September, the bird is commonest, but wintering Greens will haunt one spot for weeks at a time. Many sandpipers perch on branches, but this is a regular arboreal nester. The eggs, rather lightly spotted on a variable ground colour, are usually laid in the old nest of another species or in a squirrel's drey.

The streaked head is greyish-brown, the back and wings greenish-brown with a bronze gloss and fine white spots. The upper tail-coverts are white, and the central tail feathers white with broad blackish-brown bands towards the tip; the outer pair are white and those between have less complete bars. Its axillaries are black with fine white chevron bars. The breast and neck are greyish-brown, the chin and rest of the underparts white. The bill is dark brown; the legs green or greenish-yellow. The white spots are smaller and fewer in winter, and the underparts are purer white, and in the immature bird the spots are buffish and the feathers of the mantle are margined with yellowish-brown. Length, 9·5 in. Wing, 5·5 in. Tarsus, 1·25 in. (*Plate 69.*)

## Wood Sandpiper                                              *Tringa glareola*

The Wood Sandpiper breeds in northern Europe and normally winters in Africa. It is a regular passage migrant through the coastal counties of east and south-east England. In recent years it has also occurred annually near the west coast of England and has become regular in Ireland. Numbers vary widely from year to year, but in a good autumn parties of a dozen may be seen in August on marshes near the East Anglian coast. The spring passage, in late April or May, is usually on a much smaller scale. There was at least one breeding record in England in the 19th century, and since 1960 one or two pairs have been nesting in the north of Scotland.

The Wood Sandpiper is a little larger than the Common and smaller than the Green, but in proportion to its size, its legs are much longer; it resembles a small, slender Green Sandpiper with very long legs. On the wing it is not so black and white in appearance, for though the upper tail-coverts show as a white patch their centres are darker, and the feathers of the tail are barred throughout, whereas in the Green the bases are white. In flight, however, the much lighter under surface of the wing is apparent. Like the Green, it haunts inland pools, streams and marshes rather than the shore, but often near the coast. In western counties, where it is more regular than books suggest, it occurs on the borders of meres and in sewage farms; the food of both Green and Wood differs little from that of other waders. On the mud it runs quickly, showing its barred flanks, and if flushed, rises smartly, often to a height, but with less twisting and dodging than the Green. The characteristic *chiff-chiff-chiff* as it rises is not as loud or clear as the corresponding flight call of the Green Sandpiper. When on the ground it dips and jerks like a Common Sandpiper.

The nest is usually a hollow on open ground, lined with a few leaves or grasses. The eggs, normally four, vary greatly in colouring, but are usually heavily blotched and spotted with brown or purple markings on a buff or greenish ground. In northern Europe they are usually laid in June.

In summer the upper parts are olive-brown, paler than the Green Sandpiper's, closely spotted with white. The head, neck and breast are streaked brown and white; there is a pale superciliary stripe. The belly and upper tail-coverts are white, the underside of the wing pale, the axillaries being white with grey specks. In winter the white speckling is faint. The bill is dark brown, the legs yellowish or olive, paler than the Green Sandpiper's. Length, 8 in. Wing, 5 in. Tarsus, 1·5 in. (*Plate 69*.)

### Solitary Sandpiper                                          *Tringa solitaria*

This American wader breeds in Canada and winters as far south as Argentina. It has occurred eight times in England and once in Scotland. It resembles the Green Sandpiper in the dark upper and under surfaces of its wings and in its olive-green legs, but it is distinguished in flight by its dark rump and conspicuous white sides to its dark tail. Length, 8·3 in.

### Common Sandpiper                                          *Tringa hypoleucos*

The Common Sandpiper is a summer visitor to the British Isles, usually arriving in April, rarely at the end of March, and generally leaving in September. It breeds throughout Europe and winters further south, occasionally reaching the Cape. It nests abundantly in Scotland and the greater part of Ireland, the northern counties of England and north and central Wales, but with the possible exception of a pair or two on Dartmoor it does not breed regularly south-east of a line from the Severn to Flamborough Head. It is well known in the south and east of England as a passage migrant.

This graceful bird, with its cheery note as it skims over the northern river, lake or loch, needs little description; the only birds with which it may be confused are the Green and Wood Sandpipers, both of which have white rumps. Many of the Common Sandpipers have left before these autumn birds appear. Though sometimes nesting on lowland streams and estuaries, this bird is *the* sandpiper of the hills, delighting in the clear trout-streams where its companions are the Dipper and Grey Wagtail. It seldom haunts the coast until early autumn. The hills are usually deserted before the end of July; indeed, in this month small parties, probably families, reach the lowland streams and shore, and early in August emigration begins. Actual migration often takes place at night, for the familiar calls of birds keeping touch with one another are not uncommon on autumn nights. Most birds leave the north before the end of August, though stragglers may pass for a month or more; and Common Sandpipers are occasionally found in winter in various parts of England and Ireland.

When the Sandpiper reaches its summer haunts it settles on its own reach of the river or stretch of lake-side; there it wades in the shallows, catching gammarids and other crustaceans, small worms and the larvae of insects. If approached it will stand jerking its tail and nodding its head. Suddenly it takes wing, its course over the water a semicircle, its wing-beats strong and decided, alternating with a sharp downward stroke when for a moment the down-bent primaries perceptibly quiver. During this characteristic flight the long rippling whistle is uttered, a call from which the bird gets two local names—Kittie-Needie and Willy-wicket; either of these, repeated quickly two or three times, gives a better idea of the note than many of the attempts to express it by a combination of letters. Courtship begins immediately after arrival. The male bird trills a love-song, either when on the wing, when the down-pointed tips vibrate rapidly but actual progress is slow, or when running, with wings stiffly uplifted, along some wall or rail. He will circle round the female in wide sweeps, alight and trip towards her, wings uplifted, or chase her over the bank and sand. The trill, especially when the excited bird sings from an elevated perch, is varied by a plaintive pipe, a single note very like the warning call to the young.

The nest is in various situations, but usually well concealed in vegetation and at no great distance from water. The four buff eggs are speckled or blotched, rather sparsely, with brown, and the shell has a decided polish; they are usually laid in May and are incubated by both sexes. The young, clothed in pale grey down, marbled with black, crouch like other juvenile waders, but often betray themselves by a feeble pipe in answer to the parental clamour.

The general colour of the upper parts is greenish-brown, the feathers of the mantle having dark centres and margins. The barred secondaries are edged with white, forming a bar, conspicuous in flight. The outer tail feathers are white, barred with brown, and the streaked breast, neck and cheeks are light brown. A line above the eye, the chin and underparts below the breast are white. The bill is brown; the legs greenish. The young bird is a darker brown. Length, 7·75 in. Wing, 4·25 in. Tarsus, 0·8 in. (*Plates 67, 69 and 169.*)

## Spotted Sandpiper                                   *Tringa macularia*

The Spotted Sandpiper is a rare vagrant from North America; only four were recorded between 1958 and 1967, three from the Scilly Isles. It is a little smaller than the Common Sandpiper, which it closely resembles, except that in summer its underparts are spotted with black. These spots disappear in winter and are absent in the young bird, but the broad brown bar on the secondaries is continuous in the Spotted Sandpiper and interrupted in the Common. The throat of the Spotted is whiter and less streaked. The bill is yellow with a black tip. Length, 7 in.

### Redshank                                                    *Tringa totanus*

The noisy, restless Redshank is a resident and abundant passage migrant and winter visitor to all parts of the coast. Abroad it breeds throughout Europe, wintering as far south as the Cape. From about 1865 to 1940 the Redshank had a period of expansion as a breeding species, during which it colonised nearly every county in the British Isles and spread far inland, whereas previously it had been regarded as a coastal bird. More recently there has been a decline in south-east England and perhaps elsewhere.

The Redshank is easily recognised. It announces its presence by a triple call—*tu, tu, ee*—or a long, plaintive *tyu*. It stands, bobbing in sandpiper fashion, dipping its head and breast as if hinged on its long red legs, and, when it takes wing, shows a white lower back and an even more distinctive broad white border to the wing, formed by the white secondaries and the white on the inner primaries. Although a greyish-brown, red-legged bird when feeding, it looks very black and white in flight. In March there is an increase of birds at the breeding stations, and in April and May a strong northward movement. In August immature birds appear on the shore, and in September southward migration is in full swing; in favourable localities large flocks remain all winter. Grasslands and saltings, mud-flats and sandy shores, even rocky coasts, are frequented, and no wader more frequently visits the sewage farms. Insects, molluscs and crustaceans are its food. Like some other waders, it throws up 'pellets'. These are small, smooth and grey, and are apparently composed of tiny fragments of the hard parts of small crustaceans, and are found on the shore. In shore pools it wades belly-deep and swims easily, but at high tide it awaits the ebb on rocks, shingle or sand, acting as a sentinel for its less wide-awake companions, for it is ever on the alert, ready to take alarm. Its flight is swift and erratic, and it calls loudly as it flies.

In nuptial flight the Redshank dances in the air, rising on quivering wings, yodelling a long trilling *tchu, tchu, tchu*, with emphasis on the *t*. It drops a few feet and rises again and again, dancing above one particular spot like a gnat in sunshine. As it descends, still trilling, gliding diagonally earthward, the wings are bowed, the tips held downward. If the nesting area is invaded the notes change to a yelping, scolding *tuik, tuik*, and it mobs the intruder long after he has passed the danger zone. Half a dozen or more Redshanks will fly yelling after a passing Harrier, a Kestrel and even a harmless Cuckoo. The nest, which is usually in a dry spot, though sometimes in wet marsh, is often well concealed by the surrounding grass or rushes; the bird interweaves the the ends of the grass so as to form a tent-like screen. Other nests are quite open; in one colony on sheep-cropped saltings all were exposed, and in another, two had thick tents, one a loose tunnel of rushes, and others had no cover. During display, when not in the air, the male will trip lightly towards the female, stiffly holding up the pointed wings, exhibiting the white under surface. Though so wary, the bird is often a close sitter; there are many recorded instances of females which would allow themselves to be taken in the hand rather than leave the eggs. The eggs, normally four, are laid in March or April; they vary, but a not unusual type is like a small egg of the Lapwing with a very light ground. The nestlings, which crouch for concealment like other waders, are rich buff, with black lines or curves on the head and back. The legs are very pale yellow, and the bill blackish-olive.

In summer the upper parts are brown, barred, speckled and streaked with darker brown; the streaked neck and breast are paler, and the flanks are barred. At all seasons and any age the lower back is white, the upper tail-coverts and tail white, barred with black, and the axillaries and under wing-coverts white. The general colour is more ashy in winter, and the underparts are purer; the upper parts of the immature bird are buffer, and the streaks are more marked on the breast and flanks; the legs are yellow. These in the adult bird are orange-red, as is the base of the bill, the tip being black. Length, 12 in. Wing, 6·5 in. Tarsus, 1·9 in. (*Plates 70 and 169.*)

## Spotted Redshank                                       *Tringa erythropus*

The Spotted or Dusky Redshank is a regular visitor on passage from its arctic breeding grounds to its winter quarters in Africa; it also occurs on the northward migration and in the winter months. It is numerous in the eastern coastal counties from the Wash to the Channel, and in August and September may be counted in dozens on some East Anglian coastal marshes. Spotted Redshanks are also regular in autumn and occasional in spring in north-west England; they are becoming increasingly frequent in the south of Scotland and in Ireland. Some individuals regularly spend the winter in the south of England and wintering birds are not infrequent in the north-west.

The Spotted is a larger, taller bird than the Common Redshank; its bill and legs are longer. It can always be told from the commoner bird by the secondaries, which are barred with black and grey-brown, so that they do not show as a conspicuous white band in flight. The central tail feathers also differ, being ashy-grey or brown, but with obscure bars. Its habits and food are similar to those of the Redshank, but it haunts the open shore less frequently and is often seen on sewage farms and marshy pools, though seldom far from the coast. Like the Greenshank, it sometimes runs through shallow water with open bill or sweeps from side to side like an Avocet. Its call note is very different from the Redshank's, a rather harsh *tchueet*.

In summer the general colour of both upper and underparts is blackish. On the back and wings, which are tinged with brown, are the white flecks which give it the name Spotted. The rump and upper tail-coverts are barred with black and white; the centre of the tail is brownish-grey, faintly barred. The base of the bill and the legs are dark red, much duller than in winter. In winter the upper parts are grey, flecked with white marks; the underparts and under surface of the wing are white. The juvenile in autumn is much browner than the adult and resembles the Common Redshank in general colour, but the bill, legs and flight pattern are still distinctive. A noticeable dark streak passes through the eye, showing up a white superciliary stripe. Length, 12 in. Wing, 6·5 in. Tarsus, 2 in. (*Plate 70.*)

### Greater Yellowlegs *Tringa melanoleuca*

This vagrant from North America has occurred about seventeen times in the British Isles, chiefly in autumn. It is larger and longer-legged than the Lesser Yellowlegs, and has a longer, stouter, slightly upcurved bill. It differs from the Greenshank, which it resembles in size, voice and habits, in its spotted mantle, speckled rump without the long white V up the back, and orange-yellow legs. Length, 14 in. Wing, 7·75 in. Tarsus, 2·5 in.

### Lesser Yellowlegs *Tringa flavipes*

This North American wader is now recorded in the British Isles nearly every autumn. It is one-third smaller than the Greater Yellowlegs and has been likened to a large Wood Sandpiper. It could be confused with an immature Redshank, but the secondaries are dark, so that no broad white wing-border shows in flight; further distinctions are that the axillaries are barred and the white on the rump forms a square patch and does not make a V-shape on the lower back. The legs are bright yellow; the bill straight and slender. The flight call resembles the Greenshank's *tew-tew*, but is weaker. Length, 10·75 in. Wing, 6·4 in. Tarsus, 2 in.

### Greenshank *Tringa nebularia*

In northern Europe the Greenshank nests south of the arctic circle, and it visits southern Europe and Africa in winter; in most parts of the British Isles it is a regular passage migrant, common in autumn but scarce in spring, joining other waders on the shore and frequently appearing on inland waters. In the north of Scotland, and on a few Scottish islands, it nests in small numbers. A few birds winter in England and Ireland and, more rarely, Wales and Scotland.

The long, slightly uptilted bill of the Greenshank is usually a character by which we can separate it from the Redshanks with which it often feeds, but it is a longer-legged, larger bird, and when it rises, though the white rump is very conspicuous, shows no white wing-border, for its secondaries are brown. Its pose, too, is different, the body being held horizontally, at right angles to its legs, which has the effect of making it look a much longer bird. Though alert enough, it has little of the nervous ducking action so characteristic of the Redshank. In winter it is a greyer and paler bird, and in summer its back is blacker. It flies quickly, and though quieter than the ever-noisy Redshank, has a clear

*Above* : Curlew, p133
*Below* : Whimbrel, p135

PLATE 66    *Above* : Woodcock, p131
*Below* : Black-tailed Godwit, p138

PLATE 67

Common Sand-
piper, p140

Photo:
J. B. and S. Bottomley

PLATE 68

Greenshank, p144

Photo:
J. B. and S. Bottomley

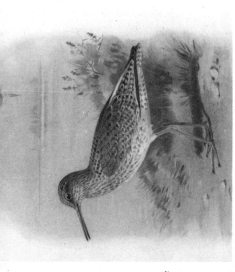

PLATE 70

*Above left :*
Redshank, p142
*Below left :* Knot
(winter), p146

*Above right :*
Spotted Red-
shank, p143
*Below right :*
Greenshank, p144

PLATE 71

Knot, p146

*Photo : J. B. and S. Bottomley*

PLATE 72

*Above :* Little Stint, p148

*Below :* Pectoral Sandpiper, p150

*Photo : J. B. and S. Bottomley*

PLATE 74    *Above*: Dunlin (summer and winter), p151
*Below*: Curlew Sandpiper (summer and
autumn), p153

*Above*: Ruffs, p156
*Below*: Reeve, p156

Photo : *J. B. and S. Bott*

PLATE 75

*Above :* Sanderling, p154

*Below :* Dunlin, p151

Photo : *J. B. and S. Bott*

PLATE 76     Avocet, p157

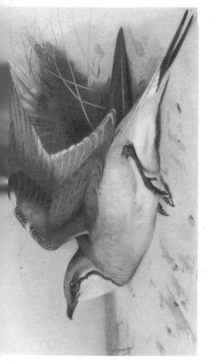
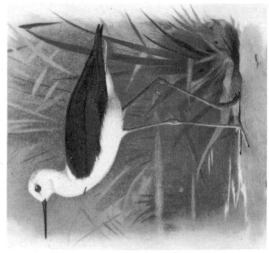

# PLATE 78

*Above left :*
Avocet, p157
*Below left :*
Cream-coloured
Courser, p164

*Above right :*
Pratincole, p163
*Below right :*
Black-winged
Stilt, p158

Photo: J. B. and S. B

PLATE 79

*Above:* Grey Phalarope, p159

*Below:* Wilson's Phalarope, p161

Photo: J. B. and S. B

PLATE 80     Arctic Skua, p166

PLATE 81

*Above left:*
Arctic Skua, p166
*Above right:*
Long-tailed Skua,
p167

*Below left:*
Razorbill, p193
*Below right:*
Pomarine Skua,
p167

and distinctive call—*choo-tchoo-tchoo*—each note well emphasised. Occasionally this is a double *chee-weet* on rising. The Greenshank reaches its Scottish breeding grounds early. Passage migration continues throughout April and May. The first autumn migrants appear in July and continue to pass until October, halting singly or in parties of a dozen or more on estuaries, marshes, sewage farms or inland pools. The usual wader diet is varied by the capture of small fish. Greenshanks frequently feed by making short dashes through shallow water with bill submerged, though they also walk more sedately, sweeping the bill from side to side or picking and probing.

The nest is a slight structure, little more than a depression in the turf, amongst rocks, in heather, or open grassland, but usually near water. The four buff, beautifully marked eggs are generally laid in May. The young in down are light buff, blotched and streaked with black. The anxious parent reveals the presence of young by flying round with wild cries, or, like the Redshank, it perches on a mound or rock and keeps up a continuous mournful warning note.

In summer the grey head is streaked with dark brown; the mantle is blackish, the rump white, and the tail is mottled and barred with brown, but never so distinctly as that of the Redshank. The underparts are white, with ashy streaks and spots on the breast and flanks. The bill is blackish, the legs olive-green. The whole of the upper parts are greyer in winter, and the underparts are a purer white. Young birds have light brown or buff fringes to the feathers of the back and mantle, and the flanks and breast are lined with blackish-grey. Length, 13 in. Wing, 7·5 in. Tarsus, 2·25 in. (*Plates 68, 70 and 168.*)

## Marsh Sandpiper                                   *Tringa stagnatilis*

The Marsh Sandpiper inhabits southern Siberia and some parts of southeastern Europe, and has been recorded in Britain some sixteen times, usually in autumn. It is not unlike a small Greenshank, but may be distinguished by its white face and forehead, thin straight bill and proportionately longer legs. It is a grey and greyish-brown bird with white underparts in winter; but in summer the breast is spotted and the upper parts show decided black marks. The bill is greenish-brown, the legs dark greenish. Length, 9 in. Tarsus, 2in.

## Terek Sandpiper                                    *Xenus cinereus*

The Terek Sandpiper breeds in north-eastern Europe and Siberia and migrates south in autumn. It has been recorded in the British Isles five times, usually in May or June. It is a noisy wader with fluty or piping polysyllabic calls. The upper parts are grey with dark markings on the back and streaks on the head; the underparts are white with dusky mottles on flanks and breast. In flight the pale rump and white trailing edge of the wing are noticeable. The long, greenish-black bill is curved upwards at the tip; the legs are yellowish-green. Length, 9 in. Tarsus, 1 in.

**Knot**                                                    *Calidris canutus*
Countless hordes of Knots visit the British Isles on passage, although they
are scarce or absent in north-west Scotland and on the west coast of Ireland,
and very large numbers remain to winter, but it was not until 1876 that any
breeding-place was discovered. The Knot has apparently a circumpolar
breeding range, but all the known haunts are far north of the arctic circle; its
winter wanderings take it to South Africa, Australia, New Zealand and
Patagonia.

In Britain the haunts of the gregarious Knot are the sea-shores where there
are wide stretches of sand or tidal mud; in favoured localities its numbers are
large in winter, immense during migration, and a fair number of non-breeding
birds remain all summer. Among the crowds of waders which feed on the
flats the Knot may be singled out by its intermediate size, considerably larger
than the Dunlin and Sanderling, shorter in leg than the Redshank, and small
beside the tall Godwits and heavy Curlew. It is a squat, short-billed, dumpy
wader, always looking plump and in good condition—in winter grey and white,
in spring and summer reddish-chestnut. Immature birds with buffer underparts mix in the autumn and winter packs. The name is said to have origin
in Canute's tidal experiences, but surely it is derived from the bird's note—
a clear *knut, knut*. When a flock settles the chorus rises as a beautiful twitter.
There is also a disyllabic flight call. On the banks no waders pack as closely
as the Knot. On the Lancashire tide-line one can see for a mile or more one
continuous ribbon of birds, varying in width from two or three feet to six or
more yards. Where the birds are thickest, and they move all in one direction
with their heads down, the impression given is of a slowly advancing grey
carpet. As they feed in these compact masses they must clear the shallowing
water and wet sand of the small marine worms, molluscs and crustaceans, the
winter food. The bird feeds with the falling tide both by day and night.

Spring passage usually begins in April, and by May many of the birds have
donned summer dress. Used though it is to exposure to weather, the Knot
evidently prefers to be out of the wind; when the flocks are resting or feeding,
birds on the windward side constantly rise, take two or three fluttering wing-
beats, and drop into the thickest place so as to obtain the shelter of their
comrades. At rest the bird stands on one leg, its head sunk in its shoulders or
with its bill in the scapulars; if approached it will, without putting down the
raised leg, hop slowly away. The rush of wings of one of the vast flocks when
disturbed is a sound to remember, the sight most impressive; the rising
cohorts form a dense curtain. The aerial movements of the flock are as complicated and well ordered as those of the Dunlin; turning and twisting, the
compact body skims out over the water, rises or descends, or thins out into a
long undulating line; often the whole body re-settles where it rose. The
Knot is strong and swift on the wing, capable of sustained flight. Many birds
leave the west coast before the end of April, but passage continues throughout
May. In the last week in July or early in August the immigrants arrive from
the north. Some adult birds, already in grey dress, may be noticed among the

buff-breasted juveniles, and the passage continues until October. The chestnut of the adult birds when gradually attaining winter grey is much deeper than the buff of the young.

The Knot occasionally occurs inland, but very rarely more than two or three together. Single birds are met with on inland waters in winter as well as in autumn.

The Knot in summer plumage is deep chestnut on the face, throat, breast and abdomen; the streaked head is browner, and the mantle much darker, spotted with chestnut and with pale edgings to many of the feathers. The white-shafted primaries and secondaries are greyish-black; the under tail-coverts are whitish, mottled with dark grey and black. The lower back and upper tail-coverts are white, barred with black and chestnut. The bill is black, legs deep olive. In winter the upper parts and breast are ashy-grey, with dark streaks on head and breast, and with the coverts neatly patterned with dark grey. There is a distinct white wing-bar. The underparts are white with grey markings on the flanks. In the young the upper parts are ashy, but marked with bars of black and buff; the breast, abdomen and flanks are suffused with buff, and the throat and breast streaked with brown. Length, 10 in. Wing, 6·5 in. Tarsus, 1·25 in. (*Plates 70 and 71*.)

## Purple Sandpiper                                    *Calidris maritima*

The breeding range of the Purple Sandpiper, though almost circumpolar and largely arctic, includes Scandinavia, Iceland and the Faeroes. Though nesting in the Shetlands is still unproved, reports that it has done so there may have foundation. In the British Isles it is a well-distributed visitor from August until June, and a few non-breeding birds remain all summer.

The Purple Sandpiper is local on our coasts simply because it is a rock-haunting species, and seldom visits sandy shores or mud flats. In small flocks it frequents tangle-covered reefs and rocky shores, feeding at low tide amid the debris at the foot of the cliffs. It shares the tastes of the Turnstone, its constant companion. A very dark, squat bird, it may be recognised by its habits as much as by its appearance; if seen at close quarters—by no means difficult, for it is absurdly indifferent to the presence of man—its short yellow legs and the white patch on the inner secondaries when it flies are distinctive characters. The ebb is the favourite feeding time of this rock bird; it then catches the molluscs, worms and crustaceans before they have hidden themselves under stones or in the thick weed; it wades in the shallowing rock pool, nipping up the retreating crab or prawn, and not refusing a small goby or other fish. Surf on the rocks does not disconcert it; at the right moment it runs like a mouse to drier rock, or leaps into the air and hovers until the breaking wave retreats. It will alight in the backwash, and if swept from its foothold swims buoyantly.

Quick on the wing, its flight is more direct than that of most sandpipers; it hurries from reef to reef as each is uncovered. At high tide a little party will stand together on the rocks out of reach of the waves but not of the spray;

there they will rest, preen the plumage, or sleep until the ebb. The bird is lethargic, deliberate, or very much in a hurry; it is a slow and systematic seeker for food, but immediately a fresh rock is exposed it hurries to reach it. In flight it has a low note, a whistle or pipe. As it flies a white patch is very distinct on its dark wing, and when it alights, and for a second holds its wings uplifted, the white under surface is very striking on so dusky a bird.

In summer the upper parts are blackish but relieved by buff and chestnut bars and spots, and white margins to the feathers. The lower back to the centre of the tail is very dark, almost black, the outer tail feathers being pale brown. The breast and flanks are greyish with dusky brown streaks and spots; the abdomen is white. In autumn and winter it is a still darker bird, glossed with purple sheen and with leaden feather edges; the breast and flanks are mottled and streaked with blackish-brown. The young bird differs from the winter adult in the decided and neat pattern caused by the white and buff feather edgings. The bill is orange at the base, dark towards the tip; the legs yellow to orange. Length, 8·25 in. Wing, 5·3 in. Tarsus, 0·9 in. (*Plate 73*.)

### Little Stint                                              *Calidris minuta*

Breeding in arctic Europe and Asia, and travelling far south to winter, the Little Stint pays short but regular visits to our shores in autumn, less frequently in spring and is occasionally seen in winter. It is a passage migrant which reaches South Africa and India.

The Little Stint is not unlike a small Dunlin; the rarer Temminck's Stint resembles a diminutive Common Sandpiper. The small size and shorter bill—roughly three-quarters the length of that of the Dunlin—are sufficient to attract attention when the bird is feeding without other shore waders; in the hand it is at all times a warmer-tinted bird than Temminck's, and the two outer pairs of tail feathers are brownish-grey, whereas in the latter they are white. It looks whiter on the breast than the Dunlins so often seen with it, and there is a suggestion of a pale collar. Passage Stints arrive in August, but early September is the time when most are noticed; they come in small parties and at first keep rather to themselves, but soon join the mixed congregations on the banks, feeding sociably with Dunlins, Sanderlings and Curlew Sandpipers. By early October most have passed on, and a November Little Stint is uncommon. Its spring visits are from April to June. Although it is a typical shore bird, overland journeys are at times taken. The occurrence inland is not merely due to wandering or storm; indeed, the repeated appearance on the sewage farms suggests intentional visits to places where food is abundant. In its behaviour when feeding, the Stint is more of a Sanderling than a Dunlin, constantly active, running smartly to pick up insects, worms and small molluscs or to chase the sandhoppers and shrimps; it will swim when the water is too deep for its short legs. At times it will push its bill into the sand to capture a retreating worm, but does not probe for food like the Snipe. It flies swiftly, often outdistancing larger companions, and when small flocks are flying together the aerial performances are skilful—rapid turns, twists and swerves, when the light underparts flash as every bird at the same instant smartly careens. The triple call, *tchik, tchik, tchik*, is sharp and quickly repeated, and birds on the sand have a lower, more twittering note.

The upper parts in summer are reddish; the forehead is white, crown streaked, and a dark line passes from lores to eye. The finely speckled breast is rufous, the rest of the underparts white. The quills are dusky, and a white bar crosses the open wing. The bill and legs are black. In winter the general colour is ashy-grey, the wings and coverts much greyer than in summer. The young have darker backs and mantles, patterned with buff and chestnut, and with white on the wings and scapulars showing as irregular streaks. The white forehead and stripe above the eye show up the grey and reddish-brown crown. The breast is tinged with buff, the underparts white. Length, 6 in. Wing, 3·5 in. Tarsus, 0·8 in. (*Plates 72 and 73.*)

**Least Sandpiper**                                    *Calidris minutilla*

This small sandpiper, formerly known as the American Stint, which breeds in arctic America, is a very rare vagrant to the British Isles. Thirteen records have been accepted, most of them from south-east England in autumn. It is darker and less rufous than the Little Stint in summer, but otherwise very similar in appearance and habits. Its call is a grating *kreet*. The outer tail feathers are light grey, intermediate between those of the Little and Temminck's Stint. In the grey winter dress the rump is still dark and the breast has dusky streaks. The fine bill is blackish-brown, the legs yellowish or greenish. Length, 5·25 in. Wing, 3·5 in. Tarsus, 0·75 in.

**Temminck's Stint**                                    *Calidris temminckii*

Temminck's Stint, even in autumn, is a rarer passage migrant than the Little Stint; it is more frequent on the south and south-east coast than elsewhere, though it has occurred in most parts of our islands. It nests in arctic Europe and winters in northern Africa. In the 20th century it has nested three times in the Cairngorms in Scotland and once in Yorkshire, but in each case unsuccessfully.

Temminck's Stint is slightly smaller than the Little Stint, and at all seasons much greyer. Its outer tail feathers are white, not grey as in the Little Stint. In the British Isles it is more of a freshwater species than the Little Stint and is rarely seen on the open shore. It frequents sewage farms and marshes, or creeks and gullies on the shore, and does not associate freely with other species. Its flight is erratic and twisting, and its call a trilling titter.

In summer the adult is greyish-brown with darker streaks and spots, but with a few chestnut bars and margins on the upper parts. Except at its dusky tip the outer primary is white; the others are brownish-grey; a narrow bar crosses the wing. The buff breast is streaked, the rest of the underparts white. The bill is black, legs greenish or yellowish. The winter plumage is ashy with indistinct dark markings and pale margins; the breast is unstreaked. The feathers of the upper parts in young birds are tipped with white, and the underparts are suffused with buff. Length, 5·75 in. Wing, 3·8 in. Tarsus, 0·6 in. (*Plate 73*.)

### Baird's Sandpiper *Calidris bairdii*

There were nineteen records of this North American wader in the British Isles up to 1967, all but two since 1950 and all but one in autumn. Baird's Sandpiper is about the size of a Dunlin, but its brown and white colouring rather suggests a Sanderling. The long wings overlap the tail; the bill is fine and rather long. Immatures have dark, patterned upper parts and white underparts with buff patches on the breast. The tail is brown with dark central feathers. The bill and legs are blackish. Length, 7 in. Wing, 4·7 in. Tarsus, 0·9 in.

### White-rumped Sandpiper *Calidris fuscicollis*

This arctic American Sandpiper, formerly known as Bonaparte's Sandpiper, is now recognised as an annual autumn visitor to the British Isles in very small numbers. On an average, four or five are recorded each year. Although occurrences are most frequent in Cornwall and Scilly the bird has been found in many parts of England, Scotland and Ireland.

This bird is not unlike a small, short-billed Dunlin in winter dress, but may always be distinguished by its white upper tail-coverts. Its note is distinctive, a low *weet*. It differs from the Curlew Sandpiper in the smaller extent of the white on the rump and in its shorter bill and legs.

The head and upper parts, including the tail but excluding the upper tail-coverts, are brown; the head is streaked, and the feathers of the back have dark centres and rufous edges. The breast and flanks are grey, dotted with brown, the rest of the underparts white. In winter the bird is greyer, and the marks on the underparts fainter. The underparts of the young are tinged with buff, and white and rufous spots show on the back and mantle. The bill is black and short; the legs dark olive. Length, 7·25 in. Wing, 4·75 in. Tarsus, 0·9 in.

### Pectoral Sandpiper *Calidris melanotos*

The Pectoral Sandpiper breeds in arctic America and visits South America in winter. Formerly regarded as a rare vagrant to the British Isles, it is now recognised as a regular autumn passage migrant in small numbers. It has been recorded from many parts of Britain, but is most regular in the south and east of England; a few are recorded annually in Ireland. Spring occurrences are much less frequent.

The Pectoral Sandpiper is not unlike a large Dunlin with a snipe-like pattern on the back and sharply defined streaked breast. In Britain it is more often seen on sewage farms and marshes than on the shore, and does not usually associate with other species. It moves slowly when feeding. When flushed it utters a thin *tirrp-tirrp* and flies off with a swift, usually zigzag flight.

The head and upper parts generally are blackish-brown with rufous streaks and feather edgings; there is a slight wing-bar. The central tail feathers are almost black, the outer ones dark brown; the upper breast is heavily streaked, and the abdomen white. A whitish superciliary stripe and a white chin set off the speckled cheek, and a dark streak runs from the bill through the eye. The bill is greenish-black; legs yellowish-brown. Length, 8 in. Wing, 5·3 in. Tarsus, 1·2 in. (*Plates 72 and 73.*)

**Sharp-tailed Sandpiper**                              *Calidris acuminata*
Formerly known as the Siberian Pectoral Sandpiper, this wader breeds in north-east Siberia and has occurred in Great Britain eight times, seven of them in autumn. It closely resembles the Pectoral Sandpiper, but in summer the breast-band is not so clean-cut and the crown is reddish. The legs are greenish-black, not yellowish as in the Pectoral Sandpiper. Length, 7·5 in. Tarsus, 1·1 in.

**Dunlin**                                                      *Calidris alpina*
Not only is the Dunlin the commonest bird of the shore, but it is one of the most abundant British birds. It has a wide range in northern Europe and Asia, and migrates in winter to northern Africa. In the British Isles it is a resident, summer visitor, winter visitor and passage migrant, for some of our home-bred birds leave in autumn and the majority of the vast hordes which may be seen in the spring and autumn on the west coast do not remain all winter. At all seasons there are Dunlins in our estuaries and on the shore, for numbers of non-breeding birds remain all summer. As a breeding bird the Dunlin is rather thinly distributed in parts of Wales, the north of England and north-west Ireland, but is more abundant in parts of Scotland and the northern isles.

In any mixed party of small waders the Dunlin predominates. It is a small, plump, fairly long-billed wader, ashy-grey with white underparts in winter, reddish-brown and black, with a large black patch on the lower breast, in summer. There is no more variable wader than the Dunlin in size as well as plumage. The smaller birds belong to the race which nests in Britain, the larger ones being winter visitors or passage migrants from further north. The length of the bill is also very variable; the shorter bills are almost straight and the longer ones slightly curved downwards towards the tip.

Sandbanks and estuarine mud-flats are the favourite haunts of the Dunlin, but it is also common along any sandy shore, and in little sandy bays on a rocky coast; saltings and maritime marshes are also frequented; it delights in the tidal gutters. On the west coast, at any rate, the bird is most abundant at times of passage. Early in February, even in January, there is usually a northward movement, possibly of birds which have never left England, and in March the numbers are greatly increased, but in April and May the flocks are immense. Towards the end of July the second increase begins, which reaches its height in September. The winter flocks are often very great, but small compared with the countless hosts on migration. In many of its movements the

Dunlin is deliberate and sedate, but it can run quickly, its short black legs twinkling, especially when chasing sandhoppers on the recently covered banks. At low water it wades in the shallow pools, its body low, its head forward and shoulders hunched, as it probes the mud; it will swim a deep pool. It is never as energetic as the Sanderling or Ringed Plover, its constant companions. When feeding it does not pack as closely as the Knot, and often the birds scatter far and wide over the banks and saltings. It is less nervous than the Ringed Plover, often running rather than taking wing. Single birds are often strikingly tame and approachable.

Flocks when feeding keep up a low twittering chorus, but the alarm note and flight call is a rather long *purre*; it is quick on the wing, swerving and rolling rather than zigzagging, and the pale outer feathers of the tail show clearly in contrast to the central pair as it flies from the watcher. Its greatest aerial skill, however, is shown by its ordered manoeuvres in large flocks. The whole body will swing out over the water, skim the waves, rise until like a cloud they show against the sky, then suddenly rain down, flashing like silvery drops if the sun be shining. A rapidly moving flock at a distance flickers, now visible, now invisible, as white breast or dark back turn towards the observer, for every bird turns at the same moment. At times the flock thins out into a line stretching across the field of vision, and undulating in regular waves; then it will bunch, and without disorder every individual, moved by some strange social impulse, dives, swerves, or sharply changes direction at the required moment. The speed of the flying Dunlin is always great, and at night coastwise wires cause numerous fatalities. The rushing sound caused by the wings of a large party resembles escaping steam, and even two or three birds hurtling past produce a remarkable rustle. When the banks are flooded the birds will repair to the marshes or fields, and after a few evolutions settle to rest or hunt for insects. All will stand, head to wind, bobbing frequently, but if the wind is high, the nearest birds constantly rise, flutter over their companions and drop behind for shelter, so that the whole party slowly shifts downwind.

The marine food is similar to that of all small waders, but when nesting, and halting inland on migration, insects are largely eaten. To the meres, reservoirs on the hills, and sewage farms the bird is a frequent visitor in winter as well as on passage; it paddles in the settling tanks, finding an abundance of dipterous larvae, and often remaining many days. On the coast it feeds with the rising and falling tide, by night as well as by day, sleeping at high water or at irregular intervals.

The Dunlin nests on the high moors, often at 2000 ft. or more, but a few pairs also breed on low marshes and saltings at sea level. On the moors the bird soars and swoops like a Snipe, trilling as it rises and falls. The breeding call, *dwee, dwee*, is quite distinct from the purr of alarm when the bird is put off the nest. The nest is a neat cup of grass, about 3 in. in diameter, often well hidden in ling or moorland grass, but at times barely screened. The four eggs are variable in ground and markings, generally brown or yellow, sometimes green, with brown, sepia and grey blotches, as a rule thickest at the larger end and often more or less oblique; they are laid in May or June. The nestling has rich buff or chestnut down, marbled with black and flecked with white; its underparts are almost white.

In summer the adult is reddish-brown mottled with black on the upper parts; the wings and some of the coverts ashy-grey, and the upper breast greyish-white and striated. The lower breast and part of the abdomen are black, the size of the area very variable; the rest of the underparts are white. The upper parts are ashy-grey in winter, and underparts, except for an indistinct band on the breast, white. The black is lost gradually in autumn. In the young the brown upper parts are mottled with rufous, buff and black, and the dark head is streaked with rich brown; the breast is suffused with buff, and the white underparts are dotted and splashed with brown. The bill and legs are black. Length, 7·5 in. Wing, 4·6 in. Tarsus, 0·8 in. (*Plates 74, 75 and 169.*)

**Curlew Sandpiper**                                                  *Calidris ferruginea*

The Curlew Sandpiper breeds in arctic Siberia, and in winter ranges as far south as the Cape. To the British Isles it is a passage migrant, irregular in numbers, but sometimes abundant. It is very rare in north-west Scotland and scarce in the west of Ireland. Exceptionally, it occurs in winter. Indeed, though it is never present in any numbers except when migration is at its height, there is no month in the year in which it has not been recorded. Autumn immigration begins in July, and often birds are about until November; spring migration lasts from March until June, and there are scattered records for the other three months. Though the largest numbers visit the east and south coasts it is by no means rare in the west, and its frequent occurrence inland, especially in September, indicates more or less regular overland migration.

In spite of the long, curved bill and the fact that its legs are longer, it is not always easy to distinguish from the Dunlin, when with this and other waders it is feeding on the shore. When, however, the flock takes wing, its white upper tail-coverts show at once if the bird flies away from the observer; they are almost as striking as the lower back of the House Martin. Immature birds, and the majority that visit us in autumn are immature, have shorter and less curved bills than those which are adult. Even in mature birds the length of the bill varies. But at all ages the absence of dark streaks on the breast distinguishes this species from the Dunlin. In spring, when the summer dress is often partially attained, there is less difficulty, for it is even redder than the Knot. Its haunts are those of the Dunlin and Sanderling—the banks, mudflats and saltings. In some seasons very few birds are noticed; probably the force and direction of wind regulates its eastern or western route.

The flight of the Curlew Sandpiper is rapid and strong, more undulating, but less erratic than that of the Dunlin; yet large flocks will indulge in complicated but well-ordered evolutions. Its call on rising sounds like *twee, twee, twee*; it has also a whistling *twer-ret*, which perhaps is the note said to resemble that of the Dunlin. When feeding, a flock keeps up a low, rather musical twitter. On the shore it often runs quickly, but at other times is as deliberate as the Dunlin, especially when working the pools at low tide. Marine inverte-brates are its food on the shore, but inland it will eat freshwater molluscs and insects. The tanks in sewage farms attract it; over a hundred have been counted in autumn on a Cheshire farm.

In breeding plumage the Curlew Sandpiper has the upper parts chestnut, variegated with black and grey; the wing-coverts show white margins; the wings are ashy-grey; upper tail-coverts white barred with black. The reddish-chestnut underparts are but slightly marked with grey; the axillaries are white. The bill and legs are black. After the autumn moult the upper parts are ashy-brown, but faintly edged with white and buff on the back; the head is streaked, and there is a pale stripe over the eye; the upper tail-coverts and underparts are white. The young have the breast and flanks washed with buff, and a considerable amount of buff shows on the greyish-brown back. Length, 7·5 in. Wing, 5·1 in. Tarsus, 1·2 in. (*Plate 74*.)

### Semi-palmated Sandpiper                                 *Calidris pusilla*

This common North American wader has been recorded eight times in the British Isles. It resembles the Least Sandpiper, but is greyer and less rufous. In winter it is hard to distinguish from the Little Stint, but the bill is thicker and upper parts paler. The bill and legs are blackish. Length, 6 in.

### Sanderling                                               *Calidris alba*

In winter the Sanderling, which nests far north in arctic Asia and America, reaches the southern limits of Africa, America and Australia; the majority of the large numbers which visit our shores are halting on the long journey. September and May are the great Sanderling months, but there are some birds on the shore at all seasons; many winter here, and a few non-breeding birds linger through the summer.

This little wader, as its name suggests, prefers sand to mud, and is com-moner on the beach than in the estuary. Inland waters are sometimes visited on passage, but only by single birds or very small parties. Dunlins and Ringed Plovers are its companions, but it will mix with other waders, and when the big packs of Knots rest at high-water mark, there are generally a few 'little birds' with them. The Knots line the ripples, the tall Godwits stand in the water, but the Dunlins and Sanderlings fringe the shore side, sheltered by their larger companions. When the feeding Dunlins sedately probe the mud, the more energetic Sanderlings, recognised by short black bills and restless activity, race to and fro, chasing the sandhoppers, and even hurrying to capture washed-up molluscs. The fact that the Sanderling may be distinguished from all other small waders by the absence of a hind toe is of small value unless the bird is in the hand. But the grey, almost pearly winter dress, is whiter than that of any other wader; in a good light, winter Sanderlings look white spots on the yellow sand. If summer plumage has been partially attained it is more like a Dunlin with a short bill, but it never has the black on the underparts.

The quick flight, often with quivering wings, is rather like that of the Common Sandpiper, but the bird is not always in a hurry to fly. A number of Sanderlings will run along the beach more quickly than a man can walk, and finally skim out over the water to settle behind the disturber. As the bird runs it will often uplift its wings, holding them with the tips pointed skyward.

The first immigrants, usually in quite small parties, arrive about the middle of July, but in August the flocks are often large. They do not cling to the tideline, but scatter over the beach at low water, working the shallow, slowly draining pools. Most of the earlier birds show warm chestnut in their dress, and the birds of the year have necks and breasts tinged with buff. Later in August the chestnut markings are lost, and for a time adult birds have very black backs. Even in October a few birds retain traces of warm colour, for like the Dunlin this bird is irregular in its changes, and often moults slowly. The returning birds arrive towards the end of March, and in April many are still grey, but by early June most are in breeding plumage. Perhaps more than other waders, the Sanderling varies its diet of marine invertebrates with vegetable fragments, picking up bits of seaweed or the buds and tender shoots of littoral plants. The note in flight is a sharp *quik*, *quik*, and on the beach a rapid *wee, wee, whit*.

The upper parts in summer are warm chestnut, streaked and speckled on the head and breast, and variegated with black, grey and white on back and wings; the lateral tail-coverts and underparts below the breast are white. In winter the upper parts are delicate French grey with darker but not very distinct shaft streaks; the quills greyish-brown. A line above the eye and the underparts are white. Young in autumn are spotted with black, white and buff on the back and wings, and have the upper breast tinged with buff. The bill and legs are black. Length, 8 in. Wing, 4·7 in. Tarsus, 0·8 in (*Plates 75 and 77*.)

### Buff-breasted Sandpiper                                    *Tryngites subruficollis*

The Buff-breasted Sandpiper nests in arctic America and winters in South America. In recent years it has been recorded annually in the British Isles in very small numbers. Most are seen in autumn, though there are records for spring and summer.

The bird looks, both in flight and plumage, like a very small Reeve with a long neck, yellow legs and white ring round the eye. It is very tame and approachable and tends to 'freeze' or run rather than fly. It has a low trill and a clicking note. It prefers grassland to shores or marshes. The upper as well as the underparts are buff, the former with black and brown spots and mottles; the outer tail feathers are barred. Most of the under surface of the wing and the axillaries are white, but the secondaries and under wing-coverts are marbled with black, as are the inner webs of the quills. No wing-bar shows in flight. On immature birds the marbling is obscure and greyer, and the upper parts show white edgings. The bill is greenish-black; the legs are yellow. Length, 8 in. Wing, 5·25 in. Tarsus, 1·25 in.

**Broad-billed Sandpiper**                                 *Limicola falcinellus*

The Broad-billed Sandpiper breeds in northern Scandinavia and Russia, so it is surprising that, unlike several waders from arctic America, it has not, so far, been shown to be a regular visitor to the British Isles. There have been about thirty records in Great Britain and Ireland, mostly in autumn. It is a small, short-legged, long-billed, comparatively slow-moving wader which on passage is usually found on coastal creeks and saltmarshes rather than the open shore. The call is a deep *chr-r-eek*. The blackish bill is flat and broad, bent down towards the tip. In summer the dark brown head and mantle are streaked with buff, snipe-like in character, and there is a white superciliary stripe, forked behind the eye. The flight and central tail feathers are almost black; the outer tail feathers pale brown. The throat and breast are buffish-white streaked and speckled with black and brown; the abdomen is white. In winter the upper parts are ashy-grey, obscurely mottled, and the underparts white, but the white throat and eye-stripe are distinctive. A faint whitish wing-bar shows in flight. Length, 6·5 in. Tarsus, 0·75 in.

**Ruff**                                                    *Philomachus pugnax*

The Ruff, formerly an abundant nesting species in Britain, was practically wiped out during the first half of the 19th century; it was good to eat, and easy to kill when obsessed with its spring madness; as soon as it was rare the collectors took care that no eggs were hatched. By 1880 very few nesting pairs remained, and though birds have occasionally attempted to nest in the present century, most of the eggs laid are in private collections. The breeding range includes much of northern Europe, and in those parts of Holland where the bird is protected it is plentiful. In Britain it is now a regular though hardly abundant passage migrant in autumn and spring. As a spring visitor it is more frequent in the eastern counties than elsewhere, but it is by no means rare in autumn in the west and has become much more common in Ireland in recent years. It now winters in some numbers in several parts of England.

When, between April and the end of June, the male is in full dress, with frill and head tufts, he is unique, but no description of plumage can include all variations of colour that he sports; he is our most variable bird. The Reeve, the female, is more stable, and in winter the Ruff resembles her; she is a little like the Redshank, but can always be told by her short bill and, in flight, by the dark secondaries and the white patches on each side of the dark tail. The neatly patterned back and wings, due to the buff and grey feather margins, are particularly striking. Though often seen on the shore, the bird is frequent by inland waters, visiting lakes, reservoirs and sewage farms on migration, and lingering where food is plentiful. It feeds largely on insects and worms. It is quick on the wing, often rising high if flushed. In autumn it utters an occasional *few-it*, but it is generally a silent bird. Its carriage when feeding is erect, and if it is suspicious the neck is straightened, but it does not jerk like a nervous Redshank. It will probe the mud, though not as deeply as a Snipe. It is largely a nocturnal feeder but also feeds quite commonly by day.

Ruffs seem to be promiscuous in their mating. Each male usually has its own display ground where it scuttles around in a crouching posture, expands its ruff and quivers its wings, and where it may be visited by two or more Reeves. Actual fighting between males is not common but does occur. The nest may be concealed in long herbage, but in Holland is usually a hollow in short grass. The Reeve is not a very close sitter, and when approached runs quietly from the nest. The four variable eggs are laid in May or June. The nestlings have buff and chestnut down, streaked and barred with black, and frosted with white.

In spring the face of the Ruff is covered with rough warty and usually yellowish skin; on the head are two erectile bunches of long feathers, and a flowing frill hangs from the neck; the tufts and frill may be purple, red, brown, black or white, plain or barred. The variation also extends to the head, breast and upper parts generally. There is a conspicuous white patch on either side of the upper tail-coverts at all seasons, and the central tail-coverts are barred. The Reeve is greyish-brown, spotted with black, the grey-edged spots forming regular streaks on the mantle. The neck, flanks and breast are greyer and mottled with black; the rest of the underparts are white. In winter the sexes are alike, except in size, the male being much the larger; the upper parts are ashy, with dark spots, and underparts white, except on the neck and breast, which are streaked. The upper parts of the young are variegated with black, brown and buff, and the breast dull buff, but the same neatness of pattern shows on the back. The white tips of the secondaries form a narrow wing-bar. The bill, sometimes distinctly decurved, is brown or black, yellowish at the base. The legs are very variable—yellow, orange, flesh-coloured or grey. Male: Length, 12·5 in. Wing, 7·25 in. Tarsus, 2 in. Female: Length, 10 in. Wing, 6 in. Tarsus, 1·75 in. (*Plate 74.*)

Family RECURVIROSTRIDAE Avocets and Stilts

*Long or very long legs; fine bill straight or upturned; chiefly black and white plumage.*

**Avocet**                                                    *Recurvirostra avosetta*

The Avocet, like the Black-tailed Godwit, owes its re-establishment as a British breeding species to the energetic measures taken by the Royal Society for the Protection of Birds to provide not only protection from interference but also favourable and controlled conditions at the main breeding colonies. The bird had become extinct as a breeder in the British Isles by the middle of the 19th century. Two pairs nested in Ireland, and probably two in England, between 1938 and 1946, but effective re-colonisation began with four or five pairs on Havergate Island, Suffolk, in 1947. In spite of setbacks a colony of sixty pairs or more has become established there, and a smaller one has been formed at Minsmere, the other R.S.P.B. reserve on the Suffolk coast. Occasional pairs have nested elsewhere in east and south-east England. In recent years winter occurrences have become more frequent in various parts of England and Ireland and are now regular in the south-west. Abroad the Avocet breeds in several widely separated areas in Europe and moves south and west in winter. So black and white a bird, with a unique uptilted bill is easily recognised. Considering the delicacy of its bill, the Avocet is a plucky bird. It will drive gulls or other intruders from the vicinity of its nest, striking at them with its wings and feet but not with its bill. The birds fly over, yelping *kloot*, with long legs dangling, or crouching with wings half-spread, head low and shoulders hunched in an injury-feigning display. At the nest the bird utters a low *cut* or *gut*, quickly repeated. The Avocet is a bird of the ooze and shallow pool; it may, perhaps, occasionally probe the mud with its needle point, but the usual method of feeding is to scoop the surface with a side-to-side action, which as it walks leaves a wavy track behind. On land, insects are captured deftly in the upturned tip. Small crustaceans are scooped from the pools or skimmed from the mud. It wades deeply, its partly webbed feet preventing it from sinking in the ooze, but it swims well, alighting on water intentionally, and 'up-ends' like a duck. On the mud it often runs with wings uplifted, perhaps ready to fly if the feet sink too deeply. Like the Redshank it is a noisy bird when alarmed.

The Avocet nests in colonies, usually on open stretches of sand or mud, sometimes on water-surrounded tussocks. Colonies are, however, sometimes on grassland. More or less—usually less—litter encircles the nest hollow; often only a few dead bents or shells are collected. The normally four buff, black-spotted eggs are not unlike small eggs of the Oystercatcher.

The plumage of the mature bird is white and black, the latter confined to the head to below the eye, the back of the neck and parts of the back and wings. The distribution on the primaries and coverts gives a black-streaked appearance to the closed wing. The back is browner and edged with rufous on the immature bird. The bill is black, the legs blue-grey. Length, 18 in. Wing, 9 in. Tarsus, 3 in. (*Plates 76, 78 and 171.*)

### Black-winged Stilt                                   *Himantopus himantopus*

The Black-winged Stilt breeds in southern Europe and Asia, ranging eastwards from Spain and the south of France. It is partly migratory and some individuals occasionally wander northwards. By no means all the records for this species in the British Isles, which are widespread though much more numerous on the south and east coasts of England than elsewhere, are autumnal. There have been many records in April, May and June, and in 1945 two pairs nested on Nottingham sewage farm and reared young.

A novice could identify this very long-legged black and white sandpiper; 10 in. of leg on a 13-in. bird is not usual. The use of these long shanks is apparent when the bird is feeding; it wades deeply in the marshy pools, for it is a bird of the open marsh, and snaps right and left at the hovering aquatic flies, or catches the beetles and tadpoles when they come up for air. In flight it is a striking bird with its outstretched neck and bill and legs trailing behind; its wings are narrow, angled and pointed. When a nesting colony is invaded the birds will hover with dangling legs, uttering repeated cries of excitement. It is a very noisy bird with a high-pitched yelping call.

Breeding takes place in marshy situations. Some nests are built up in shallow water, while others are mere hollows in a tussock or on the ground, with the addition of a few scraps of material. Three or four dull, clay-coloured eggs with black spots and blotches are laid in May or June.

The back and wings of the adult male are glossy greenish-black and its tail greyish; the rest of the plumage is white except for a dark patch on the back of the head. This is absent in the female, which has dark brown upper parts. Juveniles and winter adults have dusky markings on the head and neck. The bill is black; the legs pink. Length, 13·5 in. Wing, 9·5 in. Tarsus, 4·7 in. (*Plate 78.*)

## Family PHALAROPODIDAE Phalaropes

*Slender bill; lobed anterior toes; regular swimmers; females larger and brighter than males.*

### Grey Phalarope                                    *Phalaropus fulicarius*

The imperfect web, forming distinct lateral lobes on the distal joints of the toes, is a character that separates the phalaropes from the other sandpipers. The Grey Phalarope has an arctic circumpolar range; the nearest breeding haunts to Britain are Greenland and Iceland. Its migration travels are often oceanic; it can rest when it wishes and find sufficient food for its needs in the surface-swimming marine organisms. On autumn migration large numbers must frequently if not regularly pass our islands, for if contrary winds—usually gales from the south-west—are encountered, many are forced upon the southern and south-western shores of England and Ireland. Spring visits, though recorded occasionally, are rare, and the bird has been noted in winter; the majority are seen between August and December.

Naturally most of the Grey Phalaropes seen in Britain are in autumn and winter dress, and a large number evidently immature. On the water the bird swims very lightly, looking more like a tiny gull than a sandpiper—a pearly-grey and white bird. So tame, or rather indifferent, it is, that inland, where it often settles to rest and feed on small ponds, it may be examined at close quarters. It swims in a zigzag course and with a quaint bobbing action of the head and neck, darting this way and that as it snaps at gnats and flies, its favourite food inland, though it will pick small molluscs from the weeds. It rises frequently, flitting rather than flying, and in the air darts from side to side like a wagtail, often hovering for a second. In these short flights the small lobed feet hang limply, but are trailed when longer distances are undertaken. The notes of the bird are variously described, but no combination of letters conveys the short, low whistle that the bird repeatedly gives when on the wing.

In winter the back is clear pearl-grey, the wings more smoky and mottled; the forehead, crown and underparts are white, and on the wing is a well-defined white bar. From the eye a dark streak runs back towards the slate nape. White edges show on the wing-coverts and dull streaks on the flanks. The bill is black, sometimes yellowish at the base; the legs dark grey. In summer the warm chestnut of the underparts is the most noticeable colour; the upper parts are brownish-black streaked with buff or chestnut. In autumn the chestnut is gradually lost. As a rule the young are redder on breast and wings than a bird which is losing breeding plumage. Length, 8·25 in. Wing, 5 in. Tarsus, 0·9 in. (*Plates 77 and 79.*)

### Red-necked Phalarope *Phalaropus lobatus*

The circumpolar breeding range of the Red-necked Phalarope is rather more southerly than that of the Grey. To a few of the northern isles of Scotland, one area on the mainland and one district in western Ireland it is a summer visitor, nesting in small and scattered colonies, but elsewhere only an uncommon passage migrant, more frequent in autumn than spring, and a rare winter visitor.

The diminutive size of the swimming Red-necked Phalarope is striking; it looks about half as big as a Dabchick. It swims as buoyantly as the Grey, with the same restless, jerky energy, darting from side to side after insects. Its slender sandpiper head and neck bob as it swims—wonderfully strongly for so small a bird. Characteristically tame or indifferent to the presence of man, it will alight on a wayside pond and feed with confidence. The colour scheme of the summer dress is very neat, a combination of slate-grey, fox-red and white. A striking feature is the contrast between the white chin and the rich chestnut throat, and the long, slender bill. The white of the underparts runs up to a peak on the breast. In winter plumage it is not easily distinguished from the Grey Phalarope, but its upper parts are rather darker and more streaked, the white wing-bar shows up more clearly in flight, and the bill is longer and thinner. In flight a long angled white stripe—the edges of the coverts—crosses the open wing. A feeding bird utters a short weak pipe—*pleep, pleep*. Other notes are described, including a trill like the Ringed Plover's when courting. On the water both Phalaropes will sometimes swing round and round as if on a pivot, the effect being to stir up the bottom or draw insects and crustaceans into the eddy formed by the movement. When bathing, the bird will swing the body to and fro, hinged on the legs, or quaintly roll from side to side, as it throws the water over the plumage.

The Red-necked Phalarope arrives at its British breeding haunts late in May and seldom remains after the end of August. It is never numerous on passage. The female usually courts and often bullies the male; but even when the male has yielded to the wiles of a successful suitor, he is not in a hurry to take over his effeminate duties; Miss Turner watched one being conducted by his mate, and whenever he strove to have a short nap she literally 'hen-pecked' him into activity. The nest is as a rule well concealed, and after the four eggs are laid, most if not all the incubation is performed by the male. The nestlings, clad at first in golden down which soon pales, have two white stripes on their darker backs. They are cared for by the cock bird, though the hen will mount guard and warn him to slip off the nest if danger threatens, when he will join her on the water and pretend to feed.

In summer the adult has head, lower neck and most of the upper parts slate-grey, darkest on the back where there are buff edges to some of the feathers. The chin, eye-spot and abdomen are white, and on the neck, extending to the lower part of the face, is a rich chestnut band. The bill is almost black; the legs blue-grey. The male is duller than the female. The autumn moult is gradual and in winter the sexes are alike. The forehead, cheeks, throat and breast are then white. The back of the head and eye-streak are dark brown, and the upper parts greyish marked with white and buff. The backs and wings of young birds are warmer—more buff and chestnut—than in old birds in winter dress. Length, 7·5 in. Wing, 4·4 in. Tarsus, 0·8 in. (*Plates 77 and 169.*)

**Wilson's Phalarope**                                                 *Phalaropus tricolor*
This Phalarope, which breeds in Canada and the United States and migrates to South America, has occurred over twenty times in the British Isles since it was first recorded in 1954. At all seasons it can be distinguished from other phalaropes by its white rump and absence of a white wing-bar. In flight it resembles the Lesser Yellow-legs, but on the ground can be identified by its shorter legs and unspotted mantle. In winter the upper parts are pale grey, underparts, rump and tail white, legs yellowish. In summer there are blackish and chestnut markings on the neck and back, duller in the male; the long slender bill is black, the thick legs dark in summer, yellowish in winter. Length, 9 in. (*Plate 79.*)


## Family BURHINIDAE Thick-knees

*Bill short and straight; legs long, with three toes united to second joint.*

**Stone Curlew**                                                     *Burhinus oedicnemus*
The Stone Curlew in many ways resembles the plovers, but in others—its choice of habitat, for instance—is more of a bustard. It is found in suitable places in central and southern Europe, and is a partial migrant. Even in

England, where it is normally a summer visitor, some remain to winter, usually in Cornwall and Devon. To Scotland and Ireland it is only a wanderer, and in eastern and southern England is decidedly local, haunting only wide, open spaces—wolds, chalk-downs and the 'brecks' of Norfolk and Suffolk. The increased use of marginal land for agriculture and forestry during and after the 1939–45 war has greatly reduced the breeding population of Stone Curlews in England, and the status of the species in several of its former strongholds is now precarious.

The large, bright yellow eye of the Stone Curlew is its most salient character; it attracts the eye when the surroundings obliterate the lines of the motionless bird. It is a long-legged, large plover, giving an impression of a round head framing a very round eye. Whether its colour hides it or gives it away depends entirely upon the nature of the ground, but in most of its usual haunts it is a very inconspicuous bird.

In flight the double wing-bar is very noticeable, and a white line along the wing is visible when the bird is at rest. If disturbed in the daytime the flight is direct and low, but at night, and especially in autumn, it is often erratic. The bird will run quickly, with head low, but neck drawn in, for a long distance before taking wing.

Birds occasionally arrive in March, but April is the usual month; most leave in October. Though not continuously gregarious, several pairs will nest in one restricted area, but in autumn, shortly before departure, the social habit becomes marked. At these autumn gatherings the birds are very lively, and go through a performance which, if in spring, would be called nuptial display; the birds run rapidly with uplifted wings or posture as if courting.

Normally the Stone Curlew is crepuscular, and, certainly on moonlight nights, nocturnal. In the daytime it is a shy, silent, secretive bird, but at dusk it becomes lively, and its weird, wailing, but musical calls are responsible for its name Curlew. It feeds on nocturnal insects, but does not refuse a frog or mouse.

The nest is a scratched hollow and the lining seldom more than a collection of rabbit-droppings, the number of these varying considerably. The ground colour of the two—seldom more—eggs, usually laid late in April, varies from buff to stone-colour, and the markings may be only specks and blotches or a network of lines. On stony ground, a favourite site, the eggs are difficult to see; indeed, from the egg onward the life of the Stone Curlew is spent in hiding itself from view. The crouching habit—that of lying still and trusting to colour and form to produce invisibility—is assumed as soon as the chick is hatched, but at first is imperfect.

The newly hatched bird is a naturally protected ball of sandy down, patterned with black, but when it lies still in the presence of an imagined enemy it crouches in the position adopted by many other young plovers, and not for some days does it flatten itself with outstretched neck in the characteristic attitude of older juveniles and adult birds. When lying prone these shammers will allow themselves to be touched or even lifted without moving. The parent birds slip away and wisely leave the motionless young, unlike many real plovers, which by their noisy or fussy behaviour reveal the presence of eggs or young.

The adult Stone Curlew of either sex is sandy-brown, streaked with dark brown; the chin, throat, a broad line below the eye and a narrow one above it, are white. The neck, breast and flanks are paler, and the abdomen almost white and unstreaked; the under tail-coverts are reddish-buff. There are two white bars along the wing, contrasting with the dark primaries. The bill is yellow, black at the tip, the legs greenish-yellow and the irides golden-yellow. Young birds have the bars on the tail more distinct than when mature. Length, 16 in. Wing, 9·5 in. Tarsus, 3 in. (*Plates 77 and 169.*)

## Family GLARIOLIDAE Pratincoles and Coursers

*Pratincoles: bill short and curved; wings long; legs long; hind toe present, middle and outer toes connected.*
*Coursers: bill short and decurved; three toes, the middle elongated.*

**Pratincole**                                    *Glareola pratincola*
As an irregular wanderer from southern Europe or western Asia, the Pratincole has occurred over forty times in England, Scotland and the northern islands. Most of the records are from southern and eastern counties. Normally it winters in Africa.

The long, narrow wings and forked tail, together with the swift, sustained flight, suggested the Swallow to Linnaeus; but in general appearance, and in its harsh angry voice if its breeding colony is invaded, it has much in common with the terns. The long legs and excellent running power of the Pratincole are those of a plover; it is a tern-like plover with a short, curved bill. The forked tail alone is enough to put it apart from other plovers, and, as if to emphasise this character, it jerks its tail up and down when at rest. The times of its appearance in Britain are varied, but most records are for spring and autumn. There is a black line bordering the dull yellow chin and upper throat. The general colour of the mature bird is clove-brown on the upper parts, yellower brown on the breast, and white on the abdomen; the tips of the secondaries and the base of the tail are also white. Under the wing the axillaries and coverts are reddish-brown, and in flight this is sufficient to distinguish it from the only other pratincole on the British list. The bill is dark brown, red at the base; the legs are blackish. Young birds have bars of black and buff on the back and wings. Length, 10 in. Wing, 7·5 in. Tarsus, 1·25 in. (*Plate 78.*)

**Black-winged Pratincole**                                    *Glareola nordmanni*
The range of the Black-winged Pratincole is rather more easterly than that of the Pratincole, though both occur in south-eastern Europe and western

Siberia. A few have been identified in the British Isles. It is difficult to distinguish from the Pratincole in the field. The main points of difference are that the axillaries and under wing-coverts are black, and the secondaries lack white tips. From above the wings look almost uniformly dark compared with the grey and white pattern of the other bird. Length, 10 in.

## Cream-coloured Courser                *Cursorius cursor*

The Cream-coloured Courser is an inhabitant of sandy deserts in Africa and southern Asia, but wanders in autumn into Europe, and some have reached the British Isles, chiefly the eastern and southern coastal counties of England. In recent years its visits have become increasingly rare, with an average of only two or three in a decade.

The English name of this bird is descriptive; it runs well and is noticeably light coloured. It is easy to identify; there is no mistaking the sandy colour, the long, almost white legs, curved bill and white and black stripes on face and neck. Being a desert bird, it naturally remains on our sandy shores; it has seldom been noticed far from the coast, where it eats insects and small molluscs. On the wing it is strong and swift, and the contrast between the black wing feathers and the rich buff upper parts when it rises is striking. The axillaries and under wing-coverts are black and show in flight. The note, uttered on the ground, either is a short *wutt* or a double *wutt-quoi*.

On the nape of the adult Cream-coloured Courser is a slate-blue patch, and the back of the head has a line of black. Below this is a white streak passing from above the eye down the side of the neck, and from the eye to the nape a blackish line. The primaries and under surface of the wing are black, contrasting with the pale, sandy body plumage. The young bird has the eye-streak buff, and the breast and back marked with wavy brown lines. The bill is dark brown, the legs creamy or dull white. Length, 9 in. (*Plate 78.*)

## Family STERCORARIIDAE Skuas

*Hook-tipped bill with cere; narrow, angled wings; usually dark plumage.*

### Great Skua                *Stercorarius skua*

Skuas differ in form and habits from gulls and terns; the strongly hooked bill has a horny 'cere', and the curved claws are sharp; the birds look predacious, though they are not regular flesh-eaters, and are piratical rather than parasitical, robbing others of their food. Largest, fiercest and most powerful is the Great Skua, a bird of the North Atlantic, nesting in Iceland, the Faeroes, Shetland, Orkney, the outer Hebrides and occasionally the Scottish mainland. In autumn these haunts are deserted and the bird becomes pelagic, only occasionally visiting the shore. On passage it may be seen off any of our shores, but more often in the North Sea and off south-west Ireland than elsewhere. The breeding stations are returned to in March or April.

The Great Skua is a large, heavily built bird, umber-brown in general colour, about the size of a Herring Gull; at a distance it might be taken for a young Herring or Lesser Black-back in mottled plumage. It is, however, darker and browner—less grey—and on the outspread wing is a large white patch, formed by the white basal inner webs of the primaries. In all the skuas the central tail feathers are elongated; in the 'Bonxie', as the bird is called in Shetland, they only just project beyond the outer ones, yet sufficiently to give a rounded appearance to the tail. The white patch may be concealed by the flank feathers when the wing is closed, but shows immediately the bird rises. Normally the Great Skua has a gull-like, drifting, aimless flight, but it becomes direct and powerful when the bird has sighted chance of food, a clamorous cloud of gulls harrying an unlucky shoal of fish. When from amongst the flock it has singled out some victim, gull or tern, its true speed and aerial agility is shown. It has also a gliding flight, often associated with courtship; with wings raised at an angle of about 45°, it floats like a harrier. The method of obtaining a meal, shared by other skuas, is to select its victim and give chase with ferocity and terrifying cries, following every turn and dodge relentlessly, threatening to strike with wing, beak and foot. As a rule, at any rate, there is no need actually to buffet the screaming fugitive, which sooner or later reluctantly disgorges its latest meal, sometimes half digested, or the fish it has just captured. Instantly the Skua stoops like a falcon, usually catching the fish before it strikes the water. The cry during the chase is *skeerr* or *skua*; from this the name is derived; in ordinary flight it has a deep gull note, and a barking cry of alarm or anger. Any gull or tern is hunted. Vicariously caught fish are not the only food of the Great Skua, for it will pick up offal, gorge on a carcase, and even slay smaller birds and devour them; it is also a robber of the eggs and young of other birds.

In Shetland the shepherds look upon it as a friend, for it boldly drives away other predatory species, even attacking and defeating the eagles; thus it unconsciously protects the flocks. The nest is usually a trodden depression in ling or rough grass, somewhat loosely built of grass, and littered around with feathers, remains of recent meals and cast-up pellets of feathers, scales and bones. Two eggs, light or dark olive-brown or buff, sparsely spotted with darker brown and grey, are laid late in May. The down of the nestlings is buffish-sepia, and is without distinct markings; the bill and legs are leaden. In defence of eggs or young the Great Skua is at its best, boldly attacking an invader of its territory, though by no means always striking, but sweeping past with a rush of wings. The legs are lowered threateningly when the screaming bird attacks.

The adult bird has its umber-brown plumage streaked and speckled with yellowish-brown, and the neck is lighter than the head and back; the underparts are more cinnamon-brown. The outer primaries are white at the base, but this is less noticeable in juveniles. The bill and legs are black. Length, 22–25 in. Wing, 16 in. Tarsus, 2·5 in. (*Plates 82, 83 and 170.*)

**Arctic Skua** *Stercorarius parasiticus*

The Arctic Skua is a circumpolar bird, but though it nests in the arctic in both hemispheres, its range extends to northern Scotland; in winter the bird inhabits warmer seas, but though recorded far south, is normally a northern species. It nests in colonies in the north of Scotland, the Orkney and Shetland Isles and some of the Hebrides. On migration it is at times noticed in extraordinary numbers, especially on the east coast, the most extensive movements being after or during stormy weather. Though usually offshore, the autumnal passage on the west coast of England from August to October is regular though less extensive than in the east.

The Arctic or Richardson's Skua, is dimorphic, having more or less stable dark and light forms which inter-breed. It is, however, a variable bird, and all manner of intermediate forms occur. The dark phase is perhaps the commoner in our seas, and in this the bird resembles a small Great Skua with much more elongated and pointed central tail feathers, projecting in adult birds about 3 in. beyond the others. It is smaller than the Pomarine, which has the elongated feathers rounded, and larger than the Long-tailed, which has very much longer streamers. Immature birds, before the tails have lengthened, are very puzzling, especially when in flight.

On the wing the Arctic Skua is graceful, its flight being steady and regular, varied with hawk-like glides, but when chasing a gull, tern or diving bird, for it victimises the Guillemot and Puffin, it is erratic, swift and powerful. When the hunted bird throws up food, the swoop of the Skua is wonderfully smart, yet if it misses the desired tit-bit it seldom tries to recover it from the water, but turns its attention to another victim. It frequently hunts in couples, one bird worrying its dupe and the other fielding the food, but often a single Skua follows a tern. When, however, a shoal of sand-eels or fry has attracted large numbers of gulls, terns and auks three or four Arctic Skuas will attend on the outskirts of the noisy crowd, commandeering whenever opportunity offers. On the moors insects and berries are eaten, and it is said that small waders are killed and devoured. A light, even white, patch may be seen at the base of the primaries of the flying bird. The ordinary call is well described as mewing, but it is sharper and more ferocious when the bird is engaged in piracy.

The Arctic Skua is a moorland nester; nests in colonies are scattered and seldom close together. The nest is little more than a hollow scraped or flattened in the grass or heather, and has very little, if any, lining. The eggs, laid at the end of May or in June, are usually two in number, and are dark or light olive-green or brown in ground, blotched and suffused with darker brown and underlying grey. An invader on the moor may be attacked and struck, usually with the feet, but 'injury-feigning' near the nest is not uncommon. As the seemingly damaged bird struggles along the ground it beats with the extended wing, exhibiting the white shafts. The nestling is greyish-brown, and shows little indication of the phase into which it will develop.

The dark phase is dark brown, with a distinct slate tinge in many examples, darkest on the head and paler beneath, but often showing yellow on the ear-coverts. The light birds have the neck and underparts white, often with a creamy or pale brown band across the breast, and at times with all the white suffused with cream. Light birds may have the back of the neck suffused or streaked with yellow. Immature birds of either form are barred and streaked with brown and reddish-buff, and the barring is most noticeable on the lower back. The bill and legs are black. Length, 18 in. Wing, 13 in. Tarsus, 1·4 in. (*Plates 80, 81 and 170.*)

### Pomarine Skua                                    *Stercorarius pomarinus*

The Pomarine or Pomatorhine Skua is another skua with an arctic circumpolar range and a southward pelagic migration in autumn. It visits our shores in autumn, rarely in spring, and young birds have been observed in summer; as a winter visitor it occurs at sea near the south coast. In the so-called skua-years many hundreds have been driven shoreward, and not a few picked up inland. Though looked upon as irregular in its visits, it appears that this and other species migrate normally at some distance from the land; adverse conditions explain their appearance on the shore.

The Pomarine is intermediate in size between the Great and Arctic Skua, and, though it occasionally exhibits dimorphism, is usually of the same brown and whitish pattern as the Long-tailed and light phase of the Arctic. The tail of the mature bird differs from that of all others, for not only are the two central feathers rounded at their tips, but they are twisted so that they are at an angle, sometimes almost a right angle, to the outer feathers. The effect is curious, and when in its chase the bird hovers over its dodging victim, the tail is expanded or closed like a fan. When open it looks square, the twist of the shafts of the streamers giving them a paddled-shaped appearance as they project beyond the fanned-out outer feathers, but the tips of these projecting feathers are not infrequently broken off. In young birds the central feathers are but little elongated. The flight is hardly as free and rollicking as that of the Arctic, nor so graceful as the Long-tailed Skua's, but its piratical habits are the same. It is said to fish at times for itself, and will feed on carrion, small birds and ships' refuse. The note is a harsh *whichyew*.

The mature bird of the light type has the head black on crown and nape, and the cheeks and neck suffused with yellow. The back, wings and tail are umber-brown; the breast and front of neck white and the lower abdomen brown. Dark phase adults have blackish-brown upper and underparts, but both types show white bases to the primaries in flight. Immature birds are brown above and below, barred and mottled with rufous and lighter markings. The bill in adults is greyish-black, browner in young birds; the legs brown. Length, 21 in. Wing, 14·5 in. Tarsus, 2 in. (*Plate 81.*)

### Long-tailed Skua                                *Stercorarius longicaudus*

The Long-tailed or Buffon's Skua has a circumpolar range and in winter is not met with far south in northern Atlantic and Pacific oceans. It is less frequent than the Pomarine and much rarer than the Arctic Skua, appearing as a passage migrant in autumn, and occasionally in spring, off our shores and inland. At times, in 'skua years', numbers arrive, stormy weather causing invasions; the greatest numbers have been observed on the east coast from Yorkshire northward, but there are scattered records from all parts.

Long-tailed Skua is a descriptive name, for the literally outstanding feature of the mature bird is the extraordinary elongation of the two central tail feathers, which project for from 6 to 9 in. beyond the others. In general colour pattern it resembles the light phase of the Arctic Skua, but is rather greyer; dimorphism has been recorded in this species, but it is less variable than the Arctic. In young birds, and all skuas take some years to attain perfect plumage, the streamers are shorter, and, according to some authorities, are more obtuse at the tip than in the Arctic, but this is difficult to see in a living bird. The rule, however, that the shafts of the two outer primaries only are white, the others dusky, holds good in most cases. The Long-tailed is the smallest and most elegant of the skuas; its flight is lighter and more graceful; it glides through the air without effort, and often hovers like a tern. Indeed, there is much that is suggestive of a tern in its build and behaviour.

The bird swims buoyantly, holding the neck straight; indeed, on land as well as water the skuas generally have an alert pose, the neck held at right angles to the horizontal body, though they are by no means nervous or shy. Piratical feeding habits are common with this species; terns and Kittiwakes are most tormented; the Long-tailed Skua enjoys the chase, and will hunt small waders and even its own kind for pure love of sport. Indeed, during one invasion of this and the Pomarine, the two were observed chasing one another and occasionally nipping off the ends of the pursued bird's streamers. On the wing the Long-tailed seems to be less noisy than other skuas. It varies its second-hand fish diet with insects, crustaceans and worms.

The mature bird has the upper parts of the head dark brown, and the back, wings and tail shading from dark grey to slaty-brown; the rest of the plumage is whitish, purest on the neck and breast, tinged with yellow on the cheeks, and with greyish-brown below the breast. The bill is blackish at the tip, blue-tinged at the cere, the legs greyish-olive. Immature birds are profusely barred with brown and grey on the upper parts, but are less rufous than Arctics. Length, 21in. Wing, 12·5 in. Tarsus, 1·8 in. (*Plate 81.*)

## Family LARIDAE Gulls and Terns

*Wings long; anterior toes webbed; bill hooked at tip (gulls), or long and pointed (terns); body plumage usually white in adults.*

### Ivory Gull                                        *Pagophila eburnea*

The Ivory Gull is a circumpolar breeding bird which is almost an arctic resident, but wanders south occasionally, and has reached most parts of our islands, though it is best known in the Orkneys and Shetlands. Though a winter visitor, it has remained as late as June; unlike the Sabine's Gull, as many mature as immature birds are met with.

This arctic gull is tern-like in its flight and in its harsh cry. Fish, lemmings, crustaceans and garbage are eaten. Like other arctic birds it is foolishly confiding when it visits Britain.

In its adult dress, whether in summer or winter, this gull is white, the white mantle distinguishing it from all others. The white of immature birds is spotted with dark grey or black to a variable degree; in some the upper parts only are sparsely spotted, but in others the underparts are similarly marked. The primaries have black tips and the tail a subterminal brown-black band. The bill is greenish-grey with a reddish-yellow tip; the legs are very dark grey; the eye-rims red. Length, 18 in. (*Plate 86.*)

## Great Black-backed Gull                                  *Larus marinus*

The Great Black-backed Gull breeds on the coasts of northern Europe and migrates south in winter, some reaching the Mediterranean. It breeds plentifully in Scotland, the Scottish islands, north and west Ireland, including some inland localities, and on the west coast of England and Wales, where it nests chiefly on islands. There has been a striking increase in breeding numbers in all these areas in the present century, but the bird is still scarce or absent as a nesting species on the east coast of Great Britain. In winter it is present in estuaries and along the coast in large numbers for there is a large-scale immigration in autumn. The migrants arrive in East Anglia from mid August, and ringing recoveries show that many of them come from Norway.

The size of the bird and its very dark mantle distinguish it from the British Lesser Black-back and all other gulls, but it is unsafe to go by the colour of the mantle alone, as it is slate-black in this species and in the Scandinavian Lesser Black-back. When resting with other gulls on the banks or sand it stands, a black-backed giant, dwarfing even the Herring Gulls, and making the Black-headeds look mere pygmies. Considering its tyrannical and predacious habits, it is extraordinary how peacefully small gulls will stand or rest beside it; it is a confirmed bird-eater. On the wing its movements are easy and deliberate; it sails lightly in spite of its bulk, and often soars to an immense height.

In recent years the Great Black-back has become increasingly common inland as a scavenger. The wintering population of the London area alone is well over a thousand, and hundreds are to be found in the industrial regions of East Lancashire, the West Riding of Yorkshire and the Midlands, feeding at refuse tips by day and flighting to neighbouring reservoirs to roost.

The hoarse, barking *agh, agh, agh*, differs from the notes of other gulls, and the deep guttural, angry barks, *ugh, ugh*, of adults in alarm near the nest are more emphatic than the normal note. The challenge, however, uttered with head raised, differs but little from that of its congeners. After this vociferous call, the bird lowers the head below the level of the raised shoulders, and peers from side to side as if expecting a reply. All gulls are omnivorous, but the

Great Black-back prefers its meals to be of flesh, either recent or ancient. A dead rat, dog or whale is alike acceptable to the 'Corpse-eater'; where the carcase is, there will the Black-backs gather, keeping the smaller fry away. This bird will pounce upon and half devour the 'cripple' before the wildfowler can gather it; it ruthlessly slays its neighbours, the Puffins and Shearwaters, tearing out their entrails and leaving the rest for the rats; it has been known to bolt whole large birds such as Redshank and Little Auk. It occasionally captures and swallows small birds on the wing.

In England and Wales this bird usually nests singly on the top of some stack or rocky headland, but in Ireland and Scotland there are some large colonies. A few pairs often nest in the centre of a colony of Lesser Black-backs, including one on the Pennines more than ten miles from the sea. The nest is an untidy collection of seaweed, thrift and grass torn up by the roots, sticks and litter, placed either on turf or the bare rock. The two or three eggs are buff or olive, usually boldly but not profusely spotted with brown and grey; they are laid in May or early June. The nestling, which is fed by regurgitation, has pale-grey, often yellowish down, boldly spotted with black. At an early age it leaves the nest and runs for shelter if approached.

The quills and scapulars of the mature bird are white tipped; the second primary usually has a 'mirror'. The rest of the wings and back are slate-black; all other parts white. The bill is yellow with red on the deeply angled under mandible; the orbits are red. The legs vary from flesh colour to dull white. In winter there are brownish-grey streaks on head and neck. In the first plumage of dappled brown and grey, the bird is paler than the young Herring Gull, but in its second year there is some indication of the dark mantle. Maturity is usually reached about the fourth year; the bill changes from blackish-grey to yellow, but during the change shows a pinkish tinge at the base. Length, 29 in. Wing, 19 in. Tarsus, 3 in. (*Plates 82, 84 and 170*.)

### Lesser Black-backed Gull
*Larus fuscus*

The status of the Lesser Black-backed Gull in the British Isles has changed to a remarkable extent since about 1940. Before 1930 it was almost entirely a summer visitor to Britain, wintering on the coasts of Spain, Portugal and north-west Africa, and only a few individuals were seen in the British Isles in midwinter. An enquiry by the British Trust for Ornithology in the winter of 1949–50 found about 300 resident birds, nearly all adults; ten years later the total had increased to 2800, and by 1964 over 7000 were reported roosting on inland waters in England alone. The great majority of these gulls spent the winter on the outskirts of big industrial areas, especially in north-west England, the west Midlands and London, where refuse and offal tips provided them with food. However, many of our birds are still migratory, and only a very small proportion of juveniles spend their first winter in the British Isles.

The largest nesting colonies are in north-west England, Wales, and the western side of Scotland and Ireland. There are colonies on moorland some distance from the sea, and for some years there was a considerable colony of mixed Lesser Black-backs and Herring Gulls on a factory roof twenty miles from the sea in south Wales; other inland nests on buildings have been recorded. This gull breeds in northern Europe as far south as Brittany. Those nesting in Scandinavia have darker wings and mantles than British birds, the same shade as the Great Black-back. Birds of this race appear as passage migrants in the British Isles, both in spring and autumn, sometimes in flocks of fifty or more on the east coast.

The Lesser Black-back is smaller and slighter in build and bill than the Great Black-back, but differs from both this and the Herring Gull, at least in spring and summer, in its yellow legs. However, it should be noticed that in winter the yellow is usually much paler and some adults as well as immatures have whitish or flesh-coloured legs. The mantle of the British Lesser Black-back is noticeably lighter in shade than that of the Great Black-back at all seasons. In immature plumage, though at first it closely resembles the Herring at the same age, the darker mantle soon becomes apparent. In spring and summer, especially near nesting colonies, this gull is common, though never as abundant as the Herring Gull, but in spring and autumn it is a far more familiar bird inland, for there are regular overland as well as coastal migratory movements. From early February to mid June birds are going north, many of the later arrivals being immature, and from June to December going south. The gulls normally travel singly or in small parties, but flocks of fifty or more are seen on some inland routes. Some migrants closely follow the coastline, especially in autumn on the east coast, but there is a heavy volume of inland migration and this seems to be increasing with the growing use of refuse tips as a source of food. Large numbers of these gulls are now seen both in spring and autumn in the West Midlands and the Trent valley.

The Lesser Black-back joins the Herring Gull in its watchful and sustained flights behind steamers, remaining on the wing for hours, also in the frenzied raids on shoals of fish, when the water is churned by the plunging and superficial dives of the excited birds, and the air rings with their cries; it is an equally useful scavenger in rivers and harbours, but it is more of a fish-eater than the Herring Gull. It is as omnivorous as the commoner bird, but has not acquired its habit of dropping shell-fish to smash them. At its nesting colonies the disembowelled corpses of Puffins and Shearwaters prove it to be almost as murderous as its larger relative. It delights, too, in a large carcase, only yielding its place to the Great Black-back. Its manner of flight, its pose on land and its habit of perching on an elevation agree with the Herring Gull, but its calls differ slightly. The loud *ky-eoh* and the angry *hak-ak-ak*, or *wow-ow-ow*, when it swoops with a rush toward the head of an intruder, sound more ferocious than the usual wails of the Herring Gull; but both birds have a wailing mew and an irate bark. The normal *ow* or *owch* is deeper and more melancholy than the call of the other bird.

Though odd pairs of Lessers nest with Herring Gulls, and there is a mixed colony of several thousand pairs of each species on Walney Island, Lancashire, it usually keeps in a colony by itself. Loud though the clamour is when a colony of the latter bird is invaded, the medley of angry voices and the frequent threatening swoop of an anxious parent is more marked on Black-back ground. The bird may be slighter in build and weaker in bill than the Herring Gull, but it is often bolder. Grassy islands and peat mosses are more usual nesting sites than steep cliffs, and on rocky coasts the Lesser Black-back nests on the cliff tops rather than with the Herring Gull on the ledges. The nests vary in size and construction, but though often smaller, closely resemble those of its constant neighbour. The eggs, two or three in number, are sometimes greenish, but usually stone-coloured or buff in ground, and boldly spotted; they are laid in May. There is no certain distinction between the mottled nestlings and those of the Herring Gull; the down, often greyish, is sometimes warm in tint, but varies greatly. At first the juveniles of the Herring and Lesser Black-backed Gulls can usually only be distinguished by close examination, which reveals the darker inner primaries of the Lesser Black-back, but after a moult or two the darker mantle becomes evident. The bill grows yellower, the black remaining on the angle until replaced by red when almost mature plumage is attained, and the banded tail becomes mottled before it is finally pure after three to four years.

The adult bird, slate-grey and white, has 'mirrors' on the first two primaries; the bill is yellow with red on the angle, the legs and irides are yellow and the orbital ring vermilion. In winter the head and neck are streaked with grey, and in many birds the leg colour fades to whitish or flesh colour. Length, 22 in. Wing, 16 in. Tarsus, 2·6 in. (*Plates 84, 85 and 170.*)

**Herring Gull**                                                    *Larus argentatus*

Though it is increasingly abundant inland, the Herring Gull is the typical gull of the British coast. It nests on all suitable cliffs and islands, on Scottish lochs and a few inland moors. There has been a remarkable increase in the number and size of breeding colonies all over the British Isles in the present century. The gulleries on Puffin Island, North Wales, and Walney Island, Lancashire, with over 10,000 pairs each, are especially noteworthy. The British Herring Gull is resident; although there is some dispersal after the breeding season very few British-ringed birds have been recovered abroad. On the other hand there is evidence of considerable immigration in autumn from northern Europe.

The Herring Gull roughly agrees with the Lesser Black-backed in size, but its mantle is pearl-grey, not dark, and its legs flesh-coloured, not yellow, as in the latter bird. Its black outer primaries have 'mirrors' like those of the Common Gull, but they have white tips and grey inner edges; the yellow bill has a red mark or splash on the angled lower mandible. Mottled brown birds in various stages of immaturity, for full plumage is not attained until the fourth or fifth year, are common at all seasons, and through an optical illusion appear larger than the grey and white old birds. Only by careful expert examination can the first-year young be distinguished from those of the Lesser Black-backed Gull, though as they grow the paler mantle serves to distinguish them.

The flight of the Herring Gull is typical of all the larger gulls, and can be studied when clouds of these birds follow in a steamer's wake. The gull drifts or sails, without noticeable wing action, even in the teeth of the wind, automatically adjusting its pose so as to benefit from every change of air current; thus it will poise above the stern, travelling exactly at the rate of the ship, and glancing with yellow eye to right or left, ready to swoop to pick up from the waves any morsel thrown over or churned to the surface by the screw. After it has settled and been left far behind it rises, and in a few strong but never hurried wing-beats recovers its position and again sails. One can frequently see birds drop one foot as if to adjust the balance while they scratch the beak with the other, and neither lose altitude nor speed. Indeed, all its graceful aerial actions are perfectly controlled. Often a number will rise for high flights, wheeling, mere specks in the sky. With the Black-headed it comes to harbours and coastal towns, wrangling amongst the fishing boats for the garbage and offal, a useful scavenger. In the Mersey it floats with the tide past the anchored liners, flying back again and again to keep a watch for the appearance of cook or steward disposing of scraps. In rows it lines the dock sheds, or perches on the chimneys and pinnacles of high buildings. On its native cliffs it will stand, looking seaward, and at towns where the houses crest the cliffs it is just as ready to use the roof parapet. In some seaside resorts—Llandudno, for example—the charity of visitors is rewarded by confident familiarity. The bird usually rests on one leg, the long body horizontal, the head sunk in the shoulders, and when on the beach, head to wind.

Many of its feeding habits are similar to those of the Common Gull: it drops crabs and molluscs to smash them; it also dances in wet sand or at the edge of the waves. It will occasionally dive for food, though somewhat awkwardly. On fields near the shore it follows the plough, but on cultivated land does not confine its attention to 'pests', for its cast-up pellets, which with broken shells and claws of crabs litter the cliff-top, often contain husks of oats or other grain. It frequents refuse tips in hundreds, even far inland, and roosts with other gulls on inland waters. All gulls are egg-robbers, looting unguarded nests of other sea-birds, and occasionally scouring the moors and fields; the Herring Gull is no exception. The bird has a loud and strident voice, which may trail off into a mournful wail; usual more cheerful notes are a plaintive, cat-like mew and a round full *hoh, hoh, hoh*. It has a defiant *kehoh*, and a harsh *ha, ha, ha*, a threat rather than alarm note when the breeding colony is invaded, but when the bird is specially annoyed this becomes a barking and rapid *wow, ow, ow*. The challenge, uttered with uplifted, wide-open beak, is clear and ringing.

The nests are in colonies on the grassy slopes and ledges of high cliffs, on grassy islands or among sand dunes. At times the nest is sheltered by a rock, but is often in the open. In some coastal towns occasional nests, and even regular colonies, are found on the roofs of houses and other buildings.

The nests are built of a variable quantity of roots, grass and seaweed, and often have a little sheep's wool mixed in the lining; they are shallow and untidy as a rule. Three is the normal number of eggs, which are dark olive or pale brown, plentifully blotched with dark brown. Incubation begins about the middle of May. The nestlings have dark markings on their brown, buff or grey down. They are fed by regurgitation, which they stimulate by pecking at the red spot on the lower mandible of the parent's bill, and long after they can fly they follow the old birds with outstretched necks, whistling demands.

The adult's plumage in summer is white except for the light grey mantle and wings and the outer primaries, which are mostly black with white tips and 'mirrors'. In winter there are ashy streaks on the head and neck. In the first autumn the mottled greyish-brown young with white, brown-banded tails, have black bills, slightly fleshy at the base, and slate-grey legs with pink webs. As the pearl-grey feathers gradually replace the brown, the colour of bill and legs changes. Length, 24 in. Wing, 17·5 in. Tarsus, 2·5 in. (*Plates 85 and 170.*)

## Common Gull                                             *Larus canus*

The Common Gull ranges over northern Europe, and, in winter, north Africa. In the British Isles it is resident, a winter visitor and a bird of passage; it breeds abundantly in Scotland and north and west of Ireland, but its only regular breeding colony in England is a dwindling one near Dungeness. It has recently begun to nest in Anglesey.

Gulls as gulls are familiar, but the various species, owing to changes of plumage and variability in size, can be difficult to identify; the name Common Gull is a frequent source of error. In most parts, especially in England and Wales, the Black-headed is the common gull, and as it loses its distinctive brown hood in winter it is confused with the present species. The Common Gull is more robust, a stouter bird than the Black-headed, but is considerably smaller than the Herring Gull, which it resembles in its white and French-grey plumage, though its back is noticeably darker. When they can be seen, the colours of bill and legs are useful distinguishing characters in gulls; in the adult Common Gull the bill is greenish-yellow, without the splash of red or orange, and the legs are yellowish-green. In the flying bird white spots or 'mirrors' show near the tips of the two first primaries; these are not present in the Black-headed Gull or Kittiwake, which approach this species in size. Except for occasional immature birds, distinguished by the black band on the tail, the Common Gull deserts England and Wales in March or April, and as a rule does not return until July or August.

Like other gulls, this bird is omnivorous, picking up garbage, animal for choice, on the shore, catching small surface-swimming fish, and searching the sand and banks at low water for molluscs, crustaceans and worms; on land it eats earthworms and insects and their larvae, and occasionally a little grain. It will paddle in shallow water or wet sand, dancing or marking time to bring worms to the surface, and regularly drops bivalves in order to smash the closed shell. When at a height of from 15 to 30 ft. it will droop the head, hold the wings motionless for a second, and deliberately drop the mollusc on hard sand or rock, stooping at once to recover its treasure. If the shell is not cracked at the first attempt it will try again; sweeping round until above the same spot, but rising to a greater height. It is less of an urban scavenger than the other British gulls, but in recent years has been appearing in increasing numbers with the other species on refuse tips. Large numbers feed on farmland, especially on the drier upland pastures, or follow the plough, and there are roosts of thousands on lakes and reservoirs. In December 1963 about 124,000 were reported roosting inland. On the shore it constantly harries waders and Black-headed Gulls to make them drop their food.

The flight of the Common Gull is leisurely, its wing-beats more deliberate than those of the Black-headed. It sails frequently, careening so as to benefit from every air current, and adjusting its balance with its tail. It swims gracefully, but only submerges itself when excited by the pursuit of a shoal of fish. Its usual calls are a sharp *kak, kak, kak,* an alarm note or threat, and a resounding *kyah,* but it has other calls difficult to express by any combination of letters. One note, however, is either a love signal or challenge, but may be heard long before the bird leaves our shores; the head is lowered and then raised, the bill pointed upwards, and, with the mandibles wide open, the bird gives vent to a series of clarion, laughing cries.

At all seasons the Common Gull is gregarious, and though isolated pairs are sometimes met with in inland localities, the nests are usually in a colony on a cliff, an island either at sea or on a loch, or on the moors, even at over 2000 ft. altitude. The nest is at times a scratching in short turf or on a ledge, but is often in thick heather or coarse herbage; it may be lined and walled with grasses, ling or rushes, and on the cliffs with seaweed. Three is the normal number of eggs, which vary greatly in ground colour and markings; a usual type is olive or buff, sparsely spotted with black. Incubation begins in May, and the first young leave the colony as a rule in July. The nestlings, which like other juvenile gulls vary greatly, are greyish-buff, mottled and streaked with black or brown.

The adult bird in summer has pale grey back and wings, and, with the exception of the black outer primaries and black-banded, white-tipped inner quills, is elsewhere snowy-white; the bill is green at the base, yellower towards the tip; the legs are distinctly greenish. In winter the head and hind neck are streaked with grey, but not blotched as in the winter Black-headed. The young have mottled brown mantles with greyish feather edges, and their heads, underparts and flanks are spotted with grey and brown; their primaries are brown and lack the white mirrors and tips, and the tail is broadly banded with black. The bill is brown, black at the tip; the legs pale brown. As they advance towards maturity the grey feathers appear in the mantle. Length, 17·5 in Wing, 14·5 in. Tarsus, 2 in. (*Plates 86, 87 and 170.*)

## Glaucous Gull                                              *Larus hyperboreus*

The pale plumage of the Glaucous Gull is suggestive of an arctic species, for not only does this gull nest north of the Arctic Circle in both hemispheres, but it often remains for the winter. It is, however, also a migrant, and wanders south as far as the Mediterranean. To the Orkneys, Shetlands and Outer Hebrides it is a regular autumn visitor. Both mature and immature birds reach the Shetlands in October, and some, mostly young, remain all winter. On the east coast it is a frequent 'hard-weather' bird, and it also occurs regularly in Ireland. Elsewhere it is an uncommon straggler; it occurs occasionally on the west coast of England.

In size the Glaucous Gull corresponds with the Great Black-back, and may be distinguished from all other large gulls, except the Iceland, by the absence of black on the primaries; the Iceland is about the size of the Herring Gull. The Glaucous is a very white-looking bird when mature, and at all ages is pale; its light grey mantle is several shades paler than that of the Herring Gull. It differs from the Iceland Gull in the relative shortness of its wings, which when closed rarely project beyond the tail and in its heavier build and bill. It differs from even the Great Black-back in its steady soaring flight, for it shows less angle in the wing than any other gull; indeed, its shape when at a height resembles rather a Buzzard or other raptorial bird. There are good and bad years for this species, and doubtless the irregularity in its numbers is due to abundance or shortness of food caused by climatic variation in the arctic. Though it delights in dead meat, and helps to dispose of the refuse turned out from the whaling stations, it is even more predacious than the Great Black-back; it worries all birds smaller and weaker than itself, ripping them to bits with its massive beak. It has been known to swallow a Golden Plover without troubling to dismember it. Its calls differ little from those of its congeners.

The adult in summer is very pale grey on the back and wings, and the rest of the plumage is white, including the tips of the quills. In winter the head is faintly streaked with brownish-grey. The bill is yellow with an orange patch at the angle; the legs are pink; the irides and eye-rims yellow. At first the young bird is pale buff, mottled, barred and streaked with ashy-brown, lighter than any other gull in corresponding plumage. With each moult the colour pales, and the bill, legs and irides, which are at first brownish, approach nearer to the colours of maturity. Length, 29 in. Wing, 18·5 in. Tarsus, 2·75 in. (*Plate 85.*)

### Iceland Gull *Larus glaucoides*

The Iceland Gull nests in Greenland and part of arctic America. Annually some reach the Shetlands, and usually other northern islands and the coast of Scotland and north-east England, but elsewhere it is a rare straggler, except during an invasion of the species, when it is met with in all parts.

The main difference between this whitish gull and the Glaucous is its smaller size and more slender bill; it is about the bulk of the Lesser Black-back. From all other gulls, except the rare Ivory Gull, which has black legs, it can be told by its whitish primaries. In its later stages of immaturity it is dull or dirty white, and though in its first winter it is said to be darker than the first-year Glaucous, it is paler looking than other young gulls. Its cry is

PLATE 82

*Above:* Great Skua, p164

*Below:* Great Black-backed Gull, p169

PLATE 83
Great Skua, p164

Photo : Eric Hosking

PLATE 84      *Above :* Lesser Black-backed Gull, p170

*Below :* Great Black-backed Gull, p169

Photo : Eric Hosking

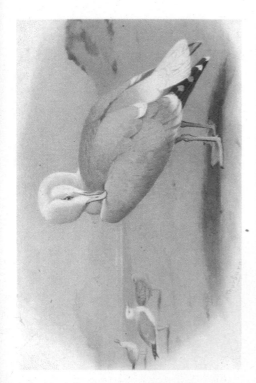

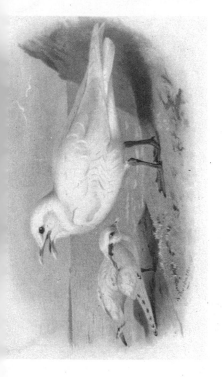

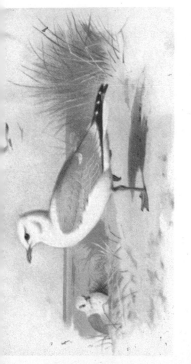

PLATE 86

*Above left:*
Common Gull,
p174
*Above right:*
Ivory Gull, p168

*Below left:*
Kittiwake, p181
*Below right:*
Sabine's Gull,
p180

Photo: *J. B. and S. Bottomley*

PLATE 87

*Above:* Mediterranean Gull, p177

*Below:* Common Gull, p174

Photo: *Sidney J. Clarke*

PLATE 88

Common and
Roseate Terns,
pp185 and 189

*Photo:*
*J. B. and S. Bottomley*

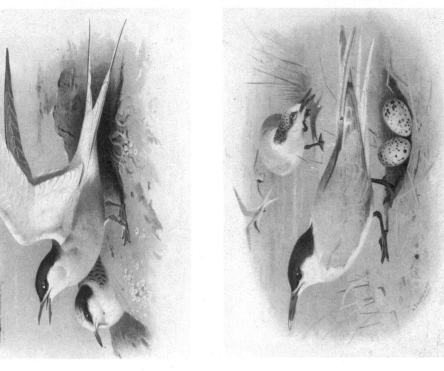

*Above* : Arctic Tern, p188
*Below* : Sandwich Tern, p191

PLATE 90    *Above* : Gull-billed Tern, p185
                 *Below* : Roseate Tern, p189

PLATE 91
Guillemot, p196

PLATE 92

*Above :* Collared Dove, p205

*Below :* Turtle Dove, p206

PLATE 93

*Above left:*
Puffin, p199
*Above right:*
Guillemot, p196

*Below left:* Little
Auk (winter), p195
*Below right:*
Black Guillemot,
p197

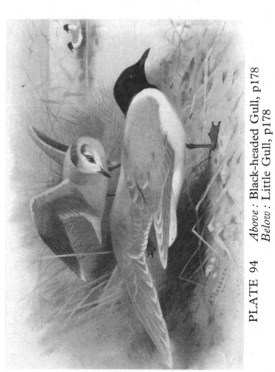

*Above* : Shore Lark, p237
*Below* : Rock Dove, p203

*Above* : Black-headed Gull, p178
*Below* : Little Gull, p178

PLATE 94

PLATE 95    Long-eared Owl, p216

PLATE 96     Barn Owl, p211

PLATE 97

*Above left :*
Stock Dove, p202
*Above right :*
Turtle Dove, p206

*Below left :* Wood
Pigeon, p204
*Below right :*
Collared Dove,
p205

shriller than the Herring Gull's. It frequently consorts with Herring or other gulls, and even feeds with them on insects and grain in the fields; it does not appear to be specially partial to carrion, and certainly is less predacious than the fierce Glaucous.

The proportionately longer wings, which project well beyond the tail when the bird is at rest, look long and narrow in flight; it flies with ease and buoyancy. The very pale grey and white bird has the head streaked with greyish-brown in winter. The yellow bill has red at the angle, but the legs are flesh-coloured, as are the eye-rims; the irides are yellow. The immature stages appear to correspond with those of the larger bird, and it is said that maturity is not reached until the fourth year. Length, 22 in. Wing, 17 in. Tarsus. 2·4 in. (*Plate 85.*)

### Great Black-headed Gull                              *Larus ichthyaetus*

The Great Black-headed Gull, a native of south Russia and central Asia, has wandered to England on six or more occasions. It is a large gull, about the size of the Great Black-back, with a black, not brown hood, and a slightly darker mantle than our small bird. The white-tipped secondaries form a bar on the wing, and the primaries are white, broadly barred with black. In winter the hood is replaced by dark streaks. The yellow bill has a black band across both mandibles; the legs are greenish-yellow. The brown-backed immature is distinguished from other large gulls of the same age by the white tail and clearly defined black sub-terminal band. The female is often much smaller than the male. Length, 26 in.

### Mediterranean Gull                              *Larus melanocephalus*

This gull, which breeds in the eastern Mediterranean, occurs annually in Britain, chiefly on the south coast of England. Most records are of immature birds in summer or autumn. It resembles the Common Gull in size, build and shape of wing, but it has longer legs and a heavy bill which appears to turn down at the tip. The adult in spring has a black hood extending down the nape and white primaries without black tips. In winter the black hood is reduced to a dark line through the eye. Immatures resemble young Common Gulls, with black band on the tail and rear edge of the wing, but at all ages the Mediterranean is paler on the mantle and shows more white on the wing. The adult's bill and legs are red; the bill of the immature bird is blackish. Length, 15·5 in. Wing, 11·75 in. Tarsus, 1·9 in. (*Plate 87.*)

### Bonaparte's Gull                              *Larus philadelphia*

Bonaparte's Gull breeds in northern America and migrates as far south as the Gulf of Mexico; it has occurred seventeen times in the British Isles. Its flight is light and tern-like; it swoops towards the water to catch insects, and flutters after them in the air. Its voice is said to be harsh and rasping.

Its size is between that of the Black-headed and the Little Gull. The hood is slate-black in summer, but in winter the head is nearly white. In its general appearance, including the white forewing and black primary tips, it resembles a small Black-headed Gull, but it differs in having a white, not dark grey underside to the primaries. The thin bill is black; the legs orange. Immatures resemble young Black-headed Gulls, but have black patches near the ends of the inner primaries and secondaries. Length, 14 in.

## Little Gull                                       *Larus minutus*

The Little Gull breeds in northern Europe and Asia and winters as far south as northern Africa. Its autumnal migrations appear to trend westward, and as within recent years it has also extended its breeding area westward, it is hardly surprising that to our eastern seaboard it is a fairly regular winter visitor or passage migrant in spring and autumn. In some years it is even plentiful. On the west coast and in Ireland it is now regular, though it usually occurs singly.

In flight this bird looks smaller and more round-winged than the Black-headed. It has been likened to a tern, but there is nothing tern-like in its much less pointed wings. In the adult bird the primaries are grey with white edges and tips; the outer primary looks white in flight, and the pale upper surface of the wing throws up the smoky under surface, as the bird loiters through the air, for it has a peculiarly hesitating, desultory flight. Its slightly forked tail is also noticeable when expanded, as it checks its speed or turns to snatch at a flying insect. It feeds on the wing much more than the common British gulls. Although usually seen near the coast it frequents fresh as well as tidal waters. Insects, even as small as gnats, form a considerable proportion of its food, though it catches small fish. Its call, sharp and harsh, is not often heard in winter.

In summer the adult has the whole head, including the nape, black; the back and wings are very pale grey, the underwing blackish and the rest of the plumage white. The bill is dark red; the legs are vermilion. In winter all that remains of the black head is a few streaks on the nape; the legs and bill are duller. In first plumage the upper parts are brown, streaked and mottled with buff, white and grey; the primaries are sooty except on the inner edge, and the under-wing is white. Later the crown is flecked with grey and the ear-coverts and a line round the eye are blackish; there is a half-collar of grey and a sooty bar on the wing similar to that on the immature Kittiwake. As the bird advances towards maturity the back becomes purer grey, and the central tail feathers white, leaving a few half-bars on the outer tail feathers. Length, 11 in. Wing, 8·5 in. Tarsus, 1 in. (*Plate 94*.)

## Black-headed Gull                              *Larus ridibundus*

The range of the Black-headed Gull extends over most of Europe and Asia and in winter includes northern Africa. It is resident in all parts of the British Isles, but many move south in autumn and others from the north and east come to winter or on passage. Amongst those whose interest in birds is superficial the fact that this is our commonest species causes confusion; they call it the 'Common Gull', and insist that its head is not black, ignoring the seasonal change of plumage. The brown hood is worn in spring and summer, though exceptionally it is retained all winter, or regained before the end of the year; most birds lose the hood in August. The Black-head is an inland as well as coastal gull; it is never pelagic and is seldom seen far from land; it nests as far from the sea as Northamptonshire, and feeds regularly in fields, sewage farms and at refuse tips all over the country. In tourist areas it has learnt to exploit picnickers at popular car parks. In recent years there has been a spectacular increase in the number of gulls feeding inland, and this species is the most numerous of all. In his report on an enquiry by the British Trust for Ornithology, R. A. O. Hickling estimated the number of Black-headed Gulls roosting on inland waters in December 1963 as 310,000, almost double the number normally roosting inland ten years before. Yet the old notion that a gull inland is a sign of bad weather dies hard. The adult bird in summer may always be recognised by the brown hood, blood-red bill and legs, and at any season by the white outer fringe of the wing contrasting with the pearl-grey of the mantle. In winter the white head is blotched with brownish-grey on the ear-coverts and near the eye; the head of the Common Gull at this season is streaked with grey. Young birds have the wings mottled with chestnut-brown.

The wing-beats of the Black-headed are quicker than in larger gulls, and its build is slimmer; there is a suggestion of relationship to terns in many of its movements. It has a desultory uncertain flight; it wavers, careens and drifts, but when migrating or hurrying often flies steadily, and a party will adopt chevron formation. When about to alight on water the bird will 'shoot' like a Rook, darting down with half-open wings, turning and twisting as it descends. The quickest flight is when in pursuit of some favourite food; a big rise of mayfly, the emergence and nuptial flight of crane-flies or winged ants excites the greedy birds. The air is a maze of dodging, screaming gulls, their white wings fluttering as they check their hurried rushes and swoops after the erratic insects. Although omnivorous like other gulls, the Black-headed is undoubtedly a useful bird, especially inland; it follows the plough, wrangling with the Rooks and Starlings, or with its companions, as it hastens to the freshly opened furrows. Stomach examination proves that though many worms and some harmless insects are eaten, great numbers of 'leather-jackets' and wireworms are taken from the newly turned ground. In rivers and on shore it devours insanitary garbage, and is a faithful attendant on the fishing fleet when the catch is sorted. A little grain is picked up, and a small percentage of fishy matter has been found in the stomach, but it is a poor fisherman, lacking speed and diving skill, though it may clumsily submerge when plunging from the air. It will paddle on mud or wet sand to bring food to the surface, like other gulls. It has been seen to pick haws and acorns from trees. Indeed both its diet and its feeding methods are extraordinarily varied and adaptable. The corvine call-note is harsh and scolding. The idea that any of its calls are 'laughing', as suggested by its scientific name, is strange; they are often peevish or quarrelsome in tone, and when a nesting colony is visited the angry *kik, kik, kik* is usually the prelude to a fierce swoop at the head of the visitor. Since the passing of the Bird Protection Bills this gull has increased enormously, in some measure owing to the checking of ruthless shooting of young birds, but the eggs are still gathered for food; the adaptability of the species is an important factor. An enquiry of the British Trust for Ornithology in 1958 showed that there were about 50,000 pairs of Black-headed Gulls nesting in 185 colonies in England and Wales. The biggest colony in the British Isles is at Ravenglass on the Cumberland coast, where some 12,000 pairs nest in the marram grass on the sand dunes. In spite of recent increases there are still comparatively few gulleries in southern and central England.

At all times the bird is sociable, consorting with waders and other gulls on shore, and with Lapwings, Golden Plovers and Rooks inland, but it is most gregarious in its nesting habits. The marshy edge of a lake, or the islands and tussocks in a shallow pool, are the most favoured nesting sites, and these may be close to the shore or on the moors at over 1000 ft. When a gullery is approached the gulls rise and whirl overhead with an angry and anxious clamour, the boldest making repeated threatening dashes, but they soon quieten down. Sudden 'dreads', like those of terns, are not uncommon; the noisy bickerings will cease, and the whole colony will fly off in a cloud with a weird hush; in a few seconds the flock breaks up, the birds drift back, and the normal clamour is resumed. Dr N. Tinbergen remarks that these flights are most frequent at the beginning and end of the breeding season and considers them an indication of the birds' sense of insecurity in the breeding habitat.

The nest is a mass of sticks, sedges, rushes or grass, often large when on wet ground; it is placed on a tussock in the water, on level dry ground, on a rock or wall, exceptionally in a tree. The eggs are two or three in number, more rarely four, and vary greatly in ground and markings; some are bluish, others olive, green, buff or brown, with blotches, spots or zones of black, grey and brown. The nestlings are almost as variable, the down being grey, buff or brown, mottled and striped with irregular lines of black and brown.

The adult in spring has a chocolate-brown hood, white neck, tail and underparts, light grey mantle, and wings light grey with black tips to the primaries and a white leading edge which is conspicuous in flight. In winter the head is white except for a dark smudge behind the eye. The bill and legs are red. The young bird is at first suffused with brown and shows but little white, most of its mottlings being on the wings and back, but by the autumn the head is whitish with bands of grey on the crown and nape and blotches on the ear-coverts; underparts and tail are white, the last crossed by a broad brown band; the back is pearl-grey, and wings and coverts tipped and mottled with grey and brown. Length, 16 in. Wing, 11·75 in. Tarsus, 1·75 in. (*Plates 94 and 171.*)

### Sabine's Gull                                                        *Larus sabini*

Sabine's gull is a circumpolar arctic species which visits western Europe in winter with some degree of regularity; it is recorded almost every autumn or winter from the east coast of England, and is frequently met with elsewhere in England, Scotland and Ireland. The majority of the birds which reach us are immature.

On the wing it is graceful and tern-like, and its forked tail is much more pronounced than that of the Little Gull. Many of its visits have been when terns were on the move, and it has been seen associating with them. Its harsh cry resembles that of the Arctic Tern.

In its nuptial dress, which is occasionally seen in England, the head and neck are slate, with a black line where the hood meets the general white plumage. The back and wings are dark pearl-grey, the outer primaries are black tipped and inwardly margined with white, and the inner primaries and secondaries are mostly white. In flight both adults and immatures show a distinctive pattern of black, grey and white triangles on the wings. The yellow-tipped bill is black; the legs are brownish-black. In winter the head is only marked with grey streaks and suffusion. Young birds have the back, wings and a patch on the side of the breast ashy-grey with brown bars; the nape is dusky and the forked tail broadly bordered with dark brown. Length, 13 in. (*Plate 86.*)

## Kittiwake                                                                *Rissa tridactyla*

The Kittiwake nests on the coasts of northern Europe and winters as far south as the Mediterranean. It is resident in the British Isles and its adjacent waters. The number and size of its colonies have increased greatly during the present century, and it is now nesting on much lower cliffs than formerly. The largest colonies are on the coasts of north Scotland and north-east England. In autumn and winter numbers of immigrants appear off our shores. Ringing recoveries show that some British-bred birds remain in home waters while others disperse widely; many, chiefly second-year birds, have been recovered in Newfoundland and Greenland.

In summer the Kittiwake is a gull of precipitous cliffs—in winter of the open sea; but in recent years some birds have been frequenting harbours and river mouths and even feeding on bread and at sewer outfalls on the Tyne. In that district they take freshwater fish and bathe in reservoirs. The Kittiwake has a clean and neat appearance, its mantle and quills bluish-grey, the rest of its plumage snowy-white except for the tips of the outer primaries which are black, and show on the open wing as a triangular black patch. On the first two or three there are neither white tips nor mirrors; thus the flying bird can at once be told from the Common Gull which it rather resembles. The bill is greenish-yellow, but the legs are usually so dark that they look black, though there is considerable variation, and some individuals show shades of grey, yellow and red. In the hand it can at once be told by the virtual absence of the hind toe, this being represented by a mere vestige. The inner primaries are white-tipped, and show on the closed wing. Immature birds, still known as 'Tarrocks', have a distinct dark half-collar, a band of mottled brown across the wings, and banded tails. The flight is easy and graceful; its gentle buoyancy hardly suggests battles with winter gales, yet, unlike other gulls, it selects the open sea for its winter home; its power of sustained flight is proved by its habit of following steamers, for it has been known to accompany liners across the Atlantic.

Surface-swimming fish and the larger crustaceans or other planktonic animals are its chief food, and for these it dives with more skill than other gulls. It beats about near the surface until it sights prey, then alights and dives, remaining below for a short time, swimming under water. Even a rough sea it rides lightly, mounting the steeply advancing waves, head to wind, and either plunging through the crest or fluttering over to avoid a crashing curl. A winter gale of long duration tries it, driving down its food; immature birds especially are weakened and driven ashore, only a few saving themselves by flying inland before the storm. After a gale the shore is often littered with corpses.

The Kittiwake is as a rule a silent bird away from the nesting colony, only uttering a sharp *kit, kit,* when wrangling for food, but is lively enough at the nesting ledges. The colonies, often very large, are in caves or on steep cliffs, the nests being stuck on most insecure-looking ledges, often many close together. Two or three colonies have now become established on buildings on the North Sea coast; at Lowestoft more than twenty pairs nest annually on a curved ledge on the pier pavilion. In March the pelagic birds begin to gather at the nesting place, but nest building is not hurried; eggs are often laid in May, but incubation seldom begins until June. The nest, a small collection of seaweed and grass, looks as if a puff of wind would dislodge it from its narrow base, but really it is a work of art. Both birds collect material, which consists of clay and mud as well as weed, and this, well trodden by the patient architects, forms when dry a firm, almost solid foundation. During courtship, nest building and incubation the colony rings with pleasant calls of *kitti-waake, kitti-waake,* with an ascending emphasis on the last syllable.

Though there is frequent sparring between the various occupants of a ledge, the paired birds are most affectionate, caressing one another and expressing their feelings in head and gulping throat movements. The male frequently feeds the female, and takes a share in incubation. In the evening when the birds change places, many exchanges of compliments and a cheerful volley of *kitti-waakes* accompany the 'relief'. About the end of August the majority of old and young are ready to depart, but for some time after that remain at sea near the cliffs. The two or three eggs are usually lighter in ground—greyish, pale buff or stone colour—than the eggs of most gulls; they are blotched and zoned with brown and grey. The nestlings are also paler than those of gulls which nest in more accessible situations; their heads are greyish-white, and the marks on the grey backs are very faint. The parent does not regurgitate and present the young with food, but allows it to fish in its open mouth for what it can find, after the manner of a Cormorant.

The adult's summer plumage is white except for the black-tipped grey wings and grey mantle. In winter the crown and nape are also grey. The bill is greenish-yellow, legs blackish and eyes dark brown. The juvenile at first has back and wings mottled with brown; in the succeeding 'Tarrock' plumage, which lasts about a year, there is a dark mark across the back of the neck, a diagonal dark band across the wing and a black band at the end of the tail. Length, 16 in. Wing, 12 in. Tarsus, 1·4 in. (*Plates 86 and 171*.)

**Black Tern**                                            *Chlidonias niger*
About 150 years ago the Black Tern bred freely in the east coast marshes, but it has only nested in England two or three times in the 20th century. Now it is a regular passage migrant, halting for food in April and May, August and September. A Black Tern in June, July or October is unusual, in other months very rare. Formerly it was chiefly seen in the south and east of England, but since about 1945 it has been much more numerous and widespread both in spring and autumn. Inland routes are largely used and occurrences are now regular in north Lancashire and central Yorkshire. It appears annually in Ireland, often in some numbers, and is not uncommon in the south of Scotland.

In summer plumage the Black Tern is a very dark bird; its slate wings, back and tail look almost pale compared with the deep blue-black of its head, neck and breast. From both White-winged and Whiskered Terns, its nearest allies, it may be told by its black bill and blackish legs, red in these birds. From the former, when both are mature, its darker wings and grey tail and tail-coverts are distinct when in flight, and the latter is a larger, paler tern with a black cap and not wholly dark head. The immature plumages are more puzzling. The Black Tern does not hurry through England, but stays for a few hours, and often days, about some inland water where food is abundant. It beats up and down with desultory flight, swooping when it sights food on or near the surface; sometimes its descents and ascents are long, graceful, swinging curves, varied with a check and flutter as it intercepts some dodging fly or gnat, but often it dives obliquely with a half turn, lightly touches the water with its bill, leaving a circle of ripples where an insect swam or drowned, and banks smartly. Its loitering flight is broken by a series of deep U-curves, but it rarely strikes the water with its body. Like the Swallow, it feeds against the wind, sweeping down wind to repeat the process when it reaches the limits of the pool. When tired it settles on some rail or mooring-post; on this it perches head to wind, its head and neck depressed, its long wing-tips crossed above its short tail and slightly raised; it tilts forward in its resting position. It is sociable rather than gregarious on migration, often flying with Common and Lesser Terns, when its even more buoyant flight is very marked. Large numbers have, on rare occasions, been recorded from the east coast, but more than fifty in a party is unusual.

The Marsh Terns, as the members of this small group are called, are inland rather than sea terns, more frequent over fresh than salt water. They seldom swim, the webs being more deeply indented between the toes than in other terns, the feet better fitted for walking. The Black Tern nests in extensive and treacherous marshes, the nest itself, built of sodden and often rotten vegetation, is frequently surrounded by water, placed on a quaking platform of dead aquatic plants. Though noisy at the nest, on migration it is usually a silent traveller.

The head, neck and breast of the mature bird are black in summer; the rest of the plumage, except for white on the carpal angle and the under tail-coverts, is slate-grey, varying in depth. The bill is black; the legs are dark reddish-brown. After the autumn moult the forehead, sides of face and neck, a collar and the underparts are white, tinged and speckled in places with grey. The greyish upper parts of young birds are suffused and mottled with brown and buff, and the face, nape and a patch on the side of the neck are dark grey; there is a dark patch on the shoulder, which is still present in the second autumn when the back and wings have lost their brown splashes. Length, 9·6 in. Wing, 8·5 in. Tarsus, 0·6 in. (*Plate 89.*)

**White-winged Black Tern**                                *Chlidonias leucopterus*
The White-winged Black Tern breeds in central and south-eastern Europe and western Asia, and winters in southern Asia and Africa, yet it wanders north-west and a few birds regularly appear in spring and autumn, chiefly in our southern and eastern counties.

There is no difficulty in identifying the adult bird in summer, for the white patch on the carpal joint is, naturally, conspicuous against the deep black head, back and breast, and more noticeable still are the white upper and under tail-coverts and tail. The rest of the plumage except the wings is blacker than in the Black Tern, and the bill and legs are strikingly red. The wings are greyish-slate, almost pearl-grey on the secondaries, and the primaries, though really blackish, are so frosted as to appear pearl-grey; thus the whole wing apart from the white patch, is considerably lighter than that of the Black Tern. This difference is reversed in the under-wing, for the under wing-coverts and axillaries in this bird are black, and in the Black Tern suffused with grey; the effect is that as the bird cants in flight the upper surface shows lighter than the under in the White-winged Tern, and *vice-versa* in the Black. Its habits, at any rate when on migration, closely agree with those of its congener; it catches insects and small fish, stooping to the water or taking the former in the air, and its flight is equally slow and desultory.

In winter the head, except for the blackish nape, the neck and underparts are white, but the tail is suffused with grey and the under-wing becomes paler. There are no dark patches on the breast as in the Black Tern. The bill is blackish. The young bird is at first mottled with brown and buff and has a dark brown 'saddle' contrasting with the pale grey wings and white rump. Length, 9·3 in. (*Plate 89.*)

**Whiskered Tern**                                          *Chlidonias hybrida*
Southern Europe and north Africa are the breeding areas of the Whiskered Tern, and it winters further south. It is a rare vagrant to the British Isles, but one or two have been recorded in most recent years, chiefly in the south and

east of England, though it has also reached Scotland and Ireland. It has occurred both in spring and autumn.

The pure white under wing-coverts are a good distinctive character, for the bird flies slowly though buoyantly and its wing-beats are deliberate; when it cants over the under-wing is visible. The food, as in other marsh terns, consists of insects, small fish and frogs, but unlike the Black Tern it regularly plunges into the water. The adult in summer differs from its congeners in having only the crown and nape black; the chin, cheeks and throat are white. The mantle and wings are slate-grey; the primaries black, frosted with pearl-grey. The underparts are dark, almost black on the belly. The bill and legs are red. After the autumn moult the mantle is lighter and the underparts and forehead white; the black on the head is streaked and spotted with white. The upper parts of young birds are at first mottled with brown. Length, 10 in.

### Gull-billed Tern                                      *Gelochelidon nilotica*

The Gull-billed Tern breeds on the western shores of Europe from Denmark to Spain; it also nests inland. It occurs from time to time in our southern and eastern counties and occasionally in other districts, chiefly in spring or summer. Records have become more frequent in recent years. A pair nested in Essex in 1950, and probably in 1949.

This tern feeds largely on insects, catching them on the wing, but it also eats fish and frogs. The call at the nesting colony is a rich, full *kurruck*, deeper than that of the Sandwich Tern, and it also has a squeaky, tremulous *kerreray* or *kerray*. Its plumage resembles that of the Sandwich Tern, but its tail is grey and less forked. The heavy angled bill is black, as are its legs, which are longer than other terns. Length, 15 in. Tarsus, 1·5 in. (*Plate 90.*)

### Caspian Tern                                      *Hydroprogne tschegrava*

One or two Caspian Terns have been recorded in Britain in most recent years, chiefly in the eastern and southern coastal counties of England, though it has also occurred in the north-west and even in Donegal. It breeds in Sweden and Finland and on the Black Sea.

It is found on both marine and inland waters and feeds chiefly on fish. It is a large, heavily built tern, as big as a Black-headed Gull, with powerful flight. Its size, its short, hardly forked tail and conspicuous heavy red bill are the most striking characteristics. The cap is black in summer, streaked with white in winter; the back and wings are light grey, the rest of the body plumage white, the underside of the primaries dark. The juvenile has a streaked cap and brown markings on the back. The bill is red; legs black. Length, 20 in. Wing, 16·5 in. Tarsus, 1·6 in.

### Common Tern                                              *Sterna hirundo*

The Common Tern breeds on most European coasts, and in winter migrates far south. In the British Isles it is certainly the commonest tern in most parts;

it nests all round our shores, least plentifully in the north, and large numbers visit us on passage.

Sea-swallow is a name given to all the commoner terns, but except in the long, pointed wings and forked tail with streamers, there is little to suggest a Swallow. The Common and Arctic Tern can with difficulty be distinguished on the wing, though in the hand the characters are clear. Broadly speaking, the bill of the Common in the breeding season is red with the distal third dusky or almost black, and that of the Arctic coral-red throughout or with only the extreme tip dark. When the birds are seen flying overhead the outer primary feathers of the Common look opaque; in the Arctic they are all semi-transparent. The Common Tern has a slightly longer tarsus, and therefore stands a little higher, but this is difficult to judge in life, as is the paler greyish suffusion of the underparts. On the average the wings of the Common are longer and its tail streamers shorter than those of the Arctic, but the position of the tips when the wing is closed varies according to the pose of the bird and is an unsafe guide. The difference in the voice can only be learnt by experience. The Common Tern is one of our best-known sea-birds. It beats over the waves with slow and deliberate but powerful strokes; the determined down-strokes look as if they should jerk the slender, cigar-shaped body upward. It poises in the air with upraised wings vibrating, tail depressed and expanded, and bill pointed seaward, then half closing its sharply angled wings, dives obliquely, often with a slight screw twist, entering the water with a splash. In a second it is up again, for frequently its wing-tips are not submerged, and rises with or without a struggling fish. It sports in the air with companions, the call *kierie*, or a sharp *kit*, often being changed to *pierre* of mock annoyance; a clamour of voices announces the discovery of a shoal of fry, and excited terns hurry from all directions, hover, a snowy cloud, and rain upon their silvery victims. Terns rest upon the shore, but walk little and badly; the crossed tips of the long wings are usually held well above the tail. They are easy though not quick when swimming, but are certainly most at home in the air.

Towards the end of April the immigrants arrive, for they are summer visitors; many travel overland and halt to feed on inland waters; there they catch insects as well as fish, swooping gracefully and taking them on the wing either from or near the water. From the middle of May until August they remain near the nest colony, but by the end of September most have left our shores, though passage birds drift through in October. Young birds when able to fly wander at first; ringed Common Terns have been recovered in their first autumn far to the north of the ternery, though others have been reported in France and Spain. The breeding colonies are in various situations, on coastal dunes, rocky islets, shingle spits or saltmarshes. There are inland colonies in Scotland, Ireland and some eastern counties of England.

Nests may be lined or unlined, eggs being laid on bare rock or soil, in neatly rounded depressions, or in nests of considerable size. The female often lays and adds lining after incubation has begun. The materials vary as much as the site and include marram, bits of stick, straw, seaweed, pebbles, shells and crab-claws. In only a few cases are these materials mixed; each bird seems to select its special decoration. The male feeds the female before and during incubation; indeed, with all terns, the presentation of a fishy offering is the most important nuptial preliminary. The male depressing its half-spread wings, and elevating head and tail, dangles his gift before the crouching, expectant female. When the ternery is first approached the birds rise and fly to and fro overhead, many at a great height, filling the air with a maze of white wings and harshly screaming voices, the most prominent being the long drawn *pieerah*, or the sharply repeated *kit, kit* of some specially anxious parent; but the tumult soon subsides and the life of the colony may be watched from close quarters. One may see, after they have settled down, the strange simultaneous departure of the birds, a habit shared by Black-headed Gulls and Sand Martins. A sudden cessation of the normal clamour is followed by an uncanny hush as all wing seaward, but before out of sight a bird calls and the whole body drifts back to resume activities.

Irate birds will dive savagely at and occasionally strike the head of anyone walking amongst the nests. Others than human trespassers are assaulted, even killed. At Ravenglass one may find the bill-pitted skulls of young rabbits and the juvenile Black-headed Gulls which have wandered from their own domain. Passing birds, innocent as well as would-be thieves, are driven off or overwhelmed, and even cattle are mobbed.

The colour of the eggs varies greatly: some are pale, greenish or buff; others deep brown in ground; and the marks of black, brown or grey may be speckles, spots or blotches. It is practically impossible to distinguish between the eggs of the Common and Arctic Tern. Three is the usual number, but clutches of two are common; only a small proportion are hatched. Eggs and nestlings are destroyed by rats, weasels and stoats at night, but diurnal robbers get a warm reception. Most eggs are laid in June. The nestlings' down varies from grey to deep brown, although sandy buff is most usual; the black markings and mottles are irregular. The nestlings are fed by the parents on small fish—sand-eels, dabs and coal-fish fry being common. The food is usually delivered to the young, when the old bird, with wings uplifted, daintily alights beside it. The young, which follow their parents with repeated insistent cries, *chik, chik, chik,* are at first much mottled with buff and slate on the upper parts, and their foreheads are buff. After the autumn moult the forehead is white, the crown speckled and the nape brownish-black; the back and mantle are then marked with grey and buff, and the shoulders show a greyish band.

The mature bird has a black cap, pearl-grey back and wings, primaries edged with dark grey, and a white tail with greyish borders to the streamers. The underparts are slightly suffused with grey, sometimes showing a pinkish blush, but they are white in winter, when the forehead is white and crown mottled. The red bill is black-tipped, the legs coral-red. Length, 14·25 in. Wing, 10·5 in. (*Plates 88, 89 and 171.*)

**Arctic Tern**                                                     *Sterna paradisea*

Few birds, if any, have a greater range than the Arctic Tern, for it nests far
north of the Arctic Circle and occurs in winter in the Antarctic. In December
1966 a bird ringed in Anglesey in June of the same year was recovered in
New South Wales. In the British Isles, almost the southern limit of its breeding range in Europe, it outnumbers the Common Tern on the west coast of
Scotland and the islands, but it has decreased in Ireland. It has only a few
colonies in England and Wales. In some of these, for instance on the Farnes,
the two species nest close together, but even there the colonies are more or
less distinct.

As a summer visitor the Arctic Tern arrives a little later than the Common;
it is often May before the birds appear, and well into June before eggs are
laid. The characters by which it can be recognised—the blood-red bill,
deeper grey underparts, short tarsus and semi-transparent outer primaries
—have been already stated. In general appearance, manner of flight, food and
feeding habits, and to some extent voice, it closely resembles the Common
Tern; its usual call is shorter—a harsh *kleeah*, with emphasis on the second
syllable. Rocky islands and stacks are more frequently occupied as breeding
colonies than sites on the mainland, but there are some large terneries on
dunes, sand and shingle, and a few on inland lakes. There has been some extension southward of its breeding range, and small parties have appeared in
terneries which previously contained only Common Terns. Though there is
variation in the site and construction of the nest, eggs are frequently laid on
bare rock, or on the ground without surrounds or lining; nests as bulky as
many of those of the Common Tern are rare. On one small group of stacks on
the Welsh coast most eggs are in cracks in jagged rock, some with a few
ripped-off strips of lichen around them, but they may be ringed by grass and
rabbit bones, both of which must have been carried from the land.

Two or three eggs in a clutch are normal. They vary quite as much as those
of the Common Tern, though the average size is smaller. The nestlings are
at least dimorphic, there being creamy-white and dusky-brown phases; they
are doubtfully distinguishable from those of the Common Tern. Like the
young of the Common Tern, they soon leave the nest, and at first stagger, but
soon run fairly quickly on their short and thick, light or dark reddish legs,
crouching under shelter of rocks or vegetation for protection if alarmed. The
parents feed them on fish, usually bringing only one at a time, but in an Irish
colony have been seen to supply them with insects, mostly crane-flies. When
leaving the colony to fish, the old birds fly low over the water, but return at a
higher level, and in Scotland are not infrequently robbed of their load by the
bullying Skua. The Arctic Skua is one of the few birds which is too much for
the terns, for in defence of the young the Arctic Tern is even bolder than the
Common; it will frequently strike the head of a human visitor to the ternery.
The violence with which the bird can strike and then recover itself without
breaking its neck is really remarkable; this power of a sudden reversal of
position is shown by its rapid emergence when diving for food.

The adult's breeding plumage is closely similar to the Common Tern's, except that the throat and breast are greyer and the flight feathers whiter. The bill is blood-red, the legs coral. In winter the bill is blackish. The juvenile has a whitish forehead and buffish neck and cheeks, whilst its back and wings are mottled with buff; but after the autumn moult, the crown is speckled and the nape brownish-black, but the pearl-grey upper parts are purer, though marked with a dusky band on the shoulders. The bill and legs are much darker than in the mature bird. Length, 14·5 in. Wing, 10 in. Tarsus, 0·7 in. (*Plates 90 and 171.*)

## Roseate Tern                                                    *Sterna dougallii*

The Atlantic breeding range of the Roseate Tern is more southerly than that of the Common Tern. In the northern part of its range it is migratory, and is a summer visitor to Britain in small numbers. Many of its former nesting haunts in the British Isles have long been deserted, but it breeds in varying numbers in a few colonies in England, Wales and Scotland, usually among larger numbers of other species. There have been some larger colonies in Ireland, but numbers fluctuate widely.

The evanescent salmon-pink tint of the underparts of the Roseate Tern is not always easy to see; in direct sunlight it is usually plain. Better characters are the much blacker bill and the noticeably long tail streamers. Among Common Terns its body looks long and slender; the wings are shorter, and the tail much longer than that of its companions. The flight appears deliberate; in the down-stroke the wings are not brought so far beneath the plane of flight as in other terns. The black hood appears to extend further on the neck than in the Common Tern. The alarm or call of annoyance is a long *aaack*, or a sharper *agh*; it has too a long *craak* or *cree*. The call-note is a clearer *chew-it*.

Persecution nearly exterminated our Roseate Terns, but protection saved the situation in some places. There are, however, other factors which make the Roseate's position unsatisfactory, the worst being its competition with more go-ahead species. On congested stacks the best sites for nests are monopolised by the earlier breeding Commons or Arctics. The Roseate arrives late in April, nests often late in June and seldom remains in British seas long after the end of August.

Most of the colonies are on rocky stacks occupied by other species, but, except for occasional pairs, the nests are in one area. Some of the now extinct colonies were on dunes or shingle banks, and recently a few pairs have nested in Common Tern colonies on the mainland. Very little nesting material or lining is used, most eggs being laid on ledges, or in cracks and hollows in the rock. Either one or two eggs are laid. Variation is less frequent than in the eggs of Common or Arctic Terns; they have a light stone or buff ground and small spots of varied browns and greys, which often form a zone towards the larger end. On the average they are slightly larger and longer than those of the Common, but many eggs would puzzle an expert. The nestling is paler buff than most juvenile terns, and its greyish-brown markings are streaks rather than mottles; the down is coarse or matted.

The adult bird has the top of the head and back of the neck black in summer and speckled with white in winter; the outer margin of the streamer is white. The white streak on the primaries, even extending round the tip, is present in the young bird, which has also a white-streaked forehead, brownish nape and crown, and ashy-brown speckles on the back and wings. The bill of the adult bird is black, except for a red patch at the base; the legs are orange-red. The length of the streamers varies greatly; in one bird they were 8 in. long, but others are much shorter. Length, 15–17 in. Wing, 9·25 in. Tarsus, 0·87 in. (*Plates 88, 90 and 171.*)

### Sooty Tern                                        *Sterna fuscata*
About twenty examples of the Sooty Tern have wandered north from tropical or subtropical seas and have been found on our shores or in inland localities. The visits have been in both spring and autumn. The crown, back of the neck and a streak through the eye of the adult bird are black; the back, wings and tail—except the outer web of the streamer—are sooty-black; the rest of the plumage is white. The bill and legs are black. The young bird has the dark back feathers tipped with white, and the underparts are sooty-brown. Length, 16 in.

### Little Tern                                      *Sterna albifrons*
The Little Tern breeds on the coasts and inland waters of northern Europe. It is a summer visitor to the British Isles, nesting in small and scattered colonies on most coasts, but is absent from the north of Scotland. Numbers have decreased in many places, owing to disturbance of beaches by holiday-makers. It reaches the south coast about the middle of April, and birds are passing north in early May; it is seldom seen after the end of September.

Apart from its size, for this is our smallest tern, it may be recognised by its broad, semi-lunar white forehead. The white extends to above the eye, and is emphasised by a black streak from the bill through the eye. The legs and bill are yellow, the latter with the tip black. Its wide wing-stretch magnifies its size, and its wing-beats are quicker than those of other terns; it beats above the waves at a height of from 10 to 15 ft., with head drooped, scanning the surface. At intervals it checks its pace, poises with wings uplifted and vibrating, and tail depressed and expanded. Its body is held well upright, and as its streamers are short, its spread tail is almost triangular. Suddenly wing movement ceases, and as the bird drops it reverses, and with wings almost closed bores through the air with a half turn, throwing up a shower of spray as it strikes. Instantly it reappears, and with a few strong strokes mounts again, but at times it checks its descent and rises without touching the water. By no means every dive brings reward: one bird averaged a catch to every six dives. Complete submersion is common, but the bird is up again before the splash has subsided. Small crustaceans as well as fish are eaten, and these, even when in shallow tide-pools, are obtained by diving, the bird checking the impetus of descent with skill. The call—*pee-e-err*—is neither so harsh nor sustained as that of the Common Tern, but the bird is very loquacious on the wing. It has, in addition, a short *zit, zit,* and a long *tirrue, tirrue, tirrue.* On migration the Little Tern often visits inland waters, fishing occasionally, but usually swooping for flying insects after the manner of the Black Tern.

The nesting colonies are small and the nests seldom close together; favourite sites are shingle banks or stretches of sand above the tide-mark. It seldom if ever nests on rock, and bare ground is preferred to grass-grown flats. Some colonies are foolishly near the water; high tides destroy many eggs, yet the bird returns annually to these danger zones, and never seems to learn by experience. Courtship gifts of fish to the female and the postures during presentation are as common with this species as with others, and a pair will indulge in high nuptial aerial chases, the air ringing with excited cries. The eggs may be placed amongst pebbles without any attempt at a nest, or laid in an unlined scoop in fine sand; only occasionally is grass or other soft lining used, though the eggs are frequently on a paving of small pebbles or broken shells. When these are collected from the immediate vicinity the denuded ground forms a distinct zone round the nest; paved nests are conspicuous when on sand. Indeed, on sand the sitting bird and even the two or three light stone-coloured eggs, spotted, blotched, or smeared with brown and grey, are easy to see, but amongst fair-sized pebbles the bird is inconspicuous, and the eggs most difficult to discover.

On returning to the nest, which it does very soon after being disturbed, the bird descends direct, and can with ease be marked down. Yet it is a plucky defender of its property, chasing away with fierce cries of *ki, ki, ki* any marauding gull, crow, or more innocent bird which approaches the colony. Like other terns, it dives at the human head, rising first to a great height, and plunging down with three or four strong beats before the wings are half closed, but with a few hurried and angry notes it sheers off without striking. Eggs are usually laid about the middle of May, and one brood is usual, but where the nests are disturbed fresh eggs in July are not uncommon. The grey or yellowish down of the young helps concealment when they crouch either on sand or amongst stones; the head is speckled with black, and there are irregular longitudinal lines on the back.

The adult in summer has a white forehead, black cap, grey mantle and wings, with black on the outer primaries, and white underparts and tail. The bill is yellow with a black tip; legs orange. Young in autumn have the back and wings mottled and barred with brown; the cap is brownish, and the white on the forehead wide; on the carpal joint is a dark patch, which persists until the second year. The bill and legs are much duller yellow than in the mature bird. Length, 10 in. Wing, 6·75 in. Tarsus, 0·6 in. (*Plates 89 and 171.*)

## Sandwich Tern                                          *Sterna sandvicensis*

The Sandwich Tern breeds in widely scattered colonies round the coasts of Europe and migrates as far south as Natal in winter. The largest colonies in

England, all now protected, are at the Farne Islands, Ravenglass and in East Anglia; there are rather more nesting groups in Scotland and Ireland, but their sites frequently change. In all colonies numbers may fluctuate widely from year to year, but in recent years there were over 1000 pairs in Norfolk and on the Farnes.

The Sandwich is the largest of our breeding terns and one of the easiest to recognise; its greater stretch of wing, shorter forked tail and heavier build, separate it at once from the slender, long-streamered birds. It is, however, graceful and easy in flight, often rising high, and in a good light a rosy tinge shows on its white underparts, for this adornment is not a monopoly of the Roseate Tern. On the ground the very black cap is striking, and as the feathers of the nape and neck are pointed they often stand out as a mane or crest, especially when raised under excitement. The black bill with a yellow tip can generally be seen on the flying bird; the legs are also black. The call—*kirr-whit* or *troo-it*—is less harsh than the notes of Common and Arctic Terns, and sounds almost musical when many are calling; the alarm or threat is a sharp *gwit* or *whut*. When hovering before a dive the tail is not, as a rule, depressed as in the other terns, and when it enters the water it is frequently submerged for an appreciable interval. The habit of the male of presenting fish to the female during courtship is very noticeable at the nesting colony; he struts with wings expanded and depressed, dangling his gift from the tip of his uplifted bill, sometimes, it is said, offering it to several females in turn until it is accepted. The upstretched neck and skyward pointed bill are characteristic attitudes of display. High, towering flights are also a feature of the courtship period. Most birds reach the breeding grounds in April, and eggs are often laid early in May; by the end of July most birds are at sea, and southward departure is in August and September. The majority of the British colonies are on sand dunes or sandy shores, but there are a few colonies on rocky stacks and, occasionally, on inland Irish loughs. Nests on sand are often mere scoops without any attempt at lining or rim, but round others a thin scattering of bents is arranged. Finished structures are uncommon. The colonies, or rather colonies within the colony, for little groups are often scattered around or even on the ground occupied by other terns or Black-headed Gulls, consist of half a dozen to several hundred nests, usually close together. At Ravenglass most of these groups of nests are on the slopes of the dunes amongst sparse marram grass. As incubation proceeds the nests become more and more evident, owing to the insanitary habits of the sitting bird, and often they are surrounded by scattered feathers.

The eggs are light in ground—creamy-white to rich buff—and are beautifully speckled, streaked, or blotched with black, brown and grey; two is the usual number, but single eggs are common. The parent birds are said to be less demonstrative in defence of eggs and young than other species, but they certainly stoop at the head of visitors to the colony with considerable show of ferocity. The nestling in down is better protected by its colour than the eggs, and though there are light and dark phases, it is on the whole lighter than other juvenile terns. The paler birds are creamy-white with a few black specks and dashes, darker ones are rich buff. When only a few days old the young leave the nest and ramble, and conceal themselves by partially burying themselves in self-made scrapes, exactly fitting their bodies, in the loose sand. The habit is most marked with the older young, the scoops being deeper. When they are about a fortnight old the young of the colony collect into a compact drove which moves about with striking cohesion before an intruder in the ternery.

The adult in breeding plumage has a black cap with a crest of longer feathers, pale grey mantle and wings and white underparts and tail. In winter plumage, which is often acquired in early autumn, the forehead is white and the crown streaked black and white. The bill is black with a yellow tip and the legs black. Immature birds in their first winter have a brownish cap and mottled back, wings and tail. Length, 15 in. Wing, 12 in. Tarsus, 1·2 in. (*Plates 90 and 171.*)

## Family ALCIDAE Auks

*Stout, short-winged, web-footed diving birds. Bills variable in shape; legs set far back and short; hind toe absent.*

**Razorbill**                                         *Alca torda*

Although the Razorbill is classed as a British resident, it is only from about the end of March to the beginning of August that it willingly comes to land; the rest of its life—day and night alike—is spent at sea. It is a pelagic inhabitant of the North Atlantic, nesting as far south as the Channel Islands. In their breeding haunts all round the British Isles the Razorbill and Guillemot are usually near neighbours. Razorbill colonies are widely distributed on cliffs round the British Isles but are absent from the English coast between Yorkshire and the Isle of Wight. Numbers have recently declined sharply in south-west England and south Wales, perhaps because of oil pollution at sea. In autumn and winter the Razorbill keeps well away from the shore, but stormy weather drives it in; after continuous rough weather, when it finds difficulty in obtaining food, large numbers of weakened birds are beaten to death by the breakers.

In the shape of its bill the Razorbill is intermediate between the two other common British auks, the Guillemot and the Puffin; it is deep and laterally compressed, far more so than the long pointed bill of the Guillemot, but shallower and less smartly decorated than that of the Puffin. It is black and transversely grooved, the deepest groove being sharply lined with white. The swimming Razorbill looks black on the back and wings, the Guillemot brown. The Razorbill floats buoyantly, tossed like a cork; its head rests easily on its stout neck; its short, pointed tail is slightly elevated. It can paddle quickly, and does so as a boat approaches, glancing back over its shoulder to judge the right moment to duck; when the curl from the bows threatens to swamp it, the bird neatly dives, leaving a trail of bubbles from its now open wings, for it flies under water. When swimming under water the bird inclines downward to react against the uplift of its air-filled body, and the wings propel it rapidly forward, the feet being only used as rudders when turning. Small fish, its chief food, are captured and swallowed under water, but when it hunts for its young, it brings them to the surface, and it is then that it has to dodge the unwelcome attention of thieving gulls. For so short-winged a bird its flight is rapid, but it splashes a little when rising from the water; when once fairly on the wing it flies straight with whirring pinions, usually near the surface, but it can rise high by a gradual ascent. No combination of letters expresses its curious and often querulous growling note; the young, when following the old birds on the water, have a plaintive whistling mew.

In February the birds return to the neighbourhood of the nesting colony, but remain on the water for some time before they visit the ledges. In April and May they line the face of the cliffs, resting on the whole of the foot—the tarsus and toes—but seldom walking, for they are poor pedestrians. The eggs are laid during May, usually late in the month, and both birds share in incubation. Before and during incubation the pair exchange compliments, rubbing and playing with one another's bill, or gently nibbling at the dense plumage; squabbles in which there is much bill biting and growling are frequent between neighbours and perhaps paired birds, but on the whole the life on the ledges is peaceful. Razorbills and Guillemots incubate in close proximity, but the latter places the egg on a more open ledge, sitting upon it in an upright position, whereas the former selects a crack or overhung ledge, and incubates with the egg lengthwise beneath the recumbent body. The cranny or sheltered ledge is usually on a steep cliff-face, but holes amongst broken rocks near the top of the cliff are sometimes occupied.

There is no attempt at a nest, the single large egg resting on the rock. It is more conical, less pyriform than that of the Guillemot, and though showing a wide range of variation, conforms a little more to regular types; a single example can give no idea of the wonderful variation of the eggs of either species. The spots, streaks, lines and blotches differ in size and quantity; the ground may be white, cream, blue, green or brown. The nestling has a short and shallow bill, a whitish head and underparts, and a velvety-brown back, but the first plumage closely resembles the summer dress of the old bird. The young is fed by the parent on fish, frequently sand-eels, and these are often brought several at once, held crosswise in the bill. After two or three weeks on the ledge the young goes to sea, and does not return to land until the following spring. The ledges are often 100 ft. or more above the sea, yet young still unable to fly may be seen with their parents on the water. The evidence indicates that they flutter down unaided, often in answer to their parents' calls from the sea below. The parents continue to feed them on the water, but the young soon learn to hunt for themselves.

The upper parts of the adult in summer are black, glossed with green; the chin and throat are dark, rich brown; the underparts, a wing-bar, and a line from the top of the bill to the eyes are white. In winter the sides of the face, chin and throat are white, and the line from bill to eye obscure. On the bill in summer there is a raised rim at the base of the upper mandible, but this is lost in winter. The bill of the young bird in autumn, when it has a plumage like the adult in winter, is short, shallow and at first ungrooved. The legs of the young are dark brown, of the old bird practically black. Length, 17 in. Wing, 8·5 in. Tarsus, 1·25 in. (*Plates 81 and 171.*)

**Little Auk**                                                   *Plautus alle*

The summer home of the Little Auk is on arctic islands and in the seas around them; the nearest of these to Britain is off the coast of Iceland. Its winter pelagic wanderings take it as far south as the Canary Islands and Azores, and almost annually a few are met with on our coasts during the colder months. Exceptionally birds in summer dress have been recorded as late as June. From time to time blizzards or fierce gales hurl hundreds upon our shores or whisk them far inland, even, during a north-easterly gale, across England from the east to the west coast; there are few counties which cannot record some of these unfortunates. It has been suggested that these casualties are birds already weakened by starvation, having strayed south of their normal range into warmer waters which are poor in their planktonic food, or the food may have been driven down beyond reach by prolonged storms.

The bird swims well, but deeply, 'by the stern'. It looks short-necked and stumpy, but neat and compact; its small size and short, conical bill prevent confusion with its congeners. It flies fast and straight, its wings whirring rapidly, and seems always in a hurry; if alarmed when swimming, it scutters along the surface and dives headlong into an advancing wave. It swims with its short wings like a penguin, steering as it turns with the spread webbed feet. Like other auks it swallows its food under water. Crustaceans and not fish seem to be the chief food of the Little Auk; at the breeding stations, its pouch-like cheeks are often loaded with small planktonic Crustacea— *Euphausia* in particular. Mysids, shrimps, prawns and small crabs are also captured, and the bird has been known to feed on offal thrown overboard from whalers and deep-sea trawlers.

During these invasions or, more correctly, 'wrecks' of Little Auks, the bird comes prominently before the public. The Little Auk comes to us to die. A few find temporary refuge on inland pools, or if more fortunate, reach quieter seas and may survive, but most if wind-driven far beyond the fatal lee shore finally drop exhausted.

In summer the upper parts are glossy-black, the lower part of the face, chin, neck and throat more sooty; a small semi-circular spot above the eye, the tips of the scapulars, a wing-band and the underparts are white. In winter the chin and throat are white, and there is a more or less marked white collar. Immature birds resemble the adult in winter, but lack the eye-spot. In spring and autumn, during plumage change, the chin and throat are mottled. The bill is black, the legs greenish-grey. Length, 8 in. Wing, 5 in. Tarsus, 0·9 in. (*Plate 93.*)

### Guillemot                                                    *Uria aalge*

The Guillemot breeds on suitable cliffs round the coasts of the British Isles, and the numbers of birds at some of the Scottish colonies are huge; but there has been a marked decline in the breeding population of England and Wales during the present century. Many Guillemots succumb to oil pollution of the sea, but deterioration in the food supply may also be a factor in the decrease. The breeding range in Europe extends as far south as Portugal.

On the water the Guillemot, besides being a browner bird, lacks the compact, plump and neat appearance of the Razorbill; it is a longer necked, more slender bird, with a long pointed bill. It swims well, and may be seen sporting on the surface, splashing and rolling, sometimes with the white underparts upward. It dives swiftly, catching and swallowing fish below the surface, and uses the wings under water, only employing the feet to assist when turning rapidly. Its flight is swift and straight, and when moving to and from distant feeding grounds parties frequently form strings or lines, skimming near the surface. In February or earlier, birds collect near the breeding cliffs, and long before the eggs are laid in May, constantly visit the ledges, quarrel for sites or posture with bobbing heads and swinging necks in nuptial preparation. In late summer the young are induced to take to the water. Throughout early autumn old and young remain near the cliffs. In winter, though some remain offshore, many appear to journey south, but a spell of rough weather brings some, mostly immature, hungry and wave-battered, and casts them dying on the beach. The note of the bird is a chattering growl, at times deep and angry in tone, at times shrill and querulous; from it the name 'Murre' is derived, though this conveys little to most ears.

On most coasts the Guillemot is more abundant than the Razorbill, and in favoured haunts, such as the chalk cliffs of Bempton and Flamborough, the rugged headlands of Wales, and the stacks and crags of Scotland and Ireland, its numbers are immense. Long rows of white-breasted birds sit upright on the ledges at dizzy heights, those sitting eggs usually with their front to the cliff, but the others, well upright, rest on the tarsus, the toes bent over the lip of the ledge, and swing their snaky necks from side to side. On the Farnes the flat tops of the Pinnacles are crowded with birds, but the brown mass is constantly in motion, disturbed by the arrival of newcomers who fight for foothold, while a stream drops off to fish. When leaving the ledge neither Guillemot nor Razorbill habitually dives seaward as frequently depicted and described, but flies off, maintaining a more or less horizontal position. The head and tail are depressed, and the arched back is held highest by the whirring wings; the bird floats outward and downward, gliding obliquely forward. No nest is made; the single large pyriform egg lies on bare rock, often on a ledge which slopes dangerously seaward.

The colour variation of the eggs is endless: the ground may be white, cream, yellow, blue, green, purple, red or brown; the spots, streaks, lines, smears or blotches of any colour, light or dark. Some eggs are blue or green without a spot; others are blotched or zoned with solid black or brown. The sitting bird is usually upright, though lack of head room may force it to lie prone; the egg is tucked lengthwise beneath the body and as much as possible of its surface brooded. When the downy young, dark brown above, greyish beneath, and with hoary heads, are hatched, the activity of the colony reaches its height. As far as the eye can reach the water is spotted with birds busily fishing; others trail off to known distant feeding grounds, or speed to join with gulls and porpoises in decimating a passing shoal of fry. The air is full of ascending and descending birds, and when a fish, for usually only one is brought at once, is carried up for the young, the captor alights on the slippery ledge with a flutter of wings as it strives to secure a balance. It is then that a bad-tempered neighbour will snatch its prize, or with a dig topple it backward and force it to make another attempt to land. Growling unamiable remarks greet these new-comers, and often with bills interlocked two will struggle for foothold. When in September the half-grown young eagerly follow their diving parents, swimming with head low and short bill pointed forward, they pipe a shrill *pee-oo, pee-oo.* The Bridled Guillemot, a sporadic variety with a white eye-rim and line towards the nape, is more numerous in the north and its frequency increases from under 1% on the south coast of England step by step to as much as 50% in northern Norway.

The adult bird in summer is slaty-brown on the upper parts, and more rufous-brown on the cheeks, chin and throat; the underparts and a narrow wing-bar are white. In winter the plumage is browner, and the sides of the face, chin and throat are white, a dark line passing through the eye to the cheeks. The first plumage of the juvenile resembles that of the adult in summer, but in autumn one more like the winter dress is attained, but the sides of the face and neck are mottled with brown. The bill is blackish-horn, the legs and feet blackish-brown. Length, 16·5 in. Wing, 7·75 in. Tarsus, 1·25 in. (*Plates 91, 93 and 172.*)

## Brunnich's Guillemot                                    *Uria lomvia*

This arctic bird has occasionally wandered to our shores. It has been recorded in Scotland, on the east coast and the Irish Sea. It is blacker than our bird and has a pale line from nostril to gape; the bill is stouter and deeper. In winter the dark cap extends well below the eye. Length, 16·5 in.

## Black Guillemot                                         *Cepphus grylle*

The Black Guillemot differs in many ways from other auks; it has a very distinct seasonal change of plumage, lays more than a single egg and is much less gregarious. It is found, seldom in large numbers, in Iceland and north-west Europe. In the British Isles it breeds locally in Scotland and the western islands, more plentifully in the Orkneys and Shetlands. It occurs round the coasts of Ireland and the Isle of Man, and a few pairs now breed in Cumberland and Anglesey. In winter, though pelagic, it wanders south and is occasionally met with in bays and inlets on all parts of the coast, but it is never common. In early spring an odd bird will remain on a rocky shore, its summer dress suggesting nuptial intentions, and it is always possible that some of its old stations may at times be occupied.

Few birds are more easy to recognise than the Black Guillemot in summer dress, for the glossy brownish-black plumage is set off by the big white patch on the wing; as it flies, even at a distance, or when like a duck it rises in the water to flap its wings, the flicker of this patch and of the white under-wing attracts the eye. Its legs are brilliant red, and when it calls, its bill, though really black, appears red, for the inside of the mouth is conspicuously orange-red. The white and black dress of winter is almost as noticeable. The plumage has a soft, blended look, the black and white bars on the upper parts merge without sharp dividing lines; the white patch on the dark wing remains unchanged. There is much variation in winter dress, for in many birds the head is almost white, merely flecked with black, but in others is well marked with dark streaks. The black dress is not invariably lost in winter and there is something in this soft, hoary plumage which suggests the doves.

Less sociable than other auks, the Black Guillemot straggles to its nesting haunts in February, but comes little to land until April. It swims lightly and dives with skill; both feet and wings are used in underwater progression. In flight its wings beat quickly; it flies close to the water as a rule, straight and with considerable speed, but finds the same difficulty in rising as other auks, splashing with feet and wings. On rocks it is more agile than the Common Guillemot, often standing on the toes alone, walking well with the body upright. When resting it sinks on to the tarsus or lies prone, the position during incubation. The common Orkney and Shetland name 'Tystie' is probably derived from its whistling cry. Fish are eaten and brought, one at a time, to the young, but crabs and other crustaceans, hunted for at the bottom or amongst the tangle of submerged rocks, are perhaps its chief food.

The eggs, usually two, are placed in a crack or fissure, seldom at any great height on a cliff-face, or are beneath loose stones in the fallen masses at the foot of a crag and sometimes in a cave. No nest is made. The colour is white or slightly tinted with green or cream, blotched and spotted towards the larger end with brown and lavender; they are laid late in May or in June. The nestling has sooty-brown down.

The adult in summer has completely black plumage except for a conspicuous white patch on the wing-coverts. In winter the head and underparts are white and the back barred blackish and white; the wing pattern is unchanged. The juvenile resembles the winter adult, but is darker and the whites are mottled with brown. The adult's bill is black; legs coral-red. Length, 13·5 in. Wing, 6·5 in. Tarsus, 1·25 in. (*Plates 93 and 172*.)

**Puffin** *Fratercula arctica*
No bird is more distinctive than the Puffin, and it is an abundant species.
It inhabits the arctic seas and north Atlantic, breeding as far south as Portugal,
and there is a wide dispersal from the breeding colonies in winter. Colonies
are scattered on suitable cliffs or islands round the British Isles, but there are
few on the east and south coasts of England; some in Scotland, Wales and
Ireland contain many thousands of birds.

There has been a very marked decrease in numbers, especially in the southern
part of the Puffin's range, in the 20th century. Brown rats are probably
responsible for the extinction of some colonies; elsewhere numbers have been
reduced by increased predation of Great Black-backed Gulls.

It is not the black and white plumage, the large parti-coloured bill, the upright carriage, or the orange legs that give the Puffin its quaint appearance,
but its eye; no bird has caused more unjustifiable hilarity than this 'big-nosed'
dumpy auk. The eye is set deeply above the round, full cheek, and from it a
conspicuous groove curves backward. Around the eye is a crimson ring, above
it a triangular steel-blue plate, and below a small bar of the same colour. As
we look at the serious birds, for they do look very serious standing in solemn
rows at the edge of the cliff or scattered over the thrift-grown turf, we unconsciously smile, but do not realise that it is the fixed expression caused by the
eye that entertains us. The Puffin is no clown, but a business-like, beautiful
little auk; it is our conceited ignorance of serviceable avian proportions which
misleads us. From its deep but shapely bill the bird receives semi-humorous
names—'Sea-parrot', 'Bottlenose', or the more descriptive 'Coulterneb';
there is something suggestive of the coulter of a plough in its shape, but
nothing to justify bottle-shape or parrot bill. It can catch and hold a slippery
fish and nip severely.

In March the far-scattered Puffins turn towards our islands. The majority
make their first landing in April, after lying offshore for some days in huge
rafts. Departure, which begins in August, often drags on until the middle of
September. Holes or burrows, not exposed ledges, are the nesting sites,
consequently the biggest colonies are on turf-covered islands, or the grassy
slopes of cliffs. At the colony the birds swarm, many loitering aimlessly,
others excavating, or attending to various domestic duties. Mated pairs
affectionately rub their bills together. Bowing, head-shaking and billing are
regular features of courtship, but coition takes place on the sea. The Puffin
stands on the toes—popularly called the foot—and does not rest upright on
the whole length of the tarsus like a Guillemot. When walking it has a nautical
roll, due to its short legs and the position of the feet, but it walks without
labour and can run quickly. A bird may often be seen chasing another with
head held low, and if the pursued is overtaken the big bills will be interlocked,
and with much growling each appears to be striving to wring its rival's neck.
On the sea near the colony the birds swim in hundreds; the brightly coloured
bill serves to distinguish them from their companions, Guillemots and
Razorbills.

The Puffin dives without effort, and under water swims with wings alone. The flight differs from that of other auks. When turned out of its burrow the bird runs down the slope towards the sea, often tumbling in its haste, and with open and quivering wings slowly rises like a starting aeroplane. When the bird rises clear the feet are gathered beneath it with 'palms' meeting, but as it descends towards the water are extended on either side of the tail. In the oblique descent they function as rudders and balancers, but are again drawn together when it skims out, perhaps for half a mile, low over the water. The pose of the body during the aerial dive is more diagonal than that of the descending Guillemot, and the wings vibrate rather than beat; the bird looks like some thick-bodied dragonfly. This curious vibrating flight is noticeable at other times, especially when clouds of birds wheel in accord; indeed, the Puffin is an active and agile bird on the wing, turning smartly with a steep heel over. The deep guttural *arr* is heard in the colony and on the water; it is a discontented and complaining sound, and has an angrier ring when the bird is rudely evicted from its burrow. The note varies or the bird has distinct calls, but all are deep. Though it will strive to shrink away from an intruding hand in its hole, the first evidence of occupation is often a savage and painful nip.

It is true that a rabbit burrow is occupied if one is handy, but most of the tunnels are excavated by the birds themselves; in a large colony the springy cushions of thrift and the turf are undermined by a labyrinth of burrows; the foot sinks into the superficial tunnels. The Puffin digs vigorously, scratching the soil backwards with its feet. A heavy, peculiar smell hangs over this densely crowded colony; the bird is not particular about sanitation. Many holes have more than one exit, and the position of the nest, when nest is made, may be a few inches from the entrance or many feet beyond reach. Holes under rocks or amongst loose stones are occupied; indeed, all the Puffin demands is a hole. The egg may be laid on the bare soil, or an untidy nest of grass, seaweed, thrift and feathers may be collected in a rounded chamber. The single egg, laid in the latter half of May, is dull white, rough in texture, and usually zoned with grey or reddish spots; it becomes much soiled from the wet feet of the incubating birds. The nestling has long sooty down, with a whitish patch on the underparts; its short bill and legs are slate-grey. It grows rapidly, and a little later has greyer down, and its legs show a pinkish tinge; it is active, runs well, and quickly bolts into its burrow if placed near the entrance. It has a piping note when handled, or when the old bird arrives with its beak full of fishes, neatly arranged in a row. R. M. Lockley, who has studied this species on the islands of west Wales, discovered that the parents desert their young one about the fortieth day, and that it then fasts for several days before it ventures out and flutters down the slope.

The adult Puffin has the upper parts and a collar greyish-black, darkest on the back; the underparts are white. The cheeks and throat are delicately shaded with grey. The basal portion of the beak is blue-grey, the outer portion orange and vermilion, more or less in transverse streaks; at the angle of the gape is a rosette of orange skin. The legs are orange, vermilion or lemon-yellow; indeed, the colours of beak and legs show considerable variation. In winter the raised rim, most of the outer covering of the bill, the rosette at the gape, and the decorations above and below the eye are shed; the bill becomes smaller and less brilliant. The young bird has the cheeks darker, and in front of the eye is a blackish patch; the bill in the young is at first short and more conical. Length, 12 in. Wing, 7 in. Tarsus, 1 in. (*Plates 93 and 172.*)

# Order COLUMBIFORMES

## Family PTEROCLIDAE Sandgrouse

*Ground birds; bill short, curved; wings long, pointed; tarsi short, feathered; toes three, united.*

**Pallas's Sandgrouse**                                    *Syrrhaptes paradoxus*
This bird breeds on the Mongolian and central Asiatic steppes and normally migrates southwards, but occasional westward irruptions have scattered birds over Europe. These abnormal movements are believed to be due to deep or hard snow depriving the birds of their diet of seeds. The last of these invasions to reach the British Isles was in 1908, when small flocks were scattered over our islands. In 1888 two or three pairs stayed to breed. Since 1909 the only records of the species are two in Ireland and one in Kent.

The birds look like light-coloured Partridges with pigeon heads, long pointed wings and tails, and remarkably swift flight recalling that of the Golden Plover. The call is *chack, chack*. The bird has short legs and feathered feet and walks awkwardly with short steps. Both male and female are sandy-brown in general colour, and have elongated central tail feathers. The head of the male is sandy-grey; his cheeks and chin rusty. His back is barred with brown, and there is a large buff patch on the wing. The lavender primaries are pointed. The breast is greyish-buff, crossed by a band of fine black markings; below the breast is a broad chocolate band. The female has smaller but more numerous markings on the upper parts; her head is streaked, and she lacks the gorget and buff wing patch. Length, 15–17 in.

## Family COLUMBIDAE Doves and Pigeons

*Wings ample, bill short, nostrils in soft, fleshy membrane; feet arboreal, toes four, tarsus short.*

**Stock Dove**                                                *Columba oenas*
In the northern part of its European range the Stock Dove is a migrant, but there is little evidence of migration in the British Isles, where the bird is a well-distributed and often plentiful resident. It has gradually extended its range during the present century and has now colonised practically the whole of Ireland, but it is still absent from the far north of Scotland. A sharp drop in numbers between 1957 and 1963, most noticeable in eastern England, was probably due to poisonous seed dressings.

The three pigeons, though superficially alike, have distinctive characters. The Stock Dove lacks the white wing-bar and half-collar of the Wood Pigeon and the white rump of the Rock Dove. The haunts of the Stock Dove are in more or less open country, for though it often nests in trees it prefers parklands to thick woods. It is common on coasts where the cliffs provide holes, and frequents sand dunes. Its flight is quick, performed by regular beats, with an occasional sharp flick of the wings, characteristic of pigeons in general. Indeed, there is much of the domestic pigeon in its bobbing gait, appearance and habits. In nuptial display it walks along a horizontal branch with swelled neck, lowered wings, and fanned tail. A male will bow to the female, with his bill almost touching the ground and his spread tail elevated vertically. During the circling spring flight the wings are smartly cracked.

The Stock Dove is sociable as well as gregarious, often consorting with Wood Pigeons. Something to its liking takes it to the shore, where it may be seen pecking at the sand on tidal banks, a common habit also of domestic pigeons. Although it eats grain at certain seasons, the seeds of weeds, especially chickweed and charlock, form an important part of its diet in winter and spring, and it does not usually compete with the Wood Pigeon in the clover leys. The short, deep, greeting call is quite distinct from the modulated cooing notes of the Wood Pigeon.

The nest, though it is seldom that any nesting material is used, is usually in a hole in a tree, a crack in a rock face, or in a rabbit-burrow, but the bird also nests in ivy, or in the thick growth round the boles of limes, as well as in deserted nests of other birds, squirrel dreys and in ruins and large buildings. Two creamy-white eggs, measuring about 1·5 by 1·15 in., are laid practically at any time between March and October. The down of the nestling is yellowish, and its bill at first dark, but later flesh-coloured. The young, like those of other doves, are at first fed on 'pigeon's milk'.

The upper parts of the adult are blue-grey, palest on the rump. The wing is crossed by two interrupted black bars, the quills are dark slate, and the tail shades from grey to almost black at the tip. The breast is pinkish and on the neck is a metallic-green and purple patch. The rest of the underparts are pale blue-grey; the under-wing is grey. The bill is brownish-yellow, pink towards the base; the legs pink with a purple tinge. The young bird has at first little lustre on the neck or sign of bars on the wing. Length, 13·5 in. Wing, 8·8 in. Tarsus, 1·1 in. (*Plates 97 and 173*.)

**Rock Dove**                                                    *Columba livia*

The Rock Dove has a restricted range in western and southern Europe; in our islands it is a local resident, even in Scotland, Ireland and the western and northern isles, which are the only areas where the bird is found in a fairly pure form. Even here there may be interbreeding with feral pigeons. There has been a marked decline in the numbers of Rock Doves during the 20th century, perhaps due to competition with the Stock Dove for the seeds which form its staple diet in the winter. This bird is the Blue Rock from which our domestic breeds are descended, and not only will the wild bird visit and feed with tame birds about the farms, but, pairing with them, induces them to cast off the fetters of domesticity.

The white lower back of the Rock Dove is its best character, but the two black bars on its pale grey wing are distinct; the tail is margined with white. It is strong and quick on the wing, dashing out from the caves, flying low over the water, its white rump showing well from above. Little parties will circle over the sea and the cliff-tops, when the white under-wing is equally conspicuous; in its flight, behaviour and voice, which is more of a dovecot *coo* than the phrase of the Wood Pigeon, it shows its relationship. Though fields are visited for grain and green food, it is nowhere so plentiful as to be a pest, and the seeds of many weeds are eaten. Like other pigeons it often drinks; Coward saw one alight on the sea and apparently drink salt water. The bowing courtship, when the metallic lustre of the neck is fully displayed, often takes place on ledges where Guillemots and Razorbills sit.

The nest is usually on a ledge in a cave; it is a slight structure of grasses, heather or seaweed. The two white eggs, more like those of the Wood Pigeon than the Stock Dove, measuring 1·5 by 1·1 in., may be laid any time between March and September, or even later. The nestling has pale yellow down and a flesh-coloured bill with a dark band. It is tended and fed on 'milk' like other doves. Two or more broods are raised.

The adult's head and neck are a darker blue-grey than the back and wings; the lower back is white. There are two black wing-bars; the under-wing is white. The green and lilac or purple patch on the side of the neck is larger than that of the Stock Dove, and the tail is more distinctly banded. The bill is leaden; the legs red. Young birds are duller and show little lustre. Length, 13·5 in. Wing, 8·5 in. Tarsus, 1·2 in. (*Plates 94 and 173*.)

**Wood Pigeon**                                        *Columba palumbus*

The Wood Pigeon, or Ring Dove, breeds throughout most of Europe and is a common resident in all regions of the British Isles; but it is always most abundant in areas of intensive agriculture. R. K. Murton, in his monograph on the species, has shown that there is no foundation for the theory of large-scale migration in Britain. A few British-ringed birds have been recovered across the English Channel, but the great majority are almost sedentary. The recovery of foreign-ringed birds in Britain is even more exceptional, and the considerable numbers that are occasionally seen to arrive on the east coast are probably 'drifted' passage migrants.

Even in the London parks the Wood Pigeon, the largest of our wild pigeons, is a familiar bird; indeed, it is there so confiding that we have excellent opportunity of studying its portly figure and beautiful plumage; in the country, where it is not beloved, it is shy. It walks, perches and bows with swelled neck and fanned tail like a dovecot bird, but has certain characters and habits of its own. It can always be told by the white patch on its neck, and when flying by the transverse white bar on the wing. The song, heard at all seasons but most frequently in the summer months, normally consists of a repetitive *cooo-coo, coo-coo*; *coo-cooo-coo, coo-coo*; but there are sometimes variations. In the territorial display flight the bird rises rather steeply with strong wing-beats, then stiffening its wings, falls and rises in a series of undulations, at the end of which there is sometimes a sharp crack, caused by a strong down-beat of the wing. Nuptial display takes various forms, including a special call accompanied by bowing with raised and fanned tail, 'nest-calling' with downward pecking, caressing of the head and neck, and courtship feeding. The Wood Pigeon drinks freely without raising the head from the water to swallow. The pectoral muscles are powerful; the bird fights with the wings, and even a 'squab' in the nest will give a smart blow.

Sportsmen declare that the Wood Pigeon is difficult to kill, the shot glancing off its feathers as if it were clad in mail; certainly its pinions sound stiff and hard when with a clatter it dashes through the branches. But it is possible that it is the softness of its plumage which presents a cushion to the shot, for few birds have softer or looser covering. The diet of the Wood Pigeon varies from one district to another, but on the arable farmland where the species is most abundant cereals are the main food from July to November, while clover and brassica and legume leaves are important in winter. Acorns and other tree fruits and the seeds and leaves of weeds may also be taken in large quantities, but the survival of numbers of the pigeons through the winter depends on the availability of grain in the stubbles and large quantities of clover. Animal food is only occasionally taken.

Murton has shown that the nesting season of the Wood Pigeon is closely linked to the food supply. There is some successful breeding in April, only a little in May and June, and a peak at harvest time in August and September, when 70% of the young leave the nest. The low hatching and fledging success in midsummer occurs when the birds are taking green food. The nest is a flimsy platform of intertwisted sticks, through which the light shows, and the eggs may be seen from below; it is built in a tree or hedge at varying height from the ground; exceptionally it is on the ground or on a ledge. The two eggs are dead white and glossier than those of the Stock Dove; they measure about 1·6 by 1·2 in. Two or even three broods are reared. The nestling or squab has sparse yellow down, and a broad, soft bill, the lower mandible broadest; it pushes its boat-shaped bill into those of its parents and sucks up the milky fluid they provide for its early nourishment.

The upper parts of the adult are bluish-grey, the wings darker, and the white-bordered quills greyish-brown. On the neck, which is shot with green and purple, are large white patches, and the white bar on the wing shows when the bird is at rest as a patch on the angle. The breast is pinkish, shading to pale lavender on the abdomen. The upper surface of the tail is blackish, but the under has a blue-grey subterminal bar. The bill is yellow, red at the base, and white over the nostrils; the legs red. The young bird has at first no white on the neck, and the wing-bar is suffused with blue. Length, 16 in. Wing, 9·5 in. Tarsus, 1·3 in. (*Plates 97 and 173*.)

## Collared Dove                                        *Streptopelia decaocto*

The speed and extent of the north-westerly spread of the Collared Dove across Europe in the mid-20th century has been a most striking and interesting phenomenon. Originally an Asiatic species, it bred in a limited area of the Balkans south of the Danube in 1900. It had reached Belgrade in 1912, Hungary in 1932, and the Baltic and North Sea by 1950. A male spent the summer of 1953 in Lincolnshire and a pair nested in Norfolk in 1955. Ten years later it had spread north into the Highlands of Scotland and westward across England and Wales to the west coast of Ireland. Its distribution in the British Isles is still uneven, but it is very abundant in many parts of England, especially in agricultural districts, although it has been slow to colonise hill country.

The Collared Dove is easily distinguished from the Turtle Dove by its uniform fawn-grey upper parts and black half-collar. Confusion with feral Barbary Doves is easier, but the Barbary is a paler, creamy-coloured bird and lacks the Collared Dove's blackish wing-tips. It should be noticed, however, that in some Collared Doves the dark primaries tend to fade in summer.

The Collared Dove is usually found in the vicinity of human dwellings, near a farm or village or in a town park. It often perches on television aerials and electricity cables, from which it flies down to feed on the ground in a poultry-run, garden, field or waste ground. It has a rolling, waddling gait, but its flight is swift and straight. In towns and villages it may become tame and confiding, but in open country it is usually rather shy and unapproachable. Outside the breeding season small parties may be seen, and sometimes considerable flocks gather at communal roosts. Although there may be some local movement the bird has no regular migration and is generally sedentary, though individuals continue the north-westerly expansion of the species. The song of the male, a distinctive *coo-cooo-cuk*, with the stress on the second syllable and an abrupt end, is heard throughout the spring and summer. The female is generally silent, but both sexes use a wheezing flight call. In the display flight the bird flutters almost vertically upward and then glides down in a semicircle with outspread wings and splayed tail.

The nest is usually at least 12 ft. from the ground, often in an evergreen; it is a rough platform of sticks, sometimes with a lining of roots and grass. Two white, rather glossy eggs are laid between March and September; both birds incubate. As many as five broods may be reared in a season.

The adult is pale grey-brown on the upper parts, rather lighter on the head, and soft grey with pinkish flush on the underparts. A narrow black half-collar at the back of the neck is edged with white. The primaries are blackish. The tail seen from below is white with black at the base; from above it is grey with whitish outer feathers. The juvenile has pale edges to the feathers, giving a slightly patterned appearance, and the collar is faint. The bill is black, legs reddish, and eye ruby-red. Length, 11 in. (*Plates 92 and 97*.)

### Turtle Dove *Streptopelia turtur*

The migratory Turtle Dove has a wide breeding range in Europe, as far north as the southern shores of the Baltic and North Sea, and winters in Africa. It has extended its summer range in the British Isles, especially on the eastern side, and now nests in south-east Scotland and one or two eastern counties of Ireland. On the west side of England, south Lancashire is its northern limit.

Smaller and slighter in build than other doves, the Turtle may be recognised by its browner colour, and the black and white striped patch on the side of its neck, but it is its tail that catches the eye when it flies from the observer; it is wedge-shaped, with a dark centre and white borders and tips. When viewed from below this pattern, owing to the white under tail-coverts obscuring the dark bases, is a blackish chevron on a white ground. This is noticeable when the bird stoops to drink, raising its spread tail. April is nearly ended before the Turtle, one of the latest migrants, appears; it often is not here until May, while passage birds travel through in June.

It is a bird of open rather than dense woodlands, and frequently feeds on the ground. The flight is often described as arrowy, but is not remarkably swift; in the open it is direct, but the turns and dodges are neat when the bird flies amongst trees. For so small a dove the flight is strong, performed with purposeful beats. The nuptial flight, high and circling, is rather like that of the Wood Pigeon, but the undulations are less decided; it is accompanied by the whip-crack of the downward flicked wings. The arrival in spring is heralded by its purring notes, a rather deep, vibrating *courrr, courrr*. Seeds of various kinds are eaten, especially those of fumitory and chickweed; grain is only a minor item in its diet. Where food is plentiful a number of birds may be seen together, but it is hardly gregarious in summer. Like other pigeons it will drink salt as well as fresh water, visiting the shore and marshes for this purpose.

The nest is even more flimsy looking than that of the Ring Dove, being built of more slender twigs, usually at no great elevation, in a tree or old untrimmed hedge. Two white eggs, about 1·2 by 0·9 of an inch, are laid late in May or in June. The 'gentle Turtle', even when a mere down-clad squab, will fight vigorously, striking with its feeble wing, pecking and snapping its soft bill in defiance.

The adult has head, neck, flanks and rump blue-grey, back and wings reddish-brown with black centres to the feathers. There is a black and white striped patch on the side of the neck. The breast is pinkish, the abdomen and under tail-coverts white. The tail is blackish with white edges and tips. The bill is black, legs and eye-rims red. The neck patch is absent in the duller juvenile. Length, 11 in. Wing, 7 in. Tarsus, 0·9 in. (*Plates 92, 97 and 173.*)

# Order CUCULIFORMES

## Family CUCULIDAE Cuckoos

*The Cuckoos have a common character, the zygodactyle foot, but in appearance
and habits they show great variation.*

### Cuckoo                                                              *Cuculus canorus*

The Cuckoo is a summer visitor to the Palaearctic regions, and winters in
tropical and southern Africa. It is an abundant summer visitor and bird of
passage in the British Isles, arriving in early April and occurring from the
coastal sandhills to the tops of the moors, but avoiding the denser woods.

The almost human tone of the Cuckoo's voice compels attention. Occasionally it reaches the south coast at the end of March, though it is usually the
second or third week of April before it is generally distributed. The voice of
the bird is more familiar than its appearance. It is a long-tailed, sharp-
winged, slate-grey bird, barred on the under surface, often, not without
reason, confused with the Sparrow Hawk. Even the small birds appear to
share this doubt, and chase and mob it persistently. Its flight may be direct
and strong, but at times curiously wavering and uncertain; it is ungainly in
its movements, and will alight on a bush with outstretched wings, using them
as hands to maintain its balance. The males arrive first and at all times
predominate; indeed, the species is polyandrous. The familiar *cuc-koo* is the
song of the male and is heard at night as well as by day from April to mid June.
Bowing forward, with swelled throat, head lowered, wings drooped and fanned
tail elevated, the male Cuckoo shouts from his perch, but almost as frequently
he calls as he flies. The so-called change of tune, when the note is triplicated,
is not heard in June alone; during courtship it is common. The female has a
bubbling chuckle, and both sexes utter a deep *kow, wow, wow*.

The greedy Cuckoo is a useful bird; it devours many larvae which other
species reject. The irritating hairs of the larvae of ermine, tiger, drinker or
gold-tail moths, which protect these caterpillars from many birds, have no
terrors for the Cuckoo; the hairs stick to the lining of its stomach or are ejected
in small pellets or balls, sometimes mixed with vegetable fibre. The protectively coloured larva of the magpie moth, and that of the gooseberry sawfly,
*Nematus ribesii*, are much sought for; as many as eight Cuckoos have been seen
in one small group of bushes when the sawfly larvae have been defoliating the
plants. The stomachs of two birds killed during a plague of these grubs were
distended with the larvae. Beetles, other insects and worms are also eaten.

About a dozen eggs are normally laid in a season by a single hen. She watches
the nest-building of prospective fosterers and lays one egg directly into each
nest, carrying away, and often swallowing, one of the original clutch. Cuckoos'
eggs have been found in the nests of a wide variety of species, but the most
frequent foster-parents are Meadow Pipits, Dunnocks, Pied Wagtails, Reed

PLATE 98
*Above left :* Barn Owl, p211      *Above right :* Tawny Owl, p215
*Below :* Tengmalm's Owl, p219

PLATE 99

Snowy Owl, p213

PLATE 100

Short-eared
Owl, p217

PLATE 101

*Above left :* Long-
eared Owl, p216
*Above right :*
Snowy Owl, p213

*Below left :* Short-
eared Owl, p217
*Below right :*
Eagle Owl, p213

PLATE 102
  *Above :* Scops Owl, p212
  *Below :* Cuckoo, p208

  *Above :* Little Owl, p214
  *Below :* Hoopoe, p227

PLATE 103    Nightjar, p220

Photo: *J. B. and S. Bottomley*

PLATE 104     Great Spotted Woodpecker (female), p230

PLATE 105
*Above :* Swift, p222
*Below :* Kingfisher, p224

*Above :* Alpine Swift, p223
*Below :* Bee-eater, p225

PLATE 106
*Above :* Green Woodpecker, p229
*Below :* Great Spotted Woodpecker,
    p230

*Above :* Swallow, p238
*Below :* Lesser Spotted Woodpecker,
    p232

Photos : John Clegg

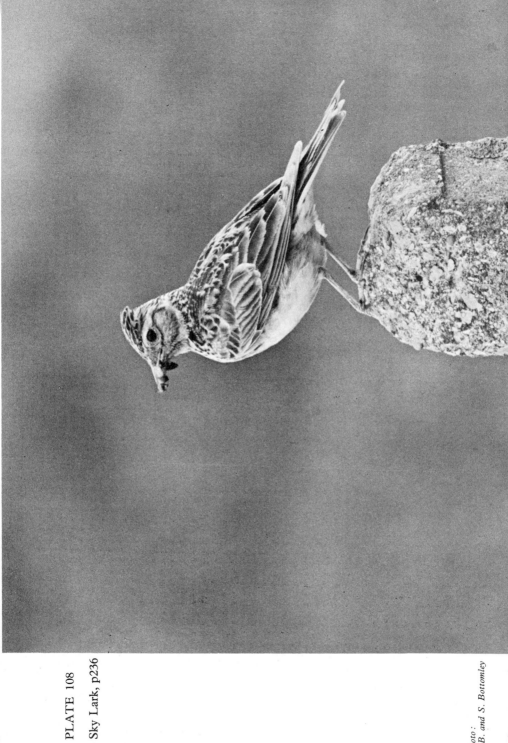

PLATE 108
Sky Lark, p236

Photo:
J. B. and S. Bottomley

PLATE 109

*Above left :*
Nightjar, p220
*Above right :*
Wryneck, p232

*Below left :*
Roller, p226
*Below right :*
Golden Oriole,
    p243

*Above :* House Martin, p240
*Below left :* Sky Lark, p236

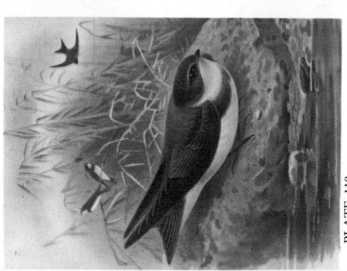

PLATE 110
*Above :* Sand Martin, p242
*Above right :* Wood Lark, p234

PLATE 111
Swallow, p238

PLATE 112    Sand Martin, p242

PLATE 113

*Above :* Raven, p244
*Below left :* Jackdaw, p249
*Below right :* Nutcracker, p251

Warblers and Robins. Each female Cuckoo usually lays all her eggs in nests of the same species. The eggs, remarkably small for the size of the bird, are speckled or blotched with brown or grey on a very variable ground colour. The incubation period is only twelve and a half days, so the Cuckoo's egg is often the first of the clutch to hatch. Though small birds instinctively mob the Cuckoo, when an egg is once in the nest and after the abnormal fledgling is hatched no attempt is made to dislodge it; indeed a bird will brood the foster-chick while her own lie slowly dying outside the nest.

When hatched the young Cuckoo, during the first few days of its naked, blind and apparently helpless existence, throws out the unhatched eggs or fellow nestlings. The bird fidgets when it feels pressure against its side, sinks to the bottom of the nest and, when egg or young roll on to its sensitive back, it at once appears to be attacked by epileptic power, stiffens its legs, stretches out its featherless wings, and using them as hands climbs backwards up the rim of the nest. With a final hitch it throws the unwelcome load over and sinks exhausted and inert back into the nest. With constant wheezy call—*chiz, chiz, chiz*—it clamours for food; when it is larger than its hard-worked foster-parents, they will stand on its back to administer food, and continue their attentions long after it has left the nest. Apparently the voice of the young Cuckoo has commanding, almost hypnotic power, for other birds than its foster-parents will feed it. The half-grown young bird, either in or out of the nest, resents interference, and will raise and lower itself on its legs, swell out its feathers until those of the crown rise like a white-rimmed frill above its head, spread its white-tipped but stumpy tail and hiss defiance. It will peck furiously at the human hand, and often at the bird which has just presented it with food. In August many of the old Cuckoos depart, but young birds are about until late in September.

The adult male is slate-grey above, with white bars on the inner webs of some of the brown quills, white bars and tips to the outer tail feathers and white spots on the shafts of the central pair. The upper breast is pale slate; the rest of the underparts are white with dark bars. The female usually shows a brownish band across the breast, and an occasional adult hen keeps the rufous juvenile plumage. The bill is slate-black; the legs, orbits and irides yellow. The young have the upper parts barred with dark brown and rufous; many of the feathers are white tipped and there is a conspicuous white patch on the nape; the white-tipped tail is also barred; the underparts are buffish-white, barred throughout with black. Length, 13 in. Wing, 8·5 in. Tarsus 0·95 in. (*Plates 102 and 173*.)

## Great Spotted Cuckoo                        *Clamator glandarius*

The large, crested Great Spotted Cuckoo breeds in Africa, southern Europe and part of western Asia; it has been recorded about ten times in England, Wales and Ireland. Its parasitic and other habits resemble those of our bird; its call is a loud *kee-ou*, and its alarm a harsh *kark*. It has a long grey crest, ash-brown, white-spotted upper parts, white-tipped tail and white underparts.

The chestnut-coloured primaries of the young bird afford a most striking aid to identification in the field. Length, 15·5 in.

## Yellow-billed Cuckoo                                    *Coccyzus americanus*

This species nests in North America and winters in South America. It has occurred at least fifteen times in England and Wales, Ireland and Scotland. It constructs a nest and incubates its eggs. The call is described as a monotonous *koo, koo, koo*. The upper parts are greyish-brown, rufous on the wings, the underparts white, tail feathers black with white tips. The upper mandible is black on the culmen; the rest of the bill is bright yellow; the legs are lead-grey. Length, 11 in.

# Order STRIGIFORMES

## Family STRIGIDAE Owls

*The Owls are separated from the diurnal Birds of Prey on account of certain structural characters, some of which are shared by certain families of the Falconiformes. The feet have the outer toe reversible; the usual position when perched is two toes in front and two behind. They are raptorial, suited for grasping or snatching prey. The bill is strongly curved and hooked; the eyes are directed forward, and usually surrounded by a well-marked facial disc. The plumage is soft and downy, noiseless in flight.*

**Barn Owl** *Tyto alba*

The Barn Owl is a resident in most parts of the British Isles, though scarce in much of Scotland and absent from the extreme north. There has been a marked decrease in nearly all districts in recent years. The Barn Owl is found throughout most of Europe, though birds of the north and east belong to a distinct race with much darker plumage. A few examples of this sub-species have been found in Britain.

Of all the owls the White or Barn Owl is perhaps the best known, for it is more frequently associated with human habitations than other species. It is often described as white, the underparts being most noticeable when, with desultory flight, it reels and wavers through the dusk. Generally crepuscular and nocturnal in its habits, it eludes observation; it appears, a noiseless shadow, and vanishes at once, for its soft pinions make no sound; but in winter, and when feeding young, it not infrequently hunts in broad daylight. It is a familiar inhabitant of old buildings, church towers, and house gables, even frequenting thickly populated suburbs. The ordinary note is a hiss, heard first when the downy young, perched outside the nesting hole, continually call for food. The old bird also hisses. In young the hiss deepens into a snore, but the usual call of the old bird is a loud, weird scream or screech, from which the bird gets the name of Screech Owl. This begins with a hiss, but continues as an accentuated combination of chirrup and snore, and has a startling effect when heard from the invisible bird. During its nightly rounds, for it has regular beats, it screeches repeatedly, a habit calculated to discount the advantage gained by its silent flight. The suggestion that small mammals are startled into movement is hardly supported by experience, for the alarmed mouse or shrew instantly 'freezes' and is then difficult to detect.

In the daytime the Barn Owl roosts in some regular spot, either in a building, hollow tree or a sheltered bank. Its pose is bolt upright, its long legs distinctly knock-kneed, its toes, if standing on the flat, point in all directions, but when perched, two are, as a rule, in front, and two behind the object grasped. The Barn Owl uses its feet for grasping its prey; they are strong and armed with sharp talons; the claw on the middle toe is pectinated. The bird fights with the feet, and will throw itself on its back ready to repel an attack;

the grip of the feet drives the sharp claws into an incautious hand. When at rest the round facial disc becomes oval, but the bird watches through slits of the apparently closed eyes, and follows the movements of the observer by turning the head without shifting the body or legs. Displeasure is shown by more grotesque contortions; an angry owl will lower the head and swing it to and fro, close to the ground, like an irate bull, or hissing, will stretch its head forward, drooping its wings, and snap its bill.

The Barn Owl is one of our most useful agricultural allies, feeding extensively on rats, mice, voles and shrews; small birds are eaten, the House Sparrow being a favourite prey. These are captured at night when at roost in ivy and evergreens. The fur and bones of the creatures devoured, together with the elytra of beetles, on which it also feeds, are regurgitated in the form of oblong pellets or 'plugs', a habit common to most insectivorous and animal-feeding birds. Barn Owl pellets are large, dark-coloured and have a smooth, almost polished surface. Mammals as large as a rat will be swallowed whole, the tail often hanging for hours from the mouth whilst digestion of the swallowed portion progresses. The tail, pelvic girdle and legs, with the almost complete skin of the rat, curiously reversed, are finally disgorged.

No nest is made, but the four to eight, or even more white eggs are often placed on a layer of dry pellets amongst the rafters of a barn, house, church tower or other building, or in a hollow tree or crevice in a rock. They are laid usually late in April, and though laid at intervals of several days, they are incubated at once; thus eggs and young of varying age are found in the nest at the same time. A second brood is usual, and eggs in December are recorded. The young at first are clad in thick white down.

The colour of the upper parts is orange-buff, vermiculated with grey, and spotted with grey and white; the underparts are white with a few dark grey spots. Round the eyes the facial disc is rusty, and the white bill is almost hidden by a double ridge of white feathers. The legs are clothed down to the feet with white hair-like feathers; the toes are dusky, the claws brown and the irides almost black. In the Dark-breasted European form the underparts are buff and more thickly spotted, the facial disc is often rusty-red throughout and the upper parts much greyer. Length, 14 in. Wing, 11·25 in. Tarsus, 2·4. in. (*Plates 96, 98 and 172.*)

## Scops Owl                                                        *Otus scops*

Scops Owl is the smallest owl which occurs in Britain, and its visits are uncertain and irregular. It is a summer visitor to southern Europe. The usual winter quarters are in Africa, but on migration the bird wanders and has frequently been met with in Europe north of its normal breeding area; in the British Isles it has occurred, for the most part in spring but also in autumn, in England, Wales, Ireland and Scotland and the northern isles.

More nocturnal than the other small owls, Scops Owl, which is distinguished from the Little Owl by its erectile horns and small head, spends the day on a branch, close to the trunk, and like the Long-eared Owl instantly straightens up its body and erects its ear-tufts if disturbed; against the bark its brownish-grey dress is inconspicuous. The monotonous call is spelt by those who have heard it as *kiu, ki-ou,* or *kee-oo.* Though it will eat small mammals, its food chiefly consists of insects.

Scops Owl is a small grey bird, mottled and vermiculated with brown and grey; on both upper and underparts most of the feathers have dark shaft streaks. The wings and tail are barred. The bill and bare toes are dark brown, and the irides yellow. Length, 7·5 in. (*Plate 102.*)

## Eagle Owl                                                        *Bubo bubo*

The Eagle Owl is a rare wanderer to Britain from the mountain forests of northern Europe. Probably those which reach the Orkneys, Shetlands and Scotland are wanderers from Scandinavia. It is doubtful if all the birds which have been recorded from different parts of England were really wild; in some cases they have been escaped captives, for the Eagle Owl is a favourite aviary bird. From size alone the Eagle Owl cannot be confused with any other. It has a loud distinctive and impressive call, *boo, boo,* and a flight note which has been likened to the cry of the Heron. Not only does it look ferocious, but it is bold and fierce, often attacking its owner when in captivity.

The ear-tufts of the Eagle Owl are long, and though occasionally drooped are less concealed than in other 'eared' owls. The upper parts are blackish-brown mottled with tawny-buff; the wings and tail are barred. The underparts are paler buff, boldly streaked on the breast, and more finely barred and streaked on the lower breast and abdomen. The bill is blackish horn and the irides orange. The female is the larger bird. Length, 24 to 26 in. (*Plate 101.*)

## Snowy Owl                                                   *Nyctea scandiaca*

As suggested by its name and white plumage, the Snowy Owl is a bird of the arctic, circumpolar in range, and migrating southward in winter. To the Orkneys and Shetlands it is an occasional winter visitor, appearing from September onwards and departing again in March and April. It not infrequently reaches the Hebrides and mainland of Scotland, and is occasionally seen in Ireland. Elsewhere in the British Isles it is a rare straggler which, it may be safely inferred, seldom escapes attention when it appears. In 1967 a pair nested in the Shetlands, far south of the usual breeding range, and succeeded in rearing five young, which were fed on rabbits and an occasional Oystercatcher. Non-breeders had been seen in the Shetlands for four preceding summers.

This large and conspicuous bird, that is, conspicuous when met with away from its snow-covered normal surroundings, cannot be confused with any other species. Its flight is with strong measured beats, but rapid; its calls, a loud *krau-au,* and its alarm *rick, rick, rick,* rapidly repeated, are rarely heard. It hunts mostly by day, and in the British Isles it will eat rabbits, mice and birds. It is described as an expert at fish-catching, waiting for them by the holes in the ice and snatching them with its feet. It nests on the ground. In

Britain it is usually seen over moorlands, marshes and other open country.

The Snowy Owl is variable in plumage, some male birds being almost entirely white with only a few brown marks on wings and tail. Most females are barred and spotted with brown except on the face and throat. The feet are feathered on soles and toes; the bill and claws are black; the irides yellow. The female is much larger than the male. Length, 22–25 in. (*Plates 99 and 101.*)

## Hawk Owl                                             *Surnia ulula*

The Hawk Owl has occurred about ten times in England and Scotland. The European subspecies, distinguished by the narrower bars on the underparts, is found in summer in northern Europe and Asia, migrating south to winter. The American race, which has also been found in Britain, breeds in northern Canada and Alaska.

The bird is hawk-like in appearance, having the facial disc incomplete, and also in its dashing flight and semi-diurnal habits. It is dark brown above, spotted and mottled with white; a broad black band borders the white disc. The tail is long and graduated, barred with brown. The underparts are regularly barred with dark brown, these bars being broader, redder, and more pronounced in the American bird. The bill is yellowish-white, the claws dark and the irides bright yellow. The female is the larger bird. Length, 14–16 in.

## Little Owl                                            *Athene noctua*

The Little Owl occurs throughout central and southern Europe. It is a sedentary species, but it is probable that genuine wanderers have reached us from its continental home, for it breeds in Holland, Denmark and Germany. But as a well-established artificial colonist the Little Owl must be included as truly British. Although the species has now colonised the whole of England and Wales and has spread into Scotland, it is thinly distributed in the northern part of its range, and there are indications that the period of expansion is now over and some recession has taken place. A general, but perhaps temporary, decrease, similar to that affecting other predatory birds, took place in about 1957, most noticeably in south-east England.

As long ago as 1843 Waterton released a few Little Owls in Yorkshire, but the attempt to establish them met with small success; later efforts, however, in Northamptonshire, Cambridge, Hertfordshire and Kent produced results which caused no small alarm amongst game preservers, for the bird spread in all directions; Lord Lilford was blamed for his repeated introduction of Dutch birds. The gamekeeper accuses it of destroying game and their eggs, but though a diurnal feeder cannot be expected to refuse an occasional Pheasant or Partridge chick, examination of its pellets reveals no serious crime. An important inquiry into the food of the Little Owl was conducted in 1936–37 by the British Trust for Ornithology. Insect food is a most important part of its diet: many beetles, crane-flies, earwigs, etc. Rodents are eaten throughout the year: rats, rabbits, mice and voles. Birds are taken mainly in the nesting season: mainly ground-feeding birds such as starlings, sparrows, etc., but game chicks rarely.

The typical call of the bird is a monotonous and far-reaching *cu, cu, cu,* and some authors speak of a mewing note; but in the spring the bird has a much more varied repertoire of calls. Though the bird usually hunts at night it is more diurnal than most owls, and will sit in bright sunshine on some gate, branch or hedge, where it suffers unwelcome attention from other birds. Its flight is erratic, uncertain in direction; its pose when perched is erect. The classical student and archaeologist is familiar with this bird of Pallas, for its figure appears on many Greek coins. The squat figure and flat-topped head are diagnostic features.

The nest is in a hollow, but without nesting material; holes in trees, walls, rocks and quarries are occupied, and sometimes the eggs are laid on the ground with hardly any shelter. Four or five white eggs are laid in April or in May, incubated by the female only. The down of the young is at first dull white, then later reddish-grey.

The upper parts of the Little Owl are greyish-brown, spotted, mottled and barred with white; the spots form streaks on the head. The wings and tail are barred white and brown; the whitish underparts streaked with brown. The bill is yellow, as are the irides; the legs and toes grey, covered with hairy down. Length, 9 in. Wing, 6 in. Tarsus, 1·1 in. (*Plates 102 and 172.*)

### Tawny Owl                                                           *Strix aluco*

Outside Britain the Tawny Owl, a sedentary species, is found in most parts of Europe. In our islands it occurs throughout Great Britain, but is unknown in the outer Scottish islands, Ireland and the Isle of Man.

The Tawny Owl is distinctly a woodland species, but is commonly found in parks and large gardens in towns as well as in more rural surroundings. It spends the day amongst trees, usually sitting bolt upright in some hollow, or on a branch with its side pressed against the trunk, and with dreamy half-closed eyes. The hearing of the owl is keen; it is practically impossible to surprise the bird at its roost. When discovered it is only necessary to move one's position to realise that the bird is really watching through the half-closed lids; without moving its feet or the position of its body it turns its neck so that the facial disc is always towards us. The dense mass of long soft feathers on the head and neck give the Tawny Owl a top-heavy appearance, and it seldom sinks the feathers so closely as to appear thin and attenuated, as does the Long-eared Owl in a similar position. It is a browner, more mottled bird than the Long-eared Owl, and the pale bars on the wings are noticeable. The voice of the Tawny Owl is the true hoot, though not the proverbial *tu-whit, tu-whit, tu-whoo.* There is a short preliminary *oo, oo,* and a long quavering and beautiful *oo-oo-oo-oo.* The note may be startling, even weird, when heard in the night, but it is certainly musical. The hoot of the young, heard in late summer or early autumn, is similar but more hissing. Tawny Owls call frequently throughout the autumn and winter, even during hard and frosty weather, not only in the woods but when on the nightly round for food. The young utter the only call which resembles *tu-wit*, a shrill sharp note quite distinct from the flight call, *ki-wik, ki-wak*, which is shared by old and young. This is a hunger call and also a cry of anger. Occasionally the bird hoots in the daytime.

The Tawny Owl, except when feeding young, seldom goes abroad in daylight, and when it does it is usually accompanied by all the smaller birds in the neighbourhood; the alarm notes of any species seem to be recognised and call together all and sundry to mob the common foe. Jackdaws and Starlings join with Robins, Chaffinches, Tits and Wrens to hustle the unfortunate owl from tree to tree. Sometimes a Blackbird or other species will discover the owl on its diurnal perch and raise a racket, but the bird, without opening its eyes, simply faces its persecutors. It never attempts to attack in these circumstances, though it will kill birds as large as a Blackbird or Starling. In addition to the usual small mammals, birds and insects, the Tawny Owl will eat young rabbits, squirrels, and even weasels; like most other owls it has occasionally been known to capture fish, including trout and bullhead. Tawny Owl pellets are light grey in colour and are soft and friable. When young are in the nest the parents often provide far more than they can eat, making a store for future use. The nest is usually in a hollow tree, not infrequently in the deserted nest of some other bird, and occasionally in holes in rocks, buildings or on the bare ground. The large white eggs, usually three or four in number, are laid at intervals and incubated as soon as laid. The first down is white, but later barred with buff. The young are fed by the parents for some weeks after they have left the nest, and are boldly protected; a Tawny with young will strike a man with its claws on the head or neck.

The Tawny Owl is a variable bird, having two distinct phases: grey and rufous. The latter, figured, is the commoner in Britain. The general colour is warm rufous-buff or greyish, mottled with dark brown; pale tips to the secondaries form light bars on the wings. The buff underparts have dark brown striations. The facial disc is grey, margined with brown; the legs are densely feathered to the toes. The bill is yellowish horn, the claws horn with black tips and the irides dark brown. Length, 15 in. Wing, 10 in. Tarsus, 2 in. (*Plates 98 and 172.*)

## Long-eared Owl                                            *Asio otus*

The range of the Long-eared Owl is practically Palaearctic, and it is more migratory than many other owls. In the British Isles it has a wide distribution as a resident, and occurs in the north and east in small numbers as a passage migrant and winter visitor. There may also be some internal movement southward in autumn, when flocks containing as many as a score of birds have been observed. There has been a marked decrease in the British breeding population during the present century and the species is now very thinly distributed in England and Wales. In Ireland and the north of Scotland it is still not uncommon in coniferous woods.

Fir woods are the favourite haunts of this species, but it also frequents the slopes of hills and open country where firs are in small clumps, and woods where conifers are absent. During the day it remains in its roost, sometimes screened by ivy, but often sitting bolt upright on a branch, pressing its apparently attenuated body close to the trunk; in this position it is difficult to detect, but when it is disturbed or the small birds discover the perch, it is mobbed without mercy. It is said that in the day the elongated feathers on the head, known as the horns or 'ear-tufts', a misleading name, are laid back, but they are raised when the bird is alarmed. At dusk it flies with wavering flight but usually silently; indeed it is a quieter bird than most owls. The hoot is a long drawn-out and quavering *oo-oo-oo-oo*, quite distinct from that of the Tawny Owl; it has a sharp quacking flight call, a yelping bark, and an anger call, *woof, woof, oo-ack, oo-ack*. The hunger call of the young resembles the creaking of an unoiled hinge. The male, when courting and also when angry, frequently 'claps' his wings, producing a dull note, *bock, bock*. Although some observers believe that the sound is produced by the wings striking together above the back, Coward was not alone in thinking that the wings do not actually meet but are struck sharply downward, with the result that the bird is lifted in the air. In its terrifying attitude, similar to that assumed by the Short-eared Owl, the secondaries are arched and meet above the back and the primaries spread wide; the wings frame the head, whilst with glaring eyes and snapping beak the bird hisses and spits defiance like an angry cat. Birds form a larger proportion of the food of this species than of the Barn Owl; decapitated and partially plucked birds lie in and round the nest. However, analysis of pellets in Lancashire showed that mammals made up at least 80% of the diet, the Wood Mouse being the most frequent victim.

The Long-eared Owl appropriates the old nest of some bird—often Jay, Magpie, Sparrow Hawk or Wood Pigeon—or a squirrel's drey in which to lay its three to five white eggs, rounder than those of the Barn Owl. Occasionally it nests upon the ground, even when apparently suitable nests are near. The eggs are laid early, in March as a rule. The young are covered at first with white down, but later the down is barred with grey and brown. In the first feathering the facial disc is blackish.

The adult has upper parts buff, marbled and vermiculated with grey and brown and with dark brown streaks; the facial disc is buff, dark close to the eye. The buff underparts are streaked with brown, and have dusky bars which form crosses or arrow-shaped markings. The bill is brownish-black, the claws dark brown and the irides bright orange. Length, 14 in. Wing, 11·5 in. Tarsus, 1·6 in. (*Plates 95, 101 and 172.*)

## Short-eared Owl                                    *Asio flammeus*

The Short-eared Owl has a very wide world range and breeds throughout Europe. In the British Isles it is a thinly distributed resident, but a fairly common winter visitor. It breeds regularly in suitable places in the north and east of England and in parts of Scotland, and pairs have nested from time to time in most counties of England and Wales. It has bred at least once in

Ireland and is known there as a winter visitor. Large numbers arrive from the Continent in autumn; many remain to winter, but others are birds of passage. The return migration is in March and April.

Open country—moors, fens, marshes, hills and even cultivated fields— are the haunts of the Short-eared Owl; it roosts and settles on the ground. It will alight on a bush, tree or fence, but it shuns woodlands. On the wing it looks a large, bullet-headed, buffish bird with long, narrow, rounded wings and tail; even at close quarters the ear-tufts are rarely visible unless the bird is excited. When hunting and during courtship the flight is uncertain, rolling and noiseless, but on migration or when flying by day, a frequent habit, it is light, slow and direct. The long pinions beat regularly, and it floats freely, with motionless wings held slightly forward, soaring and wheeling like a Buzzard. It has a harsh flight call, and the note of anger is a savage, barking *whowk*, but in winter it is generally silent. Under excitement it produces a crack with the wings; even when this is inaudible, owing to distance, the sharp down-ward stroke, distinctly lifting the bird's body, is plainly visible. Coward records that when an angry bird was flying just above him, near the nest, it frequently brought its wings almost if not quite together directly under the body, shaking them with a curious excited quiver. The bird sometimes travels at a great height.

The food—small mammals, birds and beetles—does not differ from that of other owls, but it is evidently partial to voles, for during the over-abundance of these destructive rodents, known as 'vole-plagues', there is always a great increase of Short-eared Owls. It often hunts by day as well as at dusk. On migration it feeds upon other avian travellers, capturing them as they fly on misty nights in the glare from the lighthouses.

The nest, always on the ground, may have a little lining, but this is usually the trodden vegetation; it is amongst the heather on the moors, reeds or sedges in the fens, between or even on the tussocks of a marsh, or on the sand amidst the marram of the dunes. Four to eight white eggs, laid at intervals, are the usual complement, but when voles devastated the sheep-runs of the Scottish lowlands, as many as thirteen or fourteen were found in one nest, and most birds had two or more broods. Nests were also found as early as February, though April is the usual time for laying. The young are at first covered with dirty white down, this appearance being caused by the white tips above sooty or barred bases. When the young bird is feathered it will if threatened assume the terrifying attitude of the Long-eared Owl, framing its head with the wings; its bright yellow eyes glare defiance; it hisses and snaps its bill, and will even jump towards the intruder. The old birds, if the young is touched, will dash at and occasionally strike a man.

The general colour of the adult bird is dark buff, though the shade varies considerably; the wings and tail are barred with brown, the upper parts are blotched and streaked, and the underparts striated with dark brown. The facial disc is buff, black round the eyes, and has a whitish frame or border. The bill is black, the legs feathered to the toes, the claws black and the irides bright golden yellow. The female, as in the other owls, is larger than the male. Length, 14–15 in. Wing, 12 in. Tarsus, 2 in. (*Plates 100, 101 and 172.*)

## Tengmalm's Owl                                                       *Aegolius funereus*

Tengmalm's Owl is a bird of the mountain forests of northern and central Europe and western Asia. In winter it descends to the lowlands and wanders; from time to time examples have reached Britain, mostly in autumn and winter. Most of these wanderers have been recorded from eastern counties, but a few have been seen in inland and western localities as well as in Scotland and the Shetlands.

In its northern haunts the bird feeds at any time, eating small mammals, birds and insects. Its call is a soft, long whistle. It may be distinguished from Scops Owl by the absence of ear-tufts, and from the Little Owl by its large round head, dark brown colour and dark-lined white facial discs. The upper parts of Tengmalm's Owl are umber-brown, mottled with white, more regularly on the crown than on the back; the tail is barred with brown. The underparts are white with brown bars and streaks; the facial disc greyish-white. The bill is yellowish-white; the irides yellow. The juvenile is dark brown and shows little white. Length, 9 in. (*Plate 98.*)

# Order CAPRIMULGIFORMES

## Family CAPRIMULGIDAE Nightjars

*Anatomically the Nightjars are very similar to the Swifts, but in the soft plumage, crepuscular or nocturnal habits, they approach the Owls. They have a pectinated or combed middle claw, and the wide gape is provided with strong bristles.*

**Nightjar** *Caprimulgus europaeus*

The Nightjar, one of our later migrants, seldom appears before the end of April or beginning of May. It occurs throughout northern and central Europe, and winters in Africa. In the British Isles it occurs in suitable localities in the south of England, but is much more local in the north and is absent from much of Scotland and Ireland. There has been a widespread decrease in many areas in recent years, sometimes because of destruction or disturbance of its breeding habitat, but often for no apparent reason.

Open heathy wastes, bracken-covered slopes and woods, hollows and corries on the hills where bracken mingles with the ling, are the haunts of the crepuscular Nightjar. The strange purring trill, its song, from which it derives some of its numerous names, is the surest means of identification. It flies at dusk, often at sundown, a long-tailed, shadowy form with easy, silent moth-like flight; its strong and deliberate wing-beats alternate with graceful sweeps and wheels with motionless wings. The beautifully variegated plumage shows relationship or similarity to the Wryneck, its wide gape and long wings to the Swift, its soft downy plumage and habits to the Owls, but in many characteristics it stands alone—a Nightjar. There is nothing grating or harsh, no 'jar' in its soft trill, which rises and falls as it vibrates on the variable evening breeze, or as the bird turns its head from side to side. The lower mandible vibrates; the throat is distended until the feathers stand out. When it churrs the bird lies or crouches along a bough or rail, but it will sing from a post, and occasionally perch across a branch. The duration of the trill may be for a fraction of a minute or for several minutes without a pause; rarely it is heard in the daytime. It is continued at intervals during summer, and occasionally may be heard in August and September, just before the bird departs.

During the day the Nightjar lies silent upon the ground, often on a heap of stones, wonderfully concealed by its plumage; it is most difficult to detect, looking like a bit of lichen-covered twig or fragment of bark. With eyes almost closed it watches through tiny slits, rising suddenly, sometimes with a croak of alarm, but usually silently, when we almost tread upon it. Its rounded head and short beak, together with its mottled dress, give it a peculiar reptilian appearance. When on the wing it has a soft call, *co-ic*, and a sharper and repeated alarm, *quik, quik, quik*; but during courtship, and occasionally at other times, it uses a mechanical signal, a sharp cracking sound. Coward noted that the wings were raised vertically and brought smartly down, and maintained that the crack was similar to that of a whip-lash; he could not believe that the soft feathers of either this bird or the Short-eared Owl could make a clapping sound. Others think the sound is produced by the striking together of the carpal regions of the wings. The male may be told from the female by the white spots on his wings and tail, and as he gracefully floats above her, with wings upraised at a sharp angle, he spreads wide his tail to show the white spots. On the ground both birds will swing the tail from side to side when excited. The Nightjar does not hunt with open mouth, as often depicted, but the huge gape opens wide for large insects, such as noctuid moths and dor-beetles, which are snapped up with avidity. Crepuscular insects are its food.

No nest is made; the two elongated and elliptical eggs, creamy-white mottled with brown, purple and liver, are placed upon the bare ground amongst bracken or stones; the brooding bird, sitting closely, is their best protection. They are seldom laid before the end of May. The female incubates during the day, but the male relieves her in the evening and probably at dawn. The female will 'squatter' away to attract attention if disturbed, rolling and fluttering in a perfect frenzy. When the down-clad young are hatched her excitement becomes intense. The newly hatched young are covered with vermiculated grey and brown down, livid blue skin showing on the naked nape and back. The note is a querulous *cheep*. Quickly they become active and the parents soon remove them if the nest has been visited. At times a second brood is reared. Emigration begins in August, and by the middle of September most birds have left.

The plumage of the adult Nightjar is lichen-grey, barred and streaked with buff, chestnut and black; the underparts are barred. White spots on primaries and white tips to the outer tail feathers are characters of the male; in the young male these are buff. The bill is black, the legs reddish-brown, the irides almost black. Length, 10·5 in. Wing, 7·6 in. Tarsus, 0·75 in. (*Plates 103, 109 and 174.*)

# Order APODIFORMES Picarian Birds

## Family APODIDAE Swifts

*The Swifts, superficially like the Swallows, have certain characters similar to those of Passerine birds, but in most points are closely allied to the Humming Birds and other Picarian groups. The four toes are directed forward, unsuited for perching but adapted for clinging to rough surfaces.*

**Swift**                                                                 *Apus apus*

Our Swift breeds in Europe and north-west Africa and winters in southern Africa. It is a late spring visitor to most parts of the British Isles, though it is a scarce breeder on the west coasts of Scotland and Ireland, where the wet, windy conditions are unsuitable for it.

April is well advanced before the first Swifts announce their arrival by loud screams as they wheel high overhead or rush at marvellous speed through the air. The black bird, with long, narrow, scimitar-shaped wings, needs no description, yet it is necessary to emphasise that it is not a Swallow, though through sharing aerial habits it has acquired similar form and appearance. It is a master of the art of flight, our most aerial species, and never seems to tire. The ordinary flight is an alternation of rapid wing-beats and long glides with outspread motionless wings, during which it loses no elevation. It races through the air. Courtship flight may culminate in coition in the air, but mating also takes place in the nest-holes. It is eminently sociable; little parties delight to career, screaming, between houses in our streets, or to wheel and soar high in the upper air. Except when it ascends for play, for play it certainly does, the altitude of flight is regulated by the height at which insects are flying, and in this way has relation to weather. Swifts will fly round the outside of a rain storm, and it has been shown that non-breeding birds may fly hundreds of miles against the wind round an area of low barometric pressure, though this may apply less to birds of British origin than to continental ones. On late May and June evenings the Swifts, or at any rate those which are not engaged in incubation, indulge in combined crepuscular flights. At dusk they mount high in the air, soaring with continuous screams, until they are mere crescentic specks in the sky. There they float, their voices faintly audible even when they are invisible. There is very strong evidence to support the belief that parties of Swifts spend the night on the wing at great heights, though breeding pairs normally roost in the nest-holes. The short legs, feathered to the toes, are useless for walking, but the bird has no difficulty in rising from a level surface. It raises the wings high above its back and with one or two sharp downward strokes lifts itself and flies off.

The food of the Swift consists of small flying insects, mostly diptera and staphylinid beetles. Dipterous and other parasites give the Swift much trouble, and during flight it will perform an evolution similar to the 'tumbling' of a

Pigeon, but without loss of elevation, when, doubtless, it is striving to get rid of the pests, scratching itself in the air.

The incoming Swifts lose no time in getting to the nesting holes, and eggs are generally laid before the end of May. The nest is under cover, frequently on rafters in a house or larger building, but occasionally in a crevice in a cliff or quarry face. The nesting material consists of dead grass and leaves or other airborne litter, glued together with a viscous salivary secretion. Both birds take part in the building, which continues throughout incubation, which they also share. Two, or occasionally three, long white eggs are laid, and there is only a single brood. David Lack discovered that partially incubated eggs and newly hatched young could survive several hours of exposure in cold weather when their parents left them unattended because of the difficulty in obtaining food. Feathered young in starvation conditions lose their body temperature at night and become torpid, an adaptation which may enable them to survive periods of bad weather. Even so there is a heavy mortality of nestlings in a cold summer. Healthy young perform wing exercises in the nest cavity, and once they have left the hole they never return to it, but apparently start almost immediately on their migration, in advance of the adults.

Towards the end of July some Swifts have started southward, and in most years all have left the midlands and north before the end of August.

The Swift is blackish-brown, with a small and variable white patch on the chin. In young birds this patch is purer. The bill is black; the feet very dark brown. Length, 7 in. Wing, 6·8 in. Tarsus, 0·55 in. (*Plates 105 and 173.*)

## Alpine Swift                                                    *Apus melba*

The Alpine Swift breeds in central and southern Europe and north Africa and winters further south in Africa. It has occurred in both spring and autumn in many parts of the British Isles as a scarce passage migrant or vagrant. In recent years four or five have been recorded annually. Its habits are similar to those of our bird, except that its flight is stronger and its voice louder. It is much larger, for whereas the outstretched wings of our Swift are just under 18 in. from tip to tip, this bird measures nearly 2 ft. It is easily recognised by the browner colour of its upper parts and breast and by its white throat and belly. The bill and feet are black. Length, 8 in. Wing, 8·45 in. Tarsus, 0·6 in. (*Plate 105.*)

# Order CORACIIFORMES

## Family ALCEDINIDAE Kingfishers

*The Kingfishers have long heavy bills, short, thick-set bodies, and for the most part brilliant plumage. The foot has the three front toes united. All of the family Alcedinidae are fish-eaters.*

**Kingfisher** *Alcedo atthis*

The Kingfisher is a well-distributed resident in the British Isles, but it does not breed in the north of Scotland and in recent years has become scarce in the Scottish lowlands and in some parts of the north of England. Abroad it occurs throughout central and southern Europe. The Kingfisher is abundant in some districts, and even visits polluted streams near towns. It is better known from its stuffed effigy under a glass-shade than as a living bird, for it is shy and rapid in its movements; a streak of blue as the bird vanishes round a bend is all that is often visible. When perched, facing the observer, its ruddy breast alone is seen, but if it turns or flies the prismatic colour of the upper parts is either blue or green according to the angle of incidence of the rays of light. The haunts of the bird are the waterside, since it feeds entirely upon aquatic animals, but it is as frequent beside lake, pond, canal or fenland dyke, as by the rapid trout-stream. In winter, especially when inland waters are ice-bound, it frequents tidal marshes and the shore, taking its stand on the mussel- or limpet-covered rocks and diving into the shallow gutters and pools. Fish it certainly captures, but aquatic insects and crustaceans, the latter either freshwater or marine, are freely eaten. Though taking toll of small trout, it is useful on a trout-stream, for it eats numerous freshwater shrimps (*Gammarus*) which are destructive to ova.

The flight of the Kingfisher is exceedingly rapid, the short rounded wings whirring until they appear a mere blur; it usually flies near the water, but during courtship the male chases the female through and over the trees with loud shrill whistles. From February onwards the male has a sweet trilling song, a modulated repetition of many whistles. He also signals with a whistle to the female when he is feeding her—his share of nesting duties; this whistle is produced when his bill is loaded with food, yet is clear and distinct. The female will reply and emerge from the nesting hole. She may fly to meet him, take the fish from him in the air, and return at once to the nest. The bird has regular perches or stands from which it fishes; these may be a few inches or many feet above the water. It sits upright, its tail pointed downwards, its head turned contemplatively as it watches the water beneath; suddenly it drops with a splash and usually returns at once with a struggling captive. If a large and lively fish, it is beaten into impotence on a bough or rail; a favourite execution block often glistens with many fish-scales. Small fish and insects are promptly swallowed. A fish is usually lifted and carried by the middle, but its position is changed, sometimes by tossing it into the air, before it is swallowed head downwards. It may be carried to the sitting hen held crossways or by the head. At times the Kingfisher hovers over the water, but not like the Kestrel: the body is held almost vertical, the tail and head bent slightly forward, the bill inclined downwards; the bird holds itself in this position by rapidly whirring wings. It will poise thus over the shallows, dropping on passing gammarids, and yet checking its descent so as not to injure itself on the stones. When perched and conscious that it is observed, the bird jerks its head and tail constantly, the latter forward, not upwards, but as a rule it is a quiet patient fisherman.

The nest is tunnelled in a sandy bank, usually though not always over water; both birds excavate, except when an old hole of Sand Martin or water vole is appropriated. Most holes incline upward for about 3 ft. before the nesting chamber is reached. There is no nest, but the six to seven or even more round pinkish-white eggs are placed on a litter of fish bones and dis-gorged pellets. Accounts differ about the condition of the nesting chamber, but W. Rowan found it clean, except for the fishy matter, though the tunnel is a running sewer of greenish liquid and decomposed fish, and smells abominably. The first clutch is usually laid in April, but second broods are often in the nest at the end of July. The young come to the mouth of the hole to be fed when old enough, but the newly hatched young utter a vibrating purr when expecting food. They are at first without down and clothed with numerous small blue pens. When they leave the nest they differ little from their parents, except that the colours are duller, the spot on the neck is buff, and the grey margins to the breast feathers give a mottled appearance; their call is then an insistent, continuous trill.

The general colour of the upper parts of the adult bird is bright metallic-blue, cobalt on the back, and showing greenish reflections on the head and wings; the ear-coverts and underparts are warm chestnut, the chin and sides of neck white. The bill is black, reddish-orange at the base; the legs are bright red. Length, 7·5 in. Wing, 2·95 in. Tarsus, 0·3 in. (*Plates 105 and 173.*)


## Family MEROPIDAE Bee-eaters

*The Bee-eaters, which have a wide range, are all brightly coloured birds with long curved bills, and often elongated central tail feathers. The feet have the toes united, two of the front toes joined for fully half their length.*


**Bee-eater**                                              *Merops apiaster*

The Bee-eater breeds in southern Europe, western Asia and northern Africa and migrates to southern Asia and Africa. It is gregarious, addicted to wander-ing, and many individuals or small parties have reached the British Isles between late spring and autumn: and it is now known as an annual visitor in very small numbers. In 1920 a pair excavated a hole near Edinburgh, and in 1955 three pairs nested in Sussex, two of them successfully.

The gorgeously coloured bird, tropical in appearance, attracts attention when it appears, especially as it is neither shy nor secretive. Bee-eaters nest in colonies in holes in sand-pits, river banks, and similar places to those occupied by Sand Martins. Like other hole-nesters they lay white eggs. The flight is easy and graceful; the note is described as *quilp*. The bird feeds on various insects and has, as the name suggests, a fondness for bees. It is so distinct in its shape and the brilliance of its plumage that it cannot be confused with any other species, except those of its own family. Its long curved bill is very noticeable. The main features of the brilliant plumage are the chestnut crown and nape shading to yellow on the back and rump, blue-green primaries and tail, yellow throat with a dark line separating it from the blue-green underparts, and the broad dark line through the eye. Projecting central tail feathers are conspicuous in adults but absent in juveniles. Length, 11 in. Wing, 6 in. Tarsus, 0·4 in. (*Plate 105*.)

## Family CORACIIDAE Rollers

*The Rollers are brightly coloured birds, allied to the Kingfishers and Bee-eaters, but have superficial similarity to Crows.*

**Roller**                                                        *Coracias garrulus*

The Roller occurs in summer throughout most of Europe, migrating for the winter to southern Africa. It occasionally wanders to Britain on migration, occurring most frequently on the south and east coasts in autumn, but has been met with in all parts, sometimes in spring; it has been recorded from Scotland and Ireland on several occasions.

This conspicuous and noisy bird usually travels in parties, but its normal migration route does not pass through Britain, and its occurrence in our islands is apparently accidental; though not infrequent, it is hardly a regular bird of passage. It may at once be recognised by its bright dress, Jay-like appearance and slightly hooked strong bill; it calls attention to itself by a noisy harsh chatter. The name is derived from its habit of 'tumbling' in the air during courtship, but as a rule its flight is easy and strong; the rolling is often the prelude to a quick 'shooting' descent towards a perch. It feeds on insects, worms and small lizards, and sits on some elevated perch—a tree, bush or telegraph-wire—watching for prey after the manner of a shrike.

The Roller is greenish-blue, slightly glossed, with a chestnut mantle. The central tail feathers and the wing-coverts are darker blue, the outer tail feathers tipped with black. The blue wing shows a black border in flight. The bill is almost black, the legs yellowish-brown. Length, 12 in. Wing, 7·7 in. Tarsus, 0.95 in. (*Plate 109*.)

## Family UPUPIDAE Hoopoes

*The Hoopoes have an erectile crest, long slender curved bills and a well-developed hind toe.*

**Hoopoe**                                                                    *Upupa epops*

The history of the Hoopoe as a British bird has too often been a disgraceful obituary. It is a striking and conspicuous species which breeds throughout the greater part of Europe, south of southern Sweden, and winters in southern Africa. Not only is it a passage migrant in spring and autumn but it has nested sporadically, usually in the south coastal counties of England. Breeding in Britain seems to take place in fine, warm summers, so it would be unduly optimistic to expect it to become regular. As a wanderer or passage bird it has occurred in all parts of the British Isles, and though most frequent in the south and east, is by no means unusual in the west, and it is now an annual passage migrant in Ireland.

The large, black-tipped erectile crest, when elevated like the head-gear of an American Indian, and the conspicuous barring of the back and wings, together with its almost stupid tameness, render the Hoopoe not only too easy to see but far too easy to shoot. Its flight is slow and undulating; its gait similar to that of the Starling, with which it freely consorts, its head bobbing to and fro as it walks. The food consists of insects of various kinds, worms, centipedes and wood-lice, and it is especially partial to coprophagous beetles and their larvae; for these it frequents manure heaps and animal droppings, digging for its prey with its long bill. Large beetles and worms are hammered to bits, beaten on the ground, but frequently it adopts a habit of the Hornbill, with which it has some affinity, of throwing its food into the air and catching it neatly before swallowing it. It has various notes. The *hoop, hoop*, from which it gets its name, is uttered when perched with crest depressed, throat expanded and head lowered. The hoop is guttural and carries for a great distance. It also utters a chatter of alarm, a warning to the nesting female, and a cat-like call.

Although showing little alarm at the presence of human beings, the Hoopoe is suspicious of a passing hawk, crow or other possible enemy, and at once assumes a protective attitude which, in the open, is said to make the bird look like a bundle of rags. A wounded young bird accidentally fell off a table and at once threw itself into this defensive position; it spread its wings, expanded and slightly raised its tail, drew back its head until it rested on its back, and pointed the bill straight upward. The result was distinctly unavian. On several occasions Hoopoes have wintered in England.

The nest is usually in a hollow tree or hole in masonry; during incubation the male regularly feeds the female. At times no nesting material is used, but generally an untidy collection of straws, litter and rags, mixed with evil-smelling filth, is the bed for the eggs and young. The eggs are unspotted white, grey or greenish, and often stained; the clutch numbers from five to ten or more.

The head, neck, upper back and most of the underparts are pinkish-brown, darkest on the crest and pinkest on the breast. The crest is tipped with black; the lower back, wings and tail are barred black and white; the rump is white. The bill is black, pinkish at the base; the legs brown. The bills of the young are shorter and less curved. Length, 12 in. Wing, 5·7 in. Tarsus, 0·8 in. (*Plate 102.*)

# Order PICIFORMES

## Family PICIDAE Woodpeckers

*Zygodactyle feet (two toes pointing forward, two backward); bill strong and pointed.*

**Green Woodpecker**                                                      *Picus viridis*

The Green Woodpecker occurs in most parts of Europe and in suitable woodlands in England and Wales it is not uncommon. Until about 1940 it was absent or very local as a breeding bird in the northern counties of England and was not found in Scotland, but there was a marked increase in Durham and Northumberland in the early 1940s and a spectacular colonisation of north Lancashire, Westmorland and Cumberland later in the same decade. In the 1950s much of southern Scotland was occupied, and the Green Woodpecker now breeds north of the Clyde and Forth. It is still absent from Ireland and the Isle of Man.

The Green Woodpecker is certainly the best known though not always the commonest of the three species; its large size, conspicuous plumage, loud call and habits render it more noticeable. Though it is a very green bird, colour is not always distinct in the field, much depending upon the light. When sunlight falls direct upon it the bird is conspicuously green with a crimson crown, but seen against the sun it looks almost black. If the underparts alone are seen as the bird passes over it looks almost yellow, and when it is flying away from the observer the yellow rump attracts attention. The usual haunts are more open than those of the other species; it frequents old timbered parks, and indeed any open country where there are ancient trees, rather than dense woodlands. Though a large and heavy bird, it has an easy, bounding flight. It alights on a trunk or bough and works upwards with diagonal or spiral course in quick jerky jumps or runs, halting occasionally with head drawn back and bill held at right angles to its body, with an alert though meditative expression; as it proceeds it taps the bark smartly, probably sounding it for hollows made by its prey. Rarely, a bird will descend for a short distance, tail foremost. Insects are captured by a rapid outward flick of the long tongue, gummed to its tip by sticky saliva. From early in the year until summer the loud ringing *plue, plue, plue,* often described as a laugh, and from which the bird gets one of its names—'Yaffle'—is a typical woodland call. Though it has been heard to 'drum' upon wood, it certainly does not use this call as frequently as the Spotted Woodpeckers. The alarm note is the laugh emphasised and harshened.

The food is similar to that of the other species, except that this bird has a passion for ants. It will attack the large nests in the woods, throwing aside the piled fir-needles with its bill and nipping up the insects with its tongue. When seeking ants it will wander to a distance from trees; it frequents open hillsides and coastal cliffs. Berries, nuts and acorns are stated to form part of its winter diet.

The nesting hole is similar to those of the other Woodpeckers but larger; it may be but a few feet above the ground or at the top of a tall tree. Five to seven glossy white eggs are laid upon wood chips late in April or early in May. Though there is only one brood, late nesting is not uncommon, for the Starling finds the larger holes made by the Green Woodpecker convenient nurseries and ousts the rightful tenant.

The plumage of the sexes is much alike, dark green above and yellowish-green below and with crown and nape crimson, but in the male the centre of the moustachial black stripe is crimson; the lores and around the eye is black in both male and female. The rump is chrome-yellow, the outer webs of the primaries barred black and white. The bill and feet are slate-grey; the irides bluish-white. The crimson at the base of the bill is present in the young of both sexes. Their upper parts are barred, and underparts barred, streaked and spotted. Length, 12·5 in. Wing, 6·4 in. Tarsus, 1·1 in. (*Plates 106 and 173*.)

### Great Spotted Woodpecker $\qquad$ *Dendrocopus major*

The Great Spotted or Pied Woodpecker is distributed throughout Europe. It nests in England and Wales, though nowhere in large numbers and sparingly throughout most of Scotland, where it has greatly expanded its range during the present century, after virtual extinction with the clearing of the old pine forests in the middle of the 19th century. It does not breed in Ireland, and the fifty or more occurrences there probably refer to the continental race, which sometimes visits Britain in large numbers in autumn. It is also absent from the Isle of Man and most of the Scottish islands.

The Great Spotted Woodpecker is an inhabitant of the woodlands and parks, depending for food and nesting sites upon old timber. It is a retiring, inconspicuous bird, in spite of the plumage, but when seen in flight has a 'cobby' appearance, owing to the shortness of its stiff-feathered tail; whether the bird is in flight or at rest the large white shoulder patch is a feature that catches the eye. From the Lesser Spotted Woodpecker it may always be distinguished by the crimson on the abdomen, and even when colours are not visible its inferior size separates it from the Green Woodpecker. When hidden by the foliage its presence is often advertised by the mechanical 'call', a loud vibrating rattle, produced by the rapidly repeated blows of its strong bill upon a trunk or branch. This is not merely a nuptial call or challenge, but a 'watchword' or signal of either sex; it may be stimulated by a mere desire to communicate or by excitement; it is a springtime activity and doubtless it represents the Woodpecker's song. It is audible from a great distance, depending, however, upon the wind and the condition of the wood, a hollow bough naturally producing a louder note than living wood. Probably the bird knows the location of the best sounding boards. The call-note is a sharp *quet, quet*, and another quickly repeated note is described the alarm, *chk*, which is heard when the bird is disturbed, especially near the nest.

In summer the food mainly consists of those insects which bore into or otherwise damage the timber of forest trees—the larvae of wood-boring moths and beetles, bark beetles and their larvae. The accusation that Wood-peckers damage timber is unfounded, since its borings are always in infected trees; large numbers of the destructive *Rhagium* beetles are devoured by the Great Spotted Woodpecker. The grub of *Andricus kollari* is hacked out of the marble gall, and there is some evidence that these galls are occasionally stored for winter consumption. There are many records of nestlings being taken, especially those of tits from nest-boxes, and the bird has been seen opening and drinking from milk bottles after the manner of Blue and Great Tits. It usually alights on the trunk of a tree, working upwards, often from side to side, but sometimes will perch in passerine fashion, when it sits well upright. During the ascent it smartly taps the bark, breaking off fragments, but often extracts its food from crevices with the tip of its sticky tongue. Its actions are jerky, and it hops rather than climbs, even when beneath a branch, leaping forward with one foot just in advance of the other. It will work round to the further side of a bole, often, apparently, to avoid observation. Though less frequently seen on the ground than the Green Woodpecker, it at times attacks the nests of ants. In winter, when the bird wanders from its breeding haunts, it will visit wood-piles and continue its hunt for wood-infesting insects, but in autumn it occasionally takes toll of fruit in garden and orchard. Beech-mast, acorns, nuts and berries are eaten when insect food is scarce. When an open space is crossed the flight is easy and undulating.

The nesting hole, neat and round, is bored in soft or decaying wood, hori-zontally for a few inches, then perpendicularly downwards; at the bottom of a shaft, usually from 6 to 12 in. in depth, a small chamber is excavated, where on wood chips the creamy-white eggs, five to seven in number, are laid in the second half of May. The hole is rarely used again, but not infrequently other holes are bored in the same tree; Coward records eighteen in one dead trunk; they are seldom at less than 12 ft. above the ground. Almost any tree, if sufficiently rotten, is used. The young, when the parents are feeding them, cluster at the mouth of the hole and keep up a continuous chatter, but when alarmed slip back into the nest. The increase of the Starling has had its effect upon the numbers of the Great Spotted Woodpecker, for this determined bird will evict the rightful owner and occupy the ready-made hole.

The upper parts of the male are glossy black, with buff on the forehead, a crimson spot on the nape and white on the sides of the face and neck; on the shoulder is a large white patch, and the flight feathers are barred with black and white. The three outer tail feathers are barred; these show when the short stiff tail is outspread, acting as a support in climbing. The underparts are buffish-white; the abdomen and under tail-coverts crimson. The bill is slate-black, the legs greenish-grey, and the irides crimson. The female has no crimson on the nape, and in the young this nape spot is absent, but the crown is crimson. Length, 9 in. Wing, 5·5 in. Tarsus, 0·9 in. (*Plates 104, 106, 107 and 173.*)

## Lesser Spotted Woodpecker                           *Dendrocopus minor*

The Lesser Spotted or Barred Woodpecker has a wide breeding range in Europe. In the British Isles it is resident in Wales and most of England, though rare or absent in the north-east. It is not found in Scotland, Ireland or the Isle of Man.

From its small size and its habit of spending most of its time in the tops of tall trees in woods and parks, this little woodpecker is often overlooked, but if sighted on a trunk it may at once be identified by the broad barring on the wings and narrower bars across the lower back. Its habits are very similar to those of the Great Spotted Woodpecker, and it has the same stumpy appearance, almost triangular, when bounding from tree to tree. Its note is a repeated *keek*, loud for so small a bird, and its vibrating rattle resembles that of the larger species. This substitute for a song may be heard most frequently when, early in the year, courtship begins. The Lesser Spotted Woodpecker is not known to feed frequently on fruits, nuts or other vegetable substances, but its insect food is similar to that of the Great Spotted; it is just as useful in attacking the larvae of *Rhagium* and the bark-boring Scolytidae, as well as the larvae of wood-leopards and clearwing moths. It will also hack out the grub, *Andricus kollari*, from the marble-gall. When hunting for wood-boring larvae it chips away the rotten wood, and the litter at the foot of a tree is often the first indication that upper branches are attacked by insects. At night it roosts in old holes, a habit certainly at times shared by the Great Spotted Woodpecker, though some writers state that it may sleep clinging to a bole.

A litter of chips is also a guide to a nesting hole, for the bird does not always carry these away when excavating. The hole is usually at a considerable height above the ground and may be as high as 30 or 40 ft.; it is a small burrow, measuring from $1\frac{1}{4}$ to 2 in. in diameter. The shaft varies, the nesting cavity being often a foot or more below the entrance. Five to eight highly polished white eggs are laid upon wood dust and chips in the latter half of May, and a single brood is the rule. Both birds help to excavate the hole, incubate the eggs and feed the young.

The male has a crimson crown, a brown forehead, a black superciliary stripe, and another from the base of the bill to the neck. The nape and upper back are black, but the lower back is barred with black and white. On the wings are broader and more conspicuous bars, and the outer tail feathers are also barred. The underparts are white with streaks on the flanks. The bill and legs are slate-grey; the irides crimson. In the female the crown is white, but the young birds of both sexes have more or less crimson on the head. There are no marked seasonal changes. Length, 5·6 in. Wing, 3·7 in. Tarsus, 0·55 in. (*Plates 106 and 173*.)

## Wryneck                                                  *Jynx torquilla*

The Wryneck is found in summer throughout the greater part of Europe; it winters in tropical Africa. It is now a very scarce and local breeding bird in

Britain. In the mid-19th century its regular breeding range extended north
to Westmorland and west to Somerset, but its numbers steadily declined until,
in the mid-1960s, the breeding population was reduced to a few pairs in
Kent, with perhaps an occasional nest in Surrey. Numbers have declined
elsewhere in western Europe, but the reasons for the change are still obscure.
As a passage migrant the Wryneck is still regular in small numbers on the
east coast, occasional on the west.

Even in its regular haunts the Wryneck is an inconspicuous and retiring
bird, but the loud, clear call, *quee, quee, quee*, heard in April, is familiarly
looked upon as an announcement that the Cuckoo will soon follow. It haunts
woods and open parkland like the woodpeckers, but is also found in lanes,
hedgerows, orchards and even gardens. Its flight is undulating and seldom
long sustained. Its 'Partridge-colouring' is more suggestive of the soft
marbling of the Nightjar, but some of its habits are those of the woodpeckers.
When on a trunk, however, the soft feathers of its tail give it no support. Its
alarm note is an angry *kit, kit, kit*, and it has been known to rattle or drum on
a bough like a woodpecker. Though its feet are adapted for climbing it
usually perches across a bough and feeds in the upper branches, whipping
insects off the leaves with its vermiform and sticky tongue, like a chameleon.
It is as fond of ants as the Green Woodpecker, and thrusts its tongue into the
burrows in the nests to draw out the white pupae, or settling on a trunk or
bough, intercepts the insects on their arboreal journeys. One bird, when on
passage, was attracted by the insects imprisoned in a street lamp in a busy
Cheshire town and, though managing to find an entrance, was itself unable
to escape. Its captor said that it raised its 'top knot' and twisted its neck
slowly round to such an extent that he feared it was injured. This snake-like
writhing of the neck, from which it gets its ordinary name is one of its pecu-
liarities; when clinging to a trunk it twists and turns its head without moving
its body. When in the nest it hisses if disturbed, and this, coupled with its
habits of darting out its tongue at an intruder, are snake-like habits sufficient
to alarm other than human foes. Since the days when Sir Thomas Browne
quaintly commented upon its apparent 'vertigo' and 'fitts', its habit of
feigning death when handled has been freely commented upon.

The nest is in a hole in a tree, steep bank or even masonry, but is seldom,
if ever, excavated by the bird itself; artificial nesting boxes are appreciated.
Seven to ten, even more, glossy white eggs are placed within the hole upon
any dust or litter which has accumulated but without the introduction of
nesting material; they are usually laid in May or June.

The upper parts of both sexes are mottled or variegated with grey, buff and
brown; the back is streaked with dark brown. The outer webs of the primaries
are barred with buff and brown, and the grey tail has distinct bars of brown
and buffish-white. The rich buff throat is finely barred, the flanks and breast
spotted and streaked with dark brown. The bill and legs are brown. The
markings on the underparts of the young are more distinct and pronounced.
Length, 6·5 in. Wing, 3·4 in. Tarsus, 0·7 in. (*Plates 109 and 173.*)

# Order PASSERIFORMES

*The Passeres are the most specialised birds. Their feet, with three toes in front and one behind, are adapted for grasping branches or perching; their vocal organs are well developed for production of song.*

## Family ALAUDIDAE The Larks

**Short-toed Lark** *Calandrella cinerea*

The Short-toed Lark, a southern European bird which winters in Africa and India, has been recorded almost annually in recent years, in spring and autumn. Most of these birds have been seen on the east and south coasts, from Shetland to Scilly, but there have been several records from Ireland and from inland localities in England.

This squat little Lark can hardly be confused with any British species. The hind claw is short and straight, the yellowish bill short and conical. The colour of the upper parts is buff or sandy-brown with darker streaks; the underparts buffish-white, palest on the throat and almost spotless. There is a characteristic dark patch on each side of the upper breast. The eye-stripe is white; the legs brown. Length, 5·5 in.

**Lesser Short-toed Lark** *Calandrella rufescens*

This bird breeds in parts of southern Europe, north Africa and central Asia. It has been recorded in Ireland on about half a dozen occasions; a flock of thirty was seen in Kerry in 1956. It is distinguished from the Short-toed Lark chiefly by its streaked upper breast, lack of dark cap and neck patches, and greyer, less rufous colouring. Length, 5·5 in.

**Crested Lark** *Galerida cristata*

Considering how many unexpected wanderers reach us from Europe and Asia, it is curious that the Crested Lark, which has a wide range in Europe, including France and the Netherlands, should so seldom be recorded in Britain. It has occurred on a few occasions on the south coast and as far north as Fair Isle. In general plumage it resembles the Sky Lark, but though a heavier bird it has shorter, rounded wings, orange-buff on the underside and lacking white above. The short tail has buff, not white, outer feathers. The crest is long and upstanding. Length, 6·8 in.

**Wood Lark** *Lullula arborea*

Over the past hundred years the breeding population of the Wood Lark in the British Isles has undergone marked fluctuations which can be at least partly linked with climatic conditions. The species has always been local, and since 1960 it has become increasingly scarce. By 1965 annual breeding was limited to Norfolk, Suffolk and the south coastal counties of England, though there may have been occasional nests in south and central Wales and in the Midlands. In Scotland and Ireland the Wood Lark is known only as a scarce passage migrant or vagrant. It breeds throughout central and southern Europe.

Considerably smaller, the Wood Lark may further be distinguished from the Sky Lark, when on the wing or ground, by its short tail without a white border. The crest is more pronounced, and the almost white eye-stripe runs back towards the nape, giving the appearance of a broad pale streak below the crest, which when the bird is feeding is frequently raised. The streaked breast and a dark brown and white mark at the edge of the wing are also characteristic. It is hardly a woodland bird though haunting tree-clad country, for in spite of its habit of singing from a branch and seeking refuge in trees it is distinctly a ground bird in its habits. The outskirts of woods, open spaces in parks or forest land, sandy wastes and rough hillsides, where birches and small oaks are scattered, are its favoured haunts. On a sunny hillside it frequently lies basking on the warm rocky outcrops. In winter it is less particular and roams in small flocks to places remote from its home; it is then not uncommon on the coastal slopes and cliff-tops.

The song, richer in tone than that of the Sky Lark but less varied, mainly the repetition of two or three sweet notes, is uttered when the bird rises in the air like its congener, or from a tree or the ground. The call-note is double or triple, *tweedlie* or *too-lui-ie*, and is often uttered in flight, though in winter the bird is more silent. The flight, when the bird is flitting about the open in spring, is slow and unique in character. The bird rises and falls in a series of sharply angled curves rather than undulations. It flutters up for a few feet, then glides with wings expanded, but before the ascent ends it closes its wings; when the momentum fails the wings are extended, and it slides earthward to repeat the performance. The height to which it rises varies considerably; the upward sweeps are irregular. On the ground the Wood Lark walks and runs, and when the feeding birds are disturbed they crouch like Sky Larks and rise one by one. The food consists of seeds and insects.

The nest, similar in materials but more compact than that of the Sky Lark, is placed upon the ground and is usually well concealed. The eggs, three or four, are smaller and less mottled than those of the Sky Lark and the spots are usually redder; they are laid in March, April and May, two broods being usual.

The general colour of the adult bird is buffish-brown, streaked with dark brown, nearly black upon the crown; the underparts of buffish-white are spotted and streaked on the breast; the outer tail feathers are brownish-white, and there are white tips to most of the others; the primary coverts are tipped with white. The bill is brown, darkest on the ridge; the legs pinkish-brown. In autumn the colour is more distinctly buff, and the underparts are tinged with olive. The young are streaked with black and buff on the upper parts, and are yellower beneath and more profusely spotted. Length, 5·5 in. Wing, 3·9 in. Tarsus, 0·8 in. (*Plates 110 and 173*.)

**Sky Lark**                                              *Alauda arvensis*

Everybody knows and appreciates the Sky Lark, which occurs in most parts of Europe and is very migratory. The bird nests throughout the British Isles; many remain all winter, but others of our home-bred stock emigrate in autumn and return in spring as summer visitors, the first reaching our shores towards the end of February. The northern and eastern coasts receive huge numbers of immigrants in autumn, some as winter visitors, others birds of passage, coasting south. Ireland receives a great autumn influx, and severe weather in winter causes westward movement of our winter flocks.

Undoubtedly the Sky Lark's fluent song and the ease with which the bird may be watched mounting high on quivering wing until it is a vocal speck in the blue, accounts for its popularity. It is not a showy bird, but its short crest, usually elevated when on the ground, and its habit of walking give it character, and, except for the Wood Lark, it stands alone among our native birds. The open country is its home; densely wooded areas are shunned, but so long as it is open it is happy on cultivated land, the seaboard marsh or the heathery moor; indeed it haunts the hilltops except when driven away by weather. The greatest outbursts of song are from February, when birds are pairing, until the young are hatched, but it sings, except when moulting, at any season and song is vigorous in October. On a warm day in winter or during hard frost if the sun is bright some Larks are sure to go up, but as a rule the winter ascents are to a lower altitude than those in spring. The bird rises with quivering wings, beginning the song when a few feet up; then its whole body vibrating with energy, it mounts higher and higher, often drifting round in a wide arc before it descends, still singing. When yet at a height, the song ceases and the bird drops abruptly, recovering itself a foot or so above the grass and skimming forward before alighting. The compass of the song is small and some belittle its beauty, but its vehemence and continuity are remarkable. Three or four minutes of continuous song are normal; an unbroken spell of eighteen minutes has been recorded. Into the song the Sky Lark weaves snatches gleaned from other birds. Singing from the ground, a rail or a wall is not uncommon, especially when the birds are pairing, and rival males sing vigorously when fighting. In summer the Lark is up long before daylight and it sings until dusk.

In winter, when the bird is gregarious, moving about the fields in straggling, seldom compact flocks, the usual note is a liquid purring trill; the flight is then strong and direct, a few rapid wing-beats followed by a shoot forward when the bird shuts its wings almost with a snap. It roosts on the ground, and if a field is crossed where birds are roosting the purring call-note as the invisible bird whirrs off in the darkness sounds every few seconds; evidently they do not crowd together on the ground. When approached, the feeding bird crouches, ready for the spring, but though many may be in sight they rise singly, each with its call. When the bird rises the white outer tail feathers show and may be recognition marks; they are exhibited in the courtship display before the female. Courtship is accompanied by many rapid chases, the birds turning and twisting when flying at great speed, but at times the male hovers singing, his quivering wings half-raised, a few feet above his mate. Swift chases and aerial skirmishes take place at this season between rival males. Insects, especially small beetles, are largely eaten in summer. In winter all kinds of seeds are picked up, and fields sown for clover are much frequented. When the young blades of ordinary grass or corn appear, and the seedling turnips top the earth, the early greens attract it; but on the whole it does little damage, and without doubt eats as many weeds as useful plants.

The nest, a simple structure of dry grass lined with finer bents, is placed upon the ground, in the footprint of some beast or a hollow scraped by the bird itself. The hen usually conceals the site by alighting a few feet away and running to the nest by a devious track through the grass. Three to five eggs, densely mottled with brown, are laid in April, and a second brood is usually reared.

The Sky Lark's food supply is cut off by snow, and before or during a storm vast numbers trail westward, crossing to Ireland if the storm continues. At such times and during migration we realise the immensity of the Lark population. During threatening weather the bird comes in at night, and in fog is often bewildered by the coastwise lights, but it is also a day migrant and little parties stream by all day long in autumn. For the most part these immigrants show little fatigue when landing, and may not even stop to rest upon the nearest fields.

The Sky Lark is a brown bird, streaked on head, back and flanks with darker brown; the eye-stripe, noticeable between the dark crown and cheeks, is pale buff. The underparts are buffish-white, with streaks and spots on the breast. The bill is black above and brown beneath; the legs reddish-brown. After the moult pale tips and edges give a more rufous shade, and the young, buff in general colour, have more pronounced streaks and breast spots. The shade, however, is exceedingly variable, as indeed is the size. Length, 7·75 in. Wing, 4·4 in. Tarsus, 0·9 in. (*Plates 108, 110 and 173*.)

**Shore Lark**                                             *Eremophila alpestris*

The Shore Lark is a scarce passage migrant and winter visitor to the British Isles, occurring regularly in small numbers on the east coast and occasionally on the west. There are a few records for Ireland. It breeds in northern Scandinavia and also in south-east Europe. The majority of the birds appear in autumn, but some pass on return migration.

As the name implies, the shore is the most likely place to meet with this conspicuous lark, though at times it visits the stubbles. High-water mark provides it with food—insects, small molluscs and crustaceans sheltering under the drifted weed; seeds, picked up on the beach or on the saltings or coastwise fields, form a considerable part of its winter diet. On the sand it runs quickly, carrying the body low, though the legs are not as short as they appear. The usual call of the wintering birds is not unlike that of the Meadow Pipit.

The male in summer is pinkish-brown on the back, pale yellow on the head and throat, and with a black crown and streak towards the nape which terminates in elongated feathers, forming a double crest; a patch below the eye and a band across the breast are black, and the rest of the underparts white with faint brown streaks on the flanks. The bill and legs are black. The female has no tufts on the head and less black, and the streaks on the back are more pronounced. In winter the black on the head is largely obscured by yellow margins to the feathers. Young birds have no yellow on the forehead. Length, 7 in. Wing, 4 in. Tarsus, 0·9 in. (*Plate 94.*)

## Family HIRUNDINIDAE The Swallows

**Swallow**                                              *Hirundo rustica*

The Swallow breeds throughout Europe, except in the far north, and is known to winter in tropical and southern Africa. In Britain the migrations of the Swallow are complicated by extensive passage movements to and from northern and central Europe, noticeable in the west as well as on the eastern seaboard. Many Swallows ringed as nestlings in Britain have been recovered in south-east Africa, chiefly in Natal. It is a common breeding bird throughout most of the British Isles, but it is scarce in north-west Scotland, the Outer Hebrides and the Shetlands.

The Swallow can be identified by its continuous blue back, chestnut and blue breast-bands and long tail streamers. The first birds arrive about the middle of March, but it is often well into April before they reach the north of England and May when they are seen in Scotland. Continuous waves of Swallows come in until early June, but the later arrivals are mostly passage birds. Normally the Swallow is a day migrant; consequently its movements can be observed, but the passage birds feed as they travel, and the ultimate direction of flight is not always plain. Thus a steady stream of birds may be travelling north, but individuals sweep back again and again to work a good feeding ground; yet the birds hawking to and fro in one spot may be miles away in a few minutes and others have taken their place. On southward migration—at its height in late September—the flight is often steadier; large parties of mature and immature birds pass over, frequently at a height, swerving but little though beating up into the wind and tacking, yet always bearing south. Here again diurnal flight and the need of rest leads to confusion, for flocks will gather from all directions at a favourite roosting place. The height at which these autumnal migrants travel depends upon wind and weather; at times it is beyond our vision. Against a strong wind the birds travel low; when crossing seas often merely skimming the waves.

So noticeable a bird is naturally recorded early and late: November, and even December stragglers are not rare. There is some support for the statement that, exceptionally, a bird unable to risk the sea-passage, has survived our winter, but none for the suggestion, founded on ancient myth, that birds seen early in the year had hibernated. That paired Swallows return at once to the nesting site is not true in most years. Some early arrivals pay an immediate but momentary call at the nesting site, but may then be absent for weeks before settling down. For days, even weeks, according to weather conditions, the first comers frequent the larger waters, marshes and sewage farms, where insect life is plentiful even in a late spring. All day they hawk for flies, and at night roost gregariously in reeds and osiers. When insect life becomes plentiful elsewhere, the birds speedily distribute themselves, though a late frost will drive them back to these haunts. The same roosts are occupied by returning birds in autumn; the evening flight of the twittering multitudes before they rain into the reeds or willow bed is a most interesting sight. These gatherings begin early in August, even in July, when the first brood is on the wing.

The twittering song of the Swallow is heard continuously during its stay; the bird sings on the wing and when perched. It is a cheery, simple song, hard to describe; Yarrell's *feetafeet, feetafeetit* gives perhaps the best impression. The call is a loud *twhit*, repeated two or three times. The clamour of the young when the parent brings food is an emphatic variant of this twitter, and the alarm, uttered when birds are mobbing a hawk or Cuckoo, sounds like an angry very rapid repetition of the *twhit*. The Swallow has very short legs but can perch, though on the ground it is less at ease than the House Martin. It will, however, alight to gather mud, and exceptionally to feed. Dipterous flies and other winged insects are its food, but it will sweep an insect off grass or the surface of water, and even pick one, when hovering, from a wall. Numbers of small beetles, especially *Aphodius* and its allies, are devoured, but these are taken on the wing when indulging in nuptial flight. Butterflies, and even large moths, such as the yellow-underwings, are hunted and captured; the last when disturbed by mowing machines or the feet of cattle. The height of the Swallow's flight varies from just above the ground or water to an altitude at which the wheeling birds appear mere specks. It is indirectly connected with weather, for insects vary their altitude according to atmospheric and seasonal conditions; the Swallow follows the food. Bundles of insects are collected for the young, and the 'packets' delivered to the offspring in turn.

Originally the Swallow nested in caves or under the shelter of rocks, and a few still use such situations, but the inside of a building is its usual home. On a beam or joist in a barn, shed or stable it constructs a saucer of mud and lines it with grass and feathers. More rarely it places the nest against a wall or beam; then it is a half-saucer, approaching in shape the nest of the House Martin beneath the eaves, but lacking buttresses. These unsupported nests often fall, though some broods are safely reared. As frequently proved by the capture of marked birds, old Swallows often return year after year to the same nest, and patch up the old cracked mud; but Swallows in their first year return to the same neighbourhood but never or very rarely to the actual building where they were born, as has been clearly shown by the examination of ringing records. The mud has at times to be brought from a distance; a little hair and straw is usually mixed with it. Both birds build, and before and during incubation the male feeds the female, either in the air or on the nest. The first clutch of four to six white eggs, speckled with reddish-brown and grey, is laid in May and two or three more may follow; indeed young may still be in the nest in October, but when migratory overcomes parental instinct they are left to perish. Fledged nestlings which have never flown before often fly strongly after their parents, when disturbed. For some time they need rest at intervals; their parents feed them as they perch on branches or buildings, and often in the air. They roost in the nest until it is needed for another brood. The nestlings are often attacked by the larvae of one of the blue-bottle flies (*Protocalliphora caerulea*). These blood-sucking larvae tend to kill off part of the brood. As autumn approaches the young birds, distinguished by their shorter tails, gather on trees, rope the telegraph wires and line the roof-trees of buildings in large numbers. From these places they take short flights, as if testing their wing-power, and gradually flock after flock moves southward.

The adult Swallow is steel-blue above with greenish gloss on wings and tail; most of the tail feathers have an oval white spot. The forehead and throat are rich chestnut, and below the latter is a band of blue; the rest of the underparts is creamy or buff. The bill and legs are black. The sexes are practically alike, though the tail of the female is usually a little shorter. The colours of the young are duller, the bands narrower and the tail noticeably short. Length, 7·3 in. Wing, 5 in. Tarsus, 0·5 in. (*Plates 106, 111 and 173.*)

### Red-rumped Swallow *Hirundo daurica*

This swallow breeds in parts of southern Europe, north Africa and Asia, and has been recorded in the British Isles fourteen times, usually in spring. It is easily distinguished from our Swallow by its buffish rump, chestnut nape and buff throat. Length, 7 in.

### House Martin *Delichon urbica*

The European range of the House Martin roughly corresponds with that of the Swallow, and it winters in South Africa. In the British Isles it is a bird of passage and a summer visitor, common in most parts, but is local in northern Scotland and the Scottish islands.

The white rump of the House Martin, very noticeable in flight, should prevent confusion with either the Swallow or Sand Martin, but we frequently hear people talk of the 'Swallows' that build under the eaves of their houses. A few days, even ten or more, after the Swallows reach us we see the first Martins, but it is often late in April before distribution is general. They travel with the later waves of incoming Swallows, and like them seldom go straight to the nesting sites, but hunt for food over large waters and roost in reeds and withies. The bird is not so constant in returning to its old haunts. It is more fickle and, though it often returns to its old nest, its numbers in a locality are

*Above* : Carrion Crow, p245
*Below* : Hooded Crow, p247

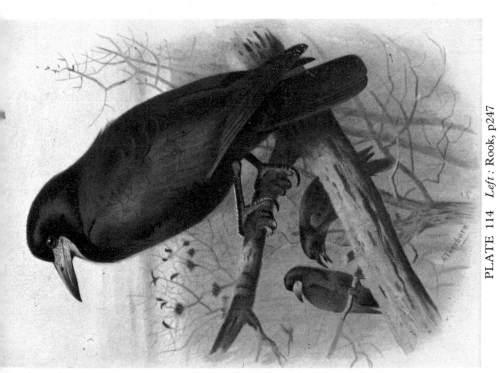

PLATE 114   *Left* : Rook, p247

PLATE 115

Jay, p251

Photo: *J. B. and S. Bottomley*

*Above:* Long-tailed Tit, p259

PLATE 116

*Below:* Marsh Tit, p257

Photo: *J. B. and S. Bottomley*

PLATE 117

*Above :* Magpie, p250
*Right :* Jay, p251
*Below :* Chough, p252

PLATE 118
*Above :* Great Tit, p253
*Below :* Crested Tit, p257

*Above :* Blue Tit, p255
*Below :* Willow Tit, p258

Photo: Eric Ho[

PLATE 119    Bearded Tit (male), p260

Photo: *J. B. and S. Bottomley*

PLATE 120    Dipper, p266

PLATE 121
*Above :* Coal Tit, p256
*Below :* Long-tailed Tit, p259

*Above :* Marsh Tit, p257
*Below :* Bearded Tit, p260

PLATE 122
*Above:* Tree Creeper, p263
*Below:* Wren, p264

*Above:* Nuthatch, p261
*Below:* Dipper, p266

Photo: *J. B. and S. Bottom*

PLATE 123     Nuthatch, p261

PLATE 124    Tree Creeper, p263

PLATE 125

*Above left :*
Fieldfare, p268
*Above right :*
Blackbird, p273

*Below left :*
Redwing, p271
*Below right :* Ring
Ouzel, p272

PLATE 126

*Above :* Song Thrush, p269
*Below :* Reed Warbler, p288

*Above :* Mistle Thrush, p267
*Below :* Marsh Warbler, p290

PLATE 127

Ring Ouzel
(male), p272

Photo:
J. B. and S. Bottomley

Photo: *J. B. and S. Bottomley*

PLATE 128     Wheatear, p275

apt to vary unaccountably. Though it travels, both in spring and autumn, with the Swallow, its haunts differ slightly; it is more a bird of the dwelling-house than the outbuilding. It is a cheerful bird; during the whole of its stay it utters a chirrupy little song, a sibilant twitter with a sound of 'z' in it, though it sings far less frequently than the Swallow; the call is a lively *tchirup*. Its food, and many of its habits, except those connected with nesting, are similar to those of the Swallow; it alights more frequently, and often aiding progression with uplifted wings, will walk a few steps when collecting mud or feeding. It has been known to perch in tree tops and pick insects off the leaves; parties sometimes perform complex aerial evolutions among the trees of a wood in pursuit of flying insects.

Undoubtedly the House Martin, before it found man providing shelter in the shape of overhanging eaves, was a cliff and cave dweller. Many large colonies of cliff-nesting Martins still exist—for instance in Yorkshire, Derbyshire, and on the sea-cliffs of Anglesey, where also a few nest in caves. Even on the bare cliff-face the bird usually builds below some overhanging rock, and on houses the nests are close under the eaves so that they may be strengthened by attachment above. The entrance is so small that the interfering Sparrow cannot invade the sanctuary when once the nest is complete. The mud, added in successive layers, is collected from ponds, streams or puddles. Both birds work at construction, but before this begins there is much play at building. A bird will fly up and dab a pellet of mud on the wall, then cling with head turned, twittering invitation to its mate, who will settle alongside and both will twitter conversationally. Then spreading their wings, they drop, perform a graceful arc and float off for aerial courtship, returning shortly to the selected spot but doing no real building. During construction there are frequent quarrels with trespassing Sparrows, but they do not usually come to grips; if the Sparrow remains in possession the Martins build elsewhere.

At all times the Martin is sociable, and many nests are built actually in contact; probably the Yorkshire instance of forty-six in a wall nine yards long represents the greatest number that could be crowded together. Four or five white eggs are laid as a rule in early June; second and third broods are common, and late nestlings are often left to starve. For weeks after leaving the nest the young congregate in ever-increasing flocks, which, as the season advances, may be seen gathering in trees or on house-tops and roping the wires with Swallows. A few days before the exodus they will wheel and dart in swarms round church towers or tall buildings; sometimes twittering hundreds collect in a tree, the centre of their aerial exercise. Towards the end of October these gatherings cease, though belated birds in November and December are not uncommon.

The adult House Martin is steel-blue above with a white rump, and white underparts; even its short legs and toes have white downy feathering. Its bill is black. The young bird is sooty-black, and some of the coverts and quills have white tips and edgings. Length, 5·3 in. Wing, 4·25 in. Tarsus, 0·45 in. (*Plates 110 and 173.*)

## Sand Martin                                                   *Riparia riparia*

The Sand Martin has a wide range in summer, embracing practically the whole of Europe and the Mediterranean countries, and it winters in south and east Africa. In the British Isles it is an abundant, though rather local summer visitor and bird of passage.

Towards the end of March, just in advance of the Swallow, the Sand Martin appears, first of its family, flitting over the larger sheets of water in search of early flies. Its brown back and small size and quicker, more jerky flight separate it at once from the two blue-backed swallows. Later parties accompany Swallows, but for a time, varying according to weather, the bird remains at these large waters and does not visit its nesting haunts. All day it flies from end to end of its selected pool, beating steadily up wind, dipping constantly to the water to pick up drifting insects, then turns and shoots down wind to repeat the process. In a strong breeze it practically remains over one small area, swerving to right or left, but neither gaining nor losing headway. When the wind is light the birds indulge in play, twittering in low tones, chasing and dodging and at times even struggling in the air. The whole party will leave the surface, rise and wheel at a considerable altitude, as if testing the wind, then drop in a body to resume the food chase. As evening approaches the flights become longer and higher until all descend to roost in the old brown reeds or other waterside vegetation. Long after the local birds have retired to nest in river bank, sand or gravel pit, often at a distance from water, fresh incursions of passage birds visit the pool, depart for the north, and are replaced by newcomers. The reeds, marshes, osiers and sewage farms are seldom entirely deserted, for a few non-breeding birds occupy them in June and July until the first batch of young come to swell the nightly gathering. The twittering song is continuous when the birds are on the wing, and becomes a conversational undertone after they have settled in the roost. The harsh alarm is heard when a passing Kestrel, Crow or other suspected enemy calls for combined action to drive it away. The food consists of small insects, mostly gnats and other flies whose early stages are aquatic.

The Sand Martin is sociable in its nesting habits; from a dozen to many hundred pairs will nest close together, according to available space. The nests are at the end of tunnels of from a few inches to 3 or 4 ft. in length, bored in sand or gravel; if the bank allows, well out of reach. Some nests are burrowed just below the turf at the top of steep marl-cliffs, and others in cracks between stones in a sandy lane only 3 ft. above the roadway. Even the softer layers of new red sandstone are pecked into by the short and feeble-looking bill; many of these tunnels are visible in the steep cuttings of the Manchester Ship Canal. Perhaps the birds do not habitually roost in the tunnels during construction, but the holes may be used as roosting places by migrating birds from other colonies. Both birds excavate, boring with the beak and scratching out the loose sand with their small feet. The actual nest is a litter of straw and feathers in a chamber at the end of the burrow; it is soon a hotbed of parasites. Four or five white eggs are laid about the middle of May, and a second brood is usual. The colony is a busy place; the young, showing their white chins, peep out of the mouth of the hole and clamorously demand food. At intervals the birds go through a strange performance, common to other colonial nesters such as gulls and terns. The air will be full of bustling, twittering birds when suddenly there is a strange hush, and all, as if by word of command, rise high into the air and leave the place deserted. After a short interval they return a few at a time and activities are resumed. This may be aerial play, but the silence and sudden departure give the impression of alarm, though no cause is apparent. The Sand Martin is victimised by the House Sparrow which sometimes occupies holes in the midst of a colony.

The Sand Martin departs early, at any rate from its more northerly haunts. In August the gatherings at the nightly roost increase enormously, though the advent and departure of passage birds causes great irregularity in numbers. It is then that the crepuscular flights become most interesting. From all directions flocks of a score or two to hundreds of birds arrive and begin aerial evolutions, wheeling in ordered companies, twittering continually. The host breaks up, the birds cross and recross one another's paths, and then re-form into long lines which undulate across the sky, like blown smoke. Often the whole body soars and after a few turns and circles begins a curious spiral descent, the leading party wheeling repeatedly, guiding the twists of a descending screw. When still some height above the reeds the birds half close their wings and shoot down diagonally, jerking from side to side, till with opened wings they check descent. Then in the waning light they skim to and fro with rapid flight, just above the reeds, into which they suddenly and imperceptibly vanish. Party follows party, but the later comers go through shorter performances and drop at once to the roost. In the south birds are noticed in October, but north of the midlands most leave early in September.

The Sand Martin is hair-brown above, white below with a narrow brown band on the breast; the bill is black, the legs brown. The young have rufous tips to the coverts and margins to the secondaries. Length, 4·8 in. Wing, 4 in. Tarsus, 0·45 in. (*Plates 110, 112 and 173.*)

## Family ORIOLIDAE Orioles

### Golden Oriole                                                           *Oriolus oriolus*

At the end of April or beginning of May some Golden Orioles reach our shores every year and pairs have nested or attempted to nest in several southern and eastern counties. At least one brood has been reared as far north as the Lake District. As an irregular visitor or bird of passage it has occurred in most parts of England, less frequently in Ireland and Scotland. It is well distributed in Europe, except in the extreme north, and in north Africa and Asia and winters far south in Africa.

The male bird is so strikingly yellow that any one can recognise it, and also has a loud clear call that attracts attention, as well as harsher notes. The female and young bird are greener, and amidst foliage are difficult to see; the male also, though conspicuous when passing from tree to tree in the open, is soon lost sight of when he dashes, as is his habit, into thick woods or foliage. The bird is an insect-feeder, but fruit is freely taken in autumn.

The nest, a fair-sized cup or saucer, is almost invariably built on a horizontal bough, slung between the branches of a fork; on either side it is firmly and cleverly bound to its supports. The eggs, usually four or five, are white or creamy with a few brown, black or purple spots, thickest towards the larger end.

The male is golden-yellow with black lores, wings and centre of the tail. Yellow and whitish tips and edges show on the closed wing, and the tail feathers are partly yellow, the black forming a graduated wedge. Bright yellow is replaced by greenish-yellow on the back and head of the female, and her lighter underparts have dark brown streaks; her wings and tail are browner. The young resemble the female, but at first are spotted on the back with pale yellow, and later are more olive in colour, whilst the flanks are distinctly yellow. The bill is dull red, legs slate-grey, and irides crimson. Length, 9·5 in. Wing, 5·9 in. Tarsus, 0·85 in. (*Plate 109.*)

## Family CORVIDAE Crows

**Raven**                                                     *Corvus corax*

The Raven has increased its numbers and range in the British Isles in recent years. In much of Wales and in parts of Scotland, the Isle of Man and the west of Ireland it is common; in England the chief strongholds are rocky coasts in the south and west, the Lake District and the northern Pennines. In the present century it has spread from Wales into Shropshire and Hereford. In the British Isles, except for occasional wandering, the bird is sedentary, but there is regular winter immigration in Scotland. The Raven has a wide distribution in Europe, though absent from densely populated and highly cultivated areas.

The Raven is the largest, most powerful and most intelligent of the crows, distinguished by its heavy bill and wedge-shaped tail.

It has been described as 'grave, dignified and sedate'; it is more, for when flying with slow but strong and measured flaps it is purposeful and determined, a great bird with heavy beak and head. When it speaks, which it frequently does, its deep croak is sufficient for identification. Variously written as *pruk*, *cruck*, *whow* and *glog*, this short, deep bark is different from any other corvine utterance. When the bird is standing on some rocky eminence the whole body lunges forward with each call, and the pointed feathers on the throat stand out like a ragged beard. Often the bird soars and wheels at a great height, its wings motionless, its flight feathers extended like fingers. It is revelling in air mastery, not seeking its prey. The food of Raven, like that of all crows, is varied; it kills small birds and mammals, especially rats and young rabbits; the weakly lamb or disabled sheep is at its mercy, but its favourite food is carrion. Round a large carcase many will gather, driving away gulls or other would-be diners. With powerful hooked bill it pierces the hides and tears the flesh. A carcase is at first approached with caution, in sidling jumps with wings half open.

The nest, a massive structure of sticks, heather stems and roots, is built upon a ledge on some rocky outcrop or precipitous cliff-face, and withstands most winter storms. The cup is lined with soft substances—wool, rabbit fur, grass or bracken. Formerly, when the bird was less persecuted, inland and lowland haunts were inhabited, and the nest was usually built in some tall and ancient tree; 'Raven trees' exist in many places from which the bird has vanished. Tree nests are now regular again in some districts, especially in Wales and on the Welsh borders. The eggs, which are laid in February or March, are from three to seven in number, and are bluish-green, blotched or streaked with brown and black.

The Raven's nuptial display is little known, although one trick, that of rolling in flight, is familiar. When descending from a height it will 'shoot' like a Rook with half-closed wings, turning and twisting with great rapidity. The roll is a cork-screw reverse when the flight is horizontal. The bird turns belly upwards and shoots forward with its own momentum, quickly recovering its normal position. Rolling is not confined to the breeding season, and is occasionally employed when the bird is attacked by a falcon. The Raven is shy and cautious rather than cowardly, and will drive gulls from the vicinity of its nest and spar with the passing Peregrine; yet Coward saw it swerve from the assault of a Kestrel and heard it cry in alarm when boldly attacked by a pair of Lapwings. Communal roosting is not uncommon, and considerable flocks of Ravens may be seen indulging in flight play over hilltops and rocky coasts at any time of year.

The plumage, legs, feet and beak are black, most of the feathers glossed with blue or green. The bill is curved and decidedly hooked. The young are duller. Length, 25 to 27 in. Wing, 15·75 to 17 in. Tarsus, 2·6 to 3 in. (*Plates 113 and 174.*)

## Carrion Crow                                           *Corvus corone corone*

The Carrion Crow and the Hooded Crow are now generally regarded as geographical races of one species, a view that is supported by the fact that where their ranges overlap they frequently interbreed and the hybrids are fertile. However, the plumage differences between the two are so conspicuous and their breeding ranges in the British Isles so well defined that they may conveniently be considered separately here.

In general appearance and many of its habits the Carrion Crow is a lesser Raven, but with a slighter, less-curved and smaller-hooked beak. Throughout

England, Wales and southern Scotland it is resident, and in spite of its unpopularity is in many places common and increasing in numbers; in the Highlands, Ireland and the Isle of Man the Hooded Crow generally replaces it. However, the Carrion Crow is extending its range northwards in Scotland at the expense of the Hooded Crow and is now not uncommon as far north as Sutherland. It has nested in Ireland, but is not a regular breeding bird there.

The Carrion can be distinguished from the Raven by size, voice and square-tailed profile in flight, and from the Hooded Crow by its black plumage, but there is frequent confusion between it and the Rook. The beak of the Crow is stouter and in consequence looks shorter, and whereas in the adult Rook the nostrils are bare, those of the Crow are covered at all ages with bristle-like feathers. The Rook is generally gregarious, the Crow solitary, but Rooks occasionally nest in isolated trees, and Crows may feed with Rooks; moreover Crows are often sociable in winter roosts. The most distinctive character is the voice, well described by a Dorset gamekeeper. 'The Rook say "caw", but t'other un der say "pawk, pawk". He's so fond of a bit of meat.' The guttural, slightly vibrant croak is distinct from any note of the Rook. The bird is garrulous, loving to perch on the top of a tree, calling three or four times in quick succession, with a slight pause between each series of croaks. The wing-beats are slower, more deliberate than those of the Rook. Though delighting in carrion of all kinds, the Crow will kill and eat any small animal it can catch, and, as the gamekeeper knows, is an inveterate egg-robber. Impudent and bold when opportunity offers, its natural caution enables it to avoid most traps. Molluscs it enjoys; when these cannot be hammered open they are repeatedly carried into the air and dropped until fractured. The Crow is more careful than gulls that the shell falls on hard ground, but seldom varies the height from which they are dropped if the first effort fails. In the fields the bird searches for worms, insects and grain. Like the Hoodie, it is a regular shore feeder. Both its diet and its feeding methods are varied and adaptable: it has, for example, been seen hovering over water and picking up fish. It frequently hides food, and there is evidence that the location of these caches is accurately remembered. Although so shy and cautious, the Crow, when free from persecution, becomes indifferent to the presence of man; it is a common London bird, roosting sociably in the parks in winter.

On cliffs and mountain crags the Crow nests on ledges or in crevices, and in some treeless lowland districts it builds on posts or electricity pylons, but the usual nest-site is a tree or tall thorn bush. The nest is similar to that of the Raven, but less bulky. The eggs, four or five in number, are seldom laid before April; they are blotched and spotted with brown on a blue or green ground and vary considerably.

The plumage is black with a green or purple sheen, but the gloss is much greener than that of the Rook. The bill, legs and feet are also black. The sexes do not vary, but the female is the smaller bird; the young are duller. Length, about 20 in. Wing, 13 in. Tarsus, 2·5 in. (*Plates 114 and 174.*)

**Hooded Crow**                                              *Corvus corone cornix*
The Hooded Crow breeds abundantly in northern Scotland, the Scottish islands, Ireland and the Isle of Man. It has also nested in some of the eastern counties of England, but it does not do so regularly. In autumn large numbers of migratory birds arrive on the east coast, many spreading over the eastern shires or proceeding inland to the midlands, where it is a well-known winter visitor. In the west of England and in Wales it is rare. The Grey Crow is, as a rule, a day migrant. In autumn birds reach our shores in small parties, following one another all day long, sometimes dropping from a height, sometimes travelling close to the waves. Abroad it breeds in northern and eastern Europe and western Asia.

The Hoodie, with its contrasted greys and blacks, cannot be confused with either the Carrion or Rook. Some authorities declare that the call-notes of the two are indistinguishable, but Macgillivray, writing of this species, says, 'its voice is not so loud or clear as that of the Carrion'. Coward supported the latter view. The flight is slow and heavy and usually straight.

The diet is similar to that of the Carrion, and its reputation as an egg-thief and destroyer of game is at least as black; it is feared and hated on the sheep-runs. Along the shore it is a constant scavenger; it takes birds from the nets of the wildfowlers and hunts for and destroys those which escape partially disabled from their guns. It drops molluscs and crabs to break them after the manner of the Carrion. On coast cliffs the eggs of gulls, Cormorants and other birds are stolen when their owners are absent, and it will enter the burrow of the Puffin with a similar purpose.

The nest is placed on or near the ground, on a cliff, in heather or a low bush, or in a tree; it closely resembles that of the Carrion, but on the coast seaweed is often interwoven in the structure. The four to six eggs are of the usual crow type, very similar to those of the Carrion; they are laid as a rule early in April.

Except for the head, throat, wings, tail and thigh feathers, which are black and mostly glossy, the plumage is ash-grey, the dark shafts giving it a streaky appearance. The bill and legs are black. The male is the larger bird; otherwise the sexes are alike. At first the young are much blacker than the parents, but in the juvenile plumage brown rather than black predominates. Length, about 20 in. Wing, 12·5 in. Tarsus, 2·25 in. (*Plates 114 and 174.*)

**Rook**                                                           *Corvus frugilegus*
Resident throughout our islands and showing partiality for association with man, the Rook is our best-known and most respected crow. It nests in colonies close to our houses; it feeds in flocks in cultivated fields. Abroad it ranges over northern and central Europe, but is rare in the south; throughout its range, including Britain, it is partially migratory. Regular migration is complicated by irregular movements in summer and winter; large numbers of immigrants reach our eastern shores in autumn and return in spring. Thus the Rook is at once a resident, a winter visitor and possibly a bird of passage. In Ireland

the movements are further complicated by short, irregular migrations across the Irish Sea, and by occasional abnormal westward flights that have sometimes ended in disaster in the Atlantic.

The feather-denuded rough skin round the base of the bill of the adult Rook, the slender and less-curved beak, blue sheen, and voice are characters which distinguish it from the Carrion Crow, but in the young bird, until a year old, the nostrils are clothed with bristles and the chin feathered. At all ages, however, the feathers of the flanks hang loosely, giving the bird a more ragged, skirted appearance round the thighs than the Crow.

The Rook is a sociable bird, amiably consorting with the Jackdaw, which joins it in the fields and the winter roosts and occasionally at the rookery. In the fields the Rook follows the plough, walking erect, with sedate, slightly rolling gait, and with occasional short flights to catch up with the tractor. The morning and evening flights, from and to the rookery or roost, are familiar to all; with steady, regular wing-beats and with frequent calls, the flock trails across the sky in loose formation. On reaching the destination, whether feeding ground or roost, the birds frequently descend in rapid, oblique flight, twisting and turning with wings half-closed; this is termed 'shooting', and is also indulged in during nuptial display. The harsh *caw*, though easily recognised, is subject to individual modulation; in most flocks one or two birds have high-pitched voices, which, however, are clearly distinct from the sharper calls of Daws. Emphasis and inflection, especially when at the rookery, suggest to our ears anger, pleasure, affection and other qualities, but the alarm note, a long harsh call, is seldom varied.

Though more of a vegetarian than other crows, the Rook is on the whole beneficial; to some extent it destroys grain and roots, but its services in checking pests, especially wireworms and 'leather-jackets', the larvae of crane-flies, usually out-weigh the damage. Infected plants and roots are torn up, and the earthen chambers in which the leather-jackets lie are dug out whole. Worms, molluscs and small mammals are eaten, and flocks frequently feed on tidal banks and the shore.

The colony or rookery is established in a clump of trees frequently close to a human habitation, and many nests may be built in one tree; nests on buildings are rare. Most of the rookeries are deserted after the young have flown, the colonies from a wide area joining forces and nightly occupying a common roost. During winter the members of a colony frequently visit the rookery, where, with much conversation, courtship display is indulged in; in February these visits, usually in the early morning, become more frequent, and destruction or reconstruction of old nests begins, but serious building is seldom started until March. In the nuptial display much bowing and tail-fanning is indulged in. Old nests are frequently repaired and added to until they become huge and unwieldy masses of sticks, but frequently the old structures are deliberately destroyed. One of a pair generally mounts guard over new foundations, for the Rook is an acquisitive and pilfering bird, ready to victimise its neighbour. Earth and small sods are used to strengthen nests, and they are lined with hair, grass and other soft material, but less wool is used than by other crows. The eggs, three to six, vary in colour, but green predominates; they are laid, as a rule, in March, and the young leave the nests in April. Shrill, infantile cries advertise the presence of the young; these change to a gobble of satisfaction when the parent unloads its distended pouch for their benefit. The young are fed in the fields long after they have left the nest; they follow the old birds with querulous calls and shivering wings.

The black plumage of the adult is glossed with blue, purple, violet and green reflections, but is duller before the moult in autumn. Down feathers clothe the chin in winter, but are lost in spring. The chin is feathered and the nostrils covered with bristles in the young, and the plumage is browner; by the following spring the greyish, warty denuded area is complete. The legs and bill are black. Length, about 19 in. Wing, 12·75 in. Tarsus, 2·25 in. (*Plates 114 and 174.*)

### Jackdaw                                                    *Corvus monedula*

The popularity of the pert and sprightly Jackdaw is evident from the prefix 'Jack', which, though not exactly a pet-name, is a diminutive given to several familiar animals. Throughout the British Isles it is resident and increasingly abundant; it has recently colonised the Shetlands, though still scarce and local in north-west Scotland. It ranges through west and central Europe, from where we receive many winter visitors in autumn. A few of our native birds appear to emigrate.

The Jackdaw, a much smaller bird than the Rook, with which it freely consorts, has a proportionately shorter and straighter beak. On the ground its movements are quick, almost fussy; it walks with a strut, jerking its body; its wing-beats in flight are rapid, readily distinguishable from those of the Rook. Its flight is less direct, more erratic, and it frequently indulges in aerial display, especially at its breeding place; here the birds of a colony will engage in combined evolutions without concerted action; each individual dodges, swerves, turns, twists or dives at pleasure. These sociable performances, most noticeable in the evening, are accompanied by incessant clamour, the sharp and shrill cries of *tchack* or *cae* blending in delightful harmony. The alarm note is similar to that of the Rook, though not so deep in tone. The food is mainly insects, worms and molluscs, but eggs and young birds are freely devoured in spring, and a little fruit and corn is taken. To obtain a favourite insect, the 'ked' or spurious sheep-tick, the Daw perches on the sheep's back and searches the wool; it will also pick hair from the backs of horses and cattle as lining for its nest.

The gregarious instinct is strongly developed in the nesting habits; solitary nests are exceptional. The highly developed social system of Jackdaw colonies has been revealed by the studies of Dr K. Lorenz. The colonies are in crag or cliff-faces, woods or ruins, and the nest is usually placed in a hole or crack in rock, tree or masonry, often down a chimney. Open nests are, however, built in trees, occasionally in rookeries; the habit of nesting, feeding and flying with

Rooks appears to be growing, and may be due to the general increase of the bird. When placed in a hole the nest may be little more than a lining, but when in branches or buildings great quantities of sticks are used. The cup is lined with wool, hair and grass. The four to six eggs are less spotted and blotched than those of most crows, and are bluer in ground colour. They are usually laid late in April.

The adult's plumage is black, glossed with blue, on the head and upper parts, duller beneath; the nape, back of neck and ear-coverts are grey. The young are browner, and the grey little noticeable until the second autumn. The bill and legs are black, and the irides bluish or greyish-white. Length, about 14 in. Wing, 9·25 in. Tarsus, 1·9 in. (*Plates 113 and 174.*)

## Magpie                                                      *Pica pica*

The Magpie is resident throughout the British Isles, and though occasionally wandering, exhibits no real migratory movements. In the north of Scotland and parts of the west of Ireland it is rare, but in most parts of the latter country it is now abundant, though introduced in the 17th century. It is found throughout Europe.

The strikingly pied plumage and long, graduated tail, as well as the loud, harsh chatter of the Magpie, prevent confusion with any other species. In the open country it commands attention as one, two, three or more birds, with rapidly moving, apparently short wings, fly in succession, chattering as they pass. When the bird alights the long tail is at once elevated and is carefully carried clear of the ground. Like other crows, its usual gait is a walk, but when attracted by food or any special object it hops quickly sideways with wings just open. The fondness of all its family for bright objects is well known. In game-preserving areas the bird, owing to incessant persecution, is shy and rare, but in London and the outskirts of the large manufacturing towns it is common: indeed, where it is not molested it courts rather than avoids the vicinity of man. In winter it becomes gregarious, wandering and feeding in small parties or flocks, and gathering at a common rendezvous to roost at night. Early in the year large numbers collect together. Darwin referred to these 'marriage' meetings, and F. J. Stubbs described the nuptial display during several of these meetings, at one of which 200 birds were present. The males rapidly raised and depressed their crests, uplifted, opened and closed their tails like fans, and conversed in soft tones quite distinct from their usual chatter. In the display the loose feathers of the flanks were brought over and hid the primaries, and the patch on the shoulders was spread so as to make the white conspicuous, presumably to attract the female eye. Short buoyant flights and chases were part of the courtship.

No animal food comes amiss to the Magpie; young birds and eggs, small mammals and insects are devoured, but acorns, grain and other vegetable substances are not despised.

Tall trees are generally selected by the Magpie for its bulky nest which is usually firmly attached to a central fork in the upper branches. The framework of the sticks is cemented with earth and clay, and a lining of the same material is covered with fine roots; above is a stout though loosely built dome of prickly branches with one well-concealed entrance. When the leaves fall these huge nests are plainly visible. Where trees are scarce, and even in well-wooded country, nests are often built in bushes and hedgerows. The eggs, small for the size of the bird, number from five to eight, and as many as ten are recorded; they show much variation in ground and marking, but a usual type is blue-green with close specks and spots of brown and grey. They are laid in April, and only one brood is reared unless disaster overtakes the first clutch.

The adult's head, neck and breast are glossy black with metallic green and violet sheen; the belly and scapulars are pure white; the wings are black, glossed with green, and the primaries have white inner webs, conspicuous when the wing is open. The graduated tail is black, shot with bronze-green and other iridescent colours. The legs and bill are black. The young resemble the parents, but are at first without much of the gloss on the sooty plumage. Length, about 18 in. Wing, 7·5 in. Tail 8–10 in. Tarsus, 1·85 in. (*Plates 117 and 174.*)

**Nutcracker**                                                    *Nucifraga caryocatactes*
The Nutcracker ranges through northern and eastern Europe and Asia, and has occurred in Britain as a rare autumn and winter visitor. In the field the bird is not unlike a Rook with a long bill. Its size, form and mottled plumage should be distinctive to any one who meets with this wanderer in the field. Seebohm describes its 'peculiar slow undulating Jay-like flight' and its harsh calls. It feeds on seeds of the cedar, nuts and acorns, and on insects.

The general colour is chocolate-brown, with large white spots except on the crown and nape; the wings and tail are almost black, the latter tipped with white. The under tail-coverts are conspicuously white. The bill is brownish-black; the legs black. The Siberian bird has a longer, more pointed and slender bill than the European form. Length, about 12·5 in. (*Plate 113.*)

**Jay**                                                            *Garrulus glandarius*
The Jay is a common resident in England and Wales, but it is rare or absent in the north of Scotland and the extreme west of Ireland and is not found in the Isle of Man. It breeds throughout Europe except in the far north.

More strictly a woodland bird than the Magpie, the vinaceous plumaged Jay is less familiar, but it is now a common bird of the London suburbs, where it has lost much of its characteristic shyness, and it even nests in some of the Royal Parks. Persecution has failed to destroy it, and today, in many areas, the Jay is increasing. Shy and wary, ever ready to take alarm, it defies the keeper's strenuous efforts. Its dress and behaviour prevent confusion with any other species, while its harsh screech, a strident *kraak, kraak,* is as distinctive. This note often calls our attention to a flash of white as the bird dodges out of sight; that is all that catches the eye. When unconscious of our presence it will sit, raising and depressing its black-streaked crest, elevating and lowering its fanned-out tail, or swinging it from side to side; it leaps rather heavily from branch to branch, constantly turning its head on the lookout for danger, or furtively seeking some unwary victim. On the ground it hops jauntily, sideways rather than forwards; on the wing, when alarmed, it flies quickly and speedily takes cover. In the open its flight is undulating and somewhat laboured; its rounded wings appear short and weak. Woods and coverts are its usual haunt. After the young have left the nest the family parties scour the woods, following one another with noisy screams, which, though really calls or notes of affection, have an angry, often distressful ring. Early in the year many gather together for courtship, and then a crooning jumble of soft and not unmusical notes make up the nuptial song; in this the imitative Jay has been heard to introduce the voices of other birds or mammals.

As its specific name implies, it is partial to acorns, beechmast and nuts. A little oats and wheat is also eaten. In spring the Jay is an egg-thief, victimising small birds and even wild ducks and Pheasants. On the other hand the bird destroys pests; Professor Newstead counted the fragmentary remains of at least 127 click-beetles—'wire-worms' in their larval stage—in the stomach of one bird killed in April, and another, shot on the nest, contained 120 larvae of the destructive winter moth. In spite of its habitual caution the Jay will raid gardens, especially when peas or fruit are ripe. One habit, shared by the Magpie and others of the group, is that of burying nuts, acorns or even inedible objects. Acorns are carried up to three-quarters of a mile. The success with which the birds find them in winter suggests that the bird remembers precisely where they were buried. A small tree, bush or hedgerow is the usual site for the nest, which is open and rather lightly built; it is lined with roots and well concealed. One brood of five to seven is reared in late April or May. A common type of the small-sized egg is light buff, finely speckled with pale brown and grey, often with a few irregular lines at the larger end.

The Jay has an erectile white crest streaked with black; the rest of the head, back and breast are pinkish-brown; the chin, throat, belly and a large area surrounding the base of the tail are pure white, this last sharply contrasting with the brown-black tail. At the base of the bill is a conspicuous black moustachial streak or patch. The wings are black, white and chestnut, with beautiful black, white and blue barred feathers on the coverts. Before the moult in autumn the general colour is browner and less pink-tinged, and the colour of the young is duller. The bill is dark horn; the legs and feet pale brown. Length, about 15 in. Wing, 7·2 in. Tarsus, 1·5 in. (*Plates 115, 117 and 174.*)

## Chough
*Pyrrhocorax pyrrhocorax*

Many of the former breeding haunts of the Chough in the British Isles are now deserted. It no longer nests in Cornwall, and the Scottish population is restricted to Argyllshire, but in Ireland, Wales and the Isle of Man the species holds its own and may even be increasing. There is little evidence to support the theory that competition with the Jackdaw, either for food or for nest-sites, is responsible for its decline in England and Scotland. Abroad it breeds in southern Europe, the Mediterranean basin and the Alps.

The Chough is distinguished from all other birds by its glossy black dress, long curved red bill and red legs. It is a gentle, sedentary, conservative bird, rarely met with far from its breeding places. The typical habitat is a coastal cliff, but there are some inland breeding sites, particularly in north Wales.

It has wonderfully buoyant and easy flight. It floats above the beetling cliffs with wide-spread primaries; the tips of these bend upwards as it curves and turns, sweeping round gracefully. With wings almost closed it shoots towards the boiling surf at the foot of the crags, then checking itself, sweeps into some wave-washed cave. Its movement on the ground is sometimes a quick run, but it will walk as sedately as a Rook. Its loud, clear notes are variously written, but *kee-aw* fits its ringing call, clearer and louder than the note of the Jackdaw; *tchuff*, from which it gets its name, is another common cry. Its food consists of insects, molluscs and other invertebrates, and, occasionally, a little corn.

Some crack or fissure in the roof or sides of a tidal cave is a usual site for the nest in the Chough's breeding haunts, and similar hollows in steep crag and cliff-faces are utilised. The nest is, as a rule, bulky, composed of roots and stems of heather, furze or other plants, and is lined with wool or hair. The eggs, laid late in April or May, and three to six in number, are spotted and speckled, not always densely, with various shades of brown and grey on a creamy or slightly tinted ground.

The plumage of both sexes is glossy blue-black, with green sheen on the wings; the bill and legs are coral-red; in the young dull orange.

Length, about 16½ in. Wing, 10·9 in. Tarsus, 2·1 in. (*Plates 117 and 174.*)

## Family PARIDAE Tits

### Great Tit                                                           *Parus major*

The Great Tit is found throughout Europe and is generally distributed in the British Isles, though it does not occur in the Outer Hebrides and the northern isles of Scotland. European birds are irregular but often abundant immigrants in autumn.

The tits as a group are perhaps our most popular birds, for they readily respond to encouragement, coming to feed on bones, suet or nuts hung up for their benefit in our gardens; the Great and Blue are the most abundant visitors. Many people, however, find difficulty in distinguishing the various species, though each has its characters—in the Great the large size, and the long black bib or waistcoat from chin to vent. Early in January, not infrequently in December, the Great Tit begins his strange song, a rasping, often squeaky, *pee-ker, pee-ker*. In April and May the male varies it by the addition of an extra note or two or by changing it into three or four sweeter sounds. The calls are varied and include a sharp *zi, zi,* and a metallic *tink,* as well as a harsh churr. For a short time in summer the bird is silent, but autumnal saw-sharpening is frequent, and in winter the constant calls are varied by occasional outbursts. In winter the sociable Great Tit joins with other species in nomadic wanderings, roaming from tree to tree with undulating flight, hurriedly examining branches, boles and buds; one moment a bird is on the ground, throwing over the dead leaves or tearing up the moss in its search for prey, the next hammering at some slumbering insect below a twig, from which it swings head downwards. From these flocks a bird will at times detach itself and flit from twig to twig just above one's head, scolding vigorously. The menu of the Great Tit is varied; spiders and insects of all kinds are eaten, and acorns, beech-mast, birch seeds and various nuts are carried to a conven-ient perch, where, holding them with one foot, the birds hacks out the contents. A favourite food is the *Andricus* larva in the marble-gall; galls with holes pecked to the central chamber lie littered under the oaks. Fungi infested with beetles and dipterous larvae are pulled to bits, and in the garden, where occasionally fruit trees are raided, sunflower seeds are much appreciated. Bud-destruction is a 'crime' of the Great Tit, but the leaf-scales are torn off to reach 'the worm in the bud'. It is even accused of murdering other small birds, driving its bill into their skulls to feed upon the brain; most of the evidence is, however, founded on cases that have occurred in aviaries. Bees are not immune from attack, and occasionally bee-keepers suffer. Like the Blue Tit, the Great Tit has become an adept at piercing the metal foil caps of milk bottles and drinking the cream.

Any hole will suit the Great Tit for its nest; the size matters little. A large cavity is filled with grass, leaves and moss, and in the woods is lined with hair, rabbit fur and feathers; a small hole contains nothing more than a felted mass of moss and hair. Holes in trees, walls, rocks and stumps are usual situations, but a letter-box, pump, or inverted flower-pot will serve. The bird sits closely, and if handled will hiss and bite, and sometimes has to be lifted before it will leave the eggs or young, which when the brood is large it cannot cover completely. Six or seven is the ordinary clutch, but ten to fifteen are some-times found. The eggs, white with few or many reddish spots, differ from those of other tits in size only; second broods are rare, and the clutch is seldom com-plete until early in May. The young are largely fed on caterpillars. From the number of visits paid in one day it has been estimated that while the young are in the nest between 7000 and 8000 grubs are destroyed.

The head, neck and a streak of varying width from the chin to the centre of the otherwise white under tail-coverts is glossy blue-black; the cheeks and ear-coverts are white; a pale, often white, nape spot shades into yellow and then olive-green on the back and mantle; the rump, tail and most of the wing are blue-grey. On the wing is a conspicuous white bar, and the outer tail feathers are white-edged. The underparts, except for the black streak, are sulphur-yellow. The bill is black, the legs and feet lead-blue. The young are duller, with the black replaced by dark brown and the white suffused with yellow. Length, 5·7 in. Wing, 2·9 in. Tarsus, 0·8 in. (*Plate 118 and 175*.)

**Blue Tit**                                                    *Parus caeruleus*

The Blue Tit is a common resident species throughout the British Isles, except in the northern isles of Scotland, and is found in all but the far north of Europe. The majority of our native Blue Tits do not migrate or wander far in winter within our islands, but large numbers of immigrants arrive in some autumns.

There are commoner but few more popular birds than the Blue Tit or Tom Tit, and this is due as much to its perky acrobatic performances as to its neat and attractive dress. There may be no bird visible in the garden when we hang up the chicken-bone or coconut, but before we have returned to the house a Blue Tit is picking bits from the denuded sternum, or its tail alone is protruding from the hole in the nut. It swings beneath the suet bag, calling up its friends with its sharp *tee, tee, tee,* and scolding them with an angry churr, its cobalt crest erected, when they come for their share. It is an irascible little bird. The song period lasts almost all the year round, but it is only from January until June that its rippling tinkle, simple but very cheerful, is heard frequently. We may hear it anywhere; the Tom-tit lives near or actually in our houses, if there is a convenient hole in the wall, but it is as common along the lanes or in the thick wood. It is at once plucky and cautious. Its reaction to handling by a 'ringer' seems to be one of anger rather than fear; it bites fiercely and often becomes a trap habitué. Blue and Great Tits are constant and apparently amicable companions in the winter flocks, and the former are the better gymnasts, feeding chiefly in the slender twigs. A Blue will often ascend a trunk in short jerky hops, imitating a Tree Creeper.

The Blue Tit is a destroyer of pests, though it has not an entirely clean sheet as a beneficial species. It is fond of young buds of various trees, and though it may pull them to bits in the hope of finding insects, the damaged and undamaged buds examined after a raid show little sign of having been previously infected. No species, however, destroys more coccids and aphids, the worst foes of many plants; examples killed when attacking ripe pears, which the Blue Tit can seldom resist, had in their stomachs a number of fruit-tree pests, including American blight, mixed up with the fruit pulp. When in August the tiny leaf-miner grubs hang from the laburnum the Blue Tit skilfully hovers and nips them from their life-lines, and when the green tortrix swarms round the defoliated oaks no bird is smarter in catching these little moths. Seeds are also eaten. The Blue Tit's habit of opening milk bottles and helping itself to the creamy top layer of the contents is now widespread, though not universal, in the British Isles. It was first noticed near Southampton in 1921, was occurring in several scattered localities in the south-east and north of England in 1939 and by 1947 had extended to Scotland and northern Ireland. The habit began with the tearing of cardboard bottle tops, but metal foil caps proved even easier to penetrate. In some years Blue Tits also become a nuisance by entering houses and tearing wallpaper, books and fabrics. This occurs chiefly in September and October and has been most noticeable in very dry autumns. No entirely convincing explanation of this behaviour has yet been offered.

The nest is in a hole in a tree, wall, stump, gate-post or pump, and few birds more readily accept the shelter of a nesting-box; the same hole is returned to year after year, and when one pair dies another takes possession. The bird is a close sitter, hissing and biting at an intruding finger. When protecting its eggs it raises its crest, but this is a sign of excitement rather than anger, for it is elevated during nuptial display. The nesting material is usually moss, wool, hair and feathers, and the eggs are laid in April or May. The number in the clutch is often very large: over twenty are sometimes recorded; seven to fifteen are normal.

The azure-blue crown and dark blue line passing through the eye and encircling the white cheeks to the chin are distinctive. The forehead, eye-streak, and a bar on the wing are also white. The nape, wings and tail are blue; the back yellowish-green; the underparts mostly sulphur-yellow with a dark line down the abdomen. The bill is black; legs bluish-grey. The young are much yellower than the old birds. Length, 4·3 in. Wing, 2·4 in. Tarsus, 0·75 in. (*Plates 118 and 175*.)

## Coal Tit                                                       *Parus ater*

The Coal Tit is a generally sedentary species found in wooded country throughout the British Isles and most of Europe. It is the commonest tit in pinewoods, and also in hill-country oakwoods.

A large white nape spot on the black head is the hall-mark of the Coal Tit; by this we may know it when it visits the garden and may pick it out when it is trooping through the winter woods with other tits. Sometimes these flocks consist of Coals alone. In acrobatic skill and restless activity it resembles other tits, though it more frequently pitches on a trunk, and in little hops imitates the Tree Creeper. Its food is similar to that of others; it is keen on beech-mast, picks out the seeds from larch and fir cones, and joins Redpolls and Siskins in birches and alders. Like the Marsh Tit, it regularly hides surplus food, especially beech-mast. During these food hunts it keeps up an incessant short flight or flock call; the song, if song it can be called, is a strident *if-he, if-he, if-he*, heard most frequently from January to June, but also in autumn. One variant of this song or call ends with a sharp *tchi*.

A favourite nesting site is a hole in a rotting tree-stump, often low down, and the nest is deep within the hole; holes in the ground, burrows of mouse or rabbit, chinks between the stones in walls, old nests of Magpies or other large birds, and squirrel dreys are also occupied. The materials, moss, hair and grass, are closely felted together, and rabbit fur or feathers added for lining; seven to eleven red-spotted white eggs of the usual tit type are laid, as a rule, in May, but second broods are rare.

The head, throat and neck are glossy blue-black, setting off the white on the nape and sides of the face; the back and wings are olive-grey shading to brownish-fawn on the rump; the white tips of the coverts show as a double bar on the wing. The underparts are white, shading through buff to rufous on the flanks. The bill is black; the legs lead-coloured. The young bird is duller, the black head having no sheen, and the whites on nape and cheeks are tinged with yellow. Length, 4·25 in. Wing, 2·4 in. Tarsus, 0·6 in. (*Plates 121 and 175.*)

## Crested Tit                                                          *Parus cristatus*

Outside its Scottish nesting area, which is centred on the Spey valley but is expanding throughout the Moray basin, the Crested Tit will not be met with in our islands, unless as a very exceptional wanderer from the Continent, for the bird is hardly migratory. But whether in Scotland or on the Continent, where it is widespread, it is an easy tit to recognise, for besides its erectile crest, the tip of which is often recurved, its gorget and collar are distinctive. It is, like other tits, talkative, and has a distinctive trilling note. The birds keep up a constant *zee, zee, zee*, similar to that of the Coal Tit. Its actions are typical of the family, and it frequently climbs on the trunks, like a Tree Creeper. The food is animal or vegetable, and it often searches the young shoots for the small pests which infest conifers in spring and summer.

The nest is in a hole in a trunk or stump, and seldom far above the ground, and the nesting materials are of the usual felted type, but in Scotland often include the hair of red deer, the fur of hare and the feathers of Grouse or Ptarmigan. The eggs, four to eight as a rule, are laid in May; they vary considerably, but are often more boldly and densely blotched than those of many tits, and these blotches are frequently very dark red.

The upper parts are buffish-brown, darker on the wings and tail; the under shade from dull white to light brown. The head is crowned by the crest in which the black feathers have white margins, giving it a speckled appearance in front but streaked towards the nape. From eye to nape a black line runs to join another which curves round the white cheeks; below this, but separated from it by a white band, is a black collar, forming in front a gorget and extending to the chin. The bill is black; the legs lead-blue. Length, 4·5 in. Wing, 2·5 in. Tarsus, 0·75 in. (*Plate 118.*)

## Marsh Tit                                                            *Parus palustris*

The Marsh Tit is absent from Ireland, the Isle of Man and Scotland, except Berwickshire, and is rare in parts of Wales. In England it is well distributed but generally less common than the Great, Coal and Blue Tits. However, in some woods, especially among yews, it is plentiful.

Marsh Tit is a misleading rather than incorrect name, for though the bird is found in damp and marshy places it is as common in dry woods and hedgerows and even occurs in gardens. The absence of the nape spot distinguishes it at once from the Coal Tit, and the glossy blue-black in favourable conditions from the duller headed Willow Tit. In mixed winter flocks seldom more than one or two Marsh Tits are present, and parties of this species alone are infrequent. Pairs often keep together through the winter, and they are usually sedentary. Its performances in the bushes and branches are just as neat and agile as those of other tits; it often hangs upside down by one leg. Like the others, it has a large range of vocal utterances. The most distinctive calls may be rendered *pitchu* and *chickadee-dee-dee*. A simple but rather variable song is heard chiefly in early spring, but also sometimes in autumn. The food is animal or vegetable; destructive weevils and other beetles, coccids and gall-insect larvae are eaten, and seeds of various kinds, including those of the thistle. When maize is provided for the Pheasants the Marsh Tit comes for a share; it carries a grain to a branch, holds it firmly and picks out the 'eye', drops the rest and flies down for another. It is a regular hoarder and stores quantities of seeds and nuts in autumn.

The nest is occasionally in a hole in the ground or a stone wall, but the bird is more of a tree species than some of its relatives. It selects a hole in a rotten willow or other trunk or stump for choice, and though it is doubtful if it ever starts a hole, it sometimes enlarges the hollow. The hole may be within a foot or two of the ground or high up in a tall tree. Wool, hair, fur and moss are felted together, and occasionally willow-down is added, but the quantity of material used is variable. Five to nine eggs of the usual tit type are laid late in April or in May. The bird sits closely and may peck savagely at an intruding hand.

The head and neck are glossy blue-black; the chin and upper throat are black, the feathers of the latter edged with white. The cheeks are white, the back is sandy-brown with an olive tinge, and the rump browner. The wings and tail are greyish, and there is no clear bar on the former. The underparts are greyish-white, shading into buff on the flanks. The bill is black; the legs lead-coloured. The young are duller. Length, 4·5 in. Wing, 2·45 in. Tarsus, 0·55 in. (*Plates 116, 121 and 175*.)

## Willow Tit                                               *Parus montanus*

The Willow Tit is widely but unevenly distributed throughout England, Wales and the south-west and central Lowlands of Scotland. It does not occur in Ireland and is apparently no longer breeding in the Scottish Highlands. It has a wide distribution in Europe.

The Willow Tit closely resembles the Marsh Tit in appearance, but in a good light, at least in winter, the light patch on the wing is very noticeable, and at all seasons the Willow has a duller black cap. Immature birds are practically indistinguishable in the field. But the species is often easier to detect by ear than by eye. Its characteristic calls include a distinctive deep, harsh *tchay*, a nasal *eez-eez-eez* and a high pitched *zi-zi-zi*. A warbling, untitlike song is occasionally heard, but a commoner form of song is a repeated *piu-piu-piu*, resembling one form of the Wood Warbler's song.

The Willow Tit excavates its own nesting hole, usually in a rotten stump or more or less decayed tree, even piercing hard bark. Waterside willows and alders in damp woods often provide nest-sites. In some cases the bird carries the chips to a distance before dropping them, but in others leaves some, at any rate, littered at the foot of the tree. The nest is a slight cup of felted material, mostly fur, hair, wood chips and feathers. The number of eggs varies from six to nine, and the reddish spots are small, or large enough to be called blotches. The food probably differs little from that of other tits.

The Willow Tit is distinguished from the Marsh Tit by a sooty-brown instead of a glossy blue-black cap; the general colour is otherwise similar, though the underparts are more buff and the flanks distinctly more rufous; the pale buff edgings to the secondaries form a light patch on the closed wing. The feathers of the crown are longer. Length, 4·5 in. Wing, 2·45 in. Tarsus, 0·55 in. (*Plates 118 and 175.*)

## Long-tailed Tit                                              *Aegithalos caudatus*

The Long-tailed Tit is rare in the north of Scotland but is a well distributed resident elsewhere in the British Isles. It is found throughout most of Europe.

This tiny but long-tailed bird is more noticeable in winter than summer; after the breeding season it sometimes joins nomadic flocks of other tits, but usually roams in family parties, advertising itself by constant thin calls, *zi, zi, zi,* but as long as the leaves are on tree and hedge it is easily hidden. It is not shy, and in winter flits with constant activity and acrobatic grace along the hedge or through the branches; now and then it utters a louder note, a double *zee-up,* difficult to imitate. The long tail assists its gymnastics, helping to balance, and as the bird shoots on whirring wings from tree to tree it functions as a rocket stick. The short wings and long tail give the bird a top-heavy appearance, but it seldom takes long flights. Seeds are occasionally eaten, but its food is mainly insects; amongst these coccids or scale insects.

The construction of the beautiful oval nest is a lengthy business which employs both birds for about a fortnight; the site may be a hedge, bush or, more rarely, high in a tree. Felting is carried to its greatest perfection in this nest, in which shredded wool, green moss, spider-silk and lichens are artfully interwoven until a thick wall and dome surround the 5-in. oval. The outside is usually decorated with lichen, giving it a black and white appearance; in a hedge it is partly concealed by the lights between the branches and leaves, or on a lichen-covered trunk it is inconspicuous; often, however, so large a nest is easy to see, and the birds, when feeding the young, make no attempt at secrecy. The entrance is above the centre, and the cup within crowded with feathers; considerably over 2000 have been counted from one nest. The white, finely red-speckled eggs, laid in April, number from eight to twelve and sometimes more. The tail of the sitting bird is held above her back; her head and the tail tip cork the entrance hole, and when she investigates eggs or young, the tail often protrudes. In spite of its fluffy plumage it is susceptible to cold; in winter balls of Long-tails, cuddled together, have been found in holes; in the winters of 1947 and 1963 many perished.

The head of the British Long-tailed Tit is dull white crossed on either side above the eye by a black band which extends to the black nape and upper back; the scapulars and rump are rosy-pink. The secondaries on the brown-black wings have white edges, and the three outer tail feathers have white margins and tips; the feathers are graduated in length. The underparts are white, with a few dusky streaks on the breast, shading to dull rose on the belly and flanks. The bill is black; the legs dark brown. The young are duller, and have no rose on the back; at first their tails are very short. Length, 5·5 in. Wing, 2·45 in. Tarsus, 0·6 in. (*Plates 116, 121 and 175.*)

Adults of the northern race, *A. c. caudatus*, have the head and neck pure white. A few individuals of this form have been recorded in Britain.

### Bearded Tit                                          *Panurus biarmicus*

Although the Bearded Tit is here placed in its traditional position in the family of Paridae, the tits, modern authorities regard it as belonging to a separate family, Panuridae, or at least a sub-family, Panurinae. Vaurie also treats the Long-tailed Tit and Penduline Tit as belonging to separate families.

The British breeding range of the Bearded Tit or Bearded Reedling is mainly restricted to East Anglia, but since 1960 small colonies have been established in Essex and Kent, and nesting has been recorded in three other counties. Although numbers are seriously reduced by a severe winter such as that of 1962–3, the population quickly recovers. The Bearded Tit breeds in Holland and very locally elsewhere in Europe. Although some individuals seem to be sedentary there is some wandering in winter and sometimes considerable immigration from Holland. Small parties have even reached west Cornwall and north Lancashire and stayed for some weeks in suitable reed-beds. It has been recorded in Wales and Ireland.

It is hardly possible to confuse the Bearded Tit with any other British bird; its tawny back, long graduated tail and the beard of the male are distinctive. At the beginning of the century, owing to restriction of its haunts through drainage, and the rapacity of collectors, it was nearly numbered among 'Lost British Birds'. Thanks to energetic protection it has not only recovered lost ground but on certain broads and Suffolk marshes is actually common. The colour of the bird harmonises with the old reeds which still remain throughout the breeding season, rather than with the young green blades. In the reed-beds one hears sharp metallic notes, *ching, ching,* like the twang of a banjo—the call of the Reedlings. Other cries of alarm or anxiety are described, but there is no true song. In windy weather the birds tend to remain out of sight on or near the ground, but in calm conditions they will climb with jerky movements to the tops of the reeds and take short flights with rapid wing-beats and a curious twisting motion of the long tail. A bird can often be seen, especially near the nest, with a reed in each foot and legs straddling wide apart.

In summer the food consists chiefly of insects and their larvae, though in winter seeds are eaten. Caddis-flies, mayflies and other four- and two-winged insects which frequent the aquatic plants, as well as caterpillars, are given to the young. The male and female roost side by side, snuggling together on the same stem, and often the cock shelters the hen with one wing. In courtship the cock raises the feathers of the crown, puffs out his beard and, elevating his tail, exposes to view the black under tail-coverts; the value of salient characters is often obscure except during nuptial display. In response to the display the hen also spreads her tail, and sometimes the two rise together for a high aerial courtship flight. In winter the birds become gregarious, wandering in little parties to broads and waterways where they do not nest.

The nest is in reeds or in beds of reedmace or sedge; it is built upon a platform of dead and decaying stems at a height of several inches above the water, and is constructed of blades of sedge or reed, lined with flowers of reed and sometimes a few feathers. The cock helps in building, incubation and care of the young. The creamy-white egg is thinly speckled with pale brown or liver spots or marked with fine wavy lines. Five to seven, occasionally more, are laid in April, and two or even more broods are reared. There are conspicuous 'recognition marks' on the palate of the nestlings—two rows of white spots or pegs on black, surrounded by vivid red.

The head of the male is blue-grey, the rest of the upper parts orange-tawny; from the lores, and partly encircling the eye, is a black patch which runs down the neck as a conspicuous moustachial streak ending in pointed feathers. The scapulars are buffish-white, and the secondaries streaked buff, black and tawny; the primaries and outer tail feathers are margined with white. The flanks are tawny, the chin, throat and breast greyish-white, with a pink suffusion on the last; the under tail-coverts deep black. The bill is orange-yellow; the legs black. The female has no black on head or tail-coverts; her head is brown and her back faintly streaked. The head and back of the young are streaked with dark chocolate, a broad band on the back being very conspicuous. Length, 6 in. Wing, 2·35 in. Tarsus, 0·75 in. (*Plates 119, 121 and 175.*)

## Family SITTIDAE Nuthatches

**Nuthatch**                                                    *Sitta europaea*

The Nuthatch, which has a wide distribution in Europe, is a common resident in England south of a line from the Mersey to the Wash, and after a recent phase of expansion now breeds in small numbers as far north as Westmorland and Northumberland. Its numbers have also increased in Wales. It has only occurred in Scotland as a vagrant and is not found in Ireland or the Isle of Man.

Old timber, especially in open parkland, is the haunt of the Nuthatch, and it climbs the boles with the same skill as the Tree Creeper, though its methods differ; it trusts to its large and powerful feet and does not make use of its stumpy tail, and it runs as quickly down as up the trunk. Its actions are jerky, spasmodic, and its route erratic; it darts from side to side, now up, now down, and uses its strong beak more as a hammer than a probe. Indeed it gives frequent woodpecker-like raps on the bark, perhaps when smashing an insect. Nevertheless it can perch, and on larches searches the young shoots for insects and picks aphids from the opening buds of other trees. Its food consists largely of insects, but, as its name implies, it is fond of nuts and seeds; these it fixes firmly in cracks in the bark and hammers until it extracts the kernel. Yew berries are favoured, and in one park Coward saw large numbers of the empty seeds, with an occasional acorn, firmly wedged in the bark of trees at some distance from a yew, for the bird has its chosen anvils to which it carries its nuts. It does not hack at them with its head and neck alone, but literally puts its back into the work, striking with the whole body hinged on the legs; often its position is head downwards during the process. It is a habitual hoarder of food; nuts and acorns are hidden in cavities in trees and then covered over with moss, lichen or wood chippings.

The Nuthatch is a noisy bird with a loud boy-like whistle; the usual note is a clear *tui, tui, tui,* but the winter call is more subdued. In spite of its gay colours, slate and chestnut, it is not very conspicuous on a grey or lichen-covered tree, but its movements catch the eye and its notes the ear. The song is a pleasant trill, not unlike a mild imitation of the Green Woodpecker's laughing call. In its pairing display it ruffles its flanks and flutters its wings to exhibit the rich chestnut, and spreads its tail to expose the white markings; at the same time it moves its raised head from side to side. With open wings and expanded tail it will float down towards the hen.

The nest, consisting of dead leaves, bits of bark, and grass, is placed in a hole, generally in the trunk or branch of a tree, but occasionally in a wall or other situation; the particular bird objects to a large entrance and blocks up all but the small hole it needs with mud or clay, and this addition is so neatly made that it is not always possible to say which is trunk and which added clay. If the mud cracks and falls away it is speedily repaired. The five to eight, or even more, eggs are white with reddish spots, varying considerably in number, but seldom thickly speckled or blotched; they are laid late in April or in May. Both birds bring material for the nest and feed the young with flies and cater-pillars.

The colour of the upper parts is clear slate-grey, and of the lower buff, shading to white on the chin and under tail-coverts and to rich chestnut-red on the flanks. Through the eye, from the base of the lead-coloured bill to the side of the neck, is a conspicuous black streak, and above the eye is a pale stripe. The central tail feathers are slate, but the others are partly black, and the outer ones have also white marks between the black and slate. The legs are reddish-brown. The female's flanks are paler than the male's, and the young have all the colours less distinct, and little or no chestnut on the flanks. Length, 5·6 in. Wing, 3·3 in. Tarsus, 0·8 in. (*Plates 122, 123 and 175.*)

## Wall Creeper                                        *Tichodroma muraria*
There are some half-dozen records of the Wall Creeper in England, and it is such a striking bird in its slate-grey plumage, with crimson on the wing-

coverts, a crimson band across the wings, and white spots on its black wings and tail, that it cannot frequently have been overlooked. It inhabits alpine areas in central and southern Europe, and has been noted as a wanderer from time to time in other parts. It climbs walls as well as rocks, and a bird in Lancashire was noticed flying round a mill chimney, the crimson bands attracting the attention of the mill-hands. Length, 6·2 in.

## Family CERTHIIDAE Tree Creepers

**Tree Creeper**                                            *Certhia familiaris*

In our islands the Tree Creeper, which has a wide distribution in central and eastern Europe, occurs everywhere in wooded country, but is nowhere abundant, though doubtless overlooked as it is small and soberly coloured. Many are astonished when they see an apparently avian mouse running up a tree. Its progress up a trunk is in a series of short murine jerks, spasmodic rather than rapid; it frequently ascends direct, starting near the ground, creeping closer to the trunk than a Nuthatch. Now and then it makes a sideways hop, attracted by some promising crack or a lateral branch; it pushes its scimitar-shaped bill into a narrow crack, delicately picks out its quarry with the needle-point, or wrestles with some clinging insect. It will twist and pull, bracing itself against the trunk with feet and stiff tail, and is seldom defeated. The protectively coloured weevil, the crouching spider clinging to its web, the cocoon-enshrouded pupa do not elude its keen eye. Reaching a branch, it travels outwards beneath it, quite as happy upside-down as when ascending; at the end it stops for a moment to utter a few lisping notes, then with a drooping flight descends to the next bole. Sometimes it climbs in a spiral, but this depends upon the set of the bark; it seldom, as is asserted, slips round to keep out of view like a squirrel, for it is an indifferent rather than a tame bird. Dense woodlands are its home, but in winter when mixed flocks of tits and Goldcrests are wandering through the woods one or two Tree Creepers usually accompany them, gleaning what the others miss. It will visit gardens and more open country. A stone wall or a rock-face likely to harbour insects is examined as well as trees and their branches, and at times it will take an insect on the wing. The Tree Creeper's habit of excavating oval roosting-holes in the soft bark of Wellingtonia trees was first recorded in Scotland in 1905. It is now regular throughout the British Isles, and there are few well-grown Wellingtonias without the characteristic hollows, often marked with droppings on the lower rim. They are usually between 6 and 15 ft. from the ground. The roosting bird has the tail pressed against the trunk and the back feathers so fluffed out that it is difficult to see the position of the head.

The usual note, uttered when it flies or when it has extracted a stubborn insect, is a shrill *cheep, cheep*, and it has a sharp call, *zit*. The song is a simple *see, see, see, sissy-pee*; it may be heard in any month of the year, though most frequently from February to May. The Tree Creeper is one of the few birds which eat the destructive coccids; the female mussel-scale, too well hidden for most birds, does not escape it. Professor Newstead found that it destroyed the turnip-flea beetle when this insect is wintering under bark, but numerous spiders and their egg-balls must be placed on the debit side of the account of a useful bird. In ordinary circumstances the flight is undulating and leisurely, but during courtship the male rapidly chases the female round and among the trees with excited cries. At this time, and after the eggs are laid, the male is attentive, constantly bringing food to the hen, who receives it, like a young bird, with fluttering wings.

An ordinary position for the nest is behind loose bark, but it is also built in cracks in trees, behind ivy-trunks on walls, or at the back of a notice-board. The size depends upon the available space; in a large crack a supporting platform of sticks is built; behind bark the shape is often oval and all available space is filled with grass, bark, moss or wool, with finer strips of bark, wool or feathers for the lining. The eggs, which number from five to even nine, are white, spotted with red or reddish-purple, at times forming a zone, and are seldom laid until May. A later brood is often reared. Both birds help in construction of the nest and care of the young, which are largely fed upon small caterpillars and flies. The bird sits closely and will hiss and peck at an intruding finger, but finally slips out sideways and will remain, clinging to the trunk a few inches from the nest before taking flight. When approaching the nest, the bird flies to the trunk and ascends, apparently feeding, then quickly slips sideways out of sight.

The characters of the Tree Creeper, adapted to its habits, are the curved bill, comparatively large feet, and stiff pointed tail feathers. Above, in both sexes, it is brown, streaked and mottled with rufous and white; beneath it is silvery-white, and as in its often zigzag progress it slips round the trunk, the gleam of the underparts catches the eye. The wings are barred with pale brown; the bill and legs are brown. In the young birds the bill is shorter and less curved. Length, 5 in. Wing, 2·5 in. Tarsus, 0·65 in. (*Plates 107, 122, 124 and 175.*)


## Family TROGLODYTIDAE Wrens

**Wren**                                          *Troglodytes troglodytes*

The Wren, found throughout the British Isles and Europe, is only migratory in the northern part of its range. The isolated populations of Wrens on St Kilda, the Shetlands and the Outer Hebrides have developed certain minor differences of size, build and plumage that have caused them to be recognised as distinct subspecies. The St Kilda Wren in particular is slightly larger than the typical bird and has a heavier bill. There is some evidence of passage migration of continental Wrens on the east coast of Great Britain.

There is little need to describe the small, stump-tailed Wren; it is almost as familiar as the Robin. Yet it is so small and mouse-like that it is easily lost sight of when it is hunting for food. It is everywhere, from the tops of mountains to the sea-coast. Its movements as it creeps or climbs are incessant rather than rapid; its short flights swift but not sustained; its tiny round wings whirr with misty vibration as they carry it from bush to bush. It is a bird of the breezy uplands, even in winter; it will slip amongst the wiry stems of the heather when snow lies thick above, vanishing into gloomy caves, a troglodyte indeed. It frequents the gardens, hopping about the flowerbeds or disappearing suddenly behind the ivy on the walls; in the farm and stack-yard it examines every nook and cranny for hidden insects; but it is quite as abundant in the thick woods, among the tree roots and tangled undergrowth. The rushes round the meres harbour a few in winter; these marshy spots provide food when other places fail.

Poets and sentimentalists talk of the shy and retiring Wren; but really it is indifferent to our presence. Its incessant activity and zeal in search for those creatures whose existence depends upon concealment take it into the depths of ivy, hedge or undergrowth, but from no desire to hide itself; indeed it will hunt readily in full view, creeping with sharp *tit-it-it* over the rockery or bank. When annoyed or excited its call runs into an emphatic churr—not unlike the reel of clockwork running down. Its song is a gushing burst of sweet music, loud and emphatic as the rattle of the Chaffinch; it has an 'enormous' voice for its size. In volume as well as quality of song individuals vary, but the efforts of a full-voiced Wren are surprising; the song often begins with a few preliminary notes, then runs into a trill, sometimes slightly ascending, and ends in full clear notes or in a second trill. At all and any season the song may be heard, though it is most noticeable during spring or at the end of winter, when with its stump erected and often with the tip pointed forward, and its whole body a-quiver with energy, it pours forth its song of love or challenge. But although territories are maintained in winter as well as spring clashes between neighbours are usually settled by song and posturing rather than actual combat. At night it often roosts in snug holes and even old nests; in winter communal roosts, with more than a dozen Wrens in a single hole, are not uncommon. For the most part small insects and spiders are its food, but in winter large pupae are swallowed, and some seeds are added. The young are fed chiefly on the larvae of moths.

In his monograph on the Wren, E. A. Armstrong gives a detailed account of its breeding cycle. The chief features of courtship are chases and 'pounces' by the male, with frequent bursts of song. Each cock builds an average of half a dozen nests, some distance apart, within his territory, and selected nests are then lined by one or more females, for the Wren is often polygamous. The normal round nest is tucked into a hole in a wall, tree trunk, crack in a rock or corner of a building, but it is often built in bushes, overhanging boughs and the litter which accumulates in branches washed by floods. It is true that the materials used often aid concealment—grass in a haystack, moss on a rock, lichens on a tree, leaves amongst litter—but this is probably un-intentional, due to the accessibility of these substances; many nests are suici-dally conspicuous. Dead leaves are largely used in the outer envelope, but the lining of moss, hair or feathers varies in quantity as well as material. On the moors the Wren builds in heather; on the cliffs in gorse; in the garden it may select a cabbage top or Brussels sprout. Five to eight or more white or slightly speckled eggs are laid in April, and second broods are reared. Incuba-tion is by the hen alone, but the cock usually helps with feeding the young.

The Wren is rufous-brown above, greyer beneath, barred with darker brown and grey, even on wings and tail. The bill is dark brown; the legs pale brown. Young are less distinctly barred. Length, 3·5 in. Wing, 1·9 in. Tarsus, 0·75 in. (*Plates 122 and 175.*)

## Family CINCLIDAE Dippers

**Dipper**                                                          *Cinclus cinclus*

The Dipper is widely distributed as a resident species in suitable habitats in the north and west of England, Wales, Scotland (except the northern Isles) and Ireland. It breeds throughout most of Europe, apart from the northern plain.

The Dipper or Water Ousel is a rotund, short-tailed bird, dark above and white-breasted, closely associated with swiftly running rivers and streams or the lakes into which these fall. On the rocks round which the water swirls and tumbles the Dipper perches with its short tail uplifted, its breast turned towards us, bobbing spasmodic curtsies. From these sudden dips it acquired its name, not from its diving habit, though it dives as well as walks into the water. The winking of the white nictitating eyelid as the bird dips is notice-able at a considerable distance. It will fly rapidly and straight, its short wings whirring swiftly and without pauses or glides, calling a shrill, *zit, zit, zit*; then either drop on the water and dive or plunge in with a little splash. From its perch it will walk into the water and deliberately submerge. At times the wings are certainly used under water, and sometimes the angle of the bird's body as it moves upstream against a swift current may help to keep it sub-merged, or it may grip moss or rock with its feet, but careful observers have recorded it walking over a sandy bottom without any of these aids to immer-sion. In this way it secures its food, the larvae of aquatic insects, including the encased caddis worms, beetles, *Limnea, Ancylus* and other freshwater molluscs. A favourite food is the small crustacean *Gammarus*, the water-shrimp, one of the worst foes of trout ova; there is no direct evidence that the bird eats ova, though it has been known occasionally to catch fry. It walks and runs on the banks and rocks, seeking terrestrial insects. It also swims, floating lightly.

The winter habits of the Dipper vary considerably and apparently individ-ually. When the swift hill-becks are frozen it is forced to descend to the low-lands and even visit the coasts, but some will remain if there is any open water.

Yet in mild winters some upland haunts are almost deserted, and at this season numbers appear on the lower stretches of the rivers and on the shores of lakes. The sweet, hurried, Wren-like lyric of the Dipper, mingling with the sound of tumbling waters, may be heard at any season, but mostly from December until May. During courtship the cock sings whilst he runs and postures before the hen, exhibiting his snowy breast, and when displaying he will take long and high flights, like those of the Kingfisher, sometimes accompanied by his mate, uttering sharp metallic calls—*clink, clink,* differing from the normal *zit.*

The nest is by the water, often under it—on the rocks beneath a fall; it is large, globular or oval, like a massive Wren's nest, built into some crack or hollow in the rock, in the masonry, or on the supports of a bridge, or more rarely in an overhanging branch. It is composed of green moss when the water splashes or actually flows over it, but on dry grey rocks it is often of dead grass and leaves. This ball, however, is merely the shelter or envelope; below the median line, usually hidden beneath a lip, is the entrance to the real nest within, a cup of grass or sedge, nearly as large as the nest of a Blackbird, lined with leaves of oak, beech or other trees. Four to six white eggs are laid in March or April, and two or three broods are reared, often in the same nest. When disturbed, the young, when hardly feathered, will at once drop into the water and dive.

The head of the adult Dipper is umber-brown, the back slate-grey mottled with black, looking quite black from a distance, and the wings and tail are brown. The throat and upper breast are white, followed by a band of warm chestnut which merges into black on the belly and flanks. The bill is almost black; the legs brown. The young are greyish-brown and have no chestnut band. Length, 7 in. Wing, 3·75 in. Tarsus, 1·1 in. (*Plates 120, 122 and 175.*)

## Family TURDIDAE Thrushes

**Mistle Thrush**                                      *Turdus viscivorus*

The Mistle Thrush is a common resident in the British Isles, and throughout most of Europe. It is partially migratory; many of our birds leave in late August or September, and continental visitors arrive from September onwards. Some of these remain as winter visitors, and others are birds of passage to winter quarters in southern Europe and northern Africa. The return northwards is noticeable in Britain in February, and continues until April.

The name, derived from its habit of feeding on mistletoe berries, where these abound, is less descriptive than another, Stormcock, which has several variants, for early in the year, when the weather is broken, the bird perches high on a tall tree and in exultant and ringing song defies the elements. In gardens, open fields, woodlands and bleak hillsides this large, conspicuous greyish thrush is equally at home; it is becoming increasingly common in parks in large towns and cities. It stands with head well raised, alert and wide awake; it hops for a foot or two, then stops with head bent sideways, keenly examining the ground, dives forward and drags out a struggling worm. It flies with strong direct flight, spreading its tail, when the spotted tips show clearly; it is larger, greyer and more distinctly spotted than the Song Thrush, and when in flight the underside of the wing and axillaries are white, at once distinguishing it from all other thrushes except the Fieldfare, from which it may be told by its yellowish-brown, not blue-grey rump. The song, which may be heard in any month, though rarely from July to September when the bird is moulting, is not as mellow as that of the Blackbird, and is more continuous and less varied than the music of the Song Thrush, but it has force and character and carries well. At times the Mistle Thrush sings as it flies, but the usual flight call is a grating scream or churr; this harsh note is modified and intensified when the bird is excited by alarm or anger. When defending its nest it is fearlessly aggressive; it will attack and drive away the Jackdaw, Rook and Kestrel. It will defeat the Sparrow Hawk and attack man. The open situation of the nest helps its foes, and Magpies steal the eggs and young. During the breeding season it has a sharp repeated challenge, *chit, chit, chit,* each note of which is accompanied by a jerk of the closed wing and expanded tail.

The food is varied; even when insects, worms or molluscs are abundant it cannot resist ripe berries of ivy, holly, yew, hawthorn or mistletoe; in autumn it raids the hills for rowans and junipers. The family parties keep together after the breeding season, and later form into flocks, which feed in the open fields with other thrushes; these flocks are often scattered over the hill pastures, and strip the yews and rowans of their berries.

The fork of a tall forest tree is a common site for the large conspicuous nest, which is at times built of noticeable material, even strips of paper. It is at varying height from the ground, often in quite a low tree or bush; in treeless districts it may be on the ground, in a stone wall, or in a quarry, on the coast in a crack in the cliff-face, or on rocks only a few feet above high-water mark. The usual materials are grass, moss, roots and wool, with a lining of caked mud, and a soft inner lining of grass. The bird nests early, and eggs are sometimes laid in February, but the first nests are often destroyed by storms. A second brood is often reared. The eggs are greenish- or brownish-white, blotched and speckled with purple-brown and violet-grey.

The upper parts are ashy-brown, the under buffish-white with conspicuous oval dark brown spots. The axillaries and under-wing are white, and the outer tail feathers have whitish tips. The bill is brown horn at the base; the legs pale brown. The young are yellower above, and the head, back and wings, especially the upper wing-coverts, are spotted with buffish-white. Length, 11 in. Wing, 6·2 in. Tarsus, 1·3 in. (*Plates 126 and 175.*)

## Fieldfare                                                            *Turdus pilaris*

The Fieldfare nests throughout Scandinavia and as far south as Hungary and Switzerland. Many birds move south and west in autumn. In the British Isles it is a winter visitor and bird of passage, arriving from about the middle of September until well into winter. Passage birds return in March, but many emigrants do not leave until April, whilst laggards are noted in June. In 1967 a pair reared three young in the Orkneys. This was the first British breeding record.

The Fieldfare is a large, distinctive bird; its slate-grey head and rump, the latter very noticeable in flight, contrast with the warm brown of its back, but even when we cannot see its colours the harsh flight call, *tsak, tsak*, is unlike the note of any other thrush. The gregarious Fieldfare frequents open country and is nomadic, its movements regulated by food supply; as long as the weather is mild and insect food abundant a flock will remain day after day in the same fields, but during frost it wanders as soon as the berries are devoured in one district. It is found in the lowlands and on the hillsides to a fair altitude, and in frost takes refuge on the shores and marshes. The bird flies direct, at no great speed, with strong wing-beats alternating with short intervals with closed wings; when moving ground the flock straggles in loose formation, and when a long flight is contemplated rises to a considerable height. In the fields the birds work steadily up wind, halting constantly to stand well erect with head uplifted, alert rather than suspicious. They fly to trees when alarmed, and perch with heads facing the wind, but if approached they rise and, turning, fly rapidly down wind with cries of alarm. In addition to the animal and berry food common to all thrushes, the Fieldfare will, when other things fail, attack turnips or other roots, and on the coast eat marine molluscs; but if there is an abundance of fruit on the hawthorns other food, even worms and insects, is neglected as long as the supply lasts. Frequently the birds chatter sociably in a tree and in spring it is not unusual to hear low warbled refrains, the first efforts at song.

In winter the slate-grey head is streaked with black, and the grey rump tinged with buff; the wings and tail are dark brown; the back and mantle warm chestnut. The rich brown throat and breast are streaked with black, and with dark brown on the flanks; the centre of the belly is white, as are the under wing-coverts and axillaries, noticeable in flight. The bill is dark brown, yellow on the under mandible, the legs dark brown. The margins, which somewhat obscure the breast markings and the grey of the upper parts, wear off during winter, and by spring the rump is a clear, uniform grey. The whole bill is now yellow. The young are at first spotted above and below, but after their autumn moult they are not unlike the adult bird, but the head and rump are grey-brown, and the underparts are more spotted. Length, 10 in. Wing, 5·75 in. Tarsus, 1·4 in. (*Plate 125.*)

## Song Thrush                                              *Turdus philomelos*

The Song Thrush is a common resident in most parts of the British Isles. As large numbers emigrate in autumn it is also a summer resident. Many of the Song Thrushes from Scotland and England migrate to Ireland, and some to the Continent, returning between February and April; but some of our birds, especially in the south of England, appear to be sedentary. The Song Thrush is found throughout Europe, except in the extreme south. Great numbers of continental immigrants reach us in September and October, some as winter visitors, others as birds of passage towards winter quarters in southern Europe and north Africa.

The Song Thrush or Throstle is one of our best-known birds; it frequents and nests in our gardens, and though found in woods and unfrequented areas, shows decided preference for inhabited and cultivated districts. The song varies individually in quality, but a good-voiced Thrush has much in common with the Nightingale, not only in the variety and tone of its phrases, but also in that it occasionally sings at night. In suitable weather the bird sings in autumn and winter, and August is perhaps its only really quiet month. The Song Thrush possesses the imitative faculty, but the notes it catches best are those which lend themselves to short-phrase repetition; it may copy the Lapwing, Ringed Plover, Redshank, Green Woodpecker, and certain notes of the Nightingale. A common call of the Thrush is *tchuck*, which, modulated or rapidly repeated, expresses various emotions; it may be shortened to *tchik* or *tic*, especially at roosting time; it can be subdued into a love-note, or hurriedly repeated in the rattling cry of alarm. It has a soft *seep* not unlike that of the Redwing, and the cock, when bringing food to the sitting hen, greets her with a hurried and anxious-sounding twitter. Early in the year the males fight frequently and will sing during the bouts.

The Song Thrush flies quickly and direct, its wings moving rapidly; on the ground it runs or hops, but seldom walks. When seeking food it holds its head on one side, as if listening, but this is due to the lateral position of the eyes; an alert and listening bird holds the head raised and the body erect. In either aggression or courtship one bird will approach another, creeping on its belly, with wings dragging and tail drooped, and with its mandibles open as if with fear. Worms, some kinds of slugs, snails and insects are its chief food; berries are eaten, but are not so eagerly sought for as by many of its congeners. Snail-stones, on which it smashes the shells of its victims, are surrounded by fragments of its feasts; on the coast a rock is often used, and in Yorkshire the hard stems of the sea-buckthorn. The young are largely fed on earthworms pecked into sections, and long after they leave the nest they call for food with a querulous *tcheep*.

The nest may be in almost any situation—in a tree, bush, evergreen, hedge, shed, hole in a wall, on a ledge, bank or the ground. The materials used are also varied—grass, leaves, moss, wool, even paper, but the lining is always a plaster of mud, generally mixed with wood chips, horse-dung or vegetable tissues; when dry this forms a solid saucer which often remains long after the outer materials have vanished. Eggs are usually laid from March onwards, but nests in February are not uncommon. Two or three broods are reared. The sitting birds do not always behave in the same manner; they usually sit closely, remaining when looked at, with the bill pointed upward and the streaks on either side of the throat showing plainly; suddenly, however, the bird leaps up and flies off with a loud rattling scream. Others slip quietly from the nest, though they usually remain near, repeating an anxious *tchuck*. The very blue, black-spotted eggs are four to five in number.

The general colour is olive-brown, with buff tips to the coverts forming an obscure wing-bar; the underparts are whitish, tinged on the breast and flanks with fulvous to rufous, and spotted with blackish-brown on the breast. The axillaries, noticeable in flight, are bright golden-buff. The bill is dark brown, the legs pale brown. During winter the tips of the feathers are abraded and the spring plumage is greyer and the spots smaller than after the moult in autumn. The young are mottled with buff on the upper parts. Length, 8·5 in. Wing, 4·5 in. Tarsus, 1·2 in. (*Plates 126 and 175*.)

### Redwing                                              *Turdus iliacus*

The Redwing breeds in the northern Palaearctic regions and winters in southern Europe. It is a regular winter visitor to our islands and many travel through towards southern Europe or north Africa; it reaches Britain in September and October, sometimes in very large numbers, and returns northward in March and April, a few at times lingering until May. Occasional nests have been found in northern Scotland, and the Redwing is now probably a regular breeder there in very small numbers.

During its stay in Britain the Redwing is distinctly gregarious, frequenting open country, feeding in the fields with Fieldfares and other birds. In these mixed flocks there are often a few Song Thrushes, from which it can be distinguished by its long pale eye-stripe and reddish flanks; when it flies the rich chestnut on the axillaries shows, much deeper than the golden-buff of the Song Thrush. The food of the Redwing is mainly worms, insects, molluscs and other small animals, and when the supply of these is cut off by hard frost or a heavy fall of snow the bird suffers; it will then take to berries, eating those of the white-thorn, yew, ivy and holly, but if these have been already stripped by the Blackbirds and Mistle Thrushes it is forced to leave or perishes. Although westward movements towards Ireland are frequent before and during heavy snowfalls, large numbers linger until they are too weak to travel, and a hard winter is usually followed by one or two years when Redwings are noticeably scarce. Although the Redwing is said not to eat berries until forced by hunger, birds which had just reached the Yorkshire coast attacked the berries of the sea-buckthorn.

The Redwing is a nocturnal migrant; its arrival is usually first noticed by its soft flight call—*see-ip*, heard even when it passes over busy towns. On the Yorkshire coast the birds will rise in a flock at dusk, mount to a great height, and then when almost invisible, make off in a southerly direction. Numbers of Redwings are killed by raptorial birds which accompany the flocks. When a feeding flock is disturbed, the birds fly off one by one, and at night they roost in evergreens and plantations, but the normal habits are those of ground birds. The strong flight is fairly rapid, a series of quick wing-beats with short intervals when the wings are closed; the flocks move in loose formation. When the birds are feeding the call is a soft *chup*, and at the roost combined twittering warbles are usual, but the song is seldom heard at its best in Britain. Shortly before departure a few begin to sing—a musical babble, very gently warbled; it is quieter and more sustained than that of the Song Thrush, and is interrupted by a *churr*, like the cry of the Mistle Thrush toned down.

In winter the upper parts are olive-brown, the under whitish; there is a pale superciliary streak, the ear-coverts are brown and the lores black. The spots on the breast and chestnut flanks form striations. The bill is dark brown; the legs pale brown. The young are spotted rather than streaked on both upper and underparts and the feathers of the back have buff central streaks. Length, 8·5 in. Wing, 4·5 in. Tarsus, 1·2 in. (*Plate 125*.)

### American Robin *Turdus migratorius*

This North American thrush has been recorded about a dozen times in the British Isles; but as numbers have recently been imported there is now a possibility of escapes. In build and carriage it resembles a Blackbird, but has dark grey upper parts, brick-red breast and white markings round the eye. The chin is white; the bill yellow. Length, about 10 in.

### Ring Ouzel *Turdus torquatus*

The Ring Ouzel is a summer resident in Scandinavia, some mountainous regions of central Europe and the British Isles, and winters in southern Europe and north Africa; with us it is also a bird of passage in spring and autumn. It has been reported as wintering occasionally.

The true home of the Ring Ouzel is moorland, amongst the rocks and heather of our wilder hills. Nowhere in England is it more abundant than on the Pennines and Peak of Derbyshire; it is common in Lakeland and on many of the Welsh mountains, and in Scotland is widely distributed; it is found on Dartmoor and other high grounds in the south-west of England. It has decreased in Ireland and is now scarce and local there. Roughly above the 1000-ft. contour the Ring Ouzel replaces the Blackbird, though often their ranges overlap and the former occurs on wild heather-clad hills even below 500 ft. It may always be distinguished by its white gorget.

The Ring Ouzel is one of our earliest spring migrants. Our resident birds appear to come straight to their moorland haunts without resting on the shores or on the way; the bird is seen in its breeding haunts, before it is noticed as an incoming migrant on the south coast, from the middle of March onwards. Birds which arrive later and are met with slowly working their way northward are probably on passage towards Scandinavia. The return journey begins in September, but many linger through October. The song is loud and clear, suggestive of that of the Mistle Thrush rather than the Blackbird; it is a wild song, in keeping with the lonely uplands. The bird sings from a rock or heather clump, and often from the rough grit walls. The quality varies considerably. The song may be heard after dark. The loud rattle of alarm resembles that of the Blackbird, but its angry *tac, tac, tac* is, if anything, harsher. The call

PLATE 130

*Top :* Bluethroat (adult and young), p284
*Centre left :* Nightingale, p282
*Centre right :* Robin, p285
*Below left :* Wheatear, p275

Photo: J. B. and S. Bottomley

Photo: *J. B. and S. Bottomley*

PLATE 132    Robin (juvenile), p285

PLATE 133
    *Above :* Barred Warbler, p294
    *Below :* Sedge Warbler, p291

*Above :* Grasshopper Warbler, p286
*Below :* Aquatic Warbler, p292

PLATE 134
   *Above:* Savi's Warbler,
          p288
   *Below:* Wood Warbler, p302

*Above:* Yellow-browed Warbler,
          p303
*Below:* Icterine Warbler, p292

*Photos : Eric Hosking*

PLATE 136
Willow Warbler,
p299

Photo:
J. B. and S. Bottomley

PLATE 137

*Above left*:
Whitethroat, p295
*Above right*:
Dartford Warbler,
p298

*Below left*: Lesser
Whitethroat, p296
*Below right*:
Blackcap, p293

PLATE 138

*Above :* Chiffchaff, p300
*Below :* Goldcrest, p304

*Above :* Willow Warbler, p299
*Below :* Firecrest, p305

PLATE 139
Goldcrest, p304

PLATE 140

Spotted Fly-
catcher, p306

PLATE 141
*Above :* Spotted Flycatcher, p306
*Below :* Garden Warbler,
p294

*Above :* Pied Flycatcher, p307
*Below :* Red-breasted Flycatcher,
p308

PLATE 142

*Left :* Meadow
Pipit, p310
*Below :* Tree
Pipit, p312

*Above :* Dunnock
or Hedge
Sparrow, p308
*Right :* Rock
Pipit, p313

PLATE 143     Pied Flycatcher (female), p307

*Photo : J. B. and S. Bottomley*

*Above :* Rock Pipit, p313

PLATE 144

*Below :* Meadow Pipit, p310

*Photo : J. B. and S. Bottomley*

PLATE 145

*Above left:*
Alpine Accentor,
p310
*Above right:*
Yellow Wagtail,
p318

*Below left:* Pied
Wagtail, p315
*Below right:*
White Wagtail,
p315

is a clear pipe. It defends its young with the boldness of the Mistle Thrush, threatening even a human intruder with ferocious noisy dashes, but at other times it is wary. The flight is strong and rapid; when flushed the bird dashes down the cloughs and gullies, skimming the rocks and dodging out of sight whenever possible. On the ground its attitudes and movements are those of the Blackbird; it elevates and spreads its tail when alighting, and droops its wings when posturing before its mate. The food, too, is similar. Whinberry, cranberry, juniper and other moorland fruits are eaten and in August, often in small flocks, it raids the mountain ashes.

The nest is at times difficult to find, well hidden in deep heather or its position screened by an overgrowing clump when it is placed on the edge of a moorland beck. At other times it is absurdly visible, on a bank, ledge or in a hollow in a stone wall. It has the same mud cup and grass lining as the Blackbird's, and the outer materials are bracken, moss, wool and stems of heather, but the majority of those on the Pennines and Peak are built of stiff, wiry moorland grass. When this is the case it almost invariably differs from the nest of the Blackbird, for the ends of the grass are left sticking out at an angle in every direction and are not twisted in. The eggs are usually laid late in April or in May; four is the ordinary number, though five or six may be found. They are similar to one type of the Blackbird, boldly blotched with reddish-brown on a blue-green ground. The male has been seen to help in building, but his chief duties are those of sentinel and guard.

In summer the male is sooty-black with pale edgings to the secondaries and with a broad white gorget; his bill and eye-rims are yellow, the former darker at the tip. The legs are dark brown. The female is browner and her narrower breast-band is tinged with brown. After the autumn moult the feathers of the breast are fringed with grey. At first the young are more or less mottled; the underparts are barred with black, brown and white. After the first moult most of these mottlings are lost but the bird retains a much greyer appearance. Length, 10 in. Wing, 5·4 in. Tarsus, 1·3 in. (*Plates 125, 127 and 175.*)

## Blackbird                                                                    *Turdus merula*

The Blackbird is found in most parts of Europe except the far north and is partially migratory, wintering in the more southerly parts of its range. In the British Isles it is at once a resident, a summer and a winter visitor and a bird of passage, for many of our nesting birds leave in autumn and large numbers come to us for winter or pass through the country, many from Scandinavia, Germany and the Low Countries. Its numbers have greatly increased in the 20th century, especially in urban areas.

Such a conspicuous and regular frequenter of the garden is naturally well known, yet the elementary fact that the hen is not black is often overlooked; she is dark brown and her rufous breast is striated and she is sometimes taken for a dark Song Thrush. Though the depth of colour of her underparts varies considerably she is never as light as a Thrush. Confusion with the Ring Ouzel is occasionally excusable, for no bird is more prone to variation; white or partially white Blackbirds are common. When the white takes the form of a band or gorget on the breast there is little difference between the two species, though the Ring Ouzel's wings are more patterned and slaty. Common as it is round houses, the Blackbird is just as plentiful in the woods and hedgerows, feeding in winter in the fields with other thrushes, though usually at no great distance from a hedge or spinney into which it retreats with screams if alarmed. On the hills its range overlaps that of the Ring Ouzel; there is a zone where both species nest. In winter, though it is seldom seen in large flocks, it is more gregarious, and on migration is sociable. The Blackbird is cautious and suspicious but hardly shy; its tail, whenever it alights, is jauntily switched upwards. During quarrels and courtship it is carried outspread almost at right angles to its back.

The song period of the Blackbird is much more restricted than that of the Song Thrush; in most years it does not sing until February, and in July the birds cease one by one and seldom sing again after the moult. On exceptionally mild days in December and January a few snatches may be heard, but autumn songs are rare. The mellow, flute-like song, though not covering a wide range, has great variety; the bird rings the changes on a series of notes. The song is loud, clear and very beautiful, but has a weak ending, almost a hissing collapse. When not in song the bird is seldom silent; its loud, startled, and often startling, rattling scream of alarm, a jumble of notes run together, is heard at all seasons. When it suddenly appears on the lawn it scares all other birds with this note uttered as chuckle, but imagined danger sends it off with a wilder scream. When flushed from the nest or merely disturbed during its investigation of the autumn litter, the clarion alarm is sounded. The attitudes assumed under nuptial excitement suggest pugnacity; the wings are drooped, the tail uplifted and the bird flirts from side to side. Half a dozen cocks will chase and fight for a hen. Few birds fight more persistently, though, so far as cocks are concerned, without serious results. Not only will the cock attack a rival with beak and claw but it will waste time on its own image in a window. Female birds also fight, probably over territorial rights.

Two familiar notes, expressive of various emotions, are a metallic *chink* or *mink*, and a rather deep *tschuck*, while at roosting time it is a monotonous and exasperating *tac, tac, tac*. The birds hop, flit and run, jerking their tails and wings, and repeating this note as if they were mobbing a cat or other foe from dusk until dark. The hunger cry of the young after they have left the nest is a piping note repeated usually two or three times in succession, not unlike early efforts at a song. The food is similar to that of other thrushes, but in summer the bird is fond of fruit; in raspberries it is very troublesome. Blackberries, junipers, rowans, haws and other wild fruit are greedily eaten, sometimes swallowed whole.

The nest is in bushes or hedgerows, in trees or on the ground; it is large and similar to that of the Song Thrush though with an additional lining of grass above the mud. Four to six greenish-white eggs, profusely speckled or blotched with reddish-brown are as a rule laid in March or April; two or more broods are usual. As a rule the cock does little to help building or incubation, but he has been seen on the nest, and assists in feeding the young; cases are recorded in which the young of a first brood have helped to feed a later brood.

The male is glossy black with orange bill and eye-rim, blackish legs and dark brown irides. The female is dark brown with a pale throat and breast streaked with black, and with spots on the lower breast; her bill and legs are dark brown. The young show pale shaft streaks on their brown plumage, and the bills of young males, which often show black backs before the heads change colour, remain very dark until the second year. Length, 10 in. Wing, 5 in. Tarsus, 1·4 in. (*Plates 125 and 175.*)

**Grey-cheeked Thrush**                                                    *Catharus minimus*

There have been five records of this North American thrush, all in autumn. It closely resembles our Song Thrush and the American Olive-backed Thrush, but it differs from the latter in the very pale buff tinge of the upper breast, its fainter eye-ring and its greyish cheeks. Length, 7·75 in.

**White's Thrush**                                                          *Zoothera dauma*

This large and strikingly marked bird is a summer visitor to eastern Siberia and winters in China. It has frequently wandered in winter into Europe and has been met with about thirty times in the British Isles, including Ireland. The general colour of White's Thrush is yellowish above and white beneath, but as most of the feathers have black margins it is speckled both above and below with black crescents. Young Mistle Thrushes might be confused with this species, but they are greyer in colour. Length, 12 in.

**Rock Thrush**                                                          *Monticola saxatilis*

The Rock Thrush breeds in south and central Europe, northern Africa and Asia, and winters in tropical Africa and southern Asia. Although it summers in parts of Germany and Switzerland it has only been noticed in England two or three times, once in the Orkneys and twice on Fair Isle in spring and autumn. It is a medium-sized short-tailed bird, both in appearance and habits more suggestive of a wheatear than a thrush. The adult male, with his slate-blue head, throat and upper back, and white band across the lower back, contrasting with rich chestnut underparts and tail, is not likely to be confused with any other species. The female also has a chestnut-sided tail, but is a browner bird barred with black and grey, and her lower back is mottled with buff. Her throat is white and the underparts buff with brown markings. Young birds are mottled with brown and slate, and have bars on the underparts. Length, 8 in.

**Wheatear**                                                              *Oenanthe oenanthe*

The Wheatear is a summer resident and passage migrant in the British Isles. Its breeding range covers practically the whole of Europe; it winters in tropical

Africa. It is generally common in open country in the north of England and in Scotland, Wales and Ireland, but is now very local and scarce as a breeding bird in the south of England, though numerous on coastal passage in spring and autumn. Birds of the slightly larger and more brightly coloured Greenland race can sometimes be identified in the field from late April to June and, with more difficulty, on their autumn passage southward.

The Wheatear can be recognised by its white rump, tail-coverts and tail, contrasting with the central feathers and black terminal band of the tail. The name is derived from this white rump and has nothing to do with wheat. It is the first real summer visitor to reach us; early in March a few males arrive on the south coast, and by the middle of the month many are in summer quarters in the north of England. Successive waves of both sexes spread during April, and in May birds of the Greenland race may linger for days or even weeks on their northward journey. The Wheatear frequents open downs, hill-sides, moorlands and mountains—nesting at over 3000 ft., rough and rocky land and coastal dunes. It is constantly on the move, flitting from stone to stone, clump to clump, repeating *chack, chack*. Its bows, tail flirts and remarks are directed at the observer as it moves ahead, flying close to the ground and halting on each little eminence for a fresh bow. Its progress is interrupted by leaps into the air and aerial turns and twists after passing flies, and it frequently sings on the wing, though seldom rising to any height. The song is pleasing, and has a greater range than that of the other chats; it has been aptly described as 'resembling the Sky Lark in its beginnings'. The full song is seldom heard after the end of June.

The Wheatear is not a gregarious bird at any season, and even when numbers are on passage in spring and autumn they are not seen as flocks, but as scattered individuals among the dunes or on the cliff-tops. Birds of the Greenland subspecies have a rather more upright stance than our natives and perch freely in trees, but our own bird will also rest on a bush or hedge when handy, and in hill country the rough stone walls are constantly used.

The food consists of small worms, insects and molluscs, especially the small helices which frequent the short sheep-cropped grass on downs and cliff-tops. Caterpillars are taken to the young. Nuptial competition leads to strange displays and furious fights. On Holy Island Coward watched two rival males combine in an attack on a cock Greenlander, whilst the hen apparently paid no attention to any one of the three. The birds dashed amongst the dunes with wonderful speed, fought in couples or all three at once, until, in the whirl of struggling wing, beak and claws, it was impossible to distinguish individuals; all the time one or more kept up florid song. At times one bird would dance and whirl by itself in a frenzy of excitement, throwing itself about in ecstatic mazes, or with drooped wings and widely fanned-out tail, would exhibit its charms. The Wheatear not only nests in holes, but bolts into them for shelter from weather or an enemy.

Rabbit burrows are the usual nesting holes on the sand dunes and downs, but on the hills stone walls, hollows under boulders and clefts in rocks and peat-stacks are used; in these a loosely built nest of grass and roots, with rabbit fur, wool, hair or feathers serves for the five to six pale blue eggs, which are usually laid in late April or early May. Most of the building and incubation is done by the hen, though the cock usually plays some part. Two broods have been recorded, but one is more usual. The young birds group themselves at the mouth of the hole when waiting for food, but scuttle back on absurdly long legs if danger threatens. Return migration, both of our birds and the larger form, lasts for many weeks, beginning in July. The main volume of migration is over by mid October, but stragglers usually continue to pass well into November.

The male in spring is pearl-grey above, with a white forehead, superciliary stripe, rump, upper tail-coverts and basal part of the tail. The white on the central tail feathers is hidden, only the black portion showing; the other feathers are mainly white with a broad terminal band of black. The lores cheeks and ear-coverts are black. The underparts are sandy-buff on the breast and flanks, and creamy-white or slightly tinged elsewhere. Greenland males have underparts a richer reddish-buff, and the grey upper parts are faintly tinged with brown. The bill and legs are black. After the autumn moult broad fringes tinge the upper parts with brown and the under with fawn; in this dress the male is very like the female; she is sandy-brown above and more buff below, but has the distinctive tail and rump. The young at first are mottled with dusky streaks and sandy-buff bars, and the pale chocolate head is faintly streaked, while the quills have broad rufous edgings. Common Wheatear: Length, 5·75 in. Wing, 3·75 in. Tarsus, 1 in. Greenland Wheatear: Length, 6 in. Wing, 4·2 in. Tarsus, 1·1 in. (*Plates 128, 130 and 175.*)

## Desert Wheatear                                      *Oenanthe deserti*

This vagrant from Africa and Asia has occurred in the British Isles fifteen times. The upper parts of the male in summer are buff; the underparts white with a buff tinge on the breast. The black on the face and throat extends to the shoulders. The best character, constant in both sexes at all ages, is that the entire tail is black to the level of the upper tail-coverts. The female is greyer above and buffer below and has no black on the throat, and in the winter plumage the black on the throat of the male is obscured by white tips. Length, 5·7 in.

## Black-eared Wheatear                                 *Oenanthe hispanica*

This Wheatear of the Mediterranean basin and the Near East has been re-corded about fifteen times in the British Isles. The male in nuptial dress has the forehead and crown white or nearly white, the mantle buff, and the wings blacker than those of the Common Wheatear; the underparts are white tinged with buff. The back, upper tail-coverts and most of the tail are white; the ear-coverts and a line from the bill, and sometimes the throat are black. In autumn and winter the head and mantle are distinctly buff, as are the under-parts, including the throat. Except the central pair, the tail feathers are much whiter than in the Common Wheatear, the white on the inner web often extending to the tip. The female is a browner bird, but has the characteristic lower back and tail, and has darker cheeks than our bird. Length, 5·7 in.

## Stonechat                                              *Saxicola torquata*

The Stonechat nests from Germany south to the Mediterranean, where it also winters. In the British Isles it is a partial migrant; some remain all winter in their nesting areas, others disperse or leave the country. There has been a widespread reduction in numbers in recent years, partly attributable to destruction of the birds' habitat and partly to the effect of such severe winters as that of 1962–63. On the coasts of Cornwall, the Isle of Man and the west of Ireland, however, it is still abundant. Inland it is now scarce and local.

The Stonechat frequents commons, rough wasteland where furze and bramble grow freely amidst the rocky outcrops, and is partial to the coast and the foot-hills and lower moors, just above the zone of cultivation. The male is a conspicuous bird with black head, white collar and shoulder-patch contrasting with a rich chestnut breast. There is great variation in the size of the white shoulder-patch and collar of male birds both in spring and autumn. This may be due to age, but cocks with greyish heads and small collars and wing-patches apparently mate freely. The male perches in full view on the top of the gorse bushes, the look-out from which he guards the nest. A telegraph wire which crosses his haunts gives a better post of vantage. If approached, he flits from bush to bush, jerking his tail, and with cries of *tsak, tsak* or *wee-tac, tac,* strives to draw us from the danger zone. The alarm note has a curious ring like the sound of pebbles struck together, and from this the bird gets its name. When perched his tail is ever in motion, and his plump and sturdy body is jerked and bobbed constantly. In autumn many usual haunts are deserted, and single birds appear in unexpected places, but the extent of the autumnal and winter wanderings is irregular. On the west coast numbers remain near the shore. Most of these wanderers are solitary males, but birds which winter on or near the sand dunes of the west coast are evidently paired. The birds return to their breeding haunts in February and March, and, at any rate in northern counties, males and females often arrive together. The male is conservative in his choice of observation post, and both male and female have particular perches when bringing food to their young, a habit noticeable in many species. The hen has also a route through the herbage by which she travels, unseen, to and from the nest.

The song is short and irregular but characteristic, a series of sweet notes rapidly repeated; it may be sung on the wing, but usually from the top of a bush or other elevated perch; it is continued from March until late in June. Flies and moths are captured on the wing, the robust little bird dodging swiftly after them with more agility than its build suggests. Seeds are occasionally eaten, but most of the food consists of insects and their larvae, small worms and spiders, and Miss Turner saw one pair bring several young lizards to the nestlings.

The nest is cleverly hidden at the foot of a gorse or other bush, in heather or a clump of grass, on or very near the ground; it is built of moss, grass and roots, with a little wool or fur added at times, and lined with fine bents, hair and a few feathers. The five to six pale blue-green eggs are often zoned with fine reddish speckles, or are clouded with red; they are laid as a rule in April, and a second brood is reared.

In spring the male has the head, throat and back black, with brown edges to some of the feathers and with rufous margins to those on the white rump; the wings and tail are brown. The sides of the neck and throat and a patch on the secondaries are white. The underparts are rich chestnut shading to buff. The bill and legs are black. The female is a browner bird with well-marked striations, and the white parts in the male are suffused with rufous. The female's throat is mottled with black and her rump is reddish-brown. In autumn (as shown in the colour plate) the male has most of the feathers edged with buff, obscuring the black and restricting the white areas. The young are spotted and streaked above and below, and have broad buff margins to the quills and tail feathers; after the first autumn moult they resemble the females and are some time in gaining full white patches and collars. Length, 5 in. Wing, 2·5 in. Tarsus, 0·85 in. (*Plates 129, 131 and 175*.)

## Whinchat                                                         *Saxicola rubetra*

The Whinchat breeds throughout northern and central Europe, and winters from southern Europe to tropical Africa. In the British Isles it is a summer visitor, usually arriving rather late in April, and has a wide though local distribution, thin in Ireland and in central and southern England. It has rarely been reported as wintering.

Open meadows in the lowlands, commons and gorse-clad wastes, marshes and rough pastures up to over 1000 ft., are the haunts of the Whinchat, a stout, short-tailed bird, less erect in carriage and robust in build than the Stonechat. The eye-stripe, white and conspicuous in the male, yellower in the female, and white patches on the wing, especially those on the primaries of the male, are points by which it may be known, but its more horizontal pose when perched and the white at the base of the outer tail feathers—not to be confused with the white rump of the other bird—are specific characters. In many tricks and habits the two birds are alike; the constantly fanned tail as it perches on a furze bush, selecting the topmost spray, or as it clings to a swaying grass-stem, and its repeated *wee-tic, tic*, remind one of the other bird, though the note is less insistent and harsh than that of the Stonechat. It will perch in a tree, and in one favourite haunt, the floral slopes of a railway-cutting, the telegraph wires make excellent look-outs. With expanded tail it balances on a wire, singing a short, rather metallic and vibrating melody, not unlike that of the Redstart. It will leave its perch for a short aerial journey, singing as it flies, or cleverly catch a dodging fly; a green caterpillar looping up a grass blade, or a beetle moving below catches its keen eye and it drops to the bank. Beetles, phytophagous and coprophagous, form a large portion of its insect diet, and the diptera over the hay-grass are diligently hunted. At dusk it chases crepuscular moths, feeding until dark. Near the nest it has a soft anxious *peep*, and this is uttered in addition to the ticking calls when both birds flit with jerking flight uneasily from plant to plant in their endeavour to draw us from their home. When thus excited the male will sing fitfully, but towards the end of June, when still feeding young, he becomes silent. As a migrant, the Whinchat travels in little parties, those in autumn apparently consisting of the family, but in spring, when spreading over the country, it will consort with other insectivorous birds.

The nest, built of grass and moss with a lining of finer bents and hair, may be at the foot of a bush or in thick cover, or simply in a hollow in the open field, well hidden by surrounding grasses; it is usually on the ground and cleverly concealed. Five to six, rarely more, greenish-blue eggs, often faintly speckled with rusty dots towards the larger end, are laid late in May, and a second brood is sometimes reared. The hen builds the nest and incubates the eggs. Towards the end of August the family parties become less noticeable, and though a few individuals remain until early October, most depart in September.

The male in spring is yellowish-brown with dark, almost black striations, black cheeks and ear-coverts, and a noticeable white superciliary stripe and line from the chin to the neck. On the brown wing are two white patches, the smaller, on the primary coverts, absent in immature birds and females. The basal half of the tail is white, though when the tail is closed the upper tail-coverts partially conceal the central portion. Rich rufous underparts shade to dull white on the belly. Buff edges, which are abraded later, dull the whole of the plumage after the autumn moult and give the bird a yellowish appearance. The bill and legs are black. The female is paler, her eye-stripe duller and her upper parts browner. The young bird is blotched and streaked, and its breast spotted with brown. The young look lighter and redder than the adult birds. Length, 5 in. Wing, 2·9 in. Tarsus, 0·9 in. (*Plates 129, 131 and 175.*)

## Redstart                                    *Phoenicurus phoenicurus*

In most parts of Britain the Redstart is a summer resident, but it is rare in Cornwall and the extreme north of Scotland and does not breed regularly in Ireland or the Isle of Man. In England and Scotland it is also a bird of passage between the northern part of its European range and its winter quarters in Africa.

Early in April the male Redstarts arrive on the south coast a few days in advance of the females, but towards the end of the month both sexes arrive simultaneously in more northern shires. The bird is often described as a frequenter of ruins, rocks and quarries, accurately enough where these occur, but in many parts the ruins it favours are those of ancient forest trees; it is a bird of the woodlands and open parkland, especially where the timber is old enough to supply cracks and crannies suitable for its nest. It is a characteristic bird of hill-country oakwoods. In many of its habits and actions the Redstart shows affinity to the Robin; it has the same general carriage, the same spasmodic bobs or duckings of its body and the jerky inquisitive behaviour in our presence. The rich chestnut tail is ever in motion, flirted suddenly upward and vibrated. It can be and is moved in any direction; in the trees it is flicked up and down; in the presence of the hen swung from side to side. The rich colour of the tail and rump attracts the eye as the bird rises to a tree or flits with jerky flight from branch to branch; no other bird except the Black Redstart has a similar tail. The white forehead of the male is also a good label, and he is more frequently noticed than his mate as he sings his short song, like some of the snatches of the Robin, but never being more than a prelude; it has an unfinished, feeble ending. Now and then the bird sings on the wing, but most of his aerial journeys are sallies after passing insects, for the Redstart is an excellent flycatcher and most of its food consists of winged insects. The widespread chestnut tail shows to advantage when the bird flits and hovers, dodging from side to side, over the long grass where flies and plant-bugs are always plentiful. The song may be heard after dark. The call is a chat-like *whee-tic tic*, and the alarm a plaintive single note, *wheet*, not unlike that of the Willow Warbler.

In its choice of a nesting site the bird is almost as catholic as the Robin. Holes in trees, cracks in rotten stumps, crannies in rocks or quarries or in stone walls are most usual, but the nest may be built in an occupied dwelling, even over the doorway, or may be tucked into a hole on the ground, but it is always well screened and hidden. It is loosely built of grass, moss, fibre, rootlets, often with a little wool added, and the cup is lined with hair and a few feathers. The five to six or even eight light blue eggs are usually laid during May, and a second brood is not uncommon. The female sits closely, and if frequently looked at gains confidence and will refuse to move unless handled. The same hole is often used year after year.

The male in summer has a slate-grey head and upper parts except the rump and tail, which, like the flanks, under wing-coverts and axillaries, are rich orange-chestnut. The forehead and a line over the eye are white; the sides of the face and throat deep black. The wings and the two central tail feathers are brown. The orange on the flanks shades to buff and to almost white on the belly. The bill and legs are black. The hen is a browner bird with paler underparts; she lacks the black and slate, and her throat is whitish. The young are mottled on both upper and underparts, but both the hen and the young have the distinctive tail. In autumn broad margins obscure the colours of the male. Length, 5·4 in. Wing, 3 in. Tarsus, 0·8 in. (*Plates 129 and 175*.)

## Black Redstart                                          *Phoenicurus ochrurus*

The Black Redstart occurs throughout Europe as far north as the Baltic and winters in southern Europe and Africa. It is a regular passage migrant in spring and autumn on the east coasts of Scotland, England and Ireland, and occurs in small numbers in a few western localities. Some birds regularly winter in south-west England, south Wales and the south of Ireland. The Black Redstart was first recorded nesting in Britain in 1923, and breeding has taken place every year since 1939. Bombed buildings provided abundant nesting sites during the war and for a few years after it, and the summer population reached a peak from 1950 to 1952, when over fifty singing males were located. By 1962 this total had declined to sixteen. Nearly all recorded breeding has occurred in east and south-east England, with the City of London and Dover as the main centres for several years, though odd pairs have nested as far afield as Cornwall, Lancashire and Yorkshire. The 'fire' of the tail labels the bird as Redstart, but it may be distinguished by its sootier appearance, even when in immature males the distinctive white wing-patch is not apparent. The male has no chestnut on the flanks and no white on the forehead. The female is greyer than the hen Common Redstart, and at any age the grey axillaries and under wing-coverts are distinctive; in the Common Redstart these are buff or chestnut.

The Black Redstart arrives in October or November and may pass on or remain to winter, returning eastward in March or April. It breeds throughout a great part of Europe. Its winter haunts differ from those of the Common Redstart. It frequents cliffs and rocky ground, clinging to the rocks, and launching out to catch passing insects or occasionally descending to the shore to hunt in the tide-wrack for flies or small crustaceans. Its quick ducks of head and body, accompanied by a flick of the wings, are robin-like, and its tail is ever jerking upwards and quivering. Its usual call is a short *tsip* or *tititic*; the song is a hurried warble, including curious rattling sounds. The nest is usually built in a hole or on a ledge in a building, though on the Continent crevices in rocks are also used. It is loosely made of dry grass and moss with a lining of hair and feathers. Four to six glossy white eggs are laid from April onwards; two broods are normally reared.

The adult male in spring has the forehead, lores, cheeks and breast black; the crown, nape and back dark slate-grey. The dark brown wings have a conspicuous white patch on the secondaries. The lower breast is black with grey bars and the belly grey. The bill and legs are black. After the autumn moult grey margins obscure the black, but these rapidly wear off and good plumage is often acquired by December. In young males the full plumage is not attained until after the second autumn moult—the white patch is inconspicuous and the underparts are smoky-grey. The female is brown, though much greyer than the hen Common Redstart; the grey underwing is a safe distinction. Length, 5·75 in. Wing, 3·4 in. Tarsus, 0·9 in. (*Plates 129 and 175*.)

### Nightingale                                          *Luscinia megarhynchos*

The Nightingale's summer range extends from England eastward to the Balkans and Asia Minor, and southward to north-west Africa. It reaches England as a spring migrant about the middle of April, and towards the end of August and during September leaves for winter quarters. In England its range is practically restricted to the area south and east of a line from the

Severn to the Humber, and in Wales to a few southern river valleys. In Ireland it is a rare vagrant.

The Nightingale is a large, handsome brown robin. It is only necessary to watch the sturdy, well-built, bright-eyed Nightingale, as it sits with head on one side examining the ground beneath, to realise its relationship. It drops to the ground, flicks its wings and dives at its quarry, warbles a few subdued notes, elevates its tail, with darker central feathers like those of the Redstart, throws over the dead leaves with spasmodic action and dives into the undergrowth. Its home is the thicket, tangled hedgerow and woodland undergrowth; it occasionally sings from a tree, but usually from hedge, bush or ground. No bird has had more rubbishy sentiment lavished upon it than the Nightingale; the very 'fire and fervour' of its wonderful song, an 'impassioned recitative', is belittled by talk of melancholy and 'melodious sorrows'. Though purely its own, there are characters in it suggestive of the varied phrases of the Song Thrush, the deep contralto of the Blackbird, the ripples of the Garden Warbler, the low call and shiver of the Wood Warbler, and the sprightly outbursts of the Robin; but it has what Warde Fowler calls 'that marvellous *crescendo* on a single note which no other birds attempt'. This, *pew, pew*, begins softly, but rising rapidly in volume and pitch, reaches a height which, to the sympathetic listener, produces a thrill, an expectant catch of the breath. Then, in the midst of surpassing music, comes a harsh croak—*kur, kur*, equally distinctive but hardly musical. This croak is also the alarm note; the call is a soft *wheet*.

The popularity of the song is due to the bird's singing at night, when most other songsters are silent, though many species, during the breeding season, sing after dark. The Nightingale is just as vocal during the day, but is then unnoticed. Bright sunshine is as welcome to the Nightingale as soft moonlight; stirred by nuptial ardour it must sing. Coward heard four or five at once in one small coppice, and saw two, with outstretched necks and bills 'on guard', and tails cocked forward like pugilistic Robins, sparring on the road and singing vigorously at each other. During song the tail quivers; indeed the whole bird shivers with energy; it sings with its body, like the Wood Warbler. The song period is short, ceasing when the young are hatched in June. There is little need to approach the 'skulking' bird with caution; a stone thrown into the bushes will startle it into song. In late summer the young warble a few notes. The male displays with outspread drooping wings, with erected feathers on his back and tail expanded. Worms, insects and berries are eaten; damp and marshy spots, where insects are always plentiful, are frequented.

The nest is either on or a little above the ground, under or in thick cover, even at the foot of a hedge. Dead leaves, chiefly oak, with a little grass are its constituents, and the lining is fine grass with some hair. Four to six olive-brown eggs are laid early in May, and there is only one brood. The nest-building and incubation are done by the hen alone.

Birds of both sexes are russet-brown above and dull white, tinged with brown, below; the tail is chestnut-brown; the bill and legs are brown. The young are more rufous, and have pale shaft-streaks and spots on the upper parts, and bars and mottles on the underparts. Length, 6·5 in. Wing, 3·35 in. Tarsus, 1 in. (*Plates 130 and 175.*)

### Thrush Nightingale *Luscinia luscinia*

This vagrant from eastern Europe and Asia has occurred seven times in the British Isles. One record is from Northumberland in September, the rest from Fair Isle in May. It closely resembles the Nightingale in appearance and song, but is rather darker in colour and at close quarters shows a brownish, mottled breast. Length, 6·5 in.

### Rufous Bush Chat *Cercotrichas galactotes*

This bird, formerly known as the Rufous Warbler, which breeds in the Iberian Peninsula, north Africa and Asia, has been recorded eight times in the British Isles. All the accepted occurrences have been in autumn and all but one in the southern counties of England and Ireland. It is a chestnut-brown bird with pale underparts, a white eye-stripe and a buff wing-bar. Its best character is its long, rounded, rich chestnut tail, with all but the central feathers with a subterminal black band and tipped with white. Length, 6 in.

### Bluethroat *Cyanosylvia svecica*

The Bluethroat breeds in northern and central Europe and winters further south. In the British Isles it is known as a regular passage migrant on the east coast in autumn, usually in very small numbers, and an occasional one in spring. On Fair Isle it is regular at both seasons.

The Bluethroat resembles the Robin in its appearance, actions and many of its habits, but at all ages and seasons it can be recognised by the reddish sides to the dark brown tail, and adults in autumn show some blue on the throat or breast. On migration it is shy and skulking, but when undisturbed will come out of cover to feed in the open, moving with robin-like hops and cocked tail, and with a noticeably erect carriage.

The upper parts of the male in spring are brown, with a white or buff superciliary stripe, and the proximal half of the tail, except the two central feathers, rich chestnut. Males of the Red-spotted subspecies, *Cyanosylvia svecica svecica*, which breeds in Scandinavia, northern Russia and Siberia, have the throat and breast blue with a broad band-like spot of chestnut, and below the blue are bands of black, white and chestnut, above its whitish underparts. The female has tawny white underparts except for a dark band across the breast. The young are at first spotted and streaked, but after the moult they resemble the female. Length, 5·7 in. Wing, 2·9 in. Tarsus, 1·1 in. (*Plate 130.*)

The White-spotted Bluethroat, *C. s. cyanecula*, is the more southern form which breeds in Europe, from Spain to the Baltic Provinces, and winters in north-western Africa. In spring males of this race have the breast-spot white, not chestnut. Several examples have been identified in England and Scotland.

## Robin                                                        *Erithacus rubecula*

The Robin is resident in all parts of the British Isles and many individuals are strictly sedentary, spending their whole lives within a few hundred yards of their birthplace. But there is also evidence of considerable migratory move-ment, and some British-ringed Robins, chiefly first-year birds from south-east England, have been recovered in France. Continental Robins, much less tame and approachable than the British, occur as passage migrants, sometimes in large numbers, in the northern islands and on the east coast. The Robin breeds throughout Europe except in the extreme north.

The Robin or Redbreast has psychological traits which are entirely its own; it has, at most seasons, absolute trust in man. It is the bird of the homestead, ever ready to attend the garden worker, perch upon the handle of his spade the moment he leaves it, or pick a worm from beneath his feet and swallow it with a low warble of satisfaction. In winter it will readily respond to encourage-ment and enter the house for food. Abundant though it is amongst houses, it is also plentiful in thick wood and coppice, in lane and hedgerow. Even in the quiet wood the clicking call of the inquisitive bird announces its arrival, and usually this is followed by a snatch of song. The Robin is a regular breed-ing bird of the oakwoods and juniper scrub in hill country and may be found at 1500 ft. above sea level. Most Robins of both sexes establish and defend a territory after the moult in August, but pairs are formed as early as December, and the territorial system does not prevent a surprising number of different individuals from visiting a known food supply such as a garden bird-table. The actions of the Redbreast are spasmodic but engaging; it hops, bobs its head and body, flicks its wings, and appears anxious to call our attention.

The song has great variety, and is a fine performance; it may be heard in summer and winter; presumably all Robins do not moult at the same time, so that even in July and August some sing. In autumn, when most other birds are silent, it is naturally appreciated. In range and some of the better notes it approaches the song of the Nightingale. The autumn song is often described as tender and sad, but it is full of exultant phrases. The Robin, as is well known, is pugnacious, fighting with his own kind and attacking other species; yet in his most furious bouts, with feathers ruffled and wings drooped like a gamecock, he will sing his challenges. The female also sings, at any rate in winter; young birds will warble a few notes, even during their first autumn moult. The explosive cry of anger, a cat-like spit, the call *tic, tic*, which when rapidly repeated becomes a skirl, and a long-drawn *seeep*, are familiar, but exactly what they mean varies with the cause of excitement. The rapidly repeated *tics*, used when mobbing a cat or other foe, are sounded at roosting time. The bird is not an early rooster; and Robins are sometimes heard singing in the dark and have even been recorded feeding late at night by the light of street lamps.

The food is animal or vegetable, for though worms, insect larvae, flies—often caught on the wing—and spiders are its main diet, it will eat soft fruit, berries and seeds. In winter it will accept most of our gifts, including breadcrumbs. In hostile display to other Robins of either sex the bird stretches up its head and neck, showing off the red breast, and may sway the body from side to side, erect the tail or flick the wings at the same time. In a series of experiments described in *The Life of the Robin*, David Lack found that Robins would react at once to the detached breast feathers of a dead adult, and that it was the red colour and not the whole bird that acted as a stimulus. The male feeds the female, who receives his gifts with quivering wings, even before nest building has begun, and continues to do so through the breeding season.

The Robin is not only catholic in its choice of a nesting site but is often eccentric. It prefers a hole in a bank, wall, tree, shed, old kettle, shoe or hat, but it will build under a shelter of grass or on a shelf in an outbuilding. A bird which built in a wooden pulpit was neither disturbed by the parson nor the organ and choir, and broods have been successfully reared in tractors and cars in regular use. The nest is bulky, built of dead leaves which form an apron at the threshold, grass and moss, and lined with hair. Five or six is the usual clutch, and two or three broods are reared. The eggs are white with reddish-brown markings, which vary from a few specks to bold blotches. The first clutch is usually laid in March or early April.

The adult bird of either sex has a narrow blue-grey margin between the olive-brown of the upper parts and orange-red of the breast; the belly is white; the under tail-coverts buff. The legs are brown; the bill and irides black. The bright brown eye is one of the bird's peculiar charms. The young are spotted and streaked with buff on a brown ground and are mottled on the breast. After their first autumn moult the breast is paler than in the adult and the red covers a smaller area. Length, 5·5 in. Wing, 3 in. Tarsus, 1 in. (*Plates 130, 132 and 175.*)

## Family SYLVIIDAE Warblers

**Grasshopper Warbler**                              *Locustella naevia*

Except in the north of Scotland the Grasshopper Warbler is a summer resident in all parts of the British Isles; it is a western European species, wintering in Africa.

Its retiring and skulking habits, without doubt, cause the Grasshopper Warbler or 'Reeler' to be overlooked; it frequents marshes in the lowlands and is found high on the moors, though seldom abundant and always local. It is not an early migrant, though it quickly spreads over the country, often reaching the north by the middle of April or early May. Its time of arrival and numbers are irregular; there are good and bad years for the species. It is sometimes numerous as a coastal passage migrant.

There is nothing to strike the eye in its sombre plumage, but the rounded tail, which is drooped and depressed when the bird is disturbed from the nest, is noticeable; indeed, we often hear but do not see the singer. The long monotonous 'reeling' song has little musical value, but it is an interesting performance, in which, with vibrating throat and wide-open bill, the bird trills one note with hardly perceptible pauses for from a few seconds to two or three minutes. So insistent is the sound that where a long trill ends suddenly the silence for a moment seems oppressive. It is a high-pitched rippling chirp, inaudible to some ears, which rises and falls, now a faint hum, now like the rattle of a distant mowing machine, now like an angler's reel, but never resembling the chirrup of the insect from which the bird gets its name. It is perhaps best heard in the early morning, but the bird sings after dusk and also in the glare of the sun at noon; in fact from the time of arrival until late in July it sings constantly in its favourite haunts. The alarm note is *twhit, twhit*; sometimes rapidly repeated; but except when the young are hatched the bird makes little fuss, flitting just above the herbage when put off the nest and dropping in a few yards to cover. Very silently it creeps back, threading its way with skill and rapidity through the stems, creeping mouse-like though without murine jerks and pauses. As far as is known the bird is insectivorous, using the word in a general sense, for spiders, wood-lice and other small animals are eaten; green caterpillars are largely given to the young. In nuptial display the male spreads wide his wings and tail and gently fans them, though he has no striking marks or colours to exhibit.

The nest is in a tussock of grass, in marshes, osier beds, or the thick vegetation near water, but it is also built in dry situations, in tangled hedgerows, gorse bushes or amongst heather on the moors. It varies in size and construction, and is made of grass or sedge, mingled with a little moss, and often lined with finer bents; it is seldom more than a few inches above the ground, and is artfully concealed. The four to six eggs are laid late in May, sometimes even in July; there are often second broods. They are closely speckled with small red spots, more rarely blotched and zoned. Emigration takes place from August onwards; birds have been noted in October.

The general colour of the upper parts is greenish-brown or russet, with streaks formed by dark centres of the feathers; the tail is faintly barred. The chin and belly are whitish, and the rest of the underparts pale brown, with a few spots on the throat. The under tail-coverts are streaked. The bill is brown, the legs pale yellowish-brown. The young are buffer on the underparts. Length, 5·4 in. Wing, 2·4 in. Tarsus, 0·8 in. (*Plates 133 and 176.*)

## Lanceolated Warbler                              *Locustella lanceolata*

This small grasshopper warbler is distinguished by its smaller size, well-defined gorget of close streaks on the upper breast and whitish chin and throat. It is a Siberian bird, wintering in southern Asia. About a dozen have been recorded in Britain, including ten on Fair Isle and one in Lincolnshire. All but one have been in autumn. Length, 4·75 in.

**Savi's Warbler**                                    *Locustella luscinoides*

After a century's absence from Britain as a breeding species, Savi's Warbler has established a very small breeding population in Kent since about 1960. Otherwise it is known in Britain only as a very rare vagrant. In Europe it breeds as far north as Holland and Poland; it winters in north Africa.

In habits it resembles the Grasshopper Warbler, but it is less shy and skulking and climbs the reeds to sing, showing itself openly. The song is like the Grasshopper Warbler's trill, but is often preceded by an accelerating sequence of ticking notes.

The nest is a deep cup, built in reed-beds, sedges or other aquatic vegetation, and is placed upon a platform of reed blades; it resembles the nest of a crake rather than a warbler. The four to six eggs are white or buff, well speckled with brown and grey.

The uniform reddish-brown of the upper parts prevents confusion with the streaked Grasshopper Warbler, and its twelve-feathered fan-shaped tail distinguishes it from some of its rarer relatives; on the tail are indistinct bars like those on our bird. Its whitish underparts are tinged with buff on the breast, flanks and under tail-coverts. Young birds have paler underparts. Length, 5·7 in. (*Plate 134.*)

**Moustached Warbler**                               *Lusciniola melanopogon*

This warbler breeds in southern Europe and north Africa. A pair nested successfully at Cambridge in 1946, and four or five others have been recorded in the British Isles. It may be distinguished, with some difficulty, from the Sedge Warbler by its blackish crown, whiter eye-stripe, dark brown cheeks and very white throat. It has a distinctive habit of cocking its tail. Length, 5 in.

**Great Reed Warbler**                              *Acrocephalus arundinaceus*

There is no evidence that the Great Reed Warbler has ever nested in Britain, but in recent years a few have been recorded annually in south-east England and some individuals have stayed for several days in spring and summer in suitable reed-beds. It breeds throughout most of Europe, including northern France, Belgium and Holland, and migrates as far south as Natal. Its song is loud and harsh; its alarm note resembles that of the Sedge Warbler. From size alone it is unlikely to be confused with any other warbler. The upper parts are dark olive-brown, throwing up the whitish superciliary stripe and the pale margins of the secondaries; the underparts are buff, whitish on throat and belly. The brown bill is noticeably long and thick. Length, 7·6 in.

**Reed Warbler**                                   *Acrocephalus scirpaceus*

Towards the end of April, sometimes not until May, the Reed Warbler arrives in England and invades the reed-beds of the southern and midland counties, spreading as far as Yorkshire and north Lancashire, where scores of pairs nest annually on the R.S.P.B. reserve at Leighton Moss. In Scotland and Ireland it is only known as a passage visitor, and it is rare in Wales and the four northern counties of England. It breeds throughout Europe to the Baltic and southern Sweden and winters in Africa.

There is nothing striking in the plain brown dress of the Reed Warbler; it is in harmony with the grey-brown of the old reeds which remain long after its arrival. It cannot be confused with the Sedge Warbler, for it has hardly any noticeable eye-stripe and lacks the distinctive head streaks and dark spotted back of this bird. It is, however, almost impossible to distinguish it in the field from the Marsh Warbler, though it is slightly darker, has more rufous on the rump and is whiter on the chin and throat. Were it not for its continuous chattering the Reed Warbler would frequently be overlooked, for though it is not shy, the reeds give concealment. As it hops from stem to stem, now with one bent leg grasping a reed, now balancing sideways with both legs flexed, its light body stirs the tops so that, though silent and invisible, its progress may be traced. It has a curious way of sidling up a reed to the top and there singing in full view. The song is a mixture of sweet and harsh notes, monotonous and deliberate, as if uttered with an effort; it is neither as varied nor loud as that of the Sedge. It normally has a rather monotonous, disyllabic rhythm, but some individual Reed Warblers have a more varied, mimetic performance which may cause confusion with the Marsh Warbler. In summer the song is heard after dark, and is frequent until the end of July and often heard in August and September. In courtship, when the male raises his crest and depresses his fanned-out tail, he will rise and sing on the wing. The male is a jealous guardian of the nest, and will drive off avian, and violently scold human intruders; his alarm note is a rasping churr.

The normal nest is a work of art, suspended or rather built round three or more reed stems, usually those growing out of water. If the young reeds are sufficiently advanced it is attached to these, and as they grow fast it rises rapidly with its supports; it may be built soon after the bird arrives in May, or not until June, and early nests are often on the old reeds. Two or three 'cocks' nests' may be built before one is finally occupied. The nest is a deep straight-sided, firmly woven structure, usually with a sound foundation of grasses, strips of reed or sedge, and with wool or reed flowers so intermingled as to render it solid and compact; in the neat cylinder of the hollow, lined with reed flowers, fine grasses and hair, eggs and young are safe when wind sways the stems, and the head of the sitting bird is often almost invisible. There is, however, great variation in the architecture, many nests being as shallow as those of the Sedge. Neither are they by any means always built in reeds nor over water. Small colonies have been found in waterside willows, even as high above the ground as 20 ft. Late nests are built with great rapidity; two or three days are enough to construct fairly good nests, and there is often a second brood. The four or five eggs are greenish-white as a rule, marbled and blotched with olive and grey; the amount of colour varies, but is usually profuse. The Cuckoo victimises the Reed Warbler; a pair may often be seen toiling to satisfy their foster-child with the small aquatic insects and caterpillars which form the normal food of their own nestlings; the growing bird bursts and flattens out the elegant nest. Young Reed Warblers, even when disturbed for the first time, are skilful in threading their way among the stems, and seldom fall into the water. As autumn approaches the old birds become silent, but their presence may be detected when a clod or stone is thrown into the reeds; the splash is followed by a short burst of expostulatory song. Towards the end of September the majority leave, but a few remain until October.

The upper parts are olive-brown, tinged rufous on the rump; there are pale edges to the secondaries. The throat and belly are white, the breast is buff and the flanks rufous. The bill is dark brown, paler at the base of the lower mandible; the legs brown. The young are more rufous on the back and rump. Length, 5·25 in. Wing, 2·5 in. Tarsus, 0·9 in. (*Plates 126, 135 and 176.*)

### Marsh Warbler                                            *Acrocephalus palustris*

The Marsh Warbler breeds in most parts of Europe south of Denmark, and winters in Africa, even at the Cape. As a wanderer on migration it has reached the Shetlands and St Kilda, but as a summer resident it is very local and nests regularly only in a very few English counties, especially Worcester and Gloucester.

So closely does the Marsh resemble the Reed Warbler that a keen eye for colour is necessary before we can separate dried skins of the two species, and when the bird is moving in the herbage the angle at which the light strikes its plumage may easily deceive the observer. It is slightly more olive than the Reed, yellower beneath, and its rump is less rufous. It haunts marshes, osier beds, and wet ditches, and is a late migrant, seldom appearing before early June; it is thought to leave in August. Its best character is its song, which has been described as like that of the Reed Warbler with the execution of the Blackcap. In its sweet and varied song it is an excellent mimic, introducing a large range of notes borrowed from other birds, even the liquid bubble of the Nightingale. The song lacks the disyllabic pattern that is a marked feature of the Reed Warbler's song. Like its congeners, it sings at night, but the duration of the song is short; usually it ends early in July. The food consists of insects, particularly those which haunt marshy ground, and, it is said, a few berries.

The nest, which is not always in marshes and has been found in cornfields, differs from most but by no means all nests of the Reed Warbler, in that it is very shallow. It is suspended from marsh plants, especially meadowsweet, willow-herb, cow-parsnip and nettles, and the stalks do not pass through the edge of the nest, but are encircled by a loop of nesting material. It has seldom more than a few rootlets and hair as a lining to its loosely woven grass structure. Four to five eggs are laid towards the end of June, and only one brood is reared. These are almost invariably whiter than the eggs of the Reed Warbler, and, boldly blotched and streaked towards the larger end with purple, violet or olive, resemble the larger eggs of the Great Reed Warbler.

The plumage is that of the Reed Warbler, with the differences already stated. Length, 5 in. Wing, 2·7 in. Tarsus, 0·9 in. (*Plates 126 and 176.*)

**Blyth's Reed Warbler**                                *Acrocephalus dumetorum*

The coloration of this Asiatic Reed Warbler so closely resembles that of the
Reed and Marsh Warbler which nest in Britain that it cannot be distinguished
in the field; it has however, a structural character, a shorter second primary.
It breeds in a wide area in central Asia and in part of Russia, and winters in
India. There have been some half-dozen British records of autumn vagrants,
all from Fair Isle or the east coast of England. Length, 5·25 in.

**Sedge Warbler**                                  *Acrocephalus schoenobaenus*

Of all the marsh-haunting warblers the Sedge Warbler is most abundant and
evenly distributed. It is found in most parts of Europe, and winters in Africa
as far south as the Transvaal. In the British Isles it is a summer resident,
arriving late in April, and a passage migrant; it is generally distributed, but
becomes rare in north-west Scotland and the Orkneys, and in the Shetlands
except on spring migration.

Except in a few localities which are unsuitable for a water-loving species,
the garrulous Sedge Warbler advertises its presence by chattering and varied
song, though, owing to the dense herbage it haunts, it is often invisible. The
presence of water, in lake, small pond, river, ditch or marsh, is all it requires,
for it feeds upon gnats, midges and other dipterous flies whose early life is
aquatic. Small molluscs and larvae of moths and beetles are eaten. The song is
varied, irresponsible and erratic; it is difficult to describe. Like many other
birds, the Sedge Warbler copies other sounds: whether melodious, sweet,
harsh or grating, high or low, does not matter. Some of the snatches are fine
productions, clear-toned, round and full; others grating chatters. It sings from
the depth of cover or from an elevated perch in full view; it has often a favourite
perch for song. In spring, at any rate, the bird is neither shy nor skulking, but
merely indifferent. When stirred by nuptial fervour it sings on the wing,
flying with tail spread and wings outstretched and quivering, making short
circular or semicircular flights. It sings frequently at night, and its richer
notes lead to its being mistaken for the Nightingale. Its explosive note, *ptree*,
scolding *pit, pit*, and harsh churr are so intermingled with its song that the
psychological meaning of its varied utterance is obscure; a bird will scold,
churr and sing loudly if startled by a thrown stone or clod, and Coward saw
one vigorously singing at a cat which it was mobbing. The song period seldom
ends before the beginning of August, and at the end of this month and in
September the bird sings a little. During August and September many depart,
but passage migrants are met with in October.

The nest is usually near water, but often in tangled overgrown ditches,
quite dry in summer; it is seldom more than 2 or 3 ft. above the ground, in
low herbage, brambles, osiers, bushes or small trees, but occasionally may be
found high up in tall thorn hedges. The statement that it is *never* suspended
but always supported is incorrect, though the latter is the rule. It is a fairly
neat, rather shallow nest of grass and moss, lined with horsehair or willow-
down or other soft vegetable tissues. It is often the middle of May before the

five or six eggs are laid; they are buff or yellowish-green, clouded, suffused or finely speckled with darker brown, and usually with a few black hair-lines.

In summer the general colour is reddish-brown with dark centres to the feathers, forming streaks on the back but not on the tawny rump. A conspicuous yellowish-white superciliary stripe is bounded above by an almost black streak, and the centre of the crown is streaked with light and dark brown; the ear-coverts are brown. Light edges show on the wing feathers. The underparts are buff, whitish on the throat, and warmest on the flanks. The bill is dark brown; the legs pale brown. After the autumn moult the eye-stripe and underparts are buffer. The young bird is redder, and has faint spots on the throat and breast. Length, 5 in. Wing, 2·5 in. Tarsus, 0·8 in. (*Plates 133, 135 and 176.*)

### Aquatic Warbler                                        *Acrocephalus paludicola*

The Aquatic Warbler breeds in the Netherlands, north Germany and scattered localities in the east and south of Europe. A few individuals are recorded in the British Isles each autumn. Most of them are seen in the southern counties of England, but there have been several occurrences in Shetland.

This bird resembles the Sedge Warbler in its song and alarm call and in its choice of habitat, but it is more skulking and secretive in its behaviour. It may be distinguished from the Sedge Warbler by the central buff streak on its crown, its buffer eye-stripe, pale cheeks, striated rump and stronger striations on its back. Length, 4·9 in. (*Plate 133.*)

### Melodious Warbler                                        *Hippolais polyglotta*

The Melodious Warbler is a slightly smaller bird than the Icterine, but its general appearance, habits and song are so similar that it is difficult to distinguish in the field. It breeds in western Europe as far north as Normandy and in north-west Africa and is now known as an annual autumn vagrant to the British Isles, chiefly to the south coasts of England, Wales and Ireland. It has also been recorded in spring and has occurred in the north of England and in Scotland.

Its prolonged babbling song is more hurried and less harsh than the Icterine's; it has a chatter like a House Sparrow's and a ticking alarm call. Its underparts are yellow; the olive-green upper parts are a little duller than the Icterine's, its crown is more rounded and its wings shorter. Length, 4·9 in. Wing, 2·5 in. Tarsus, 0·85 in.

### Icterine Warbler                                        *Hippolais icterina*

The Icterine Warbler is now looked upon as a scarce but regular bird of passage, occurring both in spring and autumn in various parts of the British Isles, especially on the east and south coasts of England and the south coast of Ireland. It is said to have nested in Wiltshire in 1907. The European range of this bird is extensive, but in western France and Spain it is replaced by the Melodious Warbler, from which it is difficult to distinguish in the field. The song is prolonged and varied but contains more harsh, discordant notes than that of the Melodious. The second primary is longer than the fifth, whereas in the Melodious it is shorter. Both birds are olive-green above, and lemon-yellow on the underparts, and have yellow lores and eye-stripes, brown wings and tail, and buff margins to the secondaries. The female is paler, and the young are browner with more pronounced buff margins. The Icterine is a slightly larger and brighter bird than the Melodious. Length, 5·2 in. Wing, 3·1 in. Tarsus, 0·8 in. (*Plate 134.*)

**Olivaceous Warbler**                                            *Hippolais pallida*
This warbler breeds in south-east Europe, western Asia and north-east Africa. Seven vagrants have been recorded in the British Isles, all in autumn. It is pale olive-brown above and white, faintly tinged with buff, below, and has an indistinct eye-stripe. Its bill is long and broad, its wing short and dark and its crown flat compared with the similar Melodious Warbler. Length, 5 in.

**Blackcap**                                                    *Sylvia atricapilla*
The Blackcap has a summer range covering all Europe except the far north, and usually winters in north Africa, though many remain in southern Europe and a few in England. In the British Isles it is a regular summer resident, and in most parts common, though in Scotland it is local, rare in the north, and in Ireland only a few widely separated groups breed, chiefly in the east. It is also a bird of passage, noticeable on the east coast in autumn.

Though frequenting thick woods the Blackcap is rather more a bird of the open than the Garden Warbler, from which it can be told at once by the black or brown cap; indeed this character puts it apart from all common warblers. In the south the immigrants often arrive in March, but are seldom widely distributed before the middle of April. Its notes are rich, clear and mellow, but the song is shorter than that of the Garden Warbler. Occasionally there is a low prelude with harsh notes suggesting the Sedge Warbler, but full notes of Blackbird-quality follow. The alarm, *tack, tack*, is loud, and it scolds like a Whitethroat. The bird sings from high trees as frequently as from undergrowth, and at intervals breaks off its song to fight with a rival. The song may be heard until late in July, but seldom in August; it has been heard from wintering birds. Although it feeds largely on insects it is also partial to berries and fruit; indeed its diet is more vegetarian than that of most warblers. The cock's courtship display is varied and striking and extraordinary antics are sometimes performed by several cocks together during the incubation period.

The nest is commonly further from the ground than that of the Garden Warbler, but this is not always the case; it is built in similar situations in brambles, thick bushes and evergreens, and is roughly but firmly woven; the materials used are grasses and sedges, lined with finer bents and a little hair. The eggs, laid late in May as a rule, are four or five in number, and vary considerably; they are mottled, marbled and clouded with yellowish- or reddish-brown on a yellowish-white or ruddy ground. The male helps to build, incubate and feed the young. In September many leave, but birds on passage have been noted throughout October, and the Blackcap is one of the few warblers which winter with us with some regularity, most commonly in south-west England, but not infrequently even in the northern counties.

The upper parts of the male are bluish-grey in spring; the back is tinged olive-brown, and the darker quills and tail have pale grey edges. The crown and nape are black. The underparts are a paler grey, whitest on the chin and belly, brownest on the flanks. The bill is dark brown, the legs lead-coloured. The black on the head is replaced by rusty-brown in the female; she is more olive-brown above and buffer below. After the autumn moult the upper parts are olive-buff, the chin is less white and the belly distinctly suffused with yellow. The young resemble the female. Length, 5·5 in. Wing, 2·75 in. Tarsus, 0·85 in. (*Plates 137 and 176.*)

## Barred Warbler                                             *Sylvia nisoria*
The European race of this species breeds east of a line from Denmark to northern Italy and migrates to tropical east Africa. In the British Isles the Barred Warbler is an annual visitor on autumn passage to the east coast of England and Scotland and to the northern isles and is now recorded with increasing frequency in other parts of England and in Ireland. The great majority of these birds are immature.

The Barred Warbler is a heavy-looking bird with thick legs and bill. It is shy and skulking in its habits. Its calls include a hard *tchack* and a grating *tcharr, tcharr*. The male is ashy-grey on the upper parts, and the greyish-white underparts are barred with brownish-grey; the wing-coverts and lower back are faintly barred. The female is browner and her bars are less distinct. The juvenile has little or no barring, but is greyer than a Whitethroat or Garden Warbler. Length, 6·2 in. (*Plate 133.*)

## Garden Warbler                                             *Sylvia borin*
Except in the extreme north and in the Mediterranean Basin the Garden Warbler is found throughout Europe; it winters in tropical and southern Africa. In the British Isles it is a common summer resident in England, Wales and parts of lowland Scotland, but is very local in Ireland and does not breed regularly in northern Scotland and the Scottish islands. There is a noticeable autumn passage, especially in the east, and it is also recorded in spring.

There is really nothing very distinctive about the Garden Warbler; it is an olive-brown bird, its buff throat distinguishing it from the Whitethroats, and the absence of a black or brown crown from the Blackcap. 'Garden' is a mis-leading title, for it is a woodland bird, frequenting thick coverts and woods where there is an abundance of undergrowth; in fruit raids it sometimes visits gardens. The song is wonderfully beautiful, a continuous mellow warble, more sustained than that of the Blackcap, but with much of the same quality, though the contralto notes, similar to those of the Blackbird and Blackcap, are not so loud. Singing from the upper branches of a tree is not uncommon, but often the bird is invisible in an evergreen. The idea that the Garden Warbler and Blackcap do not frequent the same wood seems to be true of certain areas, but certainly is not universal. The length of the warble varies, and when the snatches are short, it is difficult to say which of the two allied species is responsible until we see the singer. The alarm note is *teck*, and like the Whitethroat the bird has a scolding *chrrr*. Insects are its food; flies are often captured on the wing, but the bird joins with other species in the search for aphids, especially on the sycamores. To obtain soft fruits and berries, to which it is also partial, it will leave the woods and venture nearer human habitations.

A low bush, evergreen shrub, rose or bramble patch, usually near an open space or the outskirts of a wood, is a common site for the frail, loosely constructed but roomy nest, built of twisted grasses lined with finer bents and hair. It is seldom many feet above the ground. Unfinished 'cocks' nests' are not uncommon. Both birds build and incubate.

The eggs are laid late in May; they often number five, and are mottled and marbled with reddish-brown or greenish-grey on a whitish ground. They vary less than the eggs of the Blackcap, and closely resemble the less red types of this species. The sitting bird slips quietly away when her nest is examined, but soon reappears from another quarter, ticking anxiously.

The Garden Warbler is one of our later migrants, and it is often well into May before the species is generally distributed; the song is continued until the early part of July, and is only occasionally heard after the moult in August. Towards the end of September the emigrants slip quietly away.

In both sexes the summer plumage is olive-brown above and white, shading into buff, beneath. The throat, breast and flanks are distinctly buff. Above the eye is a hardly noticeable pale streak, and the sides of the face are ashy-grey. The bill is dark brown, paler at the base; the legs are leaden. After the moult the upper parts are darker, the under more buff, and the young are still further suffused with buff on the throat and breast. Length, 5·5 in. Wing, 3·15 in. Tarsus, 0·8 in. (*Plates 141 and 176*.)

## Whitethroat                                   *Sylvia communis*

The Whitethroat is a summer visitor, nesting throughout the British Isles except in the extreme north. In Europe it is well distributed, and it winters in southern Africa; in spring and autumn passage migrants travel along our coasts.

The two Whitethroats are slender, active, brownish-grey birds, distinguished from other warblers by their very white throats and chins, but not always easy to tell from one another in the field. The larger bird has the back and wings distinctly more rufous and there is little noticeable difference between the grey on the head and cheeks of the male, whereas in the Lesser Whitethroat the ear-coverts are decidedly darker than the crown.

About the middle of April, as a rule, we hear the persistent song of the Common Whitethroat and see the bird slipping in and out of the hedgerows. Untrimmed hedges and bramble tangles along the lanesides are its haunts; ever on the move, it appears one moment on the top, swelling its white throat in song, then slides into the shelter of the leaves, reappearing at the side some yards before us with conversational *whit, whit, whit*. Its movements are rapid, but it often halts to reach up for an insect above it, or will suddenly shoot into the air, just long enough for it to utter its short song, and descend with open wings, dancing up again, then falling into the bush or hedge. From its skill in traversing dense herbage, it is known as the 'Nettle-creeper'. The short but rapid song is uttered with emphasis and assurance; it has a character purely its own, not by any means always sweet, though its quality varies. In some birds the opening notes are round and full, mellow as those of the Garden Warbler, but the song tails off into a rather harsh warble, generally with an abrupt finish. When in July the moult begins, the song is hushed, but not infrequently it is resumed in August, and early in September most of the birds depart. Until late in October migrants are passing along the coasts.

Even before the nest is built the birds greet an intruder with a peculiar scolding note, a harsh churr, but when the nest is threatened they flutter round with sharp ticking cries. If young are in the nest a bird will shuffle near the ground, feigning lameness, but when eggs are still unhatched the sitting bird slips silently away, threading her course through the dense herbage. The food during spring and summer chiefly consists of insects, large numbers of dipterous flies being captured, but in late summer and autumn small berries and soft fruit are added; elder-berries are favoured, and in gardens raspberries and currants are attacked.

The nest is built in a hedgerow, bramble clump, low-growing herbage, a thick bush or the stocks of cut osiers, and is seldom many inches above the ground. Grass and roots are the usual nesting material, and the deep cup is lined with hair, but some nests are made entirely of rootlets and fibre. Four to six eggs are laid late in May. Greenish-white is the usual ground colour of the grey-speckled egg, but white or brown grounds and red spots and blotches are not uncommon. Both sexes help with building, incubation and feeding the young. There is often a second brood.

The general colour of the male in spring is greyish-brown, greyest on the head and tail-coverts; the wings are a warm brown. The outer feathers of the sepia tail are margined with white. The chin and throat are conspicuously white, but the remainder of the underparts are white, tinged with brown and with pinkish on the breast. The bill is dark brown, the legs pale brown. The female is brown on the head and tail-coverts as well as on the back and her underparts are whiter than those of the male. After the autumn moult the male resembles the female. The young are darker brown on the back and the throat is a duller white. Length, 5·5 in. Wing, 2·8 in. Tarsus, 0·5 in. (*Plates 137 and 176*.)

### Lesser Whitethroat                                    *Sylvia curruca*

The Lesser Whitethroat breeds in central and parts of northern Europe and winters in north Africa. In England it is generally a common summer resident, but is scarce in the extreme north and west and in Wales. In Scotland and Ireland it normally occurs only as a passage migrant.

Though the song is the best distinction between the two Whitethroats, the Lesser is a greyer brown; it looks a grey and white bird, and its brown-tinged grey ear-coverts are much darker than its crown. It arrives late in April, often not until May, and frequents thick hedgerows, bramble thickets and trees; it is far more arboreal than its relative, and though it is by no means shy, the foliage lends concealment. That portion of the song usually heard and described is a loud and rapid metallic rattle, sometimes resembling the song of the Chaffinch, but more closely that of the Cirl Bunting. A preliminary short prelude, a swallow-like twitter, is often audible, but the true song, a subdued, melodious warble, an improved echo of the emphatic Common Whitethroat, can only be heard at close quarters. This crooning warble usually ends in the clanging rattle, which some have considered its call-note. The song may be uttered on the wing. Until well into July, even when the weather is sultry, and with special vehemence if thunder threatens, the song is continued, and after the moult it may be heard late in August. By the end of September most birds have left, though it has been noted in November. There is a marked passage migration on the east coast in both spring and autumn. The note of alarm is a rapid *tic, tic,* frequently heard if the nest is near. The Lesser Whitethroat captures insects on the wing, but its usual methods are careful hunts amongst the foliage; it has also a hovering nuptial flight in May. Insects are its main food, but soft fruit is eaten, especially red currants.

The nest is frail and shallow, built of grass and rootlets and lined with fibres or hair. It is placed in a tall hedge, a tangled bramble patch or a bushy tree, and is usually higher above the ground than that of its relative. At times it is not supported beneath, but hangs suspended like that of the Reed or Marsh Warbler. The eggs, four to six, are usually creamy-white in ground with brownish spots or blotches and underlying violet-grey markings; buff grounds are not uncommon, also markings in a regular zone. Eggs are sometimes laid very soon after the birds arrive in May, but young may still be in the nest in early August.

The male in spring is slate-grey, with a brownish tinge on the back, and brown wings and tail. The cheeks are dark and tinged with brown. The edges of the secondaries are grey, not rufous; the outer tail feathers are bordered with white. The chin, throat, belly and under tail-coverts are white; the breast and flanks are pale brown. The axillaries and under wing-coverts, noticeable in flight, are white, though smoky in the Common Whitethroat. The bill and legs are bluish-grey. The breast and flanks are browner after the autumn moult. The young bird is even browner than the adult in autumn, and its underparts more dingy. Length, 5·25 in. Wing, 2·6 in. Tarsus, 0·75 in. (*Plates 137 and 176.*)

## Subalpine Warbler                                                    *Sylvia cantillans*

The Subalpine Warbler is a summer visitor to the Mediterranean countries of Europe and has been recorded nearly thirty times in the British Isles from

Shetland to the south coast. Spring occurrences are more numerous than autumn ones. The male is a handsome and distinctive warbler with light blue-grey upper parts, pinkish-orange breast and narrow white moustachial stripe. The white outer tail feathers are often conspicuous. Females and juveniles are duller and paler, especially on the breast, and the moustachial stripes are faint. Length, 4·75 in.

## Dartford Warbler                                    *Sylvia undata*

The Dartford Warbler is a local and non-migratory resident in a few localities in the south of England. The population was drastically reduced by the severe winter of 1962–63, after which, breeding was restricted to Dorset, Sussex and the New Forest, with a total of less than thirty pairs. It has a restricted range in western and southern Europe.

This small dark warbler is unlike any of its relatives in habits as well as appearance, for they seldom brave our winters, whereas the Dartford Warbler, though it suffers severely in hard weather, does not emigrate. The male looks very dark, and his constantly erected crest and long fan-shaped tail render him very conspicuous when, in the breeding season, he shows himself on the tops of furze bushes. As a rule, however, the bird is skulking and secretive, remaining unseen in the gorse thickets on the open commons which it frequents. The male has a subdued liquid warble. The note is often described as *pit-it-chou*, but under excitement it is a rapid *tirr, tirr*, often a scolding Whitethroat churr. When the young are in the nest both birds will flutter round, jerking their tails, calling *tic, tic*. The tail, as a rule, is carried well clear of the foliage, but during nuptial display the male droops and spreads it and at the same time drags his half-open wings. The flight from bush to bush is undulating, the short rounded wings whirring rapidly, and the bird suddenly drops into cover. Insects—moths are specially noticed—are its food in summer, but wild fruits and small berries are eaten in the colder months. Though severe winters and destruction of its habitat have no doubt helped to reduce its numbers, the rapacity of collectors is partly to blame.

The nest is a neat structure, well hidden in gorse or heather, though the male builds flimsy 'cock's nests'. It is composed of young furze shoots, *Galium* stems, ling, moss, grass, wool and feathers, lined with finer bents, feathers and hair. The three to five eggs are usually yellowish- or greenish-white speckled with underlying grey and more decided brownish markings, often taking the form of a zone. There are two broods: the first eggs are laid in April and the second clutch, as a rule, in June or July.

In summer the male has dark brown upper parts, shading to slate-grey on the head, and the brown wings are shown up by paler edgings on the secondaries; the two outer tail feathers have white margins and tips, conspicuous when the tail is fanned out. The underparts are rufous-chestnut. The bill is blackish; the legs yellow; the irides, and a ring round the eye, reddish-orange. In autumn the underparts, especially on the throat, are streaked with white. The female is paler above and beneath, and lacks the ruddy tints.

The young are darker above and buff on the underparts. Length, 5·1 in. Wing, 2·2 in. Tarsus, 0·75 in. (*Plates 137 and 176.*)

## Willow Warbler                                                *Phylloscopus trochilus*

The Willow Warbler, or Willow Wren, is the most abundant of all our summer residents; it is common throughout the British Isles, and great numbers, as birds of passage, travel along our coasts in spring and autumn. It is found in summer throughout central and northern Europe; some winter in the south of Europe, but most in Africa.

Three leaf-warblers, as the birds are called on account of their habits, are summer residents in Britain, and all are greenish-yellow birds. The Willow Warbler is smaller and less yellow than the Wood Warbler, but is so similar to the Chiffchaff that it is difficult to see the greener back and paler legs in a poor light or when the active bird is amongst the foliage; the songs, however, are quite characteristic. The Willow Warbler often reaches the south coast at the end of March, and by the second week in April has spread far north; the arrival is frequently noted in a succession of waves, when thousands will stream in for days together. For a few days there may be only odd birds about, then one morning the song is heard everywhere. The statement that the males arrive some days before the females and are at first silent may be true of the south coast, but if the weather is suitable the birds sing on arrival, and court-ship begins at once in more northern counties. The immigrants quickly spread over woods, lanesides, and gardens in the lowlands, and to the spinneys and even bushes high on the hills.

The song, though simple, is wonderfully sweet; Burroughs described it as a 'tender, delicious warble' with 'a dying fall. It mounts up round and full, then runs down the scale, and expires upon the air in a gentle murmur'. By the middle of April in a normal year it is the dominant song in the woods; its persistence and vehemence rather than its volume swamps the loud rattle of the Chaffinch and the strong notes of the Song Thrush. Like all songs, it varies; some birds between the snatches give a low sparrow-like chatter, and in August, after the moult, for the bird often sings in autumn, a subdued version of the true song may be heard. The alarm note is a plaintive *hweet*, and the note of anxiety a double *loo-ee*.

Small insects are skilfully captured on the wing, but most of the food is daintily picked from the leaves and twigs. Aphids are largely eaten, and beetles, including weevils, while the young are often fed on the caterpillars of small moths. In April and May the male chases the female through the trees, flying very swiftly, the lighter underparts flashing as they turn and dodge. In display he will droop his wings and puff out his feathers, or clinging to a twig or stem, gently fan his open wings, frequently one wing at a time; during this performance he usually sings, and then with tail raised and expanded, and with quivering wings slightly uplifted, floats obliquely towards his mate.

The nest is partly domed and usually built on the ground, distinguishing it from the normal nest of the Chiffchaff, which is above the ground, but in both species there is individual variation, and a Willow Warbler's nest at a height above ground is not uncommon. Grass is the usual material, but moss and dead bracken are sometimes added; a nest so constructed is hidden in the winter litter before the 'crosiers' have unfolded, and when the fronds unfold it is almost impossible to find. When disturbed the bird usually flies straight off and occasionally feigns injury. As a rule, long before the nest is reached, one or both birds begin plaintive notes of anxiety. The six to eight eggs are laid in May; they are white blotched with red, rather like the eggs of tits, and with paler markings than those of the Chiffchaff. A second brood is sometimes reared. Emigration begins in August, but the majority leave during September.

The upper parts in spring are yellowish-olive, yellowest on the eye-stripe and rump; the wings are browner, the feathers margined with greenish-yellow. The underparts are yellowish-white, the colour deepest on the flanks, and the axillaries are distinctly yellow. The bill and legs are brown; the legs are much paler than those of the Chiffchaff. After the autumn moult the birds are yellower, whilst the young are still more yellow. In the Willow Warbler the first to fifth primaries are emarginate; in the Chiffchaff the sixth is included. Length, 4·25 in. Wing, 2·5 in. Tarsus, 0·7 in. (*Plates 136, 138 and 176.*)

### Greenish Warbler                                        *Phylloscopus trochiloides*

The Greenish Warbler is a summer visitor to north-east Europe, where it has recently expanded its range, and to northern Asia. It was only recorded once in the British Isles before 1945, but thirty-eight times between 1958 and 1967. The great majority of records have been in autumn, though it has occurred in winter, spring and early summer. Most occurrences have been on the east coast of England or on Fair Isle, Scilly or Cape Clear. The Greenish Warbler closely resembles the Chiffchaff and Willow Warbler, but has less yellow underparts, a short whitish wing-bar and a more marked pale superciliary stripe. This stripe, however, is less pronounced than in the Arctic Warbler, which has greener upper parts. The legs are dark grey-brown. Length, 4·25 in.

### Chiffchaff                                              *Phylloscopus collybita*

The Chiffchaff breeds throughout the greater part of Europe and winters in south and west Europe and north Africa. It is widely but unevenly distributed throughout England, Wales and Ireland. In Scotland it breeds locally in the south, but north of Perthshire is known only as a passage migrant, chiefly on the east coast. Some birds usually spend the winter in the British Isles, chiefly in south-west England or Ireland, but occasionally also in the north.

The Chiffchaff closely resembles the Willow Warbler, except in its song. It is a little browner, its eye-stripe rather fainter and its legs usually noticeably darker, but none of these distinctions is easy to detect in the field. In the hand it can be identified by the wing formula, as explained in the description below.

About the middle of March, not long after the Wheatear and about the same time as the Sand Martin, the Chiffchaff reaches the south coast, one of the pioneer summer birds; in mild springs it reaches the northern counties of England before the end of the month, some days, often over a week, before the Willow Warbler. It sings more from the tree-tops than that bird, but is less arboreal than the Wood Warbler; when the weather is cold, however, it is first heard from the undergrowth. The song is simple, a deliberate, throbbing repetition of two or, some say, three notes, from which it gets its name. It is a steady pulsating song, neither particularly sweet nor harsh, rather suggestive of the throb of a stationary engine. Certainly some of the very early reports of its song are due to confusion with the Great Tit, but the notes of that bird are more varied in tone and usually rapidly repeated. Rarely, there is a secondary song, an interlude between snatches of ordinary song: a low, deep *chif, chif, chif*, quite distinct in tone, followed by the ordinary notes. Occasionally a male utters a sweet little warble, suggestive of a feeble Willow Warbler. The plaintive call, *hoo-it*, is like that of the Willow Warbler. The song continues, with a short pause in individuals during moult, until the birds leave in October. The majority, no doubt, go south before this month, but the song may be heard from passing birds late in September and in October. These autumn birds slowly travel south, feeding as they go, visiting spots far removed from their woodland haunts.

The insect food largely consists of aphids, small larvae and spiders, picked from the leaves and twigs, and flies are cleverly caught on the wing. The typical Chiffchaff habitat in most parts of Britain is a wood with some tall trees and plentiful undergrowth, but in Cornwall and parts of Ireland the birds are found commonly in low scrub. When the nesting site is selected the male Chiffchaff jealously guards it, driving away other birds larger and more powerful than itself.

Normally the domed nest is above the ground, but the height varies from a few inches to many feet; it is built in herbage, bushes, heaps of hedge-cuttings, the litter which collects on the branches of conifers, in evergreens or trees. Dead leaves, moss and grass are used, and the lining is of rootlets, grass and a profusion of feathers. The five to seven eggs, laid early in May, are smaller than those of the Willow Warbler, and are white, thinly spotted with purple or dark brown. Second broods are recorded in the south, but one appears to be normal in the north. The hen alone builds the nest and incubates the eggs.

The olive-green upper parts, yellowish on the rump, and white underparts, tinged grey on the breast and suffused with yellow, closely resemble the plumage of the Willow Warbler. The superciliary stripe is whitish and short; the axillaries are yellow. There are two moults, that in spring being often incomplete, but the autumn plumage varies little from that of spring. The bill is brown; the legs so dark as to look black in the field. In the young the upper parts are browner, the under more yellow and the breast is duller. In the hand the birds can be distinguished by the wing formula, apart from the emargination of the sixth primary; the second primary is shorter than the sixth; in the Willow Warbler it is equal to or longer than the sixth. Length, 4·25 in. Wing, 2·35 in. Tarsus, 0·8 in. (*Plates 138 and 176.*)

## Wood Warbler                                        *Phylloscopus sibilatrix*

As a summer resident the Wood Warbler or Wood Wren comes late and departs early, reaching the south about the middle of April, but seldom generally distributed before May. It occurs in suitable woodlands in most parts of Great Britain, but is absent from the extreme north of Scotland and the Scottish islands, except as a passage migrant, and it does not breed regularly in Ireland. In recent years there has been a marked decrease in many parts of England. It is found throughout most of Europe, except the extreme north and south, and winters in Africa.

Of our three native leaf-warblers this is the most arboreal and, from the nature of its haunts, the most local; it delights in the more open woodlands and parks, where oaks and beeches predominate and undergrowth is sparse, and in hilly districts occurs far up the slopes of wooded valleys, even where beeches are absent and oaks and birches stunted. It is larger, more slender and graceful than the dainty Willow Warbler and Chiffchaff; its longer, more pointed wings make flight and actions deliberate but easy. Added to this, the bright yellow throat and breast and white belly prevent confusion with its congeners. The young foliage is well advanced when the Wood Warbler reaches its haunts, and the greenish-yellow dress blends with the leaves; it is seldom detected until it begins its distinctive shivering song. Hudson describes this as a 'long passionate trill—the woodland sound which is like no other'; there are a few preliminary notes which glide into a rapid, descending, silvery shiver, certainly like no other in tone unless it be the more deliberate song of the Blue Tit, but, from the way its whole body, wings and tail vibrate as it sings, suggestive of the vehemence of the energetic Wren. Every few moments the song is repeated as the bird flits from branch to branch and, as it crosses to a fresh tree, the opening notes may be sounded on the wing, but the trill when it has regained a perch. An alternative song, less frequently used but by no means uncommon, consists of a liquid *piu* repeated up to a dozen times or more. The most assiduous singers are unmated cocks, which seem to be exceptionally numerous in this species. Between the snatches it is not idle; now it sails out and intercepts a passing fly, now poises in the air with rapidly whirring wings as it neatly picks an insect from the underside of a leaf, now pauses to utter its clear mellow call. The alarm is a plaintive *pee-oo.*

It is almost safe to say that the nest is always on the ground unless it is in the ground, for a hollow or depression is often utilised; a favourite spot is the slope of a bracken-covered bank, where it is wonderfully hidden by the spreading fronds. Domed like that of its relatives, it is built of dry grass, withered leaves and moss, and lined with finer bents and hair, but seldom if ever with feathers. The male, who at times helps to build, indulges in graceful nuptial flights, sailing with wide expanded wings and tail, the former quivering as he descends in a slight spiral. The five or six eggs are not often laid before the middle of May; they are larger than those of the Willow Warbler and are thickly speckled, often forming a zone, with darker, more purplish, red and violet. Early in July the song ceases, and, though the presence of the bird is difficult to detect when it is silent amongst the full summer leafage, the majority appear to leave before the beginning of September.

The plumage above is yellowish-green; beneath, white with a marked sulphur-yellow suffusion on the throat and breast, thighs and axillaries. The broad sulphur-yellow eye-stripe, reaching to the nape, and the edgings to the feathers of the wings are very noticeable. The bill and legs are brown. The juvenile is yellower than the adult. Length, 5·2 in. Wing, 3·1 in. Tarsus, 0·7 in. (*Plates 134 and 176.*)

**Bonelli's Warbler**                                              *Phylloscopus bonelli*
This bird is a summer visitor to the south and west of Europe and has recently extended its range northward in France and Germany. Although it was not recorded in the British Isles until 1948, one or two are now seen in autumn most years, chiefly in the south of England. Bonelli's is more grey and white than the other leaf-warblers. Yellow at the carpal joint and on the wing and rump contrasts with the otherwise greyish upper parts and pale grey head. Length, 4·5 in.

**Arctic Warbler**                                                  *Phylloscopus borealis*
The Arctic Warbler is a summer visitor to northern Europe and Siberia and winters in south-east Asia. Recently one or two have been recorded almost annually in the British Isles, chiefly on the east coast and on Fair Isle in autumn. This is a large active leaf-warbler, bigger than a Chiffchaff and further distinguished by a conspicuous pale yellow superciliary stripe and a dark mark through the eye. The upper parts are greyish-green and usually show a narrow whitish wing-bar. The legs are pale yellowish. Length, 4·7 in.

**Yellow-browed Warbler**                                      *Phylloscopus inornatus*
Systematic study of migrants at the Scottish lighthouses and on northern islands proves that the Yellow-browed Warbler is a regular autumn visitor and bird of passage. It has also occurred not infrequently on the east coast of England and the Scilly Islands, as well as in Ireland, and it has occasionally been noticed in spring in England and Scotland. Its home is Siberia, where several ornithologists have referred to its song. Miss Haviland says that on the Yenesei, 'its little monotonous song tinkled on without ceasing from every bush'. Its normal winter quarters are India and south-eastern Asia.

Its size, simple song and double lemon-yellow wing-bars rather suggest a Goldcrest, but it is a typical leaf-warbler, olive-green and yellowish-white; its salient character is the long yellowish eye-stripe, extending from the base of the bill to the nape, with a darker line through the eye. There is a faint lighter streak down the centre of the olive crown. Length, 3·8 in. (*Plate 134.*)

**Pallas's Warbler** *Phylloscopus proregulus*

This vagrant from southern Siberia was recorded in the British Isles only once before 1951, but there were twenty occurrences between that date and 1967, all at stations on the east and south coasts, from Shetland to Scilly, in late autumn. Its small size and habit of hovering are reminiscent of the Firecrest. It is distinguished from the Yellow-browed Warbler by its greener upper parts, broad yellow stripe on the crown enclosed by dark bands, yellow forehead and eye-stripe, double yellow (not whitish) wing-bar and yellow rump. Length, 3·7 in.

**Radde's Bush Warbler** *Phylloscopus schwarzi*

There have been seven British records of this summer visitor to southern Siberia, all in October. It resembles the Dusky Warbler in its generally brown and white rather than greenish colouring, but has a stouter bill and legs. It has olive-brown upper and creamy-white underparts, a blackish streak from the bill through the eye, and a long creamy superciliary stripe. Length, 5 in.

## Family REGULIDAE Goldcrests or Kinglets

**Goldcrest** *Regulus regulus*

Although the Goldcrest suffers severe losses in exceptionally hard winters its numbers usually recover within two or three years, and normally it is an abundant breeding bird in all parts of the British Isles except the extreme north. It is found in most parts of Europe and many migrants reach us in autumn, while some of our native birds move south.

The long oversea migration of the smallest European bird has always caused wonder, but there is only a slight difference between its size and weight and that of many warblers, and an aerial journey on a suitable air-current requires little extra exertion. At times it meets with difficulties, adverse winds, and comes down exhausted, while many perish at sea.

The Goldcrest is an inhabitant of fir woods in summer, but in winter it wanders, joining with various tits and other birds; Coward saw fifty or more Goldcrests feeding in the heather on a Welsh hillside in January. Immigrants reach the east coast, sometimes in immense numbers, in September and October. At all times the Goldcrest is indifferent to the presence of man, but these newly arrived birds, even when showing no sign of fatigue, slip amongst the marram grass and buckthorn at one's very feet. When feeding, the Goldcrest calls continuously a shrill, penetrating, though not loud *si, si, si*, and the simple song, the repetition of two notes, is high pitched, but by no means inaudible. One variation of the song of the Coal Tit is not unlike it, though in a lower key and louder. The song may be heard in winter as well as summer. The actions are those of a warbler rather than a tit, though occasionally it will

PLATE 146
*Above :* Blue-headed Wagtail, p319
*Below :* Starling (winter),
   p323

*Above :* Grey Wagtail, p317
*Below :* Rose-coloured Starling,
   p325

PLATE 147
Red-backed
Shrike, p322

Photo : Eric Hosking

Photo: *J. B. and S. Bottomley*

PLATE 148　　Greenfinch, p326

PLATE 149
*Above* : Woodchat Shrike, p321
*Below* : Great Grey Shrike, p320

*Above* : Waxwing, p319
*Below* : Red-backed Shrike, p322

PLATE 150
*Above:* Hawfinch, p325
*Below:* Siskin, p329

*Above:* Goldfinch, p328
Below: Serin, p333

PLATE 151
Twite, p330

PLATE 152
Crossbill, p334

Photo : Eric Hosking

**PLATE 153**
*Above :* Linnet, p329
*Below :* Mealy Redpoll, p331

*Above :* Twite, p330
*Below :* Lesser Redpoll, p331

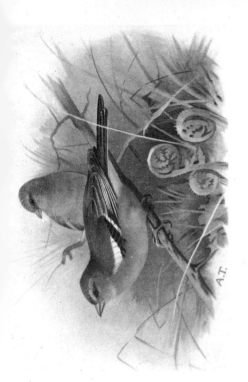

PLATE 154

*Above left :*
Bullfinch, p333
*Above right :*
Chaffinch, p335

*Below left :*
Crossbill, p334
*Below right :*
Brambling, p337

PLATE 155
Bullfinch, p333

PLATE 156
Yellowhammer
(female), p338

Photo:
J. B. and S. Bottomley

PLATE 157

*Above left :* Greenfinch, p326
*Above right :* Lapland Bunting, p343
*Right :* Snow Bunting (winter), p344

PLATE 158
*Above :* Ortolan Bunting, p341
*Below :* Corn Bunting, p339

*Above :* Cirl Bunting, p340
*Below :* Yellowhammer, p338

PLATE 159     Brambling (female), p337

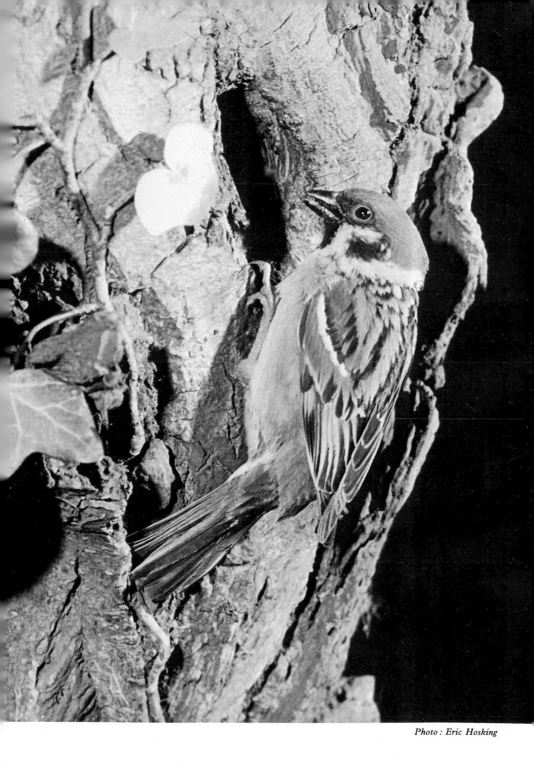

PLATE 160    Tree Sparrow, p347

PLATE 161

*Above :* Reed Bunting, p342
*Below :* House Sparrow, p345

*Above :* Little Bunting, p342
*Below :* Tree Sparrow, p347

hang beneath a leaf-stalk or branch; as a rule it flies gracefully from twig to twig, craning its neck and carefully examining every bud or leaf, but spending only a moment at each; in winter it feeds in the bare hedgerows and visits gardens. The insects captured are often small; it feeds freely on the 'American blight' on fruit trees, and other aphids are taken. The male, when displaying, droops his wings, puffs out his feathers, and expands the feathers bordering the crest so as to expose to the view of the hen the orange-yellow central streak.

The nest is a wonderfully neat hammock of moss, lichens and cobwebs, suspended beneath a branch of a conifer, usually with the moss wound round needles or twigs. It may be but a foot or two above the ground, or high in the branches of a tall fir; occasionally it is built in other situations, such as ivy or a furze bush. Feathers are largely used for the lining, and in these the tiny eggs are almost buried; these are often seven or eight, but ten or more are found at times. They are laid in April or May, and a second brood is not unusual. In colour they are buffish-white with minute reddish spots, which may form a zone towards the larger end.

The Goldcrest is olive-green above and creamy-buff beneath. The forehead, chin and throat are buff, and a black line from the forehead passes on either side of the chrome-yellow crest, the posterior portion of which, in the male, is deep chrome or orange. The wing has two white bars and a dark band. The bill and legs are brown. The young are duller in colour and have no yellow in the crest. Length, 3·5 in. Wing, 2·1 in. Tarsus, 0·7 in. (*Plates 138, 139 and 176.*)

## Firecrest                                                      *Regulus ignicapillus*

The Firecrest nests in Europe as far north as the Baltic and occurs in eastern and southern England with some degree of regularity; it is a winter visitor, arriving with the immigrant Goldcrests and often joining them in their nomadic rambles. North of Yorkshire it is only an occasional straggler; it has very rarely occurred in Ireland. Successful breeding was proved in the New Forest at least twice in the 1960s. No doubt owing to its similarity to the Goldcrest, it is often overlooked, but some observers are misled by the difference in the crest of the male and female Goldcrest and imagine that the orange on the former is the 'fire'. The most obvious distinguishing features are the white superciliary streak and the dark mark through the eye. Its call resembles that of the Goldcrest, but is lower in pitch. Its habitat preference is more catholic than the Goldcrest's, and it is often found in low undergrowth, bracken and marshy ground as well as in coniferous and deciduous woods. The nest is much like the Goldcrest's.

The adult is green on the upper parts, whitish below, with a bronze patch at the side of the neck; the wing has two white bars and one dark one. The male has an orange crown, bordered by black, the female's is lemon-yellow and the juvenile's green. All have a white stripe over the eye and a dark mark through it, dividing the whitish face. Length, 3·5 in. Wing, 2·1 in. Tarsus, 0·7 in. (*Plate 138.*)

## Family MUSCICAPIDAE Flycatchers

**Spotted Flycatcher** *Muscicapa striata*

The Spotted Flycatcher is one of the last of the summer visitors to arrive in Britain; it is often absent until early May. Except in the extreme north, it breeds throughout Europe and in north-west Africa; its known winter quarters extend as far south as Natal. In the British Isles it is well distributed, nowhere abundant, but, except in some of the northern islands and parts of Ireland, is nowhere uncommon. In the Orkneys, where it has bred, and Shetlands it is mainly a bird of passage.

Many birds capture flying insects, but none so adroitly as the Spotted Flycatcher. Its grey-brown plumage is inconspicuous and it is not really spotted; it is, too, a silent bird, yet its neat upright figure, perched on post, railing or dead branch, is noticeable. Its short aerial sallies attract the eye; sometimes it swoops obliquely with unerring aim upon some insect flying below, but usually, after many smart twists and turns, it cuts short the career of a dodger. Then, as a rule, it returns to its observation post, though often it will have two look-outs to which it flies in turn. On the wing it is a spry little bird, but when perched has an air of studied indifference; it is not the watchful sentinel like the Shrike. Yet little escapes its bright eye; its flights are timed with such precision that it seldom misses its quarry. Naturally the look-out is best where the space in front is open; thus the Flycatcher frequents the border of a lawn, the outskirts of a wood or edge of a clearing, or the branches of willow or alder overhanging a stream. The call *zit* or *zit-chic* is not loud, but is more frequently noticed than the slight low song in May and June, a few repeated soft notes. It is often stated, on the strength of habits observed abroad, that berries are sometimes eaten, but in England all its time is occupied flycatching. Butterflies, moths, beetles and aphids are taken, but most of its captures are two-winged dipterous flies. Bees and wasps are frequently taken.

For a nesting site the Spotted Flycatcher shows preference for buildings— dwelling houses and outhouses, and it will often return again and again to a favourite site in spite of repeated discouragement. The ledge or moulding of a window, the end of a projecting beam, a hole in a wall, trellis-work or creepers are all favoured, but in the woods it will nest in ivy or a cleft in a tree. Old nests of other species are frequently made use of, sometimes immediately the late occupants have flown; as a rule a slight lining of hair, grass or feathers is added. The remains of a Swallow's nest on a beam is not infrequently transformed. The nest itself is slight and usually loosely put together; it is composed of grass, moss and wool, interwoven with cobwebs. The four to five eggs, dull white with reddish spots and blotches, are seldom laid before the beginning of June; second broods are sometimes reared, but are not regular. By the end of September most of the birds have gone.

The upper parts of the adult bird are hair-brown with darker brown stripes on the crown; the underparts are greyish-white, but the flanks and breast are sandy-brown, and on the latter there are noticeable striations. The bill is brown, the legs black, and the irides dark brown. The young are more deserving of the title spotted, for their backs are mottled with buff. Length, 5·8 in. Wing, 3·4 in. Tarsus, 0·55 in. (*Plates 140, 141 and 176*.)

## Pied Flycatcher                                                    *Ficedula hypoleuca*

The Pied Flycatcher is a local summer resident in Great Britain and a regular passage migrant, often numerous in autumn on the east coast. It breeds in hill country in Wales, the north of England and the south of Scotland, and very locally in other areas. In parts of Wales and the central Lake District it is abundant. There was a general increase in numbers and some extension of range between 1940 and 1952, but this process seems to have been halted in recent years, although provision of nest-boxes can still produce local increases. In Ireland it is only known as an occasional passage migrant. It is widely distributed in summer in northern and central Europe and winters in Africa.

The male Pied Flycatcher arrives some days before the female, usually late in April or early in May, and being conspicuously black and white, is often noticed in places remote from its breeding haunts. Judging, however, from the date of first appearance in the south compared with its passage and arrival further north, the journey is rapidly performed; it may stop to feed for a few hours, but soon passes on. The conspicuous black and white cock in spring is unmistakable, but the mousy-coloured female, the male in autumn and the juvenile are much less distinctive. However, they differ from the Spotted Flycatcher in build and in showing a whitish wing-bar and outer tail feathers in flight. It is a smaller, stouter-built bird than the Spotted Flycatcher, and its attitude when perched is less erect; its movements are quicker and more tit-like, and its tail is constantly in motion, at times jerked upwards, but often more deliberately swayed up and down. It has a sharp, rather metallic call and a lively little song, frequently uttered. Saunders renders this as *tzit, tzit, tzit, trui, trui, trui*. The song is seldom heard after June. The predatory efforts on the wing fall short of those of the commoner bird, and it frequently drops from its perch to pick insects from the herbage; indeed it depends less upon flying game than on caterpillars and beetles. Though less silent than the Spotted Flycatcher, it is not demonstrative; it will drop again and again and return to the tree, though seldom to the same perch, without uttering a note. The alarm is not unlike that of its relative, but a chaffinch-like *whit* is also often heard. The males go straight to the old haunts, often to the old nesting hole. The characteristic breeding habitat is a hillside oakwood, but it also nests in gardens or scattered deciduous trees of any kind.

The nest is occasionally found in masonry, but a hole in a tree or stump is the usual site; the entrance is small except when the old hole of a Woodpecker is used. Nest-boxes are often occupied. The nest is often, but certainly not always, near running water. The nesting material, dead leaves, moss and strips of honeysuckle bark, with a lining of bents and hair, is loosely interwoven. Five to eight pale blue eggs are laid in the latter half of May or early in June. Both old and young disappear from their nesting haunts as soon as the latter are fledged. Early in August some of the birds are moving south and migration continues through September.

There are two moults; that in early spring being partial, but altering the bird's appearance considerably. The male in summer is black on the upper parts, with the forehead, border of the tail, a large but variable patch on the wing and the whole of the underparts white. The bill and legs are black. The parts black in the male are olive-brown in the female; she has no white on the forehead, and the patch on the wing is smaller; her underparts are less pure and are tinged with buff on the breast and flanks and slightly spotted with brown. After the autumn moult the sexes are similar, dark brown replacing the black of the male; his white spots are partly obscured and the underparts are suffused with buff. The young have the upper parts mottled with buff. Length, 4·7 in. Wing, 3·1 in. Tarsus, 0·6 in. (*Plates 141, 143 and 176*.)

### Collared Flycatcher                                    *Ficedula albicollis*

A summer visitor to parts of southern and central Europe, the Collared Flycatcher has been recorded five times in the British Isles. In spring the male is distinguished from the Pied Flycatcher by a white collar, whitish rump and more extensive white on the wing; in autumn the black is replaced by brown and the white on collar and wings is reduced. The female resembles the female Pied Flycatcher, but has greyer upper parts and may show traces of the white collar. Length, 5 in.

### Red-breasted Flycatcher                                  *Ficedula parva*

The Red-breasted Flycatcher breeds in central Europe from Denmark eastward into western Siberia, and is known to winter in India.

This neat little Flycatcher, with, in the male, a ruddy breast and brown back suggesting a small Robin with white in its tail, has been observed most frequently on the east and south coasts from the Shetlands to the Scilly Islands; it also reaches the lights on the Irish coast, so that it may be concluded that there is a west as well as east coast passage. The alarm note of the Red-breasted Flycatcher is *pink, pink*, suggesting the call of the Chaffinch.

The adult male is ashy-brown on the crown and back, bluish-grey on the face and neck, warm orange on the chin and throat, and the rest of the underparts shading from buff to white. The bill is brown and the legs black. The female (upper bird, *Plate 141*) has no slate or orange, and her underparts are whiter, tinged with buff. The white tail-patches are a most distinctive feature. Length, 4·5 in.

## Family PRUNELLIDAE Accentors

### Dunnock or Hedge Sparrow                               *Prunella modularis*

The Dunnock or Hedge Sparrow is a resident and partial migrant in most parts of Europe, including the British Isles. Although the majority of British birds are strictly sedentary there is some southward movement in autumn, chiefly noticed on the east coast, and some migration is also usually observed in spring.

Though it is described as peaceful, inoffensive, shy, inconspicuous and quiet, the name 'sparrow' proves that it is familiar. In build, thin bill and habits, as well as structure, it has nothing in common with the Sparrow, though in the garden in winter it joins this and other mendicants. It is common in the hedgerows, roadside spinneys, farmyards and gardens, in juniper scrub high up on mountainsides and even on bare hillsides and islands. Its sombre browns, its well-streaked back and slate-grey head give it some protection as it rootles among autumnal litter at the hedge foot. Largely a ground feeder, it disappears under the cabbage leaves or other protective shelter, not to hide but because beneath their shade it finds food. To call it quiet and peaceful is even further from the mark. The short, musical, high-pitched song, constantly repeated, is not commanding but insistent. Though most vigorous in spring it may be heard at almost all seasons, and at night as well as by day. Excitement provokes the vocal energies; it will sing vigorously at a rival, and if its slumbers are disturbed wakes with a snatch of melody. The call, a monotonous shrill piping *peep*, betrays the presence of the 'shy, quiet' bird everywhere and at all seasons. In winter it jerks, with fussy little flicks of its wings, through the hedge-bottoms, now in the lower twigs, now peering under the fallen leaves on the ground, piping perpetual remarks. In December, when courtship begins, the note gains vehemence as it fights furiously with a rival, or flits with flicking wing, and tail sawed up and down, after the hen. The flirts become a shiver as it leaps or flits from twig to twig, often rising to the top of a hedge or tree, but on the ground, when feeding, it hops. The hop differs from that of many other birds; the Dunnock makes short jerky jumps forward, but the breast is held low and the legs are bent, one foot in advance of the other.

Insects, spiders and other small invertebrates are sought for in the fallen leaves, lurking in moss or clinging to the twigs, but the Dunnock is not good at aerial fly-catching. When the laburnum-moth larvae or the caterpillars of the oak tortrix hang by threads from the trees, Blue Tits, Willow Warblers and Robins hover and snatch them in the air, but the Dunnock shuffles along the ground in search of those that have dropped. Weevils and other destructive beetles, hiding under dead plants, are discovered, and in winter many seeds, chiefly of weeds, are eaten.

A hedge, evergreen, bush, faggot-stack or bank is a usual situation for the nest, but many other sites are selected, including dead bracken and bilberry scrub. On a slight foundation of twigs a neat nest of grass and moss is constructed, lined with hair or wool. Four or five clear blue eggs, blue as a summer sky, are laid in March or April, and two or more broods are reared. The female builds the nest and incubates the eggs, which are sometimes covered by the nest lining before incubation begins. The Cuckoo is said to prefer the Hedge Sparrow for a foster-parent for its young, but in the north of England the Tree or Meadow Pipit, Wagtail or Robin are more favoured.

The colour of the adult is rufous-brown with dark brown streaks; the head, throat and breast are slate-grey; the bill and legs are brown. The young are browner and more spotted, and they have no slate on the head. Length, 5·8 in. Wing, 2·8 in. Tarsus, 0·8 in. (*Plates 142 and 175.*)

## Alpine Accentor                                      *Prunella collaris*

The Alpine Accentor is a bird of the high mountains of central and southern Europe, and closely allied forms occur in Asia. It is not looked upon as a regular migrant, but winter forces it from the high altitudes and it wanders, appearing in various parts of Europe. It has occurred over thirty times in Britain, from Cornwall to Fair Isle. Its actions are similar to those of the Dunnock; it has the same 'creeping' hop, and the song and call-note have a distinct family relationship. It may be distinguished from the Dunnock by its speckled throat, two white wing-bars and rich chestnut flanks, as well as by its greater size. Length, 7 in. (*Plate 145.*)

## Family MOTACILLIDAE Pipits and Wagtails

## Meadow Pipit                                          *Anthus pratensis*

Though a regular migrant and an abundant summer visitor the Meadow Pipit is also a resident, for many remain all winter in the British Isles. Large numbers of winter visitors and birds of passage arrive from various parts of Europe and from Iceland in autumn, when our birds are leaving the south coast. The range abroad extends across northern and central Europe, and the winter quarters are in southern Europe and Africa. Emigrants leave from September until the end of November, and the first returning birds are noted in February. More birds travel northward along the west coast and through western counties than by the eastern route. Passage birds continue to be noticeable until the middle of April, travelling with various wagtails and Reed Buntings, and roosting with them in reed-beds, though in their moorland haunts they sleep on the ground. As a rule the resident birds leave the high moors and mountains in autumn and return early in the year. Some residents return to the moors in early February before the migrants have arrived; other British-bred birds undoubtedly go abroad, since many ringed examples have been recovered.

The Meadow Pipit or Titlark is the most abundant upland bird, nesting on the highest moors and mountain slopes, where on a warm spring day dozens may be seen fluttering up from the heather for their short nuptial flight, and the air is full of their trilling songs, quick repetitions of sharp notes, as they ascend and float down with outspread pinions. The songs are less frequent than the alarm notes, *peep, peep, peep,* of the anxious parents when the safety of the nest is threatened; the birds flit before the intruder, settling on the rocks or heather and calling persistently; the flight, jerky rather than undulating, is only for a few yards. In his anxiety the cock betrays the presence of the nest, but the hen is a close sitter and leaves reluctantly. When migrating the flocks are often very large and remain for days in suitable feeding grounds. Many hundreds frequent the sewage farms of large towns, roosting in osiers and feeding by day on the mud of empty tanks. Salt marshes are resorted to, and when these are flooded by spring tides the birds follow the receding water, apparently feeding on marine worms, Crustacea or small molluscs. Many winter on the sewage farms, but in reduced numbers; indeed the winter flocks are small.

A favourite winter haunt is the rushy margin of a large sheet of water, where the birds, if disturbed, rise one after the other with the characteristic *peep*. Severe weather drives them to the stack-yards, for at this season the bird is nomadic. Though said to perch but little, feeding birds will take to the trees if alarmed, but often the whole flock flies to and fro aimlessly, each bird apparently striving to jerk itself higher, though the elevation of the party does not alter; after undecided sallies right and left the flock returns whence it rose. On the ground it runs or walks, but the actions, both of head and tail, are more jerky and less graceful than those of a wagtail.

The nest is built on the ground, well concealed in the roots of heather, a bunch of rushes, beneath an arch of rough grass, or in marram on the sand-hills. It is built of the nearest grasses to be found, and lined with finer bents and hair, the cup being small and neat. The first eggs are laid in April, but second or late clutches may be found in August. The eggs are five or six in number, and a common type is dark reddish-brown, closely speckled and with one or two hair-lines. No bird more frequently tends the young Cuckoo. On the moors and sand dunes the Cuckoo is usually mobbed by a pair of Meadow Pipits, which follow it with constant cries, and alight near it when it settles.

After the spring moult the plumage is olive-brown above and almost white below, streaked as in the Tree Pipit, but the back is more olive and the breast whiter. The outer tail feathers are white. The colour in winter appears to be darker and distinctly greener above, but there is much individual variation at all seasons. Juveniles are strongly marked on the back and yellowish on the underparts. Length, 5·75 in. Wing, 3·2 in. Tarsus, 0·85 in. (*Plates 142, 144 and 176.*)

## Richard's Pipit                                        *Anthus novaeseelandiae*

The breeding range of Richard's Pipit is Asiatic, but it has frequently travelled westward and occurs almost annually in Shetland or on our south and east coasts. It has also reached Wales and Ireland. It is a large, long-legged pipit, noticeable by its size and height from the ground; the hind claw is exceptionally long. It is slightly larger and more erect in stance than the Tawny Pipit and has a shorter bill; its call is said to be harsher and louder. The upper parts are brown with darker striations, the breast buff with a few bold streaks. Length, 7 in. Tarsus, 1·2 in.

### Tawny Pipit *Anthus campestris*

The Tawny Pipit is a European and north African bird which winters in tropical Africa. On autumn migration it occurs annually in the British Isles, chiefly on our east and south coasts, but there are also several records for Ireland and a few spring occurrences. It is a bird of the sandy wastes, and is sandy-brown or tawny in general colour, tinged with grey and lightly streaked on the back but with few or no markings on the buffish-white breast, throat and flanks. It has a noticeable pale eye-stripe. The young in autumn have streaks on breast and back and are not easy to distinguish in the field from Richard's Pipits. Length, 6·5 in. Tarsus, 1·1 in.

### Tree Pipit *Anthus trivialis*

The brown plumaged pipits, closely allied to the wagtails, are, as far as the rarer species are concerned, a very puzzling group, but the three familiar kinds can be distinguished by their habits, voices and the length and shape of the claw on the hind toe. The Tree Pipit is a regular and well-distributed summer visitor and bird of passage to and from northern Europe. It breeds in northern and central Europe, and winters from the Mediterranean basin to far south in Africa. In Great Britain, except in treeless areas, the Tree Pipit is a common bird, but in Ireland it is only known as a scarce visitor on passage.

Thick woods do not attract the Tree Pipit, but parks, the outskirts of woods or hillsides where there is plenty of timber are favourite haunts. On the bare hills and moorlands the Meadow Pipit replaces it, but the Tree Pipit nests at over 1000 ft. in open oakwoods or among scattered trees on a mountainside, and it is, in fact, one of the most characteristic breeding birds of the Lake District and north and central Wales. In general appearance the two are much alike, but the Tree is larger, and has a much shorter and more curved hind claw, well suited for its arboreal habits. One of our later migrants, it seldom reaches England before the first week of April, and, travelling slowly, is often unnoticed in the north until the third or last week; the rush is frequently in the first week of May, when its arrival is heralded by its characteristic flight and song. Both Tree and Meadow Pipit have a shuttlecock flight, mounting up rapidly for 20 ft. or more, trilling gaily, then, after a few moments of hovering flight, descending, still singing, with wings and tail outspread. But whereas the Meadow Pipit makes these aerial excursions from the ground and returns to the ground, the Tree Pipit starts from the topmost branches of a tree and usually descends to the same perch. The song of the Tree is far superior to that of the Meadow and ends with a number of deliberately repeated rather plaintive notes, *see-er, see-er, see-er*, the last of which are often uttered after the bird has settled. The song period usually ends about the middle of July; by the end of September most of the birds have departed. The alarm note, an anxious *peet*, is uttered continually when the neighbourhood of the nest is invaded. Like other pipits, it is insectivorous, though seed is occasionally eaten.

The nest, always on the ground, is often concealed under dead bracken or other vegetation, and is seldom far from a tree, from which the male soars singing at intervals until the young are hatched. It is built of grasses and lined with finer bents, and the eggs are laid, as a rule, early in May. The four to six eggs are subject to great variation, but may be grouped into three or four types, ranging from pale grounds with a few dark mottles to dark brown or red grounds thickly marbled or speckled with reds or purples.

In summer adults are light brown, striated with darker brown on the head, back, mantle, breast and flanks, but not on the rump; on the underparts the brown shades from yellowish on the breast to impure white on the belly. The outer tail feathers are white. From the brown bill a dark moustachial streak borders the unstriated throat. The legs are pinkish-brown. After the autumn moult the colours are richer and buffer. Young birds are buffer above and below, and the streaks on the back are more pronounced. Length, 6 in. Wing, 3·42 in. Tarsus, 0·8 in. (*Plates 142 and 176*.)

## Petchora Pipit                                             *Anthus gustavi*

This northern Russian and Siberian species has been recorded on Fair Isle sixteen times and on Spurn Head once, in each case in autumn. Its plumage pattern is similar to the Tree Pipit's, but two pale streaks show on the back and the outer tail feathers are buffish, not white. The breast and rump are boldly streaked. The call, a hard *pwit*, is said to be distinctive. Length, 5·8 in.

## Red-throated Pipit                                         *Anthus cervinus*

The Red-throated Pipit, which breeds in north-east Europe and Siberia, now occurs in Great Britain, from Shetland to Scilly, almost annually, and there are several records for Ireland. It has appeared as often in spring as in autumn. This bird closely resembles the Meadow Pipit, but its calls, described as a hoarse *tzeez* and a soft *teu*, are distinctive, and the chin and throat are reddish-chestnut in summer—at most they are tinged with pink in the Meadow Pipit— while the eye-stripe is better defined and is rufous-buff. It has darker upper parts than the commoner bird and a boldly streaked rump. Length, 5 in.

## Rock Pipit                                           *Anthus spinoletta petrosus*
## Water Pipit                                        *Anthus spinoletta spinoletta*

The Rock Pipit and Water Pipit are fairly distinctive geographical races of the same species. The Rock Pipit is an entirely coastal subspecies, breeding on the shores of north-western Europe, while the Water Pipit is a native of the mountains of southern and central Europe.

The Water Pipit is a regular visitor to the south of England and has been not infrequently recorded elsewhere, including Ireland. It occurs as a spring and autumn passage migrant and as a winter visitor, frequenting watercress beds, reservoirs and sewage farms. It is a shy bird and flies off with a harsh monosyllabic call when approached. In the winter plumage, normally seen in Britain, the Water Pipit can be distinguished from the Rock Pipit by its whitish, not buff, underparts, its prominent white outer tail feathers, pale eye-stripe and greyish-brown, lightly streaked head and mantle. It differs from the Meadow Pipit in its unstreaked underparts, more upright stance, larger size and dark legs. In spring Water Pipits have greyish backs and pinkish underparts, and in this plumage could be confused with some specimens of the Scandinavian race of the Rock Pipit, which also occurs in the British Isles as a passage migrant, though normally only on or very near the coast.

On the rocky portions of our coastline the Rock Pipit is resident, and as numbers leave us in autumn and return in spring it is also a summer visitor.

In summer this coast-loving bird is never far from rocks, but in winter it wanders to mud-flats, sandy shores and estuaries. Whether at the foot of storm-beaten precipitous crags or on the tangle-covered rocks exposed at low tide it is equally at home, and on stacks and islets dwells amongst the waders and gulls. Indeed when it is feeding along the tide-line or on rocks over which the surf is rolling it frequently wades, running swiftly back from advancing waves. It flutters along the shore before us, with its short rather metallic call-note, *phist, phist*, corresponding to the *peep* from which the pipits get their name. When we have advanced too far it rises and after beating up into the wind with jerky, erratic flight, slips swiftly down wind and alights again to feed. It often dances above our heads, calling constantly, especially if the nest is not far away. When disturbed on the mud-flats it makes for some stone, wall or embankment, and if these are available chooses them for its resting place at high tide. Its song flight is similar to that of other pipits, a musical ascent and descent with open wings, and in quality the notes are intermediate between those of the Meadow and Tree, lacking the rich fullness of the latter. It feeds on insects, especially the numerous flies which settle on decaying weeds, and picks small molluscs from the rocks or crustaceans and worms from shallow pools. In its habits it more nearly approaches the shore-haunting waders than any 'land bird'.

The nest is seldom far above the reach of the tide and is often spray-splashed; it is sometimes on a bank, under a clump of thrift or other maritime plant, but more commonly in a hole or crack in the rock. It is neatly built of grass and frequently a little seaweed, and a nest may be entirely composed of dry weed; the lining is of fine grass, hair, or occasionally feathers. The bird nests late and eggs are seldom laid until May, but a second brood is often reared; the number is usually four or five, and they are closely speckled with grey or reddish spots, so densely indeed as often to form a zone of colour round the widest part or near the larger end. The female is a close sitter, but the over-anxious male betrays her presence by his continuous calls and fluttering flight.

The Rock Pipit is larger and has a longer bill than the Meadow Pipit, and the striations and spots on both upper and underparts are less distinct. In summer it is olive-brown, striated, except on the browner rump, on the upper parts, and there is an indistinct whitish-buff eye-streak. The outer tail feathers are marked with smoky-grey and not with white, which distinguishes the bird from the Water Pipit. The chin is whitish and the rest of the under-parts sandy-buff, slightly spotted on the breast and faintly streaked on the flanks. The bill is dark brown; the legs reddish-brown. The sexes are alike. The upper parts are greener and the under more suffused with yellow after the autumn moult. The young bird is more streaked and spotted than the adult in winter dress. (*Plates 142, 144 and 176*.)

The Scandinavian bird, *A. s. littoralis*, has a warmer, more vinous breast, and the spots on the underparts are often hardly perceptible. Length, 6·5 in. Wing, 3·5 in. Tarsus, 1 in.

### Pied Wagtail                               *Motacilla alba yarrellii*
### White Wagtail                              *Motacilla alba alba*

The Pied and White Wagtails are two geographical races of the same species. The males of the two subspecies are strikingly different in spring, as the back of the Pied is black from crown to tail, while the White has a pearly grey back and rump. The juveniles and the adults in autumn are less easily distinguished (*see* description). The Pied Wagtail is the native British bird, which also breeds in western France, Belgium and southern Norway. Numbers of our birds remain throughout the winter, but the majority migrate in autumn to winter on the Atlantic coasts of France and the Iberian peninsula. Others, especially in mild winters, only travel as far as the southern counties of England.

The White Wagtail has also nested occasionally in the British Isles, but it is normally known as a regular and sometimes abundant passage migrant, chiefly on the western side of Great Britain. It occurs on both east and west coasts of Ireland and breeds over the greater part of Europe. The largest numbers of passage migrants follow the coastline, but it is by no means un-common inland; birds are travelling north from late March to the end of May, and the return movement lasts from August to October. A few Whites often associate with migrating Yellow Wagtails and may linger for several days on the borders of lakes or on sewage farms.

Water Wagtail, and the more vernacular 'Dish-washer', are descriptive names, for the bird delights in water and loves to paddle in the shallows; many of the gnats and flies on which it feeds are aquatic. It is constantly to be seen on the bank of a river or stream, the sandy edge of a lake, the muddy margin of a pond, the settling tank in a sewage farm, or in the puddles on the road, running swiftly here and there, leaping into the air or taking a short flight in its hunt for the chironomid gnats or other small diptera which form the bulk of its food. The long tail is carried horizontally, clear of the mud or wet, and is constantly and rapidly though gracefully elevated and depressed; it is not 'wagged', if by that a lateral movement is implied. The presence of water is not necessary for the Pied Wagtail; indeed it is less aquatic than the Grey; it darts fearlessly under the legs of the grazing cattle after flies, and is a constant attendant when ploughing is in progress, its quarry being larvae rather than perfect insects. The farmyard, where the warmth of manure and other litter encourages winter flies, is a favourite haunt, and there it runs nimbly along the roof-tree of the cowshed, constantly calling, and shooting into the air when it sights a passing fly.

The Pied Wagtail is a pioneer summer visitor, usually returning early in March, but often as soon as the beginning of February. Much though not all of the plumage is moulted in spring in addition to the complete moult in autumn, and apparently this spring moult is accomplished earlier abroad than in England, for the returning birds are noticeably cleaner-looking and smarter than those which have wintered here. The spring flocks feed in the fields with Meadow Pipits and Reed Buntings, their travelling companions, and at night roost with these birds in reed-beds or other waterside vegetation. Large roosts in greenhouses and on moored boats are sometimes reported. On the ploughed land they are conspicuous, as the very black and white males run for a moment along a ridge, then dip out of sight into a furrow, or take short bounding wave-like flights, with frequent calls of *tschizzik*, to overtake the plough. When gathering at the roost a few male birds often join in a short evensong, simple but melodious, a twittering chorus not unlike that of the Swallow.

The bank of a stream, especially where herbage overhangs, is a common site for the nest; but it is often built in a hole in a building or rocks, among the roots of a tree, or even under a clod in an open field; as a rule it is sheltered or concealed. Grass, roots and leaves are firmly matted together, the bulk varied according to the accommodation, and the nest lining is of hair or wool, with often a few feathers. The eggs, generally four to six, are finely speckled with ashy-grey on a whitish ground, but are subject to variation, and may be boldly streaked or have a few irregular hair-lines; they are laid in April, and second or third broods are reared.

For the sake of comparison the plumages of the two races are given together. The males in summer are white from forehead to neck, with crown and nape black, but in the Pied the black extends over the upper parts to the upper tail-coverts, whilst this area is pearl-grey in the White. White covert tips produce a double wing-bar and the inner secondaries are margined with white. In the Pied the quills are blackish, in the White they are browner; the tail is similar in both, blackish with most of the two outer pair of feathers white. Both have a black throat, but in the Pied this is usually sharply angled into the white of the neck, and the breast-band joins with the black on the shoulders; in the White the bib is more rounded and shoulders grey. Both have white underparts, but the flanks of the Pied are sooty, of the White pale grey. The bill, legs and feet are black. The females have a shorter tail and less black on the head and breast. In the Pied the back is grey, though not so pure as that of a male White, and is indistinctly streaked; the grey of the White is duller than that of her mate. When flying the female Pied looks darker than the more uniform grey-backed White. After the autumn moult Pieds closely resemble Whites by becoming greyer on the back and losing the black chin and throat, leaving only a crescentic band of black on the breast. At all seasons, however, the rump of the Pied is black, or very dark indeed, and of the White grey. The young in both have the face suffused with yellow and the wings browner; the grey is less pure than in adults, but in distribution of colour they resemble females. Length, 7·5 in. Wing, 3·6 in. Tarsus, 0·9 in. (*Plates 145 and 177.*)

**Grey Wagtail**                                                    *Motacilla cinerea*

In summer the Grey Wagtail is found throughout most of Europe, and in winter it ranges to tropical Africa. In Britain it is resident in suitable places, a summer visitor, for numbers leave in autumn, and a bird of passage. It is very local in south-east England.

The Grey is more of a water bird than the Pied, and running water, especially turbulent hill becks and streams, are most favoured; these it haunts from their first bound over the escarpments to the wooded gorges and valleys, but seldom frequents the lowlands in spring. Really a little smaller than the Pied, it appears bigger on account of its longer tail; it is a slimmer, more graceful bird, with more deliberate caudal gestures, which reach their highest perfection during nuptial display, when fanned, elevated and depressed to show to advantage the contrast between the whites and blacks. Along the stream margin the bird runs nimbly or walks more sedately with head and neck dipping forward at every step; in the stream it flickers from stone to stone, careless if the water flows over its feet, and darts upwards to snatch a fly. Like other wagtails, it feeds on insects, but in the shallows catches the crustaceans *Gammarus* and *Asellus*, or picks from the stones a small *Limnea* or the river-limpet *Ancylus*. It perches freely, and where trees overhang the stream uses the branches as look-out posts from which to sally, flycatching, over the water. When winter approaches it leaves the uplands and is met with by lakes, ponds, slow-flowing rivers or the coast, and at this season many move southward, and some emigrate. The call is a soft *tzissi*, and in spring it has a low plaintive love-note; but it is not much of a songster, though its short twittering melody occasionally mingles with the music of the stream. The flight is decidedly undulating, and as the bird alights it almost invariably spreads and raises its tail.

The nesting site is usually in some crevice in a rock, wall or bank, sheltered above, and close to running water. Rootlets, moss and a little grass are the outer materials, and hair forms the lining. Four to six eggs, speckled or marbled with grey and brown and often with one or two hair-lines, are laid late in April, and a second brood is sometimes reared.

In spring the male has upper parts mainly blue-grey, wings blackish, rump and upper tail-coverts greenish-yellow, cheeks grey with a white line above and below the eye, tail black with white outer feathers. The chin and throat are black, breast and underparts yellow. The female has little black on the throat and her upper parts have a greenish tinge. In winter the male resembles the female. Young birds are like winter adults, but upper parts are browner and underparts pale yellow. Length, 7 in. Wing, 3·25 in. Tarsus, 0·85 in. (*Plates 146 and 177.*)

**Citrine or Yellow-headed Wagtail**                     *Motacilla citreola*

This species from Russia and central Asia has been recorded eight times in the British Isles, from Fair Isle, Suffolk and Hampshire. The head, neck and underparts are canary-yellow, upper parts blue-grey with a black half-collar on the back of the neck. The female is browner and lacks the collar.

**Yellow Wagtail**                                           *Motacilla flava*

The Yellow Wagtail has a wide distribution in Europe and Asia, and in different parts of its breeding range geographical races have developed which are chiefly distinguished by the colour of the head of the male in breeding plumage. This is, however, a very variable species, and 'mutants' may occur in a local population, showing the characteristics of a geographically remote subspecies; for example birds indistinguishable from the west Siberian race, *Motacilla flava beema*, Sykes's Wagtail, have nested in the south of England on many occasions. Generally speaking, the British Yellow Wagtail, *M. flava flavissima*, which also breeds locally in northern France, Belgium and Holland, is distinguishable in the field from the central European Blue-headed Wagtail, *M. f. flava*, at least in spring (*see* description). A few pairs of Blue-headed Wagtails breed regularly in Kent and Sussex and occasional nests have been found in other counties; it is not uncommon as a passage migrant. The Yellow Wagtail breeds throughout most of England and in the east of Wales and is locally abundant, but it is rare in the extreme west. It breeds only in the Clyde area in Scotland, and although it has nested in Ireland it is now chiefly known there as a scarce passage migrant.

All wagtails are dainty, delicate birds, but the Yellow is the most graceful and fairy-like of them all; in March and April, when the flocks appear in our pastures, the males are wonderfully brilliant. As they run nimbly through the growing herbage their slight bodies are often hidden, but the bright colours, gold as the dandelions, catch the eye. The open country, meadowland or cultivated field, common or marsh, is the haunt of the Yellow Wagtail; it feeds amongst the grazing cattle and follows the plough, ever on the look-out for insects and their larvae or small snails in the grass. For no apparent reason a flock will rise suddenly and fly to the nearest trees, but after perching for a few moments the members drop back one by one into the grass. In courtship the male, with quivering wings and tail fanned, will hover a few feet above the feeding female, and occasionally utter a short but cheery song, though as a rule he is a silent bird. At the roost, which is frequently a reed-bed both in spring and autumn, there is a continuous soft twitter, but as other species are usually present it is not easy to analyse the notes. The call, a sibilant *tissik*, is constantly uttered during the undulating flight. The activities of the parents are most noticeable when flycatching for the nestlings; the birds fill their beaks with flies, yet always seem able to snatch another without dropping any of their load. They visit manure heaps in the farms and fields, hovering above them, dancing in the air, snapping right and left; they run across the floating weeds on ponds, fluttering their wings when in danger of sinking, or taking a flight of a few feet. When on the ground the expressive tail is ever in motion and the head moves rhythmically with the rapid steps; when alighting after a flight the tail is elevated and spread.

The nest, of grass, moss or any convenient material, and lined with hair, fur, rootlets or feathers, is built on the ground in a meadow or cornfield, and is usually partially sheltered by a clod of earth or clump of grass; in some districts potato fields are favoured, the nests being on the slope of the furrow. The eggs are laid in May, a second clutch usually following the first; four to six is the number, and they are densely speckled with reddish-brown or grey, usually with one or more hair-lines near the larger end.

The male in spring is greenish-olive on the upper parts, yellowest on the tail-coverts, with brown-black wings and tail, the former with buffish edges, forming bars, and the latter with the two outer pair of feathers mainly white. Above and below the eye and the whole of the underparts are canary-yellow; the bill and legs are black. The female is browner, her eye-stripe and wing-bars are buff, and her chin and throat whitish; her underparts are paler. In autumn, when flocks are passing preparatory to departure in September or October, the general colour of the old birds is paler and of the young browner, with buff-tinged chins and buff breasts. Length, 6·5 in. Wing, 3·25 in. Tarsus, 0·9 in. (*Plates 145 and 177.*)

The male Blue-headed Wagtail in nuptial plumage has the crown, nape and ear-coverts bluish-slate; above the eye is a distinct white eye-streak and a less conspicuous whitish streak usually, though not invariably, passes through the ear-coverts, below a dark line through the eye. The chin is white. The female is slightly bluer on the crown than the normal Yellow, and her chin and eye-stripe are pure white or very faintly tinged with yellow; the underparts are paler than in the male. In autumn both old and young closely resemble Yellows at the same season, but they are still rather greyer on the crown and whiter on the chin. (*Plate 146.*)

The male Grey-headed Wagtail, *M. f. thunbergi*, the northern race of which a few individuals have occurred fairly frequently in Britain, chiefly in the northern isles, lacks a superciliary stripe.

## Family BOMBYCILLIDAE Waxwings

**Waxwing**                                                       *Bombycilla garrulus*

The breeding range of the Waxwing is circumpolar. When there is a poor crop of rowan berries on the breeding grounds in north-east Europe large numbers of Waxwings move south-west in autumn. If the berry failure coincides with a peak in breeding population an 'invasion' of the British Isles by several thousand birds may take place, as happened, for example, in October and November 1965. The first arrivals are usually in October; few birds remain after early April. Numbers are normally greater on the east side of

Britain, but since the invasion of 1946–47 Waxwings have occurred regularly in varying numbers in several western counties. It has also become a frequent winter visitor to Ireland.

At close quarters the Waxwing, with its crest and striking wing and tail patterns, is unmistakable, but when a flock is seen at a distance in wheeling flight or perched at the top of tall trees the birds can easily be taken for Starlings. In invasion years flocks of over a hundred may be seen, but single birds or small parties are more usual. The Waxwing is often tame and approachable and feeds readily in town and village gardens. In Britain the staple diet is berries, especially hawthorn, yew, cotoneaster and rose hips, but on mild October days the bird will take short hawking flights in pursuit of flying insects. When feeding on berries it will hang from the twigs in tit-like postures. It drinks frequently when water is accessible. In winter it is generally a silent bird, but a thin trilling call is sometimes heard.

The general colour of both upper and underparts is vinaceous brown; a line from the forehead above and behind the eye, and the chin and upper throat are black. On the forehead the long erectile crest is distinctly chestnut, as are the cheeks and under tail-coverts. The upper tail-coverts and rump are dove-coloured; the centre of the abdomen is grey. A conspicuous white bar crosses the blackish wings, and the inner edge of the primaries is white, whilst the outer is yellow, as is a broad band at the tip of the tail. The bill and legs are black. The young bird is browner and is without black on the throat. Length, 7·7 in. Wing, 4·5 in. Tarsus, 0·8 in. (*Plate 149.*)

## Family LANIIDAE Shrikes

### Great Grey Shrike

*Lanius excubitor*

The Great Grey Shrike is a bird of northern Europe and Asia which occurs in our islands as a winter visitor and a regular autumn and occasional spring bird of passage. It is less frequent on the west side of Britain and it seldom reaches Ireland.

Anyone who sees this bird perched in its characteristic upright attitude on the topmost branch of a tree, or on a telegraph pole, will understand Linnaeus's epithet, *excubitor*; nothing which moves is missed by the keen eye of the watchful 'sentinel'. It turns its head sharply to follow the flight of a bee, then swoops, hawk-like, and snaps it on the wing, returning with its quarry and, holding it down with one foot, tears it to bits; it looks down sideways, attracted by the chirrup of the grasshopper, and drops lightly to the grass and the insect is no more. It pounces on birds on the ground or perched in trees, seizes them with its feet and kills them by biting the neck; aerial pursuits are usually unsuccessful. It generally kills small mammals without using its feet, and carries prey either in the bill or the claws. The victims captured are impaled upon some sharp point—the thorn of whitethorn, the stout spines of buckthorn on the east coast, and, not infrequently, the barbs of wire railings, Thus secured they can be ripped with the strong hooked bill, but its feet are not suited for tearing. When, after a sally, it returns to its observation post, it bends forward, regaining its balance with expanded and uplifted tail; it is then that the graduated black and white pattern shows to advantage. Its flight is undulating but rather heavy, but its dash is straight and determined. When disturbed its alarm note is a harsh Jay-like *skake, skake,* and its call is described as *truii.* The pleasant warbling song has been heard in England as early as December, for the bird, which usually arrives in October and November, sometimes remains to winter with us; it has been met with in all months from August until May and occasionally in June and July. As a rule the bird is solitary, and when several reach our shores at the same time they speedily spread, each mapping out its hunting ground and reducing the numbers of the immigrants with which it has travelled.

The general colour of the upper parts is pearl-grey; a stripe above the eye and the cheeks and chin are white, and a deep black streak extends from the forehead, through the eye, to the ear-coverts. The scapulars are white and the wings black and white, with one or two white bars. The underparts are white, slightly tinged with grey. The bill is nearly black, pale at the base of the under mandible; the legs blackish. In the female the underparts are greyer, and are faintly barred with greyish-brown. Young birds are greyish-brown, with conspicuous bars on the underparts. Length, 9·5 in. Wing, 4·3 in. Tarsus, 1 in. (*Plate 149.*)

## Lesser Grey Shrike                                      *Lanius minor*

This summer visitor to the south and east of Europe was formerly considered a very rare vagrant to the British Isles, but it has recently been recorded almost annually. The occurrences have been widely scattered over the country, and spring records are as frequent as autumn ones. This bird closely resembles the Great Grey Shrike, but its slightly smaller size, proportionately longer wings, shorter tail and shorter, deeper bill are diagnostic. Its food and habits resemble those of other shrikes, though it is said but seldom to impale its victims. The male has a wide black band on the forehead, and its scapulars as well as back and other upper parts are grey; the underparts are suffused with rose-pink on the breast and flanks. The white wing-bar and outer tail feathers are conspicuous. The bill and legs are blackish. The female has a narrower bar on the forehead; the young bird has none, and its back is brown and barred, its underparts yellowish. Length, 8 in.

## Woodchat Shrike                                       *Lanius senator*

The Woodchat, a conspicuous black and white shrike with a chestnut-red crown, is found in summer from Germany southward to the Mediterranean basin and in winter in tropical Africa. It is an uncommon visitor to the British Isles on migration; it is recorded annually in fluctuating numbers, varying from one or two to over twenty, chiefly at the coastal observatories. It occurs in both spring and autumn. As it nests so near our shores as Normandy its visits on migration are not surprising. Its note is a harsh chatter, and the male has a short warble in which, as in other shrikes, notes of various birds are introduced. Its food and habits are similar to those of the family.

The male has the crown and nape ferruginous; the lores are white, and the forehead, ear-coverts, sides of neck and back black, the scapulars being conspicuously white. There is a white bar on the black wings. The rump is grey, shading to white on the upper tail-coverts, and the underparts are white tinged with buff on breast and flanks. The bill is black; the legs brown. The female is duller and her upper parts are more rufous; the young bird is reddish, streaked and mottled on the upper parts and barred on the under. Length, 7·1 in. Wing, 3·8 in. Tarsus, 0·95 in. (*Plate 149*.)

### Red-backed Shrike                                    *Lanius collurio*

The Red-backed Shrike is a summer visitor to most of Europe. It comes as a rather late migrant to England. Its breeding range has steadily contracted over the past hundred years and it is now restricted to the south and east of England. Even there it is becoming increasingly scarce. As a bird of passage in spring and autumn it visits the east coast and even the Orkneys and Shetlands, but is a rare vagrant to Ireland.

The Butcher Bird seldom arrives before early May, and its stay is short, most leaving before September; during its residence it does not court concealment. The handsome cock, with distinctive red back and grey head, selects a good look-out post near the site selected for the nest, and from this makes predatory sallies. The top of a hedge, tree, post or telegraph wire is his favourite perch; he does not always stand erect, but rests with flexed legs, the breast feathers hiding his feet; his head moves from side to side, or, without shifting his position he turns his neck, looking upward, his chin toward his tail, which is constantly in motion, raised and deflected to maintain his balance, or, under excitement, swung rapidly from side to side. He launches into the air and dodges after a passing insect, but often his flight is rapid and direct, with head held forward with determination; the prey when captured is carried to the perch, held with the foot and dismembered. Now and then an insect is lifted, parrot-like, to the bill, or a beetle will be held and hammered on the ground; bees, wasps and other insects with lethal weapons are smartly smashed into impotence. Mice and small birds are suddenly dashed upon and struck down, for in fair competition of speed either can evade him; he will beat along the hedgerow like a hawk, poising with vibrating wings above a likely bush, then glide on. Mice, lizards, small birds and large insects are, for convenience, impaled upon a thorn or barbed wire before butchery; the spike is generally driven through the neck. Where there is a convenient array of hooks the shambles become the 'larder', but it is doubtful if the bird often revisits the remains when the choice bits are extracted. Nestlings of various species are slain, and the domineering bird will make passes at Thrushes or other birds which he really dare not tackle, but often he is mobbed and driven off by the pluck of small birds. The flight is jerky and uneven, and the harsh *tchack*, from which the name is derived, is frequently uttered. The male has also a sharp chirp, and in summer, during courtship, he has a short, pleasant warbling song. In nuptial display the male adopts alternating upright and horizontal postures, showing off his richly coloured breast and back to the female. Frequent gifts are brought to the female at this time, which she receives with quivering wings and low crooning notes.

The nest is large and not over neat; grass, roots, moss and wool, lined with hair, rootlets and wool are the usual materials. It is placed, well concealed, in a thick hedge, bush or mass of brambles, but the guardian male betrays its situation. The four to six eggs vary considerably, but conform to certain types; the ground is white, grey, buff or salmon-pink; the spots or blotches, often in a zone, are mostly towards the thicker end, and are red or grey. They are seldom laid until late in May or early June, and a second brood is rare.

The male has the crown, nape and rump slate-grey, the back and scapulars warm chestnut-red, and the flight feathers black. A black frontlet extends through the eye to the ear-coverts, and over the eye is a white streak. The sides of the neck and chin are white. The tail is brownish-black, with no white on the central feathers, but the others have white bases increasing in size until the outermost are mainly white. Most of the underparts are rosy-buff. The legs and bill are black. The female is without black on the head and is russet-brown above with darker crescentic bars; her underparts are buff with semi-lunar grey markings; her superciliary streak is buff. The young has hardly any eye-stripe, and is browner and duller with more distinct barring. Length, 7 in. Wing, 3·7 in. Tarsus, 0·95 in. (*Plates 147, 149 and 176.*)


## Family STURNIDAE Starlings

**Starling**                                                              *Sturnus vulgaris*

Although it is one of our best-known birds, the status of that avian humorist the Starling is complicated; its range extends over most of Europe. Our birds are resident, with us at all times, while vast hordes come from the north and east to winter here, and some, travelling further south, are birds of passage. As a breeding bird it is scarce or absent in parts of Ireland.

The beauty of the metallic-hued Starling is little appreciated; it is often smoke-begrimed or in immature or winter dress, but in early spring, when the buff or white tips that concealed its glories have worn off, it is in a good light a wonderfully beautiful species. The male, with its neck and throat distended, its wings trailing or shivering, perches erect on tree-top or chimney, whistling and chuckling, proud of his charms. His song is a medley of sweet and soft whistles and croons, with cheery laughing bubbles, chatters, chuckles and clicks; the notes of other birds or animals or merely mechanical sounds are introduced by the imitative bird. It can copy the Blackbird's mellow tones, the Curlew's wild call, the Dunlin's purr, or even a bicycle bell. Its alarm cry is harsh, a rasping scream, and the anger note, too frequent when the birds should be feeding amicably, is as unpleasant. Immediately the young have left the nest the Starling becomes gregarious; indeed throughout the nesting season, when breeding birds are scattered, flocks of young or unmated birds are common. The family parties join forces, and by autumn large flocks are formed which keep together all day. In the evening these flocks, reinforced by the immigrants from the Baltic countries, congregate at a common roost, some plantation or reed-bed as a rule, where countless thousands rope the branches or bend the tough reeds. These roosts draw the Starlings from a wide area— sometimes from as much as several hundred square miles. The birds usually collect in isolated clumps of trees, where they whistle and chatter in concert; then, as if by word of command, all rise and perform complicated aerial evolutions. The flock fans out or closes up, wheels or turns sharply, forms into a compact mass or trails off into a long waving line or wreath of birds, until as one body it dives, rains down, or drifts into the roosting trees or reeds. There are also large roosts on buildings in towns. The usual flight of the Starling is direct; the triangular wings beat very rapidly, then are held whilst the bird glides, losing but little altitude. The wings are not brought far forward; the bird's form is that of a wide-barbed arrow-head. When, however, high-flying beetles or other insects are on the wing, the Starling hawks after them like a Swallow; it turns and twists, dodges and swoops with considerable agility. On the ground it runs or walks, but seldom hops unless hurried.

In spring insects and other invertebrates are eaten, and the bird destroys large numbers of weevils and other beetles; larvae, including grass-devouring wireworms and the grubs of flies, are successfully sought for; it is a farmer's friend. In summer and autumn, however, it raids fruit crops and is particularly harmful when pears are ripe. When the young are in the nest it is always in a hurry; its arrival at the nesting hole is the signal for wheezy and impatient cries from the expectant brood. When these have left the nest they follow their parents until the woods ring with their insistent demands. In the fields the flocks are restless, settling in a body, scouring a particular area, working outwards from the centre; but if one bird takes a short flight, the others immediately follow as if fearing to miss something it has discovered. The flocks feed in gardens, pastures, ploughed land, marsh or mud-flat; anywhere and everywhere is visited for food; but long before dusk in winter the whole party rises and wings straight for the roost. The Starling retires early, but not for sound sleep; long after dark the peevish notes of expostulation may be heard as birds jostle one another on the crowded perches.

In its choice of a nesting site the Starling is catholic. The nest is almost invariably in a hole, but this may be under the eaves of a house, in a chimney, or the hollow left by a missing brick, in an old barn or ruin, in a haystack, on some wild coast cliff, in a peat-stack on a lonely moor, in tree in field or wood, or in a nesting-box. The nest is an untidy litter of straw with a lining of feathers or other soft material. From five to seven pale blue eggs are laid in April, and a second brood is sometimes reared; eggs dropped on the ground are not uncommon.

The summer plumage is metallic, purple, green and blue; these iridescent colours have different sheen when seen from various angles. In autumn they are replaced by buff and white-tipped feathers, which give the whole bird a spotted appearance, and the lemon-yellow of its bill changes to dull brown. The legs and irides are brown. The female is slightly less showy than her mate, and has shorter pointed feathers on the neck. The young, until their first autumn, are light brown with pale margins to the feathers of wings and tail; they become spotted as they grow older. Length, 8·5 in. Wing, 5 in. Tarsus, 1·2 in. (*Plates 146 and 176.*)

### Rose-coloured Starling                                         *Sturnus roseus*

The movements of the Rose-coloured Starling are erratic and uncertain. In its normal range in south-eastern Europe and western Asia it will swarm for a period in one district and suddenly leave it for no apparent reason. From time to time parties come wandering north and west, and not infrequently a few birds appear in Britain; indeed, throughout our islands there are few counties without records of vagrants, though there are few recent records from Ireland, and there is often the possibility that reported birds may have escaped from captivity. Most of the occurrences are in late summer and autumn. In food, habits, notes, and to some extent in appearance, it is a Starling, and it is not surprising that when wanderers reach our islands they generally consort with our birds. It is largely a feeder on insects, but is not free from the charge of fruit destruction. In spite of its similar flight and behaviour an adult bird can be detected by its crest and colour when flying with Starlings, but with the young it is not so easy.

In summer the adult's head, neck, breast, wings and tail are glossy black, the rest of the plumage salmon-pink. After the autumn moult much of the gloss and pink is obscured by brown tips to the feathers, which wear off by abrasion in spring. The male has a long and ample crest, partially erectile; the crest of the female is shorter and her colours duller. The young are brown, paler than young Starlings. The bill is pink, black at the base, the legs yellowish-pink. Length, 8·5 in. (*Plate 146.*)

### Family FRINGILLIDAE Finches

### Hawfinch                                        *Coccothraustes coccothraustes*

The Hawfinch is now a well-distributed resident throughout most of England, though still absent from Cornwall. In Wales and southern Scotland it is very local and it does not occur in northern Scotland. There has only been one breeding record for Ireland. Little is known about its migratory movements, but it has been noted on migration and as a winter visitor. Within recent years the Hawfinch has not only increased but extended its range considerably, and some of the occurrences in unexpected places may be attempts to colonise.

In spite of its peculiar appearance, due to its huge bill and head and short tail, calculated to command attention, the Hawfinch is looked upon as rare in places where it is really common. It is shy and secretive, and avoids man but not his dwellings, less so his gardens when fruit or peas are ripe. Split cherry stones and empty pods reveal the fact that a raid has been made before anyone was about. It occurs not infrequently in thickly populated suburban districts, even nesting in large gardens. When in flight the bird looks stumpy and top-heavy; when perched it is unlike any other bird, sitting well upright and constantly turning its huge head from side to side. The flight is often described as straight and rapid, but this is only when alarmed; the normal flight is undulating, almost bounding, far more so than that of the Greenfinch. The white patch on the wing is conspicuous when flying and when at rest. Its sudden, penetrating whistle is also distinctive; it is either a call or warning note, but not an alarm, and is usually heard when the bird is seeking safety in flight. It has a simple song, but this is seldom heard.

The massive bill is strengthened internally by horny pads; the pulp of fruit is rejected and the stones cracked to get at the kernel. Fruit stones are turned in the bill so that, when crushed, they will split in half, and the litter of split cherry, damson, holly, yew, hornbeam or haw seeds, all neatly in halves, often reveals the unsuspected presence of the bird. Pea pods are split along the hinge, crushed until they open, and the empty pods show the marks of the strong bill. In winter the Hawfinch is somewhat gregarious and occasionally gathers in large flocks.

The nest is built in a tree or bush, often on a horizontal bough at a fair height above the ground; it may be in a tall holly or other evergreen in a garden, in a fruit tree in an orchard or a forest tree in a dense wood. It is flat, composed of twigs and roots, lined with finer roots, hair or fibre, and frequently has lichens added to the outer materials. The eggs, four to six in number, are almost bunting-like in their bold irregular streaks and blotches on a buff, white or tinged ground. They are laid in late April or May.

The general colour of the adult bird is reddish-brown, shading to greyish-white on the belly and under tail-coverts. The nape is grey; the lores, throat and a line at the base of the bill are black. A conspicuous white shoulder-patch contrasts with the blue-black wings, and the short tail is white-tipped with a rufous tinged centre. The inner primaries are notched and curved like a bill-hook and are white on the inner web. The huge bill is lead-blue in spring, yellowish in winter, the legs light brown. The female is paler and less rufous than the male. The juvenile has the throat pale buff, the breast and flanks speckled and barred with brown, and the head and neck greenish-yellow. Length, about 7 in. Wing, 4 in. Tarsus, 0·9 in. (*Plates 150 and 177.*)

## Greenfinch                                                  *Carduelis chloris*

Though resident throughout the British Isles the Greenfinch is also migratory; its movements are erratic in winter. Home-bred birds are largely sedentary, though with some there is a tendency to a southward movement in autumn. In autumn passage migrants and winter visitors reach our northern, eastern and even western shores; the return migration is in March and April, but flocks, possibly north-bound immigrants, appear in February. Certain areas are deserted in winter, but wandering flocks may be met with anywhere. The Greenfinch is distributed throughout most of Europe.

In March the male Greenfinch begins his monotonous long-drawn *dwee*, which many describe as his call-note. It is also the main part of his song; he perches repeating it persistently as a love-note or challenge throughout the breeding season, and does not tire until summer is well advanced. In addition he has a pleasant twittering song, often interrupted by the droning *dwee*; he will rise with light uncertain hovering flight to utter this twitter on the wing, returning almost immediately to his perch. Although it is a common bird, many people fail to realise how smart the Greenfinch is in his summer dress; they are astonished by the brilliant yellow flash of the wing-edges and tail when the bird flies. Distinctly sociable at all times, the Greenfinch will nest in small colonies in a hedge or plantation, and when the young are on the wing they follow their parents, with much twittering, for a short period and then join forces with others of their kind. By autumn the flocks are often considerable, and at that season and in winter the birds consort with sparrows and buntings in the fields. The Greenfinch is a hanger-on rather than an associate of man; it will nest in large gardens and feeds freely in cultivated land. In the stubbles, from which the flocks rise with a whirr of wings, it picks up a certain amount of wasted grain, but also hunts for the seeds of spurrey and other weeds; those of the charlock are much favoured. As is the case with all finches, the young are largely fed on insects, but are also supplied with a quantity of crushed seed. Though some grain is eaten and in spring buds are nipped off, the services of the Greenfinch in keeping down weeds of cultivation should not be forgotten. The flight of the bird is undulating; its wings move rapidly for a second or two and then are closed for a moment, during which time the bird loses a little elevation, but the bounds are not so marked as in the larks and wagtails. During summer the pleasant twitter of the Greenfinch flocks is a familiar sound; it is conversational and interspersed with questioning calls of *pee-wee*?

The nest, loosely constructed of fine twigs, moss, grass and wool, and lined with moss, hair or feathers, is built in untrimmed hedges, evergreens or on the flat boughs of conifers; four to six eggs, white or creamy in ground with speckles or blotches of brown, red or purple towards their larger end, are laid in April or May, and a second or even a third brood is reared.

The male in summer is bright yellowish-green with slate-grey on the head, flanks and belly; the wings shade from slate-grey to brownish-black and have a bright yellow margin; the base of the forked tail is also bright yellow. The female is duller and less yellow. After the autumn moult the whole plumage is partially obscured by brown tips. The young are greyer, with brown streaks on the back and breast. The bill and legs are flesh-coloured. Length, 6 in. Wing, 3·5 in. Tarsus, 0·7 in. (*Plates 148, 157 and 177*.)

# Goldfinch                                    *Carduelis carduelis*

At the beginning of the 20th century the Goldfinch seems to have been scarce throughout the country, but there has been a marked increase in numbers since the capture of wild birds for caging became illegal. The Goldfinch is now well distributed, and in many places numerous, in England, Wales and Ireland, but it is still rare in the north of Scotland. Some of our birds may emigrate in autumn, and birds ringed in Spain and France have been re- covered in England, but these movements seem to be on a small scale. The Goldfinch breeds throughout Europe except in the far north.

The striking red, white and black head, and the broad gold band on the wing, prevent confusion with any other finch. Though lively enough in captivity, its charms are lost when confined; in the open it is a fairy bird, light and buoyant on the wing, active as a tit when feeding. Even in the nesting season it is sociable. The song, clear, sweet, and loud for so small a bird, is a combination of modulations of its liquid call, *twit*. It flies with a 'drooping', jerky flight, and a 'charm', as a flock is aptly called, twitters conversationally on the wing; amongst its favourite food-plants—knapweeds, thistles, ragworts and other weeds—it is restlessly active, flitting from plant to plant like a butterfly. In nuptial display the male, drooping his wings, turns from side to side to show his golden bar to perfection. In April, when our residents are building, flocks of Goldfinches consort with Redpolls, Chaffinches and Bramblings. The Goldfinches frequently sing in wonderful chorus. The young, calling for food, twitter in a feeble imitation of their parents. The song is continued throughout the summer.

Seeds of weeds, especially those most troublesome on the farm, form the main diet. 'Dirty' fields and untilled wastes are what it loves. It is a most useful check on weed distribution; thistle seeds are specially favoured.

Insects are largely eaten in spring; the April flocks visit larches, feeding on the larvae of *Coleophora* and other insects that attack young shoots.

The neat, Chaffinch-like nest, compactly built of fine roots and bents filled in with moss and lichens and lined with thistledown and wool, is often in an orchard tree or far out on a branch of a sycamore or chestnut. Farms, orchards and gardens attract it. Four to six eggs are laid in May; they are similar to but rather smaller than those of the Greenfinch. A second brood is often reared.

The crimson and black on the face and throat contrast with the bands of white. Except for a small white patch on the neck, the upper parts are wood- brown, shading into white. The black wings are crossed by a broad bright yellow band, and the feathers are tipped with white. There are white tips and spots on the black tail feathers. The under tail-coverts and belly are white; the flanks buff. The young, which lack the head markings, are greyish-brown, with more or less distinct streaks of darker brown. The bill is white, tinged with pink; the legs flesh-coloured. Length, 5 in. Wing, 3 in. Tarsus, 0·6 in. (*Plates 150 and 177.*)

**Siskin**                                                     *Carduelis spinus*

Although a resident, nesting with increasing frequency in England and Wales, especially in northern counties, and regularly in certain localities in Scotland and Ireland, the Siskin is best known as a winter visitor. The migrants arrive in September or October, leaving again in April or May. It breeds in northern, and in mountainous parts of central Europe.

As a winter visitor the Siskin is sporadic; in some winters it is common, in others scarce or absent. Tits and Goldcrests are at times its companions, but the Redpoll is its greatest favourite. With Redpolls it frequents birches and alders, returning day after day to the same group of trees, where its greenish plumage and short forked tail, as well as the black head of the male bird, serve to distinguish it from its companions. As acrobatic as a tit, it hangs for choice upside down when picking at the alder cones or birch seeds. In March and April it is found in larches, doubtless attracted by bud-destroying insects. Seeds of knapweed, ragwort and groundsel are eaten, but those of trees are most favoured. All the time that the birds are in the trees and when they fly in straggling parties to fresh feeding-grounds, they keep up a continuous simple twitter; but the call-note, *tsyzi*, is distinctive. The song is sweet but simple.

The summer home of the Siskin is the firwood; the nest is usually built on a horizontal bough of a fir at a considerable elevation, and dead fir twigs, especially those covered with lichens, are largely used in its construction. To these moss and roots are added, and the lining is generally of hair or feathers. The four to five eggs are a little bluer than the usual type of the egg of the Goldfinch, and are rather more profusely spotted with lilac and brown. The first eggs are laid in April and frequently a second clutch in June.

The general colour of the male in winter is olive-green, darkest on the back and shading to yellow on the rump; it is yellowish-white on the flanks, and white on the belly. The crown, chin and lores are greyish-black, and the back and flanks streaked with brown. A distinct yellow stripe above the eye joins the yellow upper breast. Two irregular greenish-yellow bars cross the wings, and the primaries are fringed with the same colour. After the grey tips are lost in spring, the colours are clearer and brighter. The female has dusky streaks on her crown and lacks the black; her underparts are paler, and she is a much greyer bird. The young are decidedly browner than the females, the whites are replaced by buff, and the streaks more pronounced. The bill and legs are brown. Length, 4·7 in. Wing, 2·8 in. Tarsus, 0·5 in. (*Plates 150 and 177.*)

**Linnet**                                                    *Acanthis cannabina*

The Linnet is resident and migratory throughout the British Isles, but local as a breeding species. It occurs throughout Europe, except in the extreme north. Immigrants reach us in autumn when emigrants are departing. Passage migrants occur in flocks in May long after our breeding birds have settled down; these often roost sociably with other species in reed-beds or osiers. There is a distinct west coast migration in September and October.

The Linnet is a bird of uncultivated rather than cultivated land, though flocks feed in the fields in winter; furze-grown commons, hillsides sprinkled with scrub, and the coast marshes and sand-hills are its haunts. Even in the field it may be distinguished from its near allies the Redpolls and Twite by its larger size, warmer brown back, and the white edges of the tail feathers; in the hand it will be found that all of the tail feathers, except the central pair, have wider white margins on the inner than the outer webs. The bird is sociable, and in spring three or four males will perch on the same bush and sing in chorus; even in winter the twitter often resolves itself into a short song. This pleasant song is not loud, but is sweet, in spite of the fact that some ears detect harsh notes. These so-called blemishes make the song peculiarly distinctive; they suggest the twang of a stringed instrument; indeed, the low notes are like the vibration of the strings of a harp. The flight note is *twit, twit*, short and sharp, uttered as the flocks pass and repass in curving sweeps, now almost halting in mid-air or rising obliquely, dancing to and fro. The call-note is a double *twe-ee*. Seeds of various plants, mostly looked upon as weeds, are eaten, and the young, though partly fed on insects, are supplied with a regurgitated mass of crushed seeds.

The favourite site for the nest is a gorse bush, but a hedge is often selected. The nest is built of a few fine twigs, grass and wool, and lined with wool, hair, thistle and willow down and sometimes feathers. Four to six eggs are laid in April, and a second brood is usually reared. In colour they are bluish-white, with faint underlying greyish markings, and with a few bolder reddish or purple streaks or blotches towards the larger end.

In breeding dress the cock Linnet's back is warm chestnut-brown; his underparts shade from fawn to almost white on the belly; his head is greyish-brown with darker mottles or streaks; his forehead, crown and breast are crimson. White edgings to the flight feathers and tail are noticeable. The bill at this season is lead-blue; the legs brown. The female is a little smaller and lacks the distinctive crimson; her general colour is duller and greyer and her whites less marked, but the striations on both upper and under surface are most distinct. After the autumn moult grey margins and tips of the feathers conceal the crimson of the male. The bill is horn-coloured. The young is like the female, but browner, the pale edgings being more buff and the white on the underparts suffused with buff; the breast is streaked and spotted with brown. Length, 5·75 in. Wing, 3·15 in. Tarsus, 0·75 in. (*Plates 153 and 177*.)

**Twite**                                         *Acanthis flavirostris*

The Twite is a local resident on some Pennine moorlands but is now rare or absent in many former haunts in the northern counties. It is common, but apparently decreasing, in parts of Scotland, chiefly the west coast and islands, and breeds locally in Ireland, especially near the west coast. Its breeding range abroad is limited, being confined to northern Scandinavia, Lapland

and Finland. Numbers reach us on migration in autumn and return in spring.

The Twite is a bird of the heather; it is often called the Mountain Linnet, and though frequenting high moorlands is also found on Scottish islands and suitable mosses in the lowlands. On the grouse-moors it replaces the Linnet, from which, when adult, it may be distinguished by the absence of red on head and breast; it is a darker bird and its longer tail, giving it a more slender appearance, further prevents confusion with the Redpolls. Its yellow bill is a distinctive character. In winter it flocks and descends from the high moors, frequenting lowland fields, marshes and the shore. The flocks fly with linnet-like indecision, dancing and wheeling over the fields, and continually twittering as they fly. The name Twite is undoubtedly derived from its call-note *twa-it*, and it has another characteristic call, *deek* or *tweek*, canary-like in sound. The song has some of the vibrating character of that of the Linnet, but is, perhaps, less varied. Weed seeds, for instance knapweed and thistle, are its chief food, but a little grain is picked up in the stubbles, and some insects are taken. In nuptial display the male by slightly opening and then closing the wings calls attention to his rosy-red rump, his one bit of bright colour.

The nest is built on the ground, in clumps of ling or other low-growing plants or in a bush; several are at times near together. Grasses, a few twigs, mosses and wool are the usual materials, and the very small cup is lined with wool, hair or down, with the addition of a few feathers. The eggs are smaller and bluer than those of the Linnet, but are of the same general type. Five to six is the number; they are laid late in May or in June, but a second brood is normal.

The general plumage of the male in summer is pale reddish-brown, shading to white on the belly and under tail-coverts. Dark brown centres to the feathers are arranged so as to give the bird a striped or streaky appearance. The brown wings are crossed by a white wing-bar and some of the feathers have white margins, very noticeable in flight, though less so than in the Linnet. The bill is pale yellow; the legs brown. After the autumn moult the plumage is dulled by pale edgings to the feathers; the wing-bars are buff. The female and young lack the rose-red rump, and have the wing-bar buff. The young is a duller, greyer bird, but otherwise like the female. Length, 5·5 in. Wing, 3 in. Tarsus, 0·65 in. (*Plates 151, 153 and 177*.)

## Redpoll                                                    *Acanthis flammea*

The Lesser Redpoll is a common though local resident in the British Isles. Redpolls also breed in the Alps and in Scandinavia. Birds of the Scandinavian race, known as Mealy Redpolls, are regular, occasionally numerous, winter immigrants, and are sometimes distinguishable in the field by their slightly larger size, paler, greyer plumage and whitish rather than buff rumps and wing-bars. Forestry plantings have produced marked local increases in the Redpoll population, especially in Wales.

The Redpoll is a lively little finch; in spring the male flies to and fro at a considerable height, trilling his simple little love-song, dancing through the air with buoyant, erratic flight. In autumn and winter it is gregarious and sociable, consorting with Siskins, tits and other birds, especially in alders and birches, where it performs gymnastic tricks as it hangs below the swaying twigs to reach the seeds. Suddenly all the birds will rise by common impulse, bounding this way and that above the trees and then as suddenly return to the feast. This is not from fear, for they pay little attention to man. When they are feeding or in flight they keep up a continuous twitter. The Redpoll also has a querulous *wheep*, and a short trilling song, often delivered in flight. Seeds of various plants and insects are its food; it will hover lightly over the grass, dropping on the dandelion 'clocks', or perched on a low twig or bramble, will reach for a flowering grass head and hold it down with one foot while it picks out the seeds. In spring it joins other birds in the hunt for aphids, both on sycamores and fruit trees, often hanging whilst it neatly pecks them from the under surface of a leaf; it also frequents the larches for their pests. Alder and willow carr, young conifer plantations and orchards are favoured habitats.

The small deep nest is built in a bush, hedge, bramble or tree at a variable height from the ground; its foundation is small sticks, to which is added moss, grass and wool, with hair, wool, vegetable down, and sometimes feathers for a lining. The four to six eggs are rather deep blue-green with speckles or spots of reddish-brown, darker and smaller than those of the Linnet. Though the first clutch is seldom laid before the middle of May, a second brood is often reared. Small colonies of Redpolls sometimes nest close together.

The Lesser Redpoll is a small, dark brown finch with a crimson forehead and crown; the mantle and back are streaked with dark brown, but the lower back is greyer than the mantle; the rump is tinged with pink. The chin is black, distinguishing it from the Linnet and Twite. The underparts are buffish-white, dark pink on the breast. Two buff bars cross the wings. The bill is horn-coloured; the legs brown. The grey tips of the new feathers after the autumn moult do not entirely obscure the pink on head and breast. The female is without the pink on the breast, but has a crimson forehead; the young has no pink and is a brown speckled bird. Mealy: Length, 5 in. Wing, 3 in. Tarsus, 0·6 in. Lesser: Length, 4·75 in. Wing, 2·75 in. Tarsus, 0·55 in. (*Plates 153 and 177.*)

### Arctic Redpoll                                          *Acanthis hornemanni*

The Redpolls breeding in the Arctic circle are now generally, though not unanimously, regarded as a separate species. They have unstreaked white rumps, pale heads, whitish and very lightly streaked underparts and con-spicuous wing-bars. Upper parts in breeding plumage look 'hoar-frosted'. The Greenland bird, *A. h. hornemanni*, is slightly larger and whiter than the European and Asiatic one, *A. h. exilipes*. A few birds apparently belonging to this species are recorded in the British Isles most years, but it is difficult to distinguish an Arctic from a pale Mealy Redpoll, *A. flammea flammea*, with certainty. Length, 5 in.

## Serin                                                              *Serinus canarius*

The Serin breeds in southern and central Europe, as far north as the Channel and Baltic coasts. A small but increasing number of these finches is now recorded each year between March and December, chiefly from the southern counties of England; a few have reached Shetland and Ireland. A pair nested successfully in the south of England in 1967. The Serin is related to the Canary and is not infrequently caged, but the recent increase in occurrences in Britain is probably not due to escapes but to the northward expansion of the breeding range of the species. Its flight and feeding habits resemble those of a Goldfinch or Linnet. When it rises from the ground, where it often feeds, its yellow rump is clearly seen. Its bill is noticeably short and thick.

The Serin is a yellowish bird, especially on the throat, breast and rump. The upper parts are olive streaked with brown, the wings and tail brown, and the flanks boldly streaked. The female is browner above and paler beneath than the male; both sexes lack the yellow outer tail feathers of the Siskin. The young bird is strongly streaked and has a brownish rump. Length, 4·5 in. (*Plate 150.*)

## Bullfinch                                                          *Pyrrhula pyrrhula*

The Bullfinch is a common resident throughout most of the British Isles, though scarce in parts of Scotland. Its numbers have greatly increased since about 1940. It has a wide distribution in Europe, and birds of the brightly coloured northern race sometimes occur in autumn and winter on our east coast and the northern isles.

The short, stout bill of the Bullfinch and the rich colour of the breast of the male prevent confusion with any other bird, but it is so retiring at most times that it has a false reputation for rarity. In summer it is chiefly a woodland species, where the only sign of its presence is often the clear soft call, *whib*, *whib*, or a fleeting vision of the white on its back; but it has recently been spreading to more open habitats. In winter it is more of a wanderer and visits gardens. Almost certainly it pairs for life, for the male and female are usually together in winter, flitting along the hedgerows or crossing the open with undulating flight. The low sub-song is accompanied by swagger on the part of the male; he moves his big head from side to side, and sways and puffs out the red feathers of his breast. Destruction of fruit buds by the Bullfinch is well known. The bird will systematically strip the twigs, starting at the tips and working inwards, showing a marked preference for certain varieties of each fruit and apparently only eating the embryonic flower. Dr I. Newton has shown that the extent of the damage done depends largely on the crop of ash seed, which in a good year provides the main late winter food. If the ash crop fails, as it usually does in alternate years, the birds turn to a diet of buds much earlier in the winter, and the destruction caused in large orchards may be very serious. In late summer and autumn seeds of birch, meadowsweet, bramble, nettle and dock are favourite foods. Some insects are taken in summer.

The nest is a cunningly interwoven flat platform of sticks, almost as frail as that of the Wood Pigeon; the shallow cup is formed of roots with a little hair in the lining; it is built in tree, hedge or bush, but usually well concealed. Four to six dark greenish-blue eggs, speckled and streaked with red and purple, are laid in April or in May, and a second brood is often reared, sometimes a third. Both parents feed the young by regurgitation on seeds and animal matter, the latter including snails and spiders. By the time they are fledged the young are feeding entirely on seeds.

The male has the head, including the chin, the secondaries and tail, glossy blue-black; the back is blue-grey, and the underparts including the cheeks are brick-red, shading to white on the under tail-coverts; the rump is pure white. The wings have a conspicuous white bar. The bill is blackish; the legs brown. The grey on the upper parts of the female is less pure and her underparts are browner; the young has no black on the head. Length, 5·75 in. Wing, 3·2 in. Tarsus, 0·7 in. (*Plates 154, 155 and 177.*)

### Scarlet Rosefinch or Scarlet Grosbeak        *Carpodacus erythrinus*

The Scarlet Rosefinch breeds in north-east Europe and Asia, and although it is a common cage bird it is considered that the annual occurrences of a few individuals, chiefly in Scotland and at the east coast observatories, are of wild vagrants. The majority are seen in autumn, but in most years there are one or two records for May. The male is a small brownish bird with rich carmine on the head, throat, breast and lower back, greyish-white beneath. Females and immatures are yellowish-brown with darker streaks. Both sexes and young have a faint double wing-bar, dark eyes and rounded heads. Length, 5·8 in.

### Pine Grosbeak        *Pinicola enucleator*

Nesting in Scandinavia, Russia and Siberia, and wintering in southern Europe, the Pine Grosbeak has been recorded eight times in England and twice in Scotland.

It is a much larger bird than the Scarlet Rosefinch, rosy-pink and slate-grey in the male, the rich colour most pronounced on the head, throat and rump. The wing has a conspicuous white bar, and a second one less noticeable. The female is much yellower, and is without the rosy tints. Length, 8 in.

### Crossbill        *Loxia curvirostra*

From time to time hordes of Crossbills leave their homes in the pine forests of northern Europe and spread south and west, many reaching Britain, where they remain to breed. In most parts of the British Isles the loose colonies formed after these invasions die out after a few years, but in East Anglia and the New Forest breeding has persisted for over fifty years. In the Scottish Highlands the Crossbill is a permanent resident, with its headquarters in the pine forests of the Spey valley.

The most striking and distinctive character of the Crossbill is indicated by its name; the tips of the mandibles cross on one side or the other; in nestlings the tips meet. The red dress of the male, the yellow and orange on young birds and females, together with a stumpy, short-necked appearance, make them easy to recognise when seen, but though not shy, they are difficult to pick out when working silently in the dark fir branches. A litter of dislocated cones beneath the trees, or a cone dropping from the branches, is often the first sign of their presence, though when moving from tree to tree, when the flight is strong and undulating, the call, *zit, zit,* or *zup,* is noticeable. In spring the males warble with a twitter like that of the Greenfinch. Their attitudes and actions are more parrot- than tit-like; they climb along the branches, often walking sideways, and swing head downwards to wrench at a cone. This is first twisted and nipped off, considerable force being used, then carried in the bill to a firm perch, where it is held, sometimes with one, sometimes with both feet, whilst the bird wrenches back scale after scale, picking out, then eating the seeds with head raised. After a cone is dropped the bird polishes its bill, probably to rub off the resin. The scales are generally split, but are seldom wrenched off or the cones stripped like those dropped by squirrels.

The nest, which is not unlike that of the Bullfinch, is placed on the branch of a conifer; a cup of grass, moss, and lichens, often with a little wool, is built on a platform of interwoven fir twigs. The Crossbill is an early but erratic nester; eggs may be laid in February or March or much later in the season. Four is the usual number, and they are of the Greenfinch type, greyish-white, spotted with reddish-brown.

The plumage of birds in a flock is usually varied; the old males are dark crimson, younger males may be blotched with orange and show yellow on the rump, and the females are mostly greenish-yellow and are more or less striped. The striations are noticeable on the greenish-grey young birds. A pale wing-bar is inconspicuous when birds are in the trees. The bill and legs are brown. Length, 5·5–6·5 in. Wing, 3·9 in. Tarsus, 0·65 in. The size is very variable. (*Plates 152, 154 and 177.*)

**Parrot Crossbill**                                        *Loxia pytyopsittacus*
This bird nests in Scandinavia and northern Russia, visiting central Europe in winter. It is normally a rare vagrant to Britain, but there was an exceptional irruption in the autumn of 1962 and a pair is believed to have nested in Surrey in 1963. It closely resembles the Scottish Crossbill both in plumage and in voice, but it is longer in the wing and its bill is deeper, broader and longer.

**Two-barred Crossbill**                                    *Loxia leucoptera*
This crossbill breeds in northern Russia and Siberia and winters in the Baltic region. It is a nomadic species and a few wanderers reach Britain from time to time, usually in autumn. It may at once be distinguished from our bird by its double wing-bar, conspicuously white, though this is least noticeable in young birds. Its habits and changes of plumage appear to be similar to those of the Common Crossbill. Length, 6 in.

**Chaffinch**                                               *Fringilla coelebs*
The familiar Chaffinch is evenly distributed throughout the British Isles; to the few Scottish islands where it is not resident it comes as a migrant. In hilly

country it is more plentiful than the House Sparrow, and though by no means shunning thickly populated districts is equally abundant in woods and open country. It is found throughout Europe. Some winter in northern Africa, but many reach us in autumn and remain as winter visitors. Our own birds flock in winter and become nomadic; there is also a marked passage migration both inland and along the coasts. Birds arrive on the east coast early in October, but on the west coast the movements are most marked from the middle to the end of the month. During severe weather in winter there are westward movements towards Ireland. Return migration begins in March and flocks pass throughout April, long after the residents have begun nesting. Linnaeus gave the bird the name *coelebs* because he thought the hens migrated and left the cocks behind, but though flocks in which one sex predominates are not uncommon, the sexes often mingle in winter where food is plentiful.

The cheery *pink, pink,* of the Chaffinch is uttered at all seasons and by both sexes. The rollicking song, often begun in February, is a rattle with an exuberant ending, which, however, varies, not only in different localities, but individually. The flight note is *chip, chip,* heard when flocks pass over with undulating flight, or when disturbed from their hunt for beech-mast. With Bramblings the birds spend much of the winter in and under beeches, but the oakwoods and conifer plantations, often thickly populated in spring, are deserted. Top-dressed fields are favoured, especially when waste hops or farmyard manure are used, but the farmyard itself has been much less frequented since the use of the combine harvester became general. At all seasons Chaffinches are found in gardens, and in tourist districts they haunt popular picnic sites, where they become extremely tame. Insects are largely eaten in spring and summer; in April, when the sycamore aphids swarm upon the saplings, the Chaffinch joins the newly arrived warblers to hunt for the small honey-dew-filled insects. As a flycatcher it is skilful, sallying from and returning to some perch by a river or road where it can see passing insects.

The spring display mainly consists of showing off its white wing-patches; the male perches stiffly with elevated crest and turns slowly from side to side. During the pairing season he is pugnacious and will sometimes fight with his own reflection in a window.

The nest is small, compact and neat, constructed of felted moss, lichens, wool and any soft substance, and lined with hair, feathers or down. The hen is the architect, but occasionally the cock brings materials; as a rule, however, he perches near and sings. It is placed in a hedge or the fork of a tree; in the latter situation the lichens often help to conceal it, but it is by no means always inconspicuous. Paper, thread and string are sometimes woven into the nest. The variable but characteristic eggs, four to six in number, are laid in April or May; often the whole egg is a rich reddish-brown with almost black irregular streaks. A second brood is unusual.

The head of the male is slate-blue on the crown and nape, pinkish-chestnut on the cheeks and round the eye; the back is warm chestnut and the rump greenish. The pink deepens on the breast and becomes lighter on the belly,

Black-throated
Diver, p2

Red-throated
Diver, p5

Little Grebe,
p11

Manx Shearwater,
p15

Great Crested
Grebe, p7

Fulmar,
p18

Storm Petrel,
p14

Leach's Petrel,
p13

PLATE 162

Bittern, p29

Heron, p25

Gannet, p20

Shag, p23

Mallard, p35

Cormorant, p22

Teal, p37

Garganey, p38

PLATE 163

Gadwall, p40

Wigeon, p41

Pintail, p43

Shoveler, p44

Tufted Duck,
p48

Pochard, p49

Eider, p57

Common Scoter,
p55

PLATE 164

Shelduck, p64

Grey Lag
Goose, p66

Red-breasted
Merganser, p59

Goosander, p61

Golden Eagle, p77

PLATE 165

Buzzard, p78

Sparrow Hawk, p80

Red Kite, p82

Hen Harrier, p86

Marsh Harrier, p84

Montagu's Harrier, p87

Peregrine, p90

Merlin, p92

Hobby, p89

Kestrel, p95

PLATE 166

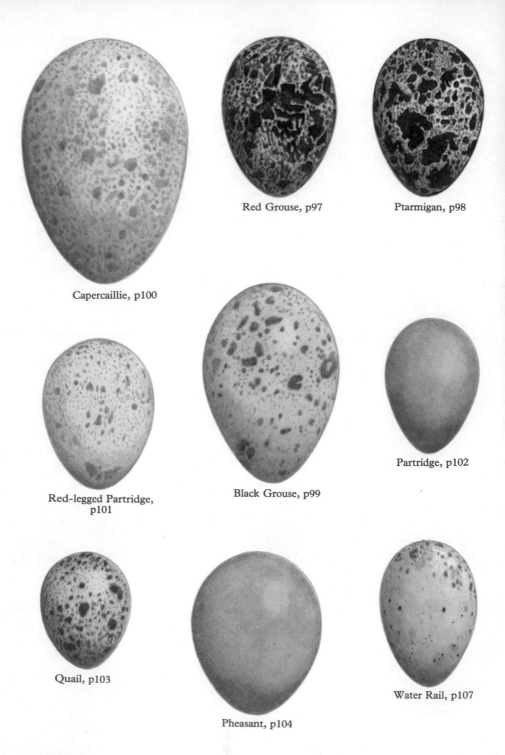

Red Grouse, p97

Ptarmigan, p98

Capercaillie, p100

Red-legged Partridge,
p101

Black Grouse, p99

Partridge, p102

Quail, p103

Pheasant, p104

Water Rail, p107

PLATE 167

Coot, p113

Oystercatcher, p117

Moorhen, p112

Dotterel, p126

Lapwing, p119

Golden Plover,
p125

Corncrake, p110

Greenshank, p145

Kentish Plover, p122

Ringed Plover, p120

PLATE 168

Whimbrel, p136

Common Snipe, p130

Stone Curlew, p162

Common Sandpiper, p141

Curlew, p135

Woodcock, p133

Redshank, p143

Red-necked Phalarope, p161

Dunlin, p152

PLATE 169

Arctic Skua,
p166

Great Skua,
p165

Great Black-backed
Gull, p170

Herring Gull, p174

Lesser Black-backed
Gull, p172

Common Gull, p175

PLATE 170

Black-headed
Gull, p180

Kittiwake, p182

Avocet, p158

Arctic Tern, p188

Sandwich Tern, p192

Razorbill,
p194

Little Tern, p191

Roseate Tern, p189

Common Tern, p187

PLATE 171

Black Guillemot,
p198

Puffin, p200

Short-eared Owl, p218

Guillemot, p197

Little Owl, p215

Barn Owl, p212

Tawny Owl, p216

Long-eared Owl, p217

PLATE 172

Wood Pigeon, p205

Rock Dove, p204

Stock Dove, p203

Turtle Dove, p207

Great Spotted
Woodpecker, p231

Lesser Spotted
Woodpecker, p232

Green Woodpecker,
p230

Swift, p223

Swallow,
p240

Cuckoo, p209

Kingfisher,
p225

House Martin,
p241

Wryneck,
p233

Wood Lark,
p235

Sky Lark,
p237

Sand Martin,
p242

PLATE 173

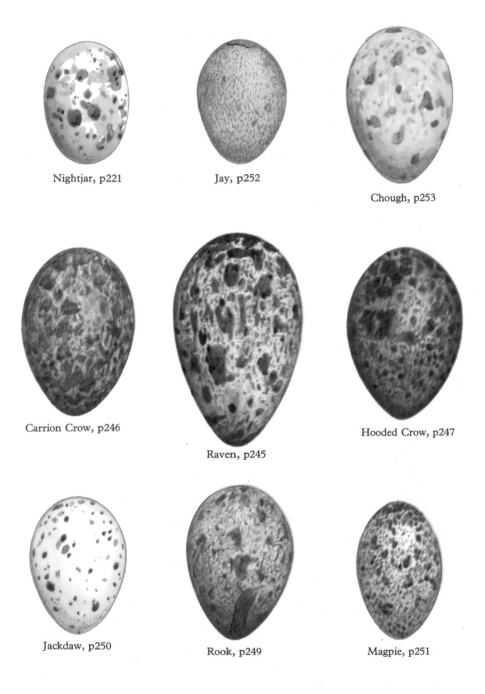

Nightjar, p221

Jay, p252

Chough, p253

Carrion Crow, p246

Raven, p245

Hooded Crow, p247

Jackdaw, p250

Rook, p249

Magpie, p251

PLATE 174

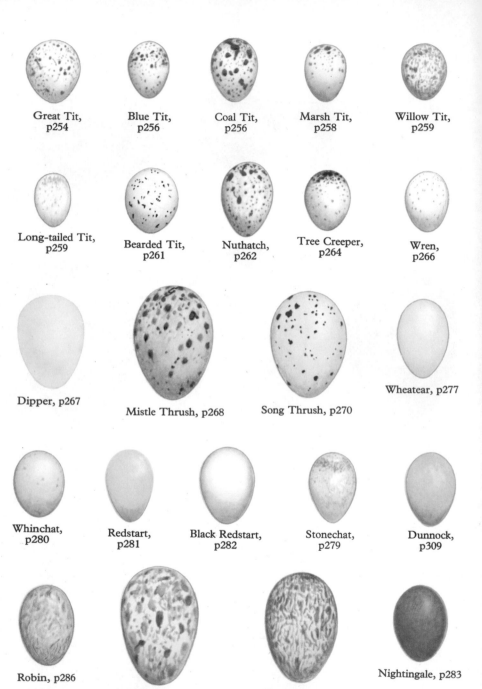

Great Tit, p254

Blue Tit, p256

Coal Tit, p256

Marsh Tit, p258

Willow Tit, p259

Long-tailed Tit, p259

Bearded Tit, p261

Nuthatch, p262

Tree Creeper, p264

Wren, p266

Dipper, p267

Mistle Thrush, p268

Song Thrush, p270

Wheatear, p277

Whinchat, p280

Redstart, p281

Black Redstart, p282

Stonechat, p279

Dunnock, p309

Robin, p286

Ring Ouzel, p273

Blackbird, p274

Nightingale, p283

PLATE 175

Reed Warbler,
p289

Marsh Warbler,
p290

Grasshopper Warbler,
p287

Wood Warbler,
p303

Sedge Warbler,
p292

Garden Warbler,
p295

Blackcap,
p293

Dartford Warbler,
p298

Chiffchaff,
p301

Willow Warbler,
p300

Whitethroat,
p296

Lesser Whitethroat,
p297

Spotted Flycatcher,
p306

Pied Flycatcher,
p307

Red-backed Shrike,
p323

Goldcrest,
p305

Meadow Pipit,
p311

Tree Pipit,
p313

Rock Pipit,
p314

Starling,
p324

PLATE 176

Pied Wagtail,
p316

Grey Wagtail,
p317

Yellow Wagtail,
p319

Hawfinch,
p326

Goldfinch,
p328

Siskin,
p329

Linnet,
p330

Twite,
p331

Redpoll,
p332

Greenfinch,
p327

Bullfinch,
p334

Crossbill,
p335

Chaffinch,
p336

Yellowhammer,
p338

Cirl Bunting,
p341

Reed Bunting,
p343

Snow Bunting,
p345

Corn Bunting,
p339

Tree Sparrow,
p347

House Sparrow,
p346

PLATE 177

shading to white. The brown wings are crossed with yellowish-white, and there is a conspicuous white patch on the shoulder. In summer the bill is lead-blue, but pinkish horn in winter; the legs are brown. The female is yellowish-brown above, greenish on the rump, and paler beneath. In winter the colours are obscured by brown or grey tips. The young are not unlike the female, but lack the greenish tints, and are paler. Length, 6·5 in. Wing, 3·45 in. Tarsus, 0·75 in. (*Plates 154 and 177.*)

## Brambling                                                    *Fringilla montifringilla*

The Brambling breeds in the pine and birch forests of northern Europe and Asia and comes to us as a winter visitor and bird of passage. Migrants arrive in large numbers on our north and east coasts late in September or in October, and return in March or April, though considerable flocks may be seen in May and laggard birds in June. It has nested at least once in Scotland.

This northern finch is the constant companion of the Chaffinch in winter, feeding in and beneath the beeches; its distribution at this season depends largely upon the abundance and fertility of the mast. Although this is its favourite diet, the Brambling is also insectivorous. Top-dressed fields are frequented, and also rough ground, where it feeds on the seeds of *Atriplex* and *Polygonum*. In April and May it frequents oaks and larches, ridding them of the larvae of small moths and the aphids that blight the young foliage. Flocks feeding on the ground rise in a body if disturbed, but the birds return singly and with caution; as they rise with twitters of annoyance, it is easy to pick out the Bramblings from Chaffinches or other companions by their white rumps, and when on the ground by their warm chestnut shoulders. The flocks when on the move fly with erratic, uncertain motion, often after many changes of direction dropping down where they rose; the flight is undulating and finch-like, several quick beats and then a shoot forward with a sharp closing of the wings. The flight note, *tscheep, tscheep*, is usually softer and longer than that of the Chaffinch, but in the trees it is a short *tuk, tuk*. The song is described as 'a short low warble', but the loud greenfinch-like call, *cree*, is frequently heard even in autumn. The nest resembles that of the Chaffinch, with lichens, moss and birch bark freely used in its construction. The eggs, usually six, are laid late in May or in June, and are similar to the lighter types of Chaffinch eggs.

The breeding male has a blue-black bill, a glossy blue-black head and neck, often with a few of the white bases of the feathers showing as flecks or markings, especially on the nape. The wing has a handsome chestnut-buff patch on the lesser coverts, followed by two white bars, and the black quills are margined with white. The chin, belly and rump are white, the throat and breast ruddy-buff. After the moult in autumn the black is obscured by broad brown tips, which give it a barred appearance, and brown tips and edgings dull the back and underparts; the bill is then yellowish with a dark tip. The female, which has none of the decided blacks and chestnuts of the male, is a browner bird, and the young are at first like the female. Length, 5·8 in. Wing, 3·5 in. Tarsus, 0·7 in. (*Plates 154 and 159.*)

## Yellowhammer                                    *Emberiza citrinella*

The Yellowhammer, or Yellow Bunting, breeds throughout Europe except in the extreme north and south. With us it is a common and well-distributed resident, and a winter visitor. Our own birds, flocking in winter, are irregular local migrants.

Though less restricted in its haunts than the Corn Bunting, it is a bird of the open country, little attracted by woodlands. It is best known as a hedgerow bird; the top of a hedge is used more often than a tree for a song platform. From this or some other elevated perch the male utters his popular song—a single *chit* repeated several times, followed by two notes, the first sharp, the last drawled out—the traditional 'Little—bit—of—bread—and—NO—cheese'. The call-note is a loud *tchick*, frequently heard from winter flocks, and this is modulated and triplicated by the amorous male in spring. February is the month when Yellowhammers begin singing, and they seldom stop before late August or September; considering that the bird sings practically all day, he must repeat the performance many thousand times a year. There is individual variation, and at times the two last notes are omitted, but as a rule each bird sticks to the same phrase and all have the same character; few songs exhibit so much sameness. This persistent song is more of a challenge than a serenade, and it is frequently interrupted by the dashing attack of a rival, for the Yellowhammer is pugnacious. Alike when perched or when flitting along the hedge, the golden and rich rufous, almost orange, adornment of the male attracts attention, and when he flies with tail half open or expands it fully on alighting, long white marks on the outer tail feathers catch the eye; in spring he opens and moves his tail to attract the eye of his mate.

In summer insects are largely eaten, but in winter the haunts vary according to the food supply; the flocks wander about the fields seeking seeds and regularly visit stubbles, where they associate with other buntings and finches. The flight is undulating; when a flock is passing over, every bird will, as if by command, suddenly dive down to a tree and settle in the branches, but at most times it is a ground rather than arboreal species. If we approach a feeding flock, the birds crouch, with the breast almost touching the ground, preparing for the upward spring if danger threatens.

The nest, built of grass and moss and lined with hair, is either on or near the ground, a hedge bank, especially when rising from a ditch, being a common site. Three to five eggs are the usual number. They are brownish- or purplish-white in ground colour, and more or less profusely lined with irregular fine or fairly thick markings. Two or even more broods are reared; the first eggs are laid towards the end of April, but young are often in the nest in September. The parent birds, when the young are hatched, will tumble about on the ground to draw attention from the nest.

The plumage of the males varies greatly in the extent and depth of the yellow. In the breeding season the head, throat and underparts are bright lemon or canary-yellow, the back, mantle and rump orange-rufous to chestnut. The head and throat are streaked with dusky-brown, and the back and flanks with rich brown. The bill and legs are brownish. The female is browner yellow, more striated on the head and underparts, and she has a distinct moustachial stripe. Pale tips and edges obscure and dull the plumage after the autumn moult, but by spring these have worn away. The young are at first like the female, but the males, after the first moult, show yellow on the head, though for a year the streaks are pronounced. Length, 6·7 in. Wing, 3·25 in. Tarsus, 0·7 in. (*Plates 156, 158 and 177.*)

## Corn Bunting                                                          *Emberiza calandra*

The Corn Bunting occurs throughout central and southern Europe as well as north Africa and western Asia. It has a wide but uneven distribution in the British Isles; there has been a very marked decrease since 1930 in Ireland, Wales, many Scottish islands and the west of England. Little change has been observed in eastern Britain, where it is still abundant in suitable agricultural districts. Many of our birds leave us in autumn and return in spring, and there are signs of passage migration on the east coast.

Largest and least showy of its group, the Corn Bunting is by no means the most frequently met with, for it is absent from woodlands and is only found in the open and usually cultivated country; where it does occur it is sometimes abundant, especially near the coast. Apart from its angled bill, a generic character, the bird is inconspicuous in its sombre dress, but noticeable by its habits and song. It delights in singing from a perch; this may be a hedge, tree or bush, but a tall weed in the centre of a field suffices; along the high roads it uses the telegraph wires, and in Wales sings from stone walls. The song is repeated every few seconds, a monotonous jingle, which, after two or three preliminary notes, *chi, chi, chi*, resembles the sound of a bunch of keys vigorously shaken. When approached it flies with heavy flight for a few yards, its legs dangling loosely, and settles again to sing. It sings early and late in the season. The call-note is a loud *chuk*, difficult to express by any combination of letters. In winter it flocks and roams, and many areas are deserted through migration. Grain and seeds are eaten in winter, but insects are devoured in spring and summer.

Although the male advertises the existence of a nest in his immediate neighbourhood, this is most difficult to find. The centre of a large field is a favourite site, and it may be built on the ground in long herbage or in a low bush. Grass, straw and moss, rather untidily put together, form the outer structure; hair is the usual lining. The four to six eggs are seldom laid before the end of May; they are of the usual bunting type, dull white, tinged purple or reddish, and scored with irregular lines with a few blotches of deep red or purple; they are subject to great variation. The male is usually polygamous; one male in Cornwall actually had seven hens.

The summer dress of both sexes is hair-brown streaked with dark brown on the head, back and breast. The eye-stripe, chin and throat are paler, and the coverts have pale edgings, as also have the feathers of wings and tail. A streak or moustachial stripe runs obliquely downwards from the base of the bill.

The bill is brown above and yellow below; the legs yellowish. The colour is browner above and slightly redder beneath after the autumn moult, and the young have more and deeper spots on the upper parts, and are buffer in tone. Length, 7 in. Wing, 3·9 in. Tarsus, 1 in. (*Plates 158 and 177.*)

## Black-headed Bunting                                    *Emberiza melanocephala*

This south European bird usually migrates east to India, but a number of vagrants have been found in the British Isles. Recent occurrences, however, may refer to escapes, as the species is now imported as a cage bird. It is apt to be confused with the Reed Bunting, which is often called the Black-headed Bunting, but besides being a larger bird its plumage is quite distinct. The black head of the male is followed by a yellow and not white collar, and there is no black on the throat and breast. The back is orange-brown and the unstreaked underparts deep yellow. The female is a lighter yellowish-brown with dark streaks on the head and back, and except on her under tail-coverts the yellow of the male is replaced by dull white. In winter the black on the head is almost hidden beneath brown feather tips, and the yellow collar and under-parts are indistinct and dull. Length, 6·8 in.

## Yellow-breasted Bunting                                       *Emberiza aureola*

Northern Russia and Siberia are the breeding grounds of this bird. Over twenty have been recorded in the British Isles on autumn migration, chiefly in Shetland or Norfolk. The mature male has a brown crown and back and a black face, chin and throat, and is pale yellow beneath, a narrow brown band crossing the breast so as to leave a yellow collar; two white bands cross the wings. In winter the bird has less black on the face and throat. The female is yellowish below with streaks only on the flanks and has a pale crown and eye-stripe. Length, 5·5 in.

## Cirl Bunting                                                  *Emberiza cirlus*

The Cirl Bunting is a southern European and Mediterranean species; its northern range extends to the more southerly parts of Britain. It nests locally in the south of England, as far north as the Malvern Hills and Chilterns. Further north and in Scotland and Ireland it only occurs as an occasional wanderer.

The bird may be distinguished from the Yellowhammer, which it resembles in many ways, by its smaller size and more squat appearance, by the olive-green on the head, and brown rump, and, in the male, by the black chin and throat and stripe through the eye. It is more of a tree-frequenting species; it often sings from the upper branches of a tall tree, where the leaves conceal it, but it will also perch on a bush or, like the Corn Bunting, a telegraph wire. The song is not unlike the rattle of the Lesser Whitethroat; the notes, though fairly rapidly repeated, are clear, distinct and metallic. When singing the bird throws up its head and opens wide its mandibles; it sings late, and may be heard in September. Its drooping flight is that of a true bunting; when rising with Linnets or other finches it is easily picked out. The food consists of insects and seeds, and in winter, when it wanders in small nomadic flocks to a distance from its usual haunts, it consorts with other birds in the stubbles.

The site of the nest is usually in a bush or hedge from a few inches to several feet above the ground, but occasionally on a bank, especially amongst the roots of a tree. The materials are practically the same as those used by the Yellowhammer, but with more moss in most cases. The three to five eggs have bolder scribbles as a rule, and are smaller and paler in ground colour; some are richly blotched and streaked with chocolate, black, or nearly black irregular markings. Two broods are reared; the first eggs are seldom laid before May.

The head of the male in summer is olive-green streaked with brown; the sides of the face are lemon-yellow with a conspicuous black line through the eye, and the throat is black. Pale yellow on the breast is followed by an olive band; the upper parts are less rufous than the Yellowhammer, and are olive on wing-coverts and rump. Below the breast is pale yellow, shading to chestnut on the flanks, which are streaked; the white on the outer tail feathers is noticeable. The bill is brown; the legs brownish-yellow. The female is duller, browner and more streaked than the male; she lacks the black on the head and chin. Her olive-brown rump distinguishes her from the female Yellowhammer. After the autumn moult pale edges obscure most of the black on the male and dull the plumage generally. The young are like the female, but less bright. Length, 6 in. Wing, 3·15 in. Tarsus, 0·7 in. (*Plates 158 and 177.*)

## Ortolan Bunting                                                 *Emberiza hortulana*

The Ortolan breeds in Europe, except in the extreme north, and in parts of the Mediterranean Basin, and is now known to be a regular bird of passage through our islands in small numbers. It occurs in both spring and autumn in the Shetlands, south-west England, Wales and Southern Ireland.

The male bird has an olive-green head and breast, and a sulphur-yellow streak running backwards from the angle of the bill, caused by the yellow chin and throat being crossed by a moustachial stripe. The wings are brown and the striated back and rump dark brown; the underparts below the band are warm chestnut. The female (the upper bird) has the head and breast streaked, and lacks the olive on the breast and yellow on the throat. Her upper parts are yellower and her under more buff. Young males have stripes on the head and rump; the bill is pink and there is a pale ring round the eye. Length, 6·5 in. (*Plate 158.*)

## Rustic Bunting                                                      *Emberiza rustica*

This bird, which has a northern European and Asiatic range, has been recorded from several different localities in England and Scotland from the south coast to the Shetlands, with a recent average of two or three a year. Most of the English occurrences have been in autumn, but in Scotland and Fair Isle it has been met with in spring. The male in breeding dress is a warm chestnut on the nape and back, and has a band of the same colour across the breast; its forehead, crown and the sides of the head are black and a white stripe extends from the eye to the nape. Its underparts are white with chestnut spots on the flanks. The female has brown instead of black on the head. In winter buff obscures much of the black on the male, and the underparts are suffused with buff. The breast-band and spots on the flanks are the best distinctive characters. Length, 5·5 in.

## Little Bunting                                        *Emberiza pusilla*

The Little Bunting inhabits arctic Russia and Siberia, migrating south in Asia and often reaching Europe in autumn. It has been recorded several times in England and more rarely in Ireland, but its passage in the Shetlands is almost regular in autumn, and it has been noted several times in spring.

In general appearance this bird is like a small female Reed Bunting, but in the male the crown and cheeks are rufous, the former bordered and emphasised by a black line extending to the whitish collar. The brown back is freely spotted in streaks. The underparts are white, shading to buff on the striated flanks. A dark streak runs downwards from the bill on either side of the chestnut throat. The head markings are less pronounced in the female and she is a paler bird; in the young the crown is buff, bordered by brown instead of black. The female may be distinguished from the Rustic Bunting by her more chestnut head and paler upper parts. Length, 5 in. (*Plate 161*.)

## Reed Bunting                                        *Emberiza schoeniclus*

Throughout Europe the Reed Bunting is resident and often migratory. With us it is at once a resident, some remaining all winter, and a summer and winter visitor, for birds from northern Europe arrive in autumn when many of our nesting birds are leaving. It is found in all parts of the British Isles. There has been a considerable increase in recent years and it has colonised some Scottish islands where it was previously unknown.

The Reed Bunting is best known as a bird of the waterside, either flowing or stagnant; it is found in the reed fringe of lakes, pools, canals and ditches, in the semi-aquatic vegetation round small ponds, in sewage farms or osier-beds, or on marshy uplands. However, it now also breeds regularly in completely dry habitats in many parts of England and Scotland, and in winter it has locally become a regular visitor to bird tables. This extension of its range of habitat probably accounts for the recent increase in numbers.

Clinging to a reed stem, one leg bent, gripping level with the breast, the other straight beneath him, the smart black-headed, white-collared male stutters and stammers his perpetual efforts to produce a song. As music it is an indifferent performance, ending after a few sharp but irregularly uttered notes with a weak, hissing finish, corresponding to the jingle of the Corn Bunting and the 'cheese' of the Yellowhammer. The song often starts in February and continues until autumn, and yet, after six months or more of effort no perfection is attained. The call is a loud *seeep*, often uttered by the bird when courting, and when the young are in the nest both birds have a short, anxious alarm or warning *chit*; they may repeat this note over and over again with beaks loaded with insects. The song is usually delivered from a perch, but the bird will at times sing on the ground, where in addition to hopping it walks when seeking food. Insects, especially tipulid flies and larvae of moths, are the chief food in summer; the young are probably fed on nothing else, but in winter seeds and a little grain are taken. The flight is jerky—a series of forward and upward shoots.

In winter a few, apparently life-paired birds, remain in their summer haunts, but the majority become gregarious and nomadic, joining with other buntings and finches in fields and farmyards as well as on marshlands. In northern England many, at any rate, leave and either wander farther south or cross the sea; but large numbers winter on the Pennine moors in Lancashire and north Staffordshire among the moor-grass, *Molinia caerulea*. Early in February some return to the nesting haunts, and the first arrivals roost sociably in reeds or withies. In March oversea birds arrive, often accompanied by Pied Wagtails and Meadow Pipits. Soon nesting begins, and the male may be seen, squatting on the ground and shuffling round but always keeping an eye on his mate, evidently suggesting building. A tuft of coarse marsh grass, the stocks of cut osiers, and the base of a clump of rushes are favoured sites for the nest which is made of any handy material: grass, reed blades, flags or moss, and lined with hair and frequently the feathery awns of the reed. Both sexes incubate, and when disturbed will struggle along the ground, feigning a helpless or wounded condition and so drawing the intruder from the nest; at times, however, the female slips away quietly and quickly. A second, often a third brood is reared; eggs are laid in April, but may still be met with in August. Four to six is the usual number in the first clutch, but late nests often contain only three. The ground colour varies from purplish-white to brown, and the streaks and spots are as a rule bolder but sparser than on the egg of the Yellowhammer.

The male in breeding dress has a black head and throat and white streak from the bill joining his snowy collar. His upper parts are mostly warm brown to chestnut, and the dark centres of the feathers form decided streaks. The outer tail feathers have broad white margins. Beneath he is whitish, streaked with brown on the flanks. His bill and legs are brown. Buff feather tips obscure the black and dull the plumage generally after the autumn moult. The female has a reddish head and no black on the breast; she has black and white streaks on either side of her dull white chin, and a buff eye-stripe and streaks on breast and flanks. The young closely resemble her. Length, about 6 in. Wing, 3 in. Tarsus, 0·8 in. (*Plates 161 and 177*.)

## Lapland Bunting                                        *Calcarius lapponicus*

The Lapland Bunting, which breeds in high latitudes in Europe, Asia and America and winters further south, was once looked upon as a vagrant to the British Isles, but the regularity of its appearance in autumn in the Shetlands and other Scottish islands, and its frequency on our east coast suggest that it is a regular bird of passage on its southern migration. In the north it is also noted in spring. Occasionally it is seen inland in autumn and winter, and on the Irish coast it is an annual autumn passage migrant in small numbers.

The Lapland Bunting is a ground-feeder, and its habit of running and long claw on the hind toe are suggestive of a pipit, but its conical yellow bill is that of a bunting. On migration it regularly perches in trees. It often associates with Sky Larks or joins mixed flocks of finches. The calls include a click and musical whistle.

The male's black head, face and throat, with the white line from above the eye round the cheeks, and the bright chestnut collar are conspicuous in spring. Below the collar the back is brown, the feathers having dark centres. Autumn females and young resemble female Reed Buntings, but have darker backs and shorter tails, showing less white on the outer feathers. Length, 6·2 in. Wing, 3·75 in. Tarsus, 0·85 in. (*Plate 157.*)

### Snow Bunting                                          *Plectrophenax nivalis*

In England, Wales and Ireland the Snow Bunting is known only as a winter visitor or bird of passage, but in Scotland a very few pairs nest in the Cairn-gorms and it has bred irregularly elsewhere. It breeds in arctic Europe and Asia and wanders south in winter.

Along the shore or on the fells in winter there are few more charming sights than a flock of 'Snowflakes' as they are aptly called. We do not meet with them in low-lying inland localities; these they seldom visit, clinging either to the coast-line or seeking the higher uplands. Suddenly the birds rise from the tide-wrack, flickering white, wheel and drift down wind, dancing before us, but soon returning to their hunt. When clouds hang low on the fells the twitter is heard before the fluttering flakes emerge from the mist; they drop on the short sheep-cropped grass, littered with broken scree, and vanish amongst the stones, some sheltering, as if in hiding, behind the rocky débris. Yet the bird is not shy, and on the shore is almost indifferent. In flight the sharply contrasted black and white of the wing renders them conspicuous, and in breeding plumage the white and black dress of the male makes him one of the most notice-able of small birds, though even he may be hidden by the presence of snow amidst dark rocks. In winter dress, tawny above and white beneath, the bird when seen upon the shore may be at first mistaken for a small wader, an error enhanced by its habit of running and seldom hopping. When a winter gale sweeps the shore the birds crouch as they feed, and if disturbed hardly rise above the sand, along which they are whirled for yards, but soon settle again.

The flight note is a Linnet-like twitter; this twitter is interrupted by a frequent call-note, a loud *tweet*. The song, often uttered from the heaped-up rocks in which the nest is hidden, has much of the indecision of the Reed Bunting, though fuller and mellower. The male will often shoot into the air like a Tree Pipit, descending in sweeping curves and singing all the time; if, however, he fears that the nest is endangered he flies round with plaintive alarm cries and settles, piping anxiously, within a few feet of the intruder. Gnats and other flies are the food in summer, but in winter various seeds and grain are eaten, those of grasses and salt-marsh plants, such as *Suaeda* and sea-aster being favoured. In the Pennines wintering flocks feed on larvae of the gall-midges that infest the tussocks of purple moor-grass and they tend to confine themselves to moorlands where this plant grows.

The nest is difficult to find. Its usual site is among disintegrating rocks and boulders, and is deeply hidden in some crack or under a stone too heavy to move. Any handy material is used: dry grass, moss, roots, with a lining of hair and feathers. In Scotland four or five eggs are usual; they vary considerably in their markings.

In breeding dress the male is a handsome white and black bird, the black being on the mantle, secondaries, primaries and tail. His bill and legs are black. These blacks are replaced by brown in the female, and her head and wing-coverts are also brown. In autumn and early winter broad chestnut tips obscure the black, and chestnut tinges the crown, ear-coverts and breast; the bill is then yellow with a dark tip. The young are much browner, especially on the wings. Length, 6·5–7 in. Wing, 4·2 in. Tarsus, 0·9 in. (*Plates 157 and 177.*)

## Family PASSERIDAE Sparrows

**House Sparrow**                                          *Passer domesticus*

Wherever man builds in our islands the House Sparrow sooner or later comes to share his abode. Though described as tame and semi-domestic, neither is strictly true; man, in the Sparrow's eye, provides food and home, but though impudently annexing his property, it remains suspicious and resents familiarity. An abundant resident, the bird is not universally common; in many hilly districts it is scarce, and it is only thinly distributed in the west of Scotland, Ireland and Wales. In cities, towns and villages, even round isolated farms, it is the most abundant bird. Our Sparrow occurs in most of Europe though replaced by allied forms in some areas; it has also followed man, intentionally or accidentally introduced, to most of his colonies—a bird of European civilisation. The House Sparrow, at least in the British Isles, is a sedentary bird. J. D. Summers-Smith, in his monograph on the species, has shown that few individuals travel more than two miles from their birth-place. Although large movements have occasionally been reported on the east coast in autumn there is no definite proof of immigration from the Continent or of unassisted emigration from the British Isles.

So familiar a bird needs little description, yet it is often confused with the smaller and slimmer Tree Sparrow, which, however, has a coppery and not grey crown, two distinct wing-bars, and a black patch on the cheeks. Gregarious at all seasons, in its nesting colonies, its feeding and bathing habits and, especially in autumn, in its communal roosting, the bird by its very abundance becomes a nuisance. Summers-Smith estimates the population of Great Britain at nine and a half million, with much the greatest density in urban areas. Cornfields in the neighbourhood of towns and villages are raided by large flocks of sparrows, at first chiefly young birds. They strip the ripening grain from a widening belt round the outside of a field and beat down the stalks with their weight. In spring our flowers, especially yellow blossoms, are attacked and torn to bits; crocuses, primroses and aconites seem to annoy it most, but strange preference is shown for certain flowers in different gardens. Seeds of weeds are certainly eaten, but seedling peas and leaves of vegetables are attacked. Were the bird more agile on the wing, it would destroy many butterflies and moths, for it never fails to hunt the passing white butterfly and even the big yellow-underwing; unfortunately it is an indifferent fly-catcher. It makes successful attacks upon aphids, and it eagerly devours saw-fly larvae. When the green tortrix attacks the oak the birds hover awk-wardly to snatch at the grubs that swing suspended by silk threads. Courtship display begins early in the year, and it is in March and April that the brief but noisy pursuits of a single female by a number of males are most frequent. In spite of these communal activities it appears that the House Sparrow is faithful for life to its mate and to its nest-hole, though if one of a pair is killed a replacement is usually soon found.

The short and incessant chirp needs no description, and its double note *phillip* is as familiar. While the young are in their nests, the old birds utter a long parental *churr*. The combined voices at dusk in the winter roosts, which, even in London and other cities, are in clumps of trees in parks and gardens, in evergreens or ivy-covered walls, have a curious effect; each individual penetrating chirp seems distinct, and yet the whole is a jumble of shrill notes. Early in August the morning twitter decreases and is hardly noticeable when the young depart. The flight is direct and bustling, but when long flights are undertaken is as undulating as that of most finches; on the ground the Sparrow hops jauntily.

From one to four broods are reared in the season. The nesting site is varied —under eaves, in holes in masonry or rocks, in ivy or creepers on houses or banks, on the sea-cliffs, or in bushes or trees, but never far from human habitations. When built in holes or ivy the nest is an untidy litter of straw and rubbish, abundantly filled with feathers, usually looted from the nearest hen-run; but large, well-constructed domed nests are built in orchard and other trees, and in treeless country in hedgerows or bushes. Before the rightful owners arrive, the old nests of House Martins and sometimes Swallows are annexed, and occasionally the Sparrow evicts a bird in occupation; the Sand Martin also suffers. The first clutch is normally laid in late April or early May. The five or six eggs, profusely dusted, speckled or blotched with black, brown or ash-grey on a blue-tinted or creamy-white ground, are variable in size and shape as well as markings. The cock regularly broods the eggs, but he does not develop incubation patches. Both sexes feed the young, the cock taking the greater share after they leave the nest.

The male in spring has a dark grey crown with chocolate-brown patches below it, meeting at the back of the neck, brown back and wings with dark streaks, white wing-bar and grey rump; it has a black throat and whitish cheeks and underparts. The bill is blue-black; the legs brown. In winter the plumage is dulled by pale edgings, and the bill is yellowish-brown. The female has no black on head nor throat, nor a grey crown; her upper parts are streaked with brown. The young are deeper brown, and the white is replaced by buff; the beak is dull yellow. Length, 6·25 in. Wing, 2·9 in. Tarsus, 0·7 in. (*Plates 161 and 177.*)

### Tree Sparrow                                                           *Passer montanus*

Although the Tree Sparrow is still local in its distribution in the British Isles and is absent from the mainland of south-west England there has been a very marked expansion of its range and increase in numbers since 1960. It is now widely distributed in England and is local but increasing in Wales and Scotland. The Irish population appeared to be extinct by 1960, but breeding colonies were widespread near the coast by 1967. Abroad it is spread over most of Europe and Siberia. Large numbers of migrants reach our east coast in autumn and return in spring; as a migrant it has occurred on many Scottish islands, including Fair Isle, and on others it breeds.

The bird is often confused with the larger and coarser House Sparrow, but its rich brown, almost coppery head, a black patch on its white cheeks, and a double white wing-bar, together with its slighter and more graceful build, are distinctive. The sexes are practically alike, an important specific character. Shy and rural in its choice of habitat, it is smarter in its movements, both on the wing and in trees, than the commoner bird. Its voice is shriller; the call is a shorter *chip*, as if the *r* is omitted from the House Sparrow's note, and is frequently repeated—*chib, tchip*, with emphasis on the second syllable. It has the double *phil-lip*, and a shrill *churr*; the song, modulated chirps, is not unmusical. Its chirrups, when gathering at the roost, for it is a sociable species, are higher pitched and more distinct than those of its congener, and the note of the young, though insistent, is more subdued. In winter it visits farms and stubbles, flocking with other sparrows and finches, or frequents, day by day, a roadside heap of manure or rubbish, or a sewage farm.

Though occasionally nesting in isolated trees, it is a gregarious bird at all seasons, and a grove of old trees with a plentiful supply of hollows, or a disused quarry, are favourite sites for the colony; what it likes is a hole in which to put its untidy nest, composed of hay, grass, wool or other material and lined with feathers. Some of the nests are not actually in holes in rock, but are built amongst roots of overhanging furze or other bushes. The haunts of man are not always shunned, for old thatch in a barn or cottage will shelter a colony, and nest-boxes are sometimes occupied. A domed nest, like that of the House Sparrow, is sometimes built in the old home of a Magpie or other bird. The four to six eggs, usually five, are smaller and, as a rule, browner than those of the House Sparrow; they vary considerably, and frequently the markings are massed at one end. In most clutches one egg is lighter and differs in markings from the others.

The crown and nape are rich chestnut, and on the white cheeks and ear-coverts there is a triangular black patch; the chin and throat are black. Two distinct though narrow white bars cross the brown wings. In summer the bill is lead-blue, in winter almost black; the legs are pale brown. Young, even in the nest, closely resemble their parents. Length, 6 in. Wing, 2·8 in. Tarsus, 0·7 in. (*Plates 160, 161 and 177.*)

# INDEX

*Acanthis cannabina*, 329, *Pls.* 153, 177
—— *flammea*, 331, *Pls.* 153, 177
—— *flavirostris*, 330, *Pls.* 151, 153, 177
—— *hornemanni*, 332
Accentor, Alpine, 310, *Pl.* 145
*Accipiter gentilis*, 81, *Pl.* 38
—— *nisus*, 79, *Pls.* 38, 166
*Acrocephalus aedon*, xv
—— *agricola*, xv
—— *arundinaceus*, 288
—— *dumetorum*, 291
—— *paludicola*, 292, *Pl.* 133
—— *palustris*, 290, *Pls.* 126, 176
—— *schoenobaenus*, 291, *Pls.* 133, 135, 176
—— *scirpaceus*, 288, *Pls.* 126, 135, 176
*Aegithalos caudatus*, 259, *Pls.* 116, 121, 175
*Aegolius funereus*, 219, *Pl.* 98
*Alauda arvensis*, 236, *Pls.* 108, 110, 173
ALAUDIDAE, 234
Albatross, Black-browed, 12
*Alca impennis*, xv
—— *torda*, 193, *Pls.* 81, 171
ALCEDINIDAE, 224
*Alcedo atthis*, 224, *Pls.* 105, 173
ALCIDAE, 193
*Alectoris rufa*, 101, *Pls.* 47, 53, 167
*Anas acuta*, 42, *Pls.* 21, 164
—— *americana*, 42
—— *clypeata*, 43, *Pls.* 21, 23, 164
—— *crecca*, 36, *Pls.* 1, 163
—— *discors*, 39
—— *penelope*, 40, *Pls.* 21, 164
—— *platyrhynchos*, 34, *Pls.* 1, 163
—— *querquedula*, 38, *Pls.* 1, 163
—— *rubripes*, xv
—— *strepera*, 39, *Pls.* 20, 21, 164
ANATIDAE, 34
*Anser albifrons*, 67, *Pl.* 30
—— *anser*, 65, *Pls.* 28, 30, 165
—— *caerulescens*, 69
—— *erythropus*, 67
—— *fabalis*, 68, *Pl.* 30
ANSERIFORMES, 34
*Anthus campestris*, 312
—— *cervinus*, 313

—— *gustavi*, 313
—— *hodgsoni*, xv
—— *novaeseelandiae*, 311
—— *pratensis*, 310, *Pls.* 142, 144, 176
—— *spinoletta*, 313, *Pls.* 142, 144, 176
—— *trivialis*, 312, *Pls.* 142, 176
APODIDAE, 222
APODIFORMES, 222
*Apus affinis*, xv
—— *apus*, 222, *Pls.* 105, 173
—— *melba*, 223, *Pl.* 105
*Aquila chrysaetos*, 76, *Pls.* 37, 165
—— *clanga*, 77
*Ardea cinerea*, 24, *Pls.* 14, 15, 163
—— *purpurea*, 26, *Pl.* 14
ARDEIDAE, 24
*Ardeola ralloides*, 27, *Pl.* 13
*Arenaria interpres*, 127, *Pls.* 55, 62
*Asio flammeus*, 217, *Pls.* 100, 101, 172
—— *otus*, 216, *Pls.* 95, 101, 172
*Athene noctua*, 214, *Pls.* 102, 172
Auk, Great, xv
——, Little, 195, *Pl.* 93
Avocet, xii, 157, *Pls.* 76, 78, 171
*Aythya collaris*, 46
—— *ferina*, 48, *Pls.* 22, 23, 164
—— *fuligula*, 47, *Pls.* 22, 164
—— *marila*, 45, *Pl.* 1
—— *nyroca*, 50, *Pl.* 25


Baldpate, 42
*Bartramia longicauda*, 133
Bee-eater, xii, 225, *Pl.* 105
——, Blue-cheeked, xv
Bittern, xii, 28, *Pls.* 16, 17, 163
——, American, 30, *Pl.* 13
——, Little, 28, *Pl.* 17
Blackbird, 273, *Pls.* 125, 175
Blackcap, 293, *Pls.* 137, 176
Bluetail, Red-flanked, xv
Bluethroat, 284, *Pl.* 130
Bobolink, xvi
*Bombycilla garrulus*, 319, *Pl.* 149
BOMBYCILLIDAE, 319
Bonxie, 165

*Botaurus lentiginosus*, 30, *Pl.* 13
—— *stellaris*, 28, *Pls.* 16, 17, 163
Bottlenose, 199
Brambling, xiii, 337, *Pls.* 154, 159
*Branta bernicla*, 69, *Pl.* 34
—— *canadensis*, 71, *Pl.* 33
—— *leucopsis*, 70, *Pl.* 34
—— *ruficollis*, 72
*Bubo bubo*, 213, *Pl.* 101
*Bubulcus ibis*, 27
*Bucephala albeola*, 50
—— *clangula*, 51, *Pl.* 25
Bufflehead, 50
*Bulweria bulwerii*, xiv
Bullfinch, 333, *Pls.* 154, 155, 177
Bunting, Black-headed, 340
——, Cirl, 340, *Pls.* 158, 177
——, Corn, 339, *Pls.* 158, 177
——, Lapland, 343, *Pl.* 157
——, Little, 342, *Pl.* 161
——, Ortolan, 341, *Pl.* 158
——, Pine, xvi
——, Reed, 342, *Pls.* 161, 177
——, Rock, xvi
——, Rustic, 341
——, Snow, xii, 344, *Pls.* 157, 177
——, Yellow, 338
——, Yellow-breasted, 340
BURHINIDAE, 161
*Burhinus oedicnemus*, 161, *Pls.* 77, 169
Bustard, xii
——, Great, 114
——, Houbara or Macqueen's, 115
——, Little, 114, *Pl.* 58
Butcher Bird, 322
*Buteo buteo*, 77, *Pls.* 32, 37, 166
—— *lagopus*, 79, *Pl.* 37
Buzzard, 77, *Pls.* 32, 37, 166
——, Honey, xii, 83, *Pl.* 34
——, Rough-legged, 79, *Pl.* 37

*Calandrella cinerea*, 234
—— *rufescens*, 234
*Calcarius lapponicus*, 343, *Pl.* 157
*Calidris acuminata*, 151
—— *alba*, 154, *Pls.* 75, 77
—— *alpina*, 151, *Pls.* 74, 75, 169
—— *bairdii*, 150
—— *canutus*, 146, *Pls.* 70, 71
—— *ferruginea*, 153, *Pl.* 74
—— *fuscicollis*, 150
—— *maritima*, 147, *Pl.* 73
—— *mauri*, xv
—— *melanotos*, 150, *Pls.* 72, 73

—— *minuta*, 148, *Pls.* 72, 73
—— *minutilla*, 149
—— *pusilla*, 154
—— *temminckii*, 149, *Pl.* 73
Calloo, 53
Capercaillie, 99, *Pls.* 50, 167
CAPRIMULGIDAE, 220
CAPRIMULGIFORMES, 220
*Caprimulgus aegyptius*, xv
—— *europaeus*, 220, *Pls.* 103, 109, 174
—— *ruficollis*, xv
*Carduelis carduelis*, 328, *Pls.* 150, 177
—— *chloris*, 326, *Pls.* 148, 157, 177
—— *spinus*, 329, *Pls.* 150, 177
*Carpodacus erythrinus*, 334
*Catharus minimus*, 275
—— *ustulatus*, xv
*Cepphus grylle*, 197, *Pls.* 93, 172
*Cercotrichas galactotes*, 284
*Certhia familiaris*, 263, *Pls.* 107, 122, 124, 175
CERTHIIDAE, 263
*Cettia cetti*, xv
Chaffinch, 335, *Pls.* 154, 177
CHARADRIIDAE, 117
CHARADRIIFORMES, 116
*Charadrius alexandrinus*, 122, *Pls.* 62, 168
—— *asiaticus*, xv
—— *dubius*, 121, *Pl.* 61
—— *hiaticula*, 119, *Pls.* 61, 168
—— *vociferus*, 122
Chat, Rufous Bush, 284
Chiffchaff, 300, *Pls.* 138, 176
*Chlamydotis undulata*, 115
*Chlidonias hybrida*, 184
—— *leucopterus*, 184, *Pl.* 89
—— *niger*, 183, *Pl.* 89
*Chordeiles minor*, xv
Chough, xii, 252, *Pls.* 117, 174
*Ciconia ciconia*, 30, *Pl.* 18
—— *nigra*, 31, *Pl.* 18
CICONIIDAE, 30
CICONIIFORMES, 24
CINCLIDAE, 266
*Cinclus cinclus*, 266, *Pls.* 120, 122, 175
*Circus aeruginosus*, 84, *Pls.* 36, 41, 166
—— *cyaneus*, 85, *Pls.* 40, 41, 166
—— *macrourus*, xv
—— *pygargus*, 86, *Pls.* 40, 42, 166
*Clamator glandarius*, 209
*Clangula hyemalis*, 52, *Pl.* 22
*Coccothraustes coccothraustes*, 325, *Pls.* 150, 177
*Coccyzus americanus*, 210
—— *erythrophthalmus*, xv

Cock, Black, 98
—— of the Woods, 100
*Columba livia*, 203, *Pls.* 94, 173
—— *oenas*, 202, *Pls.* 97, 173
—— *palumbus*, 204, *Pls.* 97, 173
COLUMBIDAE, 202
COLUMBIFORMES, 202
Coot, 112, *Pl.* 58, 168
*Coracias garrulus*, 226, *Pl.* 109
CORACIIDAE, 226
CORACIIFORMES, 224
Cormorant, 21, *Pls.* 10, 12, 163
——, Green, 23
Corncrake, xii, 109, *Pls.* 57, 168
CORVIDAE, 244
*Corvus corax*, 244, *Pls.* 113, 174
—— *corone cornix*, 247, *Pls.* 114, 174
—— —— *corone*, 245, *Pls.* 114, 174
—— *frugilegus*, 247, *Pls.* 114, 174
—— *monedula*, 249, *Pls.* 113, 174
*Coturnix coturnix*, 103, *Pls.* 57, 167
Coulterneb, 199
Courser, Cream-coloured, 164, *Pl.* 78
Crake, Baillon's, 108, *Pl.* 57
——, Carolina, 108
——, Little, 109, *Pl.* 57
——, Spotted, 107, *Pl.* 54
Crane, 106, *Pl.* 54
Creeper, Tree, 263, *Pls.* 107, 122, 124, 175
——, Wall, 262
*Crex crex*, 109, *Pls.* 57, 168
Crossbill, xii, 334, *Pls.* 152, 154, 177
——, Parrot, 335
——, Two-barred, 335
Crow, Carrion, 245, *Pls.* 114, 174
——, Hooded or Grey, 247, *Pls.* 114, 174
Cuckoo, 208, *Pls.* 102, 173
——, Black-billed, xv
——, Great Spotted, 209
——, Yellow-billed, 210
CUCULIDAE, 208
CUCULIFORMES, 208
*Cuculus canorus*, 208, *Pls.* 102, 173
Curlew, 133, *Pls.* 63, 66, 169
——, Black, 32
——, Eskimo, 136
——, Stone, xii, 161, *Pls.* 77, 169
*Cursorius cursor*, 164, *Pl.* 78
*Cyanosylvia svecica*, 284, *Pl.* 130
*Cygnus bewickii*, 74, *Pls.* 31, 33
—— *cygnus*, 73, *Pls.* 31, 33
—— *olor*, 72, *Pl.* 33

Dabchick, 10, *Pls.* 6, 8, 162

Daw, 249
*Delichon urbica*, 240, *Pls.* 110, 173
*Dendrocopus major*, 230, *Pls.* 104, 106, 107, 173
—— *minor*, 232, *Pls.* 106, 173
*Dendroica coronata*, xvi
—— *petechia*, xvi
*Diomedea melanophrys*, 12
DIOMEDEIDAE, 12
Dipper, 266, *Pls.* 120, 122, 175
Dish-washer, 315
Diver, Black-throated, xii, 1, *Pls.* 2, 3, 162
——, Great Northern, xii, 2, *Pls.* 2, 4
——, Red-throated, xii, 4, *Pls.* 4, 5, 162
——, White-billed, 4
*Dolichonyx oryzivorus*, xvi
Dotterel, 125, *Pls.* 62, 168
Dove, Collared, 205, *Pls.* 92, 97
——, Ring, 204, *Pls.* 97, 173
——, Rock, 203, *Pls.* 94, 173
——, Rufous Turtle, xv
——, Stock, 202, *Pls.* 97, 173
——, Turtle, 206, *Pls.* 92, 97, 173
Dowitcher, Long-billed, 128, *Pls.* 59, 65
——, Short-billed, 128
Duck, Black, xv
——, Ferruginous, 50, *Pl.* 25
——, Long-tailed, xiii, 52, *Pl.* 22
——, Ring-necked, 46
——, Tufted, 47, *Pls.* 22, 164
——, Wild or Mallard, 34, *Pls.* 1, 163
Dunlin, 151, *Pls.* 74, 75, 169
Dunnock, 308, *Pls.* 142, 175

Eagle, Golden, xii, 76, *Pls.* 37, 165
——, Spotted, xii, 77
——, White-tailed, or Sea-, xii, 82, *Pl.* 41
Egret, Cattle, 27
——, Great White, 26
——, Little, 26
*Egretta alba*, 26
—— *garzetta*, 26
Eider, 56, *Pls.* 26, 164
—, King, 58, *Pl.* 26
——, Steller's, 56
*Emberiza aureola*, 340
—— *calandra*, 339, *Pls.* 158, 177
—— *cia*, xvi
—— *cirlus*, 340, *Pls.* 158, 177
—— *citrinella*, 338, *Pls.* 156, 158, 177
—— *hortulana*, 341, *Pl.* 158
—— *leucocephala*, xvi
—— *melanocephala*, 340
—— *pusilla*, 342, *Pl.* 161

*Emberiza rustica*, 341
—— *schoeniclus*, 342, *Pls.* 161, 177
*Eremophila alpestris*, 237, *Pl.* 94
*Erithacus rubecula*, 285, *Pls.* 130, 132, 175
Erne, xii, 83, *Pl.* 41
*Eudromias morinellus*, 125, *Pls.* 62, 168

*Falco columbarius*, 91, *Pls.* 45, 166
—— *naumanni*, 94
—— *peregrinus*, 89, *Pls.* 42, 43, 166
—— *rusticolus*, 91, *Pl.* 45
—— *subbuteo*, 88, *Pls.* 49, 166
—— *tinnunculus*, 94, *Pls.* 43, 49, 166
—— *vespertinus*, 93, *Pl.* 49
Falcon, Gyr, 91, *Pl.* 45
——, Red-footed, 93, *Pl.* 49
FALCONIDAE, 76
FALCONIFORMES, 76
*Ficedula albicollis*, 308
—— *hypoleuca*, 307, *Pls.* 141, 143, 176
—— *parva*, 308, *Pl.* 141
Fieldfare, 268, *Pl.* 125
Finch, Citril, xvi
Firecrest, 305, *Pl.* 138
Flamingo, Greater, 33
Flycatcher, Brown, xv
——, Collared, 308
——, Pied, 307, *Pls.* 141, 143, 176
——, Red-breasted, 308, *Pl.* 141
——, Spotted, 306, *Pls.* 140, 141, 176
*Fratercula arctica*, 199, *Pls.* 93, 172
*Fregata magnificens*, xiv
Frigate Bird, Magnificent, xiv
*Fringilla coelebs*, 335, *Pls.* 154, 177
—— *montifringilla*, 337, *Pls.* 154, 159
FRINGILLIDAE, 325
*Fulica atra*, 112, *Pls.* 58, 168
Fulmar, 17, *Pls.* 11, 13, 162
*Fulmarus glacialis*, 17, *Pls.* 11, 13, 162

Gadwall, 39, *Pls.* 20, 21, 164
*Galerida cristata*, 234
GALLIFORMES, 96
*Gallinago gallinago*, 129, *Pls.* 60, 65, 169
—— *media*, 130, *Pl.* 65
*Gallinula chloropus*, 111, *Pls.* 58, 168
Gallinule, Purple, xv
Gannet, 19, *Pls.* 14, 163
Garganey, xiii, 38, *Pls.* 1, 163
*Garrulus glandarius*, 251, *Pls.* 115, 117, 174
*Gavia adamsii*, 4

—— *arctica*, 1, *Pls.* 2, 3, 162
—— *immer*, 2, *Pls.* 2, 4
—— *stellata*, 4, *Pls.* 4, 5, 162
GAVIIDAE, 1
GAVIIFORMES, 1
*Gelochelidon nilotica*, 185, *Pl.* 90
*Geothlypis trichas*, xvi
*Glareola nordmanni*, 163
—— *pratincola*, 163, *Pl.* 78
GLARIOLIDAE, 163
Glead, 81
Godwit, Bar-tailed, 136, *Pl.* 69
——, Black-tailed, xiii, 138, *Pls.* 64, 66
Goldcrest, 304, *Pls.* 138, 139, 176
Goldeneye, xiii, 51, *Pl.* 25
Goldfinch, 328, *Pls.* 150, 177
Goosander, 60, *Pls.* 27, 29, 165
Goose, Barnacle, 70, *Pl.* 34
——, Bean, 68, *Pl.* 30
——, Brent, 69, *Pl.* 34
——, Canada, 71, *Pl.* 33
——, Grey Lag, xiii, 65, *Pls.* 28, 30, 165
——, Lesser White-fronted, 67
——, Pink-footed, 68, *Pl.* 30
——, Red-breasted, 72
——, Snow, 69
——, White-fronted, 67, *Pl.* 30
Goshawk, xii, 81, *Pl.* 38
Grebe, Black-necked, xii, 9, *Pl.* 6
——, Great Crested, 6, *Pls.* 5, 7, 162
——, Horned, 8, *Pls.* 6, 8
——, Little, 10, *Pls.* 6, 8, 162
——, Pied-billed, xiv
——, Red-necked, 7, *Pl.* 6
——, Slavonian, xii, 8, *Pls.* 6, 8
Greenfinch, 326, *Pls.* 148, 157, 177
Greenshank, xii, 144, *Pls.* 68, 70, 168
Grosbeak, Pine, 334
——, Rose-breasted, xvi
——, Scarlet, 334
Grouse, Black, 98, *Pls.* 44, 50, 167
——, Red, 96, *Pls.* 50, 167
——, Willow, 96
GRUIDAE, 106
GRUIFORMES, 106
*Grus grus*, 106, *Pl.* 54
Guillemot, 196, *Pls.* 91, 93, 172
——, Black, 197, *Pls.* 93, 172
——, Bridled, 197
——, Brunnich's, 197
Gull, Black-headed, 178, *Pls.* 94, 171
——, Bonaparte's, 177
——, Common, 174, *Pls.* 86, 87, 170
——, Glaucous, 175, *Pl.* 85
——, Great Black-headed, 177

Gull, Great Black-backed, 169, *Pls.* 82, 84, 170
——, Herring, 172, *Pls.* 85, 170
——, Iceland, 176, *Pl.* 85
——, Ivory, 168, *Pl.* 86
——, Laughing, xv
——, Lesser Black-backed, 170, *Pls.* 84, 85, 170
——, Little, 178, *Pl.* 94
——, Mediterranean, 177, *Pl.* 87
——, Ross's, xv
——, Sabine's, 180, *Pl.* 86
——, Slender-billed, xv
*Gyps fulvus*, xv

HAEMATOPODIDAE, 116
*Haematopus ostralegus*, 116, *Pls.* 51, 58, 168
*Haliaeetus albicilla*, 82, *Pl.* 41
Harrier, Hen, xii, 85, *Pls.* 40, 41, 166
——, Marsh, xii, 84, *Pls.* 36, 41, 166
——, Montagu's, xii, 86, *Pls.* 40, 42, 166
——, Pallid, xv
Harlequin, 56
Hawfinch, 325, *Pls.* 150, 177
Hawk, Sparrow, xii, 79, *Pls.* 38, 166
Hen, Grey, 98
Heron, Common or Grey, 24, *Pls.* 14, 15, 163
——, Buff-backed, 27
——, Great White, 26
——, Night, 27, *Pl.* 17
——, Purple, 26, *Pl.* 14
——, Squacco, 27, *Pl.* 13
*Himantopus himantopus*, 158, *Pl.* 78
*Hippolais caligata*, xv
—— *icterina*, 292, *Pl.* 134
—— *pallida*, 293
—— *polyglotta*, 292
*Hirundapus caudacutus*, xv
HIRUNDINIDAE, 238
*Hirundo daurica*, 240
—— *rustica*, 238, *Pls.* 106, 111, 173
*Histrionicus histrionicus*, 56
Hobby, xii, 88, *Pls.* 49, 166
Hoopoe, xii, 227, *Pl.* 102
*Hydrobates pelagicus*, 13, *Pls.* 9, 162
HYDROBATIDAE, 12
*Hydroprogne tschegrava*, 185

Ibis, Glossy, 32, *Pl.* 18
*Icterus galbula*, xvi

*Ixobrychus minutus*, 28, *Pl.* 17
Jackdaw, 249, *Pls.* 113, 174
Jay, 251, *Pls.* 115, 117, 174
*Junco hyemalis*, xvi
Junco, Slate-coloured, xvi
*Jynx torquilla*, 232, *Pls.* 109, 173

Kestrel, 94, *Pls.* 43, 49, 166
——, Lesser, 94
Killdeer, 122
Kingfisher, 224, *Pls.* 105, 173
Kite, Black, 82
——, Red, xii, 81, *Pls.* 35, 46, 166
Kittiwake, 181, *Pls.* 86, 171
Knot, 146, *Pls.* 70, 71

*Lagopus lagopus*, 96, *Pls.* 50, 167
—— *mutus*, 97, *Pls.* 53, 167
LANIIDAE, 320
*Lanius collurio*, 322, *Pls.* 147, 149, 176
—— *excubitor*, 320, *Pl.* 149
—— *minor*, 321
—— *senator*, 321, *Pl.* 149
Lapwing, 117, *Pls.* 52, 62, 168
LARIDAE, 168
Lark, Bimaculated, xv
——, Calandra, xv
——, Crested, 234
——, Lesser Short-toed, 234
——, Shore, 237, *Pl.* 94
——, Short-toed, 234
——, Sky, 236, *Pls.* 108, 110, 173
——, White-winged, xv
——, Wood, 234, *Pls.* 110, 173
*Larus argentatus*, 172, *Pls.* 85, 170
—— *atricilla*, xv
—— *canus*, 174, *Pls.* 86, 87, 170
—— *fuscus*, 170, *Pls.* 84, 85, 170
—— *genei*, xv
—— *glaucoides*, 176, *Pl.* 85
—— *hyperboreus*, 175, *Pl.* 85
—— *ichthyaetus*, 177
—— *marinus*, 169, *Pls.* 82, 84, 170
—— *melanocephalus*, 177, *Pl.* 87
—— *minutus*, 178, *Pl.* 94
—— *philadelphia*, 177
—— *ridibundus*, 178, *Pls.* 94, 171
—— *sabini*, 180, *Pl.* 86
*Limicola falcinellus*, 156
*Limnodromeus griseus*, 128
—— *scolopaceus*, 128, *Pls.* 59, 65
*Limosa lapponica*, 136, *Pl.* 69
—— *limosa*, 137, *Pls.* 64, 66

Linnet, 329, *Pls.* 153, 177
——, Mountain, 331
*Locustella certhiola*, xv
—— *fluviatilis*, xv
—— *lanceolata*, 287
—— *luscinoides*, 288, *Pl.* 134
—— *naevia*, 286, *Pls.* 133, 176
Loon, 3
*Loxia curvirostra*, 334, *Pls.* 152, 154, 177
—— *leucoptera*, 335
—— *pytyopsittacus*, 335
*Lullula arborea*, 234, *Pls.* 110, 173
*Luscinia luscinia*, 284
—— *megarhynchos*, 282, *Pls.* 130, 175
*Lusciniola melanopogon*, 288
*Lymnocryptes minima*, 131, *Pl.* 65
*Lyrurus tetrix*, 98, *Pls.* 44, 50, 167

Magpie, 250, *Pls.* 117, 174
Mallard, 34, *Pls.* 1, 163
Martin, House, 240, *Pls.* 110, 173
——, Sand, 242, *Pls.* 110, 112, 173
*Melanitta fusca*, 53, *Pl.* 26
—— *nigra*, 54, *Pls.* 26, 164
—— *perspicillata*, 54, *Pl.* 29
*Melanocorypha bimaculata*, xv
—— *calandra*, xv
—— *leucoptera*, xv
Merganser, Hooded, 62
——, Red-breasted, 58, *Pls.* 24, 29, 165
*Mergus albellus*, 61, *Pl.* 29
—— *cucullatus*, 62
—— *merganser*, 60, *Pls.* 27, 29, 165
—— *serrator*, 58, *Pls.* 24, 29, 165
Merlin, xii, 91, *Pls.* 45, 166
MEROPIDAE, 225
*Merops apiaster*, 225, *Pl.* 105
—— *superciliosus*, xv
*Micropalama himantopus*, xv
*Milvus migrans*, 82
—— *milvus*, 81, *Pls.* 35, 46, 166
*Mniotilta varia*, xv
*Monticola saxatilis*, 275
Moor-fowl, 96
Moorhen, 111, *Pls.* 58, 168
*Motacilla alba*, 315, *Pls.* 145, 177
—— *cinerea*, 317, *Pls.* 146, 177
—— *citreola*, 318
—— *flava*, 318, *Pls.* 145, 146, 177
MOTACILLIDAE, 310
Murre, 196
*Muscicapa latirostris*, xv
—— *striata*, 306, *Pls.* 140, 141, 176
MUSCICAPIDAE, 306

*Neophron percnopterus*, xv
*Netta rufina*, 45, *Pl.* 22
Nighthawk, American, xv
Nightingale, 282, *Pls.* 130, 175
——, Thrush, 284
Nightjar, 220, *Pls.* 103, 109, 174
——, Egyptian, xv
——, Red-necked, xv
*Nucifraga caryocatactes*, 251, *Pl.* 113
*Numenius arquata*, 133, *Pls.* 63, 66, 169
—— *borealis*, 136
—— *phaeopus*, 135, *Pls.* 66, 169
Nutcracker, 251, *Pl.* 113
Nuthatch, 261, *Pls.* 122, 123, 175
*Nyctea scandiaca*, 213, *Pls.* 99, 101
*Nycticorax nycticorax*, 27, *Pl.* 17

*Oceanites oceanicus*, 12
*Oceanodroma castro*, xiv
—— *leucorrhoa*, 12, *Pls.* 9, 162
*Oenanthe deserti*, 277
—— *hispanica*, 277
—— *isabellina*, xv
—— *leucura*, xv
—— *oenanthe*, 275, *Pls.* 128, 130, 175
—— *pleschanka*, xv
Oriole, Baltimore, xvi
——, Golden, xii, 243, *Pl.* 109
ORIOLIDAE, 243
*Oriolus oriolus*, 243, *Pl.* 109
Osprey, xii, 87, *Pls.* 39, 46
OTIDIDAE, 114
*Otis tarda*, 114
—— *tetrax*, 114, *Pl.* 58
*Otus scops*, 212, *Pl.* 102
Ousel, Water, 266
Ouzel, Ring, 272, *Pls.* 125, 127, 175
Owl, Barn, White or Screech, xii, 211,
    *Pls.* 96, 98, 172
——, Eagle, 213, *Pl.* 101
——, Hawk, 214
——, Little, 214, *Pls.* 102, 172
——, Long-eared, 216, *Pls.* 95, 101, 172
——, Scops, 212, *Pl.* 102
——, Short-eared, 217, *Pls.* 100, 101, 172
——, Snowy, xii, 213, *Pls.* 99, 101
——, Tawny, 215, *Pls.* 98, 172
——, Tengmalm's, 219, *Pl.* 98
Oystercatcher, 116, *Pls.* 51, 58, 168

*Pagophila eburnea*, 168, *Pl.* 86
*Pandion haliaetus*, 87, *Pls.* 39, 46
Panuridae, 260

*Panurus biarmicus*, 260, *Pls.* 119, 121, 175
PARIDAE, 253
Partridge, Common or Grey, 102, *Pls.* 53, 167
——, Red-legged or French, 101, *Pls.* 47, 53, 167
*Parula americana*, xvi
*Parus ater*, 256, *Pls.* 121, 175
—— *caeruleus*, 255, *Pls.* 118, 175
—— *cristatus*, 257, *Pl.* 118
—— *major*, 253, *Pls.* 118, 175
—— *montanus*, 258, *Pls.* 118, 175
—— *palustris*, 257, *Pls.* 116, 121, 175
PASSERIDAE, 345
PASSERIFORMES, 234
*Passer domesticus*, 345, *Pls.* 161, 177
—— *hispaniolensis*, xvi
—— *montanus*, 347, *Pls.* 160, 161, 177
*Passerella iliaca*, xvi
—— *melodia*, xvi
Peewit, 118
*Pelagodroma marina*, xiv
PELECANIFORMES, 19
*Perdix perdix*, 102, *Pls.* 53, 167
Peregrine, xii, 89, *Pls.* 42, 43, 166
*Pernis apivorus*, 83, *Pl.* 34
Petrel, Bulwer's, xiv
——, Capped, xiv
——, Collared, xiv
——, Frigate, xiv
——, Kermadec, xiv
——, Leach's, 12, *Pls.* 9, 162
——, Madeiran, xiv
——, Storm, 13, *Pls.* 9, 162
——, Wilson's, 12
PHALACROCORACIDAE, 21
*Phalacrocorax aristotelis*, 22, *Pls.* 10, 12, 163
—— *carbo*, 21, *Pls.* 10, 12, 163
Phalarope, Grey, 159, *Pls.* 77, 79
——, Red-necked, xii, 160, *Pls.* 77, 169
——, Wilson's, 161, *Pl.* 79
PHALAROPODIDAE, 159
*Phalaropus fulicarius*, 159, *Pls.* 77, 79
—— *lobatus*, 160, *Pls.* 77, 169
—— *tricolor*, 161, *Pl.* 79
PHASIANIDAE, 101
*Phasianus colchicus*, 104, *Pls.* 53, 167
—— *torquatus*, 104
Pheasant, 104, *Pls.* 53, 167
*Pheucticus ludovicianus*, xvi
*Philomachus pugnax*, 156, *Pl.* 74
PHOENICOPTERIDAE, 33
PHOENICOPTERIFORMES, 33
*Phoenicopterus ruber*, 33

*Phoenicurus ochrurus*, 281, *Pls.* 129, 175
—— *phoenicurus*, 280, *Pls.* 129, 175
*Phylloscopus bonelli*, 303
—— *borealis*, 303
—— *collybita*, 300, *Pls.* 138, 176
—— *fuscatus*, xv
—— *inornatus*, 303, *Pl.* 134
—— *proregulus*, 304
—— *schwarzi*, 304
—— *sibilatrix*, 302, *Pls.* 134, 176
—— *trochiloides*, 300
—— *trochilus*, 299, *Pls.* 136, 138, 176
*Pica pica*, 250, *Pls.* 117, 174
PICIDAE, 229
PICIFORMES, 229
*Picus viridis*, 229, *Pls.* 106, 173
Pigeon, Wood, 204, *Pls.* 97, 173
*Pinicola enucleator*, 334
Pintail, 42, *Pls.* 21, 164
*Pipilo erythrophthalmus*, xvi
Pipit, Meadow, 310, *Pls.* 142, 144, 176
——, Olive-backed, xv
——, Petchora, 313
——, Red-throated, 313
——, Richard's, 311
——, Rock, 313, *Pls.* 142, 144, 176
——, Tawny, 312
——, Tree, 312, *Pls.* 142, 176
——, Water, 313
*Piranga rubra*, xvi
*Platalea leucorodia*, 31, *Pls.* 17, 19
*Plautus alle*, 195, *Pl.* 93
*Plectrophenax nivalis*, 344, *Pls.* 157, 177
*Plegadis falcinellus*, 32, *Pl.* 18
Plover, Caspian, xv
——, Golden, 124, *Pls.* 56, 61, 168
——, Green, 118
——, Grey, 123, *Pl.* 61
——, Kentish, 122, *Pls.* 62, 168
——, Lesser Golden, 125
——, Little Ringed, xii, 121, *Pl.* 61
——, Ringed, 119, *Pls.* 61, 168
——, Silver, 123
——, Sociable, 117
*Pluvialis apricaria*, 124, *Pls.* 56, 61, 168
—— *dominica*, 125
—— *squatarola*, 123, *Pl.* 61
Pochard, 48, *Pls.* 22, 23, 164
——, Red-crested, 45, *Pl.* 22
——, White-eyed, 50
*Podiceps auritus*, 8, *Pls.* 6, 8
—— *cristatus*, 6, *Pls.* 5, 7, 162
—— *grisegena*, 7, *Pl.* 6
—— *nigricollis*, 9, *Pl.* 6
—— *ruficollis*, 10, *Pls.* 6, 8, 162

PODICIPITIDAE, 6
PODICIPITIFORMES, 6
*Podilymbus podiceps*, xiv
*Polysticta stelleri*, 56
*Porphyrula martinica*, xv
*Porzana carolina*, 108
—— *parva*, 109, *Pl.* 57
—— *porzana*, 107, *Pl.* 54
—— *pusilla*, 108, *Pl.* 57
Pratincole, 163, *Pl.* 78
——, Black-winged, 163
*Procellaria diomedea*, 16
PROCELLARIIDAE, 14
PROCELLARIIFORMES, 12
*Prunella collaris*, 310, *Pl.* 145
—— *modularis*, 308, *Pls.* 142, 175
PRUNELLIDAE, 308
Ptarmigan, 97, *Pls.* 53, 167
PTEROCLIDAE, 202
*Pterodroma hasitata*, xiv
—— *leucoptera*, xiv
—— *neglecta*, xiv
Puffin, 199, *Pls.* 93, 172
*Puffinus assimilis*, 16
—— *gravis*, 16, *Pl.* 9
—— *griseus*, 17, *Pl.* 13
—— *puffinus*, 14, *Pls.* 9, 162
*Pyrrhocorax pyrrhocorax*, 252, *Pls.* 117, 174
*Pyrrhula pyrrhula*, 333, *Pls.* 154, 155, 177

Quail, xii, 103, *Pls.* 57, 167

Rail, Land, 109, *Pls.* 57, 168
——, Sora, 108
——, Water, 106, *Pls.* 48, 54, 167
RALLIDAE, 106
*Rallus aquaticus*, 106, *Pls.* 48, 54, 167
Raven, 244, *Pls.* 113, 174
Razorbill, 193, *Pls.* 81, 171
*Recurvirostra avosetta*, 157, *Pls.* 76, 78, 171
RECURVIROSTRIDAE, 157
Redbreast, 285, *Pls.* 130, 132, 175
Redpoll, Arctic, 332
——, Lesser, 331, *Pls.* 153, 177
——, Mealy, 331
Redshank, 142, *Pls.* 70, 169
——, Spotted or Dusky, 143, *Pl.* 70
Redstart, 280, *Pls.* 129, 175
——, Black, xii, 281, *Pls.* 129, 175
Redwing, 271, *Pl.* 125
Reedling, Bearded, 260

Reeler, 286
Reeve, 156
REGULIDAE, 304
*Regulus ignicapillus*, 305, *Pl.* 138
—— *regulus*, 304, *Pls.* 138, 139, 176
*Remiz pendulinus*, xv
*Rhodostethia rosea*, xv
*Riparia riparia*, 242, *Pls.* 110, 112, 173
*Rissa tridactyla*, 181, *Pls.* 86, 171
Robin, 285, *Pls.* 130, 132, 175
——, American, 272
Roller, xii, 226, *Pl.* 109
Rook, 247, *Pls.* 114, 174
Rosefinch, Scarlet, 334
Ruff and Reeve, xii, 156, *Pl.* 74

Sanderling, 154, *Pls.* 75, 77
Sandgrouse, Pallas's, 202
Sandpiper, Baird's, 150
——, Broad-billed, 156
——, Buff-breasted, 155
——, Common, 140, *Pls.* 67, 69, 169
——, Curlew, 153, *Pl.* 74
——, Green, 138, *Pl.* 69
——, Least, 149
——, Marsh, 145
——, Pectoral, 150, *Pls.* 72, 73
——, Purple, 147, *Pl.* 73
——, Semi-palmated, 154
——, Sharp-tailed, 151
——, Siberian Pectoral, 151
——, Solitary, 140
——, Spotted, 141
——, Stilt, xv
——, Terek, 145
——, Upland, 133
——, Western, xv
——, White-rumped or Bonaparte's, 150
——, Wood, 139, *Pl.* 69
Sawbill, 60
*Saxicola rubetra*, 279, *Pls.* 129, 131, 175
—— *torquata*, 278, *Pls.* 129, 131, 175
Scaup, xiii, 45, *Pl.* 1
SCOLOPACIDAE, 128
*Scolopax rusticola*, 131, *Pls.* 66, 169
Scoter, Common, xiii, 54, *Pls.* 26, 164
——, Surf, 54, *Pl.* 29
——, Velvet, xiii, 53, *Pl.* 26
Sea-parrot, 199
Sea-pie, 116
Sea-swallow, 186
*Seiurus noveboracensis*, xvi
Serin, 333, *Pl.* 150
*Serinus canarius*, 333, *Pl.* 150

*Serinus citrinella*, xvi
Shag, 22, *Pls.* 10, 12, 163
Shearwater, Audubon's, 16
——, Balearic, 16
——, Black, 17
——, Cory's, 16
——, Great, 16, *Pl.* 9
——, Little, 16
——, Manx, 14, *Pls.* 9, 162
——, Sooty, 17
Shelduck, 63, *Pls.* 25, 165
——, Ruddy, 65, *Pl.* 25
Shovelard, 31
Shoveler, 43, *Pls.* 21, 23, 164
Shrike, Great Grey, 320, *Pl.* 149
——, Lesser Grey, 321
——, Red-backed, xii, 322, *Pls.* 147, 149,
176
——, Woodchat, 321, *Pl.* 149
Siskin, 329, *Pls.* 150, 177
*Sitta europaea*, 261, *Pls.* 122, 123, 175
SITTIDAE, 261
Skua, Arctic or Richardson's, 166, *Pls.* 80,
81, 170
——, Great, 164, *Pls.* 82, 83, 170
——, Long-tailed or Buffon's, 167, *Pl.* 81
——, Pomarine or Pomatorhine, 167, *Pl.*
81
Smew, 61, *Pl.* 29
Snipe, Common, 129, *Pls.* 60, 65, 169
——, Great, 130, *Pl.* 65
——, Jack, 131, *Pl.* 65
——, Red-breasted, 128
Snowflake, 344
*Somateria mollissima*, 56, *Pls.* 26, 164
——, *spectabilis*, 58, *Pl.* 26
Sparrow, Fox, xvi
——, Hedge, 308, *Pls.* 142, 175
——, House, 345, *Pl.* 161, 177
——, Song, xvi
——, Spanish, xvi
——, Tree, 347, *Pls.* 160, 161, 177
——, White-throated, xvi
Spoonbill, xii, 31, *Pls.* 17, 19
Starling, 323, *Pls.* 146, 176
——, Rose-coloured, 325, *Pl.* 146
STERCORARIIDAE, 164
*Stercorarius longicaudus*, 167, *Pl.* 81
—— parasiticus, 166, *Pls.* 80, 81, 170
—— *pomarinus*, 167, *Pl.* 81
—— *skua*, 164, *Pls.* 82, 83, 170
*Sterna albifrons*, 190, *Pls.* 89, 171
—— *anaethetus*, xv
—— *dougallii*, 189, *Pls.* 88, 90, 171
—— *fuscata*, 190

—— *hirundo*, 185, *Pls.* 88, 89, 171
—— *maxima*, xv
—— *paradisea*, 188, *Pls.* 90, 171
—— *sandvicensis*, 191, *Pls.* 90, 171
Stilt, Black-winged, xiii, 158, *Pl.* 78
Stint, American, 149
——, Little, 148, *Pls.* 72, 73
——, Temminck's, xiii, 149, *Pl.* 73
Stonechat, 278, *Pls.* 129, 131, 175
Stork, Black, 31, *Pl.* 18
——, White, 30, *Pl.* 18
Stormcock, 267
*Streptopelia decaocto*, 205, *Pls.* 92, 97
—— *orientalis*, xv
—— *turtur*, 206, *Pls.* 92, 97, 173
STRIGIDAE, 211
STRIGIFORMES, 211
*Strix aluco*, 215, *Pls.* 98, 172
STURNIDAE, 323
*Sturnus roseus*, 325, *Pl.* 146
—— *vulgaris*, 323, *Pls.* 146, 176
*Sula bassana*, 19, *Pls.* 14, 163
SULIDAE, 19
*Surnia ulula*, 214
Swallow, 238, *Pls.* 106, 111, 173
——, Red-rumped, 240
Swan, Bewick's, xiii, 74, *Pls.* 31, 33
——, Mute, 72, *Pl.* 33
——, Whooper, xiii, 73, *Pls.* 31, 33
Swift, 222, *Pls.* 105, 173
——, Alpine, 223, *Pl.* 105
——, Little, xv
——, Needle-tailed, xv
*Sylvia atricapilla*, 293, *Pls.* 137, 176
—— *borin*, 294, *Pls.* 141, 176
—— *cantillans*, 297
—— *communis*, 295, *Pls.* 137, 176
—— *curruca*, 296, *Pls.* 137, 176
—— *hortensis*, xv
—— *melanocephala*, xv
—— *nisoria*, 294, *Pl.* 133
—— *undata*, 298, *Pls.* 137, 176
SYLVIIDAE, 286
*Syrrhaptes paradoxus*, 202


*Tadorna ferruginea*, 65, *Pl.* 25
—— *tadorna*, 63, *Pls.* 25, 165
Tanager, Summer, xvi
*Tarsiger, cyanurus*, xv
Teal, 36, *Pls.* 1, 163
——, Blue-winged, 39
——, Cricket, 38
——, Green-winged, 37
Tern, Arctic, 188, *Pls.* 90, 171

Tern, Black, xiii, 183, *Pl.* 89
——, Bridled, xv
——, Caspian, 185
——, Common, 185, *Pls.* 88, 89, 171
——, Gull-billed, 185, *Pl.* 90
——, Little, 190, *Pls.* 89, 171
——, Roseate, xiii, 189, *Pls.* 88, 90, 171
——, Royal, xv
——, Sandwich, 191, *Pls.* 90, 171
——, Sooty, 190
——, Whiskered, 184
——, White-winged Black, 184, *Pl.* 89
*Tetrao urogallus*, 99, *Pls.* 50, 167
TETRAONIDAE, 96
Thrasher, Brown, xv
THRESKIORNITHIDAE, 31
Throstle, 270
Thrush, Black-throated, xv
——, Dusky, xv
——, Eye-browed, xv
——, Grey-cheeked, 275
——, Mistle, 267, *Pls.* 126, 175
——, Olive-backed, xv
——, Rock, 275
——, Siberian, xv
——, Song, 269, *Pls.* 126, 175
——, White's, 275
*Tichodroma muraria*, 262
Tit, Bearded, xiii, 260, *Pls.* 119, 121, 175
——, Blue or Tom, 255, *Pls.* 118, 175
——, Coal, 256, *Pls.* 121, 175
——, Crested, xiii, 257, *Pl.* 118
——, Great, 253, *Pls.* 118, 175
——, Long-tailed, 259, *Pls.* 116, 121, 175
——, Marsh, 257, *Pls.* 116, 121, 175
——, Penduline, xv
——, Willow, 258, *Pls.* 118, 175
Titlark, 310
Towhee, Rufous-sided, xvi
*Toxostoma rufum*, xv
*Tringa erythropus*, 143, *Pl.* 70
—— *flavipes*, 144
—— *glareola*, 139, *Pl.* 69
—— *hypoleucos*, 140, *Pls.* 67, 69, 169
—— *macularia*, 141
—— *melanoleuca*, 144
—— *nebularia*, 144, *Pls.* 68, 70, 168
—— *ochropus*, 138, *Pl.* 69
—— *solitaria*, 140
—— *stagnatilis*, 145
—— *totanus*, 142, *Pls.* 70, 169
*Troglodytes troglodytes*, 264, *Pls.* 122, 175
TROGLODYTIDAE, 264
*Tryngites subruficollis*, 155
TURDIDAE, 267

*Turdus eunomus*, xv
—— *iliacus*, 271, *Pl.* 125
—— *merula*, 273, *Pls.* 125, 175
—— *migratorius*, 272
—— *obscurus*, xv
—— *philomelos*, 269, *Pls.* 126, 175
—— *pilaris*, 268, *Pl.* 125
—— *ruficollis*, xv
—— *sibiricus*, xv
—— *torquatus*, 272, *Pls.* 125, 127, 175
—— *viscivorus*, 267, *Pls.* 126, 175
Turnstone, 127, *Pls.* 55, 62
Twite, 330, *Pls.* 151, 153, 177
Tystie, 198
*Tyto alba*, 211, *Pls.* 96, 98, 172

*Upupa epops*, 227, *Pl.* 102
UPUPIDAE, 227
*Uria aalge*, 196, *Pls.* 91, 93, 172
—— *lomvia*, 197

*Vanellus gregarius*, 117
—— *vanellus*, 117, *Pls.* 52, 62, 168
*Vireo olivaceus*, xv
Vireo, Red-eyed, xv
Vulture, Egyptian, xv
——, Griffon, xv

Wagtail, Blue-headed, 318, *Pl.* 146
——, Citrine or Yellow-headed, 318
——, Grey, 317, *Pls.* 146, 177
——, Grey-headed, 319
——, Pied or Water, 315, *Pls.* 145, 177
——, Sykes's, 318
——, White, 315, *Pls.* 145, 177
——, Yellow, 318, *Pls.* 145, 177
Warbler, Aquatic, 292, *Pl.* 133
——, Arctic, 303
——, Barred, 294, *Pl.* 133
——, Black-and-White, xv
——, Blyth's Reed, 291
——, Bonelli's, 303
——, Booted, xv
——, Cetti's, xv
——, Dartford, xiii, 298, *Pls.* 137, 176
——, Dusky, xv
——, Garden, 294, *Pls.* 141, 176
——, Grasshopper, 286, *Pls.* 133, 176
——, Great Reed, 288
——, Greenish, 300
——, Icterine, 292, *Pl.* 134
——, Lanceolated, 287

Warbler, Marsh, xiii, 290, *Pls.* 126, 176
——, Melodious, 292
——, Moustached, 288
——, Myrtle, xvi
——, Olivaceous, 293
——, Orphean, xv
——, Paddyfield, xv
——, Pallas's, 304
——, Parula, xvi
——, Radde's Bush, 304
——, Reed, 288, *Pls.* 126, 135, 176
——, River, xv
——, Rufous, 284
——, Sardinian, xv
——, Savi's, 288, *Pl.* 134
——, Sedge, 291, *Pls.* 133, 135, 176
——, Subalpine, 297
——, Thick-billed, xv
——, Willow, 299, *Pls.* 136, 138, 176
——, Wood, 302, *Pls.* 134, 176
——, Yellow, xvi
——, Yellow-browed, 303, *Pl.* 134
Waterthrush, Northern, xvi
Waxwing, 319, *Pl.* 149
Wet-my-feet or Wet-my-lips, 103, *Pls.* 57, 167
Whaup, 134
Wheatear, 275, *Pls.* 128, 130, 175
——, Black, xv
——, Black-eared, 277
——, Desert, 277
——, Isabelline, xv
——, Pied, xv

Whimbrel, xiii, 135, *Pls.* 66, 169
Whinchat, 279, *Pls.* 129, 131, 175
Whistler, 124
Whitethroat, 295, *Pls.* 137, 176
——, Lesser, 296, *Pls.* 137, 176
Wigeon, 40, *Pls.* 21, 164
——, American, 42
Wind-hover, 94
Woodcock, 131, *Pls.* 66, 169
Woodpecker, Great Spotted or Pied, 230, *Pls.* 104, 106, 107, 173
——, Green, 229, *Pls.* 106, 173
——, Lesser Spotted or Barred, 232, *Pls.* 106, 173
Wren, xiii, 264, *Pls.* 122, 175
——, Willow, 299
——, Wood, 302
Wryneck, xiii, 232, *Pls.* 109, 173

*Xenus cinereus*, 145

Yaffle, 229
Yellowhammer, 338, *Pls.* 156, 158, 177
Yellow-legs, Greater, 144
——, Lesser, 144
Yellowthroat, xvi

*Zonotrichia albicollis*, xvi
*Zoothera dauma*, 275